Cases in the Management of Information Systems and Information Technology

Cases in the Management of Information Systems and Information Technology

Richard J. Lorette
RJL and Associates
and James Madison University

H. Charles Walton
Gettysburg College

Homewood, IL 60430
Boston, MA 02116

© RICHARD D. IRWIN, INC., 1990

Sponsoring editor: Lawrence E. Alexander
Project editor: Paula M. Buschman
Production manager: Ann Cassady
Cover designer: Robyn E. Basquin
Artist: Precision Graphics
Compositor: Harlan Typographic
Typeface: 10/12 Times Roman
Printer: R. R. Donnelley & Sons Company

Library of Congress Cataloging-in-Publication Data

Cases in the management of information systems.
ISBN 0-256-07122-5 (pbk)
   1. Business—Data processing—Case studies.
2. Management information systems.   3. Information technology.   I. Lorette, Richard J. II. Walton, H. Charles.
HF5548.2.C36   1990   658.4'038   89–19805

Printed in the United States of America

1 2 3 4 5 6 7 8 9 0 D O 7 6 5 4 3 2 1 0

To Edmond, Janet, and Spring

Preface

The cases in this book are aimed at two student populations: (1) business students and (2) information systems students. For business students, the cases should help provide an understanding of information systems technology and the implementation of change in a technical environment, and techniques for managing and dealing with information systems and information systems personnel. For information systems students, the cases should contribute a greater understanding of techniques of implementation of information systems and of managerial concerns about information technology and information systems personnel. Our intent is for this book to help both kinds of students obtain a better understanding of the overall framework for information services as it relates to the corporate environment and to the components within information services.

The cases are from actual business situations and are representative of problems that will be encountered by functional and information systems managers. While the cases present differing information technologies, with special emphasis given to the core technologies of database and teleprocessing, the significant problems are those of implementation of the technology. Technical problems are presented with appropriate recommendations from technical personnel; thus, information jargon and technical information are reinforced so that the student becomes familiar with terms and technology. However, the case problems are managerial in emphasis.

The cases have been used in the core of a business curriculum and with information systems majors. Students with little prior case analysis experience and instructors that have different case teaching techniques have successfully used the cases.

For graduate students, especially business school MBAs, we attempted to find difficult, more taxing cases that reflect the pragmatic, real-life environment of those students who are about to enter management positions for the first time or are already working as lower-level to middle-level managers; therefore, the personalities in our cases do not stress subjects such as the use of technology in Executive Information Systems (EIS), competitive edge, and strategic relevance (although these subjects are not ignored). The cases we have selected reflect a greater concern with the impact of people and human failings on system productivity, the rapid pace of technological innovation, the competitive pressures to innovate or catch up with the competition, and the day-to-day difficulties of dealing with and managing change—often by organization restructuring that is ineffective.

In most instances, our graduates and MBAs have been part-time students whose full-time jobs did not permit them to devote the amount of time they would like to spend on case analysis; so our cases are not as long, demanding, or complex as some found in other IS casebooks. Throughout, we have tried to choose cases that stress the practical, applied side of business issues and problems.

This casebook is intended to be a supplement to a standard Information Systems (IS) text and could be used in an MBA program having only one required Information Systems/Information Technology (IS/IT) course, a core level undergraduate information systems course, an undergraduate course in analysis and design, a capstone course for undergraduate IS majors, or an undergraduate program for computer science majors requiring only one course on the management aspects of IS/IT. Though not required, a basic understanding of business data processing ("bits and bytes," etc.) is recommended, while an understanding of management is essential.

Instead of using the casebook to supplement a standard text, professors might consider adopting the casebook plus a book of readings; we found that approach to be satisfactory at the graduate level. We used our own collection of what we considered to be classic articles plus a contemporary selection of articles addressing technological advances. Another option is to use the casebook to support several texts in an undergraduate IS/IT major curriculum, choosing some of the cases for the analysis and design course, others for the database course, and so on.

All but two of the cases—Case A, Automated Procurement Project, and Case 2–1, Arnold Electronics—were written by teams of MBA students and are based on observing and recording actual practice and events. The cases have been edited, updated, and substantially revised; 21 have been disguised by the student writers or the casebook authors. In addition, all cases have been revised further in accordance with comments from students and reviewers. All of the cases have been used in class at least twice; we have found that they convey current, germane issues and often induce spirited discussions.

The cases selected for the book were chosen for their ability to help IS/IT teachers do six things:

1. Train students in problem solving by requiring a systematic approach when analyzing several cases.
2. Examine technical subjects such as local area networks and systems analysis techniques (data flow diagrams, for example).
3. Focus on people and organizational elements.
4. Expose students to business problems in the major functional areas of business: Finance, Marketing, Production, Personnel, Accounting, and Distribution.

5. Familiarize students with DP/IS terminology.
6. Improve the students' writing and speaking skills—since IS planning, design, and implementation problems often reflect communication issues.

The cases are organized conceptually in a sequence that we consider chronologically sound if one is presenting an undergraduate capstone course or a graduate survey course. However, since each case describes a rather large view of an IS element and its parent organization, often with a multiplicity of issues and problems, individual professors may decide to modify the order of presentation. Additionally, it is not suggested that all the cases be used in a one-semester course.

In the Course Introduction and Chapter 1, Introduction to Information Management, the two cases depict an overview of current issues in the management of information systems. The two cases of Chapter 2, Database, provide an opportunity either to use dBASE III + and develop a database on a microcomputer, or to gain some familiarity with system flow charts and data flow diagrams. Chapter 3, Telecommunications and Local Area Networks, introduces local area networks as well as potential legal pitfalls inherent in a network designed to support an organization whose requirements are changing. The cases in Chapter 4, Office Automation, provide a timely opportunity to gauge the practicality of seeking to implement the ''paperless office'' across a large corporation. In Chapter 5, Planning and IS, we have three cases that describe problems with IS planning and the integration of different complex systems in a public utility, a large manufacturing conglomerate, and a large transportation organization. The three cases of Chapter 6, Organizing for IS, portray serious challenges awaiting those who attempt to control IS in regulated industries and large organizations using matrix management. Chapter 7, Acquisition—Hardware and Software, has three cases that provide opportunities to review company requirements processes and evaluate their equipment selection procedures. Chapter 8, Controlling Development and Implementation, is one of the larger chapters, and addresses requirements determination, internal marketing of IS, and the use of consultants. Chapter 9, Audit and Security, has two cases that look closely at the problems of safeguarding data and equipment, as well as building an IS audit capability in a large company. Chapter 10, Multinational IS Issues, has the only international case; it portrays problems of conversion and personnel following the takeover of an American firm by a foreign corporation. Chapter 11, Capstone Case, concentrates on databases and the stages of their implementation.

Problems of planning, organizing, staffing, and controlling IS departments and development projects are present in all the cases. Due to the inherent nature of case writing, which seeks to illustrate a total IS environment over time, many of the cases could be used in more than one part of the text.

One of our goals is to reinforce college computer systems programs (CIS, IS, IT, MIS, and Computer Science) by providing an approach to teach a process for solving IS/IT management problems. Therefore, the *Instructor's Manual* includes many memos describing how to analyze cases, one comprehensive sample case analysis (solution) or one sample analytical framework for each case, and discussion questions—as well as the typical teaching notes and assignment questions. Where appropriate, case financial statements and other exhibits are examined for critical information needed to arrive at logical conclusions and recommendations. We hope the *Manual* will be useful as well as thought provoking.

We wish to acknowledge the significant contributions made by our Senior Editor, Larry Alexander, and his Editorial Assistant, Lena Buonanno; they were responsive and energetic in reviewing and editing our work. We also wish to thank Paula Buschman, who managed the production of the casebook and Rosalyn Sheff, the manuscript copy editor.

Several faculty members reviewed our prospectus and the draft manuscript; their comments were constructive and specific, making the revision task considerably less arduous and stressful than it might otherwise have been. The reviewers were: Donald L. Amoroso, University of Colorado; Lloyd J. Buckwell, Jr., Indiana University Northwest; Jane Fedorowicz, Boston University; Richard T. Pokryfka, The Citadel; and Noel Taylor, University of California at Los Angeles.

Dave Kroenke very generously allowed us to include his excellent database development case, Case 2–1, Arnold Electronics, which we modified slightly to fit our needs.

We are also very grateful to the many firms that opened their files and also permitted our students to conduct lengthy interviews with members of their organizations. It would not have been possible to prepare this book without their cooperation.

Finally, we wish to thank the students at the University of Baltimore and Loyola College (Baltimore) who analyzed the cases and submitted written abstracts and analyses; these were particularly valuable material for the *Instuctor's Manual*.

We are very interested in receiving comments and suggestions to improve the cases. Also, since publishing a book of current cases is especially difficult in our dynamic field, we would appreciate receiving new cases to be considered for use in a revision to this text.

Dr. R. J. Lorette
Dr. H. Charles Walton

Contents

Coping with Change

A critical concern of managers today is how to cope successfully with advances in Information Systems (IS) hardware, software, and management concepts. Contending with change may mean taking advantage of new technology in order to assure a competitive edge or increase market share; for some firms, however, the survival of the business or organization may actually be at stake.

Managers at all levels, in government and nonprofit organizations, as well as the private sector, are deciding how to (1) measure user requirements, (2) design and acquire automated systems, and (3) install, implement, and maintain new hardware and software applications. For managers of Data Processing (DP) and IS, budget constraints, personnel turnover, and the ever-changing demands of users combine to produce a jumble of complex, exhausting problems.

SOCIETY'S DEPENDENCE ON COMPUTERS

Today, it would be difficult to perform many routine activities without computers; airline reservations, bank withdrawals, weather forecasts, insurance benefits, and payroll disbursements all now rely on large, expensive, minicomputers, main-frames, and supercomputers. Automobiles, home heating systems, and even gravel pits are halted when their computers "go down." And if the information system is strategically relevant,[1] being inoperable for 24 hours (or however long it takes to get the computer "up" again) can have major negative competitive implications.

---

[1] From James I. Cash, Jr., F. W. McFarlan, J. L. McKenney, and M. R. Vitale, *Corporate Information Systems Management: Test and Cases,* 2nd ed., Chapter 11 (Homewood, Ill., Richard D. Irwin, 1988): Where IS/IT [Information Systems/Information Technology] is "an area of great strategic importance . . . Not only does IT need the guidance of corporate goals but the achievement of these goals can be severely impacted by IT performance and capabilities (or lack thereof)."

Clients, consumers, and the general public have demanded faster and faster responses to their needs; as a result, DP/IS expenses have ballooned with hardware, software, and personnel increases. Business functional managers have seized on microcomputers as a solution to problems at all levels in their organizations. To the mainframe DP managers, the advent of powerful micros has meant a loss of authority and control over organizational computing resources and decisions; end-users now may select, purchase, and install their own hardware and software, particularly when mainframe application development exceeds two or three years. As end-users gained knowledge and experience, early arguments by DP managers — that end-users were not competent to develop systems, write code, or input sensitive data—lost legitimacy and became less effective in slowing the end-user's rise to power.

ORGANIZATIONAL CULTURE

Organizational culture has a strong influence on IS personnel's ability to manage change. Cash, McFarlan, McKenney, and Vitale state that, ''The values of senior management, the approaches to corporate planning, the corporate philosophy of control, and the speed of technological change in the company constitute one set of determinants'' of the corporate culture.[2]

For IS managers, the point is that the IS leadership and staff must play the organizational and political game within the rules that have already been established, perhaps prior to the existence of computers in some old-line firms. That may be difficult when top executives (1) refuse to use microcomputers,[3] (2) question the commitment, team play, and organizational loyalty of DP technical experts, and (3) insist nevertheless that they want, need, and must have the latest technology immediately.

More specifically, Davis and Olson wrote that, ''Within the organizational culture, having information available is a symbol of competence and inspires confidence in decision-making abilities.''[4] No one has ever doubted that functional and general managers need information; the problem for IS managers is how to market their product internally, how to persuade top management that the IS department should be supported with funds and staffing priorities. The latter is more difficult to achieve when planning staffs complete the overall corporate strategic plan without considering the potential impact on IS resources, both machines and people.

---

[2]Cash et al., *Corporate Information Systems Management*, Chapter 1.

[3]Robin Nelson, ''CEOs: Computing in High Places,'' *Personal Computing*, April 1989.

[4]Gordon B. Davis and Margrethe H. Olson, *Management Information Systems: Conceptual Foundations, Structure, and Development*, 2nd ed., Chapter 8 (New York: McGraw-Hill, 1985).

IS AND ITS ENVIRONMENT

The organizational culture is only one element of the IS environment. The hier-archical structure—for example, of a centralized versus decentralized firm—is another factor. If overall planning and decision making is decentralized, why should IS project approval and budget allocations be vested in the headquarters DP group?

For many years, especially before the arrival of powerful microcomputers and local area networks, the mainframe DP managers, operators, and programmers were the experts; they were permitted to make all decisions relative to setting priorities and developing automated systems. In some cases, DP managers argued against the acquisition of new systems, often a reasonable stand when mainframe capacity was underutilized; they made enemies of powerful functional executives. Subsequently, the DP experts have learned that corporate culture and corporate memory exist side by side; functional managers didn't get mad—they waited and watched for the chance to get even.

THE AUTOMATED PROCUREMENT PROJECT

Case A, Automated Procurement Project, the true case history of the development of an automated system in a large federal agency, focuses on many of the factors described above. Much space has been devoted to describing personal experiences and conversations so that the realism of the organizational conflict and the collision of personalities is preserved.

Automated Procurement Project is only one of many cases that reveals a major, widespread dilemma—the inability, or unwillingness, of IS/IT technical person-nel and functional area managers and staff to communicate productively and reach reasonable accommodations over interests common to each other as well as to the overall organization.[5]

Case A Automated Procurement Project

The setting is a procurement office of a large federal agency in Washington, D.C., in the spring of 1985. Thornton Jenks, the deputy procurement executive and number two person in the agency's Procurement and Contract Management di-

---

[5]In Case 1–1, Chapter 2, Bolle Navigation Systems, a similar communication gap is featured, although the technical expert versus user confrontation occurs at a lower level in a large corporation.

This case was prepared by H. Charles Walton. Names, locations, and financial data have been disguised.

vision, is placing the final touches on his report to the agency administrator. The agency has the reputation of being the most competent in the federal government, due in large part to its effective procurement and project management activities. Procurement is requesting authorization to develop—outside of the control of the Automated Data Processing (ADP) division—a complex automated procurement system. Since the objective of this request is so out of character with the way the agency normally functions, Thornton is laboring over every detail to insure its accuracy. ADP is vigorously opposing this action. It is rare in this agency for top-level executives to have such strong disagreements.

MANAGEMENT BACKGROUND

Fred Marley is the procurement executive and head of Procurement and Contract Management. He and Thornton have known each other for many years. They were classmates at a service academy and later had worked on many projects together. While in the service, both had completed MBA degrees at Harvard University, although not at the same time. Thornton had become interested in automated systems at Harvard. This was fortunate since his next service assignment, after graduating from Harvard, involved the development of an automated inventory system.

Fred and Thornton retired from the service as flag (general-admiral rank) officers. After his retirement, Fred accepted an offer from the agency to be the procurement executive and two years later asked Thornton to be his deputy procurement executive. Fred told Thornton that the office needed his strong systems background to complement Fred's management background. Thornton accepted Fred's offer. They are at ease together; each respects the other's opinions, and they work well as a team.

While examining his division's situation, Thornton had reviewed a case study prepared by two college professors for the National Contract Management Association. The case, Automated Procurement at the Department of A, was an actual account of a federal government department's attempt to automate its procurement system.

AUTOMATED PROCUREMENT AT THE DEPARTMENT OF A

In the late 1970s, difficulties in the Department of A's procurement process forced a reorganization, and James Walter was appointed the new procurement executive. Walter believed that he could get the department's procurement activities in shape. He was a retired general with extensive procurement experience and an MBA from The George Washington University.

Walter listed his procurement goals for the department in a memo to all procurement personnel; the goals were:

1. The department would be brought up to compliance with Federal Procurement Regulations.
2. The professionalism of procurement department officers would be upgraded.
3. Procurement activities would be standardized.
4. A comprehensive automated procurement system would be developed.

Walter knew the automated procurement system was a large, complex, highly structured process but with a much lower level of technology than the department had often dealt with in the past. The system would be all-encompassing and was to automate the procurement process from the time of congressional authorization to obligate funds until completion of the necessary contractual actions.

PROJECT BACKGROUND

Walter contacted the Automated Data Processing (ADP) department within the Department of A about his automated procurement system. Harlan Kahn, the ADP executive, informed him that ADP had a large backlog of system requests and a four-year backlog of approved new projects; he also warned Walter that maintenance of the current systems used 70 percent of the available personnel's time. Despite the ADP backlog, Harlan agreed to provide support to the project and assigned Nazim Ahmed to be the project leader for the initial study.

Nan James, a contracting officer with a library science degree, was the procurement area's representative assigned to assist Nazim, ADP's project leader. Walter also assigned Jack Nelson and Rudy Henry, two experienced policy officials from Procurement, to the project team. They were to be consultants to the project and would also serve as the liaison between Nan and Walter.

Nazim had worked his way up through the ADP ranks from operator, to systems programmer, to analyst. He had been taught and believed in the value of following the department's Systems Development Procedure manual.

PROJECT START

Once the study team had been formed, Nazim called Nan to schedule a one-hour meeting in his office for the following week.

In his meeting with Nan, he explained that the systems development manual and its techniques were used on all new projects. Then, he explained the phases of the project (see Exhibit 1).

Nazim told Nan the proposal submitted by Procurement was not in the accepted format; she would have to write the preliminary survey in the manner prescribed in the systems manual. He also explained that the preliminary study required a

---

EXHIBIT 1   System Development Phases

---

1. Preliminary survey.
    a. Project scope and purpose.
    b. Concept approval.

2. Feasibility study.
    a. Feasibility document.
    b. Benefits and costs.

3. Analysis.
    a. Budget and schedule.
    b. Physical requirements.
    c. User requirements.
    d. Functional specification.

4. Preliminary design.
    a. Configuration and performance needs.
    b. System specification.

5. Hardware study.
    a. Final configuration.
    b. Hardware purchase order.

6. Detailed design.
    a. Packaged design and coding.
    b. Administrative procedures.
    c. Control design and procedure.
    d. Testing plan.

7. Implementation.
    a. Training.
    b. Conversion.
    c. Acceptance.

---

detailed project scope and objectives. He concluded by saying that he would not be available for the next seven weeks; he would be tied up for three weeks due to previous project commitments, and then he was going on leave to visit his parents in India. Nazim was excited about his promotion and recent graduation from The George Washington University's Master of Science in Operations Research program.

Nan met with Jack and Rudy, the experienced procurement officials, to begin the process. Jack had serious reservations about the comprehensive scope of the proposed system. He addressed the heart of his concerns when he said, "Most of our contracting officers can't even spell *computer,* and the bureau managers know even less. The field procurement officers like the old systems because they are in control. This system will be seen as threatening their jobs, and they will feel micromanaged. Also, don't forget those field officers are not responsible to the Office of the Procurement Executive; they report through their district procurement administrators to their bureau managers, who are responsible directly to the Secretary of A."

Rudy interrupted to advise Nan, "I don't believe that what the field thinks matters; Walter has decided that he wants this system, so you'd better design it for him. He has already said that he wanted headquarters to monitor field activities closely. He feels that with this system the number and grade of contracting officers can be reduced."

Nan suggested the field offices be contacted for input. Jack replied that Walter preferred an initial plan be developed to which the field officials could respond. Rudy agreed. He said, "This is to be a top-down approach."

Nan submitted her preliminary survey. The scope of the project was to follow a contract from the time of legislative enactment until the completion and audit of the project. The objectives were to:

1. Provide information for management control.
2. Automate and standardize the procurement process.
3. Bring the procurement process into compliance with Federal Procurement Regulations.
4. Increase the professionalism of the procurement officials.

Nan stressed statutory requirements and intangible benefits as reasons for this new project.

Harlan sent word to Nazim, down through the ADP chain of command, to accept the preliminary study and to proceed with the system design. Harlan did not want ADP to lose control of such a large, important project. Nazim's preliminary estimates were for a three-year development at a cost of $5 million. Although he had never worked on a project that was half—or even a quarter—that large, he was confident that ADP could do it.

Nazim hurriedly instructed Nan in the procedures the department used for documenting system designs and loaned her a worn copy of De Marco's *Structured Analysis and System Specification,* commenting that it was "old but still one of the best books I've found on structured analysis."[1] However, since Nazim was too busy on other matters to help her, Nan proceeded on her own, trying to follow De Marco's definition of structured analysis (Exhibit 2)[2] and the accompanying data flow diagram (Exhibit 3).[3] She worked for eight months on the logical design of the current manual system, using statutory requirements and regulations as well as consulting with Rudy and Jack for their understanding of current policy and practice. She developed data flow diagrams and data types of the current system.

---

[1] Tom De Marco, *Structured Analysis and System Specification,* 1st rev. (New York: YOURDON, Inc., 1979).

[2] De Marco, *Structured Analysis,* Chapter 2.

[3] Revised from Figure 6, p. 26, De Marco, *Structured Analysis.*

EXHIBIT 2 The Seven Component Studies of Structured Analysis

- Study of the current physical environment, resulting in its documentation by a current physical data flow diagram.
- Derivation of the logical equivalent of the current environment, resulting in a current logical data flow diagram.
- Derivation of the new logical environment, as portrayed by the new logical data flow diagram plus supporting documentation.
- Determination of certain physical characteristics of the new environment to produce a set of tentative new physical data flow diagrams.
- Quantification of cost and schedule data associated with each of the possibilities represented by the set of new physical data flow diagrams.
- Selection of one option, resulting in one selected new physical data flow diagram.
- Packaging of the new physical data flow diagram and supporting documents into the structured specification.

Nazim suggested that she validate her preliminary current system logical design results in a walkthrough with the user. A contracting officer at the department's headquarters was selected to be a representative user. He examined the charts prepared by Nan carefully; then, after a 45-minute explanation of documentation and data flow diagramming techniques, he concluded, "Although I am not familiar with these techniques, it looks right to me."

With the user validation in hand, Nazim assigned three programmer-analysts to convert Nan's logical data flow diagrams to a logical equivalent of the new system. Two months later, ADP sent an expanded logical model of the new system to Nan for user validation. Nan attached a memo documenting the system progress, and forwarded the logical design of the system—along with functional specifications, physical requirements, and the budget—to Walter for his approval. Walter promptly sent it to Jack and Rudy for their inspection, which would constitute user validation.

The final paragraph of Nan's efforts concluded that the system would require six programmer-analysts, an upgraded mainframe, new communications programs, a new database management system, and an extensive terminal network. Her estimated total budget (development and operations) was $7 million.

The budget was approved, and hardware purchase orders were prepared. Five programmer-analysts were hired to develop the preliminary physical design of the new system, which they completed in six months.

Nan was given the preliminary physical design to do a walkthrough with contracting officers selected from three test sites. The contracting officers' reactions —and those of their superiors, the district administrators—were very loud and all negative. Some of the objections to the system's design were:

EXHIBIT 3   Data Flow Diagram of Structured Analysis

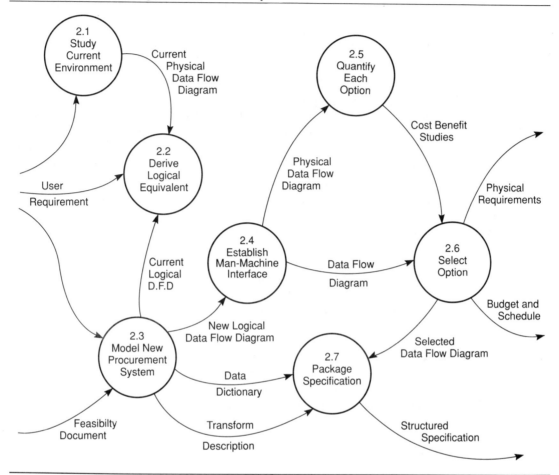

1. The system was incomplete and did not accurately represent the current environment.
2. The system did not reflect changes in statutes and regulations that occurred during its development.
3. The system did not address local issues.
4. The system transferred control of the work to be done away from those — district officials — responsible for it.
5. The system would be incomprehensible to the average contracting officer.

For two years, changes were made in the system design to rectify the problems noted by the contracting officers. A prototype was delivered to two sites. At both sites, the contracting officers refused to use the system. They contended:

1. The system was difficult to use.
2. The hardware was incompatible with local hardware.
3. Communications equipment was difficult to use.
4. The system did not produce a contract that met their needs.

Because of the resistance to the system, data collection discipline was poor; the data gathered was useless. Finally, the district administrators informed the two test sites to disregard the new system.

Nelson Tarduff, the Secretary of A, decided to ''redirect'' the effort and reduce the scope of the project. The final cost of the abandoned project was $14 million.

Walter left the department ''to pursue other opportunities.''

ASSESSING THE DEPARTMENT OF A CASE

After reading the Department of A case, Thornton put it down and breathed a heavy sigh. Although he thought his agency's personnel were much more professional, he wanted to learn from the case and avoid making the same mistakes. His project, he thought, would be done correctly.

AUTOMATED PROCUREMENT AT THE AGENCY

The procurement processes of the agency worked well overall; however, Fred felt that an automated system would add efficiency to the operation. From his service experience, he was confident that an automated system could be successfully installed; besides, he had complete confidence in his deputy Thornton's ability to do the job. As he saw them, Fred's two functions in assisting Thornton were reviewing the final version of the automated procurement system requirements document and guarding Procurement's political flanks.

The purposes of the automated procurement system were outlined in the agency's planning document (Exhibit 4).

Thornton assigned Jean, a contracting officer interested in computer systems, to manage the project. Jean, an extremely bright contracting officer, had worked for the agency one year. She had joined the agency after finishing her law degree at Harvard. Thornton and Fred praised her work highly.

Jean was told that the procurement automation activities would have to compete with other agency projects for ADP funds. Since her preliminary survey indicated that the project was feasible and that senior management support for the project was solid, she asked Thornton to organize a proposal committee.

He agreed and immediately established a committee of senior contracting officers, one from each district. Jean met with the committee members to develop

---

EXHIBIT 4 Purposes of the Automated Procurement System

---

1. Be more responsive to project officers.
   Reduce the time necessary to award contracts.
   Provide a contract better suited to meet a project's needs.

2. Assist the contracting officers.
   Reduce paperwork.
   Furnish a branching logic decision tree, including the impact of recent changes, for decision support.

3. Adhere to regulations.
   Standardize the required contract language to be consistent with the current Federal Acquisition Regulations (FAR) and the agency supplement.

4. Allow greater productivity.

5. Generate vendor lists.
   Provide assistance with small business and 8(a) (minority) contractor participation requirements.

6. Assist with local contracting provisions.

7. Ease the paperwork requirements for tracking of large projects.

8. Simplify the reporting requirements for contract administration control.

9. Reduce development costs by centralizing and standardizing software development efforts.

---

the user requirements and also with the ADP analyst to discuss the system requirements. In Jean's opinion, little progress had been made after several weeks because the committee could not come to closure on anything.

Following the fifth meeting, Jean reported the lack of progress to Thornton. As they discussed the situation, both smiled. Jean said, "The committee members may not know much about automated systems, but they are expert bureaucrats." The two agreed that Thornton needed to assume control of the project. While he was not an expert, Thornton had attended a database seminar by James Martin (the database expert), had read several of Martin's books, and had attended a Harvard Business School Executive Seminar on Information Systems; he believed he'd at least be able to ask critical questions.[4]

Brad Boswell, the agency's ADP executive, added to the committee closure problems when he informed Thornton that ADP did not have the time to develop

---

[4]"James Martin, a computer visionary who has been promoting the use of 4GL [fourth-generation languages] for several years, estimates that by 1990 users will be doing 50 percent of their own program development. This level of self-sufficiency has already been met, and exceeded, by some firms. The sales forecasting department of Pet Foods, for example, develops 80 percent of their projects." From Raymond McLeon, Jr., *Management Information Systems*, Chapter 11, 3rd ed. (Chicago: Science Research Associates, 1986).

the project as Thornton envisioned it. He proposed that automated procurement system design be modified to fit more easily into the ADP schedule.

After Thornton's discussion with Brad, Thornton recommended to Fred that, unless there were significant changes in ADP's attitude, Procurement should develop the system without the assistance of ADP. Thornton, Fred, and Brad met to try to resolve the impasse. Finally, Thornton recommended that the procurement division should contract for system development services from a vendor. Brad was opposed; he did not feel that the Procurement staff had sufficient experience to develop a new system. He also insisted that all data processing projects should be controlled by the ADP division.

Thronton perceived ADP to be the weak link in the agency and knew that many of the other operating divisions had the same opinion. ADP people were unresponsive, and they hindered alternative solutions by maintaining a "closed shop" mentality.

Thornton admitted leaning toward a philosophy of user dominance, which had started with his exposure to James Martin.[5] His argument to Fred was, "We couldn't be any worse off doing the job ourselves; at least, our compromises will be made by Procurement people, with the best interests of the project and Procurement at heart. It is time to meet ADP head-on." Fred concurred with Thornton's recommendation, and, after two more unproductive meetings with ADP, was ready for a "no holds barred" confrontation.

The recommendation, to allow Procurement to manage the development of the automated procurement process, reached the agency administrator, Tom Ault. As he reviewed Procurement's report, he thought of the precedent his response — should he concur in cutting ADP out of the development process pattern — would set.

THE PROJECT BEGINS

With permission to develop the system from Tom Ault, Thornton Jenks proceeded with a several weeks-long study that recommended selection of a large computer vendor as the contractor to develop the automated procurement system. A six-member project team from the vendor started work. They developed an overall system design and then began a study of the eight regional procurement offices

---

[5]"Increasingly, some end users are likely to create their own applications with user-friendly fourth generation languages. Where they do not build the application themselves, we would like them to sketch their needs and work hand in hand with an analyst (perhaps from an information center), who builds the application for them. User-driven computing is a vitally important trend for enabling users to get their problems solved with computers." From James Martin, *Application Development without Programmers* (Englewood Cliffs, N.J.: Prentice-Hall, 1982); and James Martin and Carma McClure, *Diagramming Techniques for Analysts and Programmers,* Chapter 1 (Englewood Cliffs, N.J.: Prentice-Hall, 1986).

that would eventually use the system. The findings of the study revealed wide variances in the practices of the regional systems. For example, the number of decision steps in their respective procurement processes varied from 6 to 30. Also, many unsound practices were discovered, such as alteration of the standard boilerplate clauses in contracts.

Following Martin's methodology closely, Thornton concentrated his efforts on marketing the application (within the agency), data administration, and conflict resolution. He controlled the project through his function as data administrator. The project team developed a data model for the agency, and Thornton required that all users comply with the definitions in the data dictionary. His development strategy centered around a powerful database and database management system, fourth-generation languages, and a strong planning process. That approach demanded a high degree of software and hardware standardization. Hardware specifications had to be detailed to include even the internal computer instruction set.

Thornton's strategy for the system's initial development was to select the three highest payoff modules in terms of end-users. The first module would produce solicitations or contracts. The menu furnished mandatory and optional clauses and provided a decision tree walkthrough of the appropriate clauses. Tom Ault, agency administrator, used a prototype in a specially conducted demonstration of the procurement system. He liked what he saw, so Fred and Thornton decided to continue the project.

DEVELOPMENT

The vendor became a big problem. Funding had lapsed, due to agency and federal constraints, and no money was available for three months. When the vendor contract was reinstated, different personnel were assigned to the project. Thornton felt they were of inferior quality, and he quickly terminated the contract.

To continue the project, an 8(a) (minority) vendor, who had been successful with Defense Department projects, was selected. Three weeks after the awarding of the contract, the main project team left the firm in a dispute over wages. The 8(a) firm's contract was terminated. A management services firm was hired to guide in-house development.

After three meetings, the agency's district procurement representatives could not agree on a new logical design. Thornton arbitrarily adopted a compromise 8-step process (as opposed to the districts' 6 to 30 steps, depending on the district). The district executives opposed the centrally mandated process, and the matter was referred to the administrator. The administrator upheld the centrally developed automated procurement system concept.

Discussing the situation several months later, Thornton indicated that a major problem was resistance to closure on decisions. His response was to act, which he admitted was not always optimal; but if he did not act, the committee would discuss and rediscuss issues but would not develop any recommendations or solutions. His method, he claimed, was based solely on political compromise. For example, the 8 decision steps in themselves were a compromise between 6 and 30. Other "balanced" decisions he made included a distributed network of managerial workstations with stand-alone software, a centralized data dictionary and database, required data reporting of some items, and fourth-generation languages for local development of local applications and query.

The system design was finally accomplished in accordance with the design of the committee and with the support of Thornton's procurement staff and the consultants. Thornton's design primarily reflected database design concepts and standardization of central applications, with distributed capabilities for local applications.

After an expenditure of $7 million and three years, the three high payoff modules were in place. Development of the other four modules continues at a reduced pace. Thornton concluded the interview with a smile, saying he hoped to reduce his involvement with automated procurement; however, he expected that he would always have responsibility for the system.

QUESTIONS

1. Did James Walter contribute to the problem? If so, how?
2. What could Harlan have done to provide assistance?
3. Do you find errors in Department A's development methodology? If so, what are they, and how would you correct them?
4. What should the agency administrator do? Why?
5. What dangers does Brad face?
6. Why did Jean have such problems? Do they seem realistic?
7. What should Thornton have learned—after reviewing the case of Automated Procurement as the Department of A—about evolving his role in system development?
8. What are the major differences in Thornton's and Walter's approaches?
9. What problems did you find in Thornton's approach?
10. What elements are required for the limited success that Thornton had?

Chapter 1

Introduction to Information Management

COMPONENTS OF AN INFORMATION SYSTEM

One question we are always asked in the first class on Management of Information Systems—usually before the instructor has had an opportunity to complete checking the enrollment—is, "Exactly what is an information system?" We have not found a better response than Kroenke's 1981 definition of a business computer system. Although he refers to a business computer system, the definition fits any computer system:

> A **system** is a collection of components that interact to achieve some purpose. A **computer system** is a collection of components, including a computer, that interact to achieve some purpose. Note the word **including.** A computer system is not just a computer; it includes a computer as one of its components. **A business computer system is a collection of components, including a computer, that interact to satisfy a business need. . . .** The five components of a business computer system are **hardware, programs, data, procedures,** and **people.** Each component is required to successfully satisfy a business need; take any of them away and the need cannot be satisfied.[1]

We prefer a slightly altered definition, changing the word *programs* to *software;* Kroenke, in the same text, also modified the people component to the term *trained people*.

Most students readily accept the idea that software is specific instructions for general-purpose computers, while procedures are instructions for people. As Kroenke adds,

> A computer must have a program, or **sequence of instructions,** to satisfy a specific

---

[1]David M. Kroenke, *Business Computer Systems: An Introduction,* Chapter 2 (Santa Cruz, Calif.: Mitchell Publishing, 1981).

need.... **Procedures** are instructions for people on the use and operation of the system. Procedures describe how people are to prepare input data and how the results are to be used. Also, procedures explain what people are to do when errors are created and need to be corrected.[2]

As for data, it is the link between the machines and their program applications (software) on the one hand and the people and their procedures on the other. Hopefully, data input is transformed into information output.

While the five components of the definition are significant, the last sentence of the quotation reveals, perhaps better than any other explanation, the cause for many system development failures: "Each component is required to successfully satisfy a business need; take any of them away and the need cannot be satisfied." Time after time, new system development projects are completed, although (1) at a cost many times greater than the budget estimate, (2) on a day, months or even years after the predicted date, and (3) with performance features and capacity well under those promised; some of these systems are never used, while others become daily reminders of development duds or personal failures.

Two such cases include a large, well-known insurance firm that invested $22 million and five years in developing a system that was delivered but never used (the cost was written off) and a federal civilian department that bought millions of dollars worth of hardware (including two minicomputers and dozens of terminals and microcomputers) that was installed but sat useless for over a year.

In the first example, the insurance application did not meet the expectations of the users; there had been too little communication between the developers and the users (who had initiated the original request) during the prolonged development and implementation process. Result? The delivered system did not meet the users' needs, which had shifted during the five-year period, to meet the realities of the marketplace. Kroenke's fifth component, people, had been neglected.

As for the federal agency, terminals gathered dust on the desks of top-level executives who refused to turn on their terminals simply to read the time and date (in fact, they were so disinterested in using computers that not one of them even requested a password when the sign-up list was circulated). Date and time was the only information available from the terminals because — incredibly — there was no data ready to be keyed in to the minicomputers. Top management had thought that they were only buying (and did buy) computer hardware and software, rather than a computer **system.** The third component—data—had been overlooked. In fact, the fifth component—trained people—had also been omitted, because the microcomputer users and database managers had not been identified nor trained prior to delivery of the equipment.

In many of the cases, which include the evolution of an IS or DP department as part of the organization background, botched system development can almost

---

[2]Kroenke, *Business Computer Systems,* Chapter 1.

always be explained, in part, by management's slighting—if not ignoring—one of Kroenke's five components.

NOLAN'S STAGE HYPOTHESIS

Understanding and appreciating the importance of a proper blend of the five components of a computer system is priceless; yet it will not guarantee a successful IS operation. Nolan and Gibson's classic EDP stage hypothesis has almost equal practical value for functional and IS managers.

In their 1974 article, Nolan and Gibson picture four different stages, not necessarily discrete, on an S-shaped curve. The stages are: initiation, expansion, formalization, and maturity. Each stage has its own management problems, computer applications, rewards, and traumata. Three sorts of growth can be identified as the DP organization emerges: computer applications, specialization of DP personnel, and formal management techniques and organizations.[3]

In the first stage, initiation, we find cost-reduction applications, personnel specialization based on computer efficiency, and loose (perhaps indifferent) management.

The early successes and reduction in the level of computer anxiety during stage 1 generates high enthusiasm and optimism, leading to stage 2, expansion. Now, there is a spread of applications to all organization functional areas, many personnel specialties are born, and management techniques are directed toward Sales. Unfortunately, the excitement and confidence of stage 2 usually generates what appears, to suddenly aware top managers, to be skyrocketing budgets and organizations; both seem out of control. Frequently, management overreacts by instituting very strong controls. Therefore, in stage 3, the organization adds personnel (whose focus is control) and control-related management procedures, while shutting down development or acquisition of new applications. Initiative and creativity of the DP staff may be stifled; some become frustrated and leave. It is unfortunate that what is usually only a temporary hold on application development comes before those applications with the greatest potential for generating increased revenues have been addressed.

With time, management's fears are somewhat allayed; the Management Information System (MIS) manager may have progressed to the upper levels of the organization and must now become adept at maintaining a stable organization while also changing to keep up with the advances of technology. Stage 4 includes the introduction of such applications as databases, matching personnel specialization in database and telecommunications, and management orientation toward DP/IS resource control and planning.[4]

---

[3]Cyrus F. Gibson and Richard L. Nolan, "Managing the Four Stages of EDP Growth," *Harvard Business Review,* January–February 1974, pp. 76-88.

[4]Gibson and Nolan, "Managing the Four Stages," pp. 76-88.

The original four-stage concept was updated by Nolan's 1979 article, "Managing the Crises in Data Processing";[5] in this article, he expanded the four stages to six, which he called initiation, contagion, control, integration, data administration, and maturity. Also, he noted—in stages 5 and 6—the increasing power of computer users and the advent and growth of strategic planning and data administration systems. A copy of the summary chart depicting the six stages from the 1979 article is included in Case 1–1, Bolle Navigation Systems.

The DP stages concept is particularly useful to managers considering the development and/or acquisition of new automated systems because they should be able to visualize where their organization is on the stage continuum. They may be able to foresee coming stages and prepare to control the possible damaging effects or take advantage of the benefits.

However, what is even more valuable is the knowledge that an organization probably has to progress step by step through the stages. Attempting to leap ahead and skip stages leads to serious disruptions because neither the DP/IS organization nor the business functional groups and corporation overall have gained the technical know-how and management experience to deal with advanced machinery and concepts.

It is also fascinating that very large, complex organizations—such as conglomerates—may have one division or subsidiary clearly in stage 2 while another is in stage 3. In fact, 10 years after the second Nolan article, in today's environment of expert systems, local area networks, powerful microcomputers, international telecommunications, CIOs, office automation, and desktop publishing, even small organizations may see themselves at stage 6 or 5 vis-à-vis data processing, stage 4 or 3 as far as databases are concerned, stage 2 in the implementation of office automation or decision support systems, and stage 1 with respect to expert systems and artificial intelligence applications. Again, the moral is that it is well to weigh the stage considerations carefully before undertaking high risk, expensive conversions to new systems, especially those employing advanced technologies beyond the experience level of the organization technical experts and users.

BOLLE NAVIGATION SYSTEMS

Case 1–1, which can be used—like Case A, Automated Procurement Process—as an introduction to IS, is a fine vehicle for discussions centering on Kroenke's five components of computer systems and Nolan and Gibson's stages of DP growth.

The primary character in the case, the director of Information Systems, also recognizes five components. Though they are not the same five, the in-depth

---

[5]Richard L. Nolan, "Managing the Crises in Data Processing," *Harvard Business Review,* March–April 1979.

presentation of his point of view provides the instructor and class with a splendid occasion to compare the two definitions and to form their own sense of what a computer system is.

In addition, the Bolle case gives the teacher two other teaching opportunities: (1) to discuss the competing strengths and weaknesses of system flow charts and data flows diagrams when used in the analysis phase of a development project, and (2) to present a brief description of configuration management, an elaborate control process used by all high-volume manufacturing suppliers of large, expensive federal systems, machinery, and equipment.

Case 1–1 Bolle Navigational Systems Division: Business Information Systems

Sheldon Haney is the director of Information Systems at Bolle Navigational Systems Division (NSD). He reports directly to the vice president of Finance in 1987; in 1986, he reported to the controller. The elevation of his position reflects the corporate acknowledgement of the growing importance of the IS group in the organizational structure. Exhibits 1, 2, and 2a illustrate this change, as well as the consolidation of the Denver group.

Exhibit 3 provides a history of Information Systems stages of growth and major accomplishments over the past 14 years. As Sheldon Haney stated, one of his major problems is the development of the next five-year plan. The IS group is just completing the last five-year plan. Under normal circumstances, his staff would be developing a new five-year plan; with the Navigational Systems Division currently on the auction block, it is impossible to engage this process. No one is certain of the future right now. Will corporate retain the division or divest it? Sheldon is currently stalling, functioning on his one-year plan until these decisions are made.

HISTORY

Bolle Navigational Systems Division (NSD) began in the 1950s as the Southwest Bay Electrical Supplies Company. In 1970 it was acquired by the Bolle Corporation, was relocated to San Bernadino, California, and started hiring new people, increasing from 200 employees to today's more than 1,600. In 1979 Southwest

---

This case was prepared by Gene Dankewicz. Names, locations, and financial data have been disguised.

EXHIBIT 1   Bolle Corporation, Navigational Systems Division, Information Systems Organization Chart (June 12, 1986)

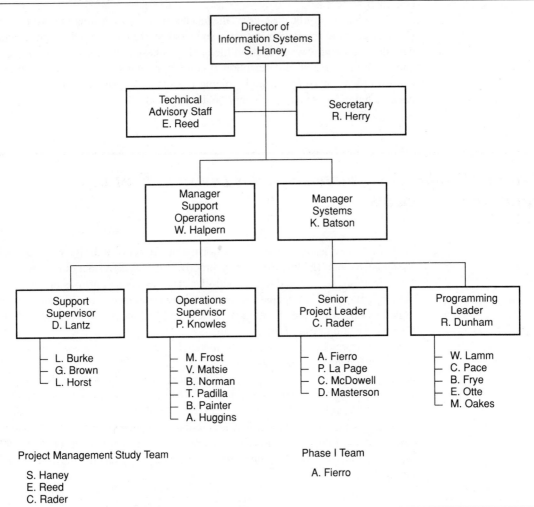

Project Management Study Team

S. Haney
E. Reed
C. Rader

Phase I Team

A. Fierro

Bay Electrical Supplies Division was renamed Bolle Electronics Division (ED) and entered a sustained growth period of about 20 percent per year in sales.

During this same period, the Bolle Corporation developed a new corporate strategy to change its image as a large sprawling conglomerate of all types of electrical supplies to a very select producer of high-technology electronic products. Bolle ED survived this change as part of the Bolle Defense Systems Group.

The Defense Systems Group was one of the most profitable in the corporation. As Bolle ED became more and more profitable, the corporate controls lessened.

EXHIBIT 2   Bolle Corporation, Navigational Systems Division, Information Systems Organization Chart (June 1, 1987)

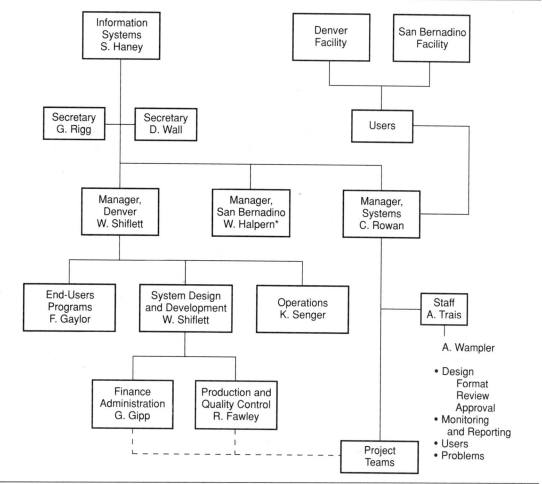

*See Exhibit 2a.

In early 1986, Bolle ED was merged with Denver's NSD to improve Denver's marketability. By combining the two groups into one division and leaving them geographically separated, Bolle introduced unique challenges for the top management as well as for the IS group. In June 1986, corporate announced its intent to divest the entire Defense Systems Group in an effort to resolve corporate cash flow problems. As of today, one of the three divisions in the defense group has been sold, and two —including NSD—remain in limbo.

Bolle Navigational Systems Division (NSD) is primarily a defense contractor whose main customers are the U.S. Navy and Coast Guard. The Denver branch

EXHIBIT 2a   Bolle Corporation, Navigational Systems Division, Information Systems Organization Chart: San Bernadino Facility (June 1, 1987)

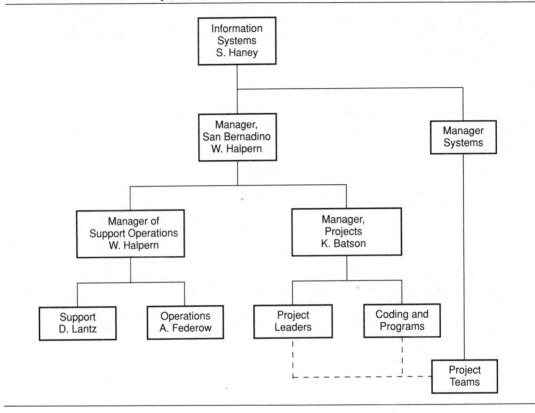

of the division is the prime supplier of attack submarine periscopes, and the San Bernadino location develops and produces ocean navigational (LORAN—Long Range Navigation) systems. Bolle currently controls about 72 percent of the market for ocean LORAN systems. Over the last three years, the defense industry has seen the phaseout of cost-plus contracts and experienced increasing pressure from the current administration to reduce costs. Almost all contracts today are awarded on a cost-competitive basis.

EXHIBIT 3   Bolle Corporation, Defense Systems Group, Bolle Electronics

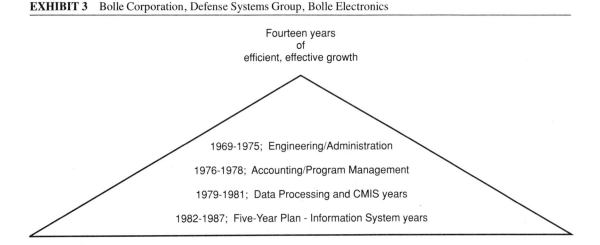

Fourteen years
of
efficient, effective growth

1969-1975; Engineering/Administration

1976-1978; Accounting/Program Management

1979-1981; Data Processing and CMIS years

1982-1987; Five-Year Plan - Information System years

BOLLE'S IS GROUP

The organization that exists today at Bolle NSD has experienced many changes since the acquisition of the Southwest Bay Electrical Supplies Company. The rapid growth and infusion of personnel from the two locations has produced a corporate culture that expects change and accepts new challenges readily. Bolle has always taken great pride in being on the leading edge of technological advancements and uses this technology advantage consistently in its marketing strategy. The Information Systems Group has evolved out of this "advancing the state-of-the-art" environment and reflects the dynamic, progressive corporate culture.

Three managers report to the director, IS: the manager of Support Operations, the manager of Systems, and the manager of the Denver facility. The manager of Support Operations is responsible for ensuring the integrity and security of the company's data and systems at all times—including installation, operation, and maintenance. The manager of Systems is responsible for the development and implementation of new systems. The manager of the Denver facility is responsible for all DP functions in Denver.

The IS group maintains a distributed processing local area network (LAN) that connects three major buildings at the San Bernadino location by means of a Ethernet coaxial cable. Major elements of the system include three HP-3000 mainframes and one VAX 11. The LAN permits a user to access any computer from a single terminal and is capable of high-speed transfer of data between CPUs. Word processing has expanded from a central group to all secretaries in the division.

The system also utilizes electronic mail, TELEX, computer graphics, CAD/CAM, FAX, and limited robotics, all of which illustrates Bolle's continued commitment to being a highly technical competitor in the electronics industry.

THE INTERVIEW WITH SHELDON HANEY

In an interview, Sheldon Haney presented a complete overview of Information Systems at Bolle NSD. Some of the key issues he addressed are:

1. IS environment at Bolle NSD.
2. Role of IS in the division.
3. IS objectives.
4. Major elements of the IS group: people, hardware, software, data, and budget.

The following paragraphs provide additional material relating to these issues.

IS Environment

"I relate my five-year plan to John Diebold's statement that, 'The organizations that will excel in the 1980s will be those that manage information as a major resource.' I really believe very strongly that this department must control its information resources, improve user relations, and increase top-management involvement.

"In terms of Richard Nolan's six stages of IS growth, Bolle NSD is solidly in the fourth stage and is beginning to exhibit some stage 5 growth.[1] Functional areas of the division are learning accountability, and some are effectively accountable. The tailored planning and control systems of stage 4 are continuing, while shared data and common systems in stage 5 have emerged. The corporate intent to divest may negatively affect the IS function. Nolan associates this stage of growth (4) with users who have accepted the cost of IS service (see Exhibit 4). As the real value is perceived, users begin to demand increased support and are willing to pay whatever it costs. At the same time, the uncertainty of the near future has capital expenditures at all-time lows; my budget is being affected negatively, just like the other departments.

"Since the current five-year plan has almost been completed, Bolle NSD has changed from batch-oriented reporting to on-line: data entry, reports, and user-generated queries. In order to accommodate general-purpose query, proper project planning and implementation must be initiated. Above all, the plan must be amenable to change as new technologies and concepts evolve. As the trend con-

---

[1]Richard L. Nolan, "Managing the Crises in Data Processing," *Harvard Business Review,* March–April 1979.

EXHIBIT 4   Six Stages of Data Processing Growth

Six stages of data processing growth

Growth Processes	Stage I Initiation	Stage II Contagion	Stage III Control	Stage IV Integration	Stage V Data administration	Stage VI Maturity
Applications portfolio	Functional cost reduction applications	Proliferation	Upgrade documentation and restructuring of existing applications	Retrofitting existing applications using data base technology	Organization integration of applications	Application integration "mirroring" information flows
DP organization	Specialization for technological learning	User-oriented programmers	Middle management	Establish computer utility and user account teams	Data administration	Data resource management
DP planning and control	Lax	More lax	Formalized planning and control	Tailored planning and control systems	Shared data and common systems	Data resource strategic planning
User awareness	Hands off	Superficially enthusiastic	Arbitrarily held accountable	Accountability learning	Effectively accountable	Acceptance of joint user and data processing accountability

Level of DP Expenditures

Transition Point

Source: Richard L. Nolan, ''Managing the Crises in Data Processing,'' *Harvard Business Review*, March–April 1979.

tinues away from batch processing, we'll see more on-line report/query and modeling systems supported by fourth-generation languages. This will also involve more detail and complexity in security, training, and interpersonal development.

"The merger with the Denver operation has added still another variable to the plan because now we have to merge their software and hardware systems over fairly significant geographical distances.

The Role of IS

"As director of Information Services at Bolle NSD, one of the first things I did was develop a report that I use to describe my department and to help define its major elements. It begins with the role of IS in the division and touches on these five major issues:

1. Become proactive rather than reactive, to effectively solve business problems.
2. Develop a charter for Information Systems.
3. Position IS as the integrator of all functional groups.
4. Provide an evolutionary path to change.
5. Create cost savings/avoidance solutions for the division to work smarter.

IS Objectives

"In IS, we're unanimous on five things we have to do:

1. Break away from the DP Mentality; that is:
   Avoid excessive paper procedures.
   Get rid of the 'we-they' attitude.
   Improve interdepartmental functionality.
2. Emphasize the systems approach.
   Interface all functional groups across the division (see Exhibit 5).
   Permit the users to have access to data on an as-needed basis.
   Permit the users to write and execute programs.
   Identify questions before providing answers.
3. Encourage user involvement by:
   Building user groups.
   Helping them to feel—and be—a part of the effort.
   Making it a work/system 'ownership' with the focus on responsibility.
4. Implement the five-year plan (see Exhibit 6).
5. Support 20 percent + compounded annual NSD gross sales growth rate.

EXHIBIT 5   Information Systems Users Group Organization Chart

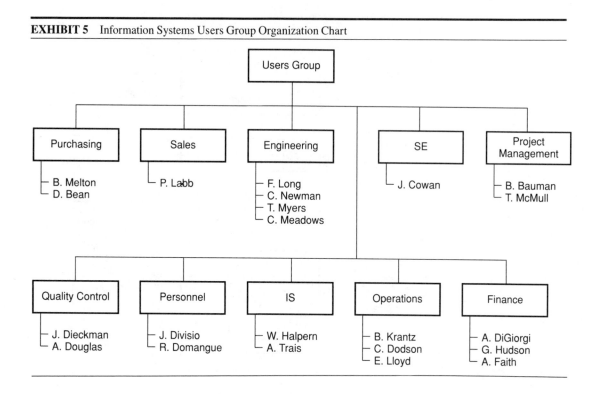

Major Elements of the IS Group

"I see five—I know, I know; everything comes in five—I see five major elements in any IS operation but not the same five that Dave Kroenke identified. His were: people, hardware, software, data, and procedures. Mine are: people, hardware strategy, software, data, and budget. Let me take those one at a time.

People.   "I believe the concept of user-friendly rapidly loses its well-intentioned meaning in a multiuser environment, with many integrated systems running on a common CPU. If manufacturing can't get the information it needs to build the products, there will be no money to pay the bills. But if finance doesn't pay the bills, then there will be no material to build the products. It's a vicious circle, and IS is squarely in the middle.

"It's a fact that users, by their very nature, tend to be selfish; they only see their own deadlines and generally have no conception about the various factors that impact on the information processing cycle. I prefer a user-responsible ap-

EXHIBIT 6   How Does the Five-Year Plan Work?

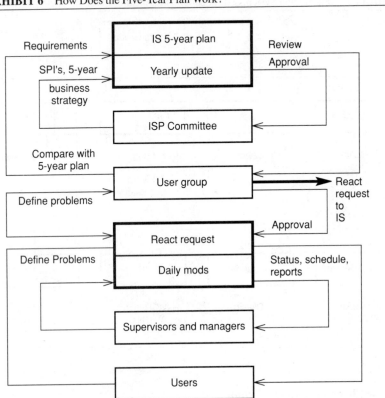

proach to this problem. I stress that, as long as systems are integrated, we have to be constantly aware of the across-the-board implications. I see user-responsibility differing from user-friendly in these ways:

1. The user is not always right. Each user might know what he or she wants, but, if satisfying one particular user's needs interferes with the operation of other systems, trying to make that first user happy may not be the way to go.
2. IS cannot always immediately respond to the needs of each user. We must evaluate the overall impact first.
3. IS must occasionally make unpopular decisions to protect the integrity of the data. Inconvenience to users to ensure data security after a power failure might be unpopular, but it's also responsible.

"I suppose the bottom line is that IS must serve many masters but really serve only one—the users as a whole. That's where the user-responsibility becomes the operating concept of the IS Department—being friendly to one user may not be responsible to the rest of the users. (See Exhibit 5.)

"Okay. That about covers the people aspect. Let's move on to hardware.

Hardware Strategy. "Our intentions and druthers, vis-à-vis hardware, go along these lines:

1. We must move toward distributed processing, which to us means:
   Centralize the management of our information resources.
   Establish corporatewide priorities, IS planning, standards, and cost reductions.
2. Continue to increase productivity/decrease overhead costs as a result of efficiency gained through office automation.
3. Choose hardware that best meets our needs from mature, stable companies and packaged software that can be run on similar equipment.
4. Improve telecommunications through the use of Telenet/Telemail.

Software. "Although it may be more efficient to purchase packaged software, we were having one devil of a time adapting some of the applications to our specific needs. We'd become involved more and more in customizing the programs, which was costing us a lot of time and expense. So, we set the following software support goals:

1. We provide full support:
   Under maintenance:

   • Our number one priority is when a system breaks.
   • Our number two priority is when the business or legal requirements change.

   Vis-à-vis development, we use project leaders to develop new systems.
   With respect to enhancements, new reports and changes to user-written reports will receive consulting support.
   To data center operations.
   Under security, we include:

   • Physical access to failures.
   • Logical access to CPUs.
   • Data backed up and archived off-site.

2. We furnish partial support to:
   Enhancements (above).
   Limited to PCs.
   Limited to OA, but with lots of training.
   Training to project leaders, user groups, and the ISP committee.

3. We give no support to:
   Data entry (phased out).
   Preparation of reports/special forms.

   "In spite of all that, our policy now on purchasing software is that wherever possible, we shall use purchased software packages to meet the needs of our users because we have found that proven packages can shrink lead times, reduce risks, and improve quality over custom-designed systems.

"Software package acquisition will follow this standardized methodology:

- Define requirements from IS user.
- Define corporate and other requirements.
- Select a package based on match.
- Install the system and then interface to other IS systems.
- Modify only if absolutely necessary.

Data.   "I suppose the magic words for data are security and responsibility. Under data, we include the following:

1. Security.
    We must have a backup plan—four generations of full backup, cross-training of people, and so on.
    Controlled physical protection of the computer room—card key, smoke detectors, halon gas, power protection, and temperature and humidity control.
    Controlled logical access to the computer data means:

    - Access onto the LAN (password).
    - Access onto each computer (44, 66, VAX).
    - Access into a particular account/application (password).
    - Registration number for each person.
    - Access into certain data (password).

2. Data responsibility.
    As we progress to on-line systems, data entry and data integrity will migrate to the user areas and become their responsibilities.

3. Data management.
    DBMS—Image, Relate, and so on.
    Database administration.
    Data communication—LAN, CPU-to-CPU.
    Understand data dependencies—each functional area has use of the division database.
    Report writer—information for users so they'll be able to generate their own reports.

4. Data sharing.
    Use hardware and software technologies conducive to interfacing.
    Employ loosely coupled systems that pass data back and forth at the daily close of business.
    Run a CRT on the computer that has all the data.
    Run similar computers closely coordinated with shared data.
    Expect users to no longer act independently, but to coordinate their actions with other users. We handle that by:

- Transferring control of data to other users.
- Negotiating definitions with users sharing the same data.

Budget.   ''Budgets have really been a problem lately, at least more so than is normally the case, for everybody. Nevertheless, we're trying to continue business as usual, pushing accountability and planning.

1. The data center has budgetary accountability. It doesn't matter that it will be a profit center (applied on chargeback or overhead basis).
2. We have to define and monitor controllable and noncontrollable items.
3. The management policies of the budget should follow corporate guidelines. Computer groups are just like any other functional group in the organization when it comes to financial planning and control.
4. Someone must determine whether computers should be acquired using capital money or lease money or rental.
5. Our budgeting techniques should be flexible and permit, where appropriate:
   Incremental budgeting (projections)—for most people.
   Zero-based budgeting using decision packages.
   Baseline budgeting (baseline budget + decision packages). Or
   Budgeting DP as a percent of Sales for the company, utilizing:

   - Guidelines.
   - International data corporation estimates.
   - *Industry Week* articles.
   - The *Datamation* yearly survey.

6. IS group must:
   Use nonprime time at ERCC.
   Increase operation efficiencies (i.e., cross-training, temporary people during peak loads, and third shift).
   Obtain new tools for programming and system development (ALERT, HPTOOLSET, ADAGER).
7. Functional groups must:
   Review their reports for possible reduction or elimination.
   Train users on systems in-place.
   Consider capital investments to reduce costs; some items to think about are:

   - Decision support for financial planning; such things as:
     HP 125 and 150 Business Assistant—forecasts, budgets, reports, presentations (color overheads).
     SEL 164 computer.
   - Fourth-generation languages that would allow users to generate their own reports.

8. Support.
   We should discuss new software techniques at the MIS manager's group meeting every six months.

There has to be closer IS support and training.

All IS cost should be brought into the in-house computers by 1988.

Summary.   ''I guess it's time to pull it all together and summarize. We think it all comes down to this: We've got to do better at working together. This means:

1. Recognize and support NSD goals and strategies.
2. Work together to clearly and completely identify business information requirements.
3. Keep each other informed, in order to:
   Minimize misunderstandings.
   Maximize productivity.
   Minimize costs, so we'll be cost effective.
   Understand each other's problems; to me, that means:

   • Support each other.
   • Work for common solutions.

Jointly, we can establish a clear and mutually acceptable working arrangement, incorporating:

   • React/Cycle/IS responsibility concept.
   • User groups.
   • Personnel interfaces.''

CONCLUSION

At the end of Sheldon Haney's interview and presentation, the researcher, a Bolle corporate-level employee, thanked him and gathered up her notes and tape recorder. As she walked back to her office, she couldn't help being impressed: Bolle really was on the leading edge of technology in the information systems field. At the same time, she wondered how Haney would solve some of the more serious issues he had raised, considering the intended divestiture and its negative affects on capital expenditures across the division. The timing was bad because users were really just beginning to appreciate the possibilities of IS and demanding more. The problems presented by the merger with the Denver facility and the growing problems associated with adapting packaged software to the functional user groups across the division only added to the complexities of the situation.

QUESTIONS

1. Where do you place the Bolle Navigation Systems Division on Gibson's six-stage continuum of EDP growth? Support your answer.
2. Where is your organization on that continuum?
3. Which definition of a computer system — Kroenke's or Dresser's — do you favor? Why?
4. Be prepared to describe your definition of a computer system and be able to explain why your version is different.
5. Discuss the five-year plan (Exhibit 6) relative to Nolan and Gibson's stage hypothesis.
6. List — in order of their importance — the most important issues and problems Jim Dresser raised and explain how you decided on their relative importance.
7. Do you agree with Jim's proposed solutions to the issues and problems? If you do, explain why. If you do not, support your reasons for disagreeing.
8. How should Jim implement his proposed solutions within the context of the five-year plan? Or must the plan be changed? If so, how should he go about making those changes?

Chapter 2

Database

DEFINITIONS OF DATA AND DATABASES

Many textbooks introduce the subject of databases in a chapter covering file structure or file organization, file access or processing, and file management. Usually, the chapter will include several pages describing embedded pointers, secondary keys, inverted lists, and hashing algorithms. Students who like programming are attracted to the technical jargon and intricate linkages that unite computer hardware and software.

Typical end users, however, have no need for that degree of technical detail. The users' supervisors and managers have even less need to understand these matters; still, they do depend on files and computers. Therefore, since the focus of this chapter is on the management of databases, which means access to and processing of files, we shall omit many of the technical details and concentrate on issues, concepts, and management systems.

Knowing the basic building blocks of a computer file makes it easier to understand what database management is attempting to do. Schultheis and Sumner describe data storage and organization as follows:

> Data stored in a computer-based, electronic filing system are usually stored in their most elementary form: binary digits or bits. These bits are then organized into characters (or bytes), the bytes into data elements, the data elements into records, and the records into files.
>
> A **data element,** or **field,** is a logical collection of characters. For example, the data element for an employee's last name is a collection of characters that make up that name.
>
> A **record** is a collection of logically grouped data elements. For instance, an employee record might contain these data elements: employee number, last name, first name, middle initial, street address, city, state, ZIP code, date hired, department, job title, and hourly rate of pay. A record is usually a collection of data elements describing an *entity.*

FIGURE 2–1 Building Blocks of a Database File System

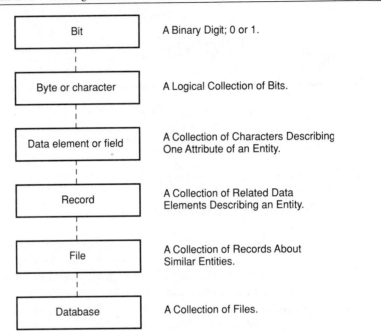

Adapted from Robert Schultheis and Mary Sumner, *Management Information Systems: The Manager's View* (Homewood, Ill.: Richard D. Irwin, 1989), p. 193.

A **file** is a collection of records of one type. For instance, a set of employee records for a firm is usually called the employee file. (See Figure 2–1.)

A **database** is a collection of files.[1]

DATA MANAGEMENT ISSUES

Deciding what a firm's database is to be —and what it is not to be—are important decisions. A number of issues must be settled before those decisions can be reached. The issues are not simple and include content, access, organization, accuracy, integrity, security, privacy, and cost.

DATABASE CONCEPTS

While managers entering the database world find themselves busy merely addressing the issues described above, they also have problems that are a result of

---

[1]Robert Schultheis and Mary Sumner, *Management Information Systems: The Manager's View,* Chapter 6 (Homewood, Ill.: Richard D. Irwin, 1989).

the firm's prior use of data processing applications and files. Most companies built their automated files over many years, usually one application at a time, employing different programmers and sometimes different programming languages as well.

Data Independence

One problem concerns data independence; that is, the way that data files are arranged to be read by programming statements. An example from Schultheis and Sumner pictures the predicament nicely:

> For example, the equipment repair application program was designed to read and write to a record with the exact fields, arranged in the exact order, with the exact field lengths that the equipment repair record contained. Other programs would be unable to read that record unless those programs were redesigned to that record's specifications.[2]

Data Redundancy

Few examples demonstrate the meaning of the term *data redundancy* better than enrolling in a university and registering for classes. Students submit applications, listing their name, home address, birthdate, and social security number (SSN); after acceptance, they apply for grants and list their name, home address (although they may now reside on campus), birthdate, class, and SSN. Some of them also apply to be College Work-Study students in the Management Information and Decision Sciences department (MI&DS); they fill out the appropriate form and state their name, home address, age, class, typing speed, word processor experience, and SSN. One student slips in a puddle on the way back from MI&SD, sprains her ankle, and is taken to the university clinic, where she fills in a form —asking for her name, home address, marital status, next of kin, campus address (if any), age, Blue Cross-Blue Shield coverage (if any), and, of course, SSN.

Obviously, there is a great deal of data redundancy; much file drawer space and computer memory is wasted.

Data Inconsistency

Less important than wasted computer space, in today's environment of portable 100 MB microcomputers, is the concept of consistency. The data redundancy example illustrates the many opportunities for information to be incorrect. If the student lived in a dormitory, successfully pledged a fraternity, and then moved into the fraternity house, all address records on the campus should be changed;

---

[2]Schultheis and Sumner, *Management Information Systems,* p. 205.

few students would bother. If a woman student married and changed her last name to that of her husband, all the campus records should be changed. Few young women ever return to make the necessary corrections—except for those receiving payroll checks for their work-study hours. All of us remember to have our check mailing address corrected.

Database systems are one solution to the conceptual problems of inconsistency, redundancy, and independence.

DATABASE MANAGEMENT SYSTEMS

Database systems are computer systems in accordance with Kroenke's five-component definition. Not giving adequate attention to hardware, software, data, procedures, and trained people can be as devastating when acquiring a database as it would be with any complex functional application. Therefore, database development, acquisition, operation, and maintenance must be managed.

Database Management Systems (DBMS) are assortments of software that "store data in a uniform way, organize the data into records in a uniform way, and allow access to data in a uniform way."[3] Components of database software programs, which are not the same for all suppliers, include: data dictionaries, data languages, teleprocessing monitors, applications development systems, security software, archiving or recovery systems, report writers, and query languages.[4]

OBJECTIVES OF DATABASES AND DATABASE MANAGEMENT SYSTEMS

One list of database objectives is provided by Everest:[5]

Database Objective	Database Description
Availability	Data should be available for use by applications (both current and future) and by queries.
Shareability	Data applications prepared by one application are available to all applications or queries. No data items are "owned" by an application.
Evolvability	The database can evolve as application usage and query needs evolve.
Data independence	The users of the database establish their view of the database and its structure without regard to the actual physical storage of the data.

---

[3]Schultheis and Sumner, *Management Information Systems,* p. 207.

[4]Schultheis and Sumner, *Management Information Systems,* pp. 209–10.

[5]G. C. Everest, *Database Management: Objectives, System Functions, and Administration* (New York: McGraw-Hill, 1985).

| Data integrity | The database establishes a uniform high level of accuracy and consistency. Validation rules are applied by the database management system. |

With a database system, data is stored only once, which reduces the redundancy problem considerably. At the same time, revisions have to be made only to one set of data, easing the update workload and decreasing the opportunities for data inconsistency and inaccuracy. The data dependence problem is diminished by breaking the link between programs and their data.

ADVANTAGES AND DISADVANTAGES OF DATABASES

The primary advantages of the database approach, as opposed to file processing, are:[6]

- Fast response to information requests.
- Multiple access.
- Lower personnel costs.
- Flexibility.
- Less storage.
- Data integrity.
- Better data management.

Disadvantages of databases include:

- High cost.
- Conversion.
- More sophisticated hardware and software.
- Higher operating expenses.
- Complexity.
- Higher vulnerability to failure.
- Recovery made more difficult.

HARDWARE AND SOFTWARE

Database systems are used on mainframes, minicomputers, and microcomputers, and software has been developed for each. The cost for mainframe database management software, such as DB2 by IBM and IDMS by Cullinet, can be in the hundreds of thousands of dollars. Microcomputer database software, such as

---

[6]Charles S. Parker, *Management Information Systems: Strategy and Action* (New York: McGraw-Hill, 1989), p. 288.

dBASE IV by Ashton-Tate, Inc. and R:Base 5000 by Microrim, can be purchased for well under $1,000 dollars.[7]

It is also possible to interconnect mainframes or minis to microcomputers and to download database information from the larger computers to the micros. Cullinet's Goldengate, for example, allows microcomputer end-users to work with its mainframe database, IDMS/R.[8]

ARNOLD ELECTRONICS AND TECHNICAL TRAINING CORPORATION

The two cases in Chapter 2 illustrate many of the problems associated with database development, design, and implementation. In Case 2–1, the Arnold case, Barbara Barlin, the manager, and Rob Hamm, the analyst, work together to find answers to the data management issues. The case also allows students to use dBASE III+ and follow through the steps Rob takes in designing the data records and screens. That Rob fails in his assignment is more a function of management style than technical incompetence.

In Case 2–2, Technical Training Corporation, a database exists but conflicts arise between the branch that maintains the database and the people who provide current data for updating the records. This case uses both system flow charts and data flow diagrams to show the flow of information within the Equipment Configuration Management Group, presenting an opportunity to compare the advantages and disadvantages of each. Again, along with the analysis and design learning objectives inherent in the exhibits, the organizational conflict demands management action.

Case 2–1 Arnold Electronics

Rob still couldn't believe it had really happened to him, even though the pink dismissal notice was right there in front of him, next to his reworked résumé. "This constitutes two-weeks' notice . . . failure to perform up to professional standards . . . in spite of frequent warnings . . . see Personnel Office for standard references . . . regret this action became necessary." Rereading the official "bureaucratise" did not ease the hurt to his ego nor lessen the growing anger at the unexpected results of the computer inventory project he had just completed.

"I've been at Arnold Electronics for five years now, worked for Barbara Barlin

---

This case was prepared by David M. Kroenke and updated by Jae Bong Yu and Janet B. Lorette.

[7]Schultheis and Sumner, *Management Information Systems,* chap. 5, p. 166.

[8]Schultheis and Sumner, *Management Information Systems,* chap. 6, p. 211.

the last three years, and now I'm out,'' he agonized to himself. ''I knew she wasn't pleased with how the micro inventory project was going, but this really floors me,'' he continued, trying to understand what had happened and why. ''Where did I go wrong? What should I have said, during one of the management reviews, that might have made the difference? Did someone have it in for me?''

THE COMPANY

Arnold Electronics is a multibillion dollar manufacturer of electronic equipment and computers. The Marketing department inventory records at one of the Arnold divisions indicates assignment of 40 personal computers, valued at $185,000, to the department. These personal computers are available typically for two- to four-week periods to personnel working on special projects. The computers differ in the amount of memory, disk storage capacity, and peripheral devices available; some have dual floppy disk drives, some are XTs, some ATs, some have color monitors, and most have graphics and communications boards.

THE MARKETING DEPARTMENT

Barbara Barlin, the manager of Marketing, has a staff of 62 people. A large part of the staff's responsibility is the processing of data on past sales, economic trends, industry forecasts, and so forth.

Employees work in teams on projects that last from 2 to 12 weeks. A typical project attempts to answer questions such as, ''Why have sales been flat on the XYZ oscilloscope in the last six months?'' The team would examine past sales, industry trends, technological change, and similar data, in an attempt to answer this question.

Clearly, the department depended heavily on the power and flexibility of its microcomputers. When Barbara Barlin took over the department four years previously, she found her staff (and Finance, Personnel, and Accounting) sharing a remote job entry station that included 10 terminals and a printer. Frequent breakdowns of the printer forced her staff to pick up printouts in the headquarters building computer center. It was through her efforts that 40 personal computers had been added to Marketing's inventory — 15 in her second and third years and 10 more at the start of the current fiscal year. However, Barbara would like to have better control over the usage of the equipment as well as over its physical location.

THE COMPUTER INVENTORY DILEMMA

First, Barbara wants to know who has what equipment, and where is it? She knows the department has 40 computers, but she cannot say, at any given moment, where they are. Peripherals such as modems and printers are another difficult problem, since there are not enough to have one of each per computer; they tend to be moved around even more than the personal computers. While the department does routinely complete a manual physical inventory of this equipment on the first Monday of each month, equipment locations are not certain between inventories.

Second, the Marketing department would like to see more efficient use of their computer equipment. Demands for more hours of computer availability have been met by buying more capacity. Some of these purchases may be unnecessary and could be met, Barbara suspects, simply by rearranging the assignments of existing computers. Individuals have claimed that ''some people around here have more capacity than they use or will ever need!''

Finally, Barbara would like to have better data on computer usage for budgeting and planning purchases. Equipment purchase, including authorization to commit the funds, takes three to four months. Unfortunately, without usage data from an allocation system, the department does not know it needs more computers until the need is imminent.

FACING UP TO THE PROBLEM

Other demands on Barbara's time took precedence until she learned about the theft of several thousands of dollars of computer equipment from another department (Inventory Security and Control). Realizing she had too little control over her own equipment and could postpone the decision no longer, Barbara asked one of her analysts, Rob Hamm, to look into the possibility of building an allocation system to track her computer inventory.

THE TASK ASSIGNMENT

When Rob was given this assignment on Friday, October 12th, he asked Barbara who would be the potential users of the system. Barbara said she would be the user. When Rob asked if she really intended to do her own data entry, she answered, ''No, I guess my secretary, Marilyn, will do that.''

''So you and your secretary will be the major users. Suppose I'm working as an analyst, and I want to know where there's a computer with enough memory to run ENABLE (a popular integrated product). Can I, as a staff analyst, use this system to find out?''

''Sure,'' said Barbara.

''OK; so the major users will be you, your secretary, and the analysts. To do this project well, I'll need input from both you and your secretary, as well as from some of the analysts. Will you make time available for me to talk to them?''

''How much time will it involve?''

Rob pondered. ''Let's say a total of three days to do requirements. A day each for you, your secretary, and one of the analysts.''

''Done,'' said Barbara. ''Now, how long will it take you to do requirements?''

"Oh, three-and-a-half days. I'll start Monday after I finish the laser rangefinder project, if that's all right."

"OK, but be sure you're allowing yourself enough time."

REQUIREMENTS DEFINITION

Rob began by identifying the project team: "I guess that's me," he muttered to himself. "I've got three days of the user's time. That and three days of my own time should get me through requirements. By then, I'll know the scope of the project, and will be able to ask for more help, if I think I need it."

USER INTERVIEWS

Rob started by arranging two-hour appointments with Barbara, her secretary, and with another of the analysts, Charlie Swartz. He picked Charlie because he and Charlie disagreed on almost everything. "That way, I'll be sure to get another opinion."

Rob prepared the interview outline shown in Exhibit 1. He conducted the interviews on Monday, and on Tuesday, he summarized his understandings of the

---

EXHIBIT 1   Rob's Interview Outline

  I. Purpose of the interview
     A. My assignment
     B. Nature of the study
     C. Why I need your help
 II. What is your perception of the problem?
     A. What ought to be
     B. What is
     C. Is it worth considering?
III. Specific requirements
     A. Questions you would like answered
     B. Reports (with format) you want
     C. Queries
     D. Need for screens
 IV. Special issues
     A. How frequently do you use this system?
     B. Time constraints?
     C. Fears and concerns?
     D. Foresee any pitfalls for me?
  V. Conclusion
     A. Thanks for your help
     B. I'll be calling for a review meeting
     C. Think of anything, call me at Ext. 2345

EXHIBIT 2   Statement of the Problem: Barlin

- I'd like to know who's got what equipment, where it's located, and how long they've had it. Right now, all I know is who had it at the start of the month.
- I'd like to know how much we use our equipment. Do we need new equipment? If so, what and when? Currently, I don't know until the need is imminent. Do we have excess equipment?

---

problem and the basic requirements. The statement of the problem is shown in Exhibit 2.

A PROTOTYPE SYSTEM

Tuesday afternoon, Rob was thinking about the best way to present the requirements. From working with microcomputers as an analyst, Rob knew how to use a microcomputer database management system (DBMS) called dBASE III + . "It shouldn't be that hard," he thought, "to build a prototype of this system. I'll define the database and build one screen and one report. Also, I'll show how to answer several queries. That will illustrate the nature of the system. I can then describe other screens and reports on paper."

Rob worked Wednesday and part of Thursday to build the prototype system. He defined a database having the structure summarized in Exhibit 3. There are two files (called *relations* in dBASE III +): (a) SYSTEM and (b) SYS–USE. Rob built a screen to input SYS–USE data (see Exhibit 4). He intended to use the screen to show Marilyn (Barbara's secretary) how to enter the data. He then typed in and loaded SYSTEM and SYS–USE data (see the Appendix at the end of this chapter). That way, he did not have to build screens for both relations. "I'll do it later, if we get that far," he thought.

Next, Rob built a System History report on the SYS–USE relation. It showed the use of each system since its purchase date (Exhibit 5). Finally, he described the dBASE query capability and used it to write several typical questions (see Exhibit 6).

On Thursday morning, when Rob saw how he was progressing, he scheduled a review meeting with Barbara, Marilyn, and Charlie for Friday afternoon. He planned to present the prototype, his understanding of the requirements, and a summary of feasibility. The meeting was set for 3:00.

Once he had the meeting scheduled, Rob finished the prototype and then typed his understanding of requirements. This was about a seven-page report (Exhibit 7 shows its table of contents). Typing the report took a little more time than Rob had expected it would. In addition, he decided to take a few minutes, after all, to build a screen for the SYSTEM relation.

Time passed very quickly Friday morning. Realizing he wouldn't be ready for the meeting at 3 PM, Rob called Marilyn at 11 AM and asked to reschedule the meeting for Monday, right after lunch. Marilyn seemed disturbed at the change,

---

EXHIBIT 3   Database Structure—Summary

(a)

Structure for database :   A:SYSTEM.dbf
Number of data records: 4
Date of last update   :   04/18/89

Field	Field Name	Type	Width	Dec
1	SYS_ID	Numeric	3	
2	CPNUM	Numeric	10	
3	MONITOR	Character	2	
4	MEMSIZE	Numeric	4	
5	NUMDSKET	Numeric	2	
6	NUMNDISK	Numeric	2	
7	PRINTER	Character	10	
8	PLOTTER	Character	10	
* * Total * *			43	

(b)

Structure for database :   A:SYS–USE.dbf
Number of data records: 6
Date of last update   :   04/20/89

Field	Field Name	Type	Width	Dec
1	SYS_ID	Numeric	3	
2	EMPNUM	Numeric	9	
3	PROJECT	Character	20	
4	STRTDATE	Date	8	
5	ENDDATE	Date	8	
* * Total * *			48	

---

mentioning that Barbara had planned to mention the project at the manager's meeting on Monday morning at 10 AM. At any rate, she promised to advise Charlie of the change and set the meeting for Monday, the 22nd, at 1 PM.

FEASIBILITY ANALYSIS

Rob was nonchalant about technical feasibility. He knew that dBASE III + (or an equivalent system) could manage the requirements as he had defined them. He also knew that one of the department microcomputers had enough memory for DBMS software and the workload. Further, there wouldn't be that much data entry—say one hour per week. Concerning disk requirements, there might eventually be as many as 300 SYSTEM records (which included project data) and 3,000–4,000 SYS–USE records. He rounded up to 5,000 records in total. If each record is 50 bytes long (rounded off from Exhibit 3b's 48 bytes), that's

---

EXHIBIT 4   Sample Screen for SYS–USE Data

@   4, 10 SAY "Press [ESC] when done with this data. . . . . ."
@   8, 37 SAY "PROTOTYPE SCREEN FOR"
@   9, 37 SAY "ENTERING SYS–USE DATA"
@ 13, 19 SAY "SYSTEM-ID:"
@ 13, 37 GET SYS–USE–>SYS_ID
@ 14, 19 SAY "PROJECT NAME:"
@ 14, 37 GET SYS–USE–>PROJECT
@ 15, 19 SAY "STARTING DATE:"
@ 15, 37 GET SYS–USE–>STRTDATE
@ 16, 19 SAY "ENDING DATE:"
@ 16, 37 GET SYS–USE–>ENDDATE

Set Up   Modify   Options   Exit

Press [ESC] when done with this data. . . . . .

                                        PROTOTYPE SCREEN FOR
                                        ENTERING SYS–USE DATA

              SYSTEM-ID: 999
              PROJECT NAME: XXXXXXXXXXXXXXXXXXXX
              STARTING DATE: 99/99/99
              ENDING DATE: 99/99/99

250,000 bytes of data—small enough to fit on a single diskette. Technical feasibility seemed certain.

As for schedule, he couldn't see any reason why it would take him more than a month (if that) to develop the system. They had the hardware already and one DBMS candidate. There wasn't that much data to convert, and the procedures, training, and documentation ought not to take that long. "Say, five weeks at the outside," he guessed.

Rob was less sure of cost feasibility. He didn't know what the value of the system would be. Most of the benefits were intangible. How do you put a dollar figure on knowing where your equipment is? Do you use equipment cost and the amount of your time it takes to locate equipment? Or can you use the value of *not* losing a system to theft, or *not* having to buy a system because of better utilization? Finally, he decided that those were questions for Barbara to decide. "I'll compute the cost of the system, and let her compute the benefits. That's why she gets paid more than I do."

System costs are summarized in Exhibit 8. Rob estimated that a total of six weeks of labor would be required to develop the system—five weeks of his time and one week of the user's time. Since Arnold's standard billing rate for one labor week of senior technical time was $2,000 (including overhead burden), this

EXHIBIT 5   System History Report

Page No.   1
04/26/89

SYSTEM HISTORY REPORT

SYSTEM ID	EMPLOYEE NUMBER	PROJECT NAME	STARTING DATE	ENDING DATE
100	111111111	Vibrator	05/01/88	05/01/88
100	222222222	Rangefinder	06/05/88	07/31/88
100	333333333	Damper	08/01/88	08/31/88
200	444444444	Waveform1	04/12/88	05/17/88
200	555555555	Voltmeter	06/01/88	06/21/88
300	111111111	Longranger	06/01/88	08/01/88

amounted to $12,000. Rob figured $200 for use of the microcomputer, $400 for a DBMS program (Arnold could buy at a substantial discount), and another $300 miscellaneous expense for paper, diskettes, and overhead.

The estimated operation costs are also shown in Exhibit 8. Machine time was calculated by assuming that one tenth of a $5,000 system would be needed. Rob also assumed that the machine needed to be amortized, on a straight-line basis, over two years. Thus, the annual cost of the computer was $250. The miscellaneous expenses were for paper, diskettes, and overhead.

Rob sat down Monday morning, sharpened all his pencils, turned on the micro, and started to review his material for the review at 1 PM. He'd spent all day Sunday reaffirming his data and checking the prototype design. Marilyn had called at 8:30 AM, asking if he'd be ready at 1 PM. He told her, "No problem, boss lady; I'm ready for anything, including Charlie Swartz."

CLASS ASSIGNMENT 1—FOR TEAMS

Each team is to prepare the briefing (10 minutes long) Rob is to present at the 1 PM meeting. Include in your submitted materials the following:

1. Your prepared revisions to Exhibits 1 and 2, plus your reasons for making the changes.
2. Your comments on the adequacy of Exhibit 7.
3. Your version of Exhibit 8 (if different from Rob's) with justification for changes.
4. Questions Rob should expect from Barbara and answers you propose for these questions.
5. A diskette with data loaded (per the Appendix) appropriate to the prototype system Rob has designed (*if a version of dBASE III (or later) is available*).

EXHIBIT 6   Query Capability—Sample Questions

1. What is in all the records in SYSTEM?
Type in:
. USE SYSTEM
. LIST

Record#	SYS_ID	CPUNUM	MONITOR	MEMSIZE	NUMDSKET	NUMNDISK	PRINTER	PLOTTER
1	100	123456	BW	256	1	1	NONE	NONE
2	200	555555	CO	256	2	0	M93	NONE
3	300	456454	BW	512	2	1	M93	J4700
4	400	789726	CO	512	2	2	M93	J4900

2. Which systems do not have a hard disk (NUMNDISK is not zero)?
Type in:
. LIST FOR NUMNDISK <> 0

Record#	SYS_ID	CPUNUM	MONITOR	MEMSIZE	NUMDSKET	NUMNDISK	PRINTER	PLOTTER
1	100	123456	BW	256	1	1	NONE	NONE
3	300	456454	BW	512	2	1	M93	J4700
4	400	789726	CO	512	2	2	M93	J4900

3. What size memory (MEMSIZE) do the color monitor systems (MONITOR = ''CO'') have and what is/are the system number(s)?
Type in:
. LIST SYS_ID, MEMSIZE FOR MONITOR = "CO"

Record#	SYS_ID	MEMSIZE
2	200	256
4	400	512

THE FIRST MANAGEMENT REVIEW

The requirements review meeting lasted two-and-a-half hours. Rob demonstrated the prototype system and then had Marilyn enter sample data. The prototype ran smoothly, and seeing it in operation gave the users greater understanding of the system Rob was proposing. Next, the group discussed Rob's requirements definition and feasibility.

The users were satisfied with the requirements definition, but Barbara had an objection to the design of the database: ''I consider computer equipment to be allocated to individuals, not to projects. So, I want an individual to be responsible, by name, for a system. I'm going to tell the staff that they are responsible for safeguarding the equipment assigned to them. And I want to know who's been assigned what. I also want the reports to show the person's building location and telephone number.''

Rob responded that this change could be made easily; if Barbara was that adamant about making individuals responsible, then a form should be developed documenting which equipment had been transferred from one person to another.

EXHIBIT 7   Table of Contents—Requirement Report

  I. Problem definition (see Exhibit 2)
 II. Specific requirements
  A. Reports needed (like Exhibit 5)
   1. Name of report
   2. Sample format
  B. List of questions to be answered by queries (like Exhibit 6)
  C. Screen formats (like Exhibit 4)
III. Constraints
  A. Hardware (use what we have)
  B. Programs (must run on our hardware)
  C. Data (don't delete used data—archive it)
  D. Procedures (simple, easy to remember, easy to follow)
  E. People (use people we have—no special personnel)
 IV. Feasibility statement
  A. Technical
  B. Schedule
  C. Cost
  V. Plan for alternative evaluation

Employees could keep a copy of these forms for their own peace of mind and protection.

Considering feasibility, there was little discussion regarding technical or schedule issues. The users agreed with Rob's statements.

Barbara was surprised that the system was so expensive to develop. Rob described the work he would have to do, and Barbara agreed that six labor weeks might be reasonable.

"Look at it this way, Barbara," suggested Rob, "over three years, the total cost of the system is twelve thousand nine plus three times twenty-eight hundred. That's twenty-one thousand—about the cost of five microsystems. With this system, can you save five micros in three years?"

"Maybe," said Barbara slowly. "Yeah, I suppose so. In any case, this system is a form of insurance, isn't it? I guess I have to pay this amount first to control the resource properly. OK; let's proceed. Look into the alternatives, and let me know what you propose."

ALTERNATIVE EVALUATION AT ARNOLD ELECTRONICS

As summarized in Exhibit 9, alternative evaluation at Arnold Electronics was simple. Since Arnold was a manufacturer of a personal computer, the AS-150, the only politically realistic choice of hardware was the AS-150. Concerning programs, Rob identified two micro DBMS products that he thought would meet the need: dBASE III+ and R:base 5000. There were no alternatives regarding

EXHIBIT 8   Computer Allocation System Costs

Development Costs		Operational Costs (annual basis)	
Labor (6 weeks)	$12,000	Labor	
Computer resource	200	Marilyn	$2,000
Computer programs	400	Barbara	200
Miscellaneous	300	Computer	250
Total	$12,900	Miscellaneous	400
		Total	$2,850

data, since the database design was simple and stipulated by requirements.

There were two alternatives regarding procedures. For one, Marilyn would do all of the data entry. No changes would be allowed by any of the staff analysts or by Barbara. When equipment was to be transferred, the analysts would complete a form indicating the transfer had taken place and send a copy of the form to Marilyn. She would use it later to create the new SYS–USE record. Analysts would only be allowed to read (access) the data.

For the second alternative, Marilyn would maintain the data about computer systems and about personnel. The staff analysts would maintain the SYS–USE data themselves. When a system was transferred from one employee to another, the analysts would access the database and change it themselves.

Rob proposed no alternatives regarding personnel. It was clear to him that Barbara, Marilyn, and the staff analysts were to be the users and that no personnel reorganization would be necessary.

CLASS ASSIGNMENT 2—FOR INDIVIDUALS

Each student is to prepare a brief half-page analysis of the strengths and weaknesses of the two alternatives. Recommend one and explain your choice.

THE SECOND MANAGEMENT REVIEW

Rob scheduled a 30-minute meeting with Barbara on the afternoon of the 24th to discuss his alternative evaluation. She listened to what he had to say and agreed with his decision. "OK," she continued, "you have not quite four weeks left. How are you going to use the time?"

"Well, I figure design will take 5 days, and implementation should take about 10 days—7 for construction and 3 for testing and installation. That will give me five days extra for delays, overages, department meetings, and so forth."

EXHIBIT 9 Summary of Alternatives for Computer Allocation System

Component	Alternative
Hardware	No choice, AS-150 must be used
Programs	dBASE III+ or R:base 5000
Data	No choice, fixed by requirements
Procedures	Analysts change SYS–USE data themselves
	or
	Centralized change of SYS–USE data
People	No choice. People and their organizational structure are fixed.

"Fine," said Barbara, "but the way I figure, it's Wednesday of the second week, so you have only a two-day pad, not five. Right?"

"Right," Rob answered reluctantly, adding, "Can we make that three?"

Barbara looked down at her desk calendar, tapped her forefinger nervously a few times, stared hard at Rob for a few seconds, and then responded. "Fine, let me know when you've finished design."

DESIGN AT ARNOLD ELECTRONICS

Data

Rob began the design stage with data. Exhibit 10 shows the format of the two reports the computer allocation system needed to produce. The Manager's Report (a) shows the specifications of each system, and the employee to whom the system is assigned. The Employee Report (b) is a sample report that shows all of the equipment that has been assigned to a particular employee.

Barbara had expressed a need to obtain information about system usage, but, when Rob examined his notes, he found them rather vague. He talked to her on the phone in an attempt to clarify what she wanted, and finally Barbara herself agreed that she didn't know exactly what she wanted in terms of data. She did know, however, what questions she wanted to be able to answer.

"How about this, Barbara," suggested Rob, "dBASE has a feature called *Assistant* that allows you to use menus to query the database. Why don't you use it for a while? It may handle your needs just fine. If not, you could tell me what you wanted, and I'd make the necessary adjustments."

"Fine," she agreed.

After he put the phone down, Rob realized the danger in letting these requirements go unspecified. Later, he might have to change the data definition; he just felt uneasy leaving part of the system so vague. "Still," he thought, "Barbara's needs are vague, and it's a waste to give her a specific report for a need even she

---

EXHIBIT 10   Sample Reports—Manager and Employee

(a)
COMPUTER ALLOCATION SYSTEM
MANAGER'S REPORT

SYSTEM ID	CPU NUMBER	EMPLOYEE NAME	LOCATION	PHONE	PROJECT
100	123455	BROWN	B205	55678	DAMPER
200	555555	SMITH	C118	98350	WAVEFORM1
300	456454	JONES	B207	55889	LONGRANGE
400	789726	JACKSON	C120	45891	WAVEFORM2

(b)

COMPUTER ALLOCATION SYSTEM
EMPLOYEE REPORT

EMPLOYEE: BROWN
The following computer systems are currently assigned to you:

System-id	Cpu number	Printer	Plotter
300	456454	M93	34700

---

doesn't understand.'' Rob wondered about taking a little more time to detail exactly what Barbara's needs were; at that moment, his phone rang, and he rushed to put out the next fire.

The needs of the analysts were easier to pin down. When analysts need a micro system for a new project, they want to know what equipment the department has, where it is, and when it will be available. As Rob thought about it, he realized that it would be great to include a reservation capability in the system. He resisted the temptation to add it, however, because it would take extra time, and besides, Barbara hadn't identified a need.

Although Rob could have defined a report that would meet many of the analysts' needs, he decided, after talking with Charlie, to let them query the database directly. Most of them knew how to use the dBASE query facilities already; finding out if there is a system with a certain plotter, so much memory, a hard disk, available after September 15, and so on, would be easier with a query language than by scanning a potentially long report. Rob reviewed his interview notes and made the list of standard questions analysts ask (see Exhibit 11).

Once the reports and queries had been designed, Rob examined them to determine what data would be needed. He realized that since Barbara wanted equipment to be allocated to specific employees, he would need three relations instead of the two he had developed in the prototype system. The three relations would be SYSTEM, SYS–USE, and a new one he'd name EMPLOYEE. The contents of these relations are shown in Exhibit 12.

EXHIBIT 11   Questions Analysts Want the Allocation System to Answer

1. Which systems have:
     A _____(type) plotter?
     Main memory greater than _____(size)?
     A color monitor?
     Two diskette units?
     A hard disk?
     A _____(type) printer?
2. Who has system _____(number)? What is their location/telephone number?
3. When will system _____(number) be available?
4. What computers are being used by the _____(name) project?

Programs

Rob had decided during alternative evaluation to use dBASE III + . Ashton-Tate, the vendor of dBASE, also sells other products that complement this system. After Rob reviewed the requirements and the Ashton-Tate sales literature, he decided that he would also need the Extended Report Writer. Since the Marketing department had already purchased rights to use this product on all of their machines, no procurement was necessary.

The next step was to plan the structure of command files. Rob decided to build three procedures for Marilyn: one to maintain the EMPLOYEE data, one to maintain the SYSTEM data, and one to produce reports. Pseudocode—which Rob preferred to flow charts when he wanted to explain programming logic—for the EMPLOYEE maintenance procedures is shown in Exhibit 13.

Hardware

The hardware for Marketing's computer allocation system was easy to specify. The system itself had to be an Arnold AS-150, since that was the only politically acceptable system. dBASE III + and related programs required 256 K of main memory, so at least that much had to be available. Rob planned to maintain the database on part of a hard disk and to back it up on diskette. Reports were to be used internally only, so a dot-matrix printer was acceptable. Either a color or a black-and-white monitor would suffice. To summarize, the hardware specification was: an AS-150, 256 K main memory (RAM), at least one hard disk, at least one diskette unit, and a dot-matrix printer.

As it turned out, these requirements were modest. Possibly as many as 8 of Marketing's 40 computers had at least this capacity, including 1 that was assigned permanently to Marilyn and Barbara. Rob checked with Marilyn, and her machine —on a table next to her desk—had quite a bit of unused capacity. In that location,

---

EXHIBIT 12   Contents of Computer Allocation Database

Relation	Contents
SYSTEM	System id, CPU number, monitor type, size of main memory, number of diskette units, number of hard disk units, printer type, plotter type.
EMPLOYEE	Name, employee number, department, location, telephone number.
SYS–USE	System id, employee number, project name, start date, ending date.

---

the analysts would have relatively easy access to the system, and Marilyn still could maintain some control. The computer was locked at night.

Procedures

Next, Rob considered procedures for the system (summarized in Exhibit 14). To maintain the database, Marilyn needed to be informed of changes in employee or system status. She also needed to know when equipment was transferred from one employee to another.

Since Marilyn was the person who typed the department's telephone roster, she was already privy to changes in employee data. Marilyn told Rob that when she typed the new roster, she could save the records of employee changes for input to the computer allocation system.

Changes in system status were a bit more difficult. System data changed when systems were purchased and sold. It also changed when analysts moved equipment (like a plotter) from one CPU to another. Rob developed a form to be executed when these events occurred (see Exhibit 15). The form would be completed by Barbara when equipment was received or sold, and it would be filled out by the analysts when equipment was moved.

Rob developed a second form (System Transfer Form) to document the transfer of a computer from one analyst to another. These forms would be sent to Marilyn for processing.

After talking with Marilyn, Rob decided that she should save employee change data, the System Change Forms, and the System Transfer Forms, and process them in a batch once per week. After making the changes, Marilyn would generate the reports.

As for backup, a dBASE III+ database consists of three files. To make a backup copy, Marilyn needed to copy these files to diskette, using the system's COPY command. According to the procedure, she was to keep backups for three

---

EXHIBIT 13   Pseudocode for Command
File to Maintain EMPLOYEE Data

Present menu with the following choices:

    Add or Change Employee Data
    Delete an Employee Record
    Print Employee List
    Exit

Dowhile not Exit
    For Add or Change:
        Present screen
        Accept choice
    For Delete:
        Obtain employee number
        Execute DELETE ROWS command
    For Report:
        Execute SELECT ALL command
    Present menu
End-do

---

weeks and rotate the diskettes after that. In addition to the backups, Marilyn was to save the forms she had used to generate changes.

For recovery, Marilyn would simply copy the three database files from diskette back to the hard disk. Then she would reprocess the changes made since the diskette copies were generated.

Procedures for the analysts were straightforward. The database was kept on the hard disk at all times. Analysts could access the database using either the dBASE III+ Assistant query facility or the direct dot prompt approach. Procedures would not have to be developed because the analysts knew how to use dBASE III+.

Analysts were precluded from changing this data by passwords. Also, for even greater security, Marilyn refreshed the database from her backup diskette each week.[1] Thus, the cycle of processing was: refresh the database from the prior backup, make changes, generate reports, backup the database, make the database available to the analysts, and repeat. In this way, Marilyn's backup was the single authorized version of the data.

Finally, Rob prepared a short menu procedure so Barbara could access the database. All she had to do was choose the name of the database when prompted to do so. At that point, she could start asking questions using Assistant. Rob provided several examples in his procedure to get her started.

---

[1]There was greater security only if the backup copy was secure.

EXHIBIT 14   Procedures for Maintaining Data in the Computer Allocation Database

---

I. Preparation
   A. Gather documents about EMPLOYEE, SYSTEM, and SYS–USE changes
   B. Start computer, go to allcatn directory
   C. Copy database files to diskette (copy 1)
      1. Put formatted diskette in drive B:
      2. Type: COPY compuse?.* B:compuse?.*
   D. Restore database from previous backup
      1. Put backup diskette in drive B:
      2. Type: COPY B:compuse?.* compuse?.*
         (If backup is bad, restore database from copy1 and proceed.)
   E. Type: dBASE (to start dBASE III + DBMS program)
II. Process employee changes
   A. Execute EMPCHNG procedure
   B. Make additions and modifications
   C. Make deletions
   D. Print EMPLOYEE List
III. Process system changes
   A. Execute SYSCHNG procedure
   B. Make additions and modifications
   C. Make deletions
   D. Print SYSTEM List
IV. Process changes in system allocations
   A. Execute ALLOCHNG procedure
   B. Make modifications
V. Generate reports
   A. Type: exit
   B. Type: xrw
   C. Type: Run MGMTRPT
   D. Type: Run EMPRPT
VI. Backup
   A. Put formatted diskette in drive B:
   B. Type: COPY compuse?.* B:compuse?.*
      (Note: three files should be copied; If not, contact Rob Hamm.)
VII. Recovery: To recover from a backup:
   A. Put backup diskette in drive B:
   B. Go to allcatn directory
   C. Type: COPY B:compuse?.* compuse?.*

People

For this simple system, there were no people to hire nor any organizational changes to implement. Rob simply needed to develop a training plan. He decided to go

---

EXHIBIT 15   Sample Form for Obtaining Data on System
Changes: Computer Allocation Database

System Change Form

Use this form when a new system is received or when
equipment is moved from one system to another. Please fill
in all the data so that we can check our records for accuracy
as we process this form. Thank you.

System id _____(enter NEW if new system)

CPU number _____

Monitor type   BW   COLOR (circle one)

Main memory size _____(in K)

Number of diskette units _____(1 or 2)

Number of hard disk units _____

Printer type _____(Model type or None)

Plotter type _____(Model type or None)

---

over Marilyn's written procedures in detail with her; then, he would show her
how to follow them. If she missed some points, there would be no great harm
because she could always ask him later.

Rob decided to schedule a one-hour meeting with Barbara once he had the
database implemented and sample data constructed. During that meeting he could
show her how to obtain answers to her usage questions with Assistant.

The analysts needed almost no training. Barbara was going to introduce the
equipment transfer form at a staff meeting once the system was finished. At that
time, she was also going to announce her new policy of considering employees
to be responsible personally for the equipment they had been assigned.

After that staff meeting, Rob planned to distribute a letter saying that the
database was available for query by the analysts. He would describe the structure
of the database in the letter (although this really wasn't necessary, since all of
the analysts knew how to obtain the structure of the database from the DBMS
itself).

Completing the people part of the design ended that stage of the inventory
system development process. Unfortunately, it was now late Friday (November
2nd), and Rob couldn't get on Barbara's schedule until 11 AM on Monday (November
5); design had taken longer than he had reckoned for Barbara, but only
two days longer. Rob took his briefcase and left, expecting to work over the
weekend, as usual.

CLASS ASSIGNMENT 3—FOR TEAMS

1. Each team is to prepare the briefing (five to six minutes long) Rob is to present to Barbara at the 11 AM meeting on Monday. Be sure to cover Exhibits 9– 15, and be prepared to support any changes you may recommend.
2. Compare pseudocode and flow charts for portraying the rationale of programming logic.
3. Design the data structure for the relation EMPLOYEE.
4. Do you agree with Rob's reasons for selecting the AS-150? Why or why not?
5. Do you agree with his reasons for selecting Ashton-Tate's dBASE III + ? Why or why not?
6. What potential problems do you see with these two decisions?
7. What questions should he expect Barbara to ask at the meeting? How should he answer?

THE THIRD MANAGEMENT REVIEW

The purpose of the meeting was to have Rob discuss progress up through the design stage with Barbara.

Rob reviewed his design with Barbara. He particularly wanted to know if she thought the reports were adequate and if she was satisfied to use the Assistant query menus to answer usage questions. He also wanted to see if she agreed with the adjustments he had made to the design since the prototype.

Barbara examined the design and was generally pleased with it. She thought the reports were appropriate, and she said she was willing to try Assistant to see if it would handle her questions. If not, she agreed that she would try to be more explicit in describing her needs.

She did have one minor problem with the design, however. "What," she asked, "is the difference between CPU number and System ID? Aren't they really different names for the same thing? Why create a separate System ID?"

"That's a good point. I hadn't really thought about it." Rob reflected. "I've constructed system numbers that are short and easy to remember. CPU numbers are long and hard to remember. That's about the only justification, I guess."

"Well, think about it. I'll go either way, but it seems unnecessary to me," responded Barbara. "Oh, one more thing. I forgot to say that I want to do a physical inventory of the equipment now and then. These checks will be irregular, but I plan about six or seven per year. Make sure the system will help me with these inventories."

Finally, she observed that Rob had taken seven days to complete design, instead of the five he had promised. Rob explained that his estimates were only estimates; while he used all his experience to come up with the days required, the process was "fuzzy" at times, and he was doing his best to meet his commitments to her. Barbara's final comment was, "Alright, I appreciate your efforts and know all about the 'magic' and 'mystery,' particularly in database design. Still, I need to be able to plan, too, so let's try a bit harder to meet our approved schedule.''

Rob left the meeting thinking that he should have been praised highly and should be feeling great, having accomplished as much as he had in the last couple of weeks. Instead, he was depressed.

IMPLEMENTATION AT ARNOLD ELECTRONICS

The implementation of the Computer Allocation System for Arnold's Marketing department was modest since, in relative terms, the system involved only a small amount of data. Also, there were only two reports to construct and a few simple procedures to document. Rob's plan was to construct, test, and install activities in sequence, calling on other analysts only for advice, and then not very often.

CONSTRUCT

It was easy for Rob to install and test the hardware and programs, although trivial problems caused occasional slight delays. Marilyn's computer was already in operation; she had been using it with other systems for some time. To prepare the micro, Rob had only to build a directory to store the programs and data.

Next, Rob obtained a copy of dBASE III+ and the Extended Report Writer from Arnold's internal microcomputer store. The store was able to purchase software and other equipment at a substantial discount because they bought in large volumes. Rob gave the store a purchase acquisition form, since the department was to be billed via the internal accounting system. Once he had the software, he simply copied the programs into the hard disk subdirectory following the vendor's instructions.

DATA DEFINITION

Next, Rob turned his attention to the data component. During design, Rob had worked backward, from reports to data definition; during construction, he worked forward, from data definition to reports. Exhibit 16[2] shows the data definition statements Rob used to create the structure of the database.

When Rob typed the Define COMPUSE command, he was in fact naming the new database COMPUSE. He then began the database definition by providing an owner password. This password determines who can change the data structure and assign other passwords. Rob had to decide who should have this password.

---

[2]Exhibit 16 is the same as Exhibit 3, with the addition of the structure for the EMPLOYEE relation.

EXHIBIT 16   Definition of Database Used

Structure for database   :   A:SYSTEM.dbf
Number of data records :   4
Date of last update   :   04/18/89

Field	Field Name	Type	Width	Dec
1	SYS_ID	Numeric	3	
2	CPNUM	Numeric	10	
3	MONITOR	Character	2	
4	MEMSIZE	Numeric	4	
5	NUMDSKET	Numeric	2	
6	NUMNDISK	Numeric	2	
7	PRINTER	Character	10	
8	PLOTTER	Character	10	
** Total **			43	

Structure for database   :   A:EMPLOYEE.dbf
Number of data records :   6
Date of last update   :   04/26/89

Field	Field Name	Type	Width	Dec
1	EMPNAME	Character	20	
2	EMPNUM	Numeric	9	
3	EMPDEPT	Character	6	
4	EMPLOC	Character	4	
5	EMPPHONE	Numeric	5	
** Total **			44	

Structure for database   :   A:SYS–USE.dbf
Number of data records :   6
Date of last update   :   04/20/89

Field	Field Name	Type	Width	Dec
1	SYS_ID	Numeric	3	
2	EMPNUM	Numeric	9	
3	PROJECT	Character	20	
4	STRTDATE	Date	8	
5	ENDDATE	Date	8	
** Total **			48	

He discussed passwords with Barbara, and she told him that he should be the owner. In addition, however, she wanted Rob to keep her informed of the current password in case of emergency.

Rob used an old phone number as the first owner password. Next, he defined the attributes (items that will be contained within the relations) of the database. At this point, Rob weighed Barbara's point about the duplication of System IDs with CPU numbers. Although he agreed with her about the duplication, he decided to keep both. CPU numbers were just to hard to work with, in his opinion.

Once all of the attributes were described, Rob defined the relations as shown in Exhibit 16. Finally, he defined a modified password for each of the three relations. He used the same value for all of them, since Marilyn would modify all three. This way, Marilyn only had to remember one password.

Next, Rob defined three screens: one each for the EMPLOYEE, SYSTEM, and SYS–USE relations. These screens, which would be used to load and change data, were developed using the dBASE screen-generation utility. They took about 30 minutes each.

Once the screens were created, he could build the command files. Using the pseudocode he had developed during design (see Exhibit 13), Rob wrote constructed sequences of dBASE commands.

At this point, Rob tested the screens and command procedures by using them to create and change test data. He found several keying errors that he had made, but basically, they worked according to his design.[3]

The next step was to build the reports using the Extended Report Writer. Rob also defined the Employee Report in a similar manner. As he examined this report, he realized that it would suffice for Barbara's new requirement regarding physical inventory. When a physical count was to be done, Marilyn could make two copies of the Employee Report. One copy would go to the employees as normal; the other would be given to Barbara for the inventory.

PROCEDURES AND PEOPLE

Manual procedures for Marilyn had been defined during design. Now, Rob documented those procedures and, as part of Marilyn's training, discussed the procedures with her. Together, he and Marilyn created and modified EMPLOYEE, SYSTEM, and SYS–USE data following the procedures and using the command files[4] and test data.

Once Marilyn felt confident with the system, Rob created an empty database to receive the operational data. Marilyn began to create the operational data from records she had been accumulating. She did this at odd moments, between other jobs. Occasionally, higher priority work forced her to skip a day or so.

Concerning Barbara's queries, Rob documented procedures for using Assistant. He then scheduled a meeting with Barbara to show her Assistant's capabilities. Some of the questions that Barbara asked—and the database responses—are shown in Exhibit 17. She was satisfied with the power and flexibility of Assistant, and, for the time being at least, she told Rob not to worry about defining reports

---

[3]See the Instructors' Manual for copies of Rob's test run for EMPCHNG.

[4]This step requires use of command files such as EMPCHNG, available in the Instructor's Manual.

EXHIBIT 17   Sample Requests

1. Show usage for all machines.
   . SELECT A
   . USE SYS–USE INDEX SYS–USE
   . SELECT B
   . USE SYSTEM INDEX SYSTEM
   . SELECT A
   . SET RELATION TO SYS_ID INTO SYSTEM
   . LIST STRTDATE, ENDDATE,B->CPUNUM

Record#	STRTDATE	ENDDATE	B->CPUNUM
1	05/01/88	05/15/88	123456
2	06/15/88	07/31/88	123456
3	08/01/88	08/31/88	123456
4	04/12/88	05/17/88	555555
5	06/01/88	06/21/88	555555
6	06/01/88	08/01/88	456454

2. Show usage for all machines and who has them.
   . SELECT A
   . USE SYS–USE INDEX SYS–USE
   . SELECT B
   . USE SYSTEM INDEX SYSTEM
   . SELECT A
   . JOIN WITH SYSTEM TO NEWDB FOR SYS_ID = B->SYS_ID
   6 records joined
   . USE NEWDB
   . INDEX ON EMPNUM TO NEWDB
      100% indexed   6 Records indexed
   . SELECT A
   . USE NEWDB INDEX NEWDB
   . SELECT B
   . USE EMPLOYEE INDEX EMPLOYEE
   . SELECT A
   . SET RELATION TO EMPNUM INTO EMPLOYEE
   . LIST STRTDATE, ENDDATE, CPUNUM, B->EMPNAME
   Command Line   I<C:>INEWDB   IRec: 1/6
   . LIST STRTDATE, ENDDATE, CPUNUM, B->EMPNAME

Record#	STRTDATE	ENDDATE	CPUNUM	B->EMPNAME
1	05/01/88	05/15/88	123456	ROGER SMITH
6	06/01/88	08/01/88	456454	ROGER SMITH
2	06/15/88	07/31/88	123456	ERIKA JONES
3	08/01/88	08/31/88	123456	BONNIE BROWN
4	04/12/88	05/17/88	555555	ANTHONY JACKSON
5	06/01/88	06/21/88	555555	GILL CARTER

3. Show machine(s) and what type monitor Bonnie Brown has out.
   . SELECT A
   . USE NEWDB INDEX NEWDB
   . SELECT B

EXHIBIT 17 (concluded)

```
. USE EMPLOYEE INDEX EMPLOYEE
. SELECT A
. SET RELATION TO EMPNUM INTO EMPLOYEE
. LIST CPUNUM, MONITOR, B->EMPNAME FOR B->EMPNAME = "BONNIE BROWN"
  Record#   CPUNUM   MONITOR   B->EMPNAME
       3    123456   BW        BONNIE BROWN
```

4. Which machines will be available after 8/15/88? Also what type monitors do those machines have, and who has them now?

```
. SELECT A
. USE NEWDB INDEX NEWDB
. SELECT B
. USE EMPLOYEE INDEX EMPLOYEE
. SELECT A
. SET RELATION TO EMPNUM INTO EMPLOYEE
. LIST B->EMPNAME, MONITOR, ENDDATE FOR ENDATE > CTOD("08/15/88")
  Record#   B->EMPNAME     MONITOR   ENDDATE
       3    BONNIE BROWN   BW        08/31/88
```

for her; he was just to do the tasks required by the previously approved requirements.

Rob prepared a letter to the analysts describing the structure of the computer allocation database. He waited to distribute the letter until after the system installation, however. Rob invited Charlie to use the test data, and Charlie had no trouble answering typical analyst queries. The construct phase had taken only eight-and-a-half days (complete on November 14th).

TESTING

Rob had tested the components of the system (hardware, programs, data, procedures, and people) during construction. He was now ready for an integrated test of all the components.

He decided to take an unusual step. Since the Computer Allocation System was simple, since all the users had been trained during construction, since he, the developer, worked in the user department, and since they were going to install in a parallel mode (with the monthly physical inventory), he decided to combine the integrated test with the parallel installation.

Normally, he would not combine the installation and test. Usually there would be a dress rehearsal, having the components operate together before the parallel installation. That sequence seemed inappropriate this time.

For one thing, Marilyn was following her procedures already and building the initial data. True, at one point, she argued about the amount of time data entry would take. She insisted keying in the data would take two to three hours a week, time she couldn't spare from her regular duties. Rob didn't want to upset her further, fearing she would perceive the separate test as busywork.

In addition, the other users were only going to query the data. Barbara had been trained, and the other analysts already knew how to use dBASE query and Assistant. A test for them would seem silly.

Therefore, Rob proceeded with installation. The decision would save some valuable time (a day or so), and he was well aware of Barbara's desire that he meet the schedule they had discussed earlier.

INSTALLATION

Rob spoke with Barbara to schedule the installation phase. "Marilyn will have all the data keyed into the system by Tuesday (November 20th)," he reported. "We can have the Employee Reports ready for your Friday (November 23rd) morning meeting. Do you want to start installation then?"

"Sure," Barbara answered, "if we're ready. Frankly, I'm more than a little concerned. This will make us even later, won't it? I'd hoped we'd have completed both test and installation by then. What happened?" she continued.

"Yeah, well, system construction went much more slowly than I expected," Rob explained, having the feeling that he'd been here before. "It seems dumb to say this," he admitted, "considering what this project is all about, but I couldn't get my hands on some equipment when I really had to have it, and Marilyn had some higher priority work to do. But, don't worry. We'll catch up!"

PREPARATION

Rob checked with Marilyn, and told her to produce two copies of the Employee Report once she had finished the data entry. "We'll give employees one copy, and I'll use the second copy to do the initial physical inventory."

He then copied a small amount of System Change and System Transfer Forms. Once he was sure they were acceptable, he'd have a larger supply printed. He then prepared an outline of his briefing to the analysts at the Friday meeting. Barbara was going to describe her new policy and then turn the meeting over to him. He would explain how the new system would work and then distribute his letter of explanation and the new forms.

On Thursday (November 22nd), Rob received the Employee Reports from Marilyn. He examined them, and they seemed OK. There was no time to have anyone else look them over. He planned to distribute them at the Friday meeting and then do the physical inventory. As he did the inventory, he would be able to get concurrence from the users regarding equipment they were assigned.

With the Employee Reports finished, he queried the database, using both the dot prompt and Assistant. As far as he could tell, all data for employees and systems had been input. Again, there wasn't time to have anyone else check his work. The system seemed ready.

THE MARKETING DEPARTMENT MEETING

Barbara announced her new policy on Friday, the 23rd. She explained that from then on, she would consider each person responsible for safeguarding the computer equipment assigned to him or her. There was some grumbling, and Charlie Swartz wanted to know if that meant Arnold was going to dock his pay if equipment turned up missing.

"No," said Barbara, "but if it happens often, some corrective action will be taken. Anything else?"

Rob took over the rest of the meeting. He explained how the system would work, discussed the new forms, and described Marilyn's role in keeping the data current. "You'll be prevented by passwords from modifying any data," he said.

Everything went smoothly until Rob distributed the initial Employee Reports. When the analysts examined them, all sorts of comments were made:

"Hey, Rob, we haven't had this system since August! This is the one that we finally palmed off on Manufacturing."

"I don't have this printer. They don't even make this printer anymore."

"We moved this plotter from this system to Andrea's system last month."

"I've never even seen this computer. Do we have it?" And so forth.

Finally, to quiet everyone down and to end the meeting, Rob said that he had used the best data he had; he acknowledged that some adjustments might have to be made. He promised to check with each person individually in the coming week.

THE RECONCILIATION

On Monday the 26th, Rob began the adjustment process and discovered Charlie Swartz had taken a two-week vacation. He visited all of the other analysts and compared their Employee Report with the equipment they actually had. A dozen or so SYSTEM records had to be changed to correct errors in capacities and peripheral equipment. Five systems could not be located. It turned out that one of them had been sent to Manufacturing, but Marketing had never been given credit. The location of the other four systems was a mystery.

Someone remarked that one of the prior analysts, Harold Johnson, who had resigned under some pressure from Barbara, had worked with a computer. Barbara called him at home, and sure enough, he still had the computer.

"I was wondering when you were going to ask for it," he said.

Barbara made arrangements to recover the computer, but there were still three complete systems not accounted for.

ACCEPTANCE

Rob lost another week and a half correcting and rechecking the SYS–USE data; he finally completed that task on December 5th. With all the changes, record length had grown to 80 bytes, and a total of 7,000–8,000 records was possible. Since he'd fallen behind two weeks, earlier in the project, there was no way he could finish on schedule.

The new system was supposed to be running in parallel with the old system; but, after the fiasco with the initial allocation data, Rob decided there couldn't be much of an old system. So he decided to run the new system alone, and take another inventory at month-end, just before the new year. He would check the processing of all transactions during the month to ensure that the system worked. Barbara was not in her office when he went to tell her of this decision.

At the end of the month, Rob found new discrepancies between the physical inventory and the SYS–USE data; old errors had been corrected, but new ones had been made. Marilyn had processed most of the transactions successfully; only fifteen would have to be keyed in again. The analysts were able to access most of the data they needed. With another week or so, Rob was certain he'd have all the "bugs" out of the system. Looking back, he wished Charlie hadn't decided to take his vacation when he did.

When he explained to Barbara, she refused to accept the system. It was December 31st, late on a cold, rainy day, and Barbara said quietly, "Rob, would you please get up and close the door? You and I have to talk."

CLASS ASSIGNMENT 4—FOR INDIVIDUALS

1. Retrace the inventory development process and determine the amount of schedule slippage experienced—from the initial assignment to Rob to the date when Barbara refused to accept the system.
2. Do you accept Rob's estimated development and operational costs (Exhibit 8)? Why or why not?
3. In addition, using Rob's cost figures, calculate the total cost of the project at the end of the case. What was the total cost overrun?
4. Evaluate Rob's actions and decisions he made. Identify any technical or managerial errors.
5. What might he have done to avoid the delayed completion of the project?
6. Did Barbara contribute to Rob's scheduling problem? How?

7. Assess Barbara Barlin as a manager and technician in the DP–IS field. What should she have done to assist Rob, if anything?
8. Give your opinion, supported with facts from the case, on Barbara's decision to terminate Rob.

Appendix

Sample List of Data in Each Database File

- USE SYS–USE
- LIST

Record#	SYS_ID	EMPNUM	PROJECT	STRTDATE	ENDDATE
1	100	111111111	VIBRATOR	05/01/88	05/15/88
2	100	222222222	RANGEFINDER	06/15/88	07/31/88
3	100	333333333	DAMPER	08/01/88	08/31/88
4	200	444444444	WAVEFORM1	04/12/88	05/17/88
5	200	555555555	VOLTMETER	06/01/88	06/21/88
6	300	111111111	LONGRANGER	06/01/88	08/01/88

- USE EMPLOYEE
- LIST

Record#	EMPNAME	EMPNUM	EMPDEPT	EMPLOC	EMPPHONE
1	BONNIE BROWN	333333333	ACCT	B789	33878
2	ROGER SMITH	111111111	ACCT	B123	11223
3	ERIKA JONES	222222222	ACCT	C113	23550
4	ANTHONY JACKSON	444444444	ACCT	B765	56466
5	GILL CARTER	555555555	ACCT	C120	34545

- USE SYSTEM
- LIST

Record#	SYS_ID	CPUNUM	MONITOR	MEMSIZE	NUMDSKET	NUMNDISK	PRINTER	PLOTTER
1	100	123456	BW	256	1	1	NONE	NONE
2	200	555555	CO	256	2	0	M93	NONE
3	300	456454	BW	512	2	1	M93	J4700
4	400	789726	CO	512	2	2	M93	J4900

Case 2–2 Technical Training Corporation: Problems with Automation

"Got a few minutes? I'd like to talk you it. It's important." Beth Jordan, branch head of Systems Analysis, peered over her spectacles and said, "Sure, Pat. Come in. What's the matter? You look upset."

Pat Ritchie was her lead analyst. She had worked for Beth for the last three years. Beth respected Pat's abilities and thought of her as a bright, competent woman. She was concerned at this moment about the look on Pat's face because usually she did not get upset at the office and rarely complained. However, she knew Pat had been under a great deal of strain due to her workload. The computer database system they had been building for the past 10 months seemed to have grown in all directions. Every day, more information was required for input and output. Beth suspected, lately, that the analysts were spending less time doing their work and more time waiting for their printouts.

"Beth, you know how I hate to complain to you about my problems, but I feel I must talk to you. I don't know where to go from here," she said carefully. "I'm not sure you realize what exactly is happening here in the office."

"I'm aware of the monster we've created with this database, Pat, if that's what you mean," she said with a grin. "But the network system we've purchased should be ready for implementation in a month or so. That should relieve the capacity and scheduling problems we've been experiencing."

"Oh, I agree," Pat responded. "I can't wait for the network. Did you know Doris came in during second shift a few days last week because Consuela wasn't able to find the time to input the data Doris needed for her meeting with the Navy last Wednesday?"

"Yes, I know. Doris asked me about it before she did it," Beth responded, as she removed her glasses wearily and rubbed her eyes. She continued, "I really felt badly about it, but the priority last week was that ECN report for the president. What could I do? I was also getting pressure from all of the program managers for that information."

"That's not really all that's bothering you, is it?" she asked Pat.

"No, it isn't, as a matter of fact," Pat replied. "We have a more important problem at this moment than the capacity of the computer. It's the attitudes of the people in this group. I don't care how efficient our computer system ever gets; it will be useless if the people who would probably benefit the most from it refuse to accept it. Or worse, refuse to use it."

This case was prepared by Illean Durkin, Janine P. Faulent, and Justine A. Pompei. Names, locations, and financial data have been disguised.

"Oh, I think they'll come around. You're expecting the worst," Beth said, half believing it herself, but thinking of nothing else to say.

"I don't know," Pat continued. "I've never worked in such a hostile environment. The tension in the air between the systems analysts and the rest of the Equipment Configuration Management Group is so heavy, I can barely breathe anymore. It was a mistake, when they created our branch last December, to plop us (System Analysis) down in a long-established organization like Equipment Configuration. They've resented us from the very beginning. It wasn't a well-thought-out decision by management. But, as usual, there was a crisis, and we needed to get our systems up and running fast," she said, sarcastically.

Pausing for a moment, she continued, speaking slowly and deliberately: "I feel extremely frustrated, Beth. I just don't know what to do anymore. Somebody had better take a few steps backward and look at the whole mess soon, or I don't know what will happen."

For a moment, neither one said anything.

Beth finally spoke. "Okay. I'll call Sam and tell him what's going on and ask him to set up a meeting for everybody involved. It will be mandatory attendance for all the people in the group. We'll get all of these problems out in the open once and for all. This resentment and hostility toward us has got to end, or we will never be effective."

"I hope it works, Beth," Pat said, as she rose and headed for the door. "I really do, but I don't have good vibes about it at all. It's really a bad situation."

COMPANY BACKGROUND

Technical Training Corporation (TTC) is a high-technology company that employs approximately 2,000 people in the Boston metropolitan area. TTC has two primary markets:

1. Military nonflight—U.S. and foreign.
2. Industrial-nuclear fossil process.

The corporation produces simulators, or trainers, that prepare people to use the real equipment. For example, a partial aircraft simulator would train military personnel to operate the sophisticated radar equipment located on the airplanes. Being in a highly competitive market and located not far from Boston's many electronic industrial parks on Route 128, TTC must struggle to stay on top of this highly technical business.

TTC has maintained steady sales and profit growth. Its stock has risen from $4 to $30 per share in the past five years. Since its inception in 1934, TTC has always provided its customers with state-of-the-art products. Its corporate culture has been highly centralized, valuing senior management's decisions on the production of products. TTC has a reputation for providing quality products, always through fair and firm customer negotiations and business dealings generally.

The top-down management approach is followed. Still, the corporation relies on feedback and suggestions from the lower levels for its decisions. Suggestion boxes are placed throughout the buildings, and they are used frequently.

TTC's primary objective is to increase growth and long-term profitability by increasing its technical leadership and developing new products in nonflight simulation to extend the business base into new markets.

A close look at TTC reveals that the majority of the business, 62 percent, is derived from its Defense Programs Division (DPD). Due to the great demand for defense products in our country, growth is obvious in military contracts. DPD provides the army and navy with simulators for their tactical maneuvers, ships, submarines, and airplanes. In 1986, the division posted a net sales figure of half a billion dollars in government contracts, making it an industry leader in defense contracts. Its innovative simulation techniques and lifelike hardware have made the company invulnerable to many of its competitors. Some individuals allege that TTC sometimes wins contracts based on the quality and performance of their past products rather than on the quality of the current winning proposal.

As for TTC's Commercial Systems Division (CSD), its nuclear power plant simulators are built to the specifications and requirements of the Nuclear Regulatory Commission (NRC). Net income for this division was $28 million dollars in 1986. Since there are few competitors in this field, the Commercial Systems Division expects to expand and grow rapidly in the future.

THE EQUIPMENT CONFIGURATION MANAGEMENT GROUP (ECMG)

Exhibit 1 shows the relationship of the Logistics Division to the TTC organization. The Product Support department is an important part of the Logistics Division.

At TTC, the Product Support department is responsible for the integrity of all products and services delivered to customers with regard to reliability, maintainability, configuration, quality, workmanship, performance, and conformance to contractual requirements.

TTC policy establishes the position of the Equipment Configuration Management Group within the Product Support department. The ECMG is composed of three branches, as shown in Exhibit 2. They are:

1. The Systems Analysis and Design branch.
2. The Drawing Release, Reproduction, and Distribution branch.
3. The Change Control branch.

Sam Metcalf is the manager of the Equipment Configuration Management Group. He has been with TTC for 35 years. Over those years, he has worked in several areas of the company. His background is mainly in manufacturing. He received a Bachelor of Science degree in Electrical Engineering from MIT several years ago through their night school program. He is well liked by his peers and

EXHIBT 1   TTC Partial Organization Chart (as of December 1987)

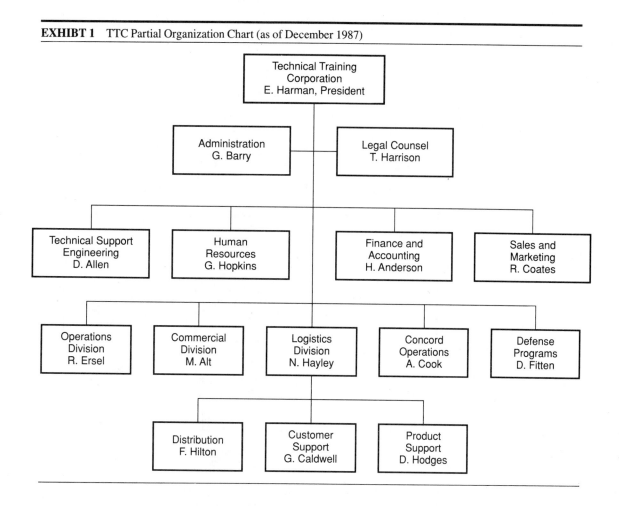

has been with the Product Support department for the past 19 years. In addition to the ECMG, he is also involved in several other areas of Product Support. He answers directly to Doug Hodges, the director of the Product Support department.

As the director of Product Support, Doug Hodges is responsible for several large sections of people, as seen in Exhibit 2. Hodges has been with TTC for 35 years, also. He has been the director of Product Support for the last eight years. He received his training in the military where he specialized in quality control.

Hodges is particularly interested in the success of the Equipment Configuration Management Group. He chose Beth Jordan to head the Systems Analysis and Design branch because he needed a strong leader to carry out the changes he had planned for the ECMG. Hodges felt Sam Metcalf was constantly bogged down with other quality control problems. Hodges recruited Beth from the old Industrial Engineering department of Tech Support Engineering, intending to make her

EXHIBIT 2 TTC Partial Product Support Organizational Chart, Equipment Configuration Management Group (as of December 1987)

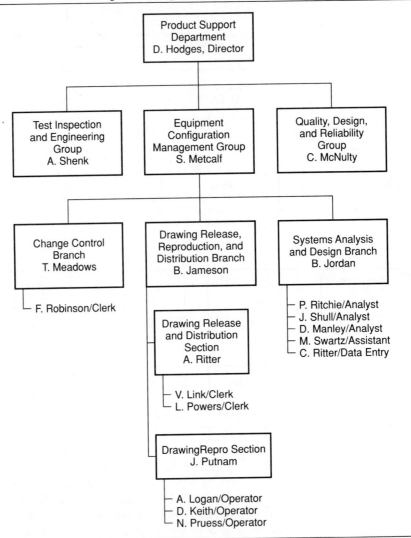

manager of the Equipment Configuration Management Group. Metcalf would then become the manager of the Quality, Design, and Reliability Group. Due to the reorganization of the company last year, however, Hodges decided to postpone this plan. Sam Metcalf remained the manager of the Equipment Configuration Management Group.

THE SYSTEMS ANALYSIS AND DESIGN BRANCH (SADB)

The Systems Analysis and Design branch was created in September 1985 to fulfill contractual configuration management requirements on all military training devices per Military Specifications (MIL SPECs). (The Technical Note at the end of this chapter describes the theory of configuration management.) Until it's inception, these requirements had been overlooked by government authorities and by TTC. A crude listing of parts and their location within the trainers had always been prepared by someone in the Product Support department. However, last year, the government began to crack down on its contractors. TTC decided to create a branch that would provide the configuration data requirements in accordance with the MIL SPECs. At the same time, Product Support would also incorporate new automated methods of developing and storing the drawing release and history records.

Doug Hodges charged Beth Jordan with the configuration data requirements task when he assigned the branch to her. Doug knew some of the procedures being used in the Equipment Configuration Management Group were outdated and redundant.

Therefore, the Systems Analysis and Design branch is directly responsible for providing the government with all configuration data for each military training device it purchases from TTC (see Exhibit 3). This data consists of the following:

1. A Configuration Status Accounting Report (CSAR), Baseline Index.
2. A Configuration Status Accounting Report, Configuration Item Identification (CII), and Released Data Summary Report.

The first report is a computerized listing of all functional items within a training device, down to the lowest replaceable item. This report also provides the following information required per MIL SPECs:

1. The Configuration Item (CI) number.
2. The TTC drawing/part number and description.
3. The current drawing revision status of the part (as ''des rev'').
4. The ''as built'' revision status of the part actually in the hardware (as ''blt rev'').
5. The TTC wiring list part number.
6. The serial number of the item.
7. The location of the part within the trainer.

The second report is also a computer-generated report, which contains the entire change history of a configured item. An example of each report is shown in the Appendix to this chapter.

To keep track and control the thousands of parts in the training devices, an IBM PC AT microcomputer (30 megabytes of memory) is used with a packaged database application program.

EXHIBIT 3 Systems Analysis and Design Branch (changed drawings and new drawings)

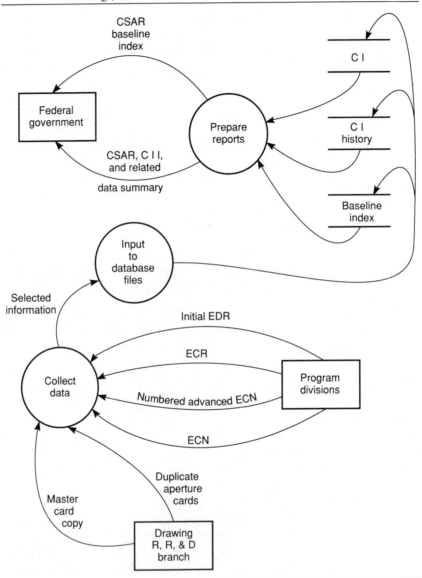

Due to the tremendous demand for computer time that analysts have experienced in recent months, a network system has been purchased; when delivered, it will consist of five terminals with the PC AT as a file server. A 100 MB external hard disk with tape backup has also been purchased to accommodate the tremendous number of records and files needed by the analysts. In addition, TTC bought a new laser printer; it will speed the printing time of the reports used and distributed by the group.

The Configuration Management Database

The database used by the analysts consists of three key files, as shown in Exhibit 4, which interact with each other to produce reports. The three files are:

1. The Configuration Identification (CI) file.
2. The CI History file.
3. The Baseline Index file.

The CI file contains all descriptive information on the configuration item (part). This information consists of the title and function of the item, its current "as designed" revision status, any applicable drawings that can be used for reference to this item (i.e., logic diagrams, wiring diagrams), and military specifications that apply to this item (i.e., soldering requirements, marking standards). Other information kept in this file includes the current and past programs that have used this configuration item in their baselines; the CI file also lists any model numbers or vendor reference numbers that apply to the item if it's not an item TTC produces.

The CI History file contains the entire change history of the configuration item. This data includes all Engineering Drawing Requests (EDRs) written against this item, the Engineering Change Notices (ECNs) that resulted, the day the ECN was released and incorporated into the hardware, the effectivity (production-line sequence number) of the ECN, and a detailed narrative description of the contents of the Change Notice.

The Baseline Index files are created for each training device that TTC manufactures. The index consists of the configuration item's TTC part number and its location within the hardware; the latest "as built" revision status, which is supplied to CM from the manufacturing floor inspectors; the serial number of the item; and, if applicable, the wiring information (wire list) and the revision that is installed in the hardware.

The Baseline Index file and the CI file are used together to produce the Configuration Status Accounting Report, Baseline Index. A relationship is established between the two files using the part number as the key field. Therefore, for every part number used in the Baseline Index file, the associated description and "as designed" revision status is retrieved from the CI file and printed to produce this report. An example of this report can be found in the Appendix.

Similarly, to produce the Configuration Item Identification and Related Data Summary Report, the CI file and the CI History file are related through the part number of the item. The two files together produce this report, which lists the entire change history of the item and all reference information needed for that item. Therefore, all pertinent information pertaining to a configuration item can be seen at a glance. The Appendix shows an example of the report.

EXHIBIT 4 TTC's Configuration Management Database Key Files and Relationships Used to Generate Reports (relationships are shown in broken lines)

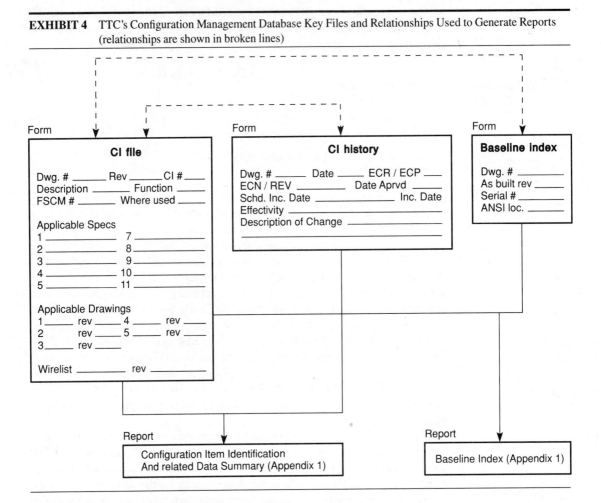

SADB PERSONNEL

The Systems Analysis and Design branch manager, Beth Jordan, is in her 40s, and has been at TTC for the last three years. She was recruited from the Tech Support Engineering (TSE) department specifically to head this section, which was formed in mid-October of 1985. Beth's background is mainly in manufacturing. She has a Bachelor of Science degree in Mechanical Engineering (still unusual for a woman) from Cornell.

The first thing Beth Jordan did when she became the branch head was recruit Pat Ritchie, also from the TSE Department. Pat was the Microcomputer manager there and was responsible for selecting the computer system now in use in TSE.

Beth believed that Pat's experience in installing a computer system would be helpful in setting up a computer system for her branch.

Pat Ritchie had no previous experience in Equipment Configuration Management before joining Jordan in her new section. She has a Bachelor of Science degree in Industrial Engineering from Penn State University. She joined the TSE department shortly before Jordan arrived. TTC is her first job since graduating from college. Presently, she is pursuing an MBA on a part-time basis at Northeastern University.

In addition to Pat, now the lead analyst, two other analysts—June and Doris—were added to the newly developed branch. Both have been with TTC for eight years but neither has any configuration management or computer experience.

June Shull had been a clerk in the Drawing Release, Reproduction, and Distribution branch before joining System Analysis and Design. She has a two-year Associate degree in Business Administration from SUNY-Binghamton.

Doris Manley is the third analyst. She has worked in several departments in her years at TTC and is especially knowledgeable about hardware used in the training devices. Manley does not have a college degree but has worked her way to this position over the last eight years.

Recently, a junior analyst position was created to provide an assistant to the analysts in their day-to-day tasks. Miriam Swartz, who is the assistant now, also is responsible for some data entry when the regular data entry person is absent or occupied. Management hopes to use this position to groom future department analysts.

The data entry clerk is Consuela Ritter. She worked in the TSE department for Beth before joining this group. Her experience in data processing is extensive. Before joining TTC, she worked in several large computer companies.

The following is Beth Jordan's view of the System Analysis and Design branch's function within the Equipment Configuration Management Group:

"Configuration management can be thought of as the 'policemen' of the design team. That is, we analyze the design of a system and determine if the design is correct per the MIL SPECs, which determine what the design criterion should be. It is more than checking, in that it involves a control aspect. We would like to be the 'tail that wags the dog' instead of the other way around. And we are making progress. For the last 10 months, we've been lagging behind and playing catch up—trying to recreate the data from the last three years on one program completely. We now have a good, centralized database of information. People are beginning to notice, too. Everyday, more people within the company are seeing our reports and are liking what they see. I was afraid, at the outset, of the reactions of the people we'd be 'policing.' Doing audits of other people's work can sometimes cause some bad feelings, but that really has not happened here. Most of them seem to appreciate the organization we have provided within our function through our computer system. In fact, the most common comments we've received are, 'It's about time' and 'I'm glad someone is finally doing it.'"

EXHIBIT 5a Drawing Release and Distribution Branch (new drawing)

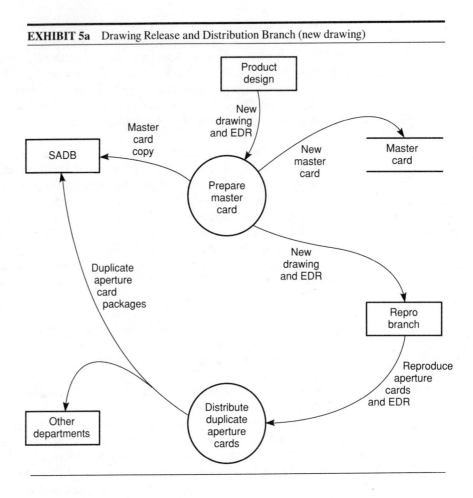

THE DRAWING RELEASE, REPRODUCTION, AND DISTRIBUTION BRANCH

The Drawing Release, Reproduction, and Distribution branch (also known as the Drawing Release branch) is responsible for releasing all TTC drawings for use throughout the company (see Exhibits 5a and 5b). The branch functions as the central point of control and distribution for all TTC drawings and any changes to those drawings. When a new drawing is created, a master card is generated by this branch. This card will serve as the history record for that drawing. Any future revisions and changes to the drawing will not be considered ''released'' until the master card is updated with the proper information. Exhibit 6 provides an example of this card.

EXHIBIT 5b   Drawing Release and Distribution Branch (changed drawing)

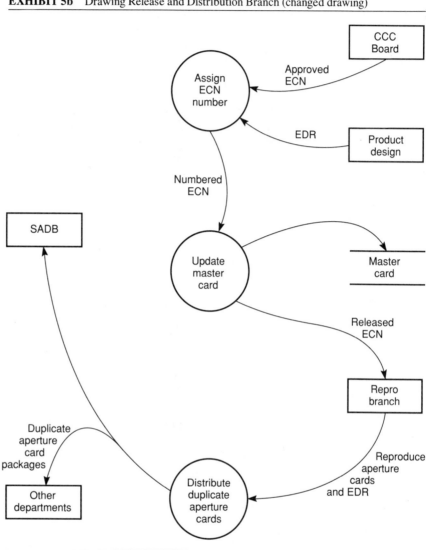

ECRs and ECNs

Any changes to a drawing must be requested from the drawing originator through a strict change control process, with the Configuration Change Control Board (CCCB) playing a vital role. This process is shown schematically in Exhibit 7.

EXHIBIT 6 Example of a Drawing Master Card

DRAWING TITLE   PANEL, BNC DISCONNECT

DWG. NO. 8667528   sht 1-2

DWG. SIZE _____ D

S.O.

RELEASE NO.	DATE	REV.	PROJECT SLIPS	NOTES AND REVISION DISPOSITIONS
24	6-18-87	—		NEW RELEASE

F-3010

EXHIBIT 7   Drawing Distribution/Change Process: (a) Drawing Change (Revision) Process, and (b) New Drawing Release Process.

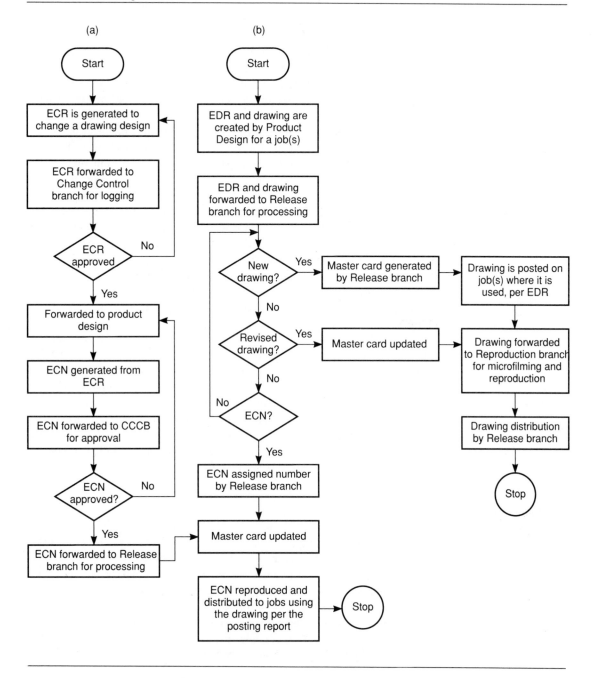

The change process begins with an Engineering Change Request (ECR), as seen in Exhibit 8. This form is processed through the Change Control branch. The ECR is then passed for approval to the program (Product Design) for which the drawing is currently being used. If the ECR is approved, the product designer generates an Engineering Change Notice (ECN), as seen in Exhibit 9. The ECN shows the change that will be made to the drawing and includes views and sections of the drawing needed to describe the change completely.

The ECN is then submitted to the Configuration Change Control Board (CCCB) for final approval. The CCCB is made up of the section head of the Change Control branch, who chairs the board, a representative from Manufacturing and Production Control, and a representative from Tech Support Engineering.

When the ECN is approved, it is forwarded to the Drawing Release branch, which assigns a number, based on the most current status of the drawing, to the ECN. For example, if a drawing is at revision status level A and has three ECNs written against the A revision, then those ECNs would be assigned B1, B2, and B3, respectively. When 10 ECNs have been written against any one revision level, then the drawing must be revised to incorporate the changes. The new revision that incorporates the ECNs mentioned in the above example would then be revision status level B. This ECN revision status information is transmitted to the Drawing Release branch through an Engineering Data Release (EDR) document as shown in Exhibit 10. EDRs are used to announce the creation of a new drawing or the revision of an existing drawing. Subsequent changes to that drawing would begin with ECN C1 and so on.

Once an ECN is assigned its number, the distribution of that ECN is carried out by the Drawing Release, Reproduction, and Distribution branch. The ECN must be distributed everywhere, on every project, where the original drawing is used. The ECN distribution process can sometimes become complex and confusing, depending on the commonality of the drawing in question and the number of people who require the information. Moreover, a standard three-day turnaround on the processing of these ECNs has been promised by the branch; in some cases, meeting that commitment requires long hours of overtime due to the volume of changes on prototype systems developed at TTC.

Ben Jamieson

Ben Jamieson became the branch chief of the Drawing Release, Reproduction, and Distribution branch two years ago. Prior to that, he was a supervisor in the Maintenance department. He does not have a college degree and had no experience in drawing release management prior to being appointed to the branch.

Jamieson oversees a supervisor—Jill Putnam—who directly supervises three operators (Section B of the branch)—Logan, Keith, and Pruess. Alice Ritter is the supervisor of the other two people, the clerks of Section A, and has been with the company for 23 years. She has been in the Drawing Release branch for

EXHIBIT 8 Example of an Engineering Change Request (ECR)

ENGINEERING CHANGE REQUEST

TO: _____ DATE: _____ CHANGE REQUEST NO: _____

PART NO: _____ PART NAME: _____ JOB NOS: _____

CHANGE REQUESTED BY: _____

DESCRIPTION OF CHANGE:

REASON FOR REQUEST:

ENGINEERING ACTION

REQUEST APPROVED: _____ DATE: _____ DISAPPROVED: _____

Signature   Signature

THIS CHANGE REQUEST IS TO BE ROUTED IN ORDER SHOWN AND RETURNED TO LIAISON GROUP AFTER COMPLETION.

	ELECTRICAL	MECHANICAL	CHG. GROUP	CHECKING	RELEASE	RETURN TO LIAISON
ROUTING						
DATE						
BRANCH LEADER						

THE FOLLOWING PROJECT SLIPS AND/OR ENG. DATA RELEASES HAVE BEEN MADE:

EXHIBIT 9   Example of an Engineering Change Notice (ECN)

the last 15 years. Vicky Link and Lorraine Powers, her two clerks, have both been in the department for over 10 years.

Jamieson's view of the Systems Analysis and Design branch follows:

"Those systems analysis people are a pain in my and my peoples' necks. They come in here, reducing my office space even more than it was before and expect us to cooperate with every improvement they suggest. Then there's that computer of theirs. I personally don't see any great benefit in having the information on it, as opposed to having it in the file drawer right in front of it. So they can make nice reports? Big deal! It doesn't help me or any of my people in our day-to-day

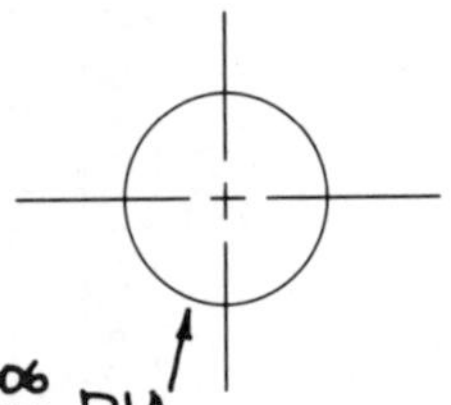

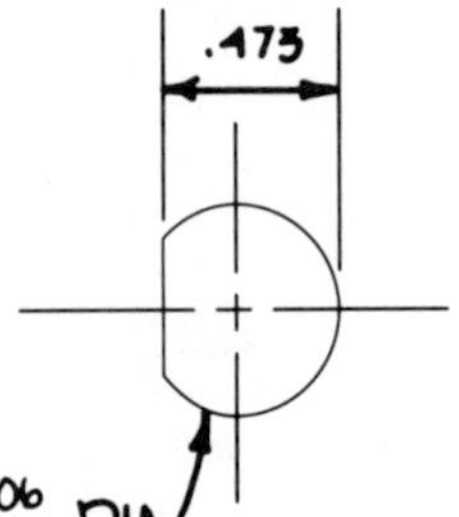

EXHIBIT 10 Example of an Engineering Data Release (EDR)

ENGINEERING DATA RELEASE		RELEASE PROCESSOR *Varlee*	DATE 6-14-87	EDR NO. →	23	27	29	
EDRFIS SCHEDULED RELEASE DATE: *1 87*	SH / OF /	DRAWN B. MILOSAVICH	DATE 87-6-17	P.E. SIG.	RPR	CAB	RAD	
		CHECKER B. MILOSAVICH	DATE 87-6-17	JOB NO. →	5151-1	5152	5153	
		PRODUCT SUPPORT D.R. Davis	DATE 6/17/87					

DWG SIZE	DRAWING NO.	CHG	REMARKS	MODEL NO. →	A47V4S 71(5)1	A47V4S 71(0)2	A47V4S 71(0)2	
D	8664203			┌→	N	N	N	
D	8667014		EDRFIS SH 21 ITEM 18	D I S P O S I T I O N C O D E S ↳	N	N	N	
D	8667015				N	N	N	
C	8669014		SH 21 ITEM 20		N	N	N	

DISPOSITION KEY:
4. CHANGE IN QTY, N/A AND/OR MODEL.
5. NO REWORK REQUIRED.

8. SCRAP PARTS MADE ORDERS TO CHANGE
14. DWG. CANCELLED
15. DWG. CANCELLED

work. In fact, they inhibit our routine. We have to have a three-day turnaround of the information we process in here, or people start screaming. With that gang trying to help us out and getting in our way, we've been turning up with late distributions; people are noticing. And all they're noticing is a lot of confusion coming out of here since the SA gang came in. Things were just fine before. We've been operating with our current system for 25 years with full government approval. I just don't buy this idea that we have to implement all this computerization because the SPECs say so. I just think that someone has a computer and wants to play with it...at our expense!''

THE DRAWING REPRODUCTION SECTION

Drawing Reproduction (Section B of Jamieson's branch) receives engineering drawings from Jamieson's Section A, Drawing Release and Distribution (see Exhibit 11). All new or revised drawings are microfilmed and placed on a computerlike punch card by a special machine. The cards, known as aperture cards, are then stored in alphanumerical order in file drawers. These cards are also duplicated on another machine and are distributed by Section A to various departments within the company. These microfilm cards can then be processed on another machine to print a hardcopy, if needed. Since the company has several of these machines, several groups can have access to drawings without the problem of storing the actual hardcopies. But, even with this distribution of aperture card duplicates to a great number of people within the company, Section B (Drawing Reproduction) is usually swamped with requests for drawing hardcopies.

Currently, there are four people working in this section, which services both the Commercial Systems and Defense Programs divisions.

Ben Jamieson is in charge of the section, as with Drawing Release and Distribution (Section A). Jill Putnam is the supervisor of the three people in this section. She has been in the position for the last 10 years. The remaining three people are strictly duplication machine operators, who fill drawing requests sent to the section.

THE CHANGE CONTROL BRANCH

The Change Control branch has only two people (see Exhibit 12). They are responsible for logging and reporting of Engineering Change Requests (ECRs) and advanced Engineering Change Notices (ECNs). An ECN can be classified as advanced only under certain conditions; a special Advanced ECN number is assigned by the Change Control branch as a temporary measure until the ECN is officially released through the Drawing Release branch.

Thad Meadows heads this branch and has been at TTC for the last 30 years. His background is mainly in production design. He was a mechanical draftsman with TTC for 20 years before he became the branch chief 10 years ago. His involvement with the other branches in the CM group is minimal. He supervises only one person, Fawn Robinson, whose function is clerical. She has a two-year degree in Business Administration from Kansas State University and has been with the branch section for over four years. She maintains several manual logs and also generates Status of ECRs and Advanced ECNs reports, which are produced and distributed to the various program offices.

EXHIBIT 11   Drawing Reproduction Section (changed drawings and new drawings)

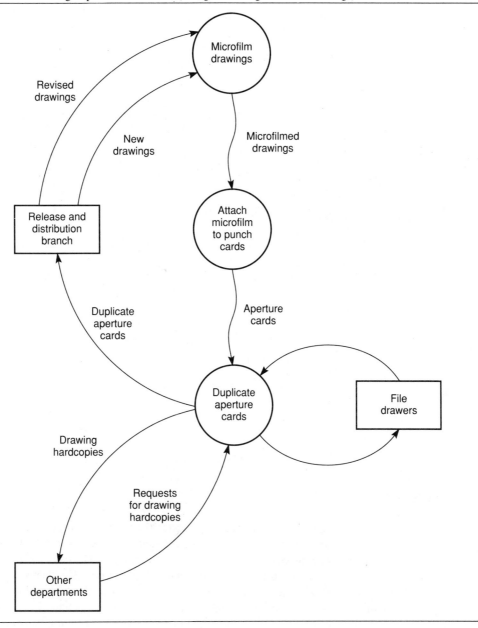

EXHIBIT 12 Change Control Branch (changed drawings)

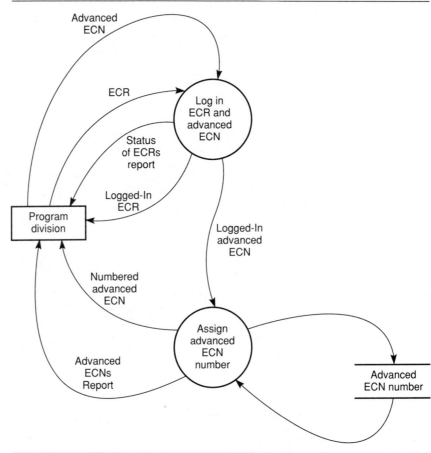

THE LUNCHEON

Sam Metcalf, Ben Jamieson, and Thad Meadows looked around the crowded dining room and spotted Beth sitting alone at the table. They started toward her. Beth sighed heavily as she saw them approaching. "This is not going to be the most pleasant lunch I've ever had," she thought to herself. She remembered the phone call she had received announcing this luncheon meeting. Doug Hodges had barked the order to be there and hung up. Doug wanted his management people to meet to discuss the scheduled departmental meeting that was planned for tomorrow morning. He was not too happy.

"Hi, Beth," Sam Metcalf said, as he sat down across from Beth. "Doug here yet?"

"No, not yet," Beth answered. She glanced up at Ben Jamieson as he sat down beside her. Ben acknowledged Beth with a quick nod of the head. Beth responded with a dry, "Hello." She did not like Ben Jamieson very much.

Ben Jamieson looked nervous and agitated as he glanced around the room. He was upset by Doug Hodges' phone call announcing this luncheon. He was afraid of Hodges and was sure that Beth had something to do with what had made Doug so angry. Jamieson did not like Beth, anyway; she was rude and pushy. Ben had received several complaints from his people about Beth. Vicky especially couldn't stand her and, as a result, had threatened to quit. Luckily, Jamieson had calmed her down before she went to Sam.

Thad Meadows greeted everyone quietly and took a seat next to Metcalf. "There's Doug now!" Sam said as he waved his arm in the air to attract his attention. Hodges moved toward them. Beth noticed Ben Jamieson take a large gulp of water as Hodges approached the table. Hodges sat down at the head of the table and gave them all icy stares.

"Good. I'm glad you're all here so we can begin," Hodges said. "I thought we should all get together at least once before we go into that damn meeting tomorrow. I understand there are some problems between the branches in the Equipment Configuration Management Group. I want to make sure we are a management team here. The problems between you people must be solved here and now," he said, angrily ramming his finger into the tabletop. "We aren't going to get the people under us to resolve anything if we, at this level, are not united. You all have got to be on the same team, not fighting one another," he continued.

"Beth," Doug said, as he turned to face her, "you brought up this meeting idea. Start us off."

Beth paused for a moment and then spoke. "I'm sorry that it's come to this, Doug. I usually try to resolve these people problems by letting them work out on their own. But things have gotten too far out of hand. I'm afraid I may lose some of my analysts if we don't do something soon. That's why I suggested the departmental meeting . . . to resolve the problems."

Metcalf spoke up, saying, "We definitely cannot afford to lose any more people. We had to layoff two women last March when we had the companywide staff reduction. Then one other woman left last June from the Reproduction section. We're running on the bare minimum. I'd hate to see anyone else leave, especially if it was over something stupid."

"Well," Beth responded, "the two branches are not getting along. It may sound stupid, but it can be quite crucial. We will never be able to implement the computerization of the Drawing Master Cards if there is no communication and understanding between the two branches. We could implement great improvements in the day-to-day running of Drawing Release, Reproduction, and Distribution sections if they would only let us."

"Ben," Hodges asked, as he turned to Ben Jamieson, "what do you have to say about this?"

Jamieson's face flushed. "I resent Beth's implication that my people are the problem here. There wouldn't be any problem if they'd just leave everything alone the way it was. My people do not want to change the way they've done things for the last 15 years. And I don't believe it's necessary. All it's causing is turmoil and disruption.''

"That's exactly the kind of attitude you should be trying to change, Ben," Beth responded bitterly, "instead of constantly reinforcing it to your people. I've heard your little sly comments on how stupid our systems are. The changes are needed and will take place. That has already been decided. There is nothing to debate on that point. We must now move on to determine how to implement the changes.''

Jamieson, becoming agitated, said, "No one ever asked me about these changes! I think I should have at least been consulted before the changes you all obviously planned behind my back. How do you expect me to react?''

"Now, Ben," Sam Metcalf interjected, "no one planned this deliberately behind your back. I agree we should have talked to you before we began to make the changes, but we honestly didn't foresee this kind of problem.''

"There have been other problems in the department besides the computer problems," Jamieson said. "That Consuela Ritter of yours has caused a lot of trouble in here. She's a troublemaker. She was responsible for Barbara leaving my area last June.''

"Now wait a minute, Ben," Beth spoke up.

"No, no, Beth. Let me finish. It's true. Barbara was having some problems with another girl in the Drawing Reproduction section and with me. Consuela kept pushing Barbara to go over my head to Personnel. Finally, it got so bad, Barbara just quit.''

Beth shook her head and smiled. "Look, I know Consuela is no shrinking violet. She stands up for what she believes, but she's a good worker. She does far more than her data entry position really requires, and she is a great aid to the analysts. Now, I agree she may not have handled her working relationship with Fawn Robinson, in Thad's branch, too well, either. Somewhere along the line, they had some argument. I have already spoken to Consuela about that.''

Thad Meadows spoke up reluctantly. "Fawn tells me that Consuela has completely refused to publish the daily advanced ECN listing on your computer. Fawn now goes to another computer system to do some of her tasks.''

Beth responded, "Thad, I know we agreed at first to help Fawn out with all of her manual tasks. But honestly, lately we have become so swamped with other priorities, that Consuela just couldn't justify stopping crucial work to type in that ECN listing. Anyway, from what they tell me, some advanced ECNs are only advanced for a day or so. If this is true, then we really don't need that listing. It was only meant for special cases of ECNs that would be delayed significantly in the release process.''

"I think we are getting off track," Hodges commented. "Let's stay on the personnel problems for now. Does anyone else have another topic that just can't wait?" he asked.

"Well, while we're here, I have another issue I'd like to comment on," Jamieson stated.

"Go ahead, Ben," Hodges responded.

"I'd just like to know why Beth's analysts are exempt from the Product Support department rules," Jamieson asked.

"How do you mean?" Hodges questioned.

"I've noticed that several of her people are not making up their time when they leave early. I've been checking the sign-out book, as I do for all of my people, and I've noticed that some of her analysts do not sign in and out when they leave the building to go out for lunch," Jamieson continued. "This makes it hard for me to enforce the rules on my people when they see Beth's people getting away with these things."

Beth responded quickly. "Look, I treat my people as the professionals they are. I will not lower myself or my people by checking their time in and out on a daily basis. If that's the way you need to manage your people, that's fine. But leave my people alone."

Sam Metcalf spoke up. "I think we are dealing with two different kinds of people in the department. There are definitely two different levels of professionalism represented. And I agree that Beth's people don't need the type of close management we are used to providing."

Hodges leaned back from the table and remarked, "That's exactly why we are having the problems between the two branches. We've got to come up with a way for these people to get along, or we're never going to have any peace within this group!"

QUESTIONS

1. Were Jamieson's complaints justified? Why or why not?
2. Do you agree with Beth Jordan? If you were in Beth's position, how would you have responded to Jamieson? Support your answer.
3. What should Hodges and Metcalf do to resolve the conflicts in the Equipment Configuration Management group? Why? How?
4. What changes would you recommend TTC implement to improve the efficiency and effectiveness of its configuration management process? Who should be responsible for making those changes and when should they be in place?
5. Draw a context diagram and Level 0 data flow diagram for the Equipment Configuration Management group.
6. Draw a data flow diagram for the processing of new drawings through the Change Control branch.
7. Write the data dictionary for ECR, ECN, and EDR.
8. Describe the relationship between DFDs and data dictionaries.

9. Compare system flow charts (such as Exhibit 6) and data flow diagrams (Exhibits 3, 10, 11, 12, and 13); what are the advantages and disadvantages of each?
10. What changes or corrections would you make to the data flow diagram set in the case? Justify your answer.

Technical Note

Configuration Management

Configuration management is probably one of the least understood management disciplines at TTC or in any industry in general. Configuration management, in its most basic terms, provides an orderly management process.

A definition of configuration says it is the complete technical description required to build, test, accept, operate, maintain, and support products. This technical description may be in the form of drawings, specifications, magnetic tapes, punched cards, manuals, vendor data, and so on.

Configuration management, therefore, is a management discipline comprised basically of four major subfunctions:

1. Configuration identification.
2. Configuration control.
3. Configuration status accounting.
4. Configuration audits.

These four functions are documented by a series of military and commercial specifications and standards that are the basis of TTC's configuration management operations.

As evidenced by past and continued major emphasis being placed on configuration management disciplines by TTC's customers and the industry in general, it is obvious to management that TTC must provide responsive, cost-effective configuration management across the board; it's mandatory if they are to remain competitive, hold their share of the marketplace, and maintain their planned, profitable growth.

To define the four functions within configuration management, one can start with configuration identification, which is the selection of the documents that identify and define the configuration baseline characteristics of an item.

Configuration control is the controlling of changes to an item after formal establishment of its configuration identification. Configuration status accounting is the recording and reporting of the information needed to effectively manage configuration, including approved configuration identification and changes thereto. And finally, configuration auditing is the checking of an item for compliance with the approved configuration identification.

The first step in implementing a configuration management program is to generate and obtain customer approval of a configuration management plan. This plan defines in detail how TTC understands contractual obligations for configuration management and how it plans to implement the configuration management program to comply with those obligations.

The next step in implementation is to identify the product in a manner that will satisfy internal needs and meet customer requirements. This identification is done through assignment of configuration item numbers, model numbers, specification numbers, drawing numbers, and serial numbers.

When the identification is pulled together, it defines the functional (how does it work and what does it do?) and physical (how does it look and fit?) characteristics of TTC products.

At this point, we must now control changes to these characteristics. This is done through internal procedures that are supplemented, when necessary, to meet a specific contract requirement. Changes to documentation and products are accomplished using an Engineering Change Notice (ECN) form that has been designed to meet internal needs and the majority of customer requirements. The configuration management function during this change processing includes Change Control Board activity, Engineering Change Proposal (ECP) generation and coordination, and ECN review and approval. The ECN is a communication link between Engineering, Manufacturing, Quality, and the customer. One of configuration management's main functions is to ensure the ECN communicates clearly.

So far, we have planned the program, identified the product, and put a control over changes. The next step is to put in place something that will record and report change processing and implementation status. This is the status accounting function of configuration management. Its primary purpose is to show the history of changes to a given product, the status of where the changes may be in the approval cycle or release process, and the actual point of implementation of the change into the product.

Once these processes are in place, TTC should have a product that meets our customer requirements and needs, with no surprises when TTC is ready to ship.

Even though there may be several testing requirements in the program, there is normally a Functional Configuration Audit (FCA) to assure the product functions as advertised. The primary objective to be met during the functional audit is to verify that test data clearly shows product performance in compliance with specification requirements.

Completion of this audit is a prerequisite to accomplishing the Physical Configuration Audit (PCA), which is the formal examination of the "as built" version of the product against its technical documentation. Successful completion of the PCA, usually conducted on first production units, establishes the production baseline. All subsequent units will be the same configuration unless there is customer approval or concurrence to change the design.

On the majority of new contracts, when the government is funding the development effort, successful completion of the FCA and PCA are prerequisites to acceptance of the product. The major function of configuration management during these audits is to coordinate company effort and cochair the audit with a government representative. The coordination effort includes ensuring hardware availability, technician availability to disassemble hardware as necessary, getting all documentation together and available, and conducting the hardware-to-drawing comparison.

Once these elements of configuration management are in place on a program, many reports are required by the customer. Typically, these reports must be updated and submitted for the life of the contract. Sample reports were shown in the Appendix.

All of the requirements discussed here are not always included in every contract. However, they are typical of large military system programs.

Appendix

Configuration Status Accounting Report: Baseline Index

NOMENCLATURE: ACOUSTIC OPERATOR TRAINER FOR AN/SQQ-89 UNDERWATER SENSOR SYSTEM
DEVICE 14E35

CONFIGURATION ITEM: N840000-01

SPECIFICATION ITEM: NAVTRAEQUIPCEN 232-115 DATED 84 10 12

DRAWING NUMBER: HN99999-1 TOP ASSEMBLY, DEVICE 14E35
DATED 84 02 21

CONTRACTOR: Technical Training Corporation
Defense Programs Division

AS OF 06/07/87

CONTRACT NUMBER N61339-82-C-0020

CONTRACT BASIC LINE ITEM SERIAL NUMBER A005

CONTRACT DATE 84 03 08

FSCM: 20551

PAGE 1

CONFIGUR. ITEM NUMBER	DRAWING NUMBER	AS DES REV	AS BLT REV	DESCRIPTION	WIRE LIST	AS DES REV	AS BLT REV	SERIAL NUMBER	(Leading zeros for ANSI report only) LOCATION
N841000-01	HN40200-1	B14	B14	EQUIP INSTL ASSY UNIT 2	HN95002	B4	B3*		02
N842003-01	HN70020-1	A8	A6*	PANEL ASSY OVERTEMP MONITOR	HN90020	A4	A3*	01132	02A01
N842005-01	HN70021-1	A4	A4	PANEL ASSY TRAINER MONITOR	HN93021	A1	A1	02854	02A02
N842006-01	HN70022-1	A5	A5	PANEL ASSY 60HZ DISTRIBUTION	HN93022	A1	A1	01346	02A03
N842002-01	HN70019-1	A5	A4	PANEL ASSY FAN/BLOWER	HN93019	A1	A1	01094	02A04
N842014-01	HN85012-1	—	—	PANEL ASSY MAINTENANCE INTERCOM					02A05
N842024-01	HN87001-1	A13	A13	PWR DISTR BOX					02A06

95

Configuration Status Accounting Report: Configuration Item ID and Related Data Summary

Descriptive Data....

CONFIGURATION ITEM NUMBER: N841000-01
DRAWING NUMBER: HN40200-1, REV B14
DESCRIPTION: EQUIP INSTL ASSY
UNIT 2
FSCM NUMBER: 20551

Applicable Specifications....		Applicable Drawings....	
1: MIL-M-13231	7:	(W/L) 1: HN95002	, REV B4 (05/13/87)
2: MIL-W-16878	8:	2:	, REV
3: MIL-T-43435	9:	3:	, REV
4:	10:	4:	, REV
5:	11:	5:	, REV
6:	12:		

Programs using this Configuration
Item: 14E35#1

TEST SPECIFICATION:

ECR/ ECP	DATED	ECN/ REV	DATE APPRVD	SCHD. INC. DATE	INC. DATE	EFFECTIVITY	DESCRIPTION OF CHANGE
						SEE WAIVER N84-01 HARD WIRED EQUIP CAB., APRVD 6/1/89	
		—	03/16/85				ORIGINAL RELEASE
		A	06/10/85				DID NOT INC. A1
		A1	04/20/85				DRAWING CLARIFICATION; NOTE: WILL BE INC. IN B REV.
		B 1	08/15/85				ENGINEERING DRAWING ERROR
		B 2	08/15/85				ENGINEERING DRAWING ERROR
		B 3	08/15/85				ENGINEERING DRAWING ERROR
		B 4	08/15/85				ENGINEERING DRAWING ERROR
		B 5	08/15/85				ADDED INFO.
		B 6	09/12/85				MFG REQUEST—TO SIMPLIFY FAB AND ASSY
		B 7	09/12/85				MFG REQUEST—TO SIMPLIFY FAB AND ASSY
		B 8	09/12/85				ENGINEERING DRAWING ERROR
		B 9	09/12/85				ENGINEERING DRAWING ERROR
		B10	11/01/85				ADDED INFORMATION
		B11	11/03/85				MFG REQUEST TO SIMPLIFY FAB ASSY
		B12	11/18/86				ENGINEERING DRAWING ERROR
		B13	03/27/86				ENGINEERING DRAWING ERROR
PA0843	***********	B14	07/02/86				ENGINEERING DRAWING ERROR

Chapter 3

Telecommunications and Local Area Networks

INTRODUCTION

A little over 25 years ago, data processing or computer experts were people who analyzed data processes, wrote computer programs, ran the big mainframes, or managed the computer center; they were called analysts, programmers, operators, and managers. Managers tried to control costs by monitoring CPU time; programmers wrote program code in FORTRAN and COBOL. Today, what we know as Information Systems and Information Technology encompasses many more personnel specializations, management techniques, technical disciplines, languages, and types of computing and peripheral equipment. Obviously, as technology and application usage has responded to demands of the market, the language of computers and information systems has changed and expanded as well.

Several factors have combined to encourage technological advances and to produce an environment that has allowed the wideranging changes to occur. Among those factors are:

- The desire of users to have greater control over their information resources.
- The inability of DP centers to respond quickly to user requests for new applications.
- Miniaturization—which has made development and production of powerful microcomputers possible at relatively low cost.
- Accounting and financial managers' needs to combine processing applications so that information can be shared (permitting input to the general ledger and financial statements, for example).
- Top executives' demands that equipment and personnel costs be restrained.
- The existence of an efficient, effective, national telephone network—*perhaps given less credit than it deserves.*

TELECOMMUNICATIONS DEFINED?

In attempting to define what we mean by the word *telecommunications,* one comes face-to-face with a lingering irritation in IS; that is, the slipshod approach to terminology, a tendency to use words—with widely accepted definitions among the general public—to mean something slightly or entirely different. For example, OEM—Original Equipment Manufacturer—is not a manufacturer of original equipment, nor of any equipment, nor even a manufacturer; and some IS texts define OEM to be an Office—or Other—Equipment Manufacturer.

A second related failing is the willingness among IS professionals to accept several different words or short phrases to mean the same thing; for example, telecommunications, teleprocessing, and data communications are all said to mean the same thing. McLeod writes, "Data communications is often referred to as *datacom.* . . . You will also hear the terms *teleprocessing, telecommunications,* and *telecom.* All of these terms can be used interchangeably."[1]

We shall attempt to categorize meanings and clarify definitions shortly. For now, however, we believe we can use the above inconsistencies as a framework to discuss communications as they relate to computers.

SIGNAL TRANSMISSION: ANALOG, DIGITAL, AND MODEMS

First, everyone should understand that most computers communicate internally with digital signals, which are electronic discrete pulses that can be on or off, or high or low. When someone thought to use telephone lines—which were already in place but used analog, continuous wave signals—to connect small, remote terminals to mainframes, a means had to be found to convert the telephone analog waves to digital pulses. Modems (abbreviation for modulator-demodulator), one of the receiving end and one at the transmission end of the message, were developed to convert the signals from analog to digital and then back again.

COMMUNICATIONS MEDIA

The signals transmitted between computers (mainframes, minis, and micros), modems, terminals, printers, CRTs, and other peripheral equipment travel through different communications media, including twisted-pair wire, fiber-optic cable, coaxial cable, microwaves, and radio waves. A long-distance telephone communications system could use several of the media plus satellites; the same applies for computer communications systems.

---

[1]Raymond McLeod, Jr., *Management Information Systems,* 3rd ed., Chapter 8 (Chicago: Science Research Associates, 1986), p. 290.

An XYZ Company manager, considering joining several microcomputers in an office, or linking several terminals to a nearby minicomputer, should consider twisted-wire pairs, coaxial cable, and fiber-optic cabling. As one progresses from the twisted wire to fiber-optic, costs increase considerably but so does system security. Another cost factor is distance between the various components.

NETWORKS

Local Area Network (LAN)

Most experts would agree that the XYZ Company manager was contemplating a local area network (LAN). The students in their dorm rooms are using a LAN, as they do when keying in their programming homework in the computer lab, where several may share one printer.

Normally chosen as a means to share expensive assets—such as a laser printer or a large, mass-storage device—within a building, the network would include microcomputer workstations (system unit, diskette unit, monitor, and keyboard), laser printer, mass-storage unit (hard disk), and cabling (very often coaxial). The topology, or physical arrangement, of the local area network is a star, ring, or bus (most frequently). If the manager wants to connect the network to another dissimilar network such as a wide area network (WAN), it would be necessary to acquire a **gateway** (which includes hardware and software).[2]

Wide Area Network (WAN)

Wide area networks allow communication between computer users over great distances, such as across the entire United States.

Hardware could comprise a host CPU, modems, multiplexers, controllers, front-end processors, terminals (both hardcopy and CRT), workstations, and concentrators. Software is also required; it would include the usual operating system software as well as other software to control the network (to poll terminals, rout and edit messages, etc.). Since the data stored within the network can be hundreds of files and thousands of records, a database management system (DBMS) will often be required.

---

[2]Charles S. Parker, *Management Information Systems: Strategy and Action,* Chapter 9 (New York: McGraw-Hill, 1989).

NETWORK MANAGER

The list of new personnel specialties mentioned in the beginning of this chapter should also contain the job title *network manager,* a position unheard of not too long ago. As with all managers, primary duties involve planning, organizing, staffing, and controlling, but also implementing and operating. He or she must work closely with analysts, programmers, the database administrator, end-users, and security specialists.

Suppose, however, that ours is a very large corporation and that we plan to reorganize our far-flung communications resources. We shall appoint a chief information officer (CIO) to provide top-level policy guidance as well as day-to-day management direction. Will one of the CIO's subordinates be the director of Telecommunications? And will the director of Telecommunications control a manager of Data Communications, a manager of Voice Communications, and a manager of Teleprocessing? Or will the CIO's subordinate be called the director of Teleprocessing and direct the activities of the managers of IS, Datacom, and Telecom, respectively? Or maybe the subordinate should be the director of MIS?

More important than titles is the question of activities and resources. What do the people working for the director of Telecommunications actually do, and what assets is the director responsible for? Who is really accountable to who and for what?

Hiring someone to fill the position of network manager shows once and for all the crisis occasioned by the terminology morass. How does one describe and advertise for such a person? Do we want someone with telecommunications or data communications background; network experience or teleprocessing experience; expertise with multiplexers, front-ends, and controllers; in-depth knowledge concerning broadband, fiber-optic cabling, and microwaves; or years with a particular LAN vendor? Certainly, no one individual can be expert in all areas. The applicant should be equally troubled about what capabilities he or she is professing to sell. Both sides would do well to approach the interview with care.

MANAGEMENT CONCERNS

While a network can represent many potential issues and problems, five of the most important are:

- **Reliability** (measured in network downtime and message error rates).
- **Response time** (most affected by signal travel distance, amount of traffic, and network channel capacity).
- **Network costs** (equipment purchase or rental, installation, network maintenance, employee training, system conversion, and equipment repair).
- **Incompatibility** (often caused by changing technology, lack of central control over hardware and software purchases, and acquisition of firms with networks already in place).

- **Access and security** (increased accessibility may mean reduced security, staff may be indifferent to proper use of log-on codes and passwords, and microcomputers accessing the host database through public, dial-up telephone lines can compromise security).[3]

SUGGESTED DEFINITIONS

We suggest that the word *network,* whether LAN or WAN, refer only to hardware and software, using the word *system* only on occasions when the speaker is referring to hardware, software, data, procedures, and trained people. Therefore, we can have data communication systems and telecommunication systems; a corporation's data communications system can include LANs and WANs. Leaving the word *teleprocessing* to be used only with *monitor,* when discussing database management software used in large networks, avoids the telecommunications = data communications = teleprocessing predicament. As for data communications (or datacom) and telecommunications (or telecom), we would reserve *telecommunications* for those times when telephones and/or telephone lines are used to access the system (such as with acoustic couplers).

CASES: MSP AND THE LAN, AND WILSON MEMORIAL HOSPITAL AND DCS, INC.

Case 3–1, MSP and the LAN, combines the five network management concerns with the decision to select a LAN vendor. MIS manager Bob Albert, the top-level executive responsible for the decision, has made his decision and presented it for the board's approval. The case with the MSP Fact Sheet permits a very technical discussion of the advantages and disadvantages of the two networks. The unpredictable moods of individual board members present Bob Albert with a quandary, quite apart from the technical features of the two networks.

Case 3–2, Wilson Memorial Hospital and DCS, Inc., portrays another difficult situation, this time involving an existing network. Some terminals are added, causing response time to drop to an unacceptable level. Neither the equipment supplier, DCS, Inc., nor the hospital can agree on an equitable resolution, and a mediator is consulted. Much of the case is a verbatim presentation of the mediator's transcripts. The *Instructor's Manual* gives the mediator's judgment.

---

[3]Robert Schultheis and Mary Sumner, *Management Information Systems: The Manager's View,* Chapter 7 (Homewood, Ill.: Richard D. Irwin, 1989).

Case 3–1 MSP and the LAN

Harold Bryce, managing partner of MSP Enterprises, is worried about the firm's decision to install a local area network (LAN) at MSP. He knows that increased automation of the firm's resources is necessary to remain competitive in the investment banking business. Still, after a great deal of negative response, he isn't sure if a LAN is the best choice. After all, LANs are a relatively new technology; though highly publicized, their widespread use has been delayed by the lack of software.

Bob Albert, having done extensive research on the subject, had made a convincing pitch at the partners' meeting. It had been such a victory convincing the majority of the partners to vote in favor of the plan. However, it appears now that he had neglected to consult others in the firm for their input. Bryce hated the thought of possibly delaying the installation of the system or of trying to change it entirely. If he faltered in his stance and requested a new vote, he might not get another chance to head up such a significant, far-reaching project.

Yet many employees have viable objections to the future network system. Bryce is ambivalent about the decision made at the partners' meeting but has very little time to change the course of action should he choose to do so. Bryce must make a final, clear-cut decision.

COMPANY BACKGROUND

MSP Enterprise (MSP), originally founded in 1825 as MSP & Company, was a collaborative effort of three brothers. Martin, Samuel, and Peterson Adams saw great opportunities on the horizon in and around the Baltimore area, particularly with the development of port facilities and construction of the Baltimore & Ohio Railroad. Outstanding opportunities included investments with the import and export merchants, as well as commercial banking demands (e.g., extending book credits to merchants, loaning capital against promissory notes, and providing banking facilities for institutions out of the state or country).

To further the commercial development of the area, MSP formed syndicates with other banking firms to finance major projects; one such project was the extension of the B&O system. In order to enhance its own growth, MSP began expanding into other cities, namely New York and Philadelphia. These larger metropolitan areas had superior port and industrial facilities, thus providing more

---

This case was prepared by Mary Lou Sigler, Susan Hornberger, and Pamela Clark; the case was updated by Eduardo Caillaux. Names, locations, and financial data have been disguised.

merchants and new companies in need of investment services. MSP also became heavily involved in municipal and government financing, helping to establish the Federal Farm Credit System.

It became obvious in 1929 that commercial banking was not the best business for MSP. Though there were no runs on the company, MSP decided to phase out its commercial banking business and deal strictly with investment banking. The firm's partners used their personal fortunes to keep the company afloat until the end of the banking crisis.

The "black days" of the stock market in 1929 posed no threat to MSP as the firm was not yet a member of any exchange. MSP did become a member of the National Association of Securities Dealers (NASD) upon its establishment, and a member of the New York Stock Exchange in 1935. The firm was later to become a member of the American Stock Exchange, the Over-the-Counter Trading System, and the Chicago Board of Options.

MSP expanded greatly throughout the 1900s through a series of mergers with smaller firms and by opening new markets. Although MSP remains a major East Coast regional firm with offices in Washington, D.C., Boston, and Atlanta, there are also branch offices in Dallas, San Francisco, and London, England. MSP & Company became MSP Enterprises in 1983, when top management decided that this conservative, old-world firm had to make the effort to keep up with its fast-changing competitors.

The year 1986 was the first of the real banner years for MSP. Net income increased 25 percent from 1985 to 1986 (a total of $1.2 million), as evidenced by the consolidated financial statements presented in Exhibits 1a and 1b. Still considered a small- to medium-sized investment banking firm, MSP decided the time was right for further expansion.

Generally, the 1986 expansion was a major office rearrangement. With several new high-rise office buildings being constructed within a few blocks of their original office building, MSP decided to lease two floors of a local commercial bank building. On completion of the building (scheduled for January of 1988), MSP would move several of its operational departments into the new space. The departments to be relocated included: Corporate Finance, Mergers and Acquisitions, Research, Institutional Sales, Trading, and Corporate Syndicate.

PHILOSOPHY

MSP Enterprises considers itself an old-fashioned, conservative firm. Though lagging behind its competitors in the area of scientific advancement, MSP believes that the firm's advanced knowledge, understanding, and experience with the financial world overcomes the technological gap.

MSP's philosophy involves dealing with people on a one-to-one basis, not just handing them over to someone down the line or turning them into a number on

---

EXHIBIT 1a   MSP Enterprises Consolidated Income Statements

MSP Enterprises
Consolidated Statements of Income
For the Years Ended December 31, 1985 and 1986
(in thousands)

	For the year ended	
	December 31, 1985	*December 31, 1986*
Revenues		
Commissions	$ 8,036	$ 6,906
Principal transactions	4,520	4,395
Investment banking	3,516	3,767
Interest and dividends	33,651	47,086
Other income	502	628
Total revenues	$50,225	$62,782
Expenses		
Partner and employee compensation	$ 8,167	$10,207
Interest	27,766	34,704
Floor brokerage, exchange, and clearance fees	613	766
Communications	510	638
Professional fees	485	610
Depreciation and amortization	1,143	1,439
Occupancy	481	607
Taxes (not on income)	122	151
Other expenses	1,546	1,914
Total expenses	$40,833	$51,036
Net income before taxes	$ 9,392	$11,746
Taxes on income (50%)	(4,696)	(5,873)
Net Income	$ 4,696	$ 5,873

---

a computer screen. Salespeople spend time with every client, talking with each one, and making sure that all needs are satisfied.

The polished rolltop desks, marble floors, and paneled walls in the branch offices underscore MSP's intention to make each customer feel that every detail of his or her account is being handled personally and with great care. Personal service and attention to detail have become the unofficial trademarks of MSP; the firm wants to keep, even boost, that reputation.

EXHIBIT 1b   MSP Enterprises Consolidated Statements of Financial Position

MSP Enterprises
Consolidated Statements of Financial Position
For the Years ended December 31, 1985 and 1986
(in thousands)

	As of	
	December 31, 1985	*December 31, 1986*
Assets		
Cash and cash equivalent	$ 542	$ 2,496
Cash and securities on deposit with clearing organizations or segregated in compliance with federal regulations	2,708	4,494
Securities purchased under agreements to resell	240,902	315,252
Receivable from brokers, dealers, and clearing organizations	35,874	63,999
Receivable from customers	58,144	64,332
Marketable securities and commodities owned at market value:		
U.S. government	276,506	334,393
State and municipal	2,572	4,161
Other	56,722	38,865
Furniture, equipment, and leasehold improvements at cost, less accumulated depreciation and amortization	880	1,498
Other assets	2,032	2,748
Total Assets	$676,882	$832,238
Liabilities and Capital		
Money borrowed	$ 19,020	$ 21,804
Drafts payable	2,775	3,662
Installment sale notes payable	4,467	2,413
Securities sold under agreement to repurchase	269,805	475,291
Payable to brokers, dealers, and clearing organizations	27,955	32,374
Payable to customers	42,575	81,559
Marketable securities and commodities owned at market value:		
U.S. government	240,835	167,529
State and municipal	271	416
Other	41,222	17,060
Accrued employee compensation and benefits	2,436	2,746
Other liabilities, accrued expenses, taxes, and reserves	8,937	9,153
	660,298	814,007
Senior subordinated notes	4,874	5,742
Other subordinated notes	338	338
Capital	11,372	12,151
Total Liabilities and Capital	$676,882	$832,238

ORGANIZATION

MSP operates as a partnership, with general, limited, and special limited partners sharing (in varying degrees) the assets and liabilities of the firm. The firm is comprised of numerous departments and holding companies. The departments include General Administration, Retail, Personnel, Special Products, Public Finance, Governments, Municipals, Mergers and Acquisitions, Research, Corporate Syndicate, Options, Corporate Bonds, and Institutional Sales. Holding companies include MSP Ventures and MSP Realty.

With a few exceptions such as New York and San Francisco, the branch offices are for retail and small institutional customers. These branch offices, along with the main office in Baltimore, deal—to a greater extent—with large institutional customers. The branch office in Columbia, Maryland, houses the Operations Center, which includes the Customer Service department, Purchase and Sales department (Billing department), Safekeeping, and MIS department.

The partners are the firm's top-level management. Major decisions (those considered to affect a substantial portion of the organization or its finances) are discussed and voted on at partners meetings usually held once a month. Individual departments are headed by one or more partners. Thus, departmental decisions can usually be made without a presentation to all the partners—unless a large capital expenditure or major structural change is involved. All departments are considered relatively equal in importance; there is no real organizational hierarchy.

MIS BACKGROUND

MIS, as a single entity, began at MSP in 1967 with the opening of the Operations Center in Columbia, Maryland. The center was established as a record and bookkeeping center. Customers' interest and dividends were collected and credited; transactions were cleared, billed, and confirmed; securities were accepted and delivered to purchase; asset control was conducted; and customers' securities were held in safekeeping. These records and transactions were maintained through the use of electronic computing and recording equipment. At the Center's inception, about two thirds of the staff worked as keypunch operators.

As part of their move toward modernization, MSP shifted the functions of the Operations Center to Automatic Data Processing, Inc. (ADP). ADP assumed many of the aforementioned functions of the Center, becoming the major retail customer information base. ADP also became responsible for posting stock transactions, retaining updated customer name and address information, and maintaining margin and cash account balances. ADP now owns and maintains all computing resources—including all physical equipment and software—at the Columbia center and manages operating personnel under a facility management site agreement. However, the conversion led to the displacement of many employees.

Keypunch operators became data entry clerks working on CRTs, and many of the managers were freed to help in the further development of MIS within the firm. The managers were assigned to liaison positions with various departments; their job was to determine the MIS needs of the departments. Bob Albert, a partner, research analyst, and now MIS manager, directed the reorganization. He hoped that new programs could be developed to strengthen the MIS function within the firm and remove some of the data processing burden from individual departments.

Problems arise in MIS because each department requires different forms of information, though it may be from the same data source. Also, the departments submit, write, and review numerous reports at any given time, and they must always have access to these various formats. For the most part, all tasks have short deadlines with little advance notice; bits and pieces of information are gleaned from numerous other reports. Though MSP also maintains a Word Processing department providing basic report assembly and storage capacity, it is not advanced enough to handle the volume of information that MSP distributes and collects.

Due to the increased demand for information services and the necessity to share DP and office resources, Albert and his constituents have decided to put certain departments on a local area network (LAN).

BOB ALBERT

After graduating from the Wharton School with a degree in Finance, Bob Albert spent three years as an assistant financial analyst for Merrill Lynch, Pierce, Fenner & Smith, Inc., in New York. During that period, he was certified as an analyst and first came into contact with MSP. Albert was offered a position with MSP as assistant financial analyst, which he accepted in 1974. Within four years, he had become one of the lead analysts in the firm, taking over as the lead analyst for the Computer Services division. Albert was made a special limited partner in 1979.

As computer services analyst, Albert had worked closely with people from numerous companies specializing in a variety of computer service areas (see Exhibit 2). Through these contacts, Albert became interested in the field of data processing and information systems management. He helped to set up the arrangement between MSP and ADP and was instrumental in the conversion to the new ADP systems installed two-and-a-half years ago. With his knowledge of many computer service companies and their programs, the firm decided Albert should be charged with the development of MSP's MIS function. Consequently, he was made MIS manager in 1985. Shortly after taking that position, Albert

EXHIBIT 2   A Partial List of Computer Services Companies Followed by MSP Enterprises

Company Name	Area of Specialization
American Management Systems	Computer services for management of large organizations
American Software, Inc.	Management software
Applied Data Research	Database management
Automatic Data Processing, Inc.	Computerized payroll and accounting systems
CCX Network, Inc.	Direct marketing databases
Certified Collateral Corporation	Computerized vehicle valuation
Cincom Systems, Inc.	Organizational software
Computer Associates International	Diversified software for micros, minis and mainframes
Focus Research Systems	Computer-based marketing research
Hogan Systems, Inc.	Software for financial institutions
IMS International, Inc.	Computer services for the pharmaceutical industry
Information Resources, Inc.	Computer-based marketing research
Integrated Software Systems	Graphics software
Planning Research Corporation	Systems analysis and data processing
SEI Corporation	Computer services for the investment industry
Safeguard Business Systems	Computer services for the accounting industry
Sterling Software, Inc.	Specialized software for IBM and IBM-compatible computers
Systems Associates, Inc.	Computer services for acute care hospitals

began tracking the development of LANs and initiated the idea of using a LAN to automate the firm's information resources.

THE PITCH

Albert felt that a LAN was the best possible solution to MSP's information resource problem. The network technology would be far easier to accommodate than the technology of conversion to a centralized mainframe. Also, with the planned move of certain operations departments to a new building, the timing for installation could not have been better. With his research backing him up, Albert made his pitch for the LAN at the partners' meeting in December of 1986. The following is a short excerpt from Albert's speech at that meeting in which he gave the reasoning behind his choice of a LAN.

Gentlemen, it is becoming obvious to all of us that, to remain a force in the investment banking business, we must make strides toward automation. Our competitors are doing more and more to outdistance us in the field of service technology. Through the computerization of their information resources, they have almost limitless information available, and they process that information at a rate that we, at present, cannot hope to match.

We can no longer do things in the same conservative, old-fashioned manner. We need the preparedness, knowledge, and speed that only computerization can give us. I am not proposing a total restructuring of every system; rather, gentlemen, I am proposing a linking of current systems to form a network of available information.

Albert's rather lengthy pitch at the meeting also included some information on LANs in general and, in particular, the one he felt was best suited to MSP's needs. Handouts were distributed showing some of the attributes of the system and also the costs involved in installation. The following is an explanation of a LAN in general and more specific terms (the choice for MSP).

LOCAL AREA NETWORKS

LANs are becoming more and more popular in industry today as companies feel the need to establish communication links between the numerous personal computers within their organizations. LANs, however, link much more than personal computers. Word processors, workstations, data storage devices, facsimile printers, intelligent copiers, computer output microfilm, and optical character readers can also be linked into a LAN. Thus, the communication system established provides for the use of electronic mail and the sharing of numerous expensive resources.

An exact definition of a LAN is difficult to find, since the various LANs on the market differ in a great many areas. There are, however, some factors common to all LANs. First of all, LANs usually operate in a small geographic area (several hundred feet to a few miles) and are considered best for operation in one specific building. However, connections between buildings, cities, and even countries can easily be effected via Telco ACCUNET T1, MEGACOM 800, and X.25 VAN/VAC lines that turn LANs into wide area networks (WANs). Also, the technology of the LANs allows for the economic use of very wide bandwidths, thus allowing for data rates of up to 400 Mbps. (Bandwidths determine data rates based on the range of frequencies expressed in cycles per second (hertz) between the highest and lowest frequencies of a band: a bandwidth, if broad enough, can be divided into one or more data, voice, or other transmission channels. See Glossary for definitions of unfamiliar terms.) LANs also allow for communication between various devices made by different manufacturers; this linking of products from various manufacturers is the latest innovation of the LANs technology and is largely due to OSI/ISO standards developed in the late 1970s. A final feature common to LANs is a low bit error rate (through the use of CRC values) which experts put at approximately 1 in 10^{12}. Some additional characteristics—which differ in varying degrees among LAN products—are summarized in Exhibit 3.

EXHIBIT 3   Additional Characteristics of Local Area Networks

Technical Characteristics

Characteristic	Description
Connectivity	Depends on the traffic patterns of the station
Point-to-point	Few stations, single routes
Switching service	Several stations, demanding alternate routing
Network services	
Speed conversion	Allows terminals or CPUs with different data rates to communicate
Protocol/code conversion	Translation of different internal protocols and codes into a standard format
Echoing support	Reduces transmission load while retaining message accuracy checks
Device-specific support	Accommodates different terminal characters
Internetwork connection	Ability to link homogeneous and heterogenous networks

Nontechnical Characteristics

Characteristic	Description
Capacity	Communication capacity should be sufficient for document transfer without extensive delay or need for extra coordination
Reliability	System must be dependable or users will continue to use old system
Flexibility	System design should not be tailored to specific equipment
Vendor support	As a new technology, it is important to choose a vendor who is dependable in terms of service and who is prepared to work for more advanced technologies

---

The classification of networks is often done along a continuum ranging from centralized to tightly coupled to decentralized. The centralized LANs are in more widespread use and are considered the older and more established networks. The centralized strategies use a central controller, usually a microcomputer acting as a Network Interface Unit (NIU). Decentralized strategies, on the other hand, do not use a central controller; rather, the control function is distributed, often passing along links of a chain (with each link containing an interface and a microprocessor located on a control board). Exhibit 4 contains a list of various network strategies; centralized, tightly coupled, and decentralized are included (see also Exhibit 5).

Network strategies are important in evaluating and selecting LANs, but there are additional secondary factors that must be considered. Data transmission, for

EXHBIT 4   Network Strategies

Centralized

Type	Description
Local nonswitched networks (LNSNs)	All communicating devices are connected through dedicated point-to-point links
Fully-connected	Direct connection between all nodes
Hierarchial	Intermediate nodes between two communicating parties (e.g., front-end processors)
Local circuit switched networks (LCSNs)	Allow one node to communicate with various other nodes as in a star configuration. These would include PBX and CBX systems
Message switched network (MSNs) and packet switch network (PSNs)	Store requested information until intended route is determined, then the stored information is transmitted (e.g., U.S. Defense Department's ARPANET and Telco's X.25 service)

Tightly Coupled

Type	Description
Shared memory systems	Provide high data rates and information availability through simultaneous memory access
Time-shared bus	Common resource is available for specified periods of time—utilizes a central controller
Daisy chaining	A line directly connects a number of systems, passing information through a series of processors until the destination is reached—utilizes a central controller
Multiported system	Processors may connect to any number of available ports—a central controller is *not* used

Decentralized

Type	Description
Rings	An architecture with minimal connectivity and unidirectional operation
Daisy chain	The previous system requires permission to transmit —dedicated wires are used
Control tokens	Permission to transmit is required, but special bit patterns are utilized in recognizing transmittal permission and destination addressing
Circulating slots	Permission is required to transmit, but while awaiting transmission, information is stored in specified slots

EXHIBIT 4 Network Strategies (continued)

Register insertion	A broken network where an information transmission is placed into a shift register and is sent only when a system is open
Contention networks	Stations compete for the use of a transmission medium
Carrier sense multiple access—collision avoidance (CSMA/CA)	The station listens to the medium and acts accordingly to avoid transmission collision. LBT (listen before talking) technology
CSMA/CA—collision detection (CSMA/CD)	The transmission is terminated if a collision is detected, the network creates a jamming signal to let all stations know of a collision, the sender then waits a random period of time prior to retransmission. LWT (listen while talking) technology

instance, can be accomplished through various media including twisted-pair wire (like telephone lines), coaxial cable (used also for TV), and fiber optics (see Glossary and Exhibit 6). LANs can be found that use combinations of these media. At times, the choice of a LAN is determined by which of these media is already available, as in the case of telephone lines.

Fiber optics are normally used for higher volumes of transactions than the current volume of MSP or even that contemplated in the near future. Therefore, MSP's choice is between twisted-pair wire and coaxial cable. Flexibility and the extent to which the LAN will be used are also important considerations; plans for later expansion or for configuration changes necessitate a more flexible system.

Finally, an issue of great importance to the users of a LAN is security. It appears, unfortunately, that LAN vendors do not generally recognize the importance of this issue; only a few vendors have installed security procedures in their systems. Of course, other organizational selection criteria will also affect the evaluation and choice of a LAN. These criteria include organizational perception of the LAN, management style, information to be included, areas to be connected, and attitudes of the participants.

MSP AND THE LOCAL AREA NETWORK

Albert had done extensive research on LANs and their capabilities. He was positive that a LAN was the answer to the information resource and access problems of the departments involved. These departments were Corporate Finance, Mergers and Acquisitions, Institutional Sales, Trading, Research, and Corporate Syndicate (see Exhibit 7 for a brief explanation of each of these departments). The biggest problem was, of course, the time it took to obtain information. Rapid retrieval of statistical information would make it possible to develop miniportfolios for institutional clients wishing to hedge against a block of stock. There

EXHIBIT 5 Network Strategies

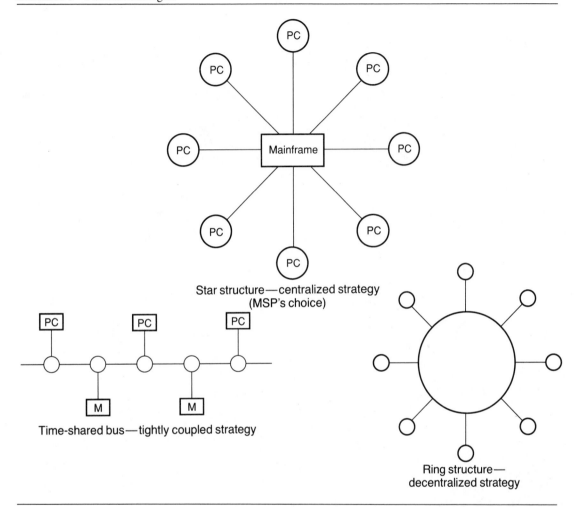

Star structure—centralized strategy
(MSP's choice)

Time-shared bus—tightly coupled strategy

Ring structure—
decentralized strategy

was also a need to track a large customer base—customers with hundreds of thousands of dollars to invest, with numerous subsidiaries and countless employees. By utilizing PCs as terminals, Albert felt that ADP data could be accessed on-line as needed. He thought this would enhance the firm's appearance of giving personal service and attention to detail by having data on each customer instantly available. Further, he knew that the PCs could also be used for other types of distributed processing such as word processing and spreadsheet applications, since it was widely acknowledged that these functions could not be economically centralized.

Team communication between MSP's salespeople, analysts, traders, and associates was also important. There were far too many people in each department

EXHIBIT 6   Types of Media

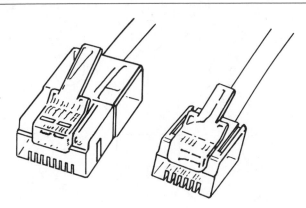

Twisted pair

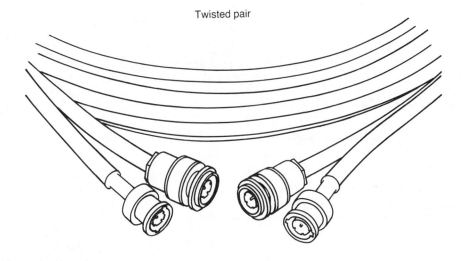

Coaxial

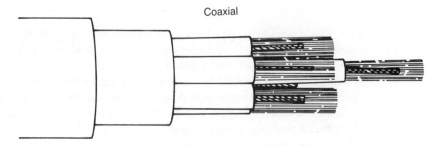

Fiber optics

EXHIBIT 7 Departmental Descriptions

Department	Description
Corporate Finance (Blake)	Works with various corporate clients to assist them in raising capital through private placements or public offerings of debt or equity securities
Mergers and Acquisitions	Works with corporate clients specifically to arrange mergers of similar companies or acquisitions of those experiencing financial or management difficulties
Institutional Sales (Hardsell)	Works with large institutional clients such as Citibank, USF&G, Morgan Guaranty in transactions involving major assets
Trading	Handles orders for NYSE, AMEX, and especially OTC (Over-the-Counter) for both retail and institutional clients
Research	Follows developments in industries and for specific companies to keep abreast of MSP's clients and competitors
Syndicate (Alexander)	Works with Corporate Finance to arrange for public offerings of new securities

for everyone to be familiar with everyone else's current information supply. There was a need for all the various types of information to be placed in, and drawn from, a central, localized, and accessible place. All of this would mean greater preparedness and service on the part of MSP and improved results for clients.

Albert knew, however, that there were still problems with the LANs. First and foremost, LAN technology was still relatively new. This meant that some important issues had yet to be dealt with to the complete satisfaction of all users; namely, security, programming/operating, and network linking (for the future). From an operational standpoint, problems arose concerning cost, software development, hardware selection, information, and user selection and logistics.

Considering all this, Albert was at a loss for a time, unable to decide from among all the available systems. LANs, such as IBM's Token Ring, Ethernet (a product of Digital Communications, Intel Corporation, and Xerox — see Exhibit 8), and Omninet (a Corvus Systems' production), were among the most popular, thus making them high on the list of options. Yet there were many other LANs available that highlighted special features; many of these were also inviting choices. Finally, late in 1986, Albert was introduced to Novell's LAN technology, which seemed to answer many of his problems. Novell, Inc.'s Advanced NetWare (software) was taking the network market — and Bob Albert — by storm (see Exhibit 9).

Novell's basic network system was S-Net, a centralized (star) strategy, utilizing one main server with several branching workstations (see Exhibit 5). This system was no different than most other centralized LANs; the difference was afforded by Advanced NetWare, Novell's latest software development. (Exhibit 10 presents some basic technical aspects of S-Net.)

Advanced NetWare is among the few LAN packages that allows LANs to be

EXHIBIT 8 Typical Configuration of an Ethernet System

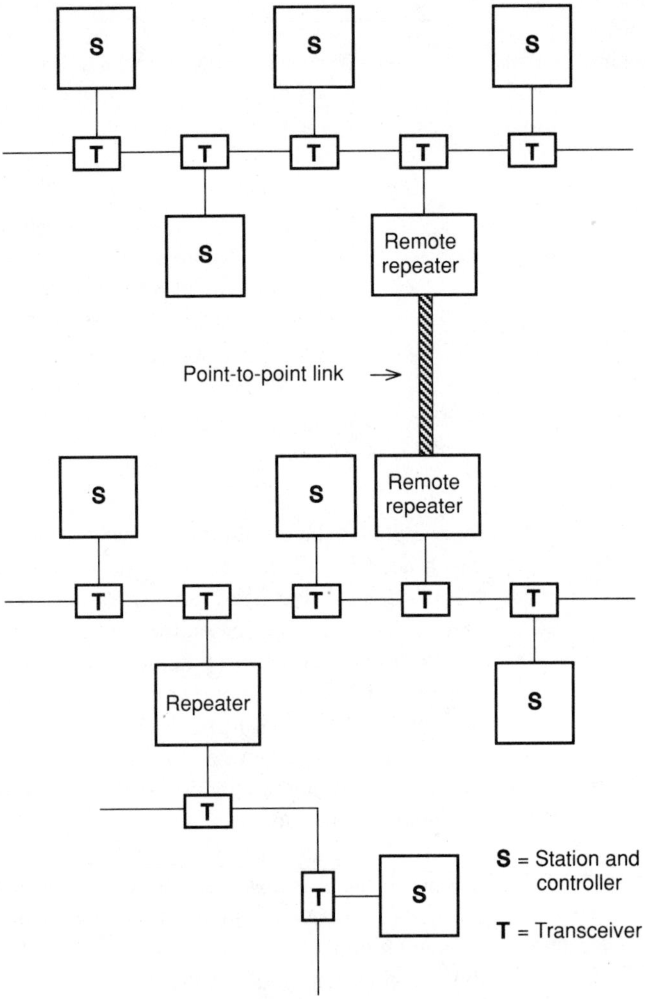
S
S
S
T
T
T
T
T
S
Remote repeater
Point-to-point link
S
S
Remote repeater
T
T
T
T
T
Repeater
S
T
T
S
S = Station and controller
T = Transceiver

linked to other LANs, providing a companywide communication system (Exhibit 11, for example). This is accomplished through the use of an IBM PC that becomes the bridge between two networks. A board from each network is installed in one PC, allowing internetwork communication and resource sharing. Once connected by the PC bridge, the network system can take whatever shape the user desires —any of the numerous network systems can be connected. Further, Advanced NetWare allows for the LAN to be connected to both IBM's BISYNC SNA/SDLC environment and DEC's ASYNC environment as well as dial-up access allowing individuals to call into the office to access the system.

EXHIBIT 9   Features of NetWare S by Novell, Inc.

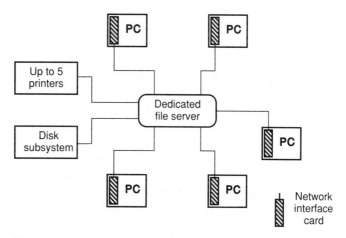

Netware S

Novell, Inc.
1170 North Industrial Park Drive
Orem, UT 84057

(800) 453-1267

Protocol — proprietary

Topology — star (24 PCs maximum)

Data Rate — 500 kbps

Medium — shielded twisted pair (1,000 meter maximum)

Computers supported — IBM PC (PC–DOS V1.1, V1.2, V2.0;
                    CP / M; CP / M-86)

Remarks — Network supports five serial printer ports from
            50 to 19.2K baud. There is a 68,000-based dedicated
            file server located at the hub of the star.

Some other features of Advanced NetWare that impressed Albert were its constant user/application interface (with the interface, users need learn only one set of commands and procedures); its multiple server capacity, allowing simultaneous log-on for up to eight servers; its placement of management responsibility on the network—not the PC workstation; and its ability to synchronize all workstations using only one device for file and space allocation.

Advanced NetWare's most outstanding feature, from Albert's viewpoint, was

EXHIBIT 10   Technical Aspects of S-Net

General	Specific
Networking media	Coaxial, twin-ax, twisted-pair, fiber optics
Network access	CSMA/CD, CSMA/CA, token passing
Data rate	600 K – 10 Mbps
Maximum number of stations	Up to 100 nodes per segment—unlimited stations
Maximum distance	1 Km without repeaters—unlimited with Telco
Computer support	IBM and IBM-compatible NIUs with BISYNC and ASYNC connectors

its security procedure. Not all departments should have access to every other department's information. To prevent compromise of department proprietary data, MSP needed some definitive security procedures.

Advanced NetWare discourages software piracy and offers controls for the number of users simultaneously running one application program. Control is accomplished through a series of copy-protection layers and usage restrictions. Specifically, servers are assigned serial numbers checked by the network's application program. If the server's identity does not match the listed identities allowed into a particular program, the network logs off the server, revokes the server's file access, and reports an error to the workstation.

The Novell network seems to be perfect. However, Novell, Inc.'s service division was opened just a few months ago; while the basic product may be very good, the service system could be too new to be trusted. Regardless, Albert was convinced that this was the best system for MSP. He presented his findings (not emphasizing the potential service problem) to a committee composed of one or two management personnel from each department and MSP's chief administrator. After reviewing the information, the committee agreed with Albert, and Advanced NetWare became MSP's hope for better information resource management.

All department managers were asked to submit specifications as to their needs for the system. The MIS department reviewed the various requests to determine what information would be placed on the network. This review was undertaken mainly to avoid duplication.

Since Novell's system will blend well with ADP's IBM equipment and the IBM PC, it was decided to use all IBM hardware and software. MSP wished to avoid writing any of its own software. Any equipment displaced by the system would either be reallocated within the firm or sold off (so as to recoup the LAN cost). The LAN would also provide word processing and electronic mail services. As a result, some other pieces of existing equipment may also become unnecessary.

The cost of the LAN was expected to be $224,825 (see Exhibit 12). Since only those departments requesting terminals would receive them, the costs were di-

EXHIBIT 11   Advanced NetWare Builds LANs Bridges

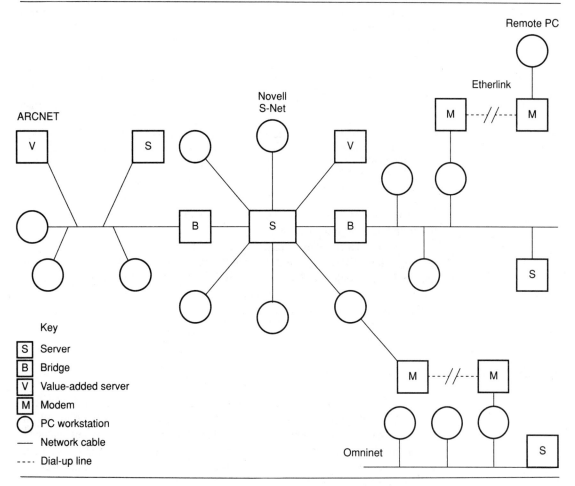

vided on a pro rata basis. Any costs incurred through the use of specific databases would be charged back to the originating department.

It did not appear that there would be any logistical problems, since it was decided that the installation of the LAN would coincide with the move of these departments to their new offices. In this way, cables and workstations would be installed at the same time as the phone cable, ADP cabling, and ADP machines.

With Advanced NetWare providing the security base, Albert set up a pyramid system for assigning serial numbers. Thus, access to the system was limited by department, preserving the confidential nature of much of the information. Mergers and Acquisitions would have total access, Corporate Finance all but Mergers

EXHIBIT 12   MSP Enterprises Cost Estimate for Installation of Novell LAN

CPUs and terminals	$145,000
Networking equipment	45,000
Printers/Plotters	10,000
Various software	15,000
AT&T ACCUNET*	1,800
Cable†	8,025
Total cost estimate	$224,825

*VAC line with three circuits with an additional monthly charge of $300.00.
†Cable costs were figured using two prices:
  1. $7.00 per foot of regular cable (775 feet total).
  2. $8.00 per foot for teflon-coated cable (325 feet total).

and Acquisitions entries, and Trading and Institutional Sales would have access to limited general information.

All in all, Albert believed this to be the best workable system for now. It was his hope that this LAN would make information and the speed of retrieval so valuable that people would come to rely heavily on the system. He hoped that the LAN would expand to other departments, thus making internetwork communication possible through the use of PC bridges and gateways as advocated by Advanced NetWare.

PERSONALITIES

Bob Albert's presentation was quite a surprise to many of the partners in that December 1986 meeting. He convinced the majority of the partners to vote in favor of his plan. Without having had a real chance to evaluate this new material, people at all levels of MSP began to question the hastiness of the decision, as well as the network proposal itself. (Refer to Exhibit 13, the organizational chart, as necessary.)

DAVID ALEXANDER

Albert was astonished that one of the objections to the system came from David Alexander, managing director of the Syndicate department. As Alexander explained it to Albert and other partners, he was not paranoid about either his position in the firm (as were some newer executives to the firm) nor about the new technology (as were some of the "computer-wary" executives). In fact, Alexander considered himself an amateur MIS expert, often helping to set up small systems throughout the firm or for partners in their homes.

Alexander felt that the firm was moving too fast in this decision and that this

EXHIBIT 13 MSP Enterprises Management Information Systems

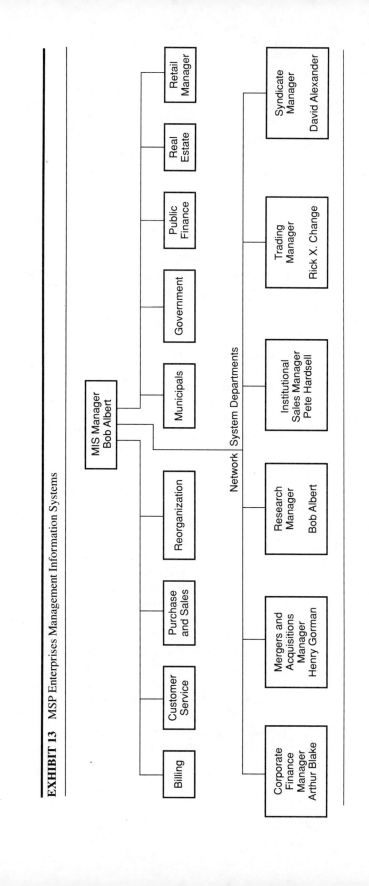

LAN would become no more than an executive's toy. All the systems and information access were already available, as were word processing and electronic mail service (provided by ADP). Alexander thus felt that more time should have been taken to evaluate the new system; however, knowing that the decision had been made, he was not sure that it should be changed or revoked at this time — so close to completion.

ARTHUR BLAKE

The manager of the Corporate Finance department, Arthur Blake, has been in his position with MSP for almost three years. At 31 years of age, Blake is rather young to be holding such a position in the firm, compared with other department managers who are in their 50s and 60s. He feels it necessary to prove himself constantly to the other managers and partners, trying to compensate for his lack of experience.

Blake's own feelings of insecurity were only increased by the decision to install the LAN. In fact, he voted against the plan when it was first submitted at the meeting of department managers. Although highly educated in his field, Blake knows nothing about data processing. He joined MSP, in fact, so that he could do what he does best and enjoys most: work with people. Blake has oriented his department around this ideal, and he feels that his network system will only undermine the people orientation of his department.

CHIP HARWOOD

Chip Harwood, manager of the Retail department in Baltimore, listened intently to Albert's sales pitch at the partners' meeting in December of 1986. He felt that Albert's system made sense for those few select departments designated as users; but he also stated the time and expense was dedicated to a project, which would serve only a few departments, and was therefore unwarranted.

Harwood is indignant because he and the people in Retail were excluded from the early phase of the decision process. Wouldn't it have been better to interview at least the managers of every department, compile a list of needs and requirements, and then go from there to determine the best possible system for everyone? If the information found on the ADP system is good enough for the Retail salespeople, it should be good enough for everyone else as well, in Harwood's opinion. On the other hand, if the ADP system is not good enough for those other departments, possibly it is not good enough for Retail, either. Any way you look at it, this new system is not fair, according to Harwood.

PETE HARDSELL

The Institutional Sales manager, Pete Hardsell, was overwhelmed but excited by the idea of fingertip availability of such quantities of information. Presently, finding information about a particular company is a tedious and time-consuming process. With this new system and its immediate information access capability, hours once spent researching can now be spent analyzing and making decisions.

Still, Hardsell is concerned about the security problem. Even with the serial access codes, he worries about how easy it might be for someone to obtain another person's access number, giving them entry to highly confidential material. Such infractions could cause serious problems in terms of the Securities and Exchange Commission rules and regulations. Albert has assured him that violations such as these will be dealt with quickly and firmly. Hardsell is still uneasy, but he favors the system.

THE SECRETARIES

Responses from the secretaries has been mixed. On the one hand, much of their footwork will be eliminated. Information input and retrieval will be much simpler. Several secretaries, however, are annoyed that they were not included in the selection process, especially in the equipment decision. They complain that management is often unaware of the most desirable features of equipment — those features making the equipment easier to use quickly. The unhappy secretaries, a vocal group though not a majority, insist that they could have chosen better, more functional equipment.

BRYCE'S FACT SHEET

Harold wanted LAN intelligence from his own sources to help him decide what actions he should take, if any, concerning the LAN. One of his administrative assistants quickly collected the following information, including the exhibits, and called it a fact sheet.

FACT SHEET

1. NOVELL is not the only LAN with security features. IBM, DEC, 3COM, AT&T, and Ungermann-Bass also have security software. Nor is NOVELL the industry leader (see Fact Sheet Exhibit 1).

EXHIBIT 1   Top Network Vendors—1987 Datapro Survey

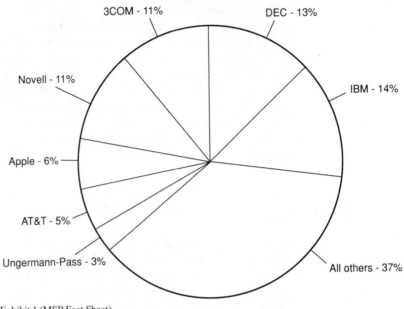

Exhibit 1 (MSP Fact Sheet)

2. In a recent Datapro survey, both AT&T and DEC scored better than NOVELL in user satisfaction, ease of installation, speed of data transmission, performance under heavy use, and overall performance. NOVELL, however, did rate higher in software performance than any other LAN in the survey.

3. The Datapro survey also indicated a recent decline in the use of LANs for mainframe and multibuilding applications (see Fact Sheet Exhibits 2 and 3).

4. Albert made no reference to any comparisons he may have made of the technical characteristics of NOVELL against other LANs. The only criterion that appeared to be under consideration was the ability to provide adequate security (see Fact Sheet Exhibits 4–8).

5. Albert apparently considered no technology but LANs. A recent breakthrough (within the last few years) for just this type of application has been the use of PBX/CBX's. These privately owned branch exchanges are installed in new and old buildings as updated phone system technologies. They allow both voice and data to be transmitted from the same workstation at the same time using only the wiring (standard twisted-pair telephone wiring) installed with the phone system. Using already installed, relatively inexpensive wiring greatly reduces the cost of installation and maintenance when compared to LANs, which use coaxial cable or fiber optics. These PBX/CBX systems provide a

EXHIBIT 2   LAN Geography — 1987 Datapro Survey

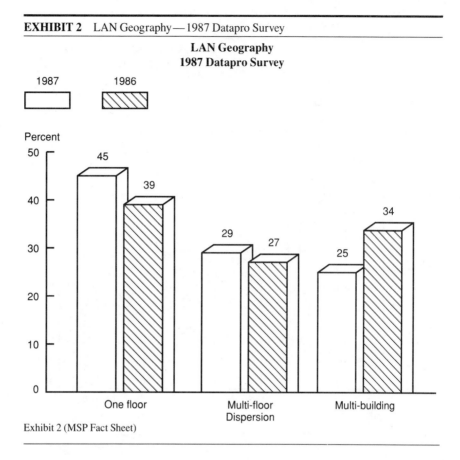

LAN Geography
1987 Datapro Survey

Exhibit 2 (MSP Fact Sheet)

link, and also furnish built-in office automation services, integrated phone/terminal workstations, word processing, business graphics, relational databases, and other features (see Fact Sheet Exhibit 9 for detailed characteristics).

6. Star Networks have been available for quite some time. They originated as a result of the telephone industry's reorganization. The advantage of the star topology is that a node does not have to decide which path to take to reach a certain destination, because there is only one route. In addition, it is easy to install this topology.

However, there are some drawbacks:

- While the computer is busy playing operator, it can perform no other duties. This restriction limits either the performance of the network or the computer as a processor—usually both.
- If the main computer fails for any reason, the entire network will be down.
- Every node requires a separate link to the hub, which can become quite

EXHIBIT 3   LAN Attachments—1987 Datapro Survey

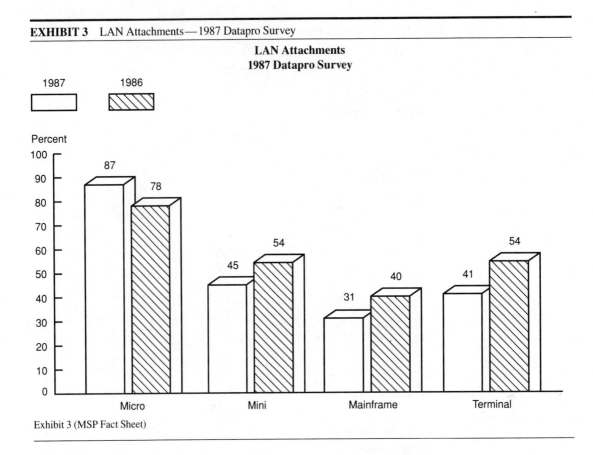

Exhibit 3 (MSP Fact Sheet)

expensive when nodes are geographically distant within the network.

7. It is not known whether Albert, or anyone else, looked, asked, or considered asking ADP if they could provide the same service as the proposed LAN.

CONCLUSION

A final thought from Bob Albert: "This system will be a great addition to the firm for information storage, retrieval, and so on. It is not, however, the 'be-all and end-all.' There are things this system will not be able to do. It may still be necessary at times to use old information sources. Changes may also be necessary in the future, but these should serve only to enhance the system's capabilities. What is most important, this system is a step into the future for MSP."

Bryce has a major decision on his hands. Overall planning for the move is well along and, unfortunately for him, installation of the new system is impending. He has little time to make this decision.

EXHIBIT 4   Novell Technical Characteristics (MSP Fact Sheet)

COMPANY   Novell, Incorporated   PHONE   (800) 453-1267

PRODUCTS   NetWare RX-Net, NP600, NetWare Ethernet, Intelligent NIC

NETWORK OPERATING SYSTEM   NOVELL Advanced NetWare

TOPOLOGIES SUPPORTED   Star, Distributed Star, Linear Bus

CABLING SCHEMES   Baseband, Broadband

ACCESS SCHEMES   Token passing, Contention

MAXIMUM CONNECTION DISTANCE   500 feet to 1 kilometer

WORKSTATIONS SUPPORTED   255 (RX-NET), 100 nodes per segment (all others)

BOARD TO HOST TRANSFER METHOD   DMA, Shared Memory and Dual Port Shared Memory

BUS INTERFACE WIDTH   16 bits (NP600), 8 bits (all others)

PRICE PER CONNECTION $350 to $800

SERVER DATA
Processor type	80286
Clock speed	6 to 8 MHz
Wait states	0 or 1
Max memory capacity	8–12 MB
Memory cycle speed	250 nsec.
Transfer channel width	16 bits
Max workstations	100 logical
Price per server	1,195 to 19,195

HARDWARE DATA
Hardware supported	All major topologies
Host operating system	MS-DOS 2.0 or higher
Emulates/runs-on-top of host operating system	Either
Disk or file server	File server based

ADDITIONAL CAPABILITIES   Electronic mail, bulletin board, asychronous communications server, SNA gateway, internal and external bridging to multiple LANs

QUESTIONS

1. Were Bob Albert's analysis and development procedures efficient and effective?
2. Comment on Bob Albert's management style in getting the LAN approved.
3. Were Alexander's, Blake's, Harwood's, and Hardsell's apprehensions about the LAN reasonable or not?
4. Is Albert correct about MSP's need for a LAN?
5. If you are familiar with networking and telecommunications, what questions would you have and where would you go for the answers?
6. If you were in Bryce's position, what, if anything, would you do now?
7. How would you implement the recommendation you chose in question 6?

EXHIBIT 5   IBM Technical Characteristics (MSP Fact Sheet)

COMPANY   IBM   PHONE   (800) IBM-2468

PRODUCTS   PC-Network and Token Ring

NETWORK OPERATING SYSTEM   IBM PC-LAN

TOPOLOGIES SUPPORTED   Star, Daisychain, Linear Bus, Ring

CABLING SCHEMES   Baseband, Broadband

ACCESS SCHEMES   Token passing, CSMA/CD

MAXIMUM CONNECTION DISTANCE   200 feet to 1,000 feet

WORKSTATIONS SUPPORTED   80 to 1,000

BOARD TO HOST TRANSFER METHOD   DMA, Shared Memory

BUS INTERFACE WIDTH   8 bits

PRICE PER CONNECTION $880 TO $1,032.50

SERVER DATA	Processor type	Specs not available
	Clock speed	Specs not available
	Wait states	Specs not available
	Max memory capacity	Specs not available
	Memory cycle speed	Specs not available
	Transfer channel width	Specs not available
	Max workstations	Specs not available
	Price per server	Specs not available

HARDWARE DATA	Hardware supported	PC-Network, baseband, broadband, token ring
	Host operating system	MS-DOS 3.1, 3.2, 3.3
	Emulates/runs-on-top of host operating system	Runs-on-top
	Disk or file server	File server based

ADDITIONAL CAPABILITIES   Messaging, saving, retrieving, send same message, editing, forwarding a
received message, skipping previously viewed messages in file log

EXHIBIT 6   DEC Technical Characteristics (MSP Fact Sheet)

COMPANY   DEC   PHONE   Contact local sales

PRODUCTS   DECNET

NETWORK OPERATING SYSTEM   DECNET

TOPOLOGIES SUPPORTED   Linear Bus

CABLING SCHEMES   Baseband, Broadband, Fiber-optic

ACCESS SCHEMES   Contention, CSMA/CD

MAXIMUM CONNECTION DISTANCE   13.5 miles

WORKSTATIONS SUPPORTED   1,063 max

BOARD TO HOST TRANSFER METHOD   Shared Memory

BUS INTERFACE WIDTH   16 or 32 bits

PRICE PER CONNECTION $645 per station

SERVER DATA
Processor type	Specs not available
Clock speed	Specs not available
Wait states	Specs not available
Max memory capacity	Specs not available
Memory cycle speed	Specs not available
Transfer channel width	Specs not available
Max workstations	Specs not available
Price per server	Specs not available

HARDWARE DATA
Hardware supported	3COM, Micom, Ethernet
Host operating system	VMS, MS-DOS, Ultrix, Tops, RSTS/E, RT-11
Emulates/runs-on-top of host operating system	Runs-on-top
Disk or file server	Either

ADDITIONAL CAPABILITIES   Electronic Mail, videotext, Vaxnotes

EXHIBIT 7 3COM Technical Characteristics (MSP Fact Sheet)

COMPANY   3COM   PHONE   (408) 562-6508

PRODUCTS   Etherlink Plus, Etherlink, Etherlink II, Token Link, Token Link II

NETWORK OPERATING SYSTEM   3 + , NOVELL NetWare, DECNET

TOPOLOGIES SUPPORTED   Star, Linear Bus, Logical Ring

CABLING SCHEMES   Baseband, Broadband

ACCESS SCHEMES   Token ring, CSMA/CD, Convention, IEEE 802.3

MAXIMUM CONNECTION DISTANCE   8,500 feet

WORKSTATIONS SUPPORTED   260 to 1,024

BOARD TO HOST TRANSFER METHOD   DMA, Shared Memory, I/O port, Bus

BUS INTERFACE WIDTH   8 or 16 bits

PRICE PER CONNECTION $495 to $895

SERVER DATA	Processor type	Specs not available
	Clock speed	Specs not available
	Wait states	Specs not available
	Max memory capacity	Specs not available
	Memory cycle speed	Specs not available
	Transfer channel width	Specs not available
	Max workstations	Specs not available
	Price per server	Specs not available

HARDWARE DATA	Hardware supported	Not stated
	Host operating system	MS-DOS 3.1, 3.2, 3.3
	Emulates/runs-on-top of host operating system	Runs-on-top
	Disk or file server	File server based

ADDITIONAL CAPABILITIES   Electronic mail, remote PC access, remote internetworking, asynchronous
gateways, 3270 emulation

EXHIBIT 8   AT&T Technical Characteristics (MSP Fact Sheet)

COMPANY   AT&T   PHONE   (800) 247-1212

PRODUCTS   Starlan

NETWORK OPERATING SYSTEM   AT&T (proprietary)

TOPOLOGIES SUPPORTED   Star

CABLING SCHEMES   Unshielded twisted-pair

ACCESS SCHEMES   Contention, CSMA/CD

MAXIMUM CONNECTION DISTANCE   800 feet

WORKSTATIONS SUPPORTED   1,200 max

BOARD TO HOST TRANSFER METHOD   Not stated

BUS INTERFACE WIDTH   32 bits

PRICE PER CONNECTION $125 to $395

SERVER DATA   Processor type   Specs not available
                 Clock speed   Specs not available
                 Wait states   Specs not available
                 Max memory capacity   Specs not available
                 Memory cycle speed   Specs not available
                 Transfer channel width Specs not available
                 Max workstations   Specs not available
                 Price per server   Specs not available

HARDWARE DATA   Hardware supported   Star, IEEE 802.3
                  Host operating system   MS-DOS 3.1, Unix,
                                              System V
                  Emulates/runs-on-top of host
                    operating system   Emulates
                  Disk or file server   Not stated

ADDITIONAL CAPABILITIES   Electronic mail

EXHIBIT 9   Northern Telecom CBX Technical Characteristics (MSP Fact Sheet)

COMPANY   Northern Telecom   PHONE   (214) 437-8000

PRODUCTS   Network Management System (NMS), Meridian DV-1

NETWORK OEPRATING SYSTEM   Unix, MS-DOS, CP/M, LAN-Link

TOPOLOGIES SUPPORTED   Star

CABLING SCHEMES   Standard twisted-pair

ACCESS SCHEMES   Circuit switched up to 2.56 Mbps

MAXIMUM CONNECTION DISTANCE   2,000 feet from node

WORKSTATIONS SUPPORTED   100 per cabinet

BOARD TO HOST TRANSFER METHOD   Not stated

BUS INTERFACE WIDTH   Not stated

PRICE PER CONNECTION   Call for price

SERVER DATA   Processor type   Specs not available
              Clock speed   Specs not available
              Wait states   Specs not available
              Max memory capacity   Specs not available
              Memory cycle speed   Specs not available
              Transfer channel width   Specs not available
              Max workstations   Specs not available
              Price per server   Specs not available

HARDWARE DATA   Hardware supported   Most micros, most minis
                                            and most mainframes,
                                            ASYNC, BISYNC,
                                            SNA/SDLC and X.25
                                            protocols. Emulates
                                            3278-2, 3274-1C, and
                                            51C cluster controller
                Host operating system   Not stated
                Emulates/runs-on-top of host
                    operating system   Emulates
                Disk or file server   Not applicable

ADDITIONAL CAPABILITIES   Data communication, electronic mail, word processing, desk-to-desk shared
                            screen, directory, time management, external relational database, third party
                            applications, virtual spreadsheet, modeling, business graphics, multiple line
                            calling, concurrent application access, electronic calendar, security pass-
                            words, and phone technology

Case 3–2   *Wilson Memorial Hospital and DCS, Inc.*

Ben Solomon has been retained to mediate a dispute over software performance. The parties are Wilson Memorial Hospital, a medium-sized general service hospital, and DCS, Inc., a small software development firm. For additional background on both Wilson Memorial and DCS, see Appendixes A and B at the end of this case.

The contract in question called for an on-line patient information system that could register patients, provide access to test results and other medical information, monitor length of stay and charge limitations, and provide the usual patient charging and general accounting functions. The system is functioning properly, but response times are consistently below those promised in the specifications. Both parties have tried several approaches to improve the response times, but they are still unsatisfactory. Further steps will require considerable expense, and the parties are unable to agree on an equitable sharing of the costs.

Ben has been asked to recommend an equitable settlement. The mediation is not binding, but both parties are committed to avoiding costly, time-consuming litigation.

A chronology of events has been provided; the facts are not disputed. Each party has also presented oral briefs to support its positions. Ben's summary of the facts follows.

JULY 1985

The hospital published a request for proposal (RFP) consisting of approximately 140 pages of detailed specifications in which the necessary functions were described. There was also considerable data on the hospital's patient volumes, the number of terminals needed, and the range of services the hospital offered. The RFP did not include an ambulatory surgery center, which was still being considered when the RFP was released. All prospective vendors were given the opportunity to visit the hospital, look over the operations, and ask questions. DCS was conscientious in seeking as much information as possible before placing a bid. The vendors were expected to include recommended hardware and its costs in the bids.

JANUARY 1987

DCS was chosen, and a contract was signed. The contract referred to the original RFP as published in July. One of the requirements agreed to was an average response time of "three seconds or less" from the time an inquiry or command

This case was prepared by David Daigle and Jeffrey Wilson and updated by David Ebelein. Names have been disguised.

is entered until the time the computer responds. Procedures for measuring the time, including sampling techniques, were established. The three-second figure was to be an average of several samples. The contract also established target dates for each of the major phases of the implementation process.

FEBRUARY 10

The hospital raised the possibility, for the first time, of adding the ambulatory surgery center. Seven additional terminals were requested. The hospital was willing to buy the terminals separately from the main contract, but they were not sure the new system would be able to process the additional load.

The installation director for DCS asked for and received estimates on the number of registrations the hospital was projecting. After consulting with his engineers and programmers, the installation director told the hospital that the system as it was being developed would be able to accommodate the additions. The contract was not amended because the installation director did not think adding the seven terminals was a material change.

MARCH 15

Hardware installation began on schedule.

APRIL 10

Training of hospital staff began. Minor "bugs" were encountered and corrected. Training was approximately a week late in starting. Response times during this period were good (2.0), but the system was not fully loaded.

MAY 1

The 90-day acceptance period began on schedule. During the 90 days, the hospital was to test the system and satisfy itself that the system was performing as expected under realistic conditions. Response times were within the three-second contractual limits, but there was little reason to be overconfident. Test samples averaged 2.9. There were no significant bugs remaining.

JUNE 1

The ambulatory surgery center was opened, and the extra terminals were put on-line. In this center, patients are registered, tests are ordered through the terminals, results are made available, surgery is performed, and the patient is discharged, in the space of five or six hours. Therefore, the demands placed on the seven terminals are more intense than is the case in many other parts of the hospital. DCS concedes that they underestimated terminal demand. Also, patient volumes proved to be higher than expected because medicare and other payors began to require that certain surgical procedures be done on an outpatient basis only. The hospital had the information necessary to forecast the outpatient volume increase accurately but failed to do the calculations. At this time, response times were perceived to be slower (more than three seconds); however, both hospital staff and vendor personnel believed user lack of expertise vis-à-vis the new system was at least partly to blame.

JUNE 7

Training was completed on schedule.

JUNE 15

Response times were substandard for the first time, with sample results averaging 3.35 seconds. This sample was the first formal measurement taken since the ambulatory surgery (short stay) center opened.

JULY 1

The hospital informed DCS that the response times were unsatisfactory. Further testing of the system confirmed that the sample test results did not meet contract specifications.

JULY 7

In their first meeting, DCS suggested three approaches that would help to spread demand more evenly, and thus improve response times.

1. Schedule the running of large management reports such as general ledger in the evening shift; while patient care demands are much lighter at night, this decision would require increasing staff on that shift by 1 or 1.5 FTEs (full-time equivalents).

2. Restrict access to terminals in nonpatient care areas during the busiest times of the day (to be accomplished by scheduling various departments to certain time slots, or "locking" certain terminals out of the system during peak periods).

3. Reduce the number of user aids available on screen. Help screens could be put into manuals for each terminal. Menu-driven programs could be altered in favor of command-driven programs.

JULY 14

The hospital agreed to proposal 1, but rejected the other two. More staff was added to the evening shift at a cost to the hospital of $29,325 a year. Response times improved marginally. Test results averaged 3.2 seconds.

JULY 25

At this meeting, the hospital reported that response times had improved but were still unsatisfactory. The vendor responded by offering to upgrade the existing CPU and the communication lines used in the system at the vendor's expense. Costs were expected to be approximately $42,000. Note: See Appendix C for response time of samples collected during the period May–July.

AUGUST 5

After the vendor's upgrades had been installed, the system still fell short of the specification performance standard. Test results for all six samples and actual and projected visits to the ambulatory surgery center are shown in the accompanying tables.

Sample Test Results, August 2, 1987

Sample Number	Response Time	Time of Day*
1	3.15	8:00 A.M.
2	3.55	10:00 A.M.
3	3.65	11:15 A.M.
4	3.05	12:00 Noon
5	3.01	2:15 P.M.
6	2.50	4:00 P.M.
Average	3.15	

*Times of the day when samples were to be taken was established in the contract; they were not selected randomly. Samples were taken only on weekdays.

Short Stay Center Visits

	Projected	Actual	Difference
June '87	60	74	23.3%
July	70	90	28.6%
August	75	99	32.0%
September	80	108	35.0%

Current capacity is approximately 120 per month.

At this point, the only solution was the replacement of the current CPU with a larger, much more expensive machine. Neither side was willing to bear the cost, nor was either side willing to discuss splitting the cost. In light of the magnitude of the costs being considered, it became clear that the parties would be unable to settle the matter on their own. Both sides agreed on mediation.

WILSON MEMORIAL'S BRIEFING TO SOLOMON

Ed Grant, director of Data Processing and coordinator for the conversion to the new system, was chosen to present the hospital's oral brief. In his early 40s, Ed had been hired by the hospital as a consultant 12 years ago (when between jobs) to prepare the RFP, oversee the selection, and monitor the installation of the old computer system; he was then asked to come aboard permanently to manage the DP operations and staff. Before the nine-month consulting task, he had been responsible for the selection and purchase of computer hardware and software to support a 500-person engineering program in a federal department. Although he had a BS in Engineering (General) from Georgia Tech, Ed's only education about computers had come from one-day seminars, community college courses, and in-house training offered by the federal agency. Ed started his presentation.

"Mr. Solomon, this case will no doubt seem to be filled with a lot of technical details and lots of finger pointing; it is not likely that an easy solution will be found. The problem in its essence is actually very simple: Wilson Memorial has spent over a million dollars on a new computer system. Parts of it work perfectly; but in one respect, it's just not good enough. When you spend two year's profit on one thing, it ought to work . . . perfectly. This system doesn't.

"The contract calls for response times of three seconds or less. After both parties have spent extra money to meet that requirement, the best we can get is 3.15. That may seem insignificant, but it's not.

"First of all, that time is supposed to be the outer limit, not the normal operating time. When you look at the most recent test samples, you find response times as high as 3.65. When you are seated at a terminal trying to get something accomplished, 3 2/3 seconds from the time you strike a key to the time the computer responds is a long, long time. Consider a clerk in our patient accounting section who is trying to post payments to a patient's bill. For each payment, she (or he) must first give the command for payment posting, and then wait. That's the first pause. Then, the clerk enters the patient's account number and waits for the computer to find that patient's account. That's the second pause. Then she enters the insurance code, a payment code, and the dollar amount. Then the computer performs some edits to see if the posting is reasonable. That's the third pause. If the entry passes the edits, it is posted to the account. If the clerk has to wait 3 2/3 seconds for every pause, that's 11 seconds idle for every single payment. We get hundreds on some days. Multiply that kind of lost time by the number of transactions that go into the computer on a weekday, and you begin to understand the magnitude of the problem. And again, at the worst time of the day, we're two thirds of a second over the limit. It could be a full second or more over a reasonable response time.

"When we discussed this system with DCS and all the other vendors, it was clear that we wanted a system that would accommodate some growth in future years. That's why we provided anticipated future volumes. This system has been slow since the day it was installed. Before the short stay center (ambulatory surgery center) was put on line, the response times were tested at 2.9. Some of that slowness might be attributable to inexperienced users, but even if you make some kind of allowance for that, it was still slow. Even if the short stay center had never come into existence, the response times would have been just barely up to specs with no room for growth. I would also remind you that DCS was late in beginning training of hospital staff because the software wasn't ready yet. I wonder how hasty and slipshod the programming work was in those last few days, when they were scrambling to make a missed deadline. That deadline is doubly significant because this system was built from preexisting modules that only need to be modified to fit a given hospital. Wilson Memorial is a fairly average, middle-of-the-road hospital. It should not have been difficult to knit well-written modules together for such an unexceptional situation.

"So here we are faced with these slow response times. In our discussions with DCS, they offered the three recommendations to reduce response times that you have already heard about. We agreed to the first one, and adding 1.5 FTEs to the evening shift will cost us almost $30,000 in the first year alone. Please note that this is a permanent, on-going expense, in contrast to DCS's one-time purchase of equipment that they probably should have gotten in the first place. Inflation and normal salary increases will only serve to increase our costs year after year.

"Their other recommendations would not have cost us any money, but they were entirely unacceptable. The recommendation that we schedule certain terminals to be used only at certain times would have negated the whole reason for having an 'on-line' system. It would have reduced it to some kind of batch operation. We don't need a million-dollar batch processing system. Some of the functions they recommended restricting have to be accessible at all times. If a patient calls up to discuss her bill, we can't tell her to call back between 2 and 4 P.M. How would you like to tell a doctor that she can only schedule her patients' admissions between 8 and 10 A.M.? Especially when she starts office hours at 11.

"The other recommendation we rejected called for a reduction of the on-screen user aids that we wanted for the sake of our people. First of all, this system was billed as being user-friendly. These modifications would have reduced that rather sharply. Now, a blank computer screen can be a pretty daunting sight to people who are uncertain about their ability to use one. Some aids to reduce the anxiety level are necessary. Also, it might be reasonable to expect certain hospital employees to know all the commands that their job requires, but it is unrealistic to expect that of the medical staff and other clinical people. They have enough to do keeping up with medicine, without taking time out to learn the ins and outs of this system. We did concur with the programming changes that allowed people to bypass menus if they didn't need them. That helped a little bit.

"But the idea of putting all the help screens in some kind of manual was ludicrous. If the people knew enough to find the right screen in the book, they could probably make do with the menus.

"When discussions with DCS began to get difficult, they started casting doubts at the accuracy of our volume data for things like patient days, outpatient visits, and general accounting transactions. First of all, the historical data was accurate. All the numbers we gave them came from reliable sources. Also, the information being used is easy to count. We're very unlikely to make a mistake on historical data.

"In hindsight, we have found that some of our projections were too conservative. Most of the growth in outpatient volume that we expected to take three years has occurred in one. The important point is that our current actual data is still within the projections we gave them. The system is supposed to be able to handle today's volumes.

"We believe the system is underdesigned because DCS did not do a very good job translating patient volumes into demands on computer time. That is the kind of expertise that they are supposed to bring to the project, and their past installations led us to believe that they had sufficient experience to do that. It should be remembered that when we were in the bidding stage, DCS asked for and received more data than was in the original RFP. They did not ask for anything that we were unable to supply. I see no way for them to complain that our data was inaccurate or insufficient.

"I expect DCS to lay the blame for this whole mess at the door of the short stay center. They'll say that it was a major modification after the contract was signed. They'll say that, if we hadn't added those seven extra terminals, there wouldn't be a problem. They may even say that we misled them by not including the short stay center in the RFP.

"First of all, the short stay center was not in the RFP because we were not sure it would ever be opened. Remember that the RFP was published in July. We had been working on it since April, and the center wasn't opened until the following June, 14 months later. Change is a constant in a hospital, and it can't be brought to a halt just because we need a new computer system. Also, a lot of this 'extra demand' you're likely to hear about is not really new. Many of these registrations are people who would otherwise have been admitted. This is merely a shift of activity from one place to another.

"The short stay center is here to stay, too. There is ample demonstrated need for such a service, and it's our responsibility to fill it. To close the center now would damage the hospital's goodwill, our reputation, and our credibility. Besides, that would be a monumental case of the tail wagging the dog. We can't inhibit our medical services just because this software can't handle it.

"Frankly, I don't see how they can complain about the short stay center at all. We asked them if the system could handle it. The installation director huddled with his technical whizzes and said that it would. He had the opportunity to say, 'No.' He had the opportunity to say, 'Yes, but you'll need a bigger CPU.' All he said was, 'Yes.'

"To sum up, I believe that the solution to this problem is simple, in the final analysis. We contracted for a system that would respond in less than 3 seconds. DCS agreed to provide it. It's time for them to do whatever it takes to do that."

DCS BRIEF TO BEN SOLOMON

Dave Caron is vice president of Integrated Systems, a department in DCS. The installation director was Jeff Baker. Dave Caron presented DCS's first formal brief to Ben Solomon following a short break after Wilson Memorial's presentation:

"Mr. Solomon, DCS and Wilson Memorial agreed to a contract entailing the installation of a hospital information system. The system installed was within the specifications of the original RFP in every way. The contract date was January 10. In February, Ed Grant (the hospital's director of Data Processing) asked us to respond to a request to install seven additional terminals in the short stay center. At that time, we were given grossly inadequate estimates of the data requirements surrounding the request. We based our decisions on the information supplied to us.

"The addition of the short stay center has resulted in system use at a level that was originally projected for 1990. The upshot of the higher usage rate is no pad or margin for growth in future years, even though the system meets all of the original specifications of the RFP. I personally feel that Wilson Memorial misled DCS by sending out an RFP that made no mention of the plans to add the short stay center.

"DCS responded to the RFP as any system integration contractor would. Wilson chose DCS for one reason: We presented the best scenario in response to their RFP. Wilson would be in their current situation, if not worse, regardless of which contractor they had chosen.

"Let's face it, we (system integration contractors) are all selling basically the same product. The fundamental differences involve the level of service provided to the customer and other very minor software distinctions that every contractor uses to differentiate the product.

"Any contractor in these circumstances would have the same problem. Wilson did not want to go to a larger CPU in the January negotiations due to cost considerations. We had suggested the larger CPU as a remedy.

"The other side of the coin is, 'Yes,' we did say that current CPU could handle the system as proposed; of course, we had not considered the short stay center area since it was not brought to our attention until after we had signed the contract.

"I find it very hard to believe that an organization the size of Wilson Memorial did not do any planning for the short stay center prior to our signing the contract. Now, because of their poor planning or even lack thereof, DCS is being told that we must pay for the hospital's mistake. That is not reasonable.

"We have already upgraded the current system at a cost, to us, of $42,000. Unfortunately, this has not lowered response time to Wilson's satisfaction. We have also recommended various alternatives. The only acceptable solution seems to be the installation of a larger CPU.

"The question is not what needs to be done, but who should pay for whose mistakes. DCS firmly believes we have responded to all problems and concerns in a professional manner. I'm not so sure that Wilson had this same level of integrity when they issued the RFP.

"We have offered to swap the current CPU for a larger one. That will cost us an additional $20,000 in removal and installation costs. We will also lose $15,000 or more on the resale of the original CPU. This is due to the fact that a computer loses value very fast when it is first put into use. Our estimate of $15,000 is very low. We are not asking Wilson Memorial to pay us for these costs. Nor did we ask them to pay for the $42,000 in original enhancements. What we are asking is that they (Wilson Memorial) pay the incremental CPU cost of $167,000 to buy the larger machine. The $167,000 represents DCS's cost of the machine, less the $300,000 paid for the original CPU. We are not looking to make any profit on the swap but instead are striving to achieve a balance whereby neither party pays for any error caused by the other.

"It would actually work out to cost less over six years if Wilson were to install the larger CPU. Wilson has already added staff to run larger jobs in the evening. This is costing them $30,000 a year plus. A larger CPU will eliminate the need for this. A savings of $30,000 a year for six years is $180,000. This is more than we are asking Wilson to pay. So, as you see, not only will the larger CPU solve the response dilemma, it will actually be more cost-effective for the hospital.

"In previous meetings, Wilson expressed concerns over hiring someone for two or three months and them having to lay off this person. I find this argument irrational for the following reasons: If they are paying someone $20,000 a year to work, a $5,000 severance payment would more than cover the goodwill costs to the hospital. In reality, the person would probably be very happy to be let go if compensated to this degree. This would provide three months' wages to carry the person until a new job was available. Wilson would still break even in six years.

"We have at no time in any of our discussions mentioned that the short stay center should be closed. I personally am insulted that anyone at Wilson could ever think that we would suggest such a thing. We are a professional corporation, and we never tell our clients how to run their businesses; by the same token, we wouldn't expect them to try to tell us how to run ours.

"As you have noticed and have been told by hospital personnel, the software and hardware system is operating without any other problems. We have delivered our product as promised, and its performance is nearly perfect except for the response time dilemma. DCS has made every conceivable effort to resolve this issue in an equitable manner. I'm sure that you will find that Wilson Memorial —not DCS—is the stumbling block to reaching an agreement. The system is 100 percent functional as is.

"We believe that the practice of issuing an RFP and then saying, after the contract has been signed—'Oh, by the way, put this in'—is amateurish, not to mention a bit inept. We have been willing to negotiate, even spend unbudgeted funds, to resolve issues caused by Wilson's overlooking one of its largest expansions to date. And we are willing to share the expense to remedy part of the mistake; we're just not willing to pay for all of it.

"We invite you to consult any of our previous customers. I think you will find that 'our word is our bond' and that we are well-respected in the business community. If you would like any additional information from us, please ask. We will be more than happy to supply it.

"On that note, I will conclude before my blood pressure rises any higher. But I have to tell you—keeping our clients happy is our foremost concern; I've never been associated with a mud-slinging contest like this in all my years with DCS —or anyone else."

WILSON MEMORIAL'S REBUTTAL

After DCS's briefing, Solomon called another short break to allow tempers to cool down before proceeding with rebuttals. Ed Grant then gave the hospital's response.

"Let me begin by reassuring you, Mr. Solomon, that our dealings with each other have not been as rancorous as might be believed by what you have heard this morning. Until the response time problem became intractable and the magnitude of the dollars involved became clear to us, our relationship had been very cordial and productive. I should also hasten to add that I did not mean to insult Mr. Caron by implying that he had recommended closing the short stay center. I merely brought it up to make the point that closing the center was not an option.

"It is also true that the system accomplishes all that it was designed to do. The problem is that it takes so long to do it.

"Before I address what has been said, let me mention some things that were not said. DCS has never offered an explanation as to why they agreed to add the terminals, and why they believed that the system would accommodate them. That seems to me to be the crux of the matter, and I have to wonder why it has not been addressed. Please bear in mind that they had every opportunity to challenge our volume estimates and to raise any expansion issues before the first piece of equipment had been installed.

"Now I will attempt to respond to Mr. Caron's statements in more or less the order they were made.

"It is true that we raised the question of adding more terminals after the contract was signed. It is also true that our volume projections were understated. Whether they were 'grossly' out of line is another matter. Since DCS was at that time less than a month into the project, we felt that was early enough for them to respond to our change with relatively little difficulty. After consultations with his experts, Jeff Baker assured us that it would be possible. I don't see anything unprofessional in our behavior because they had every opportunity to raise any problems they might have had with the revision. The fact is, they didn't recognize them.

"While we were preparing the RFP, the short stay center was still in the feasibility stage. We considered including it in the RFP but, at that point, did not know enough about its eventual configuration or viability. We had to choose whether to include a program that might never come into being or leave it out. We believed that, by stressing expandability of the system, we made accommodations for future demands on capacity. This was not, as was so snidely stated, a question of integrity, but one of judgment.

"Caron said that any other vendor would be in the same predicament. I submit to you that DCS did not really understand the limitations of the system they had designed, so they did not recognize a change that would overload the system. I question whether another vendor would have made that error.

"When Caron talks about the $42,000 spent on upgrading the current CPU, he makes it sound like they did it out of the goodness of their corporate hearts. I consider it an admission that the CPU should have been larger in the first place. According to their figures, before all this is over, and assuming the hospital buys the larger CPU, DCS will have spent $42,000 on upgrades, $20,000 on reinstallation costs, and will have lost $15,000 on resale of the original CPU. When's the last time you saw a company willing to spend $77,000 on someone else's mistake? What they're hoping to do is limit the consequences of their own failings.

"Now we come to the mythical 'savings' of the new CPU. What they have done is to take the $30,000 a year we are spending on extra staff (an expense that should not have existed in the first place) and multiply it by six. This unnecessary $180,000 suddenly becomes a savings by spending $167,000 right away. That logic reminds me of the man who murdered his parents and then begged for mercy from the court because he was an orphan!

"Next is the question of what to do with the staff we so recently hired to make up the failings in the system. First of all, we are dealing with two individuals, not one. Secondly, and most importantly, this is a question of equity, not economics. What we are concerned about here is the effect on our employees, their families, and their careers. That can't be measured in dollars, and it can't be solved with dollars. What will be done for these people who came to work for us in good faith has not been settled yet.

"Finally, since DCS believed that they could accommodate the short stay center in February, I can only deduce that they would have felt the same way before the contract was signed in January. The lateness of the addition is irrelevant, if in fact it is not a red herring. DCS has not done what they have contracted to do, and it's high time they did. If that means that they have to provide a bigger CPU, so be it."

DCS'S REBUTTAL

Dave Caron also presented DCS's rebuttal subsequent to another short break and after some brief private discussions with Jeff Baker and the other DCS people present.

"Mr. Solomon, it is an unfortunate turn of affairs that have brought us before you. I stand here telling you one version, and Ed is over there telling you another. In retrospect, I probably cast a few more aspersions than I intended.

"But masked in all this disagreement is a very real problem. We all know what the problem is, and neither party is disputing the facts surrounding the issue. With this in mind, I'd like to address Ed's concerns and then add a few more of my own.

"Ed seemed to question our ability concerning the software. True, we were a week late in starting the training, due to a small delay in the customization of the modules, but this delay has little bearing on the central issue in my mind.

"Ed has conceded, and we agree, that the software itself functions as promised. I'm sure that Ed does not recognize the significant effort and expertise required to accomplish this. Yet, very few companies, and I mean very few, can claim that their software functions as promised immediately. Our results speak for themselves in this area.

"Wilson Memorial's belief that the system design failure lies in our translating the patient volumes into demands on computing time is wrong. The failure occurred when DCS opted to install the smaller CPU in the original contract negotiations. I believe Ed may have been under pressure to hold the entire system cost to the lowest possible level.

"It was a poor decision on our part to allow Wilson Memorial to trim down the price of the system by using a smaller CPU. We at DCS were aware that the agreed upon CPU would be operating at near capacity levels in future years— if the volume estimates given to us by Wilson were accurate. DCS also realized that this new configuration left very little room for growth should any changes occur. We were not aware at that time that the actual usage rate would far exceed the projections given to us in the RFP.

"In light of what I just stated and with the advantage of hindsight, our decision to install additional terminals in the short stay center was another poor decision. But you have to remember the shoes we stand in; our prime concern is to satisfy our customer. We try as much as possible to provide what the customer wants, be it a lower price or more functions and equipment. If we cannot satisfy our customers, we would not be in business. That is why we are always ready to spend additional monies of our own to try to satisfy a client. This is also why we have offered the deal for a CPU swap to them.

"However, I am certain you appreciate I can only stretch so much before I have to say, 'No.' As it currently stands, we are not making very much profit on the contract. With the CPU swap proposal, we will be lucky to break even on direct cost before considering any company overhead costs. From a business standpoint, even that is OK, since we are growing in this area of the business; it is currently more important to us to have a satisfied customer in the long run than it is to make a lot of money in the short run. As I said just a second ago, though, I can only go so far with this philosophy before I have to step back and say, 'Come on, wait a minute; let's be a little reasonable here!'

"Ed mentioned that they asked us about the short stay center, and all we said was, 'Yes.' I do not dispute that; but if we had said, 'Yes, but you'll need a bigger CPU,' do you really think Wilson Memorial would have said, 'No thanks; we'll wait a while'?

"I hardly think so, when Ed has been swearing over his name signed in blood to all of us about how important the short stay center has become to the hospital's strategic future. We said, 'Yes,' based on the information we had, which turned out to be largely understated.

"The way I see it, Ed is covering his bases. The hospital, operating at the projected future patient volumes in the short stay center, now finds itself with a new CPU already at near capacity levels. The hospital must have known that, once they started exceeding the highest future projected levels, a new and larger CPU would be necessary.

"Unfortunately for Ed, the total expected growth has occurred almost overnight. Now, Ed must go back to his bosses and say, 'Sorry guys, I miscalculated our future needs and I'll need another $150,000 to $200,000 to cover my mistake.' His other option is to go after DCS, saying it is our fault, and that we should pay to correct the problem.

"I understand his predicament, but I don't agree with the solution he has chosen. Normally, of course, the hospital would need a larger CPU in time. Unfortunately for everyone involved, due to understated future projections by the hospital and a poor decision by DCS in trying to satisfy the customer, the larger CPU is needed now; Ed is left holding the bag. The current situation provides Ed with an opportunity to acquire a larger CPU, ease his supervisors' concerns, and cover his own mistakes—if only he can get DCS to pay for it. Sounds simple, and for him, I'm sure it is; but for us, that cure is out of the question.

"I would like to point out that we are open to suggestions. We have offered a proposal; all Ed has said is, 'No, it costs too much!' He has not provided any alternatives. His intentions are pretty obvious.

"We at DCS, on the other hand, are committed to resolving the problem in an equitable manner. DCS will be more than happy to entertain any proposals you may suggest. I'm confident a practical solution will be found. I only hope that Wilson Memorial is also committed to this same goal."

QUESTION AND ANSWER PERIOD FOLLOWING BRIEFS AND REBUTTALS

After both sides had presented their briefs and rebuttals, Ben asked a number of questions to clear up certain facts and to establish the reasons for some of the decisions that had been made.

Ben

Dave, when the hospital chose the smaller of the two CPUs, did you tell them that the system would be close to capacity?

Dave

Yes, we did.

Ben

Do you remember exactly how you phrased it?

Dave

We said "close to capacity." We also said there would not be much room for expansion.

Ben

Did you give them a percentage of capacity used?

Dave

No.

Ben

Ed, how did the hospital go about projecting the volume for the short stay center?

Ed

We used medical records to see how many of certain kinds of procedures were performed here in the last year.

Ben

Did you consider the changes in medicare regulations that now require certain kinds of procedures be done on an outpatient basis?

Ed

We considered them, but we only made an estimate. We did not have the right kind of historical data to do more than that.

Ben

Did you consult any outside sources?

Ed

No. We believe our people are as qualified as any outside consultants.

Ben

Dave, how did you go about deciding that the current system would handle the seven additional terminals?

Dave

Well, to make a long story short, Jeff Baker took the hospital's volume estimates to our systems analysts and hardware specialists. They researched the issue, and told Jeff that it was feasible at those volumes, but that the quality of the estimates was critical. If volumes were much larger, the system would be overtaxed. Jeff brought this to senior management (including me) for our approval. We gave him conditional approval dependent on the hospital's reaffirmation of these estimates, knowing how critical they were.

Ben

Dave, what did the hospital say when Jeff asked for reaffirmation of these estimates?

Dave

Jeff never did. He just told them it was OK.

Ben

Ed, I'm still not clear why you didn't mention the short stay center until February.

Ed

We did not get final board approval until their January meeting.

Ben

When did you start to study the short stay center seriously?

Ed

It was in August or September of '84.

Ben

So by the time you were in negotiations in January, it must have been pretty far along?

Ed

Yes, but we hadn't committed ourselves to it yet.

Ben

Dave, let me see if I understand why you were willing to spend your money on upgrading some of the hardware. What was your biggest single reason?

Dave

We were trying to protect our reputation.

Ben

Ed, why was the hospital willing to add the additional staff?

Ed

We thought it would be a quick and relatively cheap solution.

Ben

Ed, why did the hospital choose the smaller CPU?

Ed

DCS's original recommendation included a larger one but the price was much higher. When we asked if there was a way to reduce the price, DCS told us that a smaller CPU would do the job but that it would leave less room for expansion. We interpreted that to mean we might want a bigger one in four or five years.

Ben

Ed, if you do get a bigger CPU and no longer need the staff you just added, what will you do with those two people?

Ed

We have enough turnover that we could probably keep them until attrition solved the problem. It would be bad for employee relations to lay them off.

Ben

Gentlemen, if neither of you has anything to add, I will give you a decision within a month.

The *Instructor's Manual* gives the mediator's judgment.

QUESTIONS

1. Who should pay for the CPU upgrade needed to meet the response time objectives of Wilson Memorial—the hospital or DCS, Inc.?
2. Why isn't the answer to the above question an adequate response to the problem described in the case? Be prepared to support your answer with specific comments.

Appendix A

Wilson Memorial Hospital

Wilson Memorial is a 250-bed, not-for-profit, full-service hospital located in a rural area of the state. It offers inpatient, medical, surgical, pediatric, obstetric, and nursery services. Outpatient services include an emergency room, pediatric and well-baby clinic, a senior health clinic, and a full range of diagnostic testing. Surgery is available on an inpatient or outpatient basis.

At Wilson, and in most other hospitals in this country, inpatient utilization has been dropping for approximately the last three years. Some of this demand has shifted to outpatient services. The decrease in patient days is a result of small declines in admissions and substantially shorter lengths of stay. Because most hospital tests, therapies, and surgery occur in the early part of a patient's stay, patient revenues have not dropped as quickly as might be expected from the reduction in patient days. The decline in revenues is usually attributed to more restrictive payment climates and changes in medical practice.

ESTABLISHMENT OF THE SHORT STAY CENTER

Since Wilson is the only hospital in the county, competition from other hospitals is limited to the fringes of its service area. However, changes in medicare, medicaid, and insurance companies' payment policies have caused the establishment of small, inexpensive urgent care centers and surgical centers that compete with the hospital for the more lucrative procedures and therapies. Although these centers have yet to cut into hospital volumes in any significant way, there is every reason to expect them to do so in the near future.

The short stay (ambulatory surgery) center is the hospital's response to these challenges. The area is set up to make a patient's visit as brief and pleasant as possible. Most diagnostic tests are performed in the immediate area; it is no longer necessary to delay surgery while patients are sent to different parts of the hospital for X rays and lab tests. There are family waiting areas and private rooms for physician consultations. Registration is in the same area, and many of the details can be taken care of before the day of surgery. In promoting the use of this center to the area's physicians, the hospital has stressed the convenience for the doctor and the patient. It has also been reminding physicians of the availability of full hospital facilities in the event of life-threatening complications, something the other small, rival centers are unable to offer. The hospital also offers a full range of diagnostic tests that are not practical for the smaller centers. Primarily because of the greater level of capital investment and the necessity to staff for the possibility of acute care, no hospital can compete with the smaller centers on price.

Promotion of the new short stay center is the hospital's first venture into marketing. As in most not-for-profit institutions, there has been a reluctance to engage in marketing, an activity that seems slightly undignified. However, hard-headed business considerations are forcing the hospital into selling. The marketing plan has not been formulated. In fact, a name for the short stay center has not even been chosen.

NEED FOR A NEW COMPUTER SYSTEM

Wilson Memorial's old computer system had been in place for approximately 12 years. While it was reasonably up-to-date at the time of installation, it had become practically archaic. There had been so many modifications and enhancements that no single person actually understood the entire system any more. Nonroutine maintenance on the aging hardware was chronic and expensive. Downtime was frequent and unpredictable.

The old system provided the following functions: general accounting, patient accounting, and patient registration. Rudimentary medical records (record number, number and times of visits) had been written in a subsystem of the patient registration system. The patient charging system provided some information on patient days, tests and therapies performed, and revenue by payor, accommodation, or type of medical service. It was also possible to determine how much revenue each doctor brought into the hospital.

Dissatisfaction with the system was evident in all branches of the organization. When senior managers were given permission by the board of directors to investigate acquiring a new system, all departments of the hospital and the attending medical staff were polled for the following information:

1. Failings of the current system.
2. Essential features of a new system.
3. Desirable features of a new system (these were to be listed in order of desirability).
4. How much time, effort, and resources the survey respondent was prepared to expend in implementing a new system?

PREPARATION OF THE REQUEST FOR PROPOSAL (RFP)

After the preliminary poll had been circulated, two user committees were established. The larger of the two consisted of department heads and a physician representative of each major medical service. The hospital's Auxiliary, a representative of the County Health Department, and representatives from local senior citizen and consumer groups were also invited, to serve as an ad hoc users' committee. From that large users' group, a small executive committee was chosen to assist in selecting the system functions and features that would be in the RFP. The full users' group numbered 45, while the executive committee had 10 members.

Before serious effort began on the list of features the new system ought to have, the director of Data Processing gave the executive committee a series of classes on the current state of the art for hospital information systems. These sessions were to give the committee a sense of the possibilities that existed and to encourage realistic expectations about what the hospital could achieve and what Wilson could most likely afford. Similar presentations were made to the board of directors.

The executive committee used the results of the users' wish-list poll to reduce the lists of "essential" features to those that were achievable using current technology and software design. Some of the features that several respondents considered essential were downgraded to the desirable list. The desirable list was then condensed to a few of the most useful functions. The full 45-member users' committee was consulted several times to provide feedback and to insure broad support for the final result. It is doubtful that any group of users found every feature they wanted on the final RFP list. The user committee did give formal approval to the list of features before the RFP was written.

The following is a summary of the features the new system was to have. Features preceded with an asterisk (*) were regarded as desirable but not essential.

General Accounting

General ledger.

Accounts payable.

Payroll.

Fixed assets.

Customized reports (including budget monitoring).

*Ad hoc reporting.

*Flexible report grouping.

Patient Accounting

Billing (includes special bill layouts for various payors).

Automatic statements.

On-line account status and history.

Aging-of-receivables reports.

Automatic bad debt and charity write-offs.

Automatic dunning letters.

Bad debts by service and payor.

*Electronic billing.

*Automatic charging for tests performed.

Patient Registration

On-line registration.

On-line patient census.

On-line registration history.

Length of stay monitoring (medicare, other).

Automatic room charges.

*Remote site registration.

*Remote site scheduling of tests.

*Concurrent length of stay monitoring.

Patient Information

On-line test ordering.

On-line test scheduling.

On-line test reporting.

*On-line diagnosis.

*On-line referrals to in-house doctors.

Medical Records

On-line history summary.

Infection analysis and summary.

Utilization pattern analysis.

Concurrent utilization review status.

Morbidity analysis.

*Complication pattern analysis.

*Abstracts for epidemiological studies.

*Track of incomplete charts (signatures, final diagnosis, etc.).

Other

Database inquiry (patient, doctor, personnel, etc.).

*Electronic mail.

*Charge-out data.

Primary users of the different functions wrote the RFP under the guidance of the director of Data Processing and a consultant. For example, the patient registration specifications were written by the Admissions and Patient Accounting managers. The final RFP consisted of 141 pages of detailed specifications and summaries of projected patient volumes, and other usage estimates such as the size of the general ledger, the number of vendors in the accounts payable system, and the number of patient accounts in receivables.

In the process of writing the RFP, the hospital made the conscious decision to choose software first and the hardware for that software second. They then decided to require vendors filing bids to include their recommended hardware to run the software. The total cost of hardware and software could then be compared as one package. The hospital reserved the right to buy the appropriate hardware from another source.

Appendix B

DCS, Incorporated

This appendix provides a background on DCS, gives some details of the system that was installed, and also expands on DCS's recommendations to reduce response times.

DCS is a software and hardware integration company specializing in the medical field. Technical personnel have developed a comprehensive hospital system based on IBM software modules that have been customized as a DCS product. IBM has given DCS a perpetual license for the original software modules DCS modified. DCS pays a yearly license maintenance fee for license. DCS is also required to pay a royalty fee for every site where DCS installs the software product. The royalty is a one-time fee paid three months after customer acceptance of the system.

DCS has been in business for 14 years. The corporation's greatest growth has been in the past seven years. Initially, the company was primarily a small-system application vendor, specializing in systems costing between $25,000 and $250,000. As the company grew, it found itself selling most of its systems to small hospitals on the East Coast. Seven years ago, the company signed an exclusive development licensing agreement with IBM that allowed DCS to convert the single application IBM modules into a comprehensive hospital package. DCS staff accomplished the conversion development efforts. IBM was not entitled to sell the product as its own.

DCS offers a superior software product for a small premium above their competitors' prices. Previous customers have been very pleased that the DCS systems have performed as advertised with no major problems. DCS offers support services similar in quality and scope to those provided by their competitors.

The company is moving to larger and larger installations and is committed to establishing itself as an industry leader. DCS is well managed, and top-level executives understand what must be done to achieve the company's goals.

DCS's revenues exceeded $25 million last year. Over half was generated by sales of large systems to medium-sized hospitals like Wilson Memorial; the balance was produced by sales of software to the microcomputer industry and the installation of smaller systems in the $200,000 to $500,000 price range. DCS's profits before taxes were $2.4 million last year and $2.0 million the preceding year. DCS estimates its current year profit before taxes to be $2.9 million.

Dave Caron has been with DCS for seven years. He was hired when the company decided to develop its own product. He has been charged with overseeing installations for two years. Before that, he was a senior installation manager for the company. Dave has a Computer Science degree (undergraduate) and a Masters Degree (awarded four years ago) in Business Administration. He is very strong technically and has good business sense. The DCS executives trust Dave completely to coordinate the company's installations. His title is vice president of Integrated Systems.

Jeff Baker was in his late 20s when he joined DCS in 1984. He started his computer career 10 years before with a small computer company, where he worked his way up from operator to programmer to systems analyst to Assistant Manager of DP. Jeff was described by one of his coworkers as being "a bit prickly around the edges." He is very bright but impatient, and tends to make decisions without consulting his vice president. However, he is very often correct in these independent decisions.

DCS recommended the following three items at the first meeting between the hospital and DCS to correct the slow response time problem:

1. Schedule purge, backup, general ledger, and report-writing functions on the evening shifts.
2. Restrict access to terminals in noncritical, nonpatient areas during peak usage times.
3. Reduce the number of user aides and help screens on line at all times. These items would be added to the manuals at each terminal site. The menu screens would be converted to command driven programs that would utilize less computing time and storage space.

Wilson Memorial rejected the second and third items, asserting they would defeat the whole purpose of the user-friendly system. They did agree to the first item, along with some concessions from DCS.

Wilson Memorial also stated that they would need additional staff on the evening shift to accomplish the first recommendation. In return, DCS agreed to upgrade the current CPU with enhancements designed to improve the usable capacity of the system. The system changes included an upgrade to the CPU and the addition of another disk drive, all at a cost of $42,000 to DCS. Wilson's additional staff would cost the hospital $30,000 in salary and fringes yearly.

These efforts improved the response times but only marginally; they were now within contractual limits 50 percent of the time.

Both parties stiffened their positions at this point and started pointing fingers at each other. Wilson Memorial said that the system did not function as stated in the original contract. DCS, on the other hand, was alleging that the data estimates were grossly in error and that the information given to Jeff Baker in February had created the dilemma. Baker maintained that the original contract itself made no reference to the short stay center; if these terminals were disconnected from the system, the specs in the original contract would have been met, he declared. He believed the addition of the short stay center was a separate agreement and not subject to the original specifications in the RFP.

SYSTEM COSTS

The cost of the system, per the original negotiated contract and subsequent meetings, was as follows:

5 printers (1 high-speed, 4 Anadex)	$ 30,000
1 central processing unit (CPU)	300,000
2 controller assemblies @ $17 K	34,000
5 disk drives @ $20 K	100,000
50 terminals	110,000
Total hardware	$574,000
Additional networking	$ 14,000
Computer room preparation	19,000
Software	340,000
Software customization	135,000
Total integration costs	$508,000
1 additional disk drive	N/C
Enhancement of the CPU	N/C
Total integrated system price	$1,082,000
Year hardware maintenance costs	$65,000

PROPOSED CPU SWAP AS PRESENTED TO WILSON MEMORIAL BY DCS

Cost of next larger CPU	$467,000
Sales price of current CPU	300,000
Price differential	$167,000

DCS proposed a CPU swap whereby they would sell a larger CPU to Wilson Memorial at DCS's cost less the amount paid for the original CPU.

DCS defined its cost as the cost of the CPU itself but not including any incidental costs to remove and install the new machine. The proposed swap would cost DCS $20,000, to remove the current CPU and install the new one. DCS also estimates an additional loss of $15,000 on the resale of the original CPU, which would be a used item.

These cost and loss figures are understated, in DCS's opinion. For example, they do not include a cost for lost profit related to the new CPU, which will require very minor program changes in the existing software. The larger CPU is expected to solve all problems related to the response time issue; in addition, its greater capacity would allow Wilson Memorial to grow and expand at a rate five times greater than what the hospital originally predicted.

The larger CPU will eliminate the need for Wilson to run jobs at night, eliminating the requirement for the additional staff—who have already been hired. The software will run on either CPU with equal success.

Appendix C

Response Time Test Results

The following table gives the test results from the response time samples taken during the installation and thereafter (May–July). The times shown do not include any samples taken by Wilson or DCS people unless both parties were represented.

Date	Time of Test						Response Time Average
	8:00	10:00	11:15	Noon	2:15	4:00	
5/1	1.4	1.9	.6	.5	1.1	1.3	1.1
5/7	1.6	1.2	.9	.7	.5	.3	.9
5/15	1.6	1.4	.8	.7	.7	.9	1.0
5/21	1.6	2.6	1.2	2.0	1.9	.9	1.7
6/1	2.1	2.0	2.2	2.8	2.9	2.3	2.4
6/7	2.5	3.0	2.7	2.8	3.1	2.9	2.8
6/15	2.8	3.6	3.4	3.2	3.6	2.9	3.25
6/21	2.8	3.4	3.2	2.9	3.0	2.8	3.0
7/1	2.6	3.8	3.6	3.9	3.4	2.8	3.35
7/7	2.5	3.7	3.6	3.7	3.5	2.9	3.3
7/15	2.7	3.4	3.5	3.3	3.4	2.9	3.2
7/20	2.6	3.3	3.2	3.1	3.4	2.8	3.1

Chapter 4

Office Automation

INTRODUCTION

The office of today, while perhaps the most labor-intensive of all American institutions, is a volatile workplace whose needs and methods change continually. Procedures to gather, process, distribute, and use information quickly become obsolete.[1]

To meet the demands for more efficient office processes, many firms are automating their routine office activities, turning to the so-called electronic office, or seeking to become a paperless office.[2]

WHAT IS AN AUTOMATED OFFICE?

In O'Brien's overview of systems in an automated office, he lists and describes:[3]

Word processing systems: Computer-assisted document and text creation and editing systems. Automated text entry through dictation and OCR systems.

---

[1] From a paper by Donna Dordai and Alexander Lim, ''Office Automation: A Study of the Implementation, Costs, and Benefits'' (Loyola College, Baltimore, Md., 1987).

[2] A good example of a step toward a paperless office is the move by bank clearinghouses to reduce the labor in clearing payroll checks: ''computers in some corporations deliver their payrolls in electronic form to a clearinghouse, and from there the money is moved to banks where the corporation employees have accounts. There is then no need to print and read payroll checks.'' James Martin, *Telematic Society: A Challenge for Tomorrow,* Chapter 10 (Englewood Cliffs, N.J.: Prentice-Hall, 1981).

[3] James A. O'Brien, *Computers in Business Management: An Introduction,* 4th ed., Chapter 13 (Homewood, Ill.: Richard D. Irwin, 1985), p. 462.

Offices communication systems: Electronic mail, voice mail, facsimile, and teleconferencing systems.

Document management systems: Document storage, reproduction, and retrieval through records management, micrographics (microfilm media), and reprographics (copying and duplicating) systems.

Office support systems: Electronic calendar, tickler file, scheduling, and task management systems.

Personal computing systems: Interactive computing, graphics, information retrieval, and modeling at intelligent workstations in offices or other sites (telecommunicating).

OFFICE AUTOMATION COMPONENTS

Hardware

Most sources today refer to workstations when discussing office automation (OA), the electronic office, the paperless office, or the office of the future. Typically, workstations include a microprocessor, keyboard, monitor (CRT), printer, and disk storage; in some cases, a telephone may be used with an acoustic coupler or direct-connect modem to interface with a company mini or national database.

Software

Most manufacturers of mainframe computers sell proprietary word processing packages; some, such as DisplayWrite IV by IBM, are available in microcomputer versions as well.

Many available software packages were designed to be used with microcomputers. Integrated packages, such as 1-2-3 from Lotus (combining electronic spreadsheets, database management, and graphics) and Ashton-Tate's Framework (combining electronic spreadsheet, word processing, telecommunications, graphics, and database management), compete with word processing applications (like WordPerfect, WordStar, and Multimate), spreadsheet packages (such as VisiCalc, SuperCalc, MBA, and Multiplan), and database packages (like dBASE IV and RBase 5000).

Similar types of software packages are available for minicomputers and mainframes.

WHAT ARE THE BENEFITS AND ADVANTAGES OF OFFICE AUTOMATION?

Benefits of Office Automation

Office automation used to mean expensive people were replaced by less expensive machines; that is, the cost-displacement or head-count reduction approach.

If the goal was not to cut personnel, then those pushing the office automation proposal claimed that individuals took less time to do their assigned tasks or that they completed more tasks in the same amount of time; the increased productivity ploy.

If neither of these is the case, there is still the value-added argument; that is, it may be true that automation frees people, especially managers and professionals, from some degree of routine clerical and paper-shuffling tasks, allowing more time for planning, creative thinking, and problem solving.

Apparently, many benefits of office automation have inherent, genuine worth that cannot be expressed easily in dollars and cents. Therefore, a major problem attached to preparing the cost-benefit analysis in some business situations is that, while the costs of hardware, software, and training are quantifiable and fairly easy to obtain and support, the benefits are not. As a result, office automation proposals with valid cost savings—or at least increased revenue potential—may be ignored.

At any rate, planned benefits will not accrue unless there are controls on the system; controls include programming documentation as well as detailed system maintenance and update procedures.

Advantages

Some advantages of automating the office include the ability to:

- Increase the productivity of secretarial personnel and reduce the costs of creating, reviewing, revising, and distributing written office communications.
- Shorten the turnaround time between the preparation and receipt of a document by moving information quickly and efficiently to people who need it.
- Reduce the frustration, expense, and errors involved in typing and retyping variable or standard text material.
- Store, retrieve, and transmit documents and other written office communications quickly and efficiently.
- Increase the productivity of executives and professionals who are heavy users of office communications.[4]

---

[4]O'Brien, *Computers in Business Management,* chap. 13, p. 483.

- Upgrade jobs and open new career paths.
- Provide individual growth opportunities.

WHAT ARE OA'S PROBLEMS AND DISADVANTAGES?

Integration and Compatibility

A significant benefit of office automation is the ability to link existing office microcomputers with each other in a local area network (LAN), so that they can share expensive resources such as laser printers and large mass-storage devices. Another benefit is the capability to download information from the organization's mainframe or minicomputer to the office microcomputers. Both of these benefits will not be achieved if IS procurement and purchasing plans do not consider carefully the future desirability of integrating mainframes and minicomputers, micros, and peripheral hardware and software (including that applicable to LANs, databases, and telecommunication devices).[5]

Acceptance of the Automated Office

Case 4–1, Freddie Mac, will show that automating the office can cause unpleasantness and stress among the members of the staff. Attitude (such as unwillingness to change) and emotional problems (fear, for one) are particularly troublesome if the individuals and groups most affected by the conversion are not involved in the decision to automate, as well as in the design, development, and implementation processes. The question that many people ask, almost immediately, is "Does this mean I'm going to lose my job?"

To allay those very normal fears, those who will be most influenced by the new electronic office must be involved in the process so they will be prepared for the coming changes in their work environment.

Training will reduce office staff reluctance and the frustrations of learning new procedures by building a solid understanding of the techniques supporting an automated office. Procedure manuals and operating guides are also valuable to system users and should be readily accessible at all times.

---

[5]As is known to many in the IS field, "Microcomputers often come to the office without much planning, which complicates their rational introduction to office functions as an integrated whole." Paul S. Licker, *Fundamentals of Systems Analysis with Application Design*, Chapter 17 (Boston: Boyd and Fraser, 1987).

Disadvantages of Office Automation

The advantages of office automation are not achieved without negative effects, which include the following:

- The cost of office automation hardware is much higher than that of the equipment (typewriters, dictaphones, desk calendars, and so on) that it replaces.
- The automated system may disrupt traditional informal work groups and environments.[6] (Boredom can be a factor if little interaction is permitted with peers.)
- Some employees of long standing, unable to adjust to the technology, may have to be terminated. (Younger workers tend to use the automated equipment and view its potential more favorably than older workers.)
- Interconnection of an organization's sensitive files can degrade security.
- Eye strain (low lighting) and body fatigue (high noise levels).
- Potential health hazards from radiation emission.

WHAT ARE THE COSTS OF OA?

The costs of office automation are the same as those of any other computing system. Hardware and software is available in many sizes, colors, and configurations with a host of attractive features. Some companies choose to lease, rent, or buy new or used equipment. The cost of cabling, when planning to use LANs with fiber-optic cabling, can be sizable.

Training costs, before and after installation of the system, should not be forgotten. A company can expect a formerly very efficient secretary to operate at approximately one third his or her former efficiency level, for several weeks, if abruptly handed a new word processor without the opportunity to be trained in its use.

HOW DO WE AUTOMATE THE OFFICE?

Planning

Solid, integrated planning—perhaps centralized—involving both IS and major functional business areas, may be the only way to assure successful integration of all hardware, software, data, procedures, and trained people.

---

[6]O'Brien, *Computers in Business Management,* chap. 13, p. 483.

Management

A firm management plan, with task priorities and target dates monitored by management and the development project team, will help unify the diverse elements of the project effort.

General implementation strategies are a function of organizational management style, nature of the business, organization design, and quality of the IS being replaced. These strategies are reflected in the plan and include organization, the value and cost of information, and the human resources pilot program.

Organization Strategy

Two organizational options are the monolithic (as in the MIS department that includes all system functions) and the bipartite (wherein the IS production/distribution group is separate from the part of the department that is responsible for applications).[7]

The organization strategy, as employed by RCA Corporation, generated four significant design decisions: (1) an emphasis on the use of DBMS technology, (2) a requirement that the portion of the system visible to the users employ a high-level, nonprocedural language, (3) the use of buffering of user-entered changes to assure that standard validation routines would be activated, and (4) the receipt and direct processing of all personnel transactions.

The Value and Cost of Information

This strategy focuses on OA's capacity to complement or enhance a professional's performance, thus leading to increased effectiveness. This restructuring of work, often overlooked by decision makers, has the potential to provide a substantial return on the dollar investment.[8]

The Human Resources Pilot Program

This final OA implementation strategy suggests that only part of the office structure be automated initially and goes on to propose that the human resources segment be installed before the financial resources segment. The human resources

---

[7]Franz Edelmann, "The Management of Information Resources—A Challenge for American Business," *MIS Quarterly,* March 1981, p. 23.

[8]Franz Edelmann, "Managers, Computer Systems, and Productivity," *MIS Quarterly,* September 1981, p. 1.

segment is simpler in structure, dimension, and complexity and therefore easier to implement; it also has the advantage of ease in measuring results and comparing those results with the firm's main objectives.[9]

CONCLUSIONS

Unquestionably, a word processor is a valuable tool for fast and accurate production of documents and correspondence. And a microcomputer is an excellent aid for designing and using spreadsheets and databases. When used properly, these basic office automation components provide rapid and efficient methods of processing and analyzing information. However, proper measures must be planned in order to realize true advances in productivity. Misuse of the machines and software packages will lead to costly inefficiency and reduced productivity.

CASES: FREDDIE MAC AND FIRST NATIONAL INSURANCE

Case 4–1, Freddie Mac, illustrates the potential for serious conflict when managers, planning to automate the office (or to replace current office automation equipment), fail to heed the interests and advice of office staff. The senior vice president for IS clashes head on with his immediate subordinate, the office automation director, in front of the organization's board of governors. Two competing office word processing systems are described and discussed by organization members.

In Case 4–2, First National Insurance, corporatewide IS/DP decisions and IS expertise were centralized in the home office. The organization encountered serious operational problems when attempting to implement a paperless office with a system designed by home office analysts and programmers. Critical end-user change requests could not be satisfied, and home office DP resources were being diverted from critical application updating and maintenance to perform rudimentary equipment repair and basic system installations in the field offices.

---

[9]Edelmann, ''The Management of Information Resources,'' p. 23.

Case 4–1 Freddie Mac: Office Automation

On February 15, 1986, Dave Malone was in a rage, drumming his fingers and smoking his cigar, when his secretary opened the door for Phil Davis. Phil, a dynamic executive in his early 40s, had been president of Freddie Mac since late 1983, and this meeting with Malone, his boss, chairman of the Federal Home Loan Bank Board, was not one he looked forward to.

Malone began, "In my five years here, I have never been so badly prepared to go before Congress as I was today. I don't think you understand the implications of what was at stake. If you did, you would have had that briefing book to my staff when it was due. What in the hell happened?"

Davis responded, "I'm sure all our people did their best. We've all known for months that it was just a matter of time before the Congress would want a share of Freddie Mac's profits—it was in the political cards. Frankly, I really don't think that anything you could have said, or not said, would have made any difference."

Malone, not wanting to let Davis have the last word, added, "Oh, I agree with you that my speech was excellent, and perhaps you're right that nothing can stop Congress from taxing Freddie Mac. However, I would like to feel that we gave it our best shot, and in this case—with the briefing book being two days late—that couldn't happen. Phil, I am holding you responsible. I expect you to see that this doesn't happen again."

GENESIS OF THE PROBLEM

Because of a relatively minor failure in the corporate office automation system, a hardware "bug" had caused part of the system to fail at a critical time. Such an event would normally have gone unnoticed or certainly been considered minor above the manager level, perhaps even the secretarial level. Nevertheless, Davis now found himself in a "buck stops here" position with his boss, forced to take the blame for an event of crucial importance to the total corporation and its future method of doing business.

Returning to his office, Davis immediately met with Josh Spencer, the senior vice president of Information Services.

After describing the heated meeting with Malone, Davis said, "Josh, that briefing book was a major document, one of strategic importance to Freddie Mac. Some of our best ideas and perhaps the finest thinking we have ever done went

---

This case was prepared by Lorraine Eisenberg, Beth Malone, and Ahni Vanek.

into those 300 pages. Unfortunately, the chairman got so bogged down because it was two days late that I don't think he was able to focus properly and make the best use of it for his testimony. You have to make damn sure that something like this never happens again.''

This disturbing conversation was the first word Spencer had on the problem. While still in Davis's office, he telephoned his Office Automation director, Susan Shepherd, asked if she had been aware of the situation, and requested specifics on what had gone wrong. Susan replied that she certainly had known about the delay; Marge, the secretary in charge of supervising the production of the briefing book, had sounded on the verge of hysterics when she had called to tell Susan the system was down.

Shepherd continued: "Josh, this was one of the points we discussed when you first came on board. Because the 8100s are on three separate processing units, when Margie's system went down, and we could not find the system hang-up, there was no way for her to access her documents from a machine on another floor. She couldn't even get to her documents in order to archive them onto floppies and transfer them to another processing unit. That "disaster waiting to happen" was the major reason for my recommendation that we follow through on the original plan to integrate all floors of the Home Office with the DISOS software program. If we'd done that, Margie could have gone to another machine and continued working.''

Spencer thanked Shepherd and told her they would continue the discussion later. Phil Davis, waiting to hear the feedback, then asked Josh to make office automation his most immediate priority and to report back to the executive committee as soon as possible.

CORPORATION BACKGROUND

The Federal Home Loan Mortgage Corporation (called Freddie Mac in the industry) was created by Congress in 1970 under the Emergency Home Finance Act. Its mission is to enhance the liquidity of mortgage investments and increase the availability of funds for mortgage lending by developing and maintaining a nationwide secondary market for conventional residential mortgages. Freddie Mac develops the market by linking mortgage lenders and capital markets through its purchase and sales functions. It buys conventional single-family (one to four units) fixed-rate and adjustable-rate loans (ARMs), FHA and VA fixed-rate loans, multi-family fixed-rate loans, and home improvement loans. While dealing principally with savings and loan institutions, Freddie Mac also buys from mortgage bankers, commercial banks, and HUD-approved mortgagees.

In the latter part of 1986, Freddie Mac was buying close to 6,000 mortgages per day. The total amount of mortgages bought as of the end of the third quarter 1986 was well over $30 billion.

Freddie Mac sells mortgage pass-through securities representing undivided interests in conventional mortgages, and, to a lesser extent, FHA and VA mortgages. In May 1984, it also introduced the Collateralized Mortgage Obligation (CMO) to the secondary market. This is basically a pay-through bond collateralized by a pool of mortgages. The bonds are issued in four to eight maturity classes. Investors receive semiannual interest payments at the coupon rate, but all payments of principal initially go to investors having the shortest maturity bonds. After these investors have received all their principal, the holders of the next maturity receive all principal payments, and so on. This process allows investors to structure their investments to fit their particular portfolio needs. To date, Freddie Mac has sold nine CMOs, with classes of the last two issued being sold in Euromarkets and Japan for the first time.

Freddie Mac was initially capitalized for $100 million through the subscription of nonvoting common stock by the 12 Federal Home Loan Banks (FHLBs). FHLBs are the central banks for the nation's thrift industry, principally savings and loan institutions. The Federal Home Loan Bank Board (FHLBB) supervises the operations of the FHLBs, regulates member institutions, and has three members, who are appointed by the president of the United States. These members serve, in a separate capacity, as Freddie Mac's board of directors (see Exhibit 1).

Freddie Mac began paying quarterly dividends to the FHLBs in 1982. Special dividends have been issued periodically. Freddie Mac also started issuing preferred stock to its member institutions in 1982, and in January 1985, this preferred stock began to be traded on the New York Stock Exchange (see Exhibits 2, 3, and 4).

Being a quasi-government agency overseen by presidentially appointed directors, Freddie Mac goes through a number of major management changes within relatively short time periods. Since 1981, Freddie Mac has changed top management three times (which included the president twice).

There are almost 700 home office employees with another 200 divided among the regions. The current organizational structure of Freddie Mac is as shown in Exhibit 5.

COMPUTER RESOURCES

Freddie Mac itself consists of five regional offices located throughout the United States (Northeast—Arlington, Va.; Southeast—Atlanta, Ga.; North Central—Chicago, Ill.; Southwest—Dallas, Tex.; and West—Los Angeles, Calif.); a branch of the western regional office located in Seattle, Wash.; and the home office, located today in downtown Washington, D.C., but with a major division—Operations Services—located in two buildings in Reston, Va. These two buildings house the corporation's main computer facilities and its operational, as opposed to developmental, computer personnel.

Freddie Mac owns an IBM 3081 AX3, an IBM 3090 (not installed yet by early

EXHIBIT 1 Freddie Mac Relationship to the Federal Home Loan Bank System

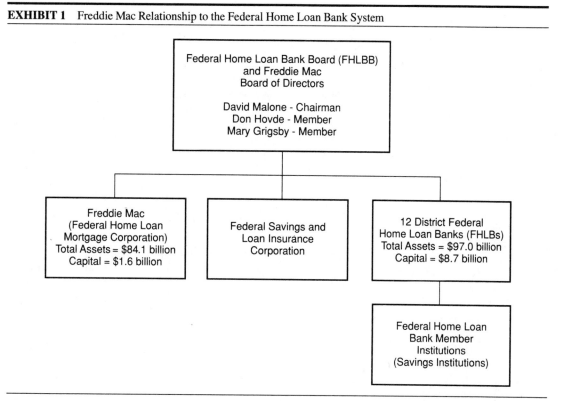

1987), a Burroughs 4800 (to be trashed when the IBM is on-line), and seven Hewlett-Packard 3000 computers. The latter seven will be sold shortly and are located as follows: one in each of the regions, one at Reston, and one in the home office. Additionally, in the home office, there are: two rented HP graphics terminals and plotters that are used mainly by Financial Strategy and Treasurer; 73 IBM PCs; and a very sophisticated graphics system — Executive Presentation System (EPS) — bought about two years ago for approximately $110,000. EPS is a stand-alone system that makes graphs and charts in color and then converts them to transparencies and slides (through a built-in camera system). The EPS is in Office Automation (OA), which requires that requests for graphs be submitted to its trained operator a week in advance.

OFFICE AUTOMATION HISTORY

In 1981, the MIS department, then called the Corporate Information Resources (CIR) department, was headed by vice president Art Cassidy and assigned organizationally to the Chief Administrative Officer (CAO). At that time, the cor-

EXHIBIT 2   Federal Home Loan Mortgage Corporation: Five-Year Financial Highlights (in millions)

December 31,	1984	1983	1982	1981	1980
Balance sheet					
Mortgage loans, net	$10,008.40	$7,476.50	$4,670.60	$5,169.70	$4,996.90
Other assets	3,144.60	1,477.60	1,353.10	1,149.80	474.80
Total assets	13,153.00	8,954.10	6,023.70	6,319.50	5,471.70
Debt securities, net	10,185.90	6,782.20	4,521.40	5,475.60	4,681.00
Other liabilities	1,372.90	1,125.80	642.10	315.00	305.70
Total liabilities	11,558.80	7,908.00	5,163.50	5,790.60	4,986.70
Capital base					
Reserve for uninsured					
principal losses	175.30	134.30	98.40	79.20	64.20
Subordinated capital	812.30	490.60	465.80	199.60	199.60
debentures					
Participating preferred stock	150.00	—	—	—	—
Common stock	100.00	100.00	100.00	100.00	100.00
Capital in excess of par value	—	100.00	100.00	100.00	100.00
Retained earnings	356.60	221.20	96.00	50.10	21.20
Total capital base	$ 1,594.20	$1,046.10	$ 860.20	$ 528.90	$ 485.00
Sold mortgage portfolio					
Mortgage participation					
certificates (PCs)	$69,521.30	$56.411.90	$41.182.10	$17.924.60	$14,785.20
Guaranteed mortgage					
certificates (GMCs)	1,398.60	1,578.20	1,770.30	1,972.80	2,177.00
Total sold mortgage					
portfolio	$70,919.90	$57,990.10	$42,952.40	$19,897.40	$16,962.20

poration's information was processed on a Burroughs system. CIR's primary function was to develop and implement the new MIDAS (Mortgage Information Direct Access Source) system, using IBM equipment. MIDAS was to include the corporate database and would provide on-line processing of loan offers, underwriting, servicing, accounting, security sales, cash management, and management support — in short, MIDAS would become a fully integrated system. Although 100 percent of CIR's resources was devoted to developing and implementing MIDAS, the system was months, or maybe years, behind schedule.

Telephone communications were the responsibility of Administration, a separate department, also under the CAO.

OFFICE AUTOMATION RESOURCES

Office Automation consisted primarily of a word processing center (WPC), a section within CIR. The center had an assortment of equipment — MICOMs, Lexitrons, Laniers, and Quixs—all stand-alone units. The word processing group

EXHIBIT 3   Freddie Mac: Five-Year Financial Highlights *(concluded)*

Year Ended December 31,	1984	1983	1982	1981	1980
Mortgage purchase and financing activities					
Mortgages					
Commitments	$32,601.00	$32,846.30	$28,178.10	$6,632.30	$3,856.10
Purchases	$21,885.10	$22,952.30	$23,671.40	$3,744.00	$3,689.80
Number of loans purchased	567,423	595,782	665,989	83,428	73,276
PCs					
Commitments	$28,938.30	$29,235.90	$28,367.90	$6,300.70	$2,425.30
Settlements	18,684.20	19,691.20	24,169.20	3,529.20	2,526.00
Long-term debt					
Issued	2,396.00	2,284.70	257.50	400.00	1,050.00
Retired	(968.10)	(682.30)	(492.70)	(388.90)	(215.10)
Net	$ 1,427.90	$ 1,602.40	$ (235.20)	$ 11.10	$ 834.90
Income statement					
Income from total portfolio	$1,344.90	$865.90	$697.90	$626.50	$493.00
Interest and related expenses	(973.20)	(609.40)	(590.70)	(557.00)	(416.50)
Net interest margin	371.70	256.50	107.20	69.50	76.50
Other expenses, net	(104.30)	(92.90)	(47.30)	(38.60)	(42.90)
Income before extraordinary item	267.40	163.60	59.90	30.90	33.60
Extraordinary item	—	(3.90)	—	—	—
Net income	$ 267.40	$159.70	$ 59.90	$ 30.90	$ 33.60
Selected financial ratios					
Return on average assets	2.4%	2.1%	1.0%	0.5%	0.7%
Return on average equity	52.0%	44.5%	21.9%	13.1%	14.7%
Debt to equity*	14:1	16:1	14:1	20:1	22:1
Leverage†	48:1	60:1	54:1	45:1	43:1
Earnings to fixed charges	1.3:1	1.3:1	1.1:1	1.1:1	1.1:1

*Total debt securities, net plus Subordinated borrowings less the sum of Cash and temporary cash investments and Mortgage securities purchased under agreements to resell, divided by Stockholders' equity.
†The sum of Notes and bonds payable: Due after one year, Collateralized Mortgage Obligations: Due after one year, Subordinated borrowings, and Contingencies divided by the sum of Reserve for uninsured principal losses, Subordinated borrowings, and Stockholders' equity.

consisted of three to four word processing people; jobs submitted for processing usually had a turnaround of one to three days, depending on the workload. Outside the CIR group, the regions and various home office departments used Quixs, MICOMs, and typewriters.

At the beginning of 1982, a pilot program of the IBM 8100 series word processing system was installed in two departments of Freddie Mac: CIR and Corporate Planning and Development (CPD). Secretaries from both departments were sent to the IBM Control Operator School for one week to become familiar with the system.

Sandy White, a secretary who worked for one of Art Cassidy's directors, was

---

EXHIBIT 4 Freddie Mac Stockholers

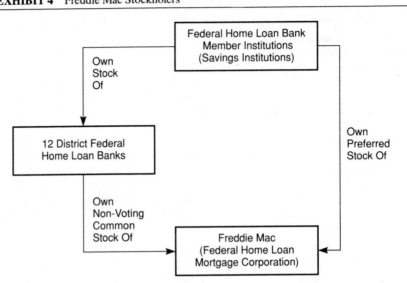

---

named the corporation's control operator for the entire system as it then existed. This duty was in addition to her already hectic workload. She thus became answerable for solving system problems (both software and hardware), acting as liaison between Freddie Mac users and IBM customer service engineers, ordering equipment, loading the corporate dictionary onto the system, and supervising the training of additional users. The WPC still existed and functioned as before.

After too many months of working 15-hour days, Sandy quit.

WORD PROCESSING EXPANSION

The 8100 word processing system was to be integrated with the existing MIDAS terminals (IBM 3278s), thus permitting access to the corporate database with the flip of a switch. All 8100 terminals would communicate with each other, and also with the regions — if the processing units were integrated. The word processor's many sophisticated features included in-context spelling, automatic hyphenation, record selecting and sorting, and math capabilities. A self-paced learning manual was handy to all departments; it took a new person approximately three days to work completely through the manual. Following that session, practical mastery of the system could be achieved in about two weeks of constant use.

EXHIBIT 5 Freddie Mac Organizational Structure

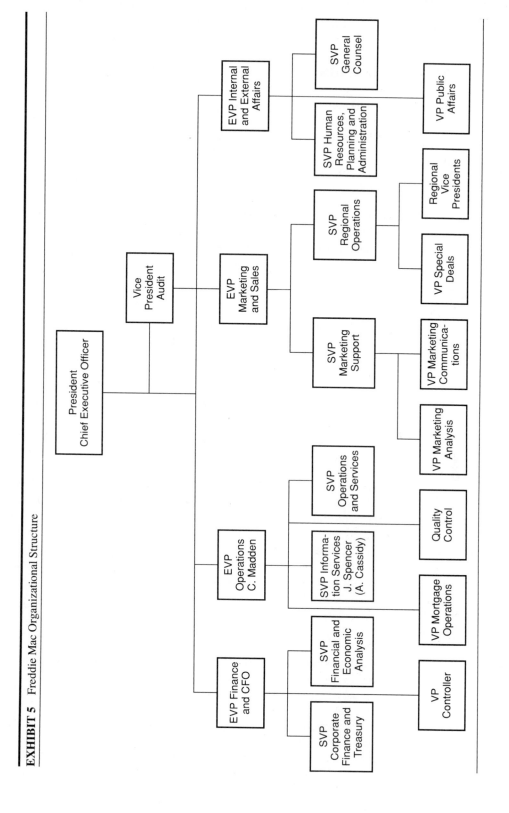

THE FIRST REORGANIZATION

One of the corporation's major reorganizations took place in August of 1982. At that time, when the new president was hired, almost half the existing officers were replaced, and Art Cassidy was promoted to senior vice president of CIR. CIR was relocated under the executive vice president of Operations. Parts of MIDAS were on line and running, but much of the system was still months behind schedule.

Also at that time, Telecommunications was reassigned to CIR, and the Office Automation section was created. The two sections were assigned to Susan Shepherd. She was promoted to director, Technology Support Systems division, and now would report to the senior vice president level.

SUSAN SHEPHERD

Shepherd has a BS in computer programming and has been in the Freddie Mac family for more than five years—a relatively long time in a company with a 25 percent annual turnover rate. She was recommended to Art Cassidy by Charles Madden, presently the executive vice president of Operations (and Cassidy's boss); Charles has been with Freddie Mac since its inception.

Susan was hired originally as a programmer; but shortly after arriving she was promoted to supervisor of the early Word Processing Center. Therefore, she was familiar with its history and the decision-making processes used to automate Freddie Mac, and was instrumental, in fact, in the initial decision to install the IBM 8100 system.

Under Shepherd's control, Office Automation began to formulate policies and procedures and to design and conduct specialized word processing classes. The classes were primarily for proficient, not occasional, users; advanced word processing features, such as math and sorting, were taught in depth. In addition, regular user meetings were held by OA approximately every two months to keep former students current on recent developments (such as new software releases) and scheduled future maintenance routines.

ADDED HARDWARE

OA began to expand the IBM 8100 system and to replace the various MICOM and Quix systems in the home office departments. The single processing unit serving the word processing system soon reached the limit of its capacity, and a new unit was added. Since the new processor was not joined electronically with the old one, only departments connected to the same processing unit could communicate directly with each other electronically. Also, since the regions were not converted to the IBM 8100, the system-to-system communication that had been present with the MICOMs (never very extensive) was lost. Panafaxing, always an option for instant communication between the regions and the home office, was now used more than ever before.[1]

SECOND REORGANIZATION

A second major reorganization took place in August 1984. Art Cassidy was fired, and a nationwide search started for a senior vice president who could integrate all phases of telecommunications within the corporation. CIR was renamed Information Services (IS).

Earlier, in the spring of 1984, the Legal department and Public Relations had both asked for IBM Display Writers (stand-alone word processing units). They believed these units would be more reliable; the 8100s had often frustrated as many as 20 users when a machine had a problem or "went down." The Display Writers were easier to learn, and would be safer for Freddie Mac's confidential material, since the documents stored on its floppy disks could be locked up at night. Also, since learning word processing seemed to be easier on the Display Writers, the OA staff expected these machines to be accepted more readily by the end-users. However, the Display Writers could not "talk" to each other, nor with the MIDAS terminals or the 8100 system. Their unit cost was also higher than the 8100s.

When Art Cassidy was fired (August 1984), the annual budget process was well underway for the following year. Not having a department head for IS, Charles Madden had been forced, for the first time, to scrutinize the budget in some detail; and he questioned the proposed increased expenses in Office Automation. Many departments were asking for the Display Writers, and more professional staff members were requesting access to the 8100 system. More CRTs and printers would have to be rented; costs were beginning to skyrocket.

SHEPHERD'S REPORT

Madden asked Susan to prepare a report for him comparing the system Freddie Mac was using to other available systems, justifying the costs, and ending with a recommendation for future automation needs. He requested this report be on his desk within two weeks.

On Shepherd's request, OA surveyed the 8100 users and compared numerous word processing systems; then, they recommended the continuation of the 8100

---

[1]Panafaxing — a term in common use when referring to facsimile transmission or reception of documents over ordinary phone lines. Users of the Panasonic facsimile equipment use the term "panafaxing" just as users of Xerox machines say "Xeroxing" rather than photocopying.

system and focused on the installation of additional equipment that would enable the system to perform as it had been intended when initially acquired.

Susan amended OA's input, recommending purchase rather than an extension of the leasing arrangements for the 8100 terminals and printers. She cited numerous reasons for this decision, among them:

- The corporation was going to IBM mainframes exclusively, and Shepherd believed the compatibility factor was important.
- IBM had done an excellent job of supporting all Freddie Mac's systems in the past.
- A great deal of time, money, and training had already been invested in the current system.
- There was now available a software package that would link not only the 8100s, but also the Display Writers and the MIDAS terminals (both of which the corporation already owned). The cost of this package was $40,000 per year.

Madden found Shepherd's reasoning logical and approved her plan and budget.

JOSH SPENCER

In September 1984, Madden hired Josh Spencer as senior vice president, Information Services. Josh was 40 years old and had a BS in Mathematics. Prior to coming to Freddie Mac, he had been vice president and manager of computer services at Central National Bank (CNB) in Cleveland from March 1979 to September 1984. At CNB, he supervised a department of 25 data processing and development staff and was in charge of reautomating CNB's banking services (for example, updating ATM services). Before working for CNB, he had been director of Business Systems and Services for Gould Ocean Systems for six years, where he had been responsible for changing office automation from an individual-user Lanier/mag card system to a word processing center using Wang office equipment. Later, he had been responsible for expanding the word processing center and developing a distributed word processing system for the entire company.

THE PLANS—SPENCER'S OR SHEPHERD'S?

After Spencer received his orders from Phil Davis to improve the OA system, and after only two or three brief meetings with Susan, he decided that the corporation's office automation needs would be better served by Wang.

Susan felt his decision was not completely thought-out and was perhaps rash. She suspected he had only briefly reviewed the situation and had not taken any of her more detailed analyses into account.

Susan's earlier analysis questioned Wang's financial stability. She had concluded that Wang was in financial trouble because it had been overambitious in trying to develop a personal computer line, to the detriment of its word processing division. Spencer, however, did not consider that element a strong factor in the analysis.

The August user survey by OA had concluded that the main tasks secretaries asked the word processor to perform were inputting, editing, spelling, hyphenation, pagination, and headings and footings.

Susan's comparison of systems concluded that, while Wang had many innovative features, it was particularly weak in the areas used most by Freddie Mac's secretaries, requiring two or three times as many keystrokes for any one function as did other word processing systems, including the IBM 8100.

Susan felt that the cost of converting documents could become a major expense of switching to any other system. She had also previously estimated that for such a massive system switch she would need about three more full-time staff members to survey user needs, conduct training, and write new policies and procedures. From her earlier discussions with Madden (confirmed later with Spencer), she knew that she would not be given the additional staff.

Another factor involved the possible relocation of the corporate headquarters. During this time, Freddie Mac was negotiating to buy two more buildings in Reston and to move most of the home office there within one year. Susan realized that Spencer was proposing to convert to the Wang system immediately, however, which would entail having two cable runs for each CRT and printer to be installed. From earlier analysis, Susan recalled that this would cost approximately $400 for each piece of equipment (approximately 200 units at this point) and recommended to Spencer that converting to any system be postponed until the firm moved to Reston.

Spencer, however, felt that there would be enough trauma involved for employees in the move itself, without their being asked to learn a new piece of equipment. He also stated that, when the move occurred, there would be a higher than normal turnover rate for the secretarial staff; he believed that it would be easier to replace them if Wang systems were in place, since Wang, he felt, was more universal.

SPENCER'S FINAL PLAN

On May 15, 1985, Spencer presented his office automation strategy plan to the executive committee, the primary decision-making body of Freddie Mac, consisting of the president and the four executive vice presidents. His 25-page plan was comprehensive and dealt with the history of Freddie Mac's office automation, strategic directions, system implementation, cost impact, and open issues and concerns.

Spencer stated, ''The major historical activities in Office Automation at Freddie Mac have centered around the installation of word processing equipment and not on its integration or effective use. No long-term goals for interconnection of various systems, document distribution, and automation directions were established. A long-range strategy has not been developed, and equipment utilization is not optimal. My plan will change that.''

Spencer felt that the specific errors and concerns of the past efforts included:

- Costly alternatives chosen (IBM 8100s, Display Writers, MICOMS).
- Word processing software on these various types of equipment was incompatible and not up to industry optimum levels.
- The learning process for this equipment was very long and required a substantial level of effort.
- Multiple workstations had been placed in close proximity to address host access, word processing, typewriting specialties, and personal computing needs.
- No long-term goals for interconnection of various systems, document distribution, and automation directions were established.
- There was limited functionality of the current word processing systems versus multiple functionality in data processing, word processing, and personal computing that was available.
- Equipment was not upgradable from one use (word processing) to another (personal computer).

During the May 15 presentation, Spencer stated, ''Office automation is the utilization of technology to improve the realization of business functions. It is an extension of the kinds of things data processing has been doing for years, updated and enhanced to take advantage of new hardware and software capabilities. Office automation can be brought beyond the traditional applications to the aid of all segments of the office by use of 'end-user oriented' systems, distributed processing to replace mail, and source data capture to reduce retyping.''

Spencer also listed his ''golden rules'' to realize the optimum results:

- Standardization of word/text processing software.
- Upgradability of office automation equipment.
- Connectability of all systems and components, including the host network.
- Ability to act as a 3270 (IBM) workstation; that is, linking equipment so that an office automation terminal can be used as a Host (MIDAS) terminal.
- Capability for graphics generation, transmission, and display.
- Ease of use.

Spencer concluded, ''The golden rules provide a strategic direction to maximize the efficient use of office automation to accomplish many future Freddie Mac office functions.''

EQUIPMENT CONFIGURATIONS

Spencer's plan was to change most of the word processing/data processing hardware environment from IBM machines to Wangs. He proposed a survey of end-users; the results would determine which of the following configurations would be employed for each individual:

1. Host on-line terminals: This class of terminals represents the largest volume of equipment installed at Freddie Mac and is used to access the Host (IBM) computers. The uses of on-line access include end-user computing (SAS, EASYTRIEVE, Financial Analysis), MIDAS processing and other on-line production systems, and program development. The standard configuration will be an IBM 3178 terminal (as is currently used).

2. Host graphics terminals: Host graphics terminals will be used for user-generated on-line graphics, primarily from the SAS and Financial Analysis systems. These are IBM Host-connected terminals and will have limited distribution within the corporation. The standard configuration will be an IBM 3279 terminal (as is currently used).

3. Word processing/office automation: This equipment will come in several configurations, and its usage will depend on the specific requirements of each individual.

   - Stand-alone word processing system: This equipment would be used specifically for word processing activities and targeted to low-volume, small-document users (five to six pages as the norm). Intermachine communication is not required, and transfer of data to another identical machine would initially be limited to manual diskette transfers (diskettes used with this machine, however, could not be used with the other OA machines). The standard configuration would be the Wang Office Assistant consisting of a display station, dual diskette drive, and a printer.
   - Attached word processing/data processing terminal: This equipment would be used for those individuals who need to communicate with other workstations in the corporation and who frequently pass data to other areas or share work with other personnel. These terminals could also be used to access data contained on the Host IBM system through the Office Automation system when linked correctly. Personnel utilizing this equipment would not necessarily have their own dedicated printer but might share either an impact or laser printer. The standard configuration would be the Wang VS terminal.

Personal computers can be configured in a variety of ways, but will essentially consist of monochrome CRT screens, hard disks, and 640 K memory. Other options include color monitors, graphics, modems, memory expansion boards, and high-speed printers. This equipment is used primarily for analysis purposes by individuals or groups within a department. The standard configuration will be IBM PCs (as currently used).

4. Printers: Printing will be provided through the following equipment:

   - Wang Office Assistant dedicated printers will be used exclusively with the WOA system.

- Laser printers, which are high-quality, high-speed page printers (12 pages per minute), will be shared among several input terminal users within a given area.
- Character printers will be shared and more closely placed with terminal users not requiring high-speed printing. Character printers are somewhat inferior to laser printers, but are more cost-effective and will be better utilized in situations not requiring high-speed/high-quality capabilities.
- Host screen image printing will continue to be performed by the IBM 3297.

SUPPORTING SERVICES

Spencer detailed four steps of support services that he felt needed to go hand in hand with hardware changes.

Word Processing Support

The first step dealt with word processing support. He said that Freddie Mac's requirements are standard for the business community, but they embody an added emphasis on numerical data and its manipulation. These requirements he addressed in terms of the main aspects of standardization in electronic information generation: training and utilization of the word processing equipment and ability to transmit documents from one system to another. Because there is a lack of standard text formatting characters in the word processing industry, miscommunication occurs when documents are transmitted to a noncompatible system.

Executive Management Support

The second support step dealt with executive management support. Numerous functional applications have been specifically tailored to meet the needs of executives and managers, and Spencer stated that Freddie Mac should be utilizing these capabilities. These functions include calendaring (where secretaries can schedule times into the system when their bosses are available for meetings, and the system will determine the impact when changes are made); messages transmission and receipt; and software packages such as 1-2-3 from Lotus (spreadsheets).

Communications Support

Spencer's third step treated communications. He stated, "Freddie Mac needs to expand its internal communication so it can electronically distribute documents from one department to another, regardless of location.

"First and foremost will be the ability to access the host information; that is, MIDAS/MIS data on the IBM mainframe. The facility to do this will be the 3270 Pass-through, which allows any terminal connected to office automation to be interconnected with the Host/IBM.

"Also vitally important is the ability for one office automation system to communicate with another. Any terminal connected to an office automation system will be able to pass data or access files on any other office automation system within the network.

"Upgrading facsimile transmissions is a third area for implementation. The Panafax technology is outdated, produces poor quality, and transmits at low speeds. My plan is to replace the Panafax with the Wang PIC.

"The fourth area I've identified is the transmission and receipt of final documents and messages. This goal will be accomplished by mail-way on the OA system.

"Finally, Freddie Mac should be able to communicate with non–Freddie Mac computers. Databases that are available for dial-up purposes through dedicated terminals (e.g., Telerate) must instead be linked with the standard office automation system." (Exhibit 6 represents a pictorial view of the communication network configuration that Spencer envisioned for OA and the Host computers.)

Data Processing Support

Spencer's fourth support step considered data processing support. He believed his plan would permit the office automation system to process today's data processing activities.

He stated, "Hewlett-Packard equipment will be replaced by either a VS computer or by PCs connected to a VS computer. Remote printing, which is also routed through the HP system and utilizes line printers, will instead be routed through the Wang system and use laser printers when software development efforts are completed. Laser printers can print at far greater speeds, are much quieter, and will provide better quality than line printers.

"End-user computing would also be available under OA, enabling the individual users to generate needed applications for their departments."

OFFICE AUTOMATION IMPLEMENTATION

Spencer proposed a phased approach for implementing his plan, with the installation of each piece of equipment within a location providing the foundation for future steps (see Exhibit 7). He also proposed that functionality of the systems be phased in beginning with word processing, followed by personal computing, and ending with office system functions. He was certain this approach would enable the users to gradually adjust to the new environment, allow IS to provide

EXHIBIT 6 Proposed Communication Network Configuration

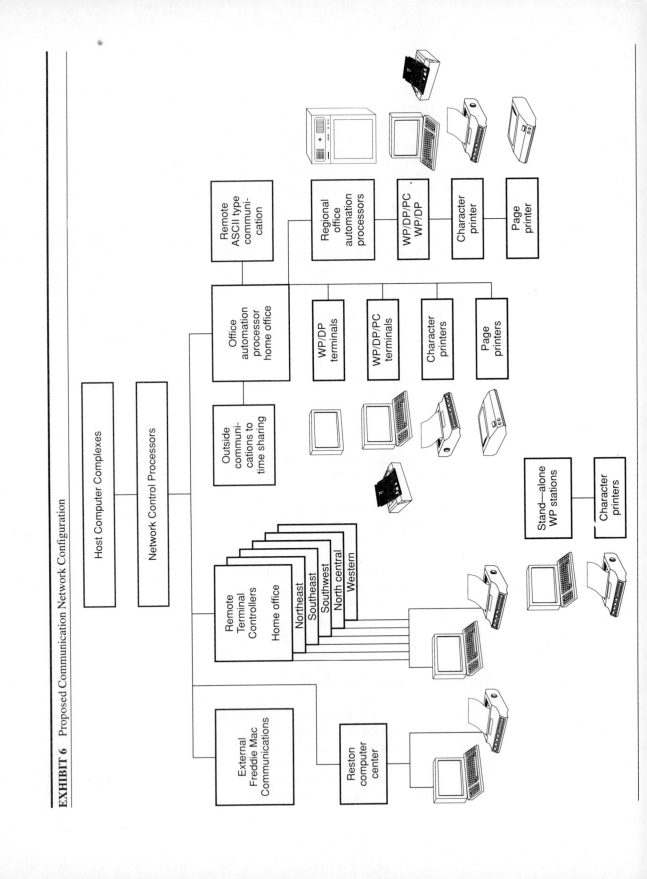

EXHIBIT 7 Corporate OA Implementation

ACTIVITIES	JAN FEB MAR APR MAY JUN JUL AUG SEP OCT NOV DEC JAN FEB

1.0   Implement OA in Retson Bldg 2
   1.1 Install work stations/printers
   1.2 Install VS–15 computer
   1.3 Install software/Wang WP
   1.4 Train the users
   1.5 Implement std. VS facilities

2.0   Implement OA in Retson Bldg 1
   2.1 Install work stations/printers
   2.2 Install VS–15 computer
   2.3 Install software/Wang WP
   2.4 Train the users
   2.5 Implement VS facilities

3.0   Set up communications

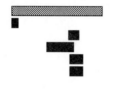

4.0   Implement OA in SE region
   4.1 Order the equipment
   4.2 Train the users on Wang PC
   4.3 Install VS–65 & hd/software
   4.4 Train users on VS–65
   4.5 Convert MICOM docs to Wang
   4.6 Perform post-implementation

5.0   Implement home office OA
     (first phase): CGR, ISD, IA
     Executives, SVP–RO, SD
   5.1 Perform the surveys
   5.2 Order the equipment
   5.3 Train the users
   5.4 Install VS–65 and all other
     equipment
   5.5 Convert IBM docs to Wang
   5.6 Perform post-implementation

6.0   Implement remaining HO:
     CON, HRD, MIM, MO, FEA,
     QC, CF&T, LEG, MC, MAD
   6.1 Perform site surveys
   6.2 Order the equipment
   6.3 Train the users
   6.4 Install VS–100 & hd/software
   6.5 Convert IBM docs to Wang
   6.6 Perform post-implementation

7.0   Implement remaining regions:
     NC, NE, SE, W
   7.1 Perform the surveys
   7.2 Order the equipment
   7.3 Train the users
   7.4 Install the hd/software
   7.5 Convert MICOM docs to Wang
   7.6 Perform post-implementation

better service at each step, and facilitate reviewing and monitoring activities.

The following are the specific steps for implementing the OA plan.

Address Corporate Guidelines and Prerequisites. Spencer felt that corporate guidelines, standards, and procedures needed to be formalized. In some cases, existing rules could be transferred from the current system, such as word processing document-naming conventions, distribution lists and files, and document retention cycles. Security procedures would also remain essentially the same. However, since this plan calls for a more comprehensive OA system, new and modified procedures would also be necessary.

Gather Requirements. Spencer proposed that each area's existing environment be inventoried and future needs addressed in terms of personnel, equipment, applications, workload, and work flows.

Configure the OA System. This step entails assessing the types and quantity of equipment needed, its physical location in the workplace, the functions and applications to be used, and the communications facilities needed.

Review the Configuration. The OA system configuration is reviewed with the user and modified, if needed. During this step, the equipment is ordered from the vendor.

Implement the OA System. Spencer saw the implementation itself as being accomplished in several phases. First, the users would be trained on both the hardware and software. Second, the equipment would be installed in the workplace. Third, system utilization was to be optimized (i.e., the applications, facilities, and hardware placement would be fine-tuned to best meet the user's needs). In some cases, a fourth step might be required: conversion of documents from one environment (MICOM, IBM) to another (Wang).

Postimplementation. Once all the preceding steps were completed for a given area, the OA system was to be reevaluated and corrective action taken when deemed necessary.

Periodic Update. On a periodic basis, each department and region will be offered follow-up training for those employees who need this service. Applications will also be reviewed to determine any new user requirements. Additionally, hardware and software enhancements will be incorporated into the OA system at this time.

As the concluding argument for his presentation, Spencer detailed the budgetary implications of using both the IBM 8100 system and the Wang system (Exhibits 8 and 9).

EXHIBIT 8 Cost of Currently Installed Equipment (as of December 1984)

	December Annualized Total	Number of Workstations	Cost per Workstation
8100s (home office)	$ 560,944	83	$6,758
Display Writers (HO)	181,608	28	6,486
MICOMs (regions)	80,115	18	4,451
HP Equipment* (regions)	254,448	44	5,783
Total	$1,077,115	173	$6,226

Note: Above costs include hardware, software, rental, depreciation, and maintenance expenses.
*Distributed printers.

CONCLUSION

Madden summed up after Spencer had finished his presentation: "First, let me say that I think you made many fine points in your presentation and that your overall concept of an integrated office environment is an idea whose time has come. However, I have here an analysis I had Susan do before your arrival at Freddie Mac, and it seems to touch on a few more details than your presentation did, particularly concerning the feelings of the users. I'm sure you're both striving for the same results, but your conclusions are totally different. Frankly, I don't know which way to go."

Phil Davis concluded the meeting with a request. "I would like the rest of the executive committee to get a copy of Susan's original study and discuss it before making this decision. Josh, I would appreciate your making yourself and Susan

EXHIBIT 9 Cost of Equipment with Fully Implemented Wang System

	Annualized Total	Number of Workstations	Cost per Workstation	Capital Expenses
Home office	$326,738	119	$2,746	$ 584,250
Reston 1	32,883	14	2,349	102,759
Reston 2	32,883	9	3,654	102,759
Northeast region	34,693	13	2,669	108,415
Southeast region	34,693	13	2,669	108,415
North central region	32,843	11	2,986	102,635
Southwest region	35,618	14	2,544	111,305
Western region	37,467	16	2,342	$117,085
Total	$567,818	209	$2,717	$1,337,623

available in case we have more questions. Hopefully, we can resolve this issue by next week.''

QUESTIONS

1. Did the briefing book problem merit the designation of office automation as an immediate priority task for Spencer? Support your answer.
2. Do you concur with Spencer's recommendation of the Wang equipment? Why or why not?
3. What is your opinion of Spencer's plan?
4. What is your opinion of Shepherd's plan?
5. What should the executive committee do?

Case 4–2 First National Insurance (FNI): The Paperless Office

Tom Lippcott, the director of Data Processing for First National Insurance (FNI), has just completed a review of the survey/interview feedback results conducted in the Personal Policy branch of the company. The feedback would help him determine the efficiency and effectiveness of Data Processing.

The survey was conducted in Personal Policy because this department is the most highly dependent on Data Processing. The survey/interview process asked for comments on current data processing service levels, satisfaction with existing systems, new system development, and planning.

Referring to the initial results of the survey/interviews, Mr. Lippcott noted, ''The users of the system are not satisfied with the way the home office has designed the system. My initial reaction is that the revisions they want will be too costly. They have no idea of what it would take to give them what they are asking for.''

COMPANY BACKGROUND

First National Insurance was incorporated in the state of North Carolina in 1920, initially offering basic fire and burglary insurance in the states of North Carolina, South Carolina, Georgia, Alabama, and Tennessee. Its written premiums at the

This case was prepared by Guy A. Davis and Carl Goetzinger. Names, locations, and financial data have been disguised.

end of the first year of operation were $480,000. The company's headquarters were in Winston-Salem, North Carolina, and branch offices were formed in the other four states. The company employed 195 people by 1923 and, through various mergers and acquisitions, grew rapidly. First National now operates in all 50 states, the District of Columbia, and some foreign countries. (The foreign operations were established for reinsurance purposes only and contribute less than 1 percent to total written premiums.)

First National now offers all lines of property and casualty insurance in each state. The company employs over 6,600 people, including 4,000 independent agents countrywide. Written premiums are estimated to reach $3 billion in 1986 and $4 billion by the end of 1988. First National is the 16th largest property and casualty insurance company in the United States.

FNI has historically produced a profit, except for the last five years; the combined loss ratio is shown in Exhibit 1. The loss ratio, a typical measure of an insurance company's profitability, is calculated by dividing the total dollar value of claims plus all expenses by total earned premium. The results at First National mirror the recent past performance of the whole industry.

The lowered profits are due to fierce price competition, which has caused overall premium income levels to decline. At the same time, claim costs such as auto repairs, health related services, and court awards in liability cases have increased greatly. The general health of the insurance industry is at risk; several firms are on the verge of insolvency. However, FNI is still financially healthy due to effective management of operating costs and a strong investment portfolio.

COMPANY OPERATING STRUCTURE

From its initial headquarters and four branch offices in 1920, the company expanded to over 50 branches by 1985. The company decision processes were highly centralized with little flexibility permitted branch offices in their day-to-day operations. In view of the tremendous growth experienced by FNI and the need to become more responsive to the dynamics of the industry, top management decided to change the operating structure. In 1981, they reorganized into 12 sectional (or regional) profit centers; each profit center was responsible for the insurance operations in assigned states. The number of branch offices remained at 50; however, each branch office reported to a specific sectional profit center. The company's organizational chart is shown in Exhibit 2.

The home office's function was to establish overall corporate policy and provide "support" to the sectional offices. Thus, each office was left on its own to operate independently of the home office within the boundaries of corporate policy. Exhibit 3 is typical of the reporting responsibilities in a sectional office.

Both the home office and the sectional offices were organized on a functional basis. The functional units were: Claims, Finance, Loss Monitoring, Marketing, Personnel, Premium Audit, Services, and Underwriting. However, throughout

---

EXHIBIT 1 FNI's Annual Loss Ratios for the Periods Indicated

Year	1981	1982	1983	1984	1985
Loss ratio	105%	112%	113%	110%	111%

Note: Loss ratio $= \dfrac{\text{Claims} + \text{Expenses}}{\text{Earned premium}}$

---

this change in structure, data processing in the company still remained centralized in the home office, with all DP-related planning, control, and decisions remaining at the home office.

DP BACKGROUND

DP, used first for financial and statistical report production, became a major factor at FNI in the late 1950s. Reports included profit/loss, production, claim data, loss ratios, and marketing information. Data was entered from entry sheets prepared by the operating divisions. The insurance information had to be translated into computer code and the amount of information to be coded was increasing tremendously. As a result, there were many problems, due mostly to major errors and late reports. It was becoming evident that the current method of processing policies and claims needed a major overhaul.

Recognizing these problems, Jim Martin, then the director of Data Processing, called for a review of DP operations; he wanted to know how FNI was processing information. In addition, the review was intended to identify weaknesses and resolve problems involving policy errors and report delays. Thus, in 1972, a committee was established that included representatives from DP and the functional user groups. They were to study the current DP problems and future requirements, and develop a new system to meet the company's needs. This review was the first conscious effort by FNI to plan DP's future.

The project was completed in 1974 and the results were as follows:

1. An automated policy-writing system was established, which would issue policies, subsequent endorsements, cancellations, and renewals.
2. On-line retrieval of policyholder information.
3. An automated claim input system, which would automatically issue claim drafts.
4. On-line retrieval of claim information.
5. Automatic preparation of marketing and financial reports from the information entered into the policy writing and claim system.

Data would be entered by the field operations via an IBM terminal CRT, and the information would be processed in batch mode by the mainframe.

For example, consider a new application received by an Underwriting depart-

EXHIBIT 2 FNI Organizational Chart

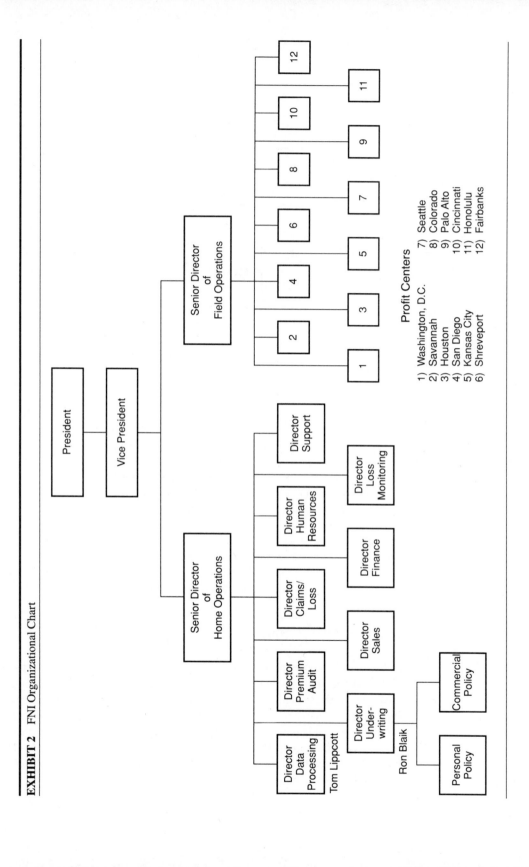

Profit Centers

1) Washington, D.C.
2) Savannah
3) Houston
4) San Diego
5) Kansas City
6) Shreveport
7) Seattle
8) Colorado
9) Palo Alto
10) Cincinnati
11) Honolulu
12) Fairbanks

EXHIBIT 3   Structure of FNI's Sectional Profit Center in Cincinnati

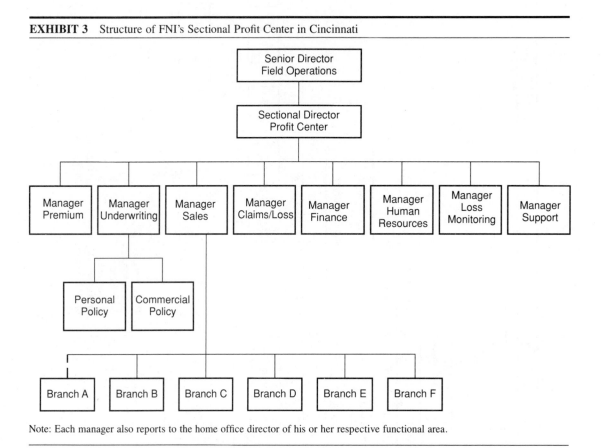

Note: Each manager also reports to the home office director of his or her respective functional area.

ment field office and sent to the Data Entry department in the same office for input. A policy would be produced and printed in the same office the next day. Also, an on-line policyholder file would be available the next day for retrieval on the terminal's CRT. A similar operation was available for claims.

PERSONAL POLICY DEPARTMENT (PPD)

The Personal Policy department, a subunit of Underwriting, is responsible for the handling of personal insurance. Each policy is somewhat standardized compared to commercial lines insurance. Thus, a large number of policies can be processed within a short period of time. Although standardized to some degree, the requirements for issuing a policy do vary by state and are subject to rapid changes in coverages and rates. In 1974, Personal Policy accounted for 42 percent of the company's written premium, 64 percent of the total policy count, and 76 percent of the total transactions.

Prior to the mechanization that took place in 1974, the Personal Policy department was a manual operation, and files were used in all aspects of day-to-day operations. All transactions were manually rated and coded. The coded sheets were then sent to a keypunch department in the home office. Since files were needed for the processing of all transactions, locating a file could be a problem; any number of individuals in the field office could have the file, either employees in the Personal Policy department or those outside the department. Additionally, once the file was located, it might take some time to decipher the contents due to the extensive amount of paperwork in any given file.

Mechanization in 1974 alleviated some of these problems. Keypunch forms no longer had to be prepared and sent to DP for entry. Rather, a request for a policy change was sent to the Data Entry department located in the respective field office. Issuance of a policy, including renewals and endorsements, was accomplished automatically. The on-line retrieval system eliminated the need, in some cases, to pull a file for services.

However, there were still several annoying problem areas. Although input of transactions was performed by the field offices, the individuals in the Data Entry department had no prior insurance experience. The information that was coded in insurance language had to be 100 percent accurate; otherwise, incorrect policies would be produced. In addition, 35 percent of the applications entered did not produce a policy the next day. The data entered was processed in batch mode every night and was run against an edit checklist that verified the validity of the data. If a particular policy did not pass all edits, an error list was produced the next day. The application was then returned to Data Entry for correction.

In the past, PPD personnel prepared the policies manually and could control their office's work flow. However, Personal Policy had no control over the Data Entry department and could not ensure that policies were processed in a timely manner. Also, files still had to be pulled for processing of changes and servicing of the policy because the on-line retrieval system did not contain all the necessary information.

PAPERLESS ENVIRONMENT IN PERSONAL LINES

In 1983, top management felt that additional cost savings and efficiencies could be obtained in the PPD policy area, particularly with the systems currently in use. A second task force, with DP and field office members, was established to study this situation (similar to the 1972 effort). The task force was charged with the following:

1. Review the current and future status of the Personal Policy department regarding DP needs.
2. Determine areas in which greater cost efficiencies can be realized and how DP can contribute.

After nine months of study, the task force recommended:

1. Move the responsibility for Data Entry to the Personal Policy department (PPD).
2. Establish a paperless file concept in PPD.

To accomplish the paperless file concept, the following was required:

1. Redesign the on-line policy information retrieval and policy-writing systems to contain all information necessary to process changes and service the policy.
2. Perform editing up front on the CRT to ensure quick correction of errors and to improve turnaround time.
3. Provide all Personal Policy underwriters with CRTs.

The task force felt that greater efficiencies and cost reductions could be realized in the following areas:

1. A reduction in the Personal Policy underwriting staff of 20–30 percent was feasible. No coding would be required, and all transactions could be processed without the actual file. Additionally, the on-line policyholder information retrieval system would make it easier to service the policy.
2. Since files would be eliminated, file room personnel could be reduced by 45–60 percent.
3. There would be improved turnaround time, and the Underwriting department would be able to control all processing of work affecting Personal Policy business.

Although the PPD would assume the additional responsibility of the data entry function, management felt that staff could still be reduced. All coding would be eliminated, and the overall handling time of a transaction would be greatly reduced due to the improved systems. The task force plan was to reduce staff through attrition. Top management approved the proposal late in 1983.

DEVELOPMENT OF THE PAPERLESS FILE SYSTEM—1984

The most difficult and time-consuming process in establishing the paperless file concept would be the redesign of the policy-writing system and on-line policyholder information retrieval system. To ensure that the system was designed properly, a staff of four Data Processing analysts and nine programmers was assigned full-time to the project, leading Jim Martin, then director of Data Processing, to comment, "Senior management gave top priority to this project, even at the expense of other projects in Data Processing. To satisfactorily implement these changes, it was necessary for us to commit as many of our resources as possible. Other projects had to be postponed. Still, management's visible support did not cause any great problems with other user groups."

The home office Underwriting division was a liaison link between Data Processing and field users. The company felt the field users needed to participate actively in the design of this new system, as they would be working with the system on a daily basis. As Ron Blaik, home office director of Underwriting, noted, ''Our staff role in the home office, as the corporate structure dictates, is one of support. Our primary function in this project is to ensure that the proper information on the system design is given to Data Processing. Thus, we will be playing the 'middle man' in this scheme. Although the field users have no background in data processing, they are in the best position to determine what they need to function efficiently and effectively. Basically, what the field wants, we will support.''

Over the next year and a half, several seminars, meetings, and surveys were held with the field offices, until the final system was designed and implemented. Testing of the system was performed by the field offices on an incremental basis; one office was used to pilot—or prototype—the entire system before countrywide implementation. The project was completed in 1985.

It was evident immediately that demand on the home office mainframe was more than the system could handle. During the first few weeks, after countrywide implementation in Personal Policy, response time became a problem. Average response time between screens when all offices were using the network was 102 seconds. Considering it took 12 screens to process a new application, response time on the system quickly became of major concern. Additionally, when one application on the mainframe went down, or the mainframe itself went down, the entire PPD operation countrywide came to a standstill.

Thus, management decided to implement a distributed processing network by installing IBM 4300 mainframes in six of the 12 sectional offices. Two offices would be connected to one 4300, thus enabling the sections to operate independently of the home office mainframe. If a 4300 went down, the two offices connected to that 4300 could easily log onto the home office mainframe.

PROBLEMS ENCOUNTERED IN THE SYSTEM DESIGN

All went smoothly in the design and implementation of the system, with a few minor exceptions. First, it was obvious that a 100 percent paperless concept could not be achieved immediately. Some of the programming required would be very time-consuming and could result in the entire project being postponed for another 9 to 12 months. However, in reviewing this problem, project managers discovered that only 3.5 percent of all existing policies would be affected. So they decided to postpone this additional programming until a later date. The 3.5 percent would have to be handled under the old manual concept. The impact on the section would be negligible.

Second, to implement a system that would perform 100 percent up-front editing would cause tremendous response time problems, given the amount of editing that was required. The project staff decided to implement only 25 percent of the editing up front. The remaining editing would be performed using the batch process. Managers felt that the policies produced the next day could be handled by the existing staff.

The third problem was more people-oriented than system-oriented. The new system would require new work skills on the part of individuals responsible for handling Personal Policies. Although extensive training on the new system was given to all users, there was still some resistance, particularly from the "old timers" who for many years were accustomed to operating under a completely manual operation.

RICK SCOTT

Commenting on the new system in 1985, Mr. Rick Scott, one of the sectional underwriting managers, noted, "I am extremely pleased with the entire process that took place in the design of the system as well as the final product itself. Involving the users from day one ensured us of a system that would meet our needs. If our involvement was not solicited to the extent it was, we would probably have been faced with a situation where a system was forced on us with a 'take it or leave it' attitude. The way this project was developed, we really have no business griping about what was done. The field users were given just about everything they wanted and even some things that they probably did not really need! Other sectional underwriting managers I've talked to feel basically as I do."

As for some of the problems encountered, Mr. Scott added, "Overall, we got what we wanted. Some of the things that DP could not come through with will not have much of a negative impact on us. I realize that some of the best laid plans can go astray. From the standpoint of the files that will have to be processed manually, I estimate that we will only need one person to handle these in my office. Most of the staff reduction will be realized. As far as some of the employee resistance, there is not much that I can do other than to offer counseling to these employees. I feel the system is here to stay, and those employees who are resisting must either learn to adapt or leave."

DP PLANNING AT FNI

From 1974 to 1985, DP planning was addressed on an as-needed basis. Changes were made only when problems occurred. No preventive measures or effective long-term planning took place.

In 1985, under the newly promoted Tom Lippcott, a structured planning procedure was proposed: DP planning was to be performed annually and completed one month before the corporate budgeting process started. Starting in October,

Mr. Lippcott would meet individually with each director (except Finance and Personnel) to discuss upcoming Data Processing requirements.

Once the new budget process got underway, these meetings would probably take several days in some cases because Lippcott would need time to educate the directors as to what was available in the market. Once the meetings were completed, the director of Finance and Mr. Lippcott would get together to determine the Data Processing capital expenditures budget for the next year. Invariably, not all of the requests of Data Processing could be satisfied within funding constraints, and it would be up to Mr. Lippcott to prioritize each request.

Once prioritized, the DP operating plan for the upcoming year would be generated by assigning project costs down the line until the money ran out. Hopefully, the projects left unattended that year would get a higher priority in the following year.

Without giving much thought to the importance of DP planning, this proposal was approved by the senior director of Operations. The same planning system is used today. Mr. Lippcott's view is that "Planning can best be done by the most experienced people. I once considered developing a steering committee with a more diverse group of people, but that would only cause delays and generate impractical ideas from people who don't understand the entire picture. Let field operations do their job, and I'll do mine. Mine is planning. Data Processing has grown stride for stride with FNI operations, and with the exception of a few minor shortcomings, the system works very well. I don't plan on changing the planning procedure anytime in the near future."

In October of 1986, Lippcott completed the planning process for 1987, which included the paperless file concept for the Claims, Loss Monitoring, and Commercial Lines departments. Subconsciously applying Rick Scott's user involvement ideas as a model, Lippcott felt he had come up with a wonderful concept. Basically, the plan was for the Claims, Loss Monitoring, and Commercial Policy departments to follow in the steps of Personal Policy. Each of the departments would undergo the following transition phases:

1. Establish a DP unit for each department that is in charge of data entry as well as file editing.
2. Redesign the on-line inquiry system to include all pertinent information. This step may require memory expansion.
3. Install a terminal CRT at each individual's desk.

In the meeting with the director of Finance, everyone agreed that in recent years DP had not received much financial support (as can be seen by the limited enhancements to the system). The DP capital expenditure budget for 1987 was set in at $2.5 million, as opposed to $1 million and $1.4 million in 1985 and 1986, respectively. The estimated costs for the 1987 plan were as shown in the accompanying table.

Redesign software:	
Claims	$ 300,000
Loss monitoring	300,000
Commercial underwriting	210,000
Total	$ 810,000
CRT additions @ $1,250/unit:	
Claims (425)	$ 531,250
Loss monitoring (245)	306,250
Commercial underwriting (125)	156,250
Total	$ 993,750
Memory expansion	$ 250,000
Total	$2,053,750

The remaining $466,250 is left for the other five functional areas requiring less Data Processing concentration.

CURRENT STATUS OF THE PAPERLESS FILE SYSTEM—EARLY 1987

After one-and-a-half years of operating under the paperless file system, 26 percent of the staff had been terminated in the PPD countrywide.

Resistance to the change has ended. However, several problems have developed that are of great concern to Mr. Scott. He described them as follows: "A year and a half ago, when this system was implemented, we all felt that it was the greatest thing since apple pie. However, I am not sure that this is now the case. First of all, we, the users in the field, have been forgotten. I do not know if the home office Underwriting department and Data Processing department realized that changes would be needed to the system. Our business changes frequently and quickly. Yet the system does not change accordingly. For instance, I needed a modification to the system that was essential for one of our states. A new coverage was introduced by the regulatory authorities, and it was mandatory that this coverage be provided. The change, to me, seemed very simple. Yet I was told that the program modification would have to be postponed for several months due to other programming priorities. Thus, policies in this state will have to be processed manually until the necessary programming changes can be made. I am still waiting for programming changes that were requested over a year ago. The number of policies awaiting manual processing has increased to 20 percent.

"I am not staffed for this type of processing. I have been told that I cannot increase staff as this would only be a temporary solution until the programming is completed. Yet, what am I to do in the meantime? Changes that are completed are not done properly. Testing of all changes is done by the home office Underwriting department, and we are assured that the testing is accurate. But why do I seem to run into problems every time a new change is implemented? Also, every change that I request must receive the approval of the home office Underwriting department. If they don't feel the change is warranted, they deny the request without any reason. The request does not even reach Data Processing. Additionally, the home office Underwriting department now requests data processing make changes to our system without consulting anyone in the field. These changes are often not needed, are not fully explained, and create problems in our daily operations. Something needs to be done to simplify this process and a mechanism put in place to ensure that our data processing needs are met. We rely on data processing extensively, but I am not sure they realize this.''

TOM LIPPCOTT

The director of Data Processing in the home office is Tom Lippcott. He was promoted to the home office staff at First National in 1985, four years after the reorganization. He liked the structure of FNI's DP because it more or less fit his personality. He is a very stubborn man who really doesn't think most people in field operations know anything about computers. Tom has his own ideas and strategies, and the system users simply have to abide by them.

Lippcott has good relations with the other directors in the home office. Ron Blaik, director of Underwriting, is one of his closest friends and a tennis companion. When asked about the home office environment, Lippcott offered the following comments: ''Environment? We have a very nice environment here at the home office. The people are relaxed and feel confident that they're doing things the best way possible. We believe in the voice of experience. At the director level alone, we have over 150 years combined experience in our fields. I've only been with this company 3 years myself but had another 14 years of experience before that. We work together, too. If Tom Bennett (director of Human Resources) over in Human Resources needs some help with his data processing requirements, I'd be happy to set up a lunch appointment with him to talk it over and likewise with him for me. In fact, the relationships between all the vice presidents are so good I asked my wife Carole, just this morning, to invite each one of them to our Christmas party next month.''

Commenting on Mr. Scott's dilemma, Mr. Lippcott noted, ''No one told us two years ago that the demand on Data Processing would be so great. It was our understanding that this system would only need periodic update and that the quantity of requests would not be large. Additionally, senior management has told us to review the possibility of implementing a paperless concept in other departments. As was the case in Personal Policy, we are devoting tremendous resources to this project. There are few resources left for changes to the system that PPD uses. Unfortunately, their dependence on us is so great that they must come to us for something as simple as a CRT connection. In fact, we send people from the home office to the various sectional offices just to install CRTs.''

To add to these problems, the company is considering removing the IBM 4300s and connecting all offices to the mainframe located in home office. Removal of the 4300s is being considered due to the expense involved in sending Data Processing people to sectional offices to perform relatively simple system maintenance.

Regarding the 4300 removal proposal, Mr. Scott had the following comments: ''If the 4300s are removed, we might as well pack up shop and go back to the old method of processing all policies manually; the response time problems that will be encountered will cause a drastic decline in service. Additionally, it is my understanding that other departments may be going to the paperless concept. What will happen when these other departments increase their demands for time on the mainframe? Things can only get worse!''

FUTURE OUTLOOK FOR FNI

A paperless file system sounds almost futuristic. Yet FNI could develop a competitive edge in the industry if they effectively bring this system on line. As the company loss ratios indicate, FNI can use any advantage it can get.

Mr. Lippcott wonders what the future holds for Data Processing. ''Structurally, the company was organized under sectional profit centers to allow those offices to operate independently of home office. Yet they are 100 percent dependent on us for any and all services pertaining to data processing.

''We have a two-fold problem. First, what can be done to improve the service we currently give to the Personal Policy department? Second, how can we avoid repeating our past problems if other departments should go paperless? I can foresee the demands on Data Processing will only increase, particularly for relatively simple changes.''

QUESTIONS

1. Evaluate the results of the 1972 and 1974 DP studies. What additional changes would you have made to each?
2. Compare the home office staff's statements with their actions (vis-à-vis the field offices) and the field people's perceptions of those statements and actions.
3. Do you agree with the approved solution and subsequent actions taken, with regard to the problems encountered in systems design?
4. Do you recommend organizational changes? If so, what and why? Who should recommend the changes you propose and who should implement them?
5. Contrast and evaluate Scott's and Lippcott's comments.
6. What is your evaluation of the new structured planning procedure?
7. Would you approve the budget?

Note: Exhibit 4, FNI's MIS Development Timetable, is the chronology of major events that occurred in FNI since 1958.

EXHIBIT 4   FNI's MIS Development Timetable

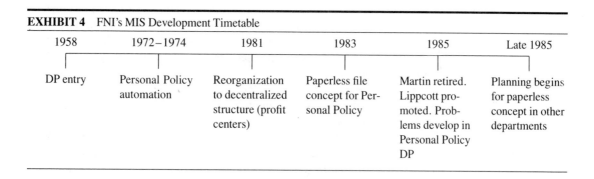

1958	1972–1974	1981	1983	1985	Late 1985
DP entry	Personal Policy automation	Reorganization to decentralized structure (profit centers)	Paperless file concept for Personal Policy	Martin retired. Lippcott promoted. Problems develop in Personal Policy DP	Planning begins for paperless concept in other departments

Chapter 5

Planning and IS

INTRODUCTION

Decision support systems (DSS), database management systems (DBMS), and telecommunications systems generate information and reports in split seconds. What is not always apparent is that those few seconds of processing time were preceded by years of development and implementation, which themselves were preceded by years of planning, analysis, and design. In this chapter, we shall be concentrating on planning.

Hussain and Hussain state that "*Planning* is a framework for orderly development of information systems,"[1] and that is especially true from the perspective of the lower-level IS managers and business functional department end-users.

However, there are also other aspects of IS-related planning that we wish to discuss. One is the fit between overall corporate strategic plan and the IS plan, focusing primarily on IS resources and how they are to be used—toward what objectives—in the coming five years. The second aspect is not a question of system development or fit but of determining what information is needed by different corporate managers and planning systems so that ISs will furnish information of the appropriate type, volume, and scope. Finally, we shall consider a third, two-part aspect of IS planning: (1) an application of computers to planning in a functional area, Materials Requirement Planning (MRP); and (2) IBM's formal IS planning process, known as Business Systems Planning (BSP).

---

[1]Donna Hussain and K. M. Hussain, *Information Processing Systems for Management,* 2nd ed., Chapter 10 (Homewood, Ill.: Richard D. Irwin, 1985).

TYPES OF PLANS

As in other organizations, IS plans can be classed as strategic, tactical, or operational. These can be reasonably equated to long-range (four to five years or longer), medium-range (two to four years), and short-range (up to one year). In addition, plans are associated with organizational level or hierarchy, in that top executives usually provide inputs to the strategic, long-range plans; middle managers are responsible for tactical or medium-range planning; and operational managers and supervisors prepare and implement operational, short-range plans.

WHO DOES IS PLANNING?

Individuals from the IS department head to the corporate information officer (CIO) (if there is one) are heavily involved with IS planning. There may also be a corporate staff planning officer or a special IS steering committee appointed to develop plans and set priorities. The committees normally are composed of functional vice presidents — who are the IS clients or users, computer center and IS department professionals, and top-level executives or their representatives.

PLANNING FOR AN INFORMATION SYSTEM

Successful development and implementation of an information system successfully depends on planning, although planning cannot guarantee success. The risks inherent in today's environment, with changing computer technology and increasing user demands, require that managers examine their position carefully before deciding to develop or acquire a new system.

A first step is to conduct a thorough investigation to be certain that there truly is a need for the system. Kroeber and Watson list the following general factors that can provide the stimulus for proposing a new system: complexity of operations, business and transaction volume, risk in highly technical ventures, business function interdependencies, and speed.[2] Ideally, these factors would have motivated corporate planners to specify a need for the system in their corporate strategic plan.

Once the system need has been established, a series of feasibility studies must be completed. The studies attempt to answer the question, ''Can this system be developed and implemented?'' and routinely include technological (can it be done?), economic (is it cost-effective?), and behavioral (should it be done?) is-

---

[2]Donald W. Kroeber and Hugh J. Watson, *Computer-Based Information Systems: A Management Approach,* Chapter 15 (New York: Macmillan, 1984).

sues. If it is decided that the system is feasible, the next step is to prepare a master plan containing subsections devoted to objectives, organization, resources, and control measures.[3]

MERGING THE IS PLAN WITH CORPORATE STRATEGY

IS must provide top-level management with two kinds of information—the first to be used in developing the strategic plan and the second to be the basis for controlling progress toward completion of the plan's goals and objectives. An IS executive, able to describe technical opportunities and to assess their feasibilities, must be included in the strategic planning process.

On completion of the plan, the IS executive, perhaps the CIO, oversees the distribution of the plan's tactical and operational subsets to middle- and lower-level IS groups; a major concern is to be certain that corporate strategic goals and objectives are properly scrutinized and expanded, down through all organizational levels, becoming tactical and operational IS goals and objectives.

INFORMATION NEEDS CATEGORIZED BY MANAGEMENT LEVEL

An organization's three levels of management—top, middle, and operational—rely primarily on three types of skills: conceptual, human relations, and technical. They also have three sets of information requirements (see Figure 5–1). Top executives must have strong human relations and conceptual skills. They are major players in strategic planning, goal formulation, and policy making. Of the three levels, top managers are the only individuals with significant internal *and* external information requirements. Note, in Figure 5–2, that the top managers of the IS planning committee must consider external inputs (such as government regulations, law, technological trends, and the competitive environment) as well as the internal inputs (corporate goals, constraints on funds, and users' needs).

Middle managers interact with management peers at their level, so they rely on mostly human relations skills (and little technical or conceptual skills). They concentrate on intermediate goals and use more summarized information.[4]

The operational level managers rely primarily on technical and human relations skills, so they need: (1) regular, detailed, internal reports, (2) current and historical data, and (3) performance status reports.

---

[3]Kroeber and Watson, *Computer-Based Information Systems*, p. 433.

[4]James A. O'Brien, *Computers in Business Management: An Introduction*, 4th ed. (Homewood, Ill.: Richard D. Irwin, 1985), p. 506.

FIGURE 5–1 Pyramid Management Model Information Requirements

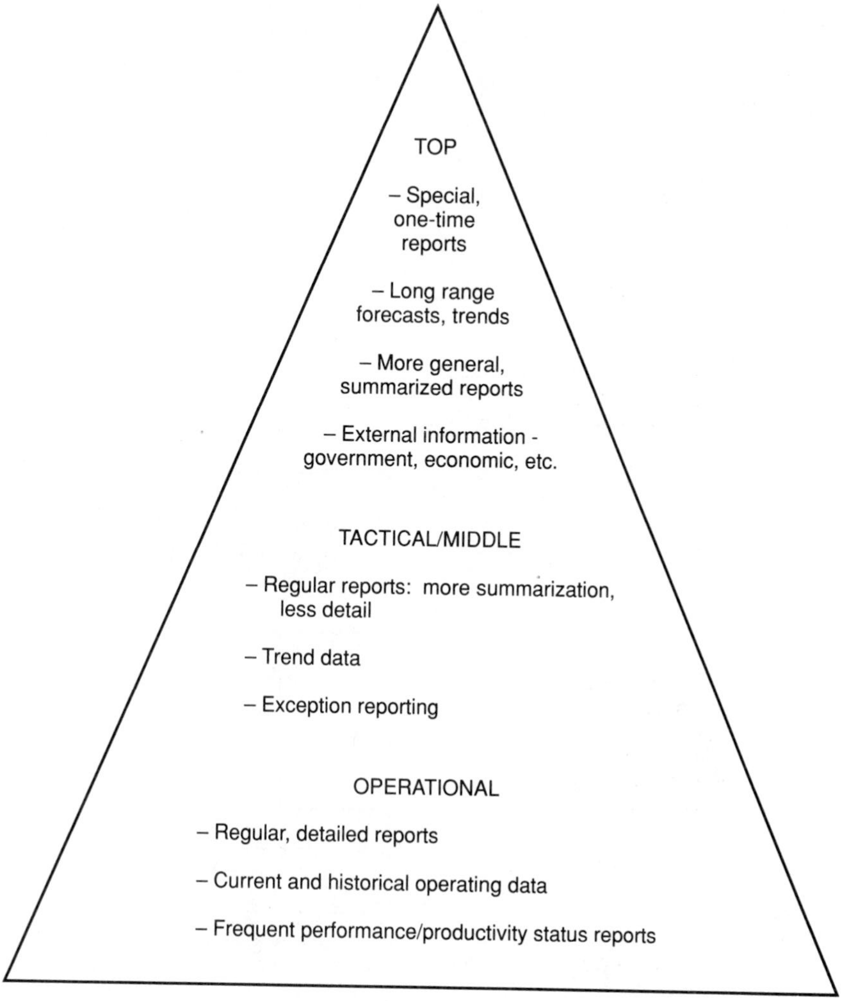

TOP

– Special,
one-time
reports

– Long range
forecasts, trends

– More general,
summarized reports

– External information -
government, economic, etc.

TACTICAL/MIDDLE

– Regular reports: more summarization,
less detail

– Trend data

– Exception reporting

OPERATIONAL

– Regular, detailed reports

– Current and historical operating data

– Frequent performance/productivity status reports

Source: Lisa Thomaidis and Larraine Clark, ''The Significance of an MIS in Supporting Strategic Planning'' (MBA paper, Loyola College, Baltimore, Md., 1985), Figure 1.

THE CHIEF INFORMATION OFFICER (CIO)

An information system must be the link between operational level information processing and top-level corporate planning. The human link is the chief information officer (CIO), who oversees the activities of the IS department staff. By

---

FIGURE 5–2   Inputs to the Planning Process

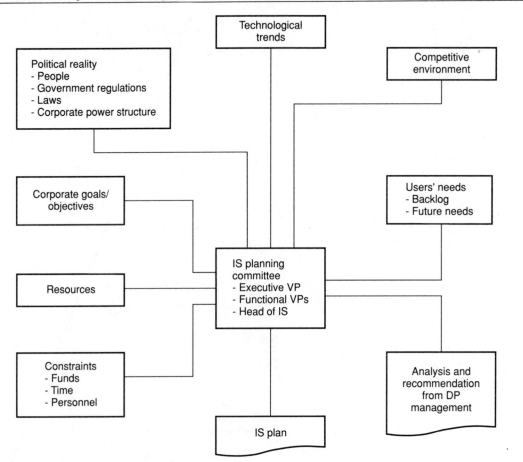

Source: Donna Hussain and K. M. Hussain, *Information Processing Systems for Management,* 2nd ed. (Homewood, Ill.: Richard D. Irwin, 1985), Figure 10–1, p. 224 (with minor changes).

virtue of being involved in the organization's strategic planning process, the CIO guarantees that information systems, where appropriate, address Critical Success Factors (CSFs)[5] at each level of management. In some organizations, the CIO is responsible for overseeing the preparation and dissemination of policies and procedure documents for new systems.

---

[5]"The CSF process effectively relates the systems plan to the organization's operations and strategies by identifying the information needs, problems, and strategies of the managers in the organization." Pran N. Wahi, K. Papp, and S. Steir, "Planning at Weyerhauser," *Journal of Systems Management,* March 1983, p. 13.

MATERIAL REQUIREMENTS PLANNING (MRP)

"The processes of identifying that stock is low, identifying the lead time to get stock from suppliers, identifying the most cost-effective order quantities, and then producing purchase orders for those stock items in the right amounts at the right time to ensure that the stock will be on hand when it is needed have become known as *material requirements planning,* or *MRP.*"[6]

MRP software, which links inventory control, bills-of-materials, and production scheduling, is readily available. Along with calculating quantities required and printing purchase orders, the software also assists managers in reducing production delays, excess stockpiles of material, and overtime associated with providing materials as they are needed.[7]

BUSINESS SYSTEMS PLANNING

Business Systems Planning (BSP) is an example of process-based methodology, which is used to develop information system master plans. The plan's information requirements start with top-level business objectives, which are used to derive lower-level business processes. The business processes, in turn, are the sources of data gathering and analysis. Executives are interviewed to identify their critical success factors and major decisions, as well as their views on current issues and problems. Based on this top-down requirements determination procedure, plus current system and proposed information architecture, planners establish application priorities and database implications.

A Business Systems Planning—Information Systems Planning Guide is available through IBM branch offices.

WHY SOME INFORMATION SYSTEMS FAIL

One reason for the failure of many management information systems is that they are designed for use at operational (lower) levels; many are based on existing information processing applications that support separate business functions. This "by-product information," when received by upper management, is out-of-date, not integrated, extraneous, and generally overwhelming (particularly in volume).[8]

---

[6]Robert Schultheis and Mary Sumner, *Management Information Systems: The Manager's View,* Chapter 10 (Homewood, Ill.: Richard D. Irwin, 1989), p. 414.

[7]Schultheis and Sumner, *Management Information Systems,* Chapter 10.

[8]Lisa Thomaidis and Larraine Clark, "The Significance of an MIS in Supporting Strategic Planning" (MBA paper, Loyola College, Baltimore, Md., 1985).

Early application designers did not perceive or portray information as an integrated corporate resource, nor did their clients 5 or 10 years ago. Today, it is not unusual for IS staffs to be asked to coordinate their operations and to arrange their support from a total corporate perspective; providing that coordination is one function of the CIO.

CONCLUSION

To provide support from a total corporate point of view, an information system must focus first on the organization's long-term goals, thereby supporting the corporation's overall strategic plan. The long-term view, however, may not show results for many years, particularly if many of the IS portfolio of applications generate intangible benefits rather than hard savings or increased revenues.[9]

If one is to successfully manage today's large organizations, the only alternative to relying solely on wisdom and intuition is strategic planning; IS's role is to assure that its activities are synchronized with the organizational critical success factors and that all are directed toward accomplishing the company's long-term goals.

CASES: SOUTHERN OHIO GAS & LIGHT, JENKINS ENGINEERING AND TECHNOLOGY, AND RANDALL INDUSTRIES, INC.

A committee studied the information needs of Southern Ohio Gas & Light and determined that the Information Services department (ISD) was overloaded with user requests; the users, finding ISD unresponsive, looked outside the company for service. Case 5–1, Southern Ohio Gas & Light, rather than presenting a significant problem for solution, offers a fine opportunity to discuss IS planning in general, and IBM's BSP in particular.

At Jenkins, a very large corporation in the transportation industry (Case 5–2, Jenkins Engineering and Technology), growth has resulted from the acquisition of other firms, many already possessing significant computer assets. Merging the systems has not produced entirely satisfactory results, and a new national telecommunications system may be required.

In trying to modernize the IS operation at Randall Industries (Case 5–3, Randall Industries, Inc.), a top executive hired a new MIS director. On arriving, the director of MIS found incompatible systems; his attempts to centralize control of the company's data processing resources caused friction with the formerly autonomous division managers.

---

[9]O'Brien, *Computers in Business Management,* 3rd ed., p. 403.

Case 5–1 Southern Ohio Gas & Light Company

Mike Murray, vice president of Corporate Planning and Services for Southern Ohio Gas & Light Company, was sitting in his office contemplating the meeting he was about to have with Bruno Mochon, director of Information Systems and Services (ISS). It was mid-June 1986, and most company employees had barely gotten used to being back to work after the long Memorial Day holiday. Mike had just finished rereading the Business Systems Planning (BSP) study and was meeting with Bruno to discuss what course of action Information Systems should take in response to the BSP.

In October 1984, Southern Ohio Gas initiated the study to analyze the current and future information needs of the company. A primary objective of the study was to develop a conceptual framework or architecture to guide Information Systems' long-range planning function. The study was completed early in April 1986.

In reviewing the study, Mike recalled how impressed he had been on his first quick scan through the report; it was truly an outstanding effort, and he was pleased, after the fact, that he had congratulated the BSP task force—in glowing terms—on a job well done. Even the company's president had expressed his appreciation to the members for their commitment to excellence and their professional team effort.

BSP STUDY (ISS PERSPECTIVE)

Traditionally, ISS's overall mission has been to plan, design, implement, and maintain all information and related telecommunications systems required by the company; also, it coordinates the company's efforts related to those activities, both in-house and with outside computer services. In carrying out this mission, ISS must assume varying rules of service, guidance, control, and coordination.

In the past, ISS has undertaken large corporate projects in addition to coordinating the company's entry into office automation. Historically, the company has used automated information systems successfully, primarily to minimize labor-intensive, repetitive processes in the day-to-day operations of the company. Although corporate projects have been staffed jointly by ISS and users, ISS has assumed control of technology selection, data management, and significant portions of project work. Therefore, ISS's control and coordination rules have been dominant.

The present environment is characterized by strong business and regulatory challenges, sufficient large-scale information systems in most company areas, and

---

This case was prepared by Glenn Decint and Bob Sweet. Names, locations, and financial data have been disguised.

continued proliferation and downward cost trends in information technology. High levels of demand within the company for information services produced large backlogs of work for ISS.

The persistent backlog continues to create opportunities and pressures within various user departments to seek alternatives to ISS-developed systems for their information needs. The tendency to bypass ISS has been strengthened by (1) the rapid growth of personal computers with user-friendly software, (2) the competitive response of large computer software vendors, (3) and the growth in computer literacy of the company work force.

In response to that three-part environment, Information Centers have been established at headquarters and the Operations Center; their function is to assist users in the development of departmental systems. The objectives of the Information Centers are to provide guidance, support, education, and access to equipment. The users are to develop systems on personal computers and, with user-friendly software, to access information stored on the mainframe.

The ISS staff has seen the changes in its roles and activities; the most recent changes will not be the final revisions. Emphasis on control is evolving into emphasis on coordination, guidance, and service. Although ISS-developed and operated systems are still the primary delivery method for the company, users have been encouraged to acquire less costly packaged software and to develop departmental systems themselves. Expanding these latter two activities will allow ISS to concentrate its resources on corporate systems, decision support applications, and needed enhancements that have been neglected due to higher priority projects.

DEVELOPMENT MATRIXES

A matrix was designed that relates the business processes to the existing corporate information systems developed by ISS and those under formulation or planned for development (see Exhibit 1). An additional matrix identifies systems independently developed or acquired by departments and relates them to the business processes. This matrix also identifies usage of external systems and databases, mini- or microcomputers (personal computers), and central company mainframe computers (see Exhibit 2).

A review of these matrixes revealed several instances of system or data duplication.

INFORMATION ARCHITECTURE

Information architecture is a model depicting the processes and data classes within an organization and the relationship between them. It provides a conceptual framework for recognizing the information systems required to support the business and its objectives. The foundation of the information architecture is the Business

EXHIBIT 1 Business Systems Planning Study: Corporate Information Systems/Business Process Matrix

Current and Proposed Application Systems Developed or Supported by Information Systems Department

Legend

E — Existing system
I — In development
P — Planned

Business Processes (columns 1–39):

1. Establish strategic plans *(Mgmt)*
2. Oversee legislative affairs
3. Determine regulatory requirements
4. Develop capacity and load forecasts
5. Perform audits
6. Assure employee and public safety
7. Provide legal services
8. Maintain & assure corporate citizenship
9. Establish organizational policies & procs
10. Forecast short-term gas demand *(Gas)*
11. Seek gas supply
12. Distribute gas
13. Prepare financial plans *(Capital)*
14. Prepare budgets & monitor expenditures
15. Obtain rate relief
16. Manage external financing
17. Manage cash
18. Process accounts receivable
19. Process accounts payable
20. Maintain financial accounts
21. Manage pension assets
22. Determine personnel requirements *(Pers)*
23. Establish personnel policies
24. Acquire work force
25. Manage employees
26. Compensate employees
27. Develop employees
28. Plan materials & supplies requirements *(Msp)*
29. Procure M&S & eqpt. and manage inventory
30. Plan, design, & constr. distr. facilities *(Plant)*
31. Manage distribution facilities
32. Plan, design, & construct general plant
33. Manage general plant
34. Plan, design, & construct production plant
35. Manage gas production plant
36. Develop & implement marketing plan *(Cust)*
37. Service customer needs
38. Maintain customer records
39. Terminate gas services

Corporate Information Systems — matrix (columns = business process numbers 1–39):

Category	System	1	2	3	4	5	6	7	8	9	10	11	12	13	14	15	16	17	18	19	20	21	22	23	24	25	26	27	28	29	30	31	32	33	34	35	36	37	38	39
Distr Mgmt	Facilities mapping																														E	E								
	Service survey inspection form																														P									
	Graphic inquiry																														P	P								
	Corrosion control priority task																															E								
	Paving order																														E	E								
	Distr. construction & maint. mgmt.																														I	I								
	T&D work management																														I	I								
	Survey management																														P									
	Main certification																															P								
	Pipeline performance																																							
	Corrosion control & planning																														P	P								
	Repair replacement																															P								
	Estimating information															E															P									
	Network logic																														P	P								
Employee	Employee information																				E																			
	Payroll																				E						E													
	Salary administration																										E													
	Jobs/positions																								E	E	E	E												
	Applicants																								E															
	Insurance																										E													
	Personnel administration																						P	P	P		P													
	Pension payroll/subsidiary payroll																								E															
Finance	Financial reporting																				E																			
	Responsibility reporting													E							E																			
	Nonjurisdictional allocation														P																									
	On-line budget data entry													P																										
	Jurisdictional acctg. & reporting													E							E																			
	Plant accounting																				E																			
	Rates and regulatory information													E																										
	Forecast data interface														P																									
Cust Info	Customer accounting						E												E		E																		E	E
	Customer inquiry																																						E	
	On-line order taking																																						E	
	Meter history & inventory																													E										
	Subsidiary billing																	I	I																					
	Hand-held meter reading																	I																						
	Service history																																					P		
	Dispatch from CRT																																					P		
	NBR tracking & reporting																														E	E			E					
Model	Cost of service allocation															E																								
	Gas sendout model				E																																			
	Corporate financial model	E												E	E		E	E																						
	Gas requirements & supply model				E																																			
	Jurisdictional modeling															I	I																							
	Subsidiary modeling															P	P																							
Mat/Eq	Materials management																				E								E	E										
	Accounts payable																			I	I																			
	Transportation management																				E												E							
	Telephone billing & inventory																																I							
	Subsidiary stores																				I																			
Misc	Stockholder info sys.						E										E	E																						
	On-line application															P																								
	Dividend reinvestment															P																								
	DP system utilization																																E							
	Computer resource chargeback																					I																		
	Legal & litigation support		P					P						P																										

EXHIBIT 2 Business Planning Study: Departmental Information Systems//Business Process Matrix

Legend

E — Existing system
I — In development
P — Planned

Business Processes (columns 1–39):

1. Establish strategic plans
2. Oversee legislative affairs
3. Determine regulatory requirements
4. Develop capacity and load forecasts
5. Perform audits
6. Assure employee and public safety
7. Provide legal services
8. Maintain & assure corporate citizenship
9. Establish organizational policies & procs
10. Forecast short-term gas demand
11. Seek gas supply
12. Distribute gas
13. Prepare financial plans
14. Prepare budgets & monitor expenditures
15. Obtain rate relief
16. Manage external financing
17. Manage cash
18. Process accounts receivable
19. Process accounts payable
20. Maintain financial accounts
21. Maintain pension assets
22. Determine personnel requirements
23. Establish personnel policies
24. Acquire work force
25. Manage employees
26. Compensate employees
27. Develop employees
28. Plan materials & supplies requirements
29. Procure M&S & eqpt. and manage inventory
30. Plan, design, & constr. distr. facilities
31. Manage distribution facilities
32. Plan, design, & construct general plant
33. Manage general plant
34. Plan, design, & construct production plant
35. Manage gas production plant
36. Develop & implement marketing plan
37. Service customer needs
38. Maintain customer records
39. Terminate gas services

Column groups: Mgmt (1–9), Gas (10–12), Capital (13–21), Pers (22–27), M&S (28–29), Plant (30–35), Cust (36–39).

Departmental Information Systems	External	Mini/micro	Mainframe	Process (col)
Appliance service				
Employee		X		E (24)
Overtime		X		E (24)
Accident		X		E (5)
Budget		X		E (14)
Premise minutes		X		E (24)
Vehicle		X		E (33)
Service route		X		E (37)
Attendance		X		E (24)
Production		X		E (24), E (31)
Inventory		X		E (31)
Meter by-pass		X		E (18)
Meter history		X		E (18), E (37), E (38)
Dual fuel		X		E (38)
Budget				
Actual capital expenditures		X		E (14)
Actual capital exp. — app. serv.		X		E (14)
Overhead rates		X		E (14)
Ratio of removal costs to improvs.		X		E (14)
Overhead rates with D&D		X		E (14)
Est. total exp. — Lima		X		E (14)
Est. total exp. — Bear Hill		X		E (14)
Comp. of detail to capital budget		X		E (14)
Active noncont. acct. listing		X		E (14)
Act. hours for contract services		X		E (14)
App. sev budget cont. serv. dollars		X		E (14)
Cont. serv budgeted — WGL		X		E (14)
Act. buildings service expense		X		E (14)
Act. postage expense		X		E (14)
Act. computer usage expense		X		E (14)
Date (time) report		X		E (14)
East station expenses		X		E (14)
T&D, gas supply labor expense		X		E (14)
T&D maintenance — Ind.		X		E (14)
Actual budget		X		E (14)
Manpower comparison		X		E (14)
Building service allocation	X			E (14)
Computer usage allocation	X			E (14)
Middletown income statement		X		E (14)
Miami income statement		X		E (14)
Bear Hill income statement		X		E (14)
Lima income statement		X		E (14)
Miami deferred taxes		X		E (14)
Middletown deferred taxes		X		E (14)
Revenues by classification — Mid.		X		E (14)
Revenues by classification — Miami		X		E (14)
Gas purchased comparison report		X		E (14)

EXHIBIT 2 *(continued)*

Legend

E — Existing system
I — In development
P — Planned

Business Processes (column key)

Group **Mgmt**
1. Establish strategic plans
2. Oversee legislative affairs
3. Determine regulatory requirements
4. Develop capacity and load forecasts
5. Perform audits
6. Assure employee and public safety
7. Provide legal services
8. Maintain & assure corporate citizenship
9. Establish organizational policies & procs

Group **Gas**
10. Forecast short-term gas demand
11. Seek gas supply
12. Distribute gas

Group **Capital**
13. Prepare financial plans
14. Prepare budgets & monitor expenditures
15. Obtain rate relief
16. Manage external financing
17. Manage cash
18. Process accounts receivable
19. Process accounts payable
20. Maintain financial accounts
21. Manage pension assets

Group **Pers**
22. Determine personnel requirements
23. Establish personnel policies
24. Acquire work force
25. Manage employees
26. Compensate employees
27. Develop employees

Group **MS**
28. Plan materials & supplies requirements
29. Procure M&S & eqpt. and manage inventory

Group **Plant**
30. Plan, design, & constr. distr. facilities
31. Manage distribution facilities
32. Plan, design, & construct general plant
33. Manage general plant
34. Plan, design, & construct production plant
35. Manage gas production plant

Group **Cust**
36. Develop & implement marketing plan
37. Service customer needs
38. Maintain customer records
39. Terminate gas services

Departmental Information Systems

System	Ext	Mini	Main	2	4	10	11	14	16	18	20	21	24	30	31	33	36	37	38
Communications																			
AP & UPI wire services	X												E						
Gas energy network	X												E						
Oh. legislative info. system	X			E															
Div. of legislative automated sys.	X			E															
Consumer relations																			
Computer aided lit. support 1		X								E									
DEC Pro 500 mgt. info. system		X																	E
Credit bureau	X									E									E
Collector work mgt.		X								E									
Corporate accounting																			
13 mon. balance sheet — WGL			X								E								
Bal. sheet by state charge			X								E								
Nonutility income statements			X								E								
Budget	X							E											
Finance charges — actuarial	X										E								
Functions for nonutility seg.			X								E								
Accounts for nonutility seg.			X								E								
Inactive functions list			X								E								
Bud. revenues & taxes — Bear Hill			X								E								
Bud. revenues & taxes — Lima			X								E								
Stats/Bear Hill condensate prod.			X								E								
Lima lease data			X								E								
Spec/gen. gas purchased & trans.			X								E								
Classification of salary & wages			X								E								
Deferred gas costs			X								E								
13 mon. balance sheet — ITC			X								E								
Corporate planning																			
Aset — adv. staffing & eval. tech.			X										E						
Advanced office controls (AOC)		X											E						
Burlington fleet	X																		
Marketing system			X														E		
T&D work management			X													E			
Corrosion work management			X											E	E				
Transportation support personnel			X												E				
NBR reporting			X													E			
Rate of return analysis			X											E	E				
Collector work management			X									E		E	E				
Normalized sales per meter	X					E													
Econometric gas demand forecast	X			(I@4)	I	I													
Distribution																			
Manpower system			X																
O&M budgeting — T&D			X				E						E						
Third-party damage			X		E				E										
NBR reporting & tracking			X																
Leak survey			X												E			E	
Service sizing system			X													E			
Map control system			X												E				
Capital budgeting — T&D	X						E												
Work management system			X											E	E				

Note: "Econometric gas demand forecast" shows an I under column 4 (Develop capacity and load forecasts) and an I under column 10 (Forecast short-term gas demand).

EXHIBIT 2   (continued)

Legend

E — Existing system
I — In development
P — Planned

Business Processes — column key:

1. Establish strategic plans
2. Oversee legislative affairs
3. Determine regulatory requirements
4. Develop capacity and load forecasts
5. Perform audits
6. Assure employee and public safety
7. Provide legal services
8. Maintain & assure corporate citizenship
9. Establish organizational policies & procs
10. Forecast short-term gas demand
11. Seek gas supply
12. Distribute gas
13. Prepare financial plans
14. Prepare budgets & monitor expenditures
15. Obtain rate relief
16. Manage external financing
17. Manage cash
18. Process accounts receivable
19. Process accounts payable
20. Maintain financial accounts
21. Manage pension assets
22. Determine personnel requirements
23. Establish personnel policies
24. Acquire work force
25. Manage employees
26. Compensate employees
27. Develop employees
28. Plan materials & supplies requirements
29. Procure M&S & eqpt. and manage inventory
30. Plan, design, & constr. distr. facilities
31. Manage distribution facilities
32. Plan, design, & construct general plant
33. Manage general plant
34. Plan, design, & construct production plant
35. Manage gas production plant
36. Develop & implement marketing plan
37. Service customer needs
38. Maintain customer records
39. Terminate gas services

Departmental Information Systems

System	Ext	Mini/micro	Mainframe	1	2	3	4	5	6	7	8	9	10	11	12	13	14	15	16	17	18	19	20	21	22	23	24	25	26	27	28	29	30	31	32	33	34	35	36	37	38	39
Distribution (continued)																																										
Leak locator work management			X																															E								
Truck driver work management			X																														E	E								
Welder work management			X																														E	E								
Machine operator work management			X																														E	E								
Capitol job control system			X																														E									
Temp. work order system			X																															E								
Corrosion work management system			X																															E								
Estimating charting system			X																														E	E								
Shops equip. & maint. systems																																				P						
DP&D budgeting		X																E																									
Internal work tracking		X																																E								
DP&D field note system			X																														E	E								
Finance																																										
CP balance & int exp by month		X																				E																				
Ave. cost of debt per month		X																		E																						
Revolving credit per month		X																		E																						
Ave. commercial paper outstanding		X																		E																						
Cumulative time-weighted returns		X																							E																	
Asset distribution		X																							E																	
Var. of portfolio div. & asset alloc		X																							E																	
Pension fund performance (SEI)	X																								E																		
Pensim (Wilshire)	X																								E																		
Financing rate analysis		X																																								E	
Five-year financing		X													E																												
Lease versus buy analysis		X																																	E							
Analysis of current financing		X															E																									
New business profitability		X																																							E	
Social security calculation		X																										E														
Master trust	X																						E																			
TRESOP trustee reports	X																											E														
Monthly cash projection		X												E				E	E																							
Analysis of financing altern.		X												E				E	E																							
Long-term debt interest exp. proj.		X												E				E																								
Gas bill projections		X												E				E																									
Storage gas projections		X												E				E																									
Financial performance & goals		X															E	E																									
Budget		X													E																											
Collection bank balances		X												E				E	E																							
Bank collection item count		X																E																								
Bank balance projection			X											E				E																									
Daily cash flow projections			X											E				E																									
Sinking fund analysis			X											E				E																									
Attachments program			X																								E														
Budget			X												E																											
Commercial paper issuance	X													E				E																								
Investment listing	X																	E																								

EXHIBIT 2 (*continued*)

Legend

E — Existing system
I — In development
P — Planned

Business Processes — Business process columns (1–39):

Mgmt
1. Establish strategic plans
2. Oversee legislative affairs
3. Determine regulatory requirements
4. Develop capacity and load forecasts
5. Perform audits
6. Assure employee and public safety
7. Provide legal services
8. Maintain & assure corporate citizenship
9. Establish organizational policies & procs

Gas
10. Forecast short-term gas demand
11. Seek gas supply
12. Distribute gas

Capital
13. Prepare financial plans
14. Prepare budgets & monitor expenditures
15. Obtain rate relief
16. Manage external financing
17. Manage cash
18. Process accounts receivable
19. Process accounts payable
20. Maintain financial accounts
21. Maintain pension assets

Pers
22. Determine personnel requirements
23. Establish personnel policies
24. Acquire work force
25. Manage employees
26. Compensate employees
27. Develop employees

M&S
28. Plan materials & supplies requirements
29. Procure M&S & eqpt. and manage inventory

Plant
30. Plan, design, & constr. distr. facilities
31. Manage distribution facilities
32. Plan, design, & construct general plant
33. Manage general plant
34. Plan, design, & construct production plant
35. Manage gas production plant

Cust
36. Develop & implement marketing plan
37. Service customer needs
38. Maintain customer records
39. Terminate gas services

Departmental Information Systems — system type columns: External / Mini-micro / Mainframe

Departmental Information Systems	Ext	Mini	Main	Business Processes (1–39)
Gas supply				
Budget preparation		X		14=E
Expense analysis		X		14=E
Task management		X		37=E, 39=E
Maintenance management		X		37=E, 39=E
Time reporting		X		26=E
Employee information		X		26=E, 27=E
Nontraditional gas volumes			X	11=E
Buckeye gas network			X	11=I
Gate station on-line control			X	12=I
Special contract customers			X	10=E
Gas prod. & storage model			X	11=E
Network analysis	X			31=E
Load factor generation	X			31=E
General services				
Address printing & list management		X		24=E
Dow Jones	X			1=E; 13=E, 14=E, 15=E, 16=E; 20=E
Dialog database	X			1–39 all = E
Gas energy network	X			1=E, 2=E, 3=E; 6=E; 13=E; 15=E; 16=E, 17=E; 20=E; 36=E, 37=E; 39=E
On-line cataloging system	X			1–39 all = E
Human resources				
Executive competencies tracking		X		27=E
Executive management training		X		27=E
Course registration tracking		X		27=E
EEO tracking		X		24=E
Applicant tracking		X		24=E
Supervisory bid tracking		X		24=E
Information systems				
Education history		X		27=E
Training budget tracking		X		14=E
MVS/Integrated control system		X		31=E
BEST1		X		31=E
Information management systems		X		31=E
EEI electronic info. services	X			31=E
Schedule of equip. installations		X		32=E
Budget req. computers & equip.		X		14=E
Micro computer usage		X		33=E
Cost by system		X		14=E
Budgets		X		14=E
Affirmative action program		X		24=E
Purchase versus lease analysis		X		29=E
Internal audit				
Audit analyzer		X		5=E
Reporting & control system		X		5=E
Customer receivables confirmation		X		5=E
EDP library listing		X		5=E
Marketing				
Enercom (GE)	X			37=E
Therm sales — Spec. contr. cust.	X			37=E

EXHIBIT 2   (concluded)

Legend

E — Existing system
I — In development
P — Planned

Column headings (Business Processes):

1. Establish strategic plans
2. Oversee legislative affairs
3. Determine regulatory requirements
4. Develop capacity and load forecasts
5. Perform audits
6. Assure employee and public safety
7. Provide legal services
8. Maintain & assure corporate citizenship
9. Establish organizational policies & procs
10. Forecast short-term gas demand
11. Seek gas supply
12. Distribute gas
13. Prepare financial plans
14. Prepare budgets & monitor expenditures
15. Obtain rate relief
16. Manage external financing
17. Manage cash
18. Process accounts receivable
19. Process accounts payable
20. Maintain financial accounts
21. Manage pension assets
22. Determine personnel requirements
23. Establish personnel policies
24. Acquire work force
25. Manage employees
26. Compensate employees
27. Develop employees
28. Plan materials & supplies requirements
29. Procure M&S & eqpt. and manage inventory
30. Plan. design, & constr. distr. facilities
31. Manage distribution facilities
32. Plan, design, & construct general plant
33. Manage general plant
34. Plan, design, & construct production plant
35. Manage gas production plant
36. Develop & implement marketing plan
37. Service customer needs
38. Maintain customer records
39. Terminate gas services

System columns: External, Mini/micro, Mainframe

Departmental Information Systems	External	Mini/micro	Mainframe	Process(es) & Code
Marketing (continued)				
Budgets		X		14: E
Five-yr. est. of serv. meters, therms		X		36: E
Emp. slaes & prospect reports		X		36: E
Cost/rev. test for new business		X		36: E
Yearly servs, meters, therms graph		X		36: E
Analysis of prosp. CNG fleets		X		36: E
Cogeneration app. studies		X		36: E
Load estimating		X		36: E
Operating cost analysis		X		36: E
Duct design		X		36: E
Piping design		X		36: E
Cooperative advertising records		X		36: E
Public utilities comm. records		X		36: E
Lead generator		X		36: E
Dual fuel			X	36: E
Thrift purchase contracts			X	36: E
Office of general counsel				
LEXIS/NEXIS	X			7: E
Computer aided lit. support 1		X		7: E; 18: E
Gas energy network	X			7: E
Payroll & stores accounting				
Social security calculation sys.		X		26: E
Rates & regulatory affairs				
Cost of service allocation — Middletown		X		15: E
Purchased gas adjustment — Middletown		X		15: E
Supplier refunds — WGL		X		15: E
Supplier refunds — Middletown		X		15: E
Lead/LAG study — Gas costs		X		15: E
Price elasticity		X		15: E
Economic studies		X		15: E
Analysis of supplier PGA		X		15: E
Supplier rate filings		X		15: E
Pro forma adjustments by month			X	15: E
Sales				36: E
Large volume sales		X		36: E
Sales calls		X		

Process/Data Class matrix (Exhibit 3), which details the relationships of the data classes and business processes.

A summary architecture (Exhibit 4) shows the major categories and the relationships among them (see Appendix 1 at the end of this chapter for details of the summary architecture). For each category, the individual business processes and data classes created are listed along with the information systems (current, in development, and planned) which support these processes. Note that a great amount of management information, in the form of direction, is required by the other categories. There are few corporate systems in place to support this information flow, which may mean that opportunities for computerization do not exist. Conversely, a noticeably small amount of capital information is needed in the other categories, while the lengthy list of corporate systems indicates significant processing requirements internal to the category.

BACKGROUND

Southern Ohio Gas & Light Company is a natural gas distribution utility company serving the metropolitan Cincinnati area. The company was founded prior to the 1900s to serve a single select customer in town. Since then, the company has grown and now serves a franchise area of approximately 4,400 square miles (surrounding and including the city) with more than 500,000 customers. The distribution system entails over 6,000 miles of gas mains. The company is regulated by three public service commissions.

Starting in 1965, the company began to recruit and train a staff of systems analysts and programmers in third-generation computer technology. The objective was to implement a database-oriented customer accounting system having terminal inquiry capability. The first third-generation equipment (RCA 3301) was installed in June 1966. Implementation of a terminal inquiry system on the RCA equipment was never completed, due to RCA hardware and software problems. At that time, most utilities were still using card systems (second-generation equipment).

In 1970, a task force of personnel from Information Systems, Accounting, and operating departments (with assistance from a consultant) conducted a study of the company's current and projected data processing requirements. The objective of the study was to identify data processing applications that would be beneficial to the company and to recommend data processing equipment that would be capable of meeting these total data processing requirements.

The study recommended a switch from RCA to IBM equipment and recommended an implementation program for the conversion of existing systems and the development of other systems identified in the study.

The first priority was to train the ISS staff on the IBM systems, followed by conversion of the hardware.

The second priority was customer service applications, such as a customer inquiry system, a customer accounting system, and a customer service and meter order system.

EXHIBIT 3 Business Systems Planning Study: Business Process/Data Class Matrix

Legend

C—Process *creates* data class
   (may also use data class)
U—Process *uses* data class

Business Processes / *Data Classes*

Data Classes (columns):

1. Organizational unit
2. Corp. policies & procedures
3. Corp. goals & objectives
4. Strategic plan
5. New legislation
6. Audits
7. Regulations
8. Long-term gas demand forecast
9. Safety policies & procedures
10. Legal requirements
11. Community programs
12. Organizational policies & procs.
13. Short-term gas demand forecast
14. Gas supplier contracts
15. Gas volumes
16. Weather
17. Distr. fac. maint work order
18. Financial plan
19. Budget & variance
20. Tariffs
21. Capital
22. Money market
23. Accounts receivable
24. Accounts payable
25. General ledger accounts
26. Pension assets
27. Job description
28. Manpower budgets
29. Personnel policies & procs.
30. Labor contracts
31. Employee description
32. Contractor
33. Employee performance
34. Employee payroll records
35. Employee training
36. M & S specifications
37. Purchase orders
38. Vendor description
39. M & S inventory history
40. Distribution facilities
41. Distr. fac. insp. & maint.
42. Gen. plant facilities & eqpt.
43. Gen. plant insp. & maint.
44. Prod. plant facilities
45. Prod. plant insp. & maint.
46. Gas production & storage records
47. Marketing plan
48. Dealer
49. Gas sale
50. Retail competitor
51. Service history
52. Customer record
53. Termination records

Business Processes (rows):

1. Establish strategic plans
2. Oversee legislative affairs
3. Determine regulatory requirements
4. Develop capacity and load forecasts
5. Perform audits
6. Assure employee and public safety
7. Provide legal services
8. Maintain & assure corporate citizenship
9. Establish organizational policies & procs
10. Forecast short-term gas demand
11. Seek gas supply
12. Distribute gas
13. Prepare financial plans
14. Prepare budgets & monitor expenditures
15. Obtain rate relief
16. Manage external financing
17. Manage cash
18. Process accounts receivable
19. Process accounts payable
20. Maintain financial accounts
21. Manage pension assets
22. Determine personnel requirements
23. Establish personnel policies
24. Acquire work force
25. Manage employees
26. Compensate employees
27. Develop employees
28. Plan materials & supplies requirements
29. Procure M&S & eqpt. and manage inventory
30. Plan, design, & constr. distr. facilities
31. Manage distribution facilities
32. Plan, design, & construct general plant
33. Manage general plant
34. Plan, design, & construct production plant
35. Manage gas production plant
36. Develop & implement marketing plan
37. Service customer needs
38. Maintain customer records
39. Terminate gas services

Left-margin process groupings (read vertically):
- **Mgmt** (processes 1–9)
- **Gas** (processes 10–12)
- **Cap** (processes 13–21)
- **Pers** (processes 22–27)
- **M S P** (processes 28–29)
- **Plant** (processes 30–35)
- **Cust** (processes 36–39)

EXHIBIT 4   Information Architecture

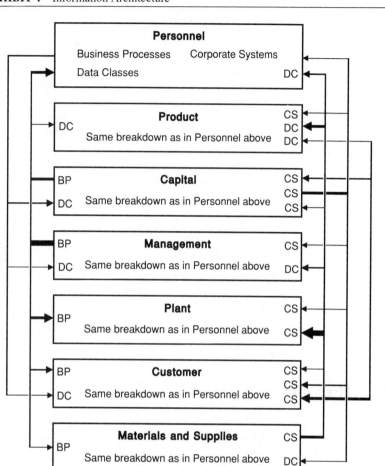

The third priority was the development and implementation of three new systems — stockholder information, financial reporting, and employee information. Additional systems were also recommended for development on completion of the above systems; they included materials management, property records, and transmission and distribution records.

As a result of the nationwide energy shortage, there was a moratorium on additional gas supplies in the natural gas industry from 1971 to 1974. Consequently, the company implemented an austerity program, and top management decided to shelve selected systems development until further notice.

With the lifting of the austerity program in 1974, projects were reinstated. ISS initiated a study to:

1. Describe the major information systems (in general terms) that had been identified to date for development.
2. Review the present status of those systems.
3. Set forth a proposed implementation plan.
4. Review steps considered prerequisites for successful and effective systems implementation.

Appendix 2 presents a summary of the development status of the identified systems at that time and shows the estimated staffing requirements and implementation time lines. Appendix 3 is the proposed implementation plan.

Between 1974 and 1984, ISS was authorized to carry out the described plan in accordance with the recommendations of the studies/reports initiated in 1970. As a result of the unhappy experiences when converting from RCA to IBM, ISS resolved never again to be a pioneer in information technology. Henceforth, its philosophy—still true today—would be to stay on the leading edge of the learning curve, but never to be the leader.

As the ISS department requirements grew, staffing (and budget) were added. Additional people came from within the company and from outside. The outside hires were technical people, chosen for their high MIS technical skills but nevertheless expected to learn the company's business. People from within came from the end-user departments. They were given computer aptitude tests, and—if accepted—were trained in MIS technology skills.

ISS progressed by following five-year plans that were reviewed and updated annually.

PERSONNEL BACKGROUND

By 1986, ISS (also referred to as ISD) had grown to a department of 173 employees with six major divisions. ISD is one of four departments within Mike Murray's responsibility area (see Exhibit 5).

Bruno Mochon heads the ISD and reports directly to Mike. Six managers, each supervising a major division of ISD, report to Bruno (Exhibit 6).

Mike Murray has been with the company for 38 years. He began his career as a clerk in the Accounting department. After 15 years in Accounting, he was promoted to executive assistant to the controller. In 1964, he received a special assignment to coordinate work on the RCA project. In 1966, he became assistant manager of the Data Processing department. In 1971, he was promoted to director of Computer Systems and Services, and—in 1974—became director of Information Systems. In 1980, Mike was promoted to vice president of Accounting and Information Systems. He received his present title of vice president of Corporate Planning and Services in 1985. He has a Business Administration Degree (undergraduate) and an MBA.

Bruno Mochon, director of Information Systems and Services, began his career in General Accounting in 1965. In 1968, he was assigned to the Data Processing

EXHIBIT 5 Vice President — Corporate Planning and Services

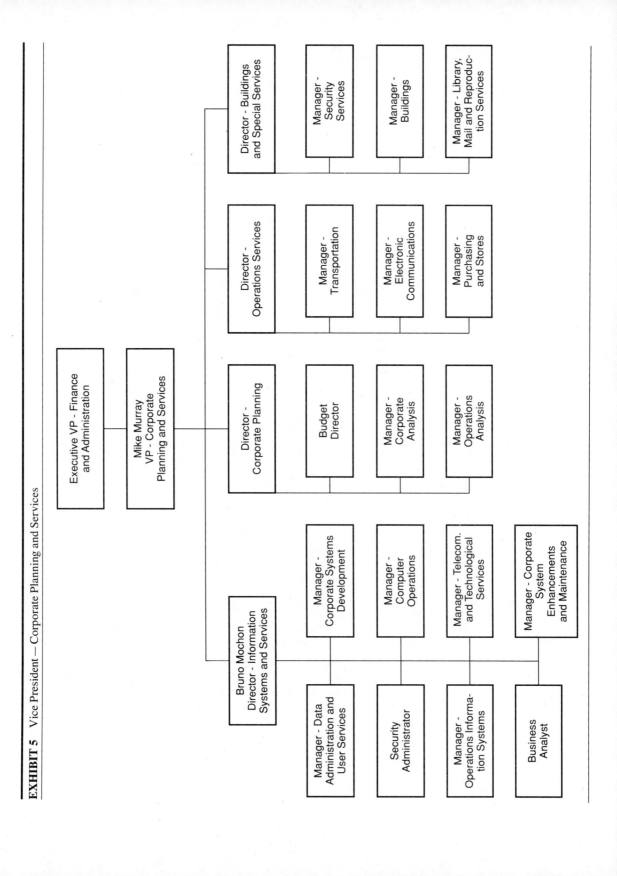

EXHIBIT 6   Information Systems and Services

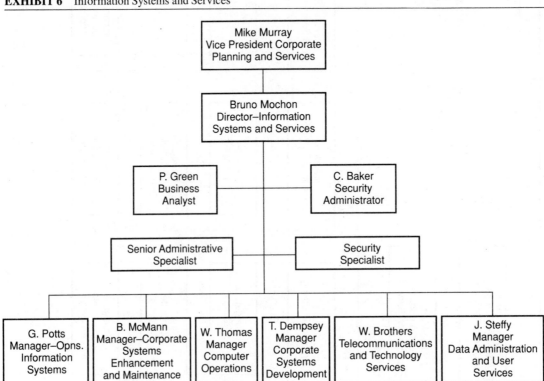

department as a programmer. He was promoted to systems analyst in 1970 and reported to Mike Murray. By 1974, Bruno was promoted to manager of Financial and Operational Information Systems. He became director of Information Systems in 1980 and received his present title in 1985. Through the entire period, starting in 1970, Bruno reported to Mike. Bruno has an undergraduate degree in Business Administration.

Terry Dempsey, manager of Corporate Systems Development, was hired in 1949 as a clerk in the Credit department. He was promoted to supervisor in 1956. In 1964, he was assigned to the task force for the RCA project as an end-user representative from the Credit department. He was promoted to senior systems analyst in 1967, and became manager of Customer and General Service Information Systems in 1971. In 1985, he received his present title. Terry has a BS in Management Technology.

Will Thomas, manager of Computer Operations, started when computer boards

EXHIBIT 6 *(continued)*

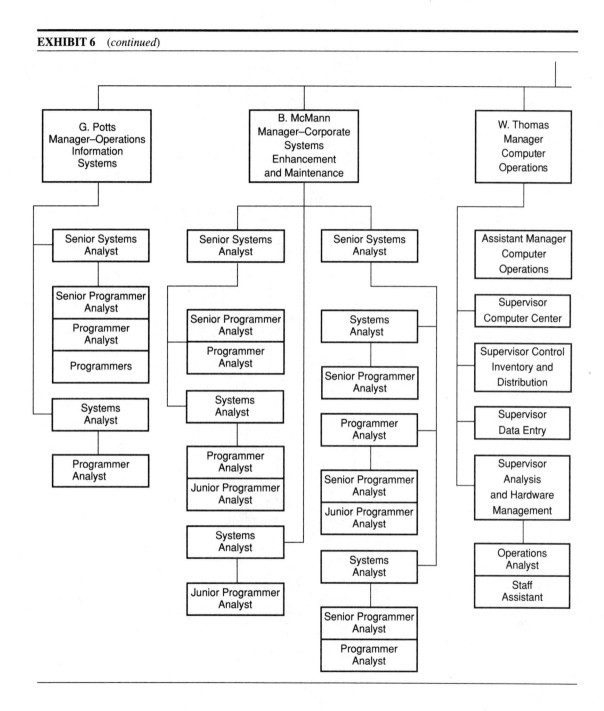

EXHIBIT 6 *(concluded)*

Organization Chart

T. Dempsey — Manager, Corporate Systems Development
- Senior Systems Analyst
  - Senior Programmer Analyst
  - Programmer Analyst
  - Programmers
- Systems Analyst
  - Programmer Analyst
- Senior Systems Analyst
- Programmer Analyst
- Systems Analyst
- Senior Programmer Analyst
- Special Projects Analyst
- Systems Analyst

W. Brothers — Telecommunications and Technology Services
- Senior Systems Programmer
- Senior Systems Programmer
  - System Programmer
- Telecommunications Administrator
  - Telecommunications Coordinator
  - Telecommunications Analyst

J. Steffy — Manager–Data Administration and User Services
- Senior Systems Analyst
  - Senior Information Systems Consultant
  - Information Systems Consultant
  - Senior Research Analyst
- Supervisor Administrative Services
  - Senior Standards and Process Analysts
  - Senior Training Specialist
  - Junior Training Specialist
- Data Base Administrator
  - Data Base Analyst

were wired. He progressed from programmer, to trainer, then to manager. He also worked on the original RCA project.

Charles Baker, security administrator, has 38 years' service and also wired boards. He first became a manager in 1971, progressing through operations to his present position.

John Steffy, manager of Data Administration and User Services, started as a programmer and worked his way up through the ranks to his present position.

George Potts, manager of Operations Information Systems, started in 1960 as a draftsman in Engineering and then transferred to Marketing. Later, he was moved to ISS to work on the RCA project. He became manager of Operations Information Systems (OIS) in 1980.

Barry McMann, manager of Corporate Systems Enhancements and Maintenance, started in Gas Supply in 1972, before transferring to ISS a few years later. Terry Dempsey is Barry's mentor.

Bill Brothers, manager of Telecommunications, also started with the RCA project. Bill is the group's expert with "hands-on" experience.

Pearl Green, business analyst, is an accountant and CPA. She is a long-time ISS employee who transferred laterally from Accounting.

CURRENT SITUATION

ISD is currently working from a five-year plan that was approved in 1984 and has been updated annually. The plan includes a corporate systems development plan with a timetable for system development, estimates of ISD staff years to completion, and a designated priority (Exhibit 7).

Working Backlog

A key variable that is often used to manage the allocation of personnel and to determine appropriate staffing levels is *work backlog* (expressed in years of work remaining at current staffing levels).

The company's backlog projections must be judged in light of the industry's backlog averages of two to four years, which are considered acceptable. The backlogs across the industry, at the end of 1984 and 1985, were two years— within the range deemed acceptable. However, at Southern Ohio Gas, the corporate systems work backlogs at the end of 1984 and 1985 were 5.3 years and 4.4 years, respectively.

EXHIBIT 7 Corporate Systems Development Plan

System Name	ISD Staff Years to Completion	Priority	Implementation Schedule
Customer and general services information systems			1984 · 1985 · 1986 · 1987 · 1988 (Q1–Q4 each)
Accounts payable	1.8	Mandated	S————F (1984 Q1 → 1985 Q4)
Subsidiary billing (1401)	2.7	Mandated	S——T————F (1984 Q1 → 1985 Q4)
Subsidiary stores (1401)	3.5	Mandated	S————F (1984 Q1 → 1985 Q4)
Transportation management	3.0	High	F (1984 Q3)
Service history	2.1	High	————F* (→ 1984 Q3)
Legal and litigation support system	4.3	Medium	S————————F† (1986 Q1 → 1987 Q2)
Dispatch from CRT (COS)	4.0	Medium	S————————F (1986 Q1 → 1987 Q2)
Meter reading workload redistribution	0.6	Low	S-F (1987 Q2)
Financial and accounting information systems			
Jurisdictional accounting and reporting—phase II	1.9	Mandated	I————F (1984 Q1 → 1984 Q4)
Plant accounting	0.8	Mandated	I——F (1984 Q2 → 1984 Q4)
Employee information phase II	3.4	Mandated	F (1985 Q3)
Retired, subsidiary payroll (1401)	3.8	Mandated	S——F (1984 Q2 → 1984 Q4)
Nonjurisdictional allocation	0.8	Mandated	S——F (1984 Q3 → 1984 Q4)

EXHIBIT 7 (continued)

System Name	ISD Staff Years to Completion	Priority	1984 Q1	Q2	Q3	Q4	1985 Q1	Q2	Q3	Q4	1986 Q1	Q2	Q3	Q4	1987 Q1	Q2	Q3	Q4	1988 Q1	Q2	Q3	Q4
Financial and accounting information systems (continued)																						
Subsidiary rental and lease disbursements (1401)	0.4	Mandated					S_F															
Bank reconciliation (1401)	0.2	Mandated					S_F															
Label-addressing (1401)	0.3	Mandated						S_F														
On-line budget data entry (RRS)	3.0	Medium								S	——F											
On-line application (SIS)	0.5	Low								S_F												
Dividend reinvestment (SIS)	3.0	Low								S	——F											
Operations information systems																						
Conversion FMS	3.9	Mandated																F				
IBM/INTERGRAPH interface	1.0	Mandated		——F																		
T&D work management	2.6	Mandated	S	———	——F																	
Service inspection form (DMS)	0.7	Mandated		S	———	F																
Distribution construction and maintenance management (DMS)	18.0	High	———	———	———	———	———	———	———	———	———	———	———	———	——F							
Graphic inquiry SDA (DMS)	0.3	High			S_F																		

Implementation Schedule

223

EXHIBIT 7 *(continued)*

	ISD Staff Years to Completion	Priority	Implementation Schedule																				
			1984				*1985*				*1986*				*1987*				*1988*			
System Name			Q1	Q2	Q3	Q4	Q1	Q2	Q3	Q4	Q1	Q2	Q3	Q4	Q1	Q2	Q3	Q4	Q1	Q2	Q3	Q4
Operations information systems (continued)																						
Main certification (DMS)	4.5	Medium				S	—	—	—	—	F											
Survey management (DMS)	6.75	Medium									S	—	—	—	—	F						
Facilities installation (DMS)	1.8	Medium														S	—	F				
Permit information (DMS)	0.7	Medium														S	F					
Estimating information (DMS)	3.25	Low																S	—	—	F	
Network logic (DMS)	4.5	Low																		S	—		
Corrosion control and planning (DMS)	11.25	Low																				
Pipeline performance (DMS)	9.0	Low																				
Repair/Replacement (DMS)	9.0	Low																				
Regulatory and planning information systems																						
RRIS—phase III	1.9	Mandated		I	—	F																
Jurisdictional modeling	1.3	Mandated			—	F																
Telephone billing and inventory	0.4	Mandated	S	—	F																	
RRIS—phase IV	3.6	High		S	—	—	—	—	—	F												

EXHIBIT 7 *(continued)*

			Implementation Schedule																	
	ISD Staff		1984				1985				1986				1987				1988			
System Name	Years to Completion	Priority	Q1	Q2	Q3	Q4	Q1	Q2	Q3	Q4	Q1	Q2	Q3	Q4	Q1	Q2	Q3	Q4	Q1	Q2	Q3	Q4
Regulatory and planning information systems (continued)																						
RRIS—phase V	0.7	Low									S——F											
Subsidiary models	12.0	Low									S——											
Teleprocessing and computer operations																						
Computer resource charge-back SDA	1.0	Mandated	S————F																			
Miscellaneous 1401 systems	0.3	Mandated	S_F																			

Legend:
S — Start of project.
F — Expected completion of project.
I — Implementation of system.
T — Temporary solutions installed.
*Scheduling is tentative pending review of SDA.
†Scheduling is tentative pending review by the Corporate Goals Committee.

225

User Demands

Just as Southern Ohio Gas is faced with increased customer expectations, ISD must cope with increased user expectations of applications for computer technology. Mandates to reduce staff have resulted in greater demand for computer resources, as user organizations have sought to compensate for the staff losses while still maintaining production levels. In 1984, the number of requests for ISD support increased by a factor of 2 over 1983.

The company faced strong business and regulatory challenges; therefore, the opportunity to achieve benefits afforded by information technology had to be exploited. The exhortation to "work smarter" created increasing user demands for information services within the company, which in turn created opportunities for a variety of technical approaches (delivery systems) to provide these information services. The principal challenge was to take advantage of these opportunities while managing the risks of uncontrolled user activities.

The BSP Study

A recommendation made in the 1984 five-year plan requested that executive management support the undertaking of a business systems plan to define an information systems architecture to include the assigning of qualified in-house staff to the study team. Later that year, the BSP study was initiated.

The methodology used to conduct the study is a planning technique developed by IBM for its internal use. BSP is a structured approach for studying an organization's short- and long-range information needs at a macro level. It is a means to translate the corporation's business strategy into an information systems plan. The BSP method focuses on the processes and the data required to operate and manage the business, as opposed to other techniques that may emphasize organizations and individuals. BSP produces descriptions of broad information needs that will support all levels of management and survive organizational restructuring (review Exhibit 1).

The Southern Ohio Gas BSP study was conducted in three phases. In the first phase, the business was analyzed at a summary level to determine and document the activities of the business, the categories of data required to support the processes, and the interrelationships of these items. The second phase was known as the management viewpoint phase. In this phase, in-depth interviews were conducted with senior management in order to benefit from their knowledge of the business and to determine their information needs. In the third phase, the task force analyzed findings of the study and developed and documented conclusions and recommendations.

THE PROBLEM

Mike Murray had completed his review of the BSP study and was ready to discuss —with Bruno Mochon—the task force findings and related revisions to the present five-year plan.

QUESTIONS

1. Was the IS department indifferent to the needs of the users? What were the users' opinions? Do you agree with the users? Why or why not?
2. Would you propose a reorganization to solve some of the problems at Southern Ohio Gas & Light? Why or why not? Provide a revised organization chart if you propose changes.
3. What are the centralization versus decentralization issues in this case?
4. What are the major facts of the backlog and user demand issues of the case?
5. Should Southern Ohio's top management discourage the tendency of user departments to go outside the company to satisfy their needs?
6. Would you change the mission, operating methods, and/or staffing of the Information Center? Why (if so) and how?
7. What is your opinion of the BSP study—strengths, weaknesses, advantages, disadvantages, and omissions?
8. What more can Southern Ohio do to resolve the backlog problem? Who should take the necessary actions, and who should implement the decision? How?

Appendix 1   Information Architecture

Personnel

Business Processes
Determine personnel requirements
Establish personnel policies
Acquire work force
Manage employees
Develop employees

Data Classes
Job description
Manpower budgets
Personnel policies and procedures
Labor contracts
Employee description
Contractor
Employee performance
Employee payroll records
Employee training

Corporate Systems
Employee information system
- Payroll
- Salary administration
- Jobs/positions
- Applicants
- Insurance
- Pension processing
- Personnel administration (P)

Product

Business Processes
Forecast short-term gas demand
Seek gas supply
Distribute gas

Data Classes
Short-term gas demand forecast
Gas supplier contracts
Gas volumes
Weather
Distribution facilities maintenance work order

Corporate Systems

Capital

Business Processes

Prepare financial plans
Prepare budgets and monitor expenditures
Obtain rate relief
Manage external financing
Manage cash
Process accounts receivable
Process accounts payable
Maintain financial accounts
Manage pension assets

Data Classes

Financial plan
Budget and variance
Tariffs
Capital
Money market
Accounts receivable
Accounts payable
General ledger accounts
Pension assets

Corporate Systems

Financial reporting system
Responsibility reporting system
• Nonjurisdictional allocation (P)
• On-line budget data entry (P)
Employee information system
• Payroll
• Plant accounting system
Customer accounting system
• Hand-held meter reading (I)
Subsidiary billing system
Materials management system
Accounts payable system (I)
Subsidiary stores system
Transportation management system
Rates and regulatory information system
• Forecast data interface (P)
Corporate financial model
• Jurisdictional modeling (I)
• Subsidiary modeling (P)
Cost of service allocation
Distribution management system
• Estimating information (P)
Stockholders information system
• On-line application (P)
• Dividend reinvestment (P)
Computer resource chargeback system (I)
Legal and litigation support system (P)

Management

Business Processes

Establish strategic plans
Oversee legislative affairs
Determine regulatory requirements
Develop capacity and load forecasts
Perform audits
Assure employee and public safety
Provide legal services
Maintain and assure corporate citizenship
Establish organization policies and procedures

Data Classes

Organizational unit
Corporate policies and procedures
Corporate goals and objectives
Strategic plan
New legislation
Audits
Regulations
Long-term gas demand forecast
Safety policies and procedures
Legal requirements
Community programs
Organizational policies and procedures

Corporate Systems

Customer accounting system
Gas sendout model
Gas requirements and supply model
Stockholder information system
Legal and litigation support system (P)

Plant

Business Processes

Plan, design, and contruction distribution facilities
Manage distribution facilities
Plan, design, and construct general plant
Manage general plant
Plan, design, and construct production plant
Manage gas production plant

Data Classes

Distribution facilities
Distribution facilities inspection and maintenance
  records
General plant facilities and equipment
General plant inspection and maintenance
  records
Production plant facilities
Production plant inspection and maintenance records
Gas production and storage records

Corporate Systems

Distribution management system
• Facilities mapping
• Paving order
• Corrosion control priority task
• Distribution construction and maintenance manage-
  ment (I)
• Graphics inquiry (P)
• Service survey inspection (P)
• Network logic (P)
• Estimating information (P)
• Repair/replace (P)
• Corrosion control and planning (P)
• Pipeline performance (P)
• Main certification (P)
• Survey management (P)
T & D work management system (I)
Customer information system
• Meter history and inventory
NBR tracking and reporting system
Transportation management system
Telephone billing and inventory (I)
Subsidiary stores system (I)
Data processing system utilization
Computer resource chargeback system (I)

Customer

Business Processes	Corporate Systems
Develop and implement marketing plan	Customer information system
Service customer needs	• Customer accounting
Maintain customer records	• Customer inquiry
Terminate gas services	• Customer order
Data Classes	• Dispatch from CRT (P)
Marketing plan	• Service history (P)
Dealer	NBR tracking and reporting system
Gas sale	
Retail competitor	
Service history	
Customer record	
Termination records	

Materials and Supplies

Business Processes	Corporate Systems
Plan materials and supplies requirements	Materials management system
Procure M&S and equipment and manage inventory	NBR tracking and reporting system
Data Classes	
M&S specifications	
Purchase orders	
Vendor description	
M & S inventory history	

Legend: (I) In development.
    (P) Planned.

Appendix 2 Information Systems Summary

Tab	System Name	Development Status			Manpower Requirements			Development Time (Months)‡
		Completed	In Process	On Queue	CS&S*	Full-Time Users†	Total	
CIS	Customer information systems							
	Customer accounting systems		X		12	3	15	5–7
	Customer inquiry system	X						
	Customer order system			X	9	2	11	20–24
SIS	Stockholder information system	X						
COSA	Cost of service allocation system	X						
FRRAS	Financial reporting and responsibility accounting system			X	6	3	9	20–24
DMS	Distribution management system			X	9	2	11	42–48
EIS	Employee information system			X	5	2	7	20–24
MMS	Materials management system			X	5	3	8	24–30
TMS	Transportation management system			X	4	2	6	12–16
PAS	Property accounting system			X	6	2	8	18–24
FINMOD	Corporate financial model		X		7	3	10	12–18
FRGASREV	Gas revenue model	X						
FMGASUSE	Gas use model	X						
OSENDOUT	Gas sendout model	X						
OLANAL	Gas leak analysis system	X						

*Excludes manpower required for system maintenance.
†Will require support from additional part-time personnel as conditions warrant.
‡Represents total estimated development time to complete project. However, where possible projects are phased so that usable segments are operational within shorter time frames.

Appendix 3   Information Systems Implementation Plan

	1985												1986								
	J	F	M	A	M	J	J	A	S	O	N	D	J	F	M	A	M	J	J	A	S
1. Training	5	8	11	10	8	5	2	2													
2. Database administration	6	6	6	7	7	7	7	7	7	7	7	7	7	7	7	7	7	7	7	7	7
3. Systems maintenance	10	4	7	7	7	2	2	2	2	2	2	2	2	9	9	9	9	9	9	9	9
4. Systems development																					
Customer accounting system conversion	5	3																			
	3																				
Corporate financial model	7	6	6	6	7	7	7	7	7	7	7	7	7	7							
	3	3	3	3	3	3	3	3	3	3	3	3	3								
Distribution management system	4	4	4	4	4	9	9	9	9	9	9	9	9	9	9	9	9	9	9	9	9
	2	2	2	2	2	2	2	2	2	2	2	2	2	2	2	2	2	2	2	2	2
Financial reporting and responsibility accounting system		3	3	3	3	3	6	6	6	6	6	6	6	6	6	6	6	6	6	6	6
		3	3	3	3	3	3	3	3	3	3	3	3	3	3	3	3	3	3	3	3
Customer order system		4	4	4	4	9	9	9	9	9	9	9	9	9	9	9	9	9	9	9	9
		2	2	2	2	2	2	2	2	2	2	2	2	2	2	2	2	2	2	2	2
Employee information system		2	2	2	5	5	5	5	5	5	5	5	5	5	5	5	5	5	5	5	5
		2	2	2	2	2	2	2	2	2	2	2	2	2	2	2	2	2	2	2	2
Materials management system																					
Transportation management system																					
Property accounting system																					
Manpower requirements:																					
CS&S		37	40	43	43	45	45	45	45	45	45	45	45	45	45	45	45	45	45	45	45
Users		8	12	12	12	12	12	12	12	12	12	12	12	12	12	12	12	12	12	12	12
Total		45	52	55	55	57	57	57	57	57	57	57	57	57	57	57	57	57	57	57	57

Revised September 1, 1974

			1987												1988												1989						
O	N	D	J	F	M	A	M	J	J	A	S	O	N	D	J	F	M	A	M	J	J	A	S	O	N	D	J	F	M	A	M	J	J
7	7	7	7	8	8	8	8	8	8	8	8	8	8	8	8	8	8	8	8	8	8	8	8	8	8	8	9	9	9				
9	9	9	9	9	19	19	16	13	13	13	13	13	13	13	13	13	13	13	15	15	15	15	15	15	15	15	23	23	30				
9	9	9	9	9	9	9	9	9	9	9	9	9	9	9	9	9	9	9	9	9	9	9	9	9	9	9	9						
2	2	2	2	2	2	2	2	2	2	2	2	2	2	2	2	2	2	2	2	2	2	2	2	2	2	2	2						
6	6	4	4																														
3	3	3	3																														
9	9	9	9																														
2	2	2	2																														
5	5	3	3																														
2	2	2	2																														
			2	2	2	5	5	5	5	5	5	5	5	5	6	6	6	6	6	6	6	6	6	6	6	6	6	6	6	6			
			3	3	3	3	3	3	3	3	3	3	3	3	3	3	3	3	3	3	3	3	3	3	3	3	3	3	3	3	3	3	3
			2	2	4	4	4	4	4	4	4	4	4	4	4																		
			2	2	2	2	2	2	2	2	2	2	2	2	2																		
						3	3	3	6	6	6	6	6	6	6	6	7	7	7	7	7	7	7	7	7	7	7	7	7				
						2	2	2	2	2	2	2	2	2	2	2	2	2	2	2	2	2	2	2	2	2	2	2					
45	45	45	45	45	45	45	45	45	45	45	45	45	45	45	45	45	45	45	45	45	45	45	45	45	45	45	45	45	45	45	45	45	
12	14	14	9	14	14	14	14	14	14	14	14	14	14	14	7	7	7	7	7	7	7	7	7	7	7	7	7	5	3	3	3	3	
57	59	59	59	59	59	59	59	59	59	59	59	59	59	59	52	52	52	52	52	52	52	52	52	52	52	52	52	50	48	48	48	48	

Case 5–2 Jenkins Engineering and Technology

The meeting had started at 9:00 A.M.; it was early October 1987, and the leaves were just beginning to turn yellow and orange in Charleston, South Carolina, headquarters of Jenkins Engineering and Technology (E & T) (see Exhibit 1). Attendees at the meeting, however, were beginning to see red. It was now almost 2:30 P.M., and they had yet to break for lunch. Everyone was hungry, tired, and frustrated.

The joint chairmen, who had called the meeting, were T. R. Townsend, vice president of Data Services (known as Jenks Data Services, or JDS, throughout the organization), and Philip C. McDaniels, E & T's vice president for Development. Both were seated at the center of the large, U-shaped, conference table and flanked by Charles M. Rhoads, the assistant vice president for Distribution, and James E. Ridenour, senior director, Transportation; both were members of McDaniel's Development organization (see Exhibit 2).

Also in attendance were two of Townsend's people—Bryan M. Pannell, director, Operations and Linda S. Hoover, director, Data Processing. Two other attendees, particularly concerned about a successful outcome to the group's efforts, were Ron W. Peale and Howard R. Malone; they were at the meeting as representatives of Jenkins Logistics Services Company (JLSC), a corporate "customer" of E & T. Peale is vice president, Marketing Services, and Malone is Peale's director of Sales, Data Services (see Exhibits 3a and 3b). Others around the table (which seated 20 comfortably) were interested members of the other major business groups under the Jenkins Distribution component—Hardware and Materials, Transportation, and Mid-America Barge Lines. On returning to their own organizations, they all expected to give a detailed briefing to their peers and superiors.

PROBLEM BACKGROUND

All of the attendees, if asked, would admit that the meeting was long overdue. Townsend, in his opening remarks, alluded to the genesis of all their difficulties —which was not news to anybody—when he covered some of the early history of Jenkins, Inc. "The merger of the Jenks System and the Walton Southern Systems Railroads in September 1981 created problems in integrating the two railroads' computer systems. We all know that Walton Southern employed IBM

This case was prepared by T. L. Dennis and J. E. Lappin. Names, locations, and financial data were disguised.

EXHIBIT 1   Jenkins Corporation Structure

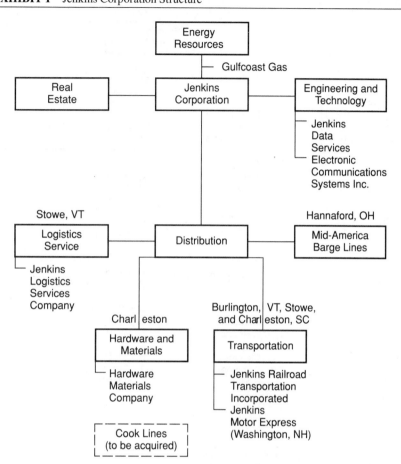

mainframes, while the Jenks System used both the Univac 1100 and the Burroughs machines.

"In addition, the two railroads had different computer concepts and philosophies; and their computer systems' data flows were not compatible. Each railroad created its own reports with its own particular revenue accounting system; it was difficult to match data."

McDaniels had added, "Right. Then, in 1984, when the new corporation was barely established, they decided to convert completely to an IBM system. We really found ourselves with a tiger by the tail. But I don't think any one of us see that as a bad decision—then or now."

Townsend continued, "Although some joint computing capability was started, no full-scale integration efforts began until 1987, when the two railroads stopped

EXHIBIT 2   Engineering and Technology

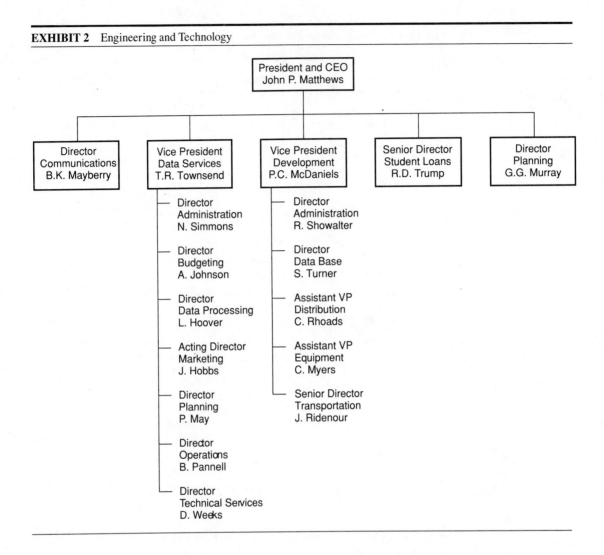

operating independently, and the entire Jenkins Corporation was restructured. As a result of the restructure, Engineering and Technology was challenged to make the two technology systems compatible, manage them effectively, and generate additional revenue through external clients.''

At this point, whether he had intended it or not, Townsend's opening statement was cut short as others joined in with their assessments of the problem. Much of the sometimes emotional, and always lengthy, discussion that followed can be summarized in the following paragraphs.

Malone, JLSC's director of Data Processing and also director of their Information Development and Management Center (IDMC), brought up one of his

EXHIBIT 3a Jenkins Logistics Services Company (JLSC)

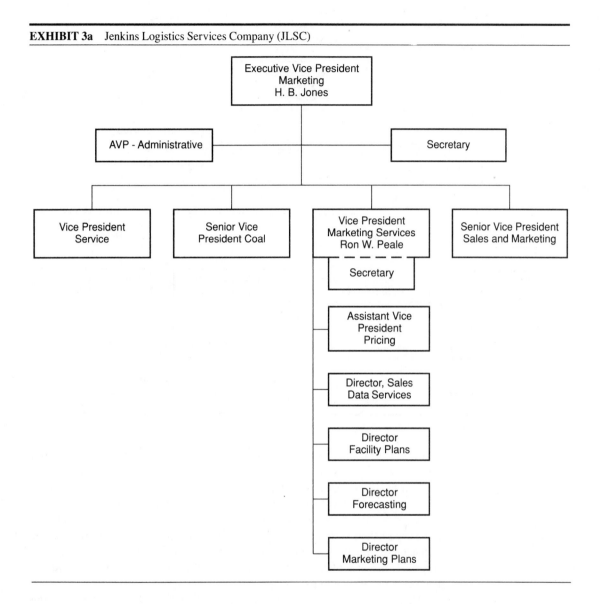

serious concerns when he asked, "Are all of you aware that, historically, application maintenance has averaged 40 percent of JDS's budget? I know that's really your bailiwick, T.R., but we're affected severely and directly by JDS's allocation of resources to application maintenance vis-à-vis development. I understand that, in the last two years, 80 percent of your budget has been allotted to new development.

"I bet most of you don't realize we're running some systems applications that

EXHIBIT 3b   Jenkins Logistics Services Company (JLSC)

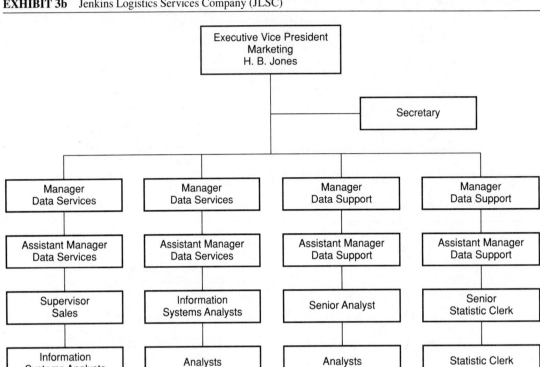

are over 20 years old. In my opinion, if they are more than 5 years old—10 at the very worst—they should be rewritten because, at that point, there's no way they can fit the current needs of the users.''

''I think you're being a mite hard on the E & T folks,'' remarked Peale. ''I've suspected for some time now that we have many users who are not truly educated in the use of their systems; I guess you'd call them unsophisticated, T.R. My bet is that there are quite a few of them who don't really know how to reap the maximum benefits of the systems that are already available to them. And yet, they continue to swamp us with requests to develop new applications.''

''That's true,'' agreed Malone, ''but I think that new IDMC training program we've worked out with BRAC (Brotherhood of Railway, Airline, and Steamship Clerks) will change all that. Everybody knows that on-the-job training is essential, but now it's going to be supplemented with more formal, classroom training.

''The computer curriculum includes basic computing, business arithmetic, word processing, number accuracy, accounting principles, typing proficiency, and even telephone skills. Courses in the more sophisticated techniques of 1-2-3 from Lotus and databases like dBASE III + , are available for advanced students. And they'll be allowed to skip areas that they understand or repeat portions that require more intensive study.

"The union is with us all the way on this; they realize that if the people they represent are going to be a part of the railroad of the future, they're going to have to prepare themselves for the evolving technology. Everyone involved is really excited about it."

Townsend, attempting to get the discussion back on track, said, "Thank you very much, Howard; I didn't realize the training program was that far along. I'd like to move on now to the subject of JDS's external interests. Not that we're deaf to the pleas of our corporate clients, but you do recall that another objective of Jenks Data Services is to acquire external clients. We have not contracted with any to date, due in part to the youth of our organization; we're just starting to get into prototyping and fourth-generation languages. At any rate, I think our top priority — yours as well as JDS's — must be to mesh the computer systems of the two railroads — Jenks Systems, Inc. and Walton Southern Rail Systems."

"I couldn't agree more," Peale quickly added. "From the point of view of an end-user in sales and marketing, the total contribution to the bottom line can't be determined when a shipment moves in the multimodal 'all in one' shipping concept, because the barge, trucking, and steamship companies all have their own revenue accounting systems.

"In addition to that, the tariffs aren't even computerized."

"Can we get back to one of our internal JDS problems?" Jim Ridenour asked. "I'd like to talk about the system development deadlines that really put us up against the wall with every new computer application. They are established by the users I work with in the Transport and Distribution business groups that Chuck and I, and our people, deal with on a daily basis. We do our darndest to get them to relax those desired completion dates; they always act like each one is set in concrete. They just don't realize the amount of effort and detail that goes into developing new systems."

"I'll second that motion," McDaniels said, "but, at the same time, I believe we have to take part of the credit for missing the deadlines, realistic or not. And I don't have a ready answer because, in some ways, we're constrained rigidly by our Life Cycle Approach (LCA). We use it in the design of almost all of our systems, and our corporate customers may not realize its shortcomings; I'm sure all of us in E & T do.

"Life Cycle automatically creates backlogs. It makes it almost impossible to meet our deadlines, and yet we all accept the need to have a structured design process.

"I intended to bring up LCA if no one else did, and so I brought along a transparency to show to our friends from the Distribution organizations. Do you suppose we have time to show this and discuss it for a couple of minutes, T.R., before we go to lunch?"

Townsend surveyed the room quickly, noting the obvious temperament of the group and appreciating the beneficial aspects of getting away from the stressful subject matter for an hour or so, and replied, "Okay, how about taking 10 more minutes maximum and then go to lunch. We can take some more time on it after if there are any questions left unanswered when you finish."

McDaniels walked over to the side of the room, dropped a transparency on the projector that displayed the 11 steps of the Life Cycle Approach (see the accompanying table).

The 11 steps of the Life Cycle Approach are:

1. User requirement.
2. Feasibility study.
3. General systems design.
4. Systems data flow.
5. Detail subsystem design.
6. Actual program specification.
7. Program unit testing.
8. System testing.
9. User acceptance testing.
10. Production installation.
11. Enhancements.

McDaniels described each of the steps in a little under a minute and then stepped back out of the way, as the group quickly left the room through the door immediately behind the projector.

COMPANY BACKGROUND

Jenkins Corporation, sometimes called "Jenkins, Inc.," was created September 4, 1981 by the merger of Jenks System, Inc. and Walton Southern Rail Systems. The central premise of the merger was that joining two strong, major rail systems could result in improved service, increased profitability, and enhanced shareholder value. The holding company, Jenkins, Inc., was created and headquartered in Asheville, North Carolina, while Jenks System continued its dual headquarters in Burlington and Stowe, Vermont with Walton Southern in Charleston, South Carolina.

JENKINS DISTRIBUTION

The two organizations, Jenks System and Walton Southern, remained separate until 1987 when Jenkins was restructured into four major components: Energy Resources, Real Estate, Engineering and Technology, and Distribution. The distribution units were reorganized internally into four business groups: Transportation, Hardware and Materials, Logistics Services, and Mid-America Barge Lines (see Exhibit 1). Each group operates independently under a chief executive officer with one purpose: to provide premier shipping services to Jenkins customers.

Under the new concept, Logistics Services is the primary interface with the shipping public and focuses on the development of service packages for satisfying customer needs. This group, which is headquartered in Stowe, Vermont, includes: Sales, Marketing, Pricing, Billing, Car Location, Special Marketing Services, and all other activities directly affecting Transportation customers. One of its major goals is to expand Jenkin's ''all in one'' shipping concept.

Jenkins Logistics Services Company (JLSC), a component of Logistics Services under the parent, Jenkins Corporation, is headquartered in Stowe, Vermont (see Exhibit 1). JLSC's executive vice president, Marketing, oversees the activities of Marketing Services, which is headed by a vice president; subordinate to him is the director of Sales, Data Services, who controls the purchase of PCs and training techniques (see Exhibits 3a and 3b). All user requests are directed to Sales, Data Services, which is the interface with Jenkins Engineering and Technology.

The Hardware and Materials group supplies and maintains the corporation's 160,000 freight car fleet, with $1.6 billion in assets, for its main customer—the Logistics Services group. It is headquartered in Charleston, South Carolina.

Mid-America Barge Lines operates barge transportation over 12,000 miles of inland waterways. Its headquarters are in Hannaford, Ohio.

Jenks Motor Express (JME), a component of the Transportation group, provides the trucking arm of the multimodal service offered by Jenkins. JME is headquartered in Washington, New Hampshire.

Cook Lines, a major steamship line, was acquired in the third quarter 1987 after receiving unanimous ICC approval on August 13, 1987. This acquisition will complete Jenkin's objective to become a complete transportation company. Cook Lines's headquarters are in Wilmington, Delaware.

JENKINS ENERGY RESOURCES

The Energy Resources group's major property is Gulfcoast Gas, which was acquired in late 1984. Under the new organization, this group continues to direct the company's activities in natural gas transmission, oil and gas exploration and development, and the management of Jenkins-owned coal reserves.

For the short-term, gas transmission appears promising, with good rates of return. The company has a strong competitive position based on its cost of service, established customer base, financial resources, and positive relationships with regulatory agencies. The principal challenges involve the need to expand facilities, services, and market reach.

The outlook for exploration is far less certain in the short-term due to price instability and excess supply. Moreover, these problems dictate a prudent approach to exploration activities. Nevertheless, clear, long-term opportunities remain for companies that have proven expertise, the ability to respond quickly, and a financial rate of return exceeding the cost of capital. Those qualities are vital to the corporation's future success in the energy business.

JENKINS REAL ESTATE

The creation of the Real Estate group signals a change in the corporation's strategy for real estate and highlights this business segment's growth potential. Jenkins Real Estate manages assets that have an estimated value of approximately $750 million, consisting of real estate interests—sales, development, and rental—as well as management of the company's hotel interest.

Historically, Jenkin's principal focus has been to convert real estate holdings from various parts of Jenkins into cash. This strategy has provided an immediate return with little risk but it obviously offers limited opportunity for the company to capitalize on significant long-term growth prospects in the real estate area. The Real Estate group will assume responsibility for all real estate activities, establishing specific financial criteria and exploring various options for development while continuing the corporation's aggressive sales program in appropriate areas.

JENKINS ENGINEERING AND TECHNOLOGY (E & T)

History and Function

The fourth group is Engineering and Technology, a separate entity, which was created in late 1986 to serve as one of the key building blocks of Jenkins. Headquartered in Charleston, South Carolina, E & T has its own president, board of directors, and financial statements.

While E & T has been a relatively small portion of the corporate total business activity, Jenkins Corporation has developed unique capabilities in information technology and communications through its systems interests and subsidiaries —Jenks Data Services (JDS) and Electronic Communication Systems, Inc. (ECSI).

Jenks Data Services is the unit of Engineering and Technology that supports Jenkins Logistics Services Company and is located in a building adjacent to the Stowe headquarters (see Exhibits 2, 3a, and 3b). Jenks Data Services (JDS) also furnishes services to the Hardware Materials Company in Stowe.

Jenks Data Services employs 204 people, and top management expects that number to double in the next five years. JDS has two people on the Strategy and

Planning board of the Jenkins Logistics Services Company; the highest ranking official of the two is a senior director.

Electronic Communication Systems, Inc. is the technology arm for the Jenkins Railroad Transportation, Inc.; both are headquartered in Charleston, South Carolina.

Engineering and Technology develops and manages computing and communications solutions for other companies as well as for Jenkins Corporation's subsidiaries. For external firms, the division offers computing resources that support financial services, particularly installment loans and student loans. It also provides processing to support loan origination, loan guarantees, and due diligence for delinquent notes.

JDS and ECSI are two of the E & T organizations that market their services externally. These capabilities enhance the company's competitive position in transportation, energy, and properties and provide significant growth opportunities. Foremost among the growth opportunities is the rapidly expanding transportation-related information market. To a great extent, this remains an untapped market that Jenkins, with its combination of transportation and information technology expertise, is uniquely prepared to serve. Engineering and Technology will continue supporting other corporate businesses, while at the same time marketing its capabilities to both government and industrial concerns in domestic as well as foreign markets.

In addition, E & T sells mainframe and personal computer software to its primary vertical markets. Occasionally, the technology organization purchases off-the-shelf applications and installs them for both Jenkins and external clients, who make up approximately 10 percent of the division's business.

Engineering and Technology's relationship with Jenkins Corporation has produced significant benefits for each organization. The parent corporation has both an effective information management strategy and an information industry subsidiary that is turning a profit. Engineering and Technology, for its part, has the strong financial backing of an extremely reliable primary customer.

As 1987 drew to a close, Engineering and Technology was ranked by *Information Week* as having the 50th largest MIS system in the United States. It is currently a $160 million company, and it has a projected annual growth rate of 20 to 25 percent.

E & T Resources

Engineering and Technology performs all of the classic IS functions for Jenkins Corporation. The group employs nearly 950 people, half of whom are programmers, with the other half serving as analyst and support personnel. In 1987, E & T spent more than $76 million to support its computing services. The group manages a total of seven IBM 3090s, using a combination of Model 200s and

Model 400s. Three 3090s are in Charleston, three in Stowe, and one at the headquarters of Jenkins Motor Express trucking and shipping subsidiary in Washington, New Hampshire. Engineering and Technology also uses IBM 4384s and 4381s and non-IBM systems that include four Digital Equipment Corporation VAX 11/780s, one Burroughs 7800, Data General Corporation processors, and a Univac 1100. All told, E & T supports some 6,500 CRTs throughout the Jenkins organization. Its computers are used primarily to support transportation management and scheduling, warehousing and inventory, as well as "internal business operations," including decision support.

The major part of Engineering and Technology's software development is database-related. Programmers typically work with well-known tools like MVS, CICS, dBASE, Focus, and IMS. Once a database is designed and implemented, the analysts spend most of their time preparing ad hoc analyses based on user requests. Very little time is available for single-thread application or report writing.

Some 240 personal computers throughout Jenkins are supported by E & T. Some are connected via networks but most are independent. Jenkins personnel, when given a menu of computing options, usually choose the features available via terminals connected to Jenkins processors and software. Those individuals generating a number of reports, or whose work involves a great many graphics, often opt for personal computers.

E & T Information Development and Management Centers

E & T uses Information Development and Management Centers (IDMCs) to provide local computer and communications management. Each major corporate group has its own IDMC, with the two largest employing 400 people each. Information Development and Management Centers are headed by a director, Sales, Data Services, who reports to the vice president, Marketing Services. The goal of the IDMCs is to combine centralized operations management with distributed development, thus allowing developers to work closely with the individual business units and to develop solutions more quickly. The IDMCs were created in 1987 to provide technical data support for end-users and also to be the interface between user and Jenkins Engineering and Technology and with the customers. Information Development and Management Centers are responsible for all terminals, PCs, training, and setting of priorities.

Jenkins Corporation revenues in 1987 were $5.04 billion, down $622 million, or 11 percent, from 1986. The 1987 net earnings were $274 million compared to $291.5 million in 1986. The declines primarily reflect lower revenues in the natural gas pipeline business due to the sharp increase in volumes handled on a transportation-for-fee basis and lower energy prices; a second degrading factor was weakness in rail merchandise traffic that resulted from the lackluster performance of the rail-served industrial and agricultural segments of the economy (see Exhibits 4a and 4b).

EXHIBIT 4a   Jenkins Corporation Financial Highlights (8/1/87)

	1986	1985	1984
		(in millions, except per share amounts)	
For the year			
Revenue	$5,642	$6,115	$4,541
Operating income:			
Before accounting change*	$729	$784	$490
After accounting change	$678	$719	$476
Earnings excluding special charge:†			
Before accounting change	$369	$358	$209
After accounting change	$340	$319	$201
Per common share			
Earnings excluding special charge:†			
Before accounting change	$3.27	$3.21	$2.11
After accounting change	$3.01	$2.85	$2.03
Cash dividends	$1.14	$1.06	$1.01
Market price range: high	$32.06	$26.41	$28.01
low	$22.49	$18.48	$15.71
At year-end			
Cash	$144	$291	$242
Working capital	$75	$178	$187
Debt ratio	32.8%	29.1%	31.8%
Return on equity before special			
charge† and accounting change	8.9%	9.3%	5.6%

*Accounting change relates to the change from the full cost to the successful efforts method of accounting for oil and gas activities.
†A $763 million pre-tax special charge as announced in September 1986. The special charge reduced net earnings by $448 million, $3.61 per share, and resulted in a net loss of $84 million, $.74 per share, for 1986.

COMPUTER HISTORY

The 1950s

In early 1955, the Jenkins Railroad Company installed a Univac I at their corporate headquarters in the Arlan Jenkins Building, Burlington, Vermont. It was the third large-scale processor to be used in the railroad industry (CSX was the first early in 1954 and Union Pacific was second in late 1954) and one of the first in non-military business use. The central processing unit alone covered 144 square feet of floor space. The machine was leased for $29,000 per month and its main purpose was revenue accounting, although it did perform some payroll functions. The memory capacity was 1,000 records of 12 characters. The system used magnetic tapes for storage and could read and punch cards. A 600-line-per-minute high-speed printer was the output device.

In 1957, the Vermont and Northern Railroad computerized its revenue ac-

EXHIBIT 4b   Jenkins Corporation: Selected Financial Ratios and Performance Data*
(8/1/87)

	1982	1986
1. Cash dividends per share	$0.89	$1.14
2. Dividends as a percent of earnings	23%	37%
3. Earnings (millions of dollars)	$450	$490
4. Earnings per share	$3.63	$3.27
5. Fixed charge coverage (pre-tax)	4.8X	4.4X
6. Return on assets	5%	4%
7. Return on capital employed	6.3%	4.9%
8. Return on equity	12.5%	9.3%

Since the corporation's formation in September 1981, Jenkins common stock has outperformed the average of its peer group of transportation and natural resource companies and the average of Standard & Poor's 500 index.

*Data in the above figures excludes special charge and accounting change.

counting with the installation of a Burroughs computer at the corporate headquarters in Stowe. The magnetic tapes alone weighed more than 40 pounds.

The 1960s

In 1961, Jenkins Railroad installed an IBM RAMAC at Asheville, North Carolina. Its purpose was to provide car location information; the system was called CLS, Car Locator System. It did not have the capacity to provide all the information expected. The Vermont and Northern installed a similar system in Stowe called CITY, Cars in the Yards.

In 1964, the Jenkins Railroad Company acquired the Vermont and Northern; to integrate their systems, the company acquired an RCA 3301 and installed it in Stowe, replacing the IBM RAMAC at Asheville. The RCA 3301 was one of the first computers able to communicate with other systems' terminals via teletype. The 3301 also had a feature called RACE (Random Access Car Equipment) and used strips of magnetic Mylar tape. Its purpose was to monitor car locations for the combined Jenkins and Vermont and Northern Railroads; RACE was not highly successful because the computer's capacity was limited.

In 1965, the Univac I in Burlington was replaced by a Univac III in Stowe. The Univac III processed revenue accounting and car location. Except for very minor upgrades, the basic system was not changed until 1986.

The 1970s

By 1973, basically all the Jenks System (the new name of the combined Jenkins/Vermont and Northern Railroads) computer applications — except for those on the RCA 3301 — were on Univac computers.

In 1975, Jenks System started a conversion to Burroughs with the acquisitions of a Burroughs B6700, B7700, and B7800. The Univac III had become obsolete, and management would not provide support for maintenance. The B6700 was used solely for systems development, a very unusual division of resources at that time. Part of the revenue accounting system was rewritten, and the Car Locator System was revised and placed on the Burroughs B7700 and B7800. The RCA 3301 was released. Since not all of the programs that were on the Univac III could be rewritten for the Burroughs, a Univac 1100 was acquired. The Univac III was junked.

In the 1970s, small processors were installed in Stowe and Asheville and other strategic locations; they were to alleviate the workload on the mainframe by assuming some of the data processing tasks. As the memory of mainframes increased and costs decreased, even these small processor systems became obsolete.

The 1980s

The merger of the Jenks System and the Walton Southern Systems Railroads in September 1981 created problems in integrating the two railroads' computer systems; Walton Southern employed IBM mainframes, while the Jenks System used both the Univac 1100 and the Burroughs machines. In 1984, the newly formed company decided to convert completely to an IBM system. The first IBM was acquired for Stowe, since the Univac was not good for analytic retrieval; also, reliable software packages were not available. A cross link between Burroughs and the IBM tube network was installed.

As of early 1987, there were three IBM 3090 mainframes in Stowe (all less than two years old), one IBM 3084, one Burroughs B7700, and one Univac 1100. At Charleston, South Carolina, there were four IBM 3090s and one IBM 3084. The Burroughs (which have processed all the revenue applications — plus 12 others) and the Univac 1100 were to be phased out by the end of 1987, thus completing the conversion to a complete IBM system. A new IBM 3090 was ordered with delivery promised in early 1988.

Two 48 KB data transmission lines connect Stowe with Charleston. The personal computers and minis are networked to the mainframe.

DEVELOPMENT OF THE MIS DEPARTMENT

In 1955, the Jenkins Railroad established a data processing (DP) function, locating the group within its Accounting department. In 1961, DP tried to automate waybills, a highly repetitive but routine procedure in coal shipments; the project failed because the Data Processing department could not impose its decisions on the Transportation department.

In 1976, the railway reorganized, this time creating an MIS department. It was not a separate entity directed by a senior vice president; instead, MIS remained under the Accounting department and continued to play a reactive role.

In the early 1980s, a crescendo of complaints and demands from mainframe users throughout the company forced top management to take action. Therefore, the Jenks System contracted with Martin-Marietta Data Services to provide time-sharing (and later on, to convert the Univac 1100 data tapes to IBM format). Jenks' time-sharing costs exceeded $800,000 per year. Martin-Marietta's obligations under the contract also included furnishing various forecasting reports for the Jenks System.

By 1987, following the merger of the two rail systems, and as a direct result of the restructuring of the new corporation, all computer organizations — their mainframes, minicomputers, and other major equipment, personnel, and other resources — were assigned to a new organization. It was called Jenkins Engineering and Technology.

COMMUNICATIONS

Communications is also an integral part of Jenkins's computing needs, since Engineering and Technology is linked to other corporate facilities by a variety of media, from DDD data circuits to T-1 carriers (between the Charleston and Stowe sites). Jenkins' extensive rail and trucking networks provide many company-owned rights-of-way, with a significant installed base of both microwave and optical-fiber links. E & T does not sell access to its communications facilities to external companies; however, on occasion, that service is provided to firms that are working with the parent corporation.

DATA TRANSFER SYSTEM (DTS)

Jenkins Corporation is aware that in today's fiercely competitive business environment, effective use of information technology creates a competitive edge — the difference for success. Jenkins is more than a railroad. It is an "all in one" shipping network comprised of rail, truck, barge, and warehousing operations and more recently an international steamship operation. Through Engineering and Technology, Jenkins provides computer hardware and software to efficiently handle data exchange between the corporation and its shippers, as well as between shippers' customers and other carriers. The centerpiece of this leading edge technology is Jenkins' Data Transfer System.

DTS is an electronic connection between the customer and the Jenkins transportation network. This connection may take the form of a terminal in the customer's office or a data link between the customer's computer and one of E & T's computer systems. Either one of these methods provides instant access to rates, equipment ordering, and shipment information. Some of the Data Transfer System's capabilities are:

- **Bills of lading:** Bills of lading exchange provides an electronic link between the customer and the freight terminal. Predefined shipment profiles stored in the computer minimize the amount of information required from the customer. After the shipment is loaded, added services such as weight reporting and notification of actual freight charges are also available.
- **Freight billing:** Electronic freight billing data exchange allows freight billing data to be transferred directly to a customer's accounting system. It enables customers to quickly produce reports that summarize transportation activity. Customers also can use Jenkins electronic funds transfer capabilities.
- **Electronic mail:** The customers can use terminals located at their offices and send messages to other offices served by Jenkins, or to any Jenkins department or individual. Electronic mail operates 24 hours a day, 7 days a week. Typical uses of electronic mail include rate quotations, billing inquiries, freight claims, and communications with freight agents. This service can also be used for equipment placement and ordering, intraplant movements, or the release of unloaded equipment.
- **Rate retrieval:** This service allows Jenkins intermodal shippers to interrogate databases for published circular and agreement rates as well as to request special price quotations. Often, shipper concurrence can be reached utilizing nothing more than computer-transmitted information.

The network that ties the PCs with mainframes, and other PCs with the corporate offices and those in outlying sales offices, is called, Automated Switching Circuit (ASC). ASC was installed in 1987 and allows communication directly between computers or to output services.

For the future, a primary concern is message switching. Engineering and Technology will spend $9.5 million over the next four to six years to develop the most cost-effective methods for high-volume message switching over diverse media. This development is expected to provide substantially greater efficiency for Jenkins, not to mention increased revenue potential for E & T.

CONCLUSION

The meeting attendees filed back into the conference room at 3:45 P.M. and found Townsend and McDaniels already waiting in their seats. In addition, John Matthews, the president and CEO of E & T, was sitting back in one corner of the room.

Townsend again opened the meeting.

"I am sure John Matthews, our president and CEO (John waved a friendly greeting) needs no introduction, so let's proceed with the meeting agenda. First, however, I'd like to try to look at the big picture, although Phil and I both realize the topics discussed earlier are important and will have to be addressed at some point in our deliberations or follow-on actions.

"First, we both feel that what we've really been talking about is the need to redesign our sytems as a result of the merger. Secondly, and there wasn't much discussion about this point this morning, we all should realize that being at 100 percent capacity, we again must consider enhanced or new systems hardware and/or combining or deleting some of the current applications.

"With those comments as the foundation for where we should go from this point, I'd like to open the discussion for some hard-headed suggestions from the group. We want to hear from everyone and request that we all be very open-minded about all comments; let's not dash water on any ideas until we've really kicked them around and are certain they are not realistic.

"Alright, where do we go from here? Who wants to start?"

QUESTIONS

1. Discuss the problem of DP personnel resource allocation to applications development versus applications maintenance. What should the allocation be?
2. Should Jenks Data Service be focusing on external clients or integrating the computer systems of Jenks Systems and Walton Southern? Why? How?
3. What are the alternatives to using the Life Cycle Approach? Is it really necessary to follow a structured design process? Explain.
4. List and discuss the problems of converting from one brand computer (such as Univac or Burroughs) to another brand (such as IBM). How can they be alleviated?
5. Do you agree with the firm's 1984 decision to convert to IBM machines? Support your answer.
6. Would you change the curriculum of the IDMC Training Center? If so, how and why?
7. If you were at the meeting, how would you respond to Townsend's final question? Take the position of all the attendees at the meeting, including Townsend. After hearing from all the other attendees, tell us what you would say if you were Matthews.

Case 5–3 Randall Industries, Inc.

Randall Industries, Inc., was incorporated in May 1940 as Randall Heavy Machine (RHM), a manufacturer of truck and machinery components. Randall acquired Cooper Chemical, a manufacturer of rubber additives and paints, in 1952. At that time, the company changed its name to Randall Industries, Inc. In 1967, Randall created the Electronics Control division as part of its effort to diversify. This outgrowth of the heavy machine manufacturing led to defense contracts and expanded offerings of solid state components to truck and auto makers. Continuing to grow, Randall acquired Pharmatech (U.K.), an emerging pharmaceutical technology company, in 1982.

Randall Industries, Inc., is organized into three divisions under the central holding company. The divisions are:

1. Randall Heavy Machine.
2. Chemical/Pharmaceuticals.
3. Electronics Control.

Strategic direction is provided by the holding company, with operational autonomy exercised by each of the divisions (see Exhibit 1).

The current business environment at Randall is intense. First, rapid technological advancements have occurred in pharmaceutical and chemical manufacturing and sales. In addition, government regulations on pharmaceutical and chemical manufacturing and sales are stringent. Similarly, restrictions on the sale of some electronic controls to foreign nations have been imposed. There is also keen competition in manufacturing and electronics markets. And finally, Randall's market share for its many products has been declining recently, perhaps emphasizing the need to modernize both manufacturing and chemicals (see Exhibit 2).

Randall has examined all aspects of its business, including MIS. Information Systems has had little central oversight or control throughout the corporation. Each division has developed financial and manufacturing systems independently. The holding company, however, has decided to upgrade the level of information and "bring the company into the 21st century" by creating more uniformity in MIS.

That decision has yet to be accepted at the division level.

This case was prepared by Gail Cooper, Tim Lepczyk, Lew Metcalf, and Steve Spotts. The case is a composite of several actual situations, with names and locations disguised.

EXHIBIT 1   Randall Industries Corporate Hierarchy

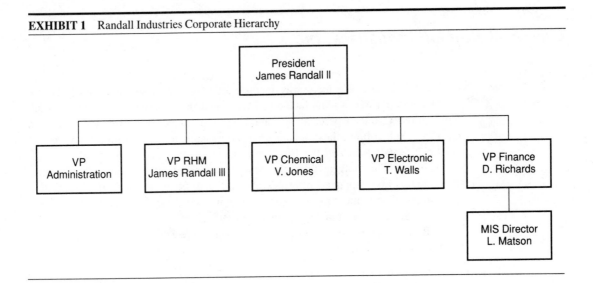

CORPORATE DP: DEPARTMENT BACKGROUND

Until recently, Randall Industries had a manager and five other employees for its entire corporate Data Processing department (DP; also referred to as EDP— Electronic Data Processing). Upper management had not been very pleased with the performance of the department and had so indicated on a number of occasions. As a result of this building pressure, the DP manager has just left the company. Donna Richards, the vice president of Finance, to whom corporate Data Processing reported, has to find an individual to replace the previous DP manager.

In discussions with the company president, James Randall II, Richards suggested that it was time to expand the corporate Data Processing department and to develop a management information area. She knew that the company needed a very strong individual with heavy information systems background.

In the past, the corporate Data Processing department had limited responsibilities and resources. Therefore, its role had been confined to preparing monthly, quarterly, and year-end consolidated financial reports, which had been a difficult, time-consuming task due to the variety of hardware in use at the various divisions (see Exhibit 3).

In addition, the divisions without computers prepared their financial statements manually and transmitted them to corporate headquarters by way of a telecopier.

EXHIBIT 2   Randall Industries, Inc., Sales History

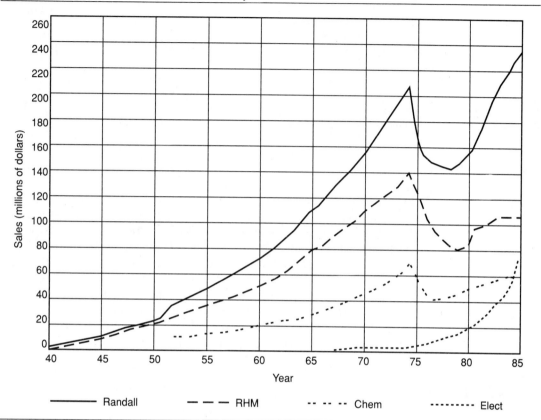

EXHIBIT 3   Randall Industries Present Hardware/Staff

Division	Hardware	EDP Staff
1. Randall Heavy Machine	Two IBM 370s	20
2. Cooper Chemical	Linked to RHM IBM; Three IBM PCs	8
Pharmaceuticals	Honeywell RL310; Foxboro Microprocessor	None
3. Electronics	Two Digital IP300As	15

LEWIS MATSON

Richards was able to recruit Lewis Matson for the opening. Lewis's education included an undergraduate degree in Accounting from Rutgers University and an MBA degree from the Wharton School of Business. He had worked for the "big eight" accounting firm of Coopers & Lybrand, where he had progressed in six years to manager of their Audit staff. In addition to his public accounting experience, he had worked as manager of Data Services for 3M for three years. After 3M, he was hired by LJM Industries to assist in the conversion from a Burroughs system to IBM equipment. This project was nearing completion when he learned that Randall Industries was looking for a director to establish an MIS department and to help in the overall process of modernization.

Matson: DP Review and Plans

Matson had been on the job for several weeks, had finished his assessment of the current status of Data Processing systems, and was preparing plans for what he felt were necessary changes. Through discussions with corporate management, as well as with executives from the various divisions of the subsidiaries, he found that Randall needed a decision-making system. In Matson's opinion, the decision system was a top priority; however, implementation would be difficult.

Another problem for Matson was the current reporting structure. The five corporate Data Processing employees reported directly to him; on the other hand, the Data Processing employees in the various divisions reported to management in their respective divisions. To gain more control of the DP function, Matson believed the reporting structure had to be changed. He was considering having all of the DP personnel in the organization report to him at corporate headquarters. He felt this step was necessary, both to gain control and to increase uniformity in DP processing throughout the corporation.

While control and uniformity would be necessary to meet future corporate goals and objectives, achieving those goals would probably cause some problems with the various divisions, he suspected. Nonetheless, Matson judged it was time to get away from the concept of operating the three subsidiaries autonomously and to begin the process of operating as one organization.

Matson: Obstacle and Tactics

Some of the divisions that needed to change or update their equipment might not understand why this was necessary. They had performed adequately for quite some time; why should they change just because corporate needed more information? Matson thought, however, that it was past time to develop a companywide management information system and believed that gaining this objective far outweighed any arguments that the divisional managements could develop. His toughest problem was going to be convincing them that the new decision-making system would allow the corporation to make quicker, smarter decisions, thus improving the profitability of the corporation as a whole (and thereby giving all individuals more job security).

Another concern for Matson was the DP budget. Before his plan to centralize control of company data processing could succeed, he would need a very large budget increase. And while a large increase in the DP budget might cause some concern and complaints throughout the divisions, Matson was confident that his plans for a unified DP department would be accepted by corporate management. Therefore, he was reasonably confident that his proposed budget would also gain approval (see Exhibit 4).

Yet another major task for Matson was devising and implementing a plan to obtain and maintain compatible data processing equipment at each of the divisions (see Exhibit 5). Matson saw this as a problem with some divisions that had newer equipment, as they would be reluctant to replace or adapt a satisfactory setup. There would also be time problems due to the installation of new software packages.

Matson hoped to persuade all parties involved in the conversion that, once the plan was in effect, there would be little additional disturbance to normality. Costs should decrease to normal levels, and time and personnel demands would stabilize.

A critical element of the plan was that Matson himself would give the final authorization on all hardware and software purchases, both for the conversion and in the future. Again, his strongest argument was the crucial need for company uniformity.

To appreciate fully the changes that Matson has proposed, we must look at the individual divisions, particularly in light of their DP requirements and the overall corporate culture.

EXHIBIT 4 EDP Budget Summary

Before Reorganization

Salaries	210,000
Hardware replacements	200,000
Software replacements	50,000
Training and education	4,000
Travel expenses	3,000
Supplies	2,000
Miscellaneous	1,000
Total	470,000

After Proposed Reorganization

Hardware replacements	3,000,000
Salaries	1,025,000
Software replacements	230,000
Training and education	50,000
Travel expenses	28,000
Supplies	12,000
Miscellaneous	2,000
Total	4,347,000

RANDALL HEAVY MACHINE (RHM)

Company Background: Pre-World War II

Randall Heavy Machine (RHM) was founded in early 1940 by James Randall, Sr., as a manufacturer of machined components for the automotive and truck industry. Randall had started his career with General Motors, Chevrolet Division, in 1923 after graduating from the University of Michigan with a degree in mechanical engineering.

During his time with Chevrolet, he had risen to the position of superintendent of Drive Train Production. While there he had seen an opportunity to start a business supplying machined components, not just to GM but to all car, truck, construction, and agricultural equipment manufacturers. In 1938, he saw his chance: The outbreak and expansion of the war in Europe was generating the need for additional suppliers of material. The inclusion of England in the conflict convinced him that the time was right.

In 1940, using the proceeds from the sale of his home in Flint, Michigan, as a down payment, he purchased a small shop in Toledo, Ohio, and started his own

EXHIBIT 5   MIS Implementation Plan

January 1986	Change reporting structure of the Data Processing department
January 1986	All hardware/software acquisitions to be approved by corporate MIS
March 1986	Complete plans for replacing noncompatible hardware/software
August 1986	Complete installation of equipment at divisions currently without Data Processing departments
September 1986	Begin parallel testing of compatible DP equipment installed at the subsidiaries
October 1986	Begin live processing of data with the new systems
June 1987	Have equipment in place so that decision-making system information is available from all divisions
February 1988	Have all necessary hardware/software changes implemented so that all divisions have standardized data processing functions

business, called Randall Heavy Machine (RHM). Randall chose that location because it was close to (1) Detroit, whose automotive plants would be the end-users of his products after the hostilities ended; (2) Cleveland, Gary, and Pittsburgh — suppliers of raw materials; and (3) the Great Lakes, whose shipping lanes would allow access to European markets.

Even though James, Sr., had little equipment, he repeatedly bid on government contracts, realizing the government would supply him with the machines and tooling required to do the jobs. The strategy worked. By July 1940, he had his first contract to supply drive shafts for trucks being sent to Great Britain. By the end of 1940, RHM had secured $2.2 million in government contracts.

By May 1941, the company had outgrown its original facility and had to be expanded. Randall purchased two adjoining structures to provide additional capacity. During the war, the company grew quickly, and sites were established in Flatrock, Michigan, and Lorain, Ohio. By the end of the war, sales were $23 million.

Post-World War II: Randall Industries

To insure the continued growth of the company and to take advantage of pent-up consumer demand, Randall secured long-term contracts with several manufacturing firms. He developed a diversification strategy in the late 1940s and positioned RHM to supply other goods to the same markets. In keeping with this strategy, the company opened manufacturing sites in Morton, Illinois, and East Gary, Indiana, and, in 1952, acquired Cooper Chemical.

In late 1952, Randall restructured the organization, forming a holding company called Randall Industries, Inc.; RHM and Cooper Chemical became operating divisions. James, Sr., appointed himself president and CEO of Randall Industries, while his oldest son, Roger, became a division vice president and the head of RHM. Roger concentrated on progressive management and manufacturing techniques to keep manufacturing costs low.

In 1965, Roger Randall succeeded his father as president and CEO of Randall Industries; James Randall, Sr., remained as chairman of the board. In turn, Roger was succeeded by his younger brother James III, who became division vice president of RHM (see Exhibit 6).

Under the leadership of James, Sr., Randall Industries expanded through the late 1950s and 60s. This growth continued until 1974 when a severe downturn in the auto industry caused a sharp drop in sales. The downturn became a downward trend that continued for nine years.

JAMES RANDALL III

During the nine low years, the only plant that stayed in the black was the Toledo Drive Train plant, which was being managed by James Randall III. James, who was educated at the University of Michigan and Harvard University, assumed the presidency of the RHM division in 1976. By 1979, he was able to stop the downward trend at RHM by applying the same methods that had succeeded at Drive Train. These methods included using, more effectively, the scheduling tools that already existed in the division and modernizing the manufacturing processes.

He had started the turnaround at Drive Train by retraining people in the use of their material requirements planning (MRP) system and by introducing computer numerical control (CNC) equipment into manufacturing. To utilize the capabilities of the CNC equipment, James visualized a group technology system in which all parts would be described by numeric code in a central database. Thus, scheduling could be based on the characteristics of the product and the availability of equipment. Machine setups would be minimized, and product information would be downloaded from the central controller directly to the machine tool. At the division level, his strategy would require large investments in capital equipment, data processing capability, and personnel.

With the rebound of some of their markets, James III saw that his two-pronged MRP/CNC strategy presented an opportunity not only to return RHM to its previous level of sales but to become dominant in the industry. Even though capital was tight, the plan progressed nicely until 1982. At that point, everyone finally realized the division didn't have the technical expertise to complete the job. The plan stalled, and so did growth.

In 1984, James formally requested that the entire company adopt the program and that each of the other divisions help RHM complete its plan, which would be expanded to include the entire corporation. He visualized a corporatewide system in which all divisions would be electronically linked, having access to the same information in the same format.

EXHIBIT 6 Randall Heavy Machine Organization Chart

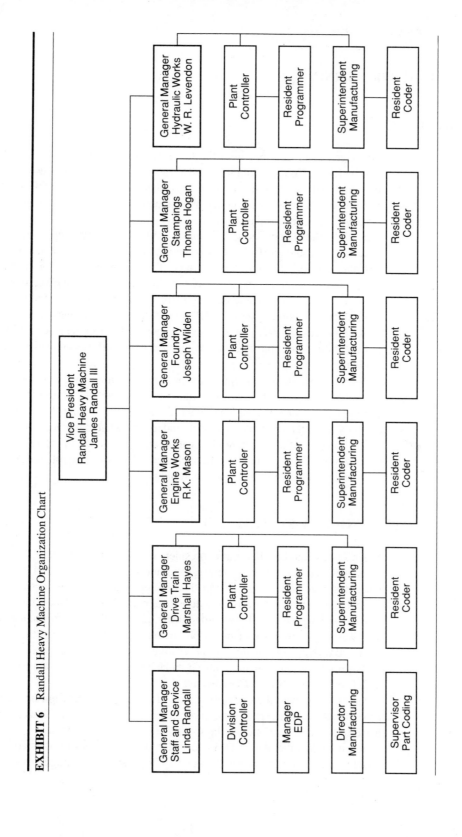

RANDALL INDUSTRIES, INC.

DP Background

DP usage began in 1965, with the lease of an IBM 1460 mainframe that was used by RHM, Cooper Chemical, and corporate offices. Original use was limited to Payroll and Accounting. In those days, there was no separate DP function for RHM or the chemical division, and all production scheduling was done manually; there were no operation applications.

In 1968, RHM and Cooper Chemical DP functions were separated from corporate offices, and an IBM 360 was purchased for the exclusive use of RHM. It was placed in the division headquarters. Though the DP function had been divorced from corporate, the systems remained compatible. RHM expanded the use of DP in 1970 to include operations-related activities, principally a material requirements planning system (MRP) for production scheduling and a distribution tracking system. In 1971, the system was modified to include machine load analysis capability, and a permanent five-member MIS staff was created at the Toledo headquarters.

While these systems were quite advanced for their time, they were never utilized beyond 50 percent of their capacity, due mostly to the lack of operator expertise and management emphasis. The underutilization was also attributed partially to the inability of the DP professionals to understand what manufacturing was doing and to the lack of technical sophistication and knowledge in the manufacturing organization. Throughout all of these changes, divisional Payroll and Accounting remained compatible with corporate systems.

RHM'S GROUP TECHNOLOGY SYSTEM (GT)

When James Randall III became president of the division in 1976, he created a divisional Manufacturing Systems group and purchased two IBM 370s. These machines were part of his plan for the development of a group technology (GT) system that would center around a divisional parts database. The database would provide part descriptions for manufacturing, along with cost information. James's idea was to promote use of new CNC manufacturing technology that would be linked to a dynamic scheduling and costing system. The linkage should reduce costs greatly because manufacturing capacities could be used more effectively and inventory levels could be lowered.

James recognized the underutilization of the 370s at RHM but he intended to expand their use to the rest of the corporation. He felt secure with this expectation because he knew that one day he would be running the company.

To implement the plan, RHM added five programmers and parts coders to its Toledo headquarters between 1976 and 1979. In spite of an augmented staff, the division was not able to meet James's timetable. Between 1979 and 1982, in an attempt to get back on schedule, another eight people—five from Chemical division—were added to the project; they were also to support system maintenance, which had suffered as more and more resources were assigned to the GT project.

Following the last staff addition, James III commented, ''I really don't understand. It seems that for each additional body we bring in, productivity drops almost proportionately. If we (RHM) are to implement this project successfully and convince the other divisions that this is the way to go, we're going to have to do a lot better.''

However, the next year was no better; nevertheless, a plan was developed to include the rest of the divisions before completion of the project at RHM. Randall proposed the following: ''If all of the divisions would work together towards a common system, dedicating all of our resources to bring this program on one division at a time, there is no doubt in my mind that it would be a success. The growth that we experienced between 1979 and 1982 could be repeated and shared by all divisions. Right now, we can't complete our program because we're short of competent technical people. I know that these people are available in the organization.

''If the other divisions would help us to get our system on-line, then we would help them to change over their systems to match ours. Everybody in this company has to start singing from the same song sheet. This means access to the same information and the same systems.

''I know that right now ours is the most developed system in the corporation, and that's why everyone else should get on board. We have more invested in hardware and software than some of our other divisions are worth. Hell, I'll admit that we don't do everything right, but we do it a lot better than most, and we have been doing it longer than anybody else.

''We have these people in Phoenix and in England who think they don't need us. That's ridiculous; we started this company, and we've carried them for years. Just because they are lucky now doesn't mean that things won't go the other way. We all work for the same company, a company started by my grandfather. This family has known what was best for the company in the past, and we know what is best for it in the future.''

COOPER CHEMICALS DIVISION (CC)

Business Background

Acquired in 1952, the Chemicals division had experienced steady growth up until 1975, when a decline in the automobile market caused a significant depression of sales. With 1984 sales at $62 million, the Chemical division represents approximately 25 percent of Randall Industries' gross sales. Although the present market outlook appears stable, Cooper Chemical would like to improve operations to meet increased competition (see Exhibit 7).

In describing the future strategic direction of Cooper, Vincent Jones, the divisional vice president, has emphasized the need for increased computer applications within the division.

Two subdivisions, Paints and Silica Additives, comprise the main Chemicals core. Two paint manufacturing facilities (Pittsburgh, Pennsylvania, and Poughkeepsie, New York) and three silica plants (Columbus, Ohio, Cincinnati, Ohio, and Parkersburg, West Virginia) were obtained in the initial acquisition. The R&D and DP functions of the two product lines were consolidated in 1965 to promote more effective plant assistance. Expansion of the existing production facilities was completed in 1969 to meet increasing customer demands.

Pharmatech, acquired in 1982, is still very much in the development stage. With only one pilot plant in Cowfold, England, it was initially under joint scientist ownership. Research centered on cancer-inhibiting vaccines for use on leukemia patients. The goal of the acquisition was to capitalize on an imminent breakthrough in this field.

DP Background

The Chemicals division (Paints and Silica) was incorporated into the Machine Tool's data processing scheme from the onset. In 1965, it had access to the IBM 1460 and progressed through all the software revisions in the 1970s. Currently, five of the eight programmer/analysts assigned to the Chemicals group have been recruited to assist in the DP modernization taking place within the RHM division. The remaining three analysts have little time for anything else except system maintenance. Consequently, not much progress has been made in development of new computer applications for the Chemicals division. Until the GT system conversion is complete, the lack of available staff will stop any attempts to utilize the present system.

All accounting, inventory control, order processing, payroll, and shipping functions for Paints and Silica are performed on the IBM system. In addition, several IBM PCs have been purchased by individual plant managers for operations tracking and local management decisions. The PCs were a direct response to the inadequate service of the IBM system.

The Pharmaceuticals plant has no DP department. Initial assistance from the Electronics division staff in 1982 enabled the staff to implement report generation and process automation from the existing computer control systems, as outlined below:

1. All process parameters are automatically controlled through a Honeywell TDC RL 310 unit coupled with a Foxboro Microprocessor for batch control.

EXHIBIT 7   Chemical Division Hierarchy

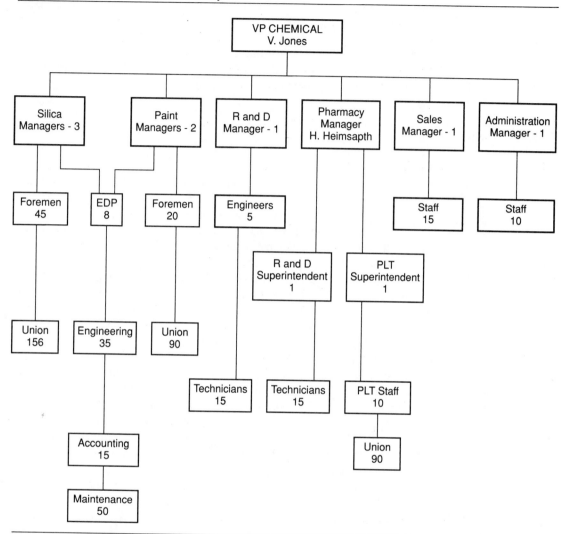

2. Report generation is implemented through use of this system.
3. All pertinent information is correlated, monitored, and printed by the TDC system. Initial programming is effected by research staff under the guidance of Electronics personnel.

The technical competence of the present Pharmatech staff is high, in contrast to the relatively limited knowledge of the Paint/Silica DP group. The DP group depends on the RHM division for guidance in instances other than routine maintenance. Consequently, development of most applications consumes much more time than would be expected, and the completed programs have limited flexibility and utility.

Past DP budgets for salaries and training have been very low. Starting with 1985, the DP budget increased substantially, reflecting corporate recognition of the importance of MIS functions (see Exhibit 8).

Future DP Goals

The DP goals of Pharmatech differ substantially from those of the core chemicals. Both, however, lean toward adding automated functions, as well as enhancing those already on hand. The Chemical plant's most immediate goal is extensive automation of manufacturing processes with investigation into compatibility of this automation with future MIS needs. The automation of operations must take place within the next 24 months to successfully combat market pressure from competitors.

Specifically, top executives in Sales have requested the implementation of a decision-making system for sales managers. Also, although the R&D staff has access to the present IBM system, many of its members have asked for more options than are currently available in-house. There also appears to be a group interested in accessing manufacturing quality data and production information.

The IBM PCs satisfy these last requests adequately. In fact, the managers with PCs have been so pleased with their flexibility and usefulness that they have seriously considered networking the PCs instead of using the IBM mainframe.

Pharmatech's goals are more hardware-specific; the primary objective is to eliminate the Foxboro microprocessor by upgrading the TDC RL 310 system to the TDC RL 520 system. The RL 520 allows internal programming and report generation. Currently, the Foxboro microprocessor performs these functions but requires an excessive amount of I/O crosswiring to do so.

Goals dependent on conversion to the 520 system include the formation of

---

EXHIBIT 8   Chemicals Division Proposed 1985 DP Budget

Supplies	$ 80,000
Personnel	300,000
Training	20,000
Maintenance (parts, labor, etc.)	250,000
RL310 modifications	
(pharmaceuticals)	530,000
Personal computer network	20,000
Total	$1,200,000

automated emergency fail-safe procedures to prevent pollution or quality violations. The 520 provides programming capability for such procedures. The degree of 520 automation will also enable a reduction in operating personnel, resulting in significant savings once the 520 is successfully on stream.

Actions Taken

Pharmatech has already ordered the new RL 520 conversion parts. Drawings and programming by operations staff is in progress. Training of all personnel on new system features is in progress. Conversion completion is scheduled for February 1987.

Chemical Plants and Silica have also taken specific steps toward achievement of their stated goals. Three meetings with DP staff and all plant superintendents have been held to determine present management information needs. Results of these meetings are outlined below. The system:

1. Must be flexible and applicable to all facets of chemicals management.
2. Must have decision-making options.
3. Should be able to access mainframe data.
4. Should be able to access future plant automated quality control systems.
5. Must have networking capability.
6. Must have optimization and scheduling functions.
7. Must be reliable with low maintenance costs.

Management's information demands reflect the success characteristics they have observed in the IBM PCs.

In an effort to determine the best means of plant automation, management hired an outside consultant, DataMachine, to do a study in July 1986. Given the time frame for plant automation, the consultants recommended an Allen Bradley PLC system within each plant.

Perceive Pressures/Outlook

Chemicals core simply wants a more effective system. The time constraint on automation is vital to survival in the present market; however, incorporation of process data into MIS functions would be valuable. At present, optimization of production parameters is more critical than compatibility with an overall MIS system, due to pressure from the competition.

Cooper Chemical executives believe the major problem with the existing IBM system is lack of internal expertise. Therefore, they are especially adamant that their new MIS system be simple, flexible, and reliable. They will forfeit extra features or special options to get a user-friendly system.

VINCENT JONES

Personal computer use coincides with Vincent Jones's directive to increase computer applications within the division. Jones is more keenly aware of the computer management systems of his competitors and senses the inadequacies of the present DP system. He believes that if he promotes a flexible, reliable system, his subordinates will be more inclined to utilize its functions to benefit operations. Unfortunately, he does not know if this logic will be strong enough to convince corporate management to allow him to break substantially with the RHM division's IBM GT system. He had problems previously just trying to get authorization to purchase the three IBM PCs already used within his division.

Another of Jones's concerns is that the consulting study did not adequately review or consider the benefits of the Pharmatech system. From all of his dealings with that particular plant, despite the distances involved, he has been able to obtain accurate, timely information in the format he desired. He was also impressed with the efficiency of Pharmatech operations. Jones hopes to use the impending facilities automation to push the information processing revisions he believes necessary for the future effectiveness of his division.

HAROLD HEIMSAPTH

Dr. (Professor) Harold Heimsapth, the general manager of Pharmatech, had quite a different problem on his mind. Had it not been for lack of funds, he would never have agreed to sell Pharmatech at so critical a point in its development. He had watched, with increasing excitement, the progress made in the past two years. It appeared that research efforts to produce a new leukemia vaccine, which he had envisioned 15 years ago, were on the verge of success. He was so enthusiastic and optimistic about the probability of success that he had concentrated all available staff and resources on the final phases of testing.

Consequently, cost and accountability controls had slipped significantly in the past six months. He was afraid that corporate imposition of time-consuming DP restrictions and standards would detract from the research applications effort. In fact, his proposed plant automation goals were specifically designed to emphasize the unique nature of the Cowfold plant, as well as to appease corporate management.

He could not expect the American-owned Randall Industries to understand the imperative nature of adequate quality assurance that his research demanded. Nor could they relate to the environmental regulations imposed on him. Although research was his paramount concern, he could not forget that an effective vaccine would generate expansion and rapid growth of new facilities. Perhaps then he might be more open to an increase in information transmission between locations, but even that depended on many considerations.

ELECTRONICS DIVISION (ED)

The Electronics division began modestly in 1967 as an outgrowth of the Heavy Machine division. The operation, based in Phoenix, was primarily a "job shop," manufacturing solid state components for the automobile industry. Business grew slowly throughout the 1960s. Then, in 1971, a new divisional vice president, Thomas Walls, was hired to direct the division (see Exhibit 9).

At one time he had been a management troubleshooter for GE. He would be sent to a plant that was plagued with poor performance and told to turn the operation around and make it profitable again. He had a remarkable success rate over the past 16 years and seemed a natural to build up this new subsidiary of Randall Industries.

Under Walls, the Electronics division took on a new strategic direction. The

EXHIBIT 9 Electronics Division Organizational Chart

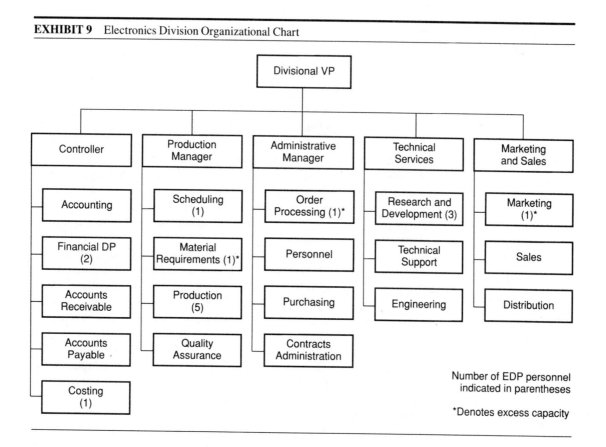

Number of EDP personnel indicated in parentheses

*Denotes excess capacity

division began to hire unemployed aerospace engineers and technicians and to develop expertise in the areas of electronic controls and microprocessors.

Since this operation was building from the ground up, Walls pushed for the development of automated systems wherever possible. Outside suppliers of this technology were limited, however, so Walls's people developed their own systems. With these developments, the division had new flexibility. With R&D and start-up costs at a minimum, they began to move into Department of Defense contracts. Soon, they had managed to obtain some sizable contracts, particularly for missile guidance systems for navy vessels.

When the bottom fell out of the automotive OEM supplier business in the early 1970s, the Electronics division remained healthy, mostly due to the defense contracts. In fact, the business grew substantially during this period, and two small facilities were opened—one in Norfolk, Virginia, and one in San Diego, California—to satisfy the requirements of the navy contracts. These new facilities were primarily technical support offices; production was still confined to the Phoenix site.

THOMAS WALLS

Beginning in 1974, sales really began to climb, growing from $5 million in 1974 to $60 million in 1984. Discussing the reasons for this success, Walls had the following comments: "Sure, we've had some luck, but we've been prepared to capitalize on available opportunities. I hired those aerospace people in the early '70s because they were talented, and they were desperate for work. I gave them a stake in the company, and they've worked hard to make it a success. Our people wear many different hats, but it's a team effort here, and everyone helps wherever there's a need. True, we run 'lean and mean,' but we've never had a layoff and hopefully never will. So far, we've been able to increase sales at a rate of 15–20 percent per year, without significantly increasing our work force, primarily due to our emphasis on automation.

"Automation has been very important to our success. It gives us the flexibility we need, and it drastically lowers our R&D and start-up costs. When we take on a new project, we strive to be up and running in less than six months, and we generally meet the goal. Automation has also given us an edge in holding down our production costs, and it allows us to respond more rapidly to new technological advances in the electronics industry."

New challenges face the Electronics division in the 1980s. As Walls tells it, "We've managed dramatic growth throughout the past 10 years in spite of the recession, but we are now entering a new era of challenge. Our defense contracts are stable, but it's very dangerous to rely too heavily on them. History tells us they come and they go—quickly. We've also seen a significant rise in the automotive OEM market as American car sales pick up again. However, we're getting more and more competitive pressure from Japanese, Korean, and Mexican electronic suppliers. Our status as a defense contractor severely limits the possibility of significant foreign trade. Thus, we must look for new domestic markets if we want to maintain our record of growth and profitability.

"That's why I thought it would be a good test to see if our DP personnel could help automate Pharmatech when Corporate asked for our help. I thought this might open up a new market for us. We were able to help Pharmatech in some areas but not in others. We just don't have the expertise to help in all areas, and I'm not sure we should get into plant automation at this time if it means hiring more people."

DP BACKGROUND AT ED

DP has been closely intertwined with the growth of the Electronics division. When it was a job shop operation, the division used an outside DP contractor (ADP) for its financial reports, accounting, and payroll. Purchasing, distribution, production scheduling, and planning were all done manually. However, under Walls, the division truly entered the computer age in the early 1970s.

DP played a critical role in the development of the automated systems presently used by the division. Walls began by hiring three programmer/analysts and purchasing a Digital mainframe. They then set out to computerize production planning and costing. Once those two jobs were completed, the three programmer/analysts—plus four new hires—went on to automate the production process. By 1977, working jointly with the engineering staff, they had developed a simple but effective point-to-point assembly robot. Again, the DP personnel expanded to 15 as more robots were developed and programmed for more and more assembly operations. During this period, the division continued to use ADP for its financial reports, accounting, billing, and payroll.

In 1980, with production automated, Walls decided to internalize the functions previously handled by ADP. A second Digital IP300A was purchased, and three members of the DP staff were put on the project of internalization using purchased software.

By 1982, all DP was done in-house, and Walls was faced with what he called "excess programming capacity" (i.e., three members of the DP staff). Because Walls disliked the idea of a layoff, he was eager to help when the corporate office asked him if he could spare some of his DP personnel to help computerize the newly acquired Pharmatech.

There is not a separate DP department within the Electronics division. Each programmer/analyst is assigned to a particular department and reports to that department's manager (see Exhibit 9). Within each department, the DP personnel specialize in certain functions; they are not restricted to that particular function, however, since their assignments depend on the needs that arise.

WALLS'S RESPONSE TO MATSON'S PLANS

When asked to comment on the activities at the corporate office, Walls offered the following: "I can understand why those guys in Toledo want to get a better grip on things. Randall Industries has become big business, and they've got to get those other two divisions to modernize if they want to remain profitable. But why should my operation, a highly successful one, suffer to help out those divisions?

"The Electronics division is highly automated and very modern. We've got things running smoothly here, so why would anyone in their right mind want us to change? My father once told me, 'If it's not broken, don't fix it.' I think those guys in Toledo could benefit from that bit of wisdom.

"I don't think they realize what it would mean to standardize on new IBM hardware. First of all, neither of my mainframes are over 10 years old, and I am not financially ready to replace them. Second, all my software is compatible with Digital, not IBM; any conversion would mean a virtual rewrite and would require years to complete.

"Sure, I have some excess capacity in the programming area, but we've been successful because we make money; we don't make work. I don't want and won't have my people spending their time on unproductive tasks, and that's just what a conversion would mean. If we were to convert, it wouldn't make us one cent more in profit, but it would cost us hundreds of thousands of dollars. That's not sound business sense.

"Then, there's that Management Information System they're talking about. I don't need MIS. I run a small operation here, and I'm deeply involved in all aspects of the business. When I want to know something, I don't wait for a report to hit my desk; I go onto the shop floor and find out firsthand. The last thing I need is more paperwork.

"Maybe they think this MIS will help them make better strategic decisions in Toledo. Well, they haven't made them in the past, so why should they now? One of the reasons I took this job was that I wanted to call all the shots. The divisions operate autonomously here, and I want it to stay that way. I'm not even sure the guys in Toledo know what we do here, let alone how we do it.

"Besides, it was my decision to automate and to reduce our reliance on automotive OEM parts. If we'd done what they wanted to do in 1974, we'd have gone right down the tubes, like every other automotive industry supplier.

"In any case, I just wish they'd leave us alone. Let them go ahead and shake up the other two divisions if they want to, but don't hamper a successful division like ours."

CONCLUSION

Matson is ready now to submit his proposal to Richards for review. Based on the diverse opinions of the various division vice presidents, their unique DP requirements, and the corporate culture of Randall Industries, Richards is faced with the difficult decision of accepting Matson's radical proposal or making major modifications. The right choice wasn't obvious.

QUESTIONS

1. How should Matson sell his common equipment approach? Should he sell it? Are there any alternatives?
2. What are the alternatives to Matson's idea? Which one do you prefer and why?
3. Discuss the differences between the information needs of the corporate staff and the information needs of the divisions. Whose needs should take precedence, and who should make that decision?
4. Is the MIS role in Randall strategic, support, factory, or turnaround? Support your answer.
5. What qualifications should Randall have sought in its MIS director?
6. Would you have hired Matson for the position? Why or why not?
7. Should Randall centralize its IS services? If so, how?
8. What should Matson do?
9. Assess James Randall III's GT system. What changes would you make, if any, and why?

Chapter 6

Organization for IS

INTRODUCTION

Microcomputers have had a profound effect on IS in at least two ways. First is an issue of centralization versus decentralization; do we centralize or decentralize our IS decision-making, information storage, and computer operations? Second is the effect of enormous amounts of information received, processed, analyzed, and transmitted to corporate locations nationwide. This is due in large measure to the almost unbelievable amount of processing power now available to millions of people in the form of 100 megabyte desktop machines and portable micros with telecommunications hookups.[1]

HISTORY

In early, first-generation computers, when what we know today as Information Systems (IS) was synonymous with Data Processing (DP), accounting functions such as payroll, billing, and general ledger were the first to be computerized; since the accounting department was the only real beneficiary, the computer and DP staff was very often directly responsible to the corporate comptroller or chief financial officer.[2]

As individuals and managers in other functional areas (marketing, finance, personnel, and so on) realized the computer's potential, they began to ask for services such as data processing and applications development.

---

[1] Jerome S. Burstein, *Computers and Information Systems,* Chapter 14 (New York: Holt, Rinehart & Winston, 1986).

[2] Sharon Hess and Bill Lawrence, ''The Developing Role of the IS Manager'' (MBA paper, Loyola College, Baltimore, Md., 1987).

In centralized organizations, with a single DP center and staff under the control of Accounting or the comptroller, demands from other areas tended to be seen as lower priority than those of Accounting. The natural conflict over DP resources led to a split from Accounting and to the establishment of a separate DP or IS department, expected now to be more responsive to the needs of all departments and divisions.

In organizations with a philosophy of decentralization, computers were located in each of the business functional departments. If the organization decided later to centralize, field organizations resisted the return of their DP resources to Accounting (or the headquarters staff).[3] Again, an independent IS function was the result.

Figure 6–1 portrays Dickson and Wetherbe's four alternative locations of the data processing or information systems function.

FIVE BASIC FUNCTIONS OF IS

Information services (or systems) groups, however organized or named, accomplish five functions or activities. They are:

1. **Systems development:** Systems development includes investigation, analysis, design, programming, implementation, and systems maintenance; O'Brien adds configuration management and communications management.[4]
2. **User services:** Providing services to users through an information center assures that they receive hardware support, software support, and people support (that is, a staff of systems analysts and programmers especially trained to help users).
3. **Data administration:** Coordinated and controlled by a database administrator (DBA) or a Database Administration department, data administration comprises database design, database operations, and database security.
4. **Operations:** The operations function—that is, the processing of data and its conversion to information—covers the major activities of data preparation and control, equipment operation, production control, and production support.
5. **Administration:** Administration of IS, like the administration of any other function, includes planning, controlling, managerial liaison, personnel management, financial management, and routine services such as supply and custodial services.[5]

---

[3]Jeffrey Wilhelm, "The Organizational Structure of Management Information Systems" (MBA paper, Loyola College, Baltimore, Md., 1987).

[4]James A. O'Brien, *Computers in Business Management: An Introduction,* 4th ed., Chapter 19 (Homewood, Ill.: Richard D. Irwin, Inc., 1985), pp. 670–71.

[5]O'Brien, *Computers in Business Management,* pp. 670–74.

EXHIBIT 6-1 Alternative Locations for the IS Function

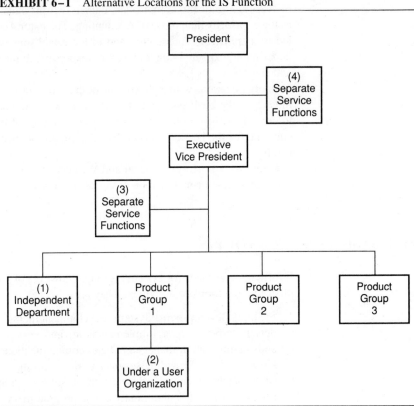

Source: Gary W. Dickson and James C. Wetherbe, *The Management of Information Systems* (New York: McGraw-Hill, 1985).

FOUR COMMON CHARACTERISTICS OF IS

Deciding where the IS function should be located in the organization and to whom its director should report are not the sole determinants of IS success. In his 1987 paper, "The Organizational Structure of Management Information Systems," Wilhelm lists four common elements of an effective IS. They are:

1. The role and the responsibility of the information system must be defined.
2. Basic parameters affecting information systems development and implementation success can be formidable; they must be identified, weighed, and respected. Three are risk aversion, flexibility, and stage of technological maturity.
3. The IS group must receive proper guidance from top management.
4. IS must work to accomplish an approved plan that includes controls to measure performance.

IS—WHERE IN THE HIERARCHY?

The establishment of separate, independent IS functions, under both centralized and decentralized organizations, did not answer the questions (1) to whom should the IS manager report, and (2) where should the organization be placed within the hierarchy?

"The director of Information Systems sits at the top of the information systems echelon in many organizations. In some very large organizations, however, the director of Information Systems reports to the Information Resource manager, who in turn may report to the chief executive officer."[6] How is this placement determined?

If the role of information systems is strategically important to the firm,[7] as in a bank or insurance company, for example, perhaps the IS manager or director should report to the president or CEO. If IS does not have strategic implications in the corporation, its manager could report to a some other senior executive such as a vice president or executive vice president.

In most large companies, it is rare today to find the IS function located under the control of a business function such as Accounting or Finance. More often, we find an information resource manager who is responsible for all the information-related technical facilities and activities of the firm. That may include —in addition to the computer center(s)—word processing, electronic mail/message systems, and other automated office devices and systems.[8]

CENTRALIZATION VERSUS DECENTRALIZATION

There can be advantages and disadvantages to centralizing or decentralizing the IS function; the strengths of one tend to be the weaknesses of the other. IS directors or managers considering a change should be specific about exactly what is to be centralized or decentralized—operations, decision making, policy determination, systems development . . . what?

A mixture of both centralization and decentralization is used by some companies. Figure 6–2 shows the variety of structures used by Multicorp.

---

[6]Burstein, *Computers and Information Systems*, Chap. 14, p. 399.

[7]See James I. Cash, F. W. McFarlan, J. L. McKenney, and M. R. Vitale, *Corporate Information Systems Management: Text and Cases*, 2nd ed., Chapter 11 (Homewood, Ill.: Richard D. Irwin, 1988). Figure 11–1, the Information Technology Strategic Grid, plus the supporting pages (pp. 622 –28) gives an excellent description of the strategic range of IS/IT activities.

[8]Burstein, *Computers and Information Systems*, Chap. 14.

INFORMATION CENTER

When users of data processing products found alternatives to the organization's centralized data processing services, they quickly chose the alternatives. The low prices and power of microcomputers, the availability and utility of user-friendly software, and, perhaps most important of all, the ability to supply much of their own data processing needs meant the end of the central DP center's monopoly control of the organization's information inventory.

Because having a microcomputer near your desk became a fad, many were bought but not used. In addition to the underutilization of micros, resources were also wasted due to duplication of programming efforts, purchases of software that had to be modified, failure of users to properly document their programs, and ineffective use of computer center technical staff. The use of corporate assets was not being coordinated.

Information centers were established to provide centralized technical computer-related support for what had become decentralized data processing.[9]

Today, the major responsibilities of information centers are to "provide users with training and consulting services. Information center personnel are responsible for defining the market for services, for providing appropriate hardware and software facilities, for offering support for application development, and for conducting training programs. Other duties of information center analysts include hardware and software evaluation, technical support, data management, hotline support, and debugging assistance."[10]

THE MANAGER OF IS

The duties and responsibilities of the IS manager have evolved as advances in technology have produced spreadsheets, databases, networks, diskettes, fiber-optic cabling, and 100 MB microcomputers. The IS manager's role has been influenced also by trends in the business environment—fast, small, cheap computers; new, user-friendly programming languages; insatiable user demands; and functional manager awareness of computer power and potential.[11]

Primary responsibilities of the IS manager involve managing—systems development, computer operations, and IS personnel—and providing security and control. His or her roles can also include information resource architect, infor-

[9]Wilhelm, "The Organizational Structure."

[10]Robert Schultheis and Mary Sumner, *Management Information Systems: The Manager's View,* Chapter 14 (Homewood, Ill.: Richard D. Irwin, 1989).

[11]Hess and Lawrence, "The Developing Role of the IS Manager."

FIGURE 6-2   Variety of Organizational Structures at Multicorp

	Centralized	*Distributed*	*Decentralized*
Equipment	Multicorp headquarters	Manufacturing plants	Computerware stores
Operations	Headquarters	At plants	Store personnel
Development	Headquarters	At plants and central consulting	In-store systems

Source: Henry C. Lucas, Jr., *Introduction to Computers and Information Systems*, Chap. 20, Figure 20–4 (New York: Macmillan, 1986).

mation resource consultant, information resource synergist, and information resource educator.[12]

RELATIONSHIPS WITH END-USERS

The relationship between end-users and computer experts has been difficult, in part because the experts sometimes tended to be arrogant and insensitive to the needs and interests of the users. Another source of conflict is the language difficulty; analysts and programmers communicate better with each other than either one does with their clients, the functional business departments. Finally, the advent of microcomputers and distributed processing has produced a reversal of power; the DP center and staff have seen their control over computer resources and activities diminish.

Organizational structuring can alleviate the expert versus user ("us versus them") problem somewhat. Hussain and Hussain pointed to the placement of EDP staffs, and the functional areas that use computers a great deal, under the direction of one top-level executive, often a vice president. They wrote:

> The vice president's title varies from firm to firm, though VP for Information Services is frequently used. This plan of organization helps coordinate teleprocessing by EDP personnel with communications under the Director of Communications, for example. It minimizes bureaucratic red tape for record managers who handle large volumes of computer output and rely on EDP equipment for retrieval and storage. A link with EDP ensures access to analysts and programmers for planners, reference service personnel, and word processor users. In deciding placement of EDP within a firm's organizational structure, the horizontal relationship of EDP with the user departments is as important as EDP's vertical integration in the organization's hierarchy.[13]

---

[12]J. Ferreira and P. R. Harris, "The Changing Roles of IRM Professionals," *Information Strategy: The Executive's Journal* 2, no. 1, pp. 18–22, 1985.

[13]Donna Hussain and K. M. Hussain, *Information Processing Systems for Management*, 2nd ed., Chapter 17 (Homewood, Ill.: Richard D. Irwin, 1985).

SUMMARY

The microcomputer revolution has been a major factor in today's dynamic IS environment. If one adds databases and local area networks to microcomputers, the three then becoming the standard configuration in office equipment, every general manager will have to become a mini-IS manager if he or she is to control routine office operations in automated surroundings. Meanwhile, IS managers (of operations, databases, microcomputers, information centers, and telecommunications) are trying to survive as organizations change to meet the pressures.

As IS departments participated in developing corporate strategies, and CEOs came to appreciate information as a corporate resource, CEOs began to spend more time in meetings about IS issues and problems. Some IS organizations and managers have been moved closer to the apex of the hierarchy triangle, sometimes as a line function, with a CIO appointed to be overall manager of all IS activities. However, most IS managers probably still serve in a staff capacity.[14]

CASES: READY LABORATORIES, SOUTHERN LODGES, INC., AND U.S. INTERNATIONAL ELECTRONICS

Ready Laboratories (Case 6–1), in attempting to compete with other laboratories, has developed and implemented an automated records transmission system. As an aftermath to the extended development process and due also to ongoing problems, the existing organizational structure is not satisfactory; a top executive has been terminated.

Southern Lodges, Inc., (Case 6–2) established its Computer Information Services division in the late 1970s and realizes that information is a strategic asset. Current major issues for the corporation are centralization versus decentralization and the relative influence and worth of users versus IS professionals. Problems are compounded by the inexperience of many IS managers.

At U.S. International Electronics (Case 6–3), the division of responsibility between two information organizations is creating communications problems and lowering IS performance. Because the corporation depends heavily on its shipping and tracking activities, two departments — IS and GIS — may have to be reorganized.

---

[14]Hess and Lawrence, "The Developing Role of the IS Manager."

Case 6–1 Ready Laboratories, Inc.: Computer Implementation

Dr. Gardner sat at his desk, reflecting on his move to the Office of the Director tomorrow and how it had come about.

Dr. Gardner

A lot has happened since I first stepped into the "old" laboratory on York Road. I was in the process of finishing my PhD when I took the graveyard shift at Redilab working on the SMAC 1260. (The SMAC is a large multichannel chemical analyzer capable of performing 28 chemistry assays on one patient sample.) Now, 10 years later, Redilab has doubled in size, and I am about to assume the role of technical director. This comes as a result of Paul Gole's "resignation" from the position of laboratory director this spring. His position is to be split into two positions: technical director and comptroller. The comptroller position is already being performed by our current administrator, Charlie McNeil. Although Charlie's job title and salary will change, he will have the same duties as before. Since my most recent position was R&D director, I will be playing a much different role. The technical director's position requires that I assume an authoritative demeanor, much more than I am comfortable with. I have worked with some of these people for close to 11 years now, and, in some instances, this new air of authority will be difficult to take on. In addition, Redilab is in the midst of a computerization project that has proven not only expensive and more time-consuming than anticipated but also disruptive to the staff. It will be my responsibility to evaluate our current status in this project and to propose a strategy to overcome the obvious problems. This is by far my most pressing challenge.

COMPANY BACKGROUND

Ready Laboratories (known informally as Redilab) was incorporated in the state of Maryland in December 1970. Thirty-two Maryland pathologists comprised the group of charter stockholders and provided the initial capitalization through purchase of stock on an equal-share basis.

The corporation is designed and managed to be self-supporting. The stock pays no dividends. All shareholders have equal stockholdings. Any operating profits are returned to the corporation in the form of expanded services and reduced charges. The officers (CEO and Administrator) and directors (Laboratory, R&D, and Personnel) comprise the Board of Directors and were elected from the general membership of 32 pathologists.

This case was prepared by Debbie Monahan and Patrick Lavery.

Redilab was formed to fill a real need in the local medical community for comprehensive, emergency toxicology services. The goal of the organization was to provide rapid, quality reference laboratory services to Maryland hospitals and laboratories at the lowest possible cost. The scope of services was dictated by demand for laboratory procedures that, by virtue of high cost, low volume, or technical difficulty, lent themselves to performance on a regional basis. Prior to its inception, hospitals had two options: (1) send the specimens to the city morgue to wait their turn, or (2) ship them to California to be analyzed. Both alternatives were costly and time-consuming. This situation produced delays due to the wait for test results. Both factors affected the cost of health care, particularly the latter, by increasing the length of hospitalization. Availability of a local reference laboratory would help avoid extra hospital per item costs that may have exceeded $100 per day and thus should provide a significant and measurable contribution to the containment of health-care costs.

Dr. King, founder and stockholder of Redilab, is a chief pathologist at Greater Baltimore Medical Center (GBMC) in Baltimore. While offering his services at the city morgue in forensic medicine, King became acutely aware of the unsatisfied market awaiting a concept such as Redilab. While at the morgue, he was able to measure the volume of specimens going through the morgue and realized that, if this volume represented only a fraction of the work out there, Redilab could survive and thrive. This conclusion prompted Dr. King to research the market more thoroughly and to begin acquiring the support of his local colleagues. King was able to convince these pathologists to invest their time and money in the concept of Redilab.

In 1971, Redilab opened its doors to the Baltimore metropolitan hospital community as the first reference laboratory to offer comprehensive, emergency toxicology services. At the time of its inception, the lab employed 11 people on various levels, ranging from drivers and secretaries to technologists and the laboratory director. The goal of Redilab since its inception has been to achieve a high level of quality, economy, and service in medical laboratory testing. Redilab has remained committed to this goal to such an extent that "Quality, Service, and Economy" form the company logo.

From 1971 to 1979, the company experienced careful but steady growth. Redilab soon outgrew the original York Road location and in 1975, on a seven-acre plot of land in Timonium, Maryland, erected a 16,000 square foot facility. The new building allowed Redilab to expand, as the board had no doubt it would, despite stiffening competition. By 1979, Redilab had expanded its services to include immunology, radioimmunoassay (RIA), special chemistry, and therapeutic drug monitoring. In 1979, Redilab's total assets had grown to $1,714,129 (with service revenues of $2,354,494 and a net income of $161,477) while maintaining a staff of 75 employees. (See Exhibit 1.)

Redilab was able to perform those assays that the hospitals could not do in-house, due to either cost-justification or technical difficulty. Therefore, Redilab

EXHIBIT 1   Redilab, Inc., Organizational Chart, 1980

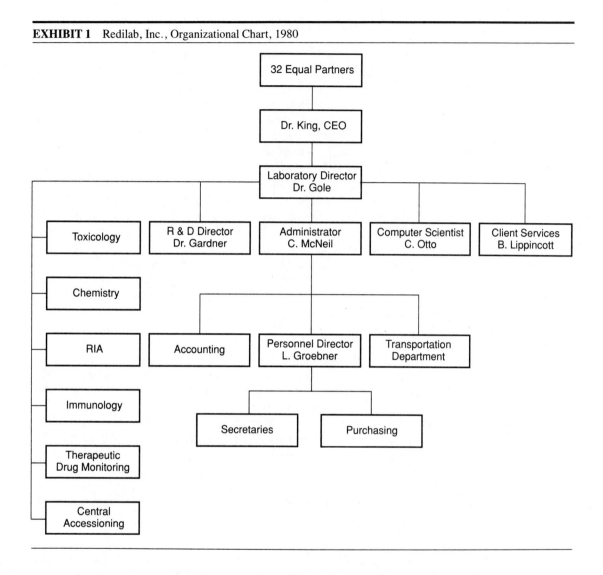

continued to function more as a service than a business, supporting hospitals in a competition-free environment.

By the late 1970s, other laboratories were beginning to compete with Redilab for the Baltimore regional market. These laboratories, both national and regional, offered similar services at competitive and sometimes lower prices. At first glance, the competition seemed formidable. Laboratory Procedures-SmithKline, a subsidiary of Upjohn, reported in 1980 that its own clinical laboratory produced 4 percent of consolidated sales of $1,771,938,000 (with a net income of

$259,854,000 on total assets of $1,554,441,000). Presently, SmithKline sends specimens to King of Prussia, Pennsylvania, for testing.

Metpath was purchased in 1981 by Corning Glass. In 1981, Metpath was the world's largest clinical laboratory (listing revenues of $88,362,000 and net income of $5,593,000 on total assets of $113,768,000). Present testing for Metpath is performed in Teterboro and Hackensack, both in New Jersey. Another large competitor, National Health Laboratories (a subsidiary of Revlon, Inc., with total assets of $2,260,260,000, net income of $196,769,000, and revenues of $2,203,324,000), operates out of Washington, D.C.

Bioscience is another large competitor in the national market. Bioscience is a subsidiary of Dow Chemicals (sales of $10,626,000,000 and a net income of $805,000,000 on total assets of $11,535,000,000). Although Bioscience operates a local laboratory in Columbia, Maryland, no toxicology services are available at that facility, and specimens must be shipped to one of Bioscience's California locations where toxicology is performed.

Notable among these national firms is their lack of local facilities for complete screening, thereby requiring time-consuming transportation of specimens to non-local sites. Mailing or shipping increases the turnaround time for results; in addition, transportation by courier or mail also increases the risk of poor specimen handling such as breakage or leakage or even specimen loss.

Maryland Medical Laboratory, Inc. (MML), however, is located just off the Baltimore beltway in the Catonsville area and appears to be Redilab's most pressing competitor. With a staff of 216 employees and sales of $5 million in 1980, MML is active in the traditional medical market, the industrial market, and also specializes in testing for veterinary medicine.

Although laboratories such as MML were gaining ground in the Baltimore area, they had not been able to loosen Redilab's hold on the hospital market. The competing laboratories were concerned primarily with the physician and industrial markets.

As Redilab continued to grow in the years between 1979 and 1981, it became increasingly apparent that computerization of the laboratory was inevitable if expansion continued at the same rate.

Dr. Gardner

> I can recall one especially stormy supervisor's meeting in 1979, when the supervisor of Central Accessioning — or Login, as we call it — lost her cool about the amount of paperwork, unnecessary phone time, and report completions that she felt were placing an unbearable burden on her staff.

As Gardner thought back to the incident, his memory was as clear as though the hassle had happened yesterday.

THE 1979 MEETING

Joyce Windsor was raising her voice and getting red. "Dr. Gole, I am sure you are aware of the fact that we are receiving close to 300 specimens daily, and I have only two people to help me process them. The current system is ancient and grossly inefficient! The requisition form is next to impossible to read. Handwritten test requests are ridiculous, for us and our clients."

Quieting down, but still clearly very angry, she had continued; "Why should clients have to refer to two different manuals for our test offerings, and then have to scribble the test they wish to order on the requisition? Half of the time, we have no idea what they want, and when we call the hospital to confirm the requests, they do not know who wrote the requisition out in the first place! Although we have requested time and time again that clients print on the requisition, only a handful are doing so, and the rest are getting sick of hearing me complain all the time. Meanwhile, here at Redilab, I've got techs screaming down my back for their specimens so they can begin the afternoon assays and try to get out of here by 5:00. I cannot be expected to satisfy the techs and also be certain that the correct test request is matched with its proper specimen. You have emphasized to me that the most important part of my job is ensuring specimen integrity, and I agree with the critical nature of proper specimen identification and documentation. Then, there is the documentation: It takes one person all afternoon just to place the Redilab six-digit identification number on all three copies of each requisition and match them with the proper specimen. It takes another person an equal amount of time to phone clients to clear up any discrepancies and to distribute the samples to the proper departments. It takes a third person the rest of the afternoon to write in the log book the patient's name, referring laboratory, patient identification numbers and location, test ordered, specimen submitted, time and date of submission, and time and date of specimen collection.

"Dr. Gole, you cannot put people under this kind of pressure. These clerks are paid a pittance over minimum wage to deal with a very high-pressure job. It's not just the amount of work, but the intensity of the work and the consequences of making a mistake. There is no continuity, and frankly, I cannot keep employees longer than a year. My turnover rate is incredible, and you know how long it takes to train a person off the streets in the technical jargon necessary for this position. Finally, we are viewed with contempt by the techs and looked down on because we are not medical technologists. They blame us for the lag time in specimen processing, and it's not us—it's the system!"

Val Indge, chief technologist, had joined in. "Wait a minute, Joyce; you cannot blame the rudeness of a few bad apples on the whole bunch. The majority of the techs understand that it is not your fault, and those who do not, I would like to know about right now. I will see to it that those attitudes come to a screeching halt.''

Then, addressing Dr. Gole, he continued, ''Dr. Gole, I agree with Joyce that something must be done. The techs are not going to be able to handle much more volume with this manual system. In this business, profits are based on costs, and costs are closely tied to volume. Immunology is here every night until 6:30 finishing reports as it is. Not only do we pay highly trained technologists to do clerical paperwork, but in doing so, we introduce human error and inaccuracy into our work. Look at the duplication of documentation that occurs. Each department takes its own specimens and logs them into a binder the same way Login does. This duplication is not unnecessary, Dr. Gole. The techs need one source for all of their work so, when a client calls looking for a result, which they often do, techs don't spend half an hour searching through old worksheets to find it.

''The real nightmare starts when the reports must go out. Not only do the techs have to handwrite results and appropriate units, they also have to include the proper normal ranges and toxic levels depending on the tests, age of the patient, type of specimen, and fasting status. For some tests, composing reports takes close to two hours!

''Dr. Gole, this system was adequate when we were performing only toxicology: Those results were either positive or negative. Now, we perform assays that require lengthy and often complicated interpretive information — we do need a new system!''

LATE 1987

Back in the present, Dr. Gardner continued:

Dr. Gardner

I remember leaving that meeting thinking that the time had come to take a hard look at a computer for Redilab. Each of the supervisors had legitimate complaints, and the office had not even had a chance to voice their concerns yet. I wondered if King would be more open to discussing a computer when he heard those complaints at the senior staff meeting? I remember guessing that he wouldn't be.

HISTORY OF DP AT REDILAB

The issue of computerization has been discussed at Redilab for close to five years; however, Dr. King was not in favor, so the idea never took off.

Dr. King

What scared me about computerization was that a system failure could destroy overnight a reputation that I have spent years to build. Our clients won't accept delays or poor service, regardless of the excuse. In fact, poor response due to systems problems at some of our larger competitors is what drove many of our clients to use our services in the first place. Our customers place quality and service above all other considerations. Price doesn't enter into the equation; they pay for reliability and accuracy. As long as I am the medical director, we will never cut corners or cheapen our product.

I know that our old manual system was time-consuming and labor intensive, but it functioned reasonably well, and our customers liked the direct personal contact with our personnel. Besides, I was not really fully convinced that an expenditure of that size would be cost-justified, or actually result in any improvement in our service at all. Too much blood, sweat, and tears had been invested in this company to throw it all away on a system that was untried and unproven in a medical application.

Dr. Gole

I remember telling King a number of times that as the volume in-house continued to build, the techs were going to have an increasingly difficult time working with the manual system. Not only that, but as reports grew more complex, report quality had deteriorated.

By 1982, King could no longer deny the need for computerization at Redilab. Bill Lippincott, the client services representative, played a big role in presenting the problem in such a way that King finally agreed. Lippincott went on a campaign to obtain client feedback concerning satisfaction with our requisitioning and reporting formats. His finding revealed a major current of client dissatisfaction with these procedures, especially considering that MML and SmithKline were currently offering computerized remote report transmission to their clients.

Bill Lippincott

We're in a service business. Our success is a direct result of responding to our customers' needs promptly using all available resources. I've spent 10 years in the medical business. The sum of that experience boils down to one tenet; the name of the game is quality and service. We've built this business from the ground up through intense personal contacts and a reputation for quality. The competition is too strong for us to take any of our accounts for granted or to be slow in responding to their needs. Out in the field, I'd been getting a lot of feedback from clients requesting clearer, more legible reports and direct transmission of results to decrease turnaround time. Although we hadn't been hit hard by our competition up 'til then, this gap in our service was going to cost us valuable clients in the long run. I had nightmares (and still do) of SmithKline moving into our local market and absconding with our larger established accounts after dazzling them with all sorts of sophisticated technology.

I'm not talking penny-ante business either; our clients average between $100,000 and $200,000 annually. If we're going to remain viable and compete, we are going to have to keep up with the times. Our customers need the improved service that computerization of test results can provide; if we were not willing to take that step, you can bet they would have gone to our competitors who were willing to respond to their needs.

Finally, King consented, begrudgingly, to support Redilab's computerization. After board approval in November of 1982, Redilab began the process of deciding whether to design a software system or to buy one of the laboratory software packages currently on the market.

Dr. Gole

It was no surprise to me that this computer decision was handled very informally; that's the way we do business around here. Redilab's loosely defined corporate structure was designed to allow King to act as the sole decision maker. Nothing involving money or technological change is ever initiated without King's stamp of approval. Lord above, we hold senior staff meetings with him every Tuesday, just so he can keep abreast of every last piece of news concerning the lab. About this hardware decision, now that I think about it, the whole thing was a bit of a charade. The decision to design our own system was predetermined; more than that, it was based on the programmer, Otto, who just happened to be working for Redilab at the time. Claude Otto had done various programming jobs for us in the past five years, small jobs on the Abbott Analyzers or the SMAC 1260. Although he began his education in physics, he obtained his masters in biomedical engineering from Johns Hopkins and was currently finishing his PhD in Computer Sciences also at Hopkins. Even with this educational background, he had never officially worked as a computer programmer. In fact, his only other job had been with St. Agnes Hospital as a R&D technician.

Dr. King

I realized Claude had never worked as a programmer, much less designed a system from the ground up before, but I felt strongly that his extensive knowledge of the laboratory would prove much more valuable to this organization in the long run. Computers were — and are — Claude's life; he had even taught graduate computer classes while working on his PhD at Hopkins. Believe me, I had inquired from his colleagues, and he had received the highest recommendations from all of them. What I'm trying to say is that I gave Claude a free hand with the project; it was to be his baby. I know we could have bought a software package and saved time, but would it suit our needs in the long run? I was very involved with GBMC's software purchase decision, and through that experience, I saw a lot of systems and learned a lot about how unique the computer needs of a laboratory are. Although I am happy with the system at GBMC, I do not feel that a reference laboratory could work within those limitations. Redilab needs a system with tremendous flexibility, adaptability, as well as reliability, and I just don't think we are going to be able to buy those things.

Early in December 1982, Claude was placed in charge of conducting a feasibility study of possible computer vendors and recommending the vendor most suitable to Redilab's computer needs, using the criteria of flexibility, reliability, and adaptability.

DP AT REDILAB

On January 20, 1983, the board approved the purchase of a Perkin-Elmer 3220 supermini mainframe based on Claude's recommendation. This project, considered high risk, also approved the hiring of Claude as computer scientist. His responsibilities would include computer systems design, computer programming and testing, computer standards and documentation, and computer operations and maintenance. At that time, no formal plan for implementation was submitted to the board for approval.

Dr. Gole

> It's strange, but this computer project was approached very casually by the board, considering the magnitude of the investment. I must admit, though, Redilab has never really viewed itself as a business, more like a service. Redilab's excellent connections with the medical community through the board of directors, senior staff, and the technical staff have pretty much eliminated the need for aggressive sales on the part of the client services representative. Many marketing functions have been performed through the well-developed channels of communication that exist between the firm and its market. Therefore, the computer project was, initially, just another innovative technological toy to add to Redilab's esoteric playpen. In the board's mind, it was not approved to maintain a competitive edge but to further upgrade the high quality of our service. When it came to quality, the decision makers at Redilab felt they had no competitors.

THE DP PLAN

Planning for the computer implementation was accomplished through weeks of meetings between King, Gole, and Claude.

Dr. King

> Dr. Gole and I knew what we wanted the computer to do for the laboratory; it was just a question of translating those needs into a workable laboratory system. We both wanted to see "paperless" tech benches. I envisioned a computer that would enable Login to enter patient demographics from the test requisition form. This entry would result in the automatic generation of assay worksheets for the individual departments. On Tuesday morning, Debbie in Immunology would simply key in Alpha Fetoprotein; a worksheet with patient ID numbers would print out, and she could go about her work. No more bulky stacks of illegible patient requisitions for highly skilled technologists to wade through. When the assay is complete, the technologist simply enters the results into the computer, they are certified by another technologist who checks for errors; with the push of a key, reports are composed and transmitted to the appropriate hospitals automatically.

Claude Otto

> I nearly had a heart attack when Dr. King first proposed such a system back in July of '82. It took me some time to get across to them that the computer would need months of manual checks by technologists to prevent any bugs from slipping through, resulting in erroneous reports, and possibly damaging the reputation for quality that Redilab values above all else. This system was ideal, but, for practicality, it would have to be accomplished in several smaller less innovative steps.

THE SCS SYSTEM

Claude outlined the system he had designed; it included a login/enter composition program, and was called the Specimen Control System (SCS)

Claude

This was to be a practical but sophisticated system designed to prevent any specimen mishandling and erroneous result entry or reporting to ever reach the client in the form of an incorrect report. When in place, the system would be absolutely crucial to the daily operations of Redilab. Our business depends on adhering to turnaround times as many of our assays are done on an ASAP or STAT basis. Once the operations became computerized, downtime would result in our inability to enter results and consequently to transmit these results to our clients.

King decided that Claude would submit a proposal for each project in the system, describing how it related to the total picture, as well as the financial and computer resources that would be necessary to achieve the plan. The proposal would include a deadline, to be approved by the senior staff, and Claude's adherence to the deadline would be monitored by Dr. Gole. It would be Gole's responsibility to manage the system development, design, and implementation, and to periodically check Claude's progress to ensure continued adherence to system goals. Gole was to report these findings to Dr. King during weekly senior staff meetings.

Dr. Gole

My control over Claude did not consist of formal weekly or monthly meetings to discuss his progress. Claude's office was right next to mine, and I saw him every day; any formalized control was really not necessary.

Claude felt that it was not necessary to design a system for accounting or accounts receivable because these functions have no unique qualities that would warrant a specially designed computer system. According to him, there was no reason why software could not be purchased for these purposes. Invoicing was another matter, however, as our test pricing is extremely complicated. The manual system presently used at Redilab depends entirely on the two secretaries who have both been with the company for over five years. They have memorized complicated client specific pricings, serial pricings, and profile or combination test pricing. Therefore, invoicing was an area that would require a separate system design effort.

Eric Gordon (senior technologist)

The computer's arrival caused a real uproar among the staff. Everyone was dying to see the computer do its first trick. The excitement was at its peak when Claude chose one representative from each department to help him determine what color screen each CRT should have. You could definitely say that in the beginning, Claude and the computer had overwhelming user support.

DP at Redilab officially began in November 1983 when the gamma counter in the radioimmunoassay section was interfaced with the computer using a protocol program. A gamma counter is used extensively in RIA procedures because the assays are based on detecting the amount of radioactivity in a patient sample. The manual system involved taking hundreds of raw counts from the gamma counter and performing many tedious mathematical calculations and graphings to obtain meaningful patient results. With the computer, the counts were fed into the computer, and patient results were calculated and printed out automatically.

From November 1983 through September 1984, Claude was busy formulating, selecting, and designing an appropriate systems approach for the SCS system. Claude's estimated completion date for this system had been June 1984. Though he'd be under considerable pressure to finish in time, Claude was against hiring a programmer to be his assistant; however, he was training Eric Gordon, one of the senior technologists, to do some of the ''grunt'' work for him.

Dr. Gole

> I felt from the very beginning that Claude was going to need some help, technical help from another programmer, not from a medical technologist who has never worked with a computer before. Claude resisted this suggestion vehemently, and Dr. King chose to go along with him.

Redilab had functioned effectively for some time using the manual system, and although there was little internal pressure to bring SCS on-line, pressure was building from the outside to computerize reports.

Lippincott, having been told that Redilab would be computerized by June 1984, had been promising clients computerized reports and remote report transmissions for almost a year. In September, three months beyond the proposed completion date, Lippincott was becoming extremely concerned about Redilab's credibility with its clients. One $300,000 account, Sacred Heart Hospital, was particularly troublesome. By November 1984, Lippincott had serious doubts about that hospital's staying power. Armed with this information, Lippincott went directly to King. At that time, King had ''about had it up to here with this whole computer project.''

It had been over a year since the computer's installation at Redilab, and Dr. King had seen only a protocol program for radioimmunoassay procedures. He had heard very little in the way of feedback from Gole; although he knew part of the blame was his, he began to wonder if this whole project was going to work. He wanted the clients to see and appreciate the benefits; and with Lippincott's information concerning Sacred Heart, he decided to give Claude an ultimatum.

Dr. Gole

> King came back and chewed me out for not keeping on top of the computer project and accused me of mismanaging Claude. King gave Claude exactly 30 days to put together a program that would allow us to transmit computer-generated reports to Sacred Heart Hospital.

Under fire, Claude decided to piecemeal or jerry-rig a program designed to produce reports solely for Sacred Heart. This was in spite of Claude's misgivings (not voiced) that such an approach would cause major integration problems in the future.

On January 1, 1985, Redilab transmitted its first report to Sacred Heart Hospital; the report-generating program was not a workable system for the entire lab by any means!

Eric

> What Claude did was to create a program called "HEART" that allowed Sacred Heart's patients to be logged in, with reports composed and transmitted by the computer. The techs would write the test results on the report for Sacred Heart, give those reports to me, and I would compose them. The system was very crude; in fact, its only benefit was it allowed us to produce a computer-generated report. It took considerably more time to compose reports using the computer than it did to compose them manually. At this time, I was the only technologist who could use the computer; the other users were the two login clerks who could operate the simple login program to enter patient demographics. A typical report would involve the following steps:
>
> **1.** I would create a file consisting of the ID numbers for Dilantin, for instance, by entering those ID numbers into the computer and giving the file a name such as "dilantin.com."
>
> **2.** I would then have to go back into the computer and call up "dilantin.com"; the computer would then give me the report's shell consisting of five lines of patient demographics on top, and Paul Gole's name and title on the bottom line.
>
> **3.** Each assay result had a file, in this instance called "dilantin. result," which inserted a line similar to the following:
> Dilantin . . . . ####mg/dl
> It would also contain the normal ranges and any interpretive information necessary for the report. I then had to manually substitute a numerical result for the hatch marks.
>
> **4.** This process had to be repeated for every report.
>
> **5.** After composing each report, I had to go back and use a very crude transmission program to transmit the reports to Sacred Heart's remote printer. The process of composing reports in this manner was more complicated with some reports than with others, but the whole process still took me close to seven hours each day.

DP staff worked from January 1985 through August 1985 to maintain and expand the program for Sacred Heart Hospital. By the end of 1985, five additional hospitals had been added to the Heart program. During 1985, several extremely cumbersome assay reports, including lengthy interpretations, were computerized.

Eric

> By the close of 1985, many of our users had begun composing their own reports on the computer using the Heart program. This was despite the fact that there had been no formal orientation program on how to use the system. Much of my time was spent explaining the procedure to the techs, which severely cut down on my productivity.

Claude Otto was sitting in his office, which was more of a glorified closet, replete with keyboards and CRT screens. Printouts were piled one on top of another on, alongside and under the desk. Along the back wall he had built a bookcase that was overflowing with Perkin-Elmer operations and software manuals. Beside the window was a large framed picture of Mickey Mouse and the rest of his band from the Magic Kingdom of Disney World. On the desk was a multicompartmented storage cabinet filled with electronic computer components that always seem to fail at the worst time. Claude didn't trust factory-trained service representatives to work on his system; he did all the service work himself.

Claude

I warned Dr. King that, once I brought an unfinished system like Heart on-line, it would require almost all of my attention for maintenance and would hinder me from bringing SCS on-line. I also predicted that the techs would request new applications that would seem justified in the short run, but in the long run would also prolong completion of SCS. My warnings were disregarded.

It wasn't until March of 1986 that the SCS program was on-line and operational. The program was still technically incomplete, however, because most reports still required manual editing during composition, and transmissions were still being done by Eric.

From March 1986 to December 1986, Claude worked primarily on minor operations maintenance and "fine-tuning the system;" in the words of Eric, "he did nothing at all." SCS still had not been completed, users still did not have access to open files, computerized invoicing had not even been started, and King had reached his limit. On December 7, 1986, King asked for Dr. Gole's resignation (see Exhibit 2).

Dr. King

I was very dissatisfied with the delays involved in implementing the system and getting it on-line. For the amount of money we invested and the manpower spent, I felt that Dr. Gole, in his role as administrator, should have made an attempt to control the situation. Never again do I want this company placed in the position of losing a valuable account due to project mismanagement.

I don't blame Claude for the situation. He is a very talented individual and also dedicated. I place the responsibility squarely on Dr. Gole's shoulders. He failed to establish effective lines of communication with Claude on the progress of the project. By not doing so he was unable to establish any effective means of control. He never realized the tremendous potential of what we were undertaking.

Jerry Gardner will be a much more effective manager than Gole. He's been with us from the beginning and has a very good rapport with the staff. Most of all, he is someone I can count on to get things done. He doesn't have to resort to pressure tactics or histrionics to make his point. That is a very important attribute when you are dealing with highly educated people with very fragile egos. I like to think of our lab as an extended family with wide open channels of communication from the top down. Gole got away from that philosophy. The situation had to be on the brink of catastrophe before he would take any affirmative action or even consult with the personnel involved.

Dr. Gole

With the advantage of 20/20 hindsight, perhaps we went about it all wrong. We were breaking new ground, and neither King nor I had any real experience with systems implementation. Our background is in medicine, not digital engineering or systems analysis. King felt that Claude knew what he was doing and trusted his judgment.

EXHIBIT 2   Redilab, Inc., Organizational Chart, 1987

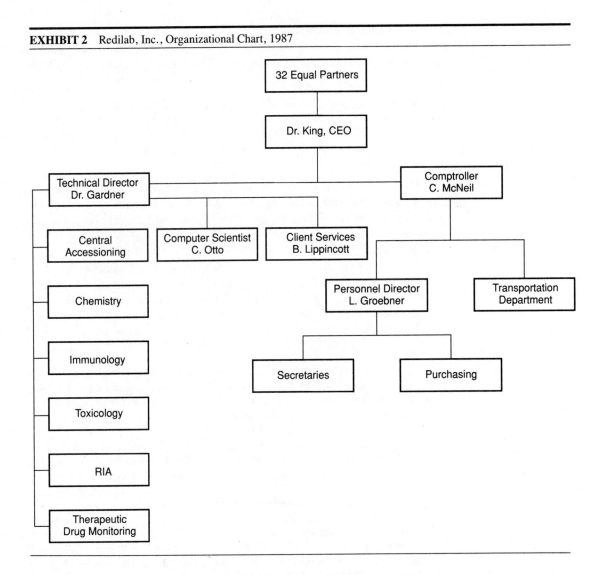

King, Claude, and I reached an informal understanding on what we needed and wanted. Because of our extensive background in toxicology and laboratory testing, we didn't feel there was a need to consult the technologists or our customers to tell us what we already knew. We trusted Claude to do the implementation. We made the mistake of letting Claude set his own timetable and manpower estimates. You must understand that Claude is a unique individual. You have to tread lightly around him, or you'll get nothing productive out of him for a week. The man's a near-genius and damn good at what he does, but I sometimes wonder if he has any comprehension of what goes on in the real world. He doesn't realize that deadlines have to be met and that benefits have to be weighed against costs. He would always insist on perfection, when we could have gotten along with "good enough" and saved time and money in the bargain.

I don't feel that the lengthy implementation process has done the company any real harm. We are still expanding within our own market niche, and our long-term relationship with our established accounts has not suffered in the least. Of course, the ultimatum from Sacred Heart shook things up a little, and we had to light a fire under Claude in order to save that account. It was his fault though, because he set the timetable and then couldn't live up to it after Lippincott had stuck his neck out to the client. Claude compressed 10 years of work into 1 to get the Heart program on-line. I was afraid the man was going to have a breakdown for a while there. Afterwards, his production did fall off dramatically, but I had more pressing matters to look after. If Claude wanted to continue reinventing the wheel until he reached perfection, more power to him; I had a lab to run. Besides, because of his close relationship to King, I tried to maintain a hands-off policy towards him and his work as best I could. If I pressed him too hard, all he had to do was pick up the phone and give King a call to get my orders overridden. I preferred to save my credibility and influence for battles that had to be won, ones that had strategic corporate importance, not the shenanigans of Claude Otto.

Jerry Gardner

As the new director, my first priority has to be this computer project. There's got to be some way to get a handle on it. My easy rapport with Claude will certainly be beneficial in establishing effective control. The question is, how do I build controls into an administrative policy that will accomplish my objective without stepping on Claude's toes?

QUESTIONS

1. Can Dr. Gardner build effective controls into his administrative policies without stepping on Claude's toes? How?
2. Should Dr. Gardner insist that he be given complete authority over Claude? How should he do this—memo, telephone, or in person?
3. What are Dr. Gardner's alternatives in dealing with Claude?
4. Was it a mistake to hire Claude in January 1983? Why or why not?
5. Should Dr. Gardner fire Claude? Support your answer.
6. Did Joyce Windsor have a legitimate complaint? How would you respond to her outburst?
7. What is your opinion of Redilab's system application development approval process and procedures? Explain.
8. Evaluate Claude's Specimen Control System (SCS). If you were Dr. Gardner and wanted to change it, how would you approach Claude?
9. How should Dr. King solve Redilab's problem, or is *he* the problem?

Case 6-2 Southern Lodges, Inc.

Early in August 1985, Dennis Bennett, the vice president of Computer Information Systems (CIS), was getting ready for his meeting with Steve Sawin, chairman of the board, Bob Walters, the controller, and Rob Bain, vice president of Finance. Bennett was concerned about the possible solutions to many CIS problems that had been piling up on his desk. He hadn't decided on one solution for a single problem. Many issues were involved, and much was at stake.

As the time for the meeting approached, more and more questions came to mind. Are my assumptions correct? Am I forgetting something crucial? Would a change in my management style be an appropriate solution for any of the problems? *Could* I change my management style? Did I make a major slip somewhere, that no one has pointed out to me? Should I tighten my control of the computer resources? Maybe it's not me at all—should I fire Rick Wallace, the director of Computer Development, or Pat Dawson, the director of Data Processing Operations, or even both of them? What should I do about the tremendous increase in user demand now, and how do I plan to handle future increases? What is the best way to plan our utilization of the computer resources we have now? What's the most effective way to serve the Finance departments and our other users?

Bennett entered the conference room for the meeting, still turning over the problems and alternatives in his mind and wondering how much to pass on to the others—how to approach them with a real can of worms.

COMPANY BACKGROUND

Southern Lodges, Inc., was founded in 1968 by its present chairman of the board, Steve Sawin. Southern Lodges, Inc., is a holding company with major investments in the health-care and hospitality industries. Through its headquarters in Washington, D.C., Southern Lodges, Inc., provides corporate and administrative staff plus legal, accounting, and data processing services to its principal subsidiaries.

The company has been growing rapidly; sales in 1985 were $454 million with net earnings of $30 million. As Exhibit 1 illustrates, only five years earlier, sales were $92 million with net earnings of $7 million. Growth has continued from year to year, with a 25 percent increase in sales in 1985 compared to 1984. Net income in 1985 was even higher, 32 percent over 1984.

The rapid expansion indicates the success of a combination of development and

---

This case was prepared by Rob Hoffman and Sandy Murray; the case was revised and updated by Eduardo Caillaux. Names, locations, and financial data have been disguised.

EXHIBIT 1 Financial and Operating Highlights, Southern Lodges, Inc., and Subsidiaries

Years Ended August 31
(in thousands, except per share data)

	1986	1985	1984	1983	1982	1981
Total revenues	$637,485	$541,643	$427,628	$386,877	$279,083	$116,307
Net income	$43,348	$36,004	$26,937	$18,972	$11,824	$8,761
Average shares outstanding	30,486	28,270	28,108	25,611	21,119	16,445
Net income per common share	1.42	1.27	.96	.72	.53	.53
Dividends per common share	.19	.17	.14	.11	.08	
Market price range: high–low	32½–14⅞	27⅝–13½	21–12½	17–6⅝	10½–6¼	8⅛–2
Funds provided from operations	$75,164	$80,767	$61,188	$40,235	$27,551	$12,514
Funds invested in property and equipment	$81,770	$60,128	$62,212	$37,511	$36,614	$8,512
Total assets	$849,713	$708,716	$616,484	$505,691	$480,422	$160,667
Long-term debt	$315,667	$346,213	$373,122	$315,640	$320,158	$91,674
Stockholders' equity	$143,489	$133,159	$116,601	$98,637	$53,360	$43,654
Financial measurements:						
Income from operations as a percent of revenue	18.7%	18.4%	17.4%	16.6%	15.5%	15.1%
Net income as a percent of revenue	6.8	6.7	6.3	5.0	4.2	7.5
Return on average assets employed	5.5	5.2	4.7	4.4	2.8	5.7
Return on average stockholders' equity	26.4	25.0	23.0	24.6	22.2	25.2
Current ratio	1.5:1	1.4:1	1.4:1	2.2:1	1.3:1	2.1
Long-term debt to equity ratio	2.2:1	2.6:1	3.2:1	3.2:1	6.0:1	2.1:1
Operating data:						
Healthcare beds in operation	20,442	19,808	19,995	14,385	14,601	4,018
Lodging:						
Franchised rooms	84,578	72,289	62,860	52,206	49,371	42,020
Company-operated or managed rooms	5,250	5,895	6,758	6,010	5,470	5,010
Number of employees	20,100	19,500	18,800	15,575	18,000	5,800

acquisitions. During 1985, Southern Healthcare Corporation added newly constructed nursing centers having 500 additional beds to the operating system. Another nursing center, containing 120 beds, is under construction in California. The board has approved plans to construct nine more new nursing centers containing 1,400 beds, and the company intends to add 600 beds in existing centers.

Hotel Franchising added 85 hotels, representing 9,500 guest rooms, during 1985; it plans to continue this aggressive selling of franchises at a pace of 10,000 plus rooms per year. In accordance with stated strategic objectives, any company-owned hotels that do not meet criteria for investment returns are sold. Five hotels were sold during 1985 for a pre-tax gain of $5 million. The cash proceeds were used to expand the operations and repay debt.

Also, in 1985, Southern Lodges increased its ownership interest in the King of Wales Hotels in the United Kingdom; therefore, it has an excellent opportunity to expand the franchise system throughout Europe.

The three major subsidiaries of Southern Lodges, Inc., are: Southern Healthcare Corporation; Southern Lodges International, Inc.; and Southern Lodges and Inns.

Southern Healthcare Corporation is a premier provider of long-term care services, operating nursing centers nationwide. It also operates acute-care hospitals, retirement living units, and pharmacy outlets. Healthcare Corporation is the fourth largest provider of long-term care services in the United States. In fiscal year 1985, it increased its revenues by 48 percent from the previous year. Exhibit 2 shows selected financial information for the Healthcare subsidiary.

Recent high rates of growth are expected to continue due to the population trends of the elderly in the United States. Southern Healthcare has a high percentage of private paying patients, which insulates the company somewhat from ever-changing government reimbursement regulations. The company's objectives in this area are to: (1) increase the private pay census and occupancy, (2) expand nursing center operations by acquisitions and new development, and (3) to provide retirement campuses.

Southern Lodges International franchises hotels in Canada, Mexico, and Europe. In 1985, Southern Lodges International had its best year, in terms of revenues, earnings, and quality improvement. Overall reservation dollar sales rose 40 percent in 1985. Exhibit 3 has selected financial data for the lodging subsidiaries.

Southern Lodges and Inns owns and operates hotels and resorts and provides managerial assistance to other owners. These hotels are located in the 48 continental United States.

Continued improvement in product quality and service is the best assurance of guest satisfaction and is also the corporation's strongest defense against the competition. Its record growth has enabled Southern Lodges, Inc., to implement a progressively demanding quality assurance program. The corporate objectives in this area are to proceed with expansion of the franchise system worldwide and to divest hotels that are not providing adequate returns.

EXHIBIT 2 Healthcare Financial Results

	Years Ending August 31, (in thousands)					
	1986	1985	1984	1983	1982	1981
Healthcare revenues	$501,188	$418,853	$316,745	$287,262	$190,641	$71,201
Income from operations	$113,770	$88,797	$67,150	$58,859	$32,650	$15,949
Healthcare operating margin	22.7%	21.2%	21.2%	20.5%	17.1%	22.4%
Number of healthcare beds	20,442	19,808	19,995	14,385	14,601	4,018
Percentage of private paying patients in nursing centers	59%	60%	59%	56%	56%	60%
Average nursing center occupancy, excluding newly opened facilities	90%	90%	93%	93%	95%	93%
Nursing center patient days	6,291,000	5,823,000	4,519,000	4,718,000	3,329,000	1,221,000

	August 31, 1986		August 31, 1985		August 31, 1984	
Facilities	Number of Units	Number of Beds	Number of Units	Number of Beds	Number of Units	Number of Beds
Nursing centers						
Owned	130	16,798	125	16,264	108	14,261
Leased	26	3,106	26	3,006	30	3,407
Managed	2	238	2	238	17	2,011
Total nursing centers	158	20,142	153	19,508	155	19,679
Acute-care general hospital	1	180	1	180	1	180
Alcoholic rehabilitation specialty hospitals	4	120	4	120	5	136
Total all facilities	163	20,442	158	19,808	161	19,995

EXHIBIT 3   Lodging Financial Results

			Years Ended August 31 *(in thousands)*			
	1986	*1985*	*1984*	*1983*	*1982*	*1981*
Lodging revenues	$136,297	$122,790	$110,883	$99,615	$88,442	$45,116
Income from operations	$19,218	$15,472	$9,314	$10,161	$12,736	$10,151
Lodging operating margin	14.1%	12.6%	8.4%	10.2%	14.4%	22.5%

Southern Lodges and its subsidiaries employ over 18,000 personnel, full- and part-time, primarily at the outlying nursing facilities. Approximately 400 employees work at the corporate headquarters, and approximately 150 more are employed at the two regional operational control centers in the Midwest and Southwest. Another 125 employees work in the Hotel Reservation Center in Los Angeles, California.

CORPORATE CULTURE

The culture of the firm stems largely from the authoritative top-down structure created by Steve Sawin, chairman of the board, when he formed the company. Sawin, then 38 years old, built the organization from the ground up by mortgaging his home to obtain the financing for several nursing facilities and partial interest in a small motel chain. The investment proved to be more and more profitable, as he plowed the profits back into the firm. In 1966, he bought out all substantial interests in the lodging chain and continued to expand the nursing centers. Due to several acquisitions, the stock price skyrocketed over the succeeding years. Totally committed to building Southern Lodges, Inc., into a profitable, ongoing business, Sawin has attempted, quite successfully, to remain active in all major decisions affecting the company.

The authoritarian structure permeates the entire company, creating an environment in which information is passed from lower and middle departmental lines to upper-level supervisors. The upper-level supervisors then pass the decisions and policy information down to subordinates in their departments. The vertical flow creates an atmosphere of extreme top-down control within the firm and seriously inhibits communication of detail between departments.

HISTORY OF CIS

Southern Lodges had no formal CIS department before the merger of the Healthcare and Lodging segments of the firm. Computer applications were applied exclusively to basic accounting functions such as payroll, accounts receivable, accounts payable, fixed assets, and general ledger, which were all contracted outside the firm on different systems. Subsequent to the merger, an IBM main-frame was purchased; some of the accounting functions, specifically general ledger, payroll, and accounts payable, were installed on the IBM. The first major acquisition (a group of 33 nursing centers) in 1980 added further to the conversions necessary to automate and standardize systems because the books, records, and all analyses for these facilities had been performed manually.

In 1981, Southern Lodges acquired 70 more nursing centers that were already partially automated in their reporting and record-keeping capabilities; with the purchase shortly thereafter of another 12 diversified, unrelated subsidiaries, top executives updated plans regarding automation and conversion of CIS systems. CIS's system development plans were complicated further by the addition of another large mainframe system included in the purchase package. Due to the nature and size of the acquired businesses, management decided that the pur-chased computer obtained in the acquisition should be moved to corporate head-quarters and utilized for all entities in the future.

Due to the numerous types of computers, operating systems, languages, and applications used during the 1980 to 1982 period, the firm decided to purchase its first personal computer, a Radio Shack TRS-80. The PC was to be a "quick and dirty" solution, consolidating figures from the various incompatible corporate group summaries, as well as performing several budgetary functions. In 1983, the first on-line operating systems were set up allowing for on-line inquiries of accounts payable, payroll, and general ledger detail balances for the 70 nursing centers acquired in 1980. By 1984, the systems for the other 85 pre-1980 nursing centers were converted. The primary corporations and operating entities within the lodging division were converted at the same time.

Currently, conversions of the systems are still in progress. The accounts re-ceivable duties for all the subsidiaries continue to be subcontracted out to external computer processing firms. Also, fixed asset and various other accounting and financial functions for certain groups of subsidiaries continue to be processed outside the company.

There are approximately 79 terminals in the corporate headquarters buildings. They provide data entry capabilities via batch processing, on-line data inquiry for current transactions, and personal computer applications subject to mainframe constraints.

Southern Lodges has 21 personal computers, primarily IBM PCs, but also including some Apples, Macintoshs, and Radio Shacks; the PCs are in the nu-merous headquarters departments, including Tax, Reimbursements, Budget, Pur-chasing, Real Estate, Construction, Office Services, Marketing, Healthcare Operations, and Lodging Operations. Although these machines are used for many functions, no one knows which applications are proper utilizations of these machines or which may be more readily performed on the mainframe system.

The responsibility for control and approval of major hardware and software acquisitions, as well as PC acquisitions, rests with the vice president of CIS.

However, these expenditures are also reviewed by the vice president of Finance and the chairman of the board. The vice president of CIS also has functional responsibility for the Lodging Reservations system.

There are two separate computer systems linked through telecommunications networks. These systems include T1 Multiplexers, Datatel Model DCP 9900s, one communications controller, four cluster controllers—IBM Model 3274, and one communications control center produced by Racal-Milgo (which controls 1200 bps modems). The telecommunications network processes in excess of 10 million calls per year, these functions being a service to the individual franchisees of the lodging division. The Reservations department reports to the vice president of Operations of Southern Inns International, Inc.; however, investment considerations and additional capital outlays for both software and hardware—as well as analysis regarding the purchase decisions—are the responsibility of the vice president of CIS.

CIS ORGANIZATION

The CIS department is headed by Dennis Bennett, vice president of CIS, who reports to Rob Bain, senior vice president of Finance. See Exhibit 4 for the organization chart. Rick Wallace, director of CIS Computer Development, and Patrick Dawson, director of CIS DP Operations, report to the vice president of CIS. See Exhibit 5 for the present organization structure of CIS.

The director of CIS Computer Development has four programming managers who report to him; this group processes requests to enhance the current CIS systems, providing solutions to problems received via problem logs, furnishing maintenance program development, and investigating new systems possibilities. Each of the four programming managers supervises four programmers, bringing the total of CIS Development personnel to 21.

The director of CIS DP Operations is responsible for all processing and scheduling of reports, as well as other functions related to operations. There are approximately 35 people in this department, from skilled operators to unskilled clerks.

An instructor at the Training Center (located in the CIS building) educates and trains the CIS users, primarily teaching programming languages and computer processing. The instructor has a BS degree in Computer Science. The Training Center, established in 1987, has two IBM personal computers and two on-line terminals; each one must be reserved on a first-come, first-served, basis.

Operations personnel from the Healthcare and Lodging divisions use the Training Center machines frequently for regular job functions and projects. Financial department personnel are typically unable to schedule training on CIS systems and IBM personal computers, due to the lack of machine availability and the distance between CIS and the departments, which are located in separate buildings.

EXHIBIT 4 Organization Chart

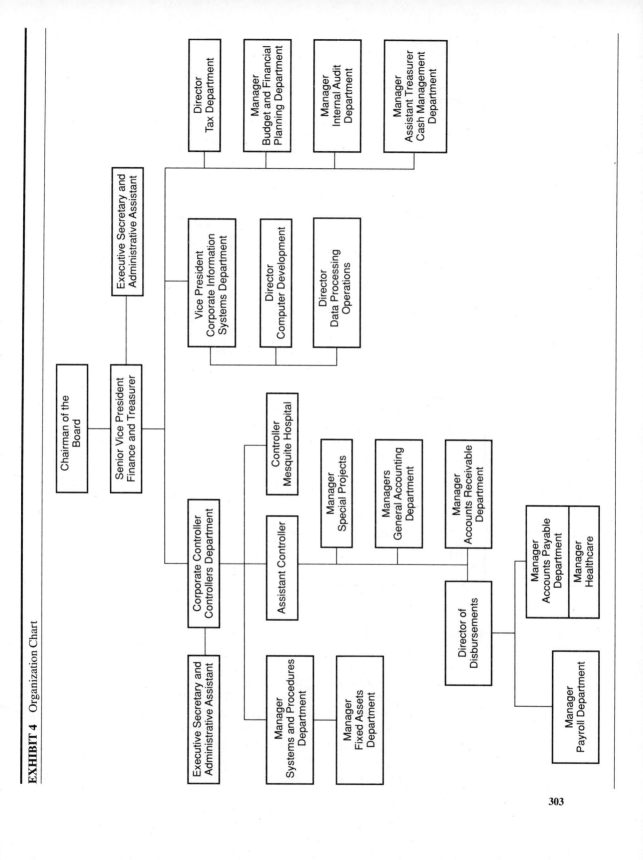

303

EXHIBIT 5   CIS Organization Chart

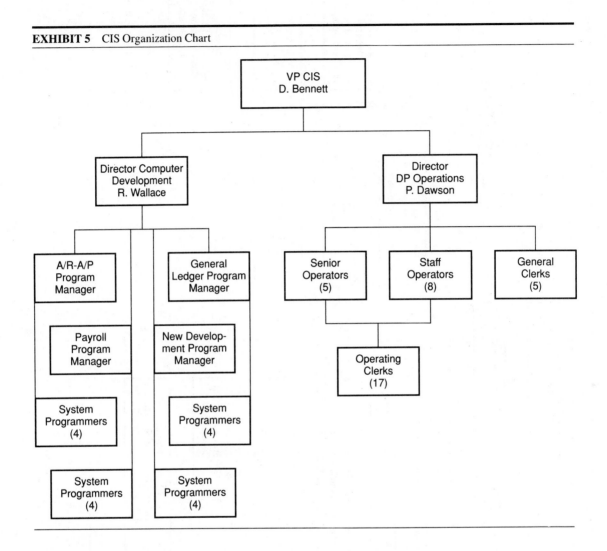

BACKGROUND OF KEY MANAGEMENT AT SOUTHERN LODGES, INC.

The controller of the firm, Bob Walters, is 39 years old and joined the firm as a special projects manager in 1975; he moved into the controller position in 1981. He had several years of experience as a senior level auditor at a regional CPA firm and holds both a CPA and an MBA. While his demeanor is dignified and serious, he appears at ease, both with his position and responsibilities.

The vice president of CIS, Dennis Bennett, is 55 years old and holds a BS degree in Computer Science, as well as an MBA that he earned in night school

15 years ago. Before his appointment as vice president of CIS two years ago, he had been the Computers Operations division supervisor for a large independent computer processing firm.

The controller and vice president of CIS both report to the senior vice president of Finance, Rob Bain, who is 58 years old and holds an MBA that he received in 1955. His exposure to CIS has been minimal except for the reports that cross his desk on a daily basis and staff meetings concerning CIS and other firm operations.

The director of Computer Development, Rick Wallace, is 36 years old and holds an MS degree in Computer Science. He has been the director for two years; for two years prior to that, he was a program manager, supervising three junior programmers. The position of director of Computer Development is new; therefore, he is the only person ever to hold that position. Prior to his employment at Southern Lodges, Inc., he was a programmer for several private software firms at various levels and positions, but he had little supervisory experience. He is currently enrolled in an MBA evening program and is well-liked and respected for his technical competence, within CIS and by other departments as well.

The director of DP Operations, Patick Dawson, is 37 years old, has been with the firm for three-and-a-half years, and was hired as the director. Previously, he was assistant supervisor for a large data processing center of a very large metropolitan bank. He has approximately 10 years' experience with the bank, starting as a computer operator. He has a BS in Computer Science. He is well-liked by his own people and other department managers. His supervision, particularly overall control and operational efficiency, has been questioned.

ACCOUNTING AND FINANCIAL FUNCTIONS PERFORMED BY CIS

Accounts payable on-line inquiry is available for determining accounts payable balances within a two-week period. Cycles of the payables are run on a biweekly basis. These reports provide transaction inquiries for the previous 60 days. The accounts payable conversion files utilize all invoice information including invoice dates, due dates, check dates, amounts, account numbers, and vendor names and numbers that are integrated throughout the accounting systems to provide general ledger as well as other operating reports.

Accounts receivable detail is processed primarily outside the firm through an independent computer processing company. Input for the accounts receivable system is submitted by mail to headquarters personnel, who transmit the data by courier to the computer processing firm. Likewise, cash receipts are coded and sent to the processing firm that calculates accounts receivable balances; from there, ledgers and schedules of accounts receivable aging are created on a bi-monthly basis. Magnetic tapes are transmitted to and from the processing firm in order to integrate accounts receivable with the company's mainframe system.

Several times, the tapes have been misprocessed or mislabeled, causing problems with the reports.

Payroll is processed entirely in-house with the payrolls of the facilities being performed on an alternative biweekly basis. The payroll system is integrated with the general ledger accounting systems. It provides W-2's as well as information required to complete payroll returns for the approximately 200 corporations that are subsidiaries of the holding company.

Monthly reports providing financial information of profit and loss are generated, indicating direct gross profit margins as well as management fees and uncontrolled costs charges to individual subsidiaries. These reports provide monthly data for current actual, budget, and prior year, as well as year-to-date data for current actual, budget, and prior year.

Communication of enhancements to the computer systems, and programs and problems occurring within the current systems, are made via enhancement requests and problem logs. These forms are sent directly to the CIS director of Computer Development and program manager for New Development through the corporate internal mail system. The forms are then logged in, prioritized, and distributed to appropriate programming managers along with estimated times required to complete the projects.

The charges back to individual departments are allocated on the basis of computer usage rather than on a project basis, unless the project is very large. Upon resolution, copies of the solution are forwarded to the user department head and also are filed within the CIS department. Examples of these forms may be found in Exhibit 6.

CIS is strategically important to the firm in both its internal and external reporting functions because a large portion of the firm's revenue is generated through reimbursements from the government medicaid/medicare programs. The forms must be accurate and supportable in order to substantiate data during audits; additionally, these reports are needed to track cash flows and to determine appropriate revenues earned. Meeting the time deadlines set by user departments has to be the primary priority. Therefore, since comprehending possible mainframe applications seem to be an insurmountable, time-consuming chore, most reimbursement analysis is being performed on personal computers.

ROLE OF THE IS INTERNAL AUDIT FUNCTION

The IS Internal Audit group develops audit programs and areas of audit examination completely independently of any functional input from user departments. Areas of concentration are selected in conjunction with financial audit work in order to assure an audit situation that is through the CIS system rather than around the system. The IS internal audit function, initiated in late 1987, has only one auditor at the present time, Caron Tate. Caron has outstanding educational and professional credentials, including a BS in Computer Science and a CPA. Also,

EXHIBIT 6 Sample Forms

Enhancement request

ORIGINATOR'S NAME   PHONE NO.   DEPARTMENT   DATE & TIME SUBMITTED

_____   _____   _____   _____ _____

DESC OF REQUEST _____

_____

_____

_____

_____

ATTACHMENTS |---|

REQUEST NO.   ASSIGNED TO   PRIORITY   CONTACT DATE   EST COMPLETE

                                                                                      /   /
_____   _____   _____   _____   _____

BRIEF DESC _____

****BUSINESS AND TECHNICAL ASSESSMENT****

EST SAVINGS   MANPOWER _____ DOLLARS _____

COMMENTS _____

_____

_____

RECOMMENDATION   APPROVE __/__/____   DISAPPROVE __/__/____   DEFER __/__/____

AUTHORIZATION   USER _____ CIS _____

LOAD DATE _____ TIME _____   CLOSED BY _____

ACTUAL MANPOWER _____   CLOSED DATE __/__/____

CIS200_____CIS20C _____CIS20D _____   CLOSED TO PROBLEM LOG NO. _____

                                                    ENHANCE REQ. NO. _____

                                                    PROJECT REQ. NO. _____

DISTRIBUTION ORIGINATOR KEEPS BOTTOM COPY   SEND OTHER COPIES TO CIS

EXHIBIT 6 *(concluded)*

Problem Log

ORIGINATOR'S NAME   PHONE NO.   DEPARTMENT   DATE & TIME SUBMITTED

_____   _____   _____   / / _____

PROBLEM DESCRIPTION _____

_____

_____

_____

_____

_____

ATTACHMENTS |--|

LOG NO.   ASSIGNED TO   PRIORITY   CONTACT DATE   EST COMPLETE

_____   _____   _____   / / _____   / / _____

BRIEF DESC _____

PERSON	DATE	****PROBLEM ANALYSIS DESCRIPTION****
	/ /	
	/ /	
	/ /	
	/ /	
	/ /	
	/ /	
	/ /	
	/ /	
	/ /	

CAUSE OF PROBLEM

_____   CLOSED BY _____

_____   CLOSED DATE _____ / / _____

_____   CLOSED TO PROBLEM LOG NO. _____

HARDWARE ____ OPERATIONS ____ OTHER _____   ENHANCE REQ. NO. _____

SOFTWARE _____ USER ERROR _____   PROJECT REQ. NO. _____

DISTRIBUTION ORIGINATOR KEEPS BOTTOM COPY   SEND OTHER COPIES TO CIS she is enrolled in a part-time MBA program. Although there is some support for her efforts and abilities, both the financial and the CIS departments remain skeptical about the true value of the IS audit function to their specific areas. The IS audit function reports to the manager of Internal Audit, Bill Jacobs, who reports to Rob Bain, senior vice president of Finance.

THE PROBLEM

Steve Sawin has been hearing many complaints about CIS services. He is beginning to compare CIS products to costs for the company and to wonder whether management of the resources is adequate. So he called two meetings for the next week. The first meeting will be with Dennis Bennett, vice president of CIS, Bob Walters, controller, and Rob Bain, vice president of Finance. To the second meeting he invited heads of all company departments, including Dennis Bennett, to discuss computer service problems, set priorities, and evaluate needs for computer services.

Dennis Bennett was worried about the coming meeting with the chairman of the board, Steve Sawin. As he tried to relax and think about what was going wrong, Bennett grabbed a notebook and started listing users' computer problems, what the CIS department was doing to solve them, and how to solve them quickly and permanently. The list was long and depressing: incorrect reports, unfulfilled needs for enhancements by users, and lack of attention to problem logs. He also noted that the system was down in peak user periods and slow the rest of the time. It was difficult to evaluate training for financial department personnel. Many users had trouble operating the systems. In addition, he understood that having accounts receivables processed by an outside company could pose problems. Furthermore, frustrated users were buying PCs and software packages to solve their computer problems; these purchases had a rolling snowball effect because nonstandard products created problems of connectivity and maintenance.

As Dennis continued to add to his list, he realized that the underlying department problems were a lack of (1) computer capacity, (2) understanding from the CIS operations side, (3) appreciation for the importance of problem solving and user satisfaction, (4) good communications with not only users but also with top management, and (5), even worse, adequate planning.

Bennett realized that his approach in the coming meeting with Sawin could very well determine his future and the future of the CIS department in the company. Sawin was a brilliant entrepreneur with high visibility who was not afraid to make tough decisions in a high-risk environment; he could fire a manager or cut an entire organization with no regrets. How could Bennett present his case in a way that would put his management of the CIS department in a more favorable light? He began writing down alternative courses of action:

- Establish better communication with the management, and prepare a plan for actual and future courses of action for the coming meeting.

- Sell the importance of the CIS department to top management and highlight the need for complete independence from the Finance department.
- Raise IS to the level of current technology. For example, the accounts receivables should be processed within the company, not only to reduce cost but also to improve efficiency.
- Offer better support to the Finance department by moving next door, if possible. In addition, training for Finance should be considered as an important matter. Any help to users to learn the system should be part of the mission.

Bennett realized he was so involved in day-to-day systems problems that he never stopped to think and plan future IS activities. He knew that the company had been growing so fast through expansions and acquisitions that services provided by the CIS department had not kept pace with users' service demands. He also realized that his type of management had to change and satisfy the company needs.

QUESTIONS

1. Prepare a response to each of the questions Bennett asked himself on the first page of this case.
2. Discuss top-down and bottom-up management in the Southern Lodges environment. Which is in effect, should it be changed, and if so, how?
3. Do you agree that IS has a strategic role at Southern Lodges? Support your answer.
4. What should be the role of IS?
5. Discuss make-or-buy, centralization versus decentralization, and the importance of users at Southern Lodges. Are these important issues?
6. Evaluate Bennett's alternatives on the last page of the case. What should he do and why?

Case 6–3 U.S. International Electronics Corporation

While studying the Shipping department's current systems layout, Jack Barnes became concerned about the methods used to develop and implement each system. After all, Gardner Systems Technology no longer supports its software, Information Systems (IS) and Group Information Services (GIS) are not following the

This case was prepared by David Weyher and Paul Blair; the case was revised by Oscar L. Salley. Names, locations, and financial data have been disguised.

existing responsibility matrix, and the systems are not sharing data or interfacing with each other. This led Barnes to propose to Bill Trapp, the manager of Shipping and Distribution, that a feasibility study and requirements definition be completed to determine if integrating all four independent systems is in the department's best interest. The integrated system would help to: (1) eliminate redundant data entry at the three stations—induction, packaging instructions, and labels; (2) allow for more efficient processing of transactions (especially at peak periods); (3) provide for future interfaces to other existing and future systems; and (4) improve data integrity and internal controls.

Trapp agreed to pay for the study, and Barnes searched outside the division to find an independent firm willing to assess the U.S. International system and propose changes. The elected firm was Romney, Reigle, and Reisling, a "big eight" accounting firm; its Systems Consulting branch spent two months interviewing and researching the Shipping department's users and their needs. However, IS and John Hale, responsible for the development of two of the four systems, were not consulted during any phase of the feasibility study or requirements definition. Yet IS will be required to convert all systems, if Shipping accepts the proposal. This bewildered Hale and the IS group and has widened the rift between GIS and IS.

COMPANY BACKGROUND

The Logistics and Maintenance Systems Division (LMSD) of the U.S. International Electronics Corporation has its headquarters in San Bernadino, California, and employs over 3,200 people. LMSD acts as a supporting arm of U.S. International's Aerospace Center for Electronics (ACE), one of the nation's leading aerospace contractors located in Los Angeles. LMSD supports such major commercial air navigational radar programs as the Boeing 747, Douglas DC-10, and Lockheed L1011; similar systems are installed on military transports such as the Air Force's C-5A. Currently LMSD is running 28 major programs serving 18 countries. The division was set up in 1970 after a recommendation by the FAA, NASA, and the U.S. Department of Commerce (DOC). Originally organized as a department, LMSD grew to become a division in 1976. As the fastest growing division in U.S. International Aerospace Systems, LMSD has doubled sales every four years (see Exhibit 1).

FUTURE GROWTH

In relation to future growth, LMSD is expected to maintain and possibly increase its average annual sales growth rate of 15 percent, due to increased spending by many airlines as they replace jetliners placed in service in the late 1970s-early 1980s. A good indication of future growth is the booking/backlog figure for 1987, which is expected to reach $1.5 billion (see Exhibit 1). These are orders that LMSD has received from all product lines, which will be taken as sales over the next two- to three-year period when products are delivered or services are performed (navigational radar systems generally have a long lead time). In addition, LMSD is currently competing for new business on many advanced electronic projects.

PRODUCT LINES

The primary objective of LMSD is to provide effective and economical support for the total life cycles of all of its air navigation projects. Providing and integrating all of these elements is a very difficult task. Support begins with logistics planning and engineering and continues with all of LMSD's product lines:

- Technical data.
- Technical training.
- Spares.
- Test equipment.
- Electronics repair (ER).
- Field engineering and support (FE&S).

Technical Data

Technical data includes writing technical manual plans, position handbooks, and equipment/system manuals, and providing this information to customers for the day-to-day maintenance of navigational radar systems and equipment.

Technical training

A second product line that supplements this data is technical training. In this area, LMSD technical instructors work directly with, and train the customer representatives, who plan courses, research equipment, and train their own technicians to receive, assemble, operate, maintain, and repair U.S. International electronic systems.

Spares

LMSD's most profitable product line is spares, which accounts for over 40 percent of the division's sales. This product line is responsible for producing, procuring, and delivering spare radar parts to the customers to replace unit parts within the

EXHIBIT 1   LMSD Financial Highlights, 1984–1987 (in millions)

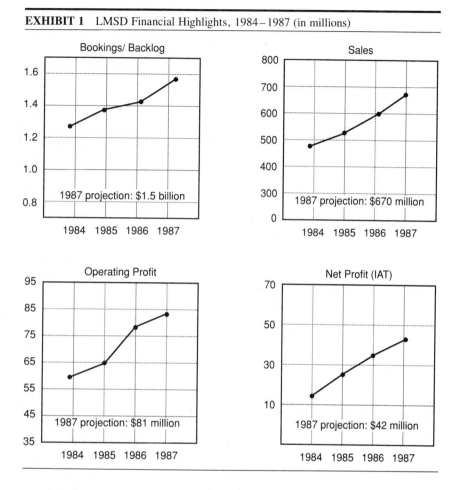

navigational radar systems. A major part of the Spares department includes a large support documentation group responsible for keeping the customers up-to-date as to the latest engineering configuration changes for all part numbers within specific radar systems.

Test Equipment

Another major product line is test equipment, which includes hardware and software used to test the radar components for quality and performance. This product line includes factory test equipment (nondeliverable equipment; located at LMSD), special test equipment (deliverable equipment; bought and used by prime contractors such as Boeing, Douglas, and Lockheed), and support equipment (deliverable equipment; purchased directly by the end-user such as TWA, Braniff, and Continental Airlines).

Electronic Repair

When electronic parts of a system are defective or damaged, they are sent to LMSD's Logistics Spares Repair Depot (LSRD) for repair. The repairs are usually done only on high-dollar items where it is more cost-effective to repair the item than to replace it with a new or reworked spare part.

Field Engineering and Support

Finally, LMSD offers field engineering and support services to customers. Professional engineers help ensure that systems perform precisely whether operating conditions involve humid, tropical airport flightlines, frigid flight temperatures at high altitudes, or the dry, sandy environment of Southwest desert landings and takeoffs. Actual operations is where product theory, design, production, and delivery come together to receive their final examinations. Services include solving operational problems and providing general maintenance, repair, and retrofit, or modification services when necessary.

MATRIX MANAGEMENT

Matrix management plays a major role at LMSD by establishing integrated organizations for each product line and program (see Exhibit 2). The three major program divisions at LMSD are AMSD (Aircraft Maintenance Services Division), ACTSD (Approach Control and Tracking Support Division), and LADSD (Logistics and Distribution Systems Division). AMSD supports airborne navigational radar systems used primarily by commercial airlines in many different jetliners. Major programs in this area include radar systems for the Lockheed L1011 and the Douglas DC-10. ACTSD is responsible for producing ground-based radars such as GSAR (Glide Slope Approach Radar) and HARTS (High Altitude Route Tracking System). LADSD primarily handles all independent and freight business and is responsible for the Boeing 747 and 737, a $430 million test and maintenance contract. The awarding of this contract to LMSD in 1980 marked the first time that the division had been chosen as the prime contractor for such a major project; previously, LMSD supplied support for ACE products. The Government department is a fourth program division that handles small defense business.

Within matrix management, functional managers decide who will perform specific tasks, how they will be accomplished, and how well they have been

EXHIBIT 2   Financial Reporting Product Lines versus Programs

	AMSD	*ACTSD*	*LADSD*	*Government*
Spares				
ER				
Test equipment				
Technical data				
Technical training				
FE&S				

accomplished. Functional areas include Engineering, Operations, and Controllers (product lines are divided under each function). In contrast, program managers decide what effort will be accomplished, when it will be performed, and how much is budgeted. Together, these managers make important joint decisions that require a large amount of cooperation and cohesiveness.

MANAGEMENT PHILOSOPHY

The basic philosophy of LMSD is that of quality and customer service. Slogans such as "At U.S. International Electronics, quality and dependability says it all" and "We do it first and do it right" appear on posters, pencils, and mugs in all buildings. Support of customer products after the production process takes place is the key ingredient for success in the future in the aircraft electronic industry where competition is strong. In addition, the future growth depends on accurately anticipating customer requirements. However, the mainspring is continued adherence to the policy of providing high-quality products combined with first-class service and support.

Important factors in motivating employees to meet future challenges are LMSD's "promote from within" and "last to layoff" policies, providing personal security to managers, professionals, and nonprofessional employees.

CONTRACTING ENVIRONMENT

For LMSD, operating in a hybrid commercial-government contractor environment is very different from a purely commercial industry. The nature of the business deals with complex electronic (radar systems) products that are sold to both national and international customers. Because these products involve high-technological theory, their product life cycle is very short. In addition, government contractors are heavily audited for accuracy and efficiency; therefore, all U.S. International's nongovernment programs are monitored very closely by federal auditors—watching overhead allocation, for example, to be certain that government programs are not unfairly charged for commercial expenses.

Since costs are charged to the government on a "job order" basis, LMSD has applied sophisticated cost accounting and charging systems across the board, which enables them to accurately allocate costs to their appropriate commercial orders, as well as to the smaller government projects. Because this accounting system allows costs to be shown on a unit basis, costs on similar civilian commercial navigational radar systems manufactured in different time periods can be compared on a cost basis.

As required by federal regulations, LMSD has set up space within its headquarters for government auditing agencies such as the DCAA (Defense Contractor Auditing Agencies) and FOFCC (Federal Office for Contract Compliance). These agencies overlook operations at LMSD and give recommendations to the government contracting officers concerning LMSD's overall performance based on recent audits. Although there is strong competition from the United States and abroad, future government business can be expected to increase for those contracting firms who strongly reflect the above characteristics of high performance and accurate charging.

Operating in highly competitive markets, LMSD must be able to meet all product delivery dates in order to gain future business. Meeting these schedules is extremely important as they are the basis for progress payments, which are funds received from commercial customers and the government to provide LMSD with cash flow needed over the total length of a program. Payments are given after evidence shows that all terms and conditions within a certain contract have been fulfilled. Primarily, evidence that performance of a contract has taken place is through delivery of goods. If delivery dates are not met in a timely fashion, progress payments for future productions may not be allowed. Contractual terms that must be met may include naming the freight company that LMSD must use to transport products, as well as the delivery of documentation that signifies performance. Therefore, packaging and distributing the products to their appropriate destination in a timely manner is the final key link to LMSD's overall success.

MANAGEMENT INFORMATIONS SYSTEMS AT LMSD

The Information Systems (IS) department was created in 1970 (along with the division—LMSD) to provide total information systems support, including the development, implementation, and control of all systems at LMSD. In addition, any department wishing to obtain a computer had to go through the IS department for permission. In the early 1970s, IS's hardware consisted of one mainframe computer, a Sperry UNIVAC system.

In mid-1978, as LMSD developed a product line concept (versus a total material concept, which existed previously), a need surfaced for an additional information systems group to determine the needs of each product line. Therefore, the Group Information Services (GIS) department was created in late 1978. Due to its product line responsibilities, GIS is a separate, integrated department from IS, and is located under the Operations group. While IS is organizationally structured under the Controller's group, GIS was organized so that each product line had its own professional IS department; the separate IS groups were responsible for understanding the operations of the existing data processing systems and working closely with the users in defining and developing new application systems.

THE IS/GIS RESPONSIBILITY MATRIX

With the creation of GIS in 1978, LMSD established a responsibility matrix approach to define the IS/GIS responsibilities in developing information systems for product lines (see Exhibit 3). This matrix has provided definite phases in the overall implementation process for which either IS or GIS are accountable; however, each department does have some input in each stage shown on the graph, although the magnitude of their inputs differs. For example, IS has very little input in the feasibility study but a great deal of say about the final implementation of a system, although final authority is given to GIS.

The matrix would work as follows:

- Initially, a need for a system or a change in an existing computer system is established by the product line users or the GIS liaison.
- Then, GIS takes over and provides the feasibility study, defines the requirements needed for the system, and decides how the system should work (that is, a functional systems definition).
- While GIS representatives are primarily analysts, IS professionals are mostly programmers. They use the information furnished by GIS to develop a working

EXHIBIT 3   IS/GIS Responsibility Matrix

GIS		IS
X	Feasibility study	
X	Requirements definition	
X	Functional systems definition	
	Computer systems definition (hardware)	X
	Programming (software)	X
X	Implementation (user manuals, training)	
X	Postimplementation and evaluation	

system—including all the hardware and software needed—under the system requirements set by GIS.

- Next, GIS provides training and manuals to the end-users with the help of IS.
- Evaluation of the system after implementation is accomplished primarily by GIS.
- Once the requirements definition is accepted by the product line manager, funds are allocated for the system in the user department's budget, and the system will be implemented.

Although the matrix represents an ideal IS/GIS process, there are exceptions. For example, in the past, GIS has asked outside firms for help with the first three stages—feasibility study, requirements definition, and functional systems definition—without getting IS's input. In addition, some product lines have developed their own small information systems groups to implement information systems unique to their own group. In this way, each product line is more responsive to its own needs; it does not have to wait for the lengthy IS/GIS process.

Frequently, product lines develop their own information systems, not to be assured of obtaining unique features but to bypass the understaffed IS department. Currently, 25 percent of the IS staff are contracted from outside IS firms.

IS/GIS ORGANIZATIONAL STRUCTURE

The present IS/GIS organizational structure (see Exhibit 4) is set up so that both departments remain separate entities, yet interact on a consistent basis. GIS is headed by Mike Hashigawa and is under Operations; IS is managed by Barry Aton, and the department reports directly to the controller. Mike Hashigawa has four managers reporting to him, three responsible for one product line each; one manager, Marie Ferenchak, is responsible for Materials and Distribution (Materials and Distribution is treated as a product line for IS/GIS purposes; Shipping is part of this group).

Each product line, including Shipping, has a systems analyst who acts as a liaison between the IS programmer and the product line; Jack Barnes is the liaison between Shipping and IS. Jack reports directly to Marie Ferenchak and has dotted line ties to the manager of Shipping, Bill Trapp.

Under IS, Barry Aton has three managers reporting to him, each responsible for particular areas, with systems programmers assigned to each area. John Hale is the IS systems programmer dedicated to the Shipping department. He has been contracted from an outside IS firm; therefore, he reports—dotted line—to Lenore Simms, manager of IS for Operations.

Currently, IS hardware consists of three mainframe systems: (1) IBM 4341, (2) Hewlett-Packard 1000, and (3) Sperry UNIVAC 1100 Series. All three systems are accessed by the Shipping department for their current operations.

EXHIBIT 4 IS/GIS Organization Structure

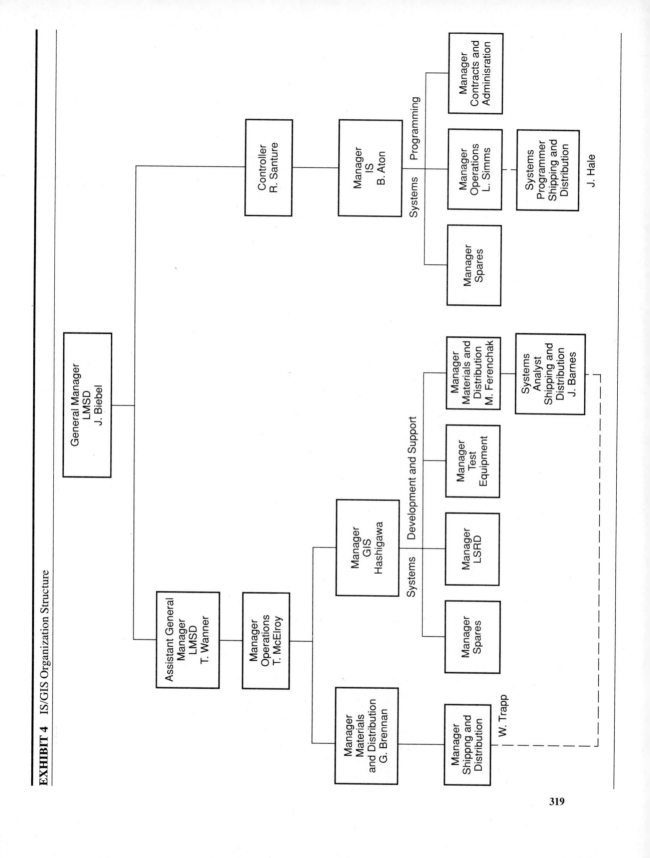

THE SHIPPING DEPARTMENT

LMSD products, once engineered and manufactured, must be delivered in safe condition and in a timely manner to support navigational radar systems on commercial jetliners as well as the ground-based approach and tracking systems installed at civilian airports. It is vital to U.S. International's customers and, even more so to U.S. International's goodwill, that these products arrive in good working condition regardless of the distribution environment—whether it be land, air, or sea—in the United States or overseas. The Shipping department, managed by Bill Trapp, is responsible for shipments of LMSD products all over the world, including Great Britain, Taiwan, Israel, and Norway. Meeting delivery schedules enhances customer satisfaction but, more importantly, allows continued progress payments; understandably, LMSD operations pushes hard to provide increased quality products on schedule.

Shipments vary immensely from very small transistors requiring special protective handling, to very large test consoles weighing as much as 3,000 lbs. Therefore, tracking LMSD products through the operation provides a clear picture of expected delivery dates, total volume of a shipment, and internal controls for operations bottlenecks. The tracking procedure is important not only to the department but also to the customers, the product lines, and upper-level management.

Computer systems (four in all) have recently been installed in the department to track LMSD products, in addition to improving production line efficiency, reducing tedious tasks, and increasing accuracy with regards to data. Jack Barnes, the GIS liaison to the department, has been instrumental in coordinating development and implementation of most of the systems; much of the time, however, he has encountered heavy resistance to change and uneasiness about new computer systems.

AUTOMATION OF SHIPPING

Bill Trapp, the man responsible for developing the Shipping department to its present size and importance, is very cautious when it comes to altering a successful, proven operation. Even so, as U.S. International has continued to expand, the move to more efficient, large-capacity operations has been inevitable. As a result, GIS, through Barnes, has targeted certain areas in desperate need of modernization. However, Trapp and his people do not believe that automation is always in Shipping's best interest. In addition, since U.S. International is very people-oriented, management listens carefully to what employees have to say; forcing change against the will of the groups most affected is unlikely. Still, four systems have been implemented for various reasons with differing degrees of management support.

The department, responsible for the transportation and distribution of millions of dollars of U.S. International products, had no real automated computer system prior to 1982. Most tasks were performed manually; many jobs were completed only through the extraordinary efforts of dedicated employees. In spite of their commitment and overtime hours, however, a degree of inaccuracy and redundancy was unavoidable.

STARTS

In 1983, Shipping could no longer cope with inventory problems and the increasing workload; for the first time, Trapp requested an automated system. The department was already in the midst of automating its production process, so Barnes suggested an automated storage and retrieval system developed by Gardner Systems Technology called STARTS (Storage and Retrieval System). At the time this system was proposed, no individual or group, outside of IS, was authorized to purchase a computer.

Barnes, however, desiring an expeditious implementation, worked around the purchasing constraint by defining the system as an automatic data storage system, not a computer. STARTS uses Hewlett-Packard H/P 2621 terminals connected to an H/P 1000 mainframe—soon to be obsolete. Gardner Systems, Barnes later found out, was unsure of this system (programmed in Pascal) and, to this date (late 1987) will not support it; nor will Hewlett-Packard maintain its obsolete hardware. The IS group refuses to even look at the system as they were not consulted to begin with.

MILAMS

The second system to be implemented in the department, a Military Label Marking System (MILAMS), became a hot item when U.S. International received a Pentagon directive requiring bar code labels for all military shipments. Trapp, complying with the military requirement, called for an immediate implementation of the MILAMS in early 1984. Due to the expedient nature of this system and the undermanned IS group, Barnes chose a local vendor, Statistical Technology, Inc. (STI), to define the system requirements (from military specifications); STI was awarded a follow-on contract to design and implement the system as soon as possible. STI developed a stand-alone system, run on an IBM PC XT, to automate the label-making process. A station on the production line is dedicated to labels. All pertinent data extracted from the shipping papers is keyed into the system to produce a complete set of labels (see Exhibit 5). A large item order, positioned at the label station, may take up to one-half hour to run all the labels. When such long runs are scheduled, smaller jobs usually take precedence or completely bypass the label station, returning prior to sealing the completed package.

Customer complaints and internal corporation (product line) criticisms regard-

EXHIBIT 5 Line Layout

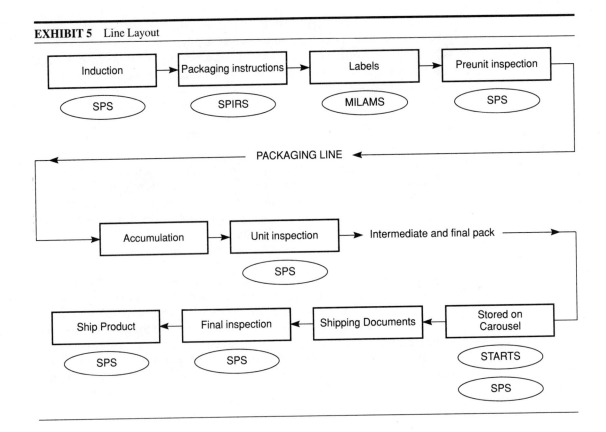

ing the whereabouts and delivery dates of a particular product prompted an inspection of the operation by the Operations manager. At his request, a Shipment Packaging System (SPS) was developed in 1985. This system, a status system, spearheaded by the IS group due to its political nature, would track LMSD products through the complete operation. With some support from GIS, IS— with John Hale in charge—quickly developed a basic system of induction and sign off of every part passing through the department. This quick-fix solution to track parts was enough to "put the fire out" but was not consistent with the department's long-range plans for an overall tracking and status system. Once the political overtones had subsided, Barnes then went back to Statistical Technology, which had provided a good working system in MILAMS, to convert SPS to a complete tracking system utilizing data collection units at strategic stations. The system utilizes Lier Stiegler ADM 22 terminals connected to an IBM PC XT accessing an IBM 4341 mainframe. SPS is now used throughout the department and is supported by GIS.

SPIRS

In 1987, the Shipping department wanted a system that could store and produce, in hardcopy, 20,000 packaging information records of parts previously shipped. Before 1986, the parts records had been kept on computer punch cards and manually processed when a part passed the station. When the department gave IS the task, John Hale took charge and defined, developed, and implemented a Shipped Parts Information Record System (SPIRS) that would bring up a packaging information record when the appropriate information from the shipping papers was keyed in by an operator. Hale, familiar with the Sperry UNIVAC system, used the 1100 series UNIVAC mainframe to process the information. Implementing a Sperry UNIVAC UTS-40 terminal at the engineering station between induction and label making provided the efficiency desired for producing packaging instructions while freeing the packaging engineers to handle the more technical end of the operation (see Exhibit 5). Shipping, knowing exactly what they wanted, went directly to Hale to provide the needed development and support. GIS had very little involvement in this project and, at one point, Barnes had no knowledge of its development. The above was not consistent with the GIS function of being a liaison to IS and does not allow GIS to maintain complete knowledge of systems implementation for future interfacing and/or additions. SPIRS, however, has provided the department with a more timely response to item orders and has increased production line efficiency sufficient to decrease turnaround time (TAT), the time required for a part to travel from induction into the system to final sign off just before shipping. Clearly, minimizing TAT is important if U.S. International delivery schedules are to be dependable, which in turn maintains customer goodwill and assures the continuation of progress payments.

A brief summary of the Shipping department's present system is listed in Exhibit 6 and diagrammed in Exhibit 7.

EXHIBIT 6 U.S. International Electronics Present Systems

System Name	Implementation Date	Requested by	Developed by	Hardware
STARTS	1983	Gardner/Trapp	Gardner Systems	H/P 1000
MILAMS	1984	Trapp	Statistical Techniques, Inc.	IBM PC XT
SPS	1985	Operations manager	IS	IBM 4341
SPIRS	1987	Trapp	IS	Sperry Univac

EXHIBIT 7   Diagram of Present Systems

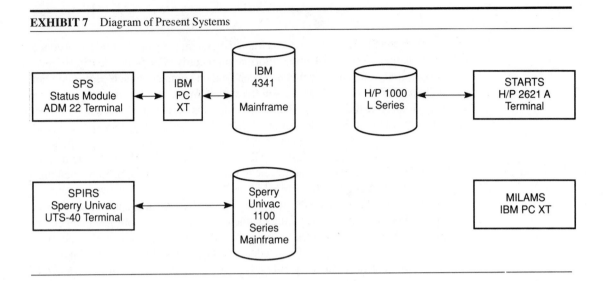

CONCLUSION

The proposal, in short, is as follows:

- To integrate SPS, SPIRS, and MILAMS so as to eliminate redundant data entry at all three stations. Presently much of the same information is inputted at these stations requiring three operations and three production line steps for each item order. The proposal would require only one station to induct and produce packaging instructions and labels by one operator (see Exhibit 8).
- To enhance SPS so as to absorb the STARTS functions; an independent STARTS station would not be needed.
- To broaden the data store so personnel may access SPS, SPIRS, or STARTS to receive information at any station throughout the department. This will help track the parts through the operation and provide up-to-date status reports when requested.

THE DILEMMA

On receiving Romney, Reigle, and Reisling's proposal for integration of the department's systems, Bill Trapp is faced with a dilemma. He is satisfied with the present systems but is losing faith in the IS/GIS systems procedure. Should Trapp accept the Romney, Reigle, and Reisling proposal for integration; or should the present IS/GIS responsibility matrix process be reviewed for this project; or should he maintain his present successful operating system?

EXHIBIT 8   Diagram of Proposed Systems

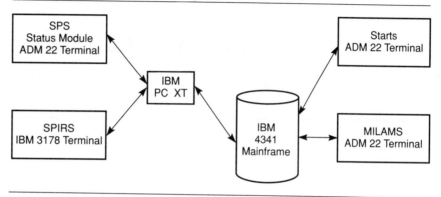

QUESTIONS

1. What should be the relationship between IS and GIS? Should they be combined into one department? If so, what would be the responsibilities of the new combined department? Who would or should head up the new department?
2. Should IS and GIS be independent groups under a common vice president? If so, what should be the split of responsibilities?
3. Who should write the annual performance evaluations for GIS personnel? Operations seniors? GIS senior administrators? IS administrators? Support your answer.
4. Did the government directives contribute to problems at U.S. International? How can similar problems be avoided in the future?
5. Is hardware a problem for U.S. International? If so, why?
6. What should Trapp do?

Chapter 7

Acquisition—Hardware and Software

INTRODUCTION

The acquisition of hardware and software is a significant capital outlay for most firms. However, purchase of powerful microcomputers and integrated software packages has decreased the percent of IS funds devoted each year to major equipment purchases.

SYSTEMS LIFE CYCLE AND LIFE CYCLE APPROACH (LCA)

The systems approach—sometimes called the scientific method—for solving problems, has been used in many industries for many years. While some definitions of the two and the number of steps may vary, the general activities listed for each are:

1. Define the problem.
2. Gather critical facts related to the problem.
3. Identify alternative solutions.
4. Evaluate and compare those alternatives.
5. Recommend one solution with facts supporting the choice.
6. Implement the decision.

A major national railroad and transportation conglomerate follows an 11-step life cycle approach[1] in its systems development; for that corporation, LCA includes:

---

[1] See Case 5–2, Jenkins Engineering and Technology.

1. User requirement.
2. Feasibility study.
3. General systems design.
4. Systems data flow.
5. Detail subsystem design.
6. Actual program specifications.
7. Program subunit testing.
8. System testing.
9. User acceptance testing.
10. Production installation.
11. Enhancements.

SYSTEMS DEVELOPMENT LIFE CYCLE

Schultheis and Sumner refer to the steps in designing an information system as the systems development methodology,[2] adding that the systems development methodology "establishes a set of procedures that conform with a life cycle."[3] They include the following key activities: problem definition, feasibility study, systems analysis, systems design, detailed design, implementation, and maintenance.[4]

When a firm plans to convert a complicated, manual process to a complex, automated process, its analysts and designers will insist on completing all the specified activities in the specified sequence. However, when several projects are waiting to be developed, the result of the technicians' dedicated commitment to the formal process is a sizable backlog — approaching two to three years (or more) is a national average. Selecting one or all of three alternatives (purchasing software packages, prototyping the design, and having users develop systems) can help reduce the backlog.[5]

---

[2]Terminology can be a problem, as we mentioned previously. Systems development life cycle, life cycle approach, systems development methodology, systems acquisition process, and possibly others all seem to refer to the means by which an organization makes the transition from not having a system to having one. The words *implementation, installation,* and *production installation* and *production* can also be troublesome.

[3]Robert Schultheis and Mary Sumner, *Management Information Systems: The Manager's View,* Chapter 16 (Homewood, Ill.: Richard D. Irwin, 1989).

[4]Schultheis and Sumner, *Management Information Systems,* Chapter 16.

[5]Schultheis and Sumner, *Management Information Systems,* Chapter 17.

REQUIREMENTS DOCUMENT

The requirements document, sometimes a package of documents, lists the problem(s) the proposed system is to correct. It is critical that the future users of the system participate in the preparation of these statements and descriptions. If the newly installed system seriously fails to meet user expectations, cooperation between developers and users—based on rapport developed in earlier joint activities—permits objective investigation and resolution of problems.

Schultheis and Sumner see the requirements document as "blueprints of the proposed system design . . . frozen once the system proposal has been approved."[6] Considering the design as frozen at almost any point is a hard position to hold in the face of user demands to change as their business environment changes.

SYSTEMS ACQUISITION PROCESS

Parker states that the acquisition process takes place at the end of the design phase, after the logical design of the new system is complete. At that point, the firm has a fairly good idea of what hardware, software, and services will meet its needs. Parker includes the following activities in the process:

1. Physical items are identified.
2. The firm's analyst gives vendors a statement of specific needs (often using a formal request for proposal (RFP)).
3. Vendors submit specific system descriptions and prices.
4. The firm (usually a team, committee, or task force) evaluates the vendor's proposals, using a vendor rating system[7] and/or benchmark tests.
5. A vendor is chosen and a contract prepared.[8]

At any rate, the systems approach should be followed whether an organization expects to buy hardware and bundled software from a vendor or intends to buy hardware and write its own application code and documentation. Similarly, most of the steps of the basic systems approach apply if the organization plans to modify the vendor's application programs; that is, to tailor the system to their own special needs.

---

[6]Schultheis and Sumner, *Management Information Systems*, Chapter 17.

[7]Charles S. Parker, *Management Information Systems: Strategy and Action*, Chapter 17 (New York: McGraw-Hill, 1989). Parker lists one weighted-criterion evaluation approach that weights functionality, ease of learning/use, speed, capacities, cost, support, and documentation.

[8]Parker, *Management Information Systems*.

USERS, COMMUNICATIONS, AND CHANGES

The user must be involved in the total process, with both user and developers responsible for learning as much about each other's business and terminology as other commitments will permit. Failing to communicate continually is almost as serious a threat to successful system development as is an inability to understand each other's language. Users must respond quickly to changing market situations and competition, as new information becomes available; and yet a design that changes daily or weekly may never reach installation and operation.

APPROVING CHANGES TO THE DESIGN

Formal procedures for approving change requests should be part of the system development process. Special committees are often formed to manage the flow of proposed changes. Here again, the users must be seriously involved; they must understand the costs and delays inherent in continually changing the approved design. In addition, since they are to be the owners and users of the system, their vote and wishes should take precedence over purely technical considerations.

MAKE–OR–BUY–OR–MODIFY DECISION (SOFTWARE)

Company management determines whether the wisest decision is to: (1) buy software packages from vendors—off the shelf, so to speak; (2) have the IS/DP staff design and write their own programs; or (3) buy applications and tailor (or modify) them to meet the organization's specific needs. In the latter option, the software costs for the tailored systems can be as much as 75 to 85 percent of the new system total costs.[9]

If the application is to be installed on a mainframe or minicomputer, the necessary analysis, design, and implementation (writing and debugging code) may be beyond the firm's capabilities—options (2) and (3); the only viable option may be to buy—option (1). One drawback to the "buy" choice is that the company may be paying for features it does not want and may not get others that it does want.

Another potential problem with in-house development involves the experience level of the staff in estimating the time and effort involved, and therefore the costs; companies must develop procedures to improve the accuracy of time and schedule estimates prepared by staffs not accustomed to making such estimates.

---

[9]James I. Cash, F. W. McFarlan, J. L. McKenney, and M. R. Vitale, *Corporate Information Systems Management: Text and Cases*, 2nd ed., Chapter 6 (Homewood, Ill.: Richard D. Irwin, 1988).

SUMMARY

There are many pitfalls in the path of those who develop, acquire, implement, install, and maintain hardware and software. Problems can be avoided if experienced IS staffs and user groups cooperate fully and communicate. Following a systems approach, using formal methodologies such as those described briefly above, is the fastest, least expensive, and most effective way to acquire a system —although it may not seem so while the process is ongoing.

CASES: COVERT COMPANY, EVANSTON INSURANCE AGENCY, AND MID-STATES GAS & ELECTRIC

Covert Company (Case 7–1) was running out of disk space with trends indicating a rising growth rate. A proposed solution is to acquire a new, more powerful system from the same vendor with a corresponding financial bonus arrangement with a very large insurance company.

Evanston Insurance Agency (Case 7–2) is a partnership, not strong on planning and risk assessment. The firm wants to move into automation but may have unrealistic expectations. The result of its efforts are serious problems when the firm attempts to install, operate, and maintain a computer system.

Mid-States Gas & Electric Company (Case 7–3) is a large utility in the Midwest, which grows through acquisitions and diversification; the number of its facilities and computer systems is immense. A recent reorganization has dismantled the Project Management department, and reassigned its sections to new divisions — except for the Computer section, which is still responsible for the management of three very large computer replacement projects.

Case 7–1 Covert Company

Carl Williams was worried. Until now, he had never realized the extent to which his business depended on computers. The Fenster F22A computer that Covert Company used primarily for accounting, sales/marketing, and on-line viewing of individual policy data was, as close as Carl could ascertain, nearly at capacity. Response time was slow. Users were complaining. Worst of all, the end-of-month accounting batch reports are now taking three days due to the voluminous data

This case was prepared by Sue Lisiewski and Michael Seldes; it was revised and updated by George Strouse. Names, location, and financial data have been disguised.

that has to be processed. This delay results in even slower response times for the users and necessitates employee overtime just to enter regular daily wrap-up data in order to be ready for the next day's business. Happily, the problem was the result of excellent company growth.

HISTORY

In 1985, Carl Williams started what is known as Covert Company in Cincinnati, Ohio. In 1977, Carl, with a Mr. Jim Covert, jointly purchased the insurance agency of McWilliams, Blanchard, & Tucker Associates — to form Covert & Williams, Inc. At that time, there were actually two agencies operating from one office: McWilliams, Blanchard, & Tucker Associates, and Covert & Williams, Inc. Later that year, Carl purchased Mr. Covert's share (and bookings) in Covert & Williams, Inc., allowing him to consolidate all operations into one agency. In seven years, the company had grown 500 percent. Premium sales were $10 million in 1984. The growth had come from both increased sales and acquisition of the other agencies.

In 1985, Covert Company grew another 20 percent, to $12 million in sales. With 6,300 customers, Covert was the fourth largest independent insurance agent in Cincinnati. Less than a year later, in April of 1986, Covert Company was serving over 7,000 customers.

When Carl originally started his business, he had a total of five employees; two were in sales. Now there are over 30 salespeople and an office staff of 24 employees, in addition to the vice president and Carl. Exhibit 1 shows the organizational structure for Covert Company.

BACKGROUND

Computer System

The current hardware system is:

1 Fenster F22A with 40 MB internal disk drive/tape backup.
11 Fenster E18 terminals.
1 Genicom printer.
1 Wordlink terminal.
1 IBM PC.
1 Diablo 630 letter-quality, daisy wheel printer.

In 1984, the Covert Company purchased the F22A with four terminals and a software package (written by TCS) from Hartford Insurance. The financing of the system was also through Hartford Insurance and was very appealing. The

EXHIBIT 1 Covert Company Organizational Structure

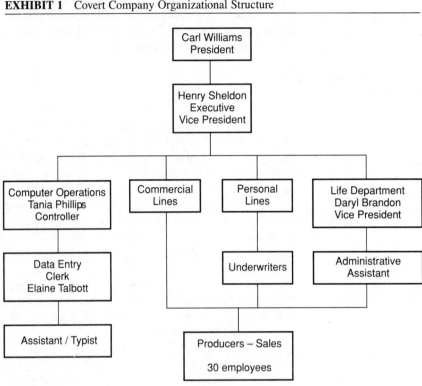

system price was $110,000, but the system was paid off by Williams through a bonus commission program of the Hartford firm. As Williams thought about the bonus arrangement, he felt that "the number of Hartford Insurance policies sold would have not been as high if we hadn't purchased the computer system from them."

The system proved very useful. In 1985, Carl purchased seven more terminals. At that time, the Fenster field service representative who performed the installation informed Carl that, as new users and applications were added, system response time would lag; a memory expansion would be required to support the additional load. He also told Carl that the system was running out of usable disk space, and printer capacity/speed might need reevaluation, also.

As close as Carl could recall, the installer had no idea how long Covert could continue to operate on the remaining 8 MB of free disk space. The man did say that as Covert's accounts grew, the remaining space would shrink. As the remaining space shrank, the system would have to work harder and longer during batch processing—creating, erasing, and recreating the temporary files it needed to do its processing.

When the seven additional terminals were added, an IBM PC was purchased to interface with the Fenster. The PC was to be used for its print screen option. Print Screen allowed billing information, tables, and individual policy management data displayed on the screen to be printed quickly. No longer would Carl's customers and salespeople have to wait for batch runs to obtain needed information (previously, customers had been asked to come back or call the following day; or the information was sent through the mail).

Carl also felt that, depending on its level of use, the IBM PC could accommodate some limited spreadsheet and word processing applications, at least on a test basis. Carl had attended a seminar on business operations analysis. While there, he had observed some really impressive "what if" analysis spreadsheet applications and word processing packages being run on an IBM PC.

The PC has not been interfaced yet; but it will be, as soon as the necessary interfacing cables arrive (the cables are backordered). Carl has no idea how much of an additional load, if any, the interfacing will add to the already heavily burdened F22A system.

The PC, back in its box, is gathering dust. Carl has simply been too busy to do anything with it. Besides, the one time he did try to use it, he discovered that making it do what he wanted was a lot more time-consuming than he'd remembered from the seminar.

Thinking back, Carl recalled that end-of-month closings were done in half a day when the F22A was new. After adding the additional terminals, things slowed down, but no one complained; they were just glad to have access.

As one of Carl's employees stated, "It just seemed that, as Covert expanded, the system contracted. As we grew, it slowed. When the seven additional terminals were added, information was suddenly at our finger-tips. We would ask for something and get a response almost immediately. Then, response began to lag as everyone started to use the system to obtain customer information. You used to be able to make a request and light up a cigarette while you were waiting. Now you can almost smoke one while you wait for a response; and at month-end, you might as well not even try. You only request information on the really important things then; the rest you just put off."

Carl felt that the obvious thing to do was to buy the additional memory and disk space Fenster's installation man had recommended. That solution would been fine, until the Fenster salesman that Carl had called arrived and showed him Fenster's new PR 5500 system with greater memory capacity and faster processing.

"In fact," thought Carl, "getting the job done 10 times faster would not only get my accounting people off my back but would probably alleviate the need for month-end overtime."

As Carl was discussing the contract with the Fenster salesman, he had a great idea: "I wonder," he thought, "what else is available out there that might be even better."

After telling the Fenster salesman he would get back to him, Carl began making phone calls to different computer companies and service bureaus. He found that everyone was more than happy to provide him with information. So much so that he booked himself solid with appointments throughout the next week.

What a week it had been! He was shown many different concepts on systems and services: buy or lease; centralized, decentralized, or networked; in-house or service bureau; IBM, DEC, DG, Unisys, ADP, and so on; there were many choices—almost too many. "Now," thought Carl, "it's time to sift through the piles of information, stacks of brochures, and estimates to decide just what Covert Company really needs."

PROCEDURES AND SOFTWARE

When Carl started the firm, the normal procedure for most local insurance agencies was to employ a computer service company called ARC. Using the outside agency had forced Covert to keep manual logs of billings to be performed, journal entries to be made, and cash to be applied to customer accounts. All invoices were produced manually. At month-end, these logs were sent to ARC, which in turn processed customer ledgers and statements, financial statements, a producer statement, and an account currency report. Turnaround time was about one week.

In the early 1980s, some insurance agencies started purchasing computers for in-house processing. In 1984, Hartford Insurance Company offered Carl the opportunity to purchase the Fenster F22A system with software from TCS, a Hartford subsidiary. Carl was still patting himself on the back for being able to pay the system off so quickly via the bonus commissions Hartford had applied against the purchase price.

Covert's original multiuser, multitasking system configuration had four CRT terminals. Covert received the system in August; by November, it was up and running.

The sequence for current system processing is as follows: When a producer has a new client, he or she contacts the Underwriting department to determine the market for that type of coverage; next, the producer selects the companies that have the most favorable terms; then, the underwriters obtain quotes, and an application is filed with the company. This same procedure is followed for change requests and endorsements.

When the actual policy is received, Elaine Talbott, the computer entry clerk, accesses the policy management section of the system software and enters:

- Customer account.
- Type of coverage.
- Policy number and company.
- Premium dollars (including last year's) and commission rates.
- Effective dates.
- Producer name.
- Policy coverage and limitations including deductible.

After receiving the input, the system asks if she wants to bill this item. If she answers, ''Yes,'' the invoice screen appears and prompts her to input:

- Billing account (if third-party billing).
- Producer for this transaction.
- Producer's commission rates.
- Amounts to be billed (for installment billings).

All of the day's invoices are printed in a batch operation at the end of the day. A hardcopy of the policy is stored in the customer file, and the customer copy and invoice is given to the producer to be verified prior to mailing. At this point, he or she checks the coverage and verifies the policy is as ordered.

When new business or endorsements are requested, the underwriters contract with the companies to obtain such coverage. When the policy arrives, the Personal Lines department receives it directly and types invoices. The department verifies all invoice data manually but the policy information is not entered into the computer. Then, the invoices are typed on a three-part form, the first copy being mailed directly to the customer. The remaining parts are given to Elaine, who enters the billing to the customer's account as a daily batch function.

When customer payments are received, they are entered under the customer's account number, and the customer's account is updated using a batch function by either the part-time accounting assistant or Tania Phillips, the assistant controller. After the batch is run, the daily monetary transaction output report is verified.

At month-end, Elaine runs two reports to be used to post closing entries to the general ledger (GL). The reports are account current (AC) and the producer statement (PS).

The account current is a listing by company of all the activity for the month. From this report, the amounts are taken for the accounts receivables (AR), the commission income (CI), and the accounts payables (AP) for posting by company for that period.

The producer statement lists all invoices for the month, with breakdowns by producer, listing the commission rate, sales for the month, year-to-date sales, percentage of year-to-date, and a comparison against last year's total sales. From this data, the commissions payable amounts are calculated and posted to the GL. The system does not interact with the AR; the above reports are used to post journal entries.

Accounts payable are input through the system, which interfaces with the GL. Payroll is not automated. If growth continues, software for payroll will have to be purchased, or a service bureau will have to be contracted for payroll production (Tania has already contacted a service bureau for a pricing estimate). After the journal entries are keyed in for the month, the system generates financial statements.

Claims are prepared manually. On a very few accounts, particularly some of the larger ones, a log is kept under policy management so that an insured's claim history is readily available.

An expiration list is generated monthly to show the producers and underwriters which policies are up for renewal. Also, an aged receivables list is run to show the customers' status on collections; it shows, for each customer, the amount outstanding for 30, 60, and over 90 days. At month-end, statements for each customer are run and printed.

Elaine and Tania are the only people at Covert Company who are knowledgeable in the use of the system. The rest of the staff use the system for the quick viewing of customer files or printing coverage binders.

PEOPLE

As previously stated, salespeople do not input data directly into the computer. They do, however, make frequent customer information inquiries. In fact, there is really only one person who inputs large quantities of data—Elaine Talbott. Besides entering data, she also initiates all reports and invoicing procedures. Her boss, Tania Phillips, is the only other person at Covert Company who has a working familiarity with the system. Carl Williams has often wondered about his vulnerability in this area, and he has often considered becoming more educated in the Fenster system. Unfortunately, he simply has not had time. Regardless, both Elaine and Tania seem happy with Covert Company and show no signs of leaving.

PROBLEM

The growth of Covert has pushed the Fenster to the edge of its capabilities. The rather limited use of the system has apparently taxed primary memory and disk space to the limit. End-of-month reports are taking three days to produce, rather than three hours as in 1984. These problems irritate Elaine and Tania, and other users are beginning to complain, also. Something has to be done.

The information the Fenster sales representative provided Carl—about obtaining additional memory and an external disk drive for the system—was limited. The drive would cost $5,000 and hopefully would provide a solution to the disk capacity problem for at least the next two years. Additional primary memory would cost $4,000. However, the salesman did not feel either of these additions would enhance processing speed. It was then that the Fenster salesman had described the new Fenster PR 5500 system and its capabilities. Of all the presentations, Carl found the Fenster, IBM, Timeshare, and Network options most appealing.

PRESENTATION

Fenster

The current machine is a Fenster F22A. An external disk drive of 40 MB could be added. This drive will have a 1 ms access time and will probably slow the system down by another 15 to 25 percent. It can, however, provide an inexpensive solution for the next two years. Additional primary storage will allow larger user areas and require less frequent paging and swapping. Only a negligible increase in processing speed would result.

Another alternative is to upgrade to the PR 5500 system. It is newer, faster, and more expandable. The system can use the F22A software. Also, the conversion time would be insignificant (two weeks at most). Most other systems would take longer, since they are not compatible and require at least two additional steps. The first step is the transfer of data from one system to another. The second step involves the time and expense for users to learn to operate the new system.

Buying the new computer (PR 5500) made sense to Carl. The necessary expansion of memory and processing capability would be provided. The response time would be almost like the old system when it was first bought in 1984, and the conversion risk (that of corrupting data and depending on a system that is unknown to Carl and his people) is almost nonexistent.

To make the $158,000 upgrade cost palatable, Hartford Insurance was offering the same bonus commission method of financing that Covert used with the F22A. The only problem with the PR 5500 is that it cannot be expanded into sales and marketing. Any new programs would be a drain on the system, and response time would probably degrade on the PR 5500, also. Only 16 terminals could be connected, which would not be enough for the projected growth of utilization in sales and finance.

IBM

IBM had another answer. Their 4341 superminicomputer could provide all capabilities needed plus more. The package they were selling with the machine supported full operations for an insurance company. The operations functions included customer profiles and portfolio processing, quick quote analysis, market trend analysis, financial processing, commission processing, claim processing, a flexible report-writing capability, and sales summary analysis for varying time periods. The system was also compatible with most insurance corporation computers. The 4341 could hook up with these other systems via a simple phone line and could transfer policy and quote data. The hookup with other computers would reduce the time delay and human labor in starting new policies or changing current ones.

Carl believes the prime consideration with the 4341 system is the degree of risk. Procedures must be changed, Covert data will have to be transferred from the Fenster to the IBM, and the setup may take three to six weeks, or more. In addition, the IBM 4341 is a complex system that will probably require an operator and several programmers if there is to be any program development and/or modification. Further, since the system will be totally new, users and operators will need an indefinite amount of time to learn the system and to "come up to speed" on its many uses.

The software package bundled with the IBM system can perform all the functions desired by Covert Company but the reports and analysis must be customized to the company's specifications, requiring additional up-front effort and expense. Overall, the conversion would take two to three months once the system is delivered. The whole conversion process produced a feeling of anxiety in Carl and left him with many unanswered questions.

In Carl's opinion, the IBM system would be a significant expense for Covert. The hardware price is only $250,000, but the software and training—plus first-year maintenance—are another $220,000. Two nagging questions Carl had immediately were: Just how much improvement in sales and information processing will be achieved? Is it worthwhile?

To resolve these uncertainties, Carl asked the IBM salesperson if he could provide any cost/benefit data or efficiency information. The salesman did not have a formal analysis but he did have some examples from other insurance companies that used IBM systems. He also told Carl that he might be able to arrange a tour of the other IBM 4341 sites for a select group of Covert people. From the examples, Carl was able to make some rough estimates of system impact (see Exhibit 2).

What did it all mean? Carl was not sure. He knew he could reduce it to just costs and a make-or-buy decision, but many of the numbers did not really tell him that much. For example, the efficiency of the salespeople may rise, but there is no certainty that sales and profit would also increase. Since producers are paid on a commission, the increase in processing capability could not be considered a direct cost savings to the company. Also, the salespeople appear to be satisfied with the current level of sales. There was more to this than just numbers. Williams had to look to the future, and he had to be realistic about the company's needs and potential for growth.

Timeshare

Another viable alternative was use of a time-sharing system. The Hartford Insurance Company has a system that it leases to its customers. This system can perform the same functions as the IBM 4341. It does not require a large initial investment, and—like the Fenster computers—it can be financed through bonus commissions.

EXHIBIT 2   System Impact—with and without IBM

- **Salespeople**
  Without system—8 old customer contacts per day.
  With system—16 old customer contacts per day.
  Without system—1 new customer contact per day.
  With system—2 new customer contacts per day.

- **Claims processing**
  Without system—16 per day.
  With system—24 per day.

- **Financial processing time**
  Without system—3 days for accounts payable and receivables reports.
  With system—less than 1 day for accounts payable and receivables reports.

- **Market studies and mailings**
  Without system—none.
  With system—up to 500,000 households can be included.

- **Commission calculations—producer report**
  Without system—1 week for the 26 producers to calculate and manually input data to
  the computer.
  With system—1 day for input and automatic preparation of the report for up to 256
  salespeople.

- **Producer salaries**
  Without system—manually done in 2 days with results from the producer report.
  With system—2- to 3-hour batch job for monthly salaries.

Yet there are certain problems associated with time-sharing systems. First, a user client is at the mercy of someone else's computer. Second, response time can vary greatly depending on user loads. Third, not even minor changes can be made to the sofware package without a time, effort, and dollar cost on the user's part, sometimes a large amount of all three. And finally, the change has to be useful or at least transparent to other users of the same system. Basically, a client loses flexibility and control.

Network

A local computer systems company, Micro-LAN, has another unique solution. By taking several IBM PCs or compatibles and linking—or networking—them with the Fenster, a very powerful local area network could be provided. This configuration would retain the F22A, with the additional 40 MB external drive acting as a central database server; meanwhile, the PCs would furnish the desired distributed processing functions.

The network would reduce the overload on the Fenster, since the Fenster would only function as a data provider and storer. Each PC would be fully devoted to its assigned task. The PCs could be located within each area of concern (e.g., Accounting), and the functional area staff would be responsible for their use and care. Also, the different types of software currently available for the PC could easily meet Covert's current needs. Further, if current trends continued, today's PCs would become as powerful as yesterday's minicomputers, and the software available for them would be voluminous.

The initial configuration would furnish all sales, invoicing, and accounting functions. Other business functions could be added later. The networking alternative would provide Covert with a flexible and powerful tool to continue and expand its operations.

The major problem Carl saw with this proposal was uncertainty. Micro-LAN has an excellent reputation with networking PCs, but the company has no experience with the F22A. Unlike IBM's proven system, the local company is unable to offer examples of its network configuration working in an insurance environment. In addition, all new software will have to be designed and written, or at least modified, to meet Covert's needs.

The time frame for the networking is also painful. The development and implementation would take about six months. The training and orientation time would probably require another month. Overall, the networking alternative would be a longer-term project.

The cost of networking, however, is relatively small. The price of the hardware and software to interface the PCs with the Fenster is only $45,000. The package includes two new PCs. The cost of the additional disk drive for the F22A is $5,000, bringing the total cost to $50,000. New PCs for the system cost about $3,000 each. About 100 PCs could be added to the network easily, providing expansion as needed, although, at this point, Carl foresees the possible purchase of no more than 16 to 24 other PCs. No cost was quoted on software packages for accounting or other functions, but several are available and relatively inexpensive.

SUMMING UP

Carl Williams now has a great quantity of information. Unfortunately, time is short. He must make a decision and resolve Covert's obvious system capacity problem, and it is his decision alone. Carl is proud of his ability to consistently make good insurance decisions for Covert. After all, it was his decisions that made Covert what it is today. Carl decides to attack this problem like he does any other. He creates a matrix (Exhibit 3) of his perceived needs by priority, also describing each system's capabilities to fulfill each need.

But somehow, the matrix falls short. There just does not seem to be enough information. No matter how he structures the problem or analyzes the information he has gathered, a solution fails to emerge.

EXHIBIT 3   Alternatives Matrix

Item	Fenster Disk Drive	PR 5500	IBM 4341	Time-sharing	Network
Cost	$15,000	$110,000	$420,000	$2,000 per month	$45,000 + $3,000 per PC + software
DP function	Same as current	Same as current	Full line	Full line	Full line
Time to order/install	0/2 weeks	2 months/ 2 weeks	3 months/ 3 months	1 month/ 1 month	6 months/ 2 months
Risk	None	Little	Some	Little	High
Memory	40 MB	100 MB +	100 MB +	Unlimited	Fenster memory
Response time (versus current)	25–50% slower	5–10 times faster	10 times faster	Varies	Fenster access; PC speed

It is getting late, as Carl sits at home sipping a Glenlivet. He is determined to make some kind of decision before the start of business tomorrow.

QUESTIONS

1. What is the main function of the system?
   Sales/Marketing? Accounting? Updating accounts?
2. How much risk is *some* or *little*? Does it matter?
3. Given the projected growth, how much memory is, and will be, needed?
4. What is the impact of slow or medium response time?
5. What do you think about the commission arrangement with Hartford?
6. What should Carl Williams do? Support your answer.

Case 7–2 Evanston Insurance Agency

Dan Grube, vice president of the Evanston Insurance Agency (EIA), and president of U.S.I.S, a subsidiary, had been awaiting this computer utilization meeting for some time now. Since 1978, the agency had been dealing with computers in some way or another, and it was now time to take stock of what has occurred and where the agency should go from here. It was mid-August 1987, and Grube was waiting for Albert Eckhart, account executive and vice president of Personnel, Polly Wright from the Claims department, Joan Helms and April Albert from Accounting, and Pauline Lupenek from the Underwriting department. Most of these people had been with Evanston for many years and were involved with the very first computer purchase and installation five years ago. Grube was very concerned that the purchased computers were not being fully utilized and that they were not providing the returns to the firm as predicted at the time of purchase. Also, since the agency's long-standing reputation was one of providing high-quality customer service, Grube was convinced there was some way the system could provide yet a higher level of service.

COMPANY BACKGROUND

In 1978, the Evanston Insurance Agency had just completed its 20th year in the agency business. Three months into the year, two senior partners had irreconcilable differences with the other members of the ownership team, and the company divided. While the Evanston Agency remained basically intact, the separating faction took approximately one third of the annualized premiums, amounting to about $4 million of business. Prior to the split, Evanston had enjoyed a large share of the insurance market in the state of Illinois; in terms of annualized premiums in this rather large market, EIA was about fourth in size. After 20 years of operation, though, EIA was faced not only with the normal serious competition from other insurance agencies but from members of its original team as well. Still, Evanston enjoyed a respected position in Illinois and decided to capitalize on its professional staff; they had reputations as good insurance people, with customer service as their very first priority.

This case was prepared and updated by David Fisher, James Scheulen, and Shawn Hopson. Names, locations, and financial data have been disguised.

PERSONNEL EXPERIENCE

After the split, two of the original Evanston partners stayed on: William Hope, president of EIA, and William Layman, vice president and secretary. Additionally, four key executives remained from the original eight: Victor Good, Albert Eckhart, J. T. Redman, and Dan Grube. These four eventually came to form the strong nucleus of the new Evanston Insurance Agency. Good, Eckhart, and Redman had extensive agency and company underwriting experience; Grube was trained in all phases of the agency business but specialized in developing business of all types for the firm. His basic training was in life insurance, employee benefits, and bonding; Good, Eckhart, and Redman had backgrounds in property and casualty. Overall, these executives presented a variety of backgrounds.

Bill Hope, prior to the split of EIA, managed a select group of business and personal lines accounts. He had grown with EIA since its beginning and knew many business owners on a personal basis, relationships developed through servicing their business and personal needs over the years. Because of this close contact, most of his accounts stayed with him after the division.

William Layman had developed a large underwriting staff in Philadelphia in the 1950s for Stewart Smith, a large London Excess insurance writer. Bill came to EIA in the early 1960s as a partner, bringing several large accounts and other contacts that proved beneficial to EIA's growth in later years.

Victor Good had 30 years of agency underwriting experience. He came to EIA in 1968 from a large Chicago agency where he specialized in property and liability insurance for large and unusual risks. Victor's specialty at EIA was administration and underwriting.

Albert Eckhart joined EIA in 1973 with a background in fire protection engineering. Prior to that, he had spent eight years with The Travelers Insurance Company working with utility companies and large-risk clients with engineering exposures.

J. T. Redman was an underwriter with the Royal Insurance Company for five years prior to coming to EIA in late 1975, prior to the split of the agency. J. T. was expected to develop the underwriting staff with the help of Victor Good. In addition, he worked with some of the larger accounts in the property and casualty area.

Dan Grube started with EIA in 1971, working in the Life and Group department as an account representative. Because of his excellent work, his rapid progression, and his experience in all areas of the insurance industry, he was made vice president in 1976.

ORGANIZATION AND CULTURE

The group of six was able to convince a total of 17 of the 26 people who originally comprised Evanston prior to the division to remain. The decision to stay was very important to all of these original staff members; many were placed in key positions during the transition and performed very well. Management supported them at every turn but these staff members really did the job expected of them.

The atmosphere at EIA that promoted employee devotion had paid off, although Evanston had long been a place where people came to work and stayed. In fact, since 1984, only two people had been hired, and they replaced long-term employees who chose to retire. This was a company where everyone knew everyone else well and approached their work as a team. Insurance is a people-oriented business, and continuity of personnel is a vital asset. Exhibit 1 illustrates the organizational chart shortly after the division, and Exhibit 2 shows the revised chart as of 1986 (the three major divisions: Illinois Leasing, International Underwriters, and U.S.I.S. will be discussed later in the case).

GROWTH AFTER 1978

As an independent agency with no outside brokers (the partners are the exclusive developers of insurance business), the new EIA emerged from the split smaller but determined to resume its leadership role in the community. Between 1978 and 1981, the Evanston Agency grew at a rate of $1 million per year, returning the firm to the premium size it enjoyed before the split. The number of employees grew from 17 to 26; since 1981, EIA has been able to maintain a rate of growth approaching $2 million per year. At the time of this meeting in 1987, Grube was delighted to see that EIA had resumed its position within the industry; it was now a $20 million insurance agency.

INSURANCE BUSINESS

The Evanston Agency conducted insurance business of all kinds—from personal lines of insurance to group insurance, property and casualty, and contract bonding. A subsidiary of EIA, International Underwriters (IU), was a special company dealing with unusual risk situations; as such, it conducted most of its business with Lloyds of London. Examples of the types of risks written by International are the major bridges and tunnels around the Chicago area. William Hope served as president of IU; Victor Good served as executive vice president and managed all the underwriting activity for this company.

The vast majority of the business, however, was conducted directly by EIA, which operated in a variety of environments. A full-service agency, EIA provides service and protection to individuals, businesses, public utilities, counties, con-

EXHIBIT 1 Organization Charts—1978

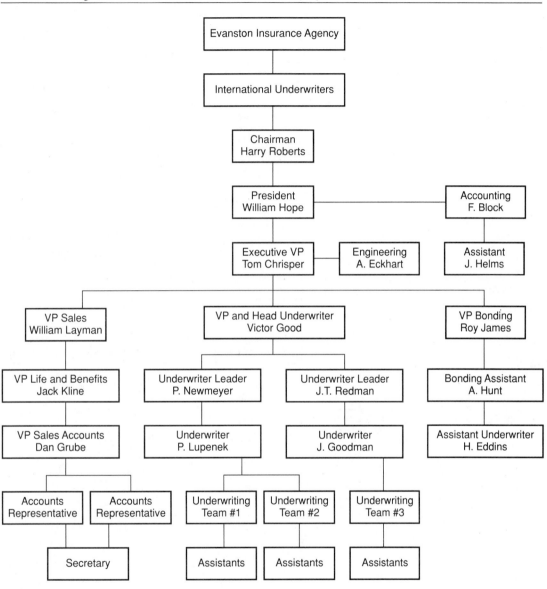

tractors, and developers, as well as to employees of many industries through its various lines of business.

The personal lines department—selling life, auto, and homeowner insurance—serves the largest number of clients but accounts for only about 5 percent of

EXHIBIT 2   Organization Chart — 1986

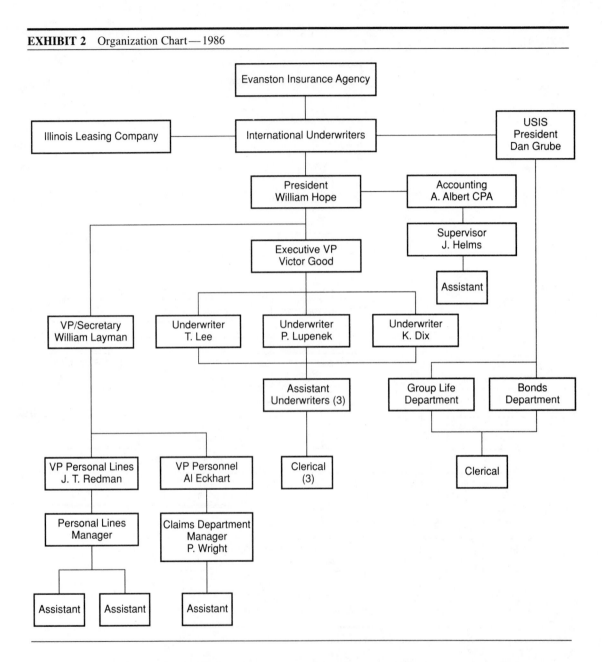

Evanston's total business in terms of premium dollars. Contract bonding (financial and performance guarantees) accounts for about 10 percent, as does the Group and Life department.

The single largest department is the property and casualty insurance for business. Major contractors, utility companies, and major developers insured equipment, buildings, and business automobiles with EIA.

Since EIA has no independent brokers (outside salespeople), most of the business is produced by Layman, Grube, and Hope and comes primarily from referrals by satisfied clients.

It is common for businesses to begin their relationship with EIA by purchasing property and casualty policies; later, when other policies are due, they switch their group policies and employee benefit packages to the Evanston Agency. It is also not unusual for individuals within these companies to purchase their personal insurance through the firm.

ACCOUNTING AND RECORD-KEEPING

In order to service clients, a number of accounting and record-keeping processes are required. Personal lines and business insurance procedures are similar and follow the same general guidelines:

1. Gather data about the client and/or equipment to be insured.
2. Judge and rate the risk to the insurance company—the rating process.
3. Complete application to develop cost from underwriters.
4. Send application to the insurance company if the cost is acceptable; client submits payment to EIA.
5. Insurance companies bill EIA each month for premiums due.
6. EIA pays bills, having already collected premiums due from clients.

BONDING

The bonding process is somewhat different. Although underwritten by insurance companies, a bond is not insurance in the true sense of the word. Rather, it is a financial and performance guarantee to the developer or financial institution that the contractor will meet all contractual responsibilities. Considering the amount of money involved in large development projects, the past performance and preceding three years' financial records of the contractor seeking a bond are scrutinized by the agency representative; that is usually Dan Grube. Before any bond is issued, Grube must be reasonably sure that the contractor will perform. This aggregate of information is then submitted to an insurance company for approval of bonding credit. Following a personal interview with the contractor, the bonding insurance company finalizes the agreement.

CLAIMS PROCESS

Like the application process, claims are managed through a series of similar steps, regardless of the type of insurance. On receiving a call regarding a claim, a Claims department employee will:

1. Gather the required information.
2. Notify insurance company providing insurance and/or directly issue a check for claims less than $750.
3. Collect damage repair estimates from clients or adjustor.
4. Notify insurance company of amount of money required.
5. Collect check from company.
6. Pass check to client.

During the claims process, it is very important that Evanston act as the client's advocate with the large insurance company. It is precisely this service that keeps independent agencies in business. So, claims service must be friendly, fast, and efficient.

The Evanston Agency provides coverage through essentially all of the major national insurance companies (Exhibit 3). However, because of rate differences, personal preferences regarding certain risks, or discounts for grouping, the majority of business is conducted through three companies: Reliance Insurance Company, the Hartford, and The Travelers Insurance.

EXHIBIT 3   Major National Insurance Companies Represented by Evanston

Largest Insurance Companies

Aetna Casualty & Surety Company	Maryland Casualty Company
The Chubb Corporation	Reliance Insurance Company
Crum & Forster Insurance Company	Rockwood Insurance Company
Fidelity & Deposit Company	Royal Insurance Company
Fireman's Fund Insurance Company	St. Paul Insurance Company
Hartford Mutual Insurance Company	The Travelers Insurance Company
The Hartford Insurance Group	Zurick-American Insurance Companies
Industrial Risk Insurers	

Excess and Surplus

All Risk, Ltd.	L. E. Harris Agency, Inc.
Waller Excess, Inc.	Markel Service, Inc.
Horan Goldman Companies	St. Paul Specialty Brokers, Inc.

COMPUTERIZATION OF EIA

Considering the nature of the industry and the recent changes in EIA, in 1978 the board of directors of the newly restructured Evanston Insurance Agency began to think about utilization of computers and computer services in their setting. While it was true that the 350 business customers and the roughly 3,500 personal lines customers were being effectively managed without computers, the board was concerned about the future. Also, many of the major competing insurance companies were beginning to think about offering computer systems to support independent agencies that gave them business. While no one really expected the companies to provide the machinery, everyone expected that the big companies would be providing some assistance in the form of equipment financing.

It was generally felt that, through programs like this, the industry was moving toward development of a paperless rating process — application, underwriting, and claims, all to be conducted electronically. While this would clearly leave significant costs for the agencies, those that could afford the investment were precisely the agencies with whom the big companies wanted to conduct business.

DATA PROCESSING AT EIA

In 1978, EIA was using a large data processing service, known as ARC, for its accounting needs. ARC, a very large service located in Texas, served the accounting needs of firms across the nation. For a fee of $500 per month, ARC provided Evanston Insurance with monthly invoices, balance sheets, and profit and loss statements. EIA's professional accounting team used ARC as a collecting and processing unit. Semiannual and year-end statements, as well as financial business planning, were provided by this professional accounting firm. For some time, ARC's service was quite acceptable; but, as the 1980s began, the turnaround times between ARC's receipt of data and the return of invoices and information to EIA grew substantially; turnaround was often as long as nine days (whereas three to four days had been the standard). The invoicing delays soon led to cash flow difficulties for EIA since their billing times were no longer synchronized with others.

LOOKING FOR A NEW SYSTEM

With little improvement expected, and the industry beginning to move toward computerization, it is easy to see why Victor Good became interested in the computer systems of agencies in nearby states. So, in the summer of 1982, when The Travelers Insurance Company approached EIA about accepting a system linked to their own, there was considerable interest at EIA. It was sparked by more than the potential accounting applications. Frankly, everyone at EIA thought that accounting alone could not provide enough utilization—but the large system demands of accounting plus claims and policy management certainly could.

For the next two to three months, representatives of EBS, a computer sales subsidiary of The Travelers, met with Good and others at EIA. At the same time, Good traveled to agencies in the surrounding states to learn about their systems. Because he managed just a few large accounts and had fallen into the role of performing the initial research, Victor Good had inherited the role of computer leader for EIA. He collected the information and reported back to the board of directors.

EBS arranged for Good and two others, Joan Helms and Pauline Lupenek, to visit an agency in Ohio that had been using a Data General system like the one proposed for EIA. During their visit, the system won good reviews from the users and certainly seemed to work well. Since the system looked good, The Travelers was a large, reliable, and important company in the industry, and the EBS financing offer was excellent, EIA chose to purchase the Data General system in November 1982. In order to maximize the 1982 tax benefits, EIA insisted on delivery before Janaury 1, 1983.

At the time of purchase, Illinois Leasing was created as a subsidiary of Evanston Insurance Agency for the purpose of owning this and other computer equipment. For the purchase price of $126,000, EIA received a Data General mainframe computer (DG S/120), nine CRTs, and one printer. One of the CRT terminals would be capable of word processing; the others would be for data entry and retrieval.

UNEXPECTED ADDITIONAL COSTS

In December, at the time of delivery, EIA executives were surprised to find that they had received less than accurate information from the EBS sales team regarding the required housing of this mainframe computer. Expected to be able to locate the machine in an open area, they were disturbed to find that they must now invest in building a separate room, costing $9,000, with air conditioning and electrical alterations. While construction plans were drawn in February 1983, Good, Helms, and Lupenek attended an EBS training program lasting five days.

With the Data General system still not operational in March of 1983 and business expanding (particularly in the personal lines), Albert Eckhart, Account Executive for Personal Lines, proposed at a monthly board meeting that EIA purchase a microcomputer to help in the rating process. Although there was presently no software to perform just this function, he was dispatched to explore the possibilities. By June, Eckhart had found both the hardware and software to perform the rating of personal line clients. While the Data General equipment was being installed, EIA purchased an Apple IIe computer in order to manage the large volume of personal line ratings.

OPERATIONAL PROBLEMS

By October of 1983, the Data General (DG) system was operational but to a very limited extent, performing only accounting duties, and those poorly. ARC, even with a nine-day turnaround, was more efficient; meanwhile, the policy database was being entered. At the same time, while displeased with the system, EIA was convinced by EBS sales representatives that these bugs would be worked out. When they were corrected, EIA would need additional CRTs for the system; therefore, nine additional CRT stations and a software upgrade were purchased. The software upgrade required additional hardware alterations, leading to a total cost of $57,000. At that point, Vince Good and Albert Eckhart decided that—since Good's interest and patience were fading, and Eckhart was becoming more involved—Eckhart would take over the computer operations for the agency.

EIA was having considerable difficulty inputting data and getting reliable output; even so, complaints and requests to EBS were met only with the suggestion that EIA personnel were obviously making some sort of error in their procedures.

In December of 1983, when the entire accounts receivable file was lost from the computer, EBS discovered that they themselves had made an error in formatting the system.

One year after purchase, in January 1984, the Data General system was finally functioning properly, performing accounting and database management; nevertheless, it was mistrusted and grossly underutilized.

CREATION OF USIS

A few months later (May 1984), Grube and Layman had succeeded in attracting a client group with over 13,000 members across the nation. After months of negotiation, EIA was chosen as the insurance agency to manage the insurance needs of the members of the National Association of Ophthalmologists. The malpractice work alone would create a substantial windfall for the firm. Since this account was so large, and was really quite different from any of the other accounts managed by EIA, EIA created the United States Insurance Service (USIS) as a subsidiary to manage this account; Grube was appointed president. This account would be large enough to justify the purchase of its own computer system for mass mailing, rating, invoicing, and accounting services.

PROBLEMS PERSIST

With the frustrations of EBS still fresh in their minds, the board decided to approach Rick Henry, a personal friend of Bill Layman (VP of EIA). Rick operated his own computer business; through him, Illinois Leasing purchased a

Seiko Computer System with four CRT terminals. As with the DG system, USIS soon found that the system had been oversold; it could not do all it was expected to do.

Mailings and ratings could not be completed efficiently together; since a large portion of servicing this account involved direct mail marketing, USIS found itself doing ratings during daylight hours and leaving the machine running at night to perform the required mailings. Users of the system found it very difficult to use, so difficult that some processes were easier done by hand.

To solve the problem, Rick Henry suggested that USIS might want to invest in a new system that would be available shortly. There were no satisfactory upgrades to the existing Seiko system, although Henry had initially said such an upgrade would be available soon. Before this decision was required, the malpractice crisis in the insurance industry became a reality. The Hartford, underwriter of the specially formatted Ophthalmology malpractice policy, informed USIS that they would no longer provide coverage. Although the Ophthalmology business had been lucrative for USIS (some $2 million in one year), they decided not to pursue the account further.

In August of 1986, The Travelers Company supplied EIA with two IBM AT computers designed to interface with The Travelers — to furnish rate quotes, handle claims inquiries, and provide electronic mail. A year later, because of hardware and software difficulties, the system was still not operating.

COMPLAINTS ABOUT THE CURRENT SYSTEM AT EIA

Exhibit 4 summarizes the computer systems now in place at EIA. Grube reflected on what a difficult road computerization had been. Because the process of computerizing the office affected so many people, Grube asked representatives of each department to submit a summary of their recollections and feelings about the systems now in place. Awaiting the arrival of his other committee members, he reviewed his summary of their submissions:

From the Underwriting Department.   ''We feel that there is now as much —if not more—paperwork than before and that the system is not used to its full potential. Data in the system is not always reliable since not all employees update files often enough. We're very concerned about the amount of downtime in system. People are still reluctant to use the system, given the prolonged period of difficulties. Also, the members of this department have learned to use the machine essentially by trial and error and by consulting another insurance agency in Missouri that uses this same DG system.''

From the Accounting Department.   ''Very mixed feelings in this group since it was here that initial implementation was to have the greatest impact. Those involved since the beginning are generally frustrated since initial training was

---

EXHIBIT 4   Evanston Insurance Agency's
Computer Equipment

---

1 Seiko 8200, 32 MB hard disk
4 Seiko 8260 CRTs
1 Toshiba P1350 printer
1 Spinwriter 3530 printer
1 Data General Eclipse S/120, 73 MB
1 Dasher D200 master CRT
19 Dasher D200 CRTs
1 Printronix printer
1 Diablo 630 printer
2 IBM Personal Computers (AT)
2 Hayes Smart Modem 1200s
2 IBM ProPrinters
1 Apple IIe, 64 K
1 Apple IIe, 1 MB
1 Okidata 93 Micro line printer

---

inadequate; the service provided by the system was clearly substandard to ARC —until very recently. In fact, some people believe the information provided by the DG system is not as good as ARC's, especially considering the huge cost differential. All feel that the system is underutilized, but most do not have the time or are afraid to experiment with other potential uses like word processing. The general feeling is that the initial training was inadequate, the initial users (and even the present users) were too overloaded with work while attempting to learn the system, and EBS still does not have adequate training programs.''

From Personal Lines.   ''Most of the Personal Line business is done on the Apple system, which generally satisfies the staff. The applications on the Apple, however, are limited to rating accounts.

''Database management of policy information is provided by the DG system. While having a computer system greatly enhances the agency's image, our people generally feel that the system has not performed adequately. Only about 80 percent of client records have been loaded, after three years of four hours per day of data inputting and updating. Today, with the system basically running well, accounts are updated first by hand, hand-recorded and filed, and then entered into the computer database.''

The board of directors has run short of patience in dealing with the Evanston computer situation. They made it clear at the last meeting that within one month, they expected a full report on the current status of systems. They also want to know where EIA is heading with information systems and how they plan to get there.

CONCLUSION

The meeting attendees arrived in a group and quickly seated themselves around the large conference table. After brief greetings to Grube and some small talk among themselves, they quieted down and looked toward Dan. He spoke.

"Ladies and gentleman, we've got some serious planning to do, starting right now. It's 1:30; we've all had lunch; I hope none of you have anything planned for the rest of the day—or evening."

QUESTIONS

1. Describe Evanston's planning process for systems development (including, at least, definition, design, acquisition, and implementation).
2. Where do you rank Evanston on the spectrum of Nolan's stages?
3. Explain Evanston's definition of an automated system and compare the definition to Kroenke's five components.
4. Should Evanston consider using a consultant? If so, what would you want the consultant to do?
5. Describe the corporate culture at EIA.
6. What was the overall reaction of the major departments in EIA to the computer systems?
7. What are EIA's options, as the case ends? Which one do you recommend and why?

Case 7–3 Mid-States Gas & Electric Company (MSG&E)

The Information Systems Center has two types of resources available to all MSG&E employees. First, there is a variety of hardware (PCs, terminals, plotters, and printers, for example) available for hands-on testing and evaluation, allowing potential user lessors-purchasers to see what type of equipment will meet their needs. Second, personnel are available to answer questions that users might have regarding problems that arise after they have obtained hardware. As yet, however, the Information Systems Center has not been well publicized to all company employees, nor has it been completely staffed. Once the availability and usefulness of the Information Systems Center's resources are known within MSG&E, new

This case was prepared by Richard Thomas and Dave Sarmir and was later revised. Names, locations, and financial data have been disguised.

requests for assistance from functional area users are likely to generate even greater staffing problems. The Management Information Services department (MISD) manager, Chris Timberlake — who also supervises the Information Systems Center—must therefore convince senior management of the importance of the Center if it is to be a success.

MSG&E's Office of the Auditor selects system automation proposals at random to verify the accuracy of the costs and savings estimated at project inception, but as yet there is no comprehensive charge-back to user departments. Timberlake is concerned about this situation and will be phasing in a limited charge-back system in 1987. This charge-back will cover only the hardware for the various proposals. None of the development or maintenance manpower costs will be charged back to the user, although Chris is considering this possibility.

COMPANY BACKGROUND

The Mid-States Gas & Electric Company (MSG&E) is a public electric and gas utility serving the central plains area. It is well known across the country as an investment offering a low level of risk to investors. The corporate bond rating by Standard & Poor's is AAA. Dividends have been very regular, with the yield averaging about 10.5 percent over the past two years. Stock recently was split two for one at approximately $50 per share (before the split). Sales for the past year were over $1.75 billion.

Mid-States Gas & Electric Company has a reputation in the Iowa/Kansas/ Missouri area as "a good place to work." Employee benefits are comparable to other large nearby corporations, and employees feel adequately taken care of by the company. The corporate managerial climate is professional and conservative. Advancement is clearly by accomplishment but knowing the right people does help to increase the visibility of individual accomplishments. The company's policy is to promote from within if possible. To this end, there is an extensive human resource development program to identify potential candidates for future openings within the company.

UTILITY DIVERSIFICATION

Many utilities in this country are beginning to diversify by investing in nonregulated areas. Subsidiaries, although not themselves under the jurisdiction of the Public Service Commission, receive and transmit funds through the parent organization. If the parent organization is itself regulated, then fund transfers through it are under regulatory oversight. The subsidiaries can become fully nonregulated, a more desirable status, by being sold off or divested from the regulated utility. Another approach is to form a holding company that owns the utility as well as the nonregulated businesses, if any. In this way, only the public utility is regulated; the holding company structure facilitates the movement of funds from one business to another, circumventing the scrutiny of the regulatory agency.

Mid-States Gas & Electric Company, however, has the distinction of being incorporated in a state that prohibits any other corporation from owning more than 12 percent of a public utility. This means that a holding company cannot be formed to own MSG&E. Therefore, any funds transfer through MSG&E can be scrutinized by the Public Service Commission overseeing MSG&E.

HOLDING COMPANY—CONTINENTAL RESOURCE MANAGEMENT

In an attempt to provide maximum flexibility to MSG&E subsidiaries, a holding company was placed between MSG&E and its wholly owned subsidiaries. Funds can be transferred among the sub-subsidiaries, as long as these funds do not pass through the MSG&E parent. Therefore, the legal restriction has not prevented MSG&E from proceeding with its strong commitment to diversify.

Diversification is an industry trend, and MSG&E is determined to be out in front. The company currently has two subsidiaries: Continental Water Power Company and Continental Resource Management. MSG&E is two-thirds owner of Continental Water Power and has been for many years. This represents merely an extension of its traditional utility operations. Continental Resource, however, is a recent acquisition for MSG&E and is itself the holding company of three distinct investments: Kansas City Capital Resources, Central City Biogas, and Central Property Management (see Exhibit 1).

EXHIBIT 1 MSG&E Corporate Structure

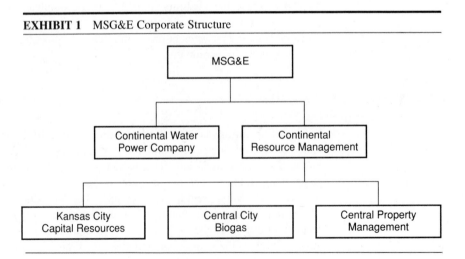

Kansas City Capital Resources is an investment concern, owning, among other things, half of three Boeing 747 jetliners with Royal Scandia Airlines. Central City Biogas is an endeavor to generate methane gas (for sale to MSG&E) from raw sewage. Central Property Management is an industrial real estate developer that started out buying fly ash from MSG&E's Riverside coal-fired generating plant for use as landfill material in a new industrial park across the street from the plant itself.

The holding company/diversification strategy has many advantages. One is that it specifically precludes a hostile takeover of MSG&E and thereby allows greater liquidity of corporate funds without management fearing for their jobs. MSG&E plans to continue seeking new avenues to diversify its expanded array of holdings in the future.

PROJECT MANAGEMENT DEPARTMENT

In 1981, the company consisted of eight divisions (see Exhibit 2, 1–8). In 1983, management found itself overcommitted in handling a number of large-scale projects. The projects ranged from the construction of a new coal-fired power plant to the replacement of their nuclear plant's computer monitoring systems. In order to control those projects more efficiently, management decided to create a new Project Management department in the Facility Construction division. The department has a few managerial-level people who work full-time in the department. Most of the remainder of the department's staff are "matrixed" individuals from other departments across the company. This matrix organization provides human resources and expertise to the Project Management department, without removing employees from their respective home departments. These individuals are on temporary or full-time assignment, but working part-time for Project Management and only for the duration of specific projects.

RECENT REORGANIZATION

As stated in a recent reorganization announcement, the Facility Construction division (consisting of the Electronics and Project Management departments), and the Logistics division (consisting of the Maintenance, Coal Power, Hydrogen Power, Quality Control, and Gas Resources departments) will be realigned, by moving functions into two newly created divisions (see Exhibit 2a). The Hydrogen Power division (HPD) will be responsible for all nuclear projects and will be based at the Big Bluff Hydrogen Power Plant, 40 miles west of the corporate offices in Kansas City. The Coal Power division (CPD) will handle all fossil power–related projects and will be located in the corporate offices. There are four departments in each division, assuming the functions of the old departments mentioned above: Each division will have an Operating department, a Mainte-

EXHIBIT 2   Mid-States Gas & Electric Company Partial Organization Chart—1986

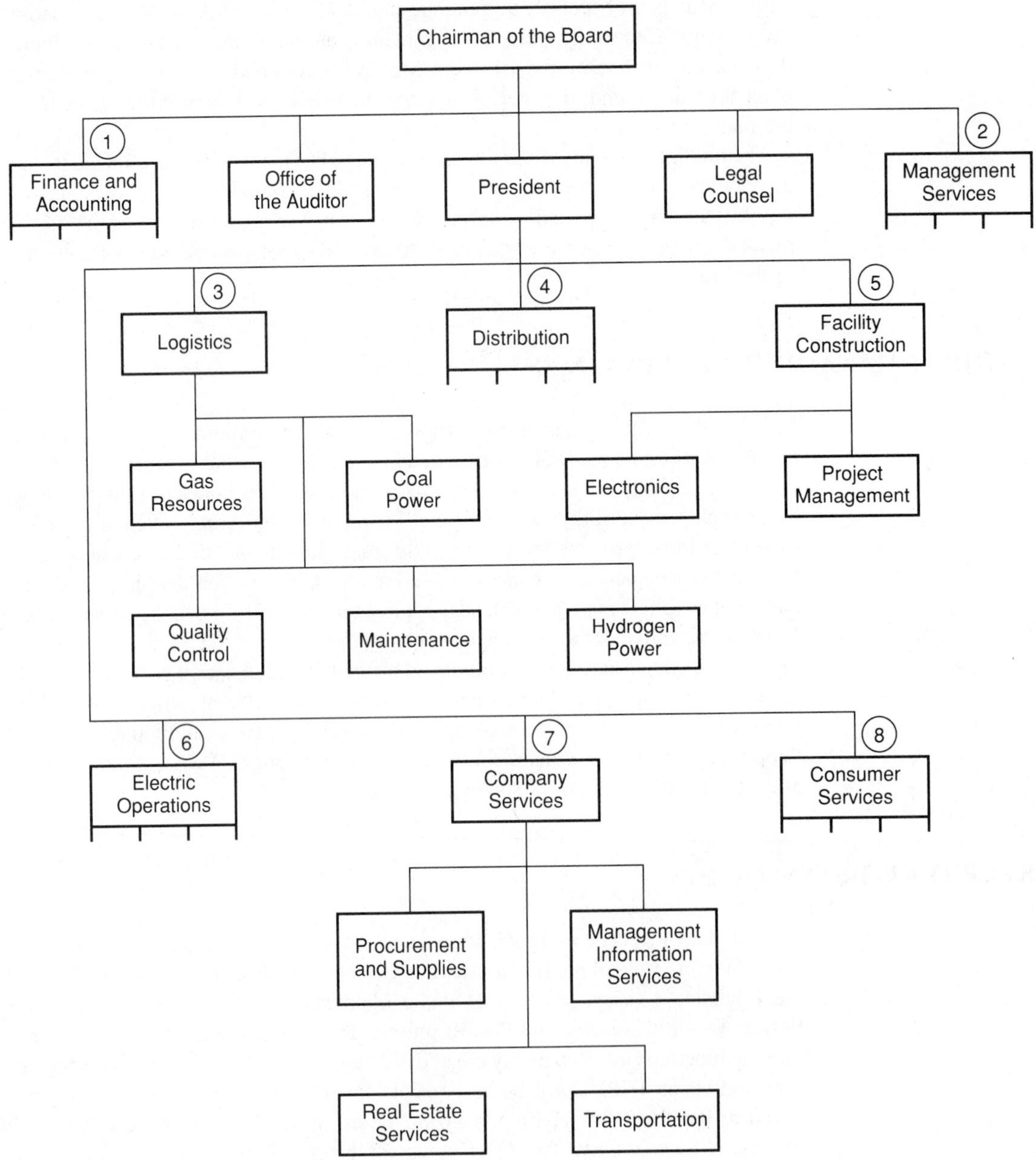

```
                          ┌─────────────────────┐
                          │ Chairman of the Board│
                          └─────────────────────┘

  ①                    ┌─────────────┐    ┌───────────┐    ②
┌───────────┐  ┌──────────────┐ │  President   │  │   Legal   │  ┌──────────────┐
│Finance and│  │  Office of   │ └─────────────┘  │  Counsel  │  │  Management  │
│Accounting │  │ the Auditor  │                   └───────────┘  │   Services   │
└───────────┘  └──────────────┘                                  └──────────────┘

        ③                    ④                       ⑤
   ┌───────────┐        ┌──────────────┐        ┌──────────────┐
   │ Logistics │        │ Distribution │        │   Facility   │
   └───────────┘        └──────────────┘        │ Construction │
                                                 └──────────────┘

   ┌───────────┐  ┌───────────┐   ┌────────────┐   ┌──────────────┐
   │    Gas    │  │   Coal    │   │Electronics │   │   Project    │
   │ Resources │  │   Power   │   └────────────┘   │  Management  │
   └───────────┘  └───────────┘                    └──────────────┘

   ┌───────────┐  ┌────────────┐   ┌────────────┐
   │  Quality  │  │Maintenance │   │  Hydrogen  │
   │  Control  │  └────────────┘   │   Power    │
   └───────────┘                   └────────────┘

        ⑥                    ⑦                       ⑧
   ┌───────────┐        ┌──────────────┐        ┌──────────────┐
   │  Electric │        │   Company    │        │   Consumer   │
   │ Operations│        │   Services   │        │   Services   │
   └───────────┘        └──────────────┘        └──────────────┘

              ┌──────────────┐   ┌──────────────┐
              │ Procurement  │   │  Management  │
              │ and Supplies │   │ Information  │
              └──────────────┘   │   Services   │
                                 └──────────────┘

              ┌──────────────┐   ┌──────────────┐
              │ Real Estate  │   │Transportation│
              │   Services   │   └──────────────┘
              └──────────────┘
```

EXHIBIT 2a   Mid-States Gas & Electric Company Partial Organizational Chart—1987

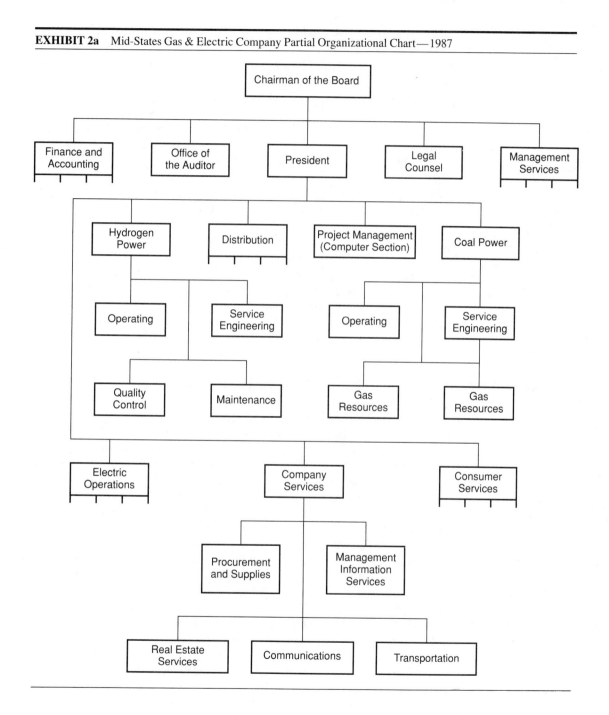

nance department, and a Service Engineering department. The Coal Power division will also have a Gas Resources department, and the Hydrogen Power division will have a Quality Control department. With the creation of the two new divisions, and reshuffling old departments into new ones, the Project Management department has become an infant mortality statistic—the various projects handled by the Project Management department have all been moved into one of the new divisions. The only section within Project Management that has not yet been reassigned to a new department or division is the Computer section, currently managing ICS and three very large computer replacement projects: The Big Bluff Plant's Information Collection System (ICS) and its Plant Computer-Replacement project are very important to the company, since Big Bluff is the source of over 60 percent of MSG&E's average annual electric generation. This low-cost source of electric power actually saves the company millions of dollars annually and saves MSG&E customers an average of $20 per month on electric bills.

In the reorganization, the Communications section of the Electronics department became a new department. This department was placed in the Company Services division along with the Management Information Services department. The new department, Communications, handles all voice and data communications in the company, and therefore, interfaces heavily with Management Information Services.

MANAGEMENT INFORMATION SERVICES DEPARTMENT

MSG&E's Management Information Services department is in the Company Services division and is considered an operating department. The department handles most of the small to medium-sized computer software and hardware projects of the company. Projects on stand-alone computer equipment that have an estimated cost of $500,000 or more are handled by the Project Management department. This rule is flexible, and the decision is still up to the discretion of senior management. Every other department has some dealings with and dependency on Management Information Services. The total Management Information Services work program (operating) budget for last year was approximately $22 million, representing about $1\frac{1}{3}$ percent of sales (see Exhibit 3). The department's capital budget was about $6 million (see Exhibit 4).

The Management Information Services department (MISD) consists of five sections (see Exhibit 5). Closest to the manager's office is the Plans Control section. Plans Control monitors and controls the work flow within the department. The department is responsible for providing reports to the manager on manpower and computer resource usage. Resource usage projections also are prepared by this section. Control procedures are designed and implemented by Plans Control, as are internal training and standards. Plans Control recently was given the responsibility for all office automation (OA) and personal computer (PC) proposals, including purchase, installation, and maintenance of the equipment. Some training

EXHIBIT 3   Company Services Division

Work Program Budget
(in thousands of dollars)

	1986 Budget	Adjustment	1986 Adjusted Budget	1987 Budget Limit	1987 Budget Request	Request Minus Limit	Percent Deviation
C1—VP Company Services	$ 41		$ 41	$ 43	$ 46	$ 3	12.2%
C2—Management Information Services	22,003	66	22,069	22,952	22,795	(157)	3.3
C3—Procurement and Supplies	10,511	62	10,573	10,996	10,977	(19)	3.8
C4—Real Estate	41,309	(7,584)	33,725	35,074	35,432	358	5.1
C5—Transportation	26,669	37	26,706	27,774	27,648	(126)	3.5
C6—Communications	0	7,702	7,702	8,010	9,240	1,230	20.0
Total	$100,533	$ 283	$100,816	$104,849	$106,138	$1,289	5.3%

is offered in standard software for the PCs, but no detailed support is provided for application software. Mid-States Gas & Electric has been experiencing a proliferation of OA and PC equipment and a corresponding expansion of user-written "semisoftware" (database and spreadsheet-type procedures). To provide the users of these systems with adequate support, while allowing them the flexibility to develop their own applications, Plans Control has set up an Information Systems Center.

INFORMATION SYSTEMS CENTER

With hardware costs declining drastically, and the cost of experienced programming and analysis staff increasing, the Information Systems Center is one method of transferring labor costs from expensive programming staff to less expensive user staff (often clerk-level personnel). The availability of quality computer personnel is relatively low. Allowing users to develop some of their own software or semisoftware frees up experienced MISD staff for projects that require their expertise. This also helps reduce the MISD budget, in lieu of a comprehensive charge-back system. Although MISD management has taken the position of encouraging users to develop software on their own, concern has risen about lack of adequate documentation and standards of such user-written software. To attack this problem, a manual of Automatic Data Processing Standards has been developed and distributed to all departments. The standards outline what the Office of the Auditor requires of user-written software, particularly in the areas of documentation and procedures.

EXHIBIT 4   Company Services Division

Capital Budget Comparison
Summary—1986 versus 1987 (28-Nov-86)

Department	1986 Capital Budget	1987 Capital Budget	Difference	Percent Change
C2—Management Information Services	$ 6,089,000	$ 7,842,000	$ 1,753,000	28.8%
C3—Procurement and Supplies	250,000	134,500	(115,500)	−46.2
C4—Real Estate	18,049,000	29,782,000	11,733,000	65.0
C5—Transportation	7,925,000	9,350,000	1,425,000	18.0
C6—Communications	2,725,000	1,271,000	(1,454,000)	−53.4
Total	$35,038,000	$48,379,500	$13,341,500	38.1%

The Systems Maintenance section (MIS-SM) has a more technical slant. One unit of the section is responsible for the support and maintenance of the two corporate IBM 3081 mainframe computers and two Hewlett-Packard 3000 mini-computers. Activities include installation and support of general use software packages, documentation of hardware problems, and subsequent contact of vendors for repair. Another unit handles the administration of databases on the company systems. A third unit maintains security by assigning passwords and file access authorizations on these systems. Although the Plans Control section handles manpower projections and planning, Systems Maintenance is responsible for capacity planning for MSG&E computer hardware resources. Systems Maintenance was deemed better able to plan future computer usage because of their technical expertise.

The Operations section (MIS-O) is responsible for the ongoing operations and processes of the company computer center. The Administration unit is responsible for the administrative tasks associated with the corporate computer center. This involves security procedures and records handling. The Operations unit (of the Operations section) handles the operation of the company computer systems. The unit's job consists of actually running the day-to-day production jobs for users of the systems, mounting of tape and disk media, and maintaining efficient distribution of system loading. This also includes Computer Output Microfilm (COM) machines, optical character readers (OCR) for reading customer bills, and the operation of two company Hewlett-Packard 3000 minicomputers. The Scheduling unit controls the scheduling of production jobs, the handling of external media (i.e., vendor tapes) to be sent to the computer center, and the distribution of computer-generated output to the various users. Finally, there are the Data Entry unit and Mail unit, whose names accurately reflect their responsibilities.

EXHIBIT 5   Management Information Services Department Summary

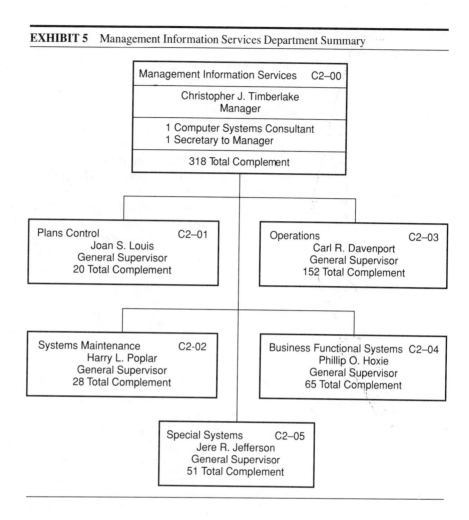

Management Information Services   C2–00
Christopher J. Timberlake
Manager
1 Computer Systems Consultant
1 Secretary to Manager
318 Total Complement

Plans Control   C2–01
Joan S. Louis
General Supervisor
20 Total Complement

Operations   C2–03
Carl R. Davenport
General Supervisor
152 Total Complement

Systems Maintenance   C2-02
Harry L. Poplar
General Supervisor
28 Total Complement

Business Functional Systems C2–04
Phillip O. Hoxie
General Supervisor
65 Total Complement

Special Systems   C2–05
Jere R. Jefferson
General Supervisor
51 Total Complement

BUSINESS FUNCTIONAL AND SPECIAL SYSTEMS SECTIONS

The remaining two sections — Business Functional and Special Systems — are both programming and development sections. These two sections are responsible for analysis, design, programming, system documentation, and ongoing programming support. The difference between the Business Functional and Special Systems sections is the type of applications that each develops and supports.

Business Functional Section

The Business Functional section (MIS-BF), as its name implies, is responsible for applications dealing with the business aspects of the company. These are systems such as customer bills, stockholder accounts, payroll, employee benefits, and accounting and finance systems. Many are on-line systems with transactions posted to the computer database one at a time, as information is keyed in on computer terminals. The real-time aspect updates the database continually. These on-line systems were develped from the older batch systems written in the mid-70s. Most of the programs are coded in COBOL. Almost all of these systems are run on the company IBM mainframe computer systems. One notable exception is the meter-reading operation, which uses an IBM minicomputer to initialize and read hand-held, automated meter-reading devices (calculatorlike machines used in the field by meter readers who key-enter meter readings directly into the device). The meter readings captured by the IBM mini are subsequently transmitted to the company mainframe for actual processing.

Special Systems Section

The Special Systems section (MIS-SS) is responsible for most other program applications within the company, including engineering modeling programs on the company mainframe, indexing/retrieval (document) systems on corporate minicomputers, electrical load forecasting and economic modeling, and tracking of radiological exposure records of nuclear plant workers. The section's duties also include maintenance of a number of real-time computer systems within the company. MSG&E defines *real-time computers* as computers connected to field sensors and controlling devices, which cannot accept any delay in responsiveness. They continually scan temperatures and pressures in operating environments and optionally send signals out to controlling devices to alter the environment (valves and pumps).

To program effectively on these computers, the programmers must become much more familiar with the operating system (or "central brain" program) of the computer. The company owns over one hundred different real-time computer systems, many made by different producers or purchased from different vendors. Programming is done in FORTRAN, assembly language, and machine langauge. Although FORTRAN (like COBOL) is very similar from one computer to the next, assembly and machine languages vary from one vendor's hardware to another and are therefore more difficult to support. The increased flexibility of these languages, however, necessitates their use for operating system functions.

CHRIS TIMBERLAKE

Chris Timberlake, the manager of the Management Information Services department, is well known and liked by the corporate management. He has a mellow personality and a flair for organizational efficiency. Chris is 46 years old and received his bachelor's degree in Electrical Engineering from Purdue. He has served in a variety of capacities within the Company Services division. He has been a general supervisor in both the Procurement and Supplies department, and Customer Service department. In the mid-70s, he served for three years on the Automatic Data Processing Coordination Committee (ADPCC).

Chris first became a department manager in the Distribution department, where he reshuffled the department's major responsibilities. Efficiency was improved, as evidenced by significant cost savings. Naturally, the cost savings were well received by upper management and may very well explain why Timberlake was moved to the Management Information Services department and became the new manager. This explanation of the transfer seems reasonable, since Chris had no prior experience with computer systems. His assignment caused some minor unrest within the department, since some people argued that more technically oriented candidates for manager were available within the department. Many staff members would have preferred any one of the more technically oriented people to Chris, whose major MSG&E experience was in business functions.

MANAGEMENT INFORMATION SERVICES STAFF

Joan Louis

Joan Louis is the general supervisor for the Plans Control section. She is in her mid-30s and has both a bachelor's and master's degree in Business Administration from the University of Dayton. She has worked her way up to her present position by spending most of her time in the Business Functional section of the Management Information Services department. She is well liked within the department, both by management and subordinates, and has a particular talent for organization and project control.

Carl Davenport

The general supervisor of the Operations section is Carl Davenport. He is 34 years old and has a bachelor's degree in Engineering (General) and two master's degrees, one in Electrical Engineering and one in Engineering Administration, all from Ohio State. He is well respected in the company. Although his roots are in Management Information Services, Carl spent several years in the Office of the Auditor. He has moved up quickly in the company and is likely to continue to do so.

Jere Jefferson

Jere Jefferson is the general supervisor of the Special Systems section of the Management Information Services department. He is 50 years old and has a bachelor's degree in Business Administration from the University of Missouri. Jere spent nine years in the Missouri Distribution department before transferring to the Management Information Services department in 1960 when the department was first started. In 1972, he went to the Office of the Auditor as the company's first computer auditor. After four years, he was back in Management Information Services as the supervisor of the Plans Control unit (later made a section). He then became the supervisor of Business Functional Systems; in 1985, he was transferred to supervisor of Special Systems. His lateral move from the Business Functional section was part of Chris's management rotation objectives. Jere is more familiar with the commercial end of the business and thus relies on his staffers for more technical advice. There was some grumbling among the ranks when Jere was assigned to the Special Systems section. The complaints were due in part to Jere's lack of technical experience (which his predecessor had); however, some measure of the unhappiness was due to a long-standing "cold war" between the Special Systems and the Business Functional sections, regarding which was the most difficult job. The old conflict is a perennial organizational problem for management, since subordinates are equally reluctant to be transferred from the Special Systems section to the Business Functional section.

Phil Hoxie

The Business Functional section is directed by Phil Hoxie. Phil is one of the few supervisors who has spent some time in both the Special Systems and the Business Functional sections, having been transferred from Special Systems to Business Functional five years ago. He is 51 years old, holding a bachelor's degree in Engineering Physics, and a second bachelor's in Industrial Management, both from Ohio State. Phil is a very laid-back individual, whose subordinates have commented on his relaxed manner. His managerial policy is that of encouragement rather than pressure.

Harry Poplar

The Systems Maintenance section is headed by Harry Poplar. Harry is 56 years old and holds a bachelor's degree in Engineering (General) from Iowa State University and a master's in Systems and Logistics from the University of Iowa. Harry began his career at MSG&E in the Power Production department as a test engineer and was then transferred to the Electronics department as a project leader. When the Automatic Data Processing department assumed responsibility for the process control computer in 1970 (and was renamed to Management Information Services department), Harry was transferred into MISD. Harry was also heavily involved in the installation of the Big Bluff Hydrogen Power Plant's first plant-monitoring computer system. Harry eventually was promoted to the general supervisor of the Special Systems section in MISD. He later served in the Project Management department (holding Ed Ames's current position) for a short time. His recent reassignment to Systems Maintenance as general supervisor is also part of Chris's rotational assignments. Although Chris is now considering eliminating Systems Maintenance as a separate section within Management Information Services (distributing the responsibilities among the other MISD sections), Harry will certainly be retained as a valuable member of the technical team.

Ed Ames

Ed Ames is the 43-year-old general supervisor of the computer section of the Project Management department. This last remaining section of the Project Management department is expected to be moved elsewhere in the organization, thus eliminating the department. Ed has both a bachelor's degree in Engineering and an MBA (University of Missouri). He is both respected and somewhat feared by his subordinates. He is a very task-oriented individual and has earned a reputation for getting the job done. Ed started with MSG&E in 1960 in the ADP department (predecessor to MISD) when it was first formed. He has worked his way up within the Management Information Services department, mostly within the Special Systems section. His experience has been with real-time process control computer equipment. He is a persistent, unyielding negotiator and has successfully negotiated several contracts with hardware and software vendors. His largest and most successful project for Management Information Services was the installation of the Power Routing and Control System (PRCS). The PRCS is a large collection of computers, workstations, displays, and mapboards in a suburb of Kansas City. The system is used to monitor, display, and control some 200 electrical substations, routing power to various customer areas as needed. PRCS also includes a Diagnostic Analysis system used to track down and identify failures in the company's distribution system. See the appendix to this chapter for an abbreviated inventory of MSG&E's computer equipment.

WORK FLOW IN MIS

The flow of work through the Management Information Services department involves both the user departments and the Management Information Services department. The processing begins when someone in the company has an idea on how to use computers to better facilitate his or her own work. Many of the ideas are prompted by some regulatory requirement or a vendor offering directly to the user. The user will contact Management Information Services using one of two forms. The first form is a Proposal for Computer Application (PCA). The Miscellaneous Computer Application (MCA) form is similar to the PCA but is used for smaller projects. These forms, which are requests for work to be done by Management Information Services, include a description of the work and an initial cost justification.

PCA Form

Management Information Services frequently assists the user in preparing the PCA by generating what is called a preliminary feasibility study for the application. The PCA (perhaps along with the preliminary feasibility study) is sent to the Plans Control section of Management Information Services. There it is recorded and sent to either the Special Systems, Business Functional, or Systems Maintenance section for a cost estimate. One of these application sections will then prepare an estimate of how much effort (dollars and manpower) the department will expend to complete the requested work. Completion of this step provides the numbers necessary to evaluate the PCA from a cost/benefit standpoint. The PCA is then returned to the Plans Control section, where the new numbers are recorded. The form then goes back to the user's manager for approval (with MISD's cost estimates included).

Automatic Data Processing Coordination Committee

Next, the PCA passes to the automatic data processing coordination committee (ADPCC). This committee is made up of one representative from each division. The committee members are charged with evaluating and prioritizing, from a company standpoint, all computer work requested of the Management Information Services department. Initially, in the early 1970s, ADPCC's charter was to constrain and manage the growth of IS throughout MSG&E.

It should be noted that the ADPCC does not see the computer work done by the Project Management department or the work done by Management Information Services employees for Project Management. Once the PCA is approved and prioritized, it is sent back to Plans Control for assignment to an application section.

When the application section staff receives the approved PCA, they place the work in their schedule and advise the user of their plan.

The ADPCC approves those proposals where the company benefit outweighs the costs. They also consider the intangible benefits (and costs) associated with proposals. Intangibles include reduction of risk, regulatory requirements, and management directives. Once the project is approved, all computer-related costs are charged to the Management Information Services department.

Problems with Large Projects

Although this method is very functional for handling the types of projects that the Management Information Services department is generally assigned, the procedure has not worked effectively with large projects (particularly those requiring software development by outside vendors). These large projects are usually handled by the Project Management department. In one instance, MISD was requested to purchase five separate software packages and associated hardware (with five separate PCAs). Since the requests were from five different users, they had to be costed, approved, and monitored separately. MISD's decision was to transfer all five proposals (PCAs) to Project Management, where they were processed as a single project, using shared hardware.

DEVELOPMENT PROCESS

User Requirements

The actual development work can be described as consisting of any number of steps, depending on how it is broken down. For our purposes, it consists of five steps: analysis, design, programming/testing, documentation, and installation/checkout.

Analysis Phase

In the analysis phase, the analyst (in MISD) works with the user to determine the functions performed in the present system and the requirements of the proposed system. It is the user's responsibility in this phase to prepare a user requirements document. This document should present all of the requirements of the proposed system from a functional level. It is written from the user's perspective, not the programmer's.

Design Phase—Programming/Testing Phase

The analyst then takes the user requirements document and begins the design phase of the project. During this phase, the analyst prepares a design specification from the requirements document. The specification document should contain all of the parts necessary for the programmer to write the code for the system. Quite often this is not the case, and the design and programming proceed somewhat simultaneously. The overlap should be expected, since unknown circumstances and restrictions frequently arise only as programming anomalies are worked out. Also, recent technological advances present opportunities not available during the earlier design phase. Programming and testing are completed by the programmer and analyst jointly, along with detailed documentation of each computer module.

Documentation Phase

Documentation is usually extensive and involves much more time than the user would anticipate. A frequent comment made by users of systems developed by Management Information Services is "I could have written that program on my PC at home in a few days, and it took MISD three months, by the time they got started." Management Information Services deems complete documentation a necessary part of the development effort in order to maintain ongoing support of the installed system. In addition, Management Information Services frequently assumes responsibility for user-written programs and then may spend up to two months just figuring out what the programs do, since there is no documentation. Furthermore, none of the current users are familiar with the programs because often they were written by people who left the company a year or two—or more —ago. Another source of frustration for the user is the backlog of work that Management Information Services has, often delaying the commencement of work on a proposal as much as two years.

Installation/Checkout Phase

At any rate, once the programming/testing work is completed, the installation/ checkout phase is begun. This phase is usually fairly short, once the system has been turned over to the user. The user identifies errors (usually, there are many) in the system, while Management Information Services makes the necessary corrections. Once the system is fully checked out by the user, it is placed into production status. If the system runs on one of the company computers, the Data Center Operations section becomes involved. The Operations section staff schedules and executes programs on the company computers. If the system runs on something other than the company computers, the Data Center Operations section need not be involved.

MISD ORGANIZATIONAL PROBLEMS

External Environment

Chris is now looking at two organizational problems. The first is Management Information Services' external organizational environment. Although he does not have the authority to decide where to locate Management Information Services within the company, Chris is expected to make recommendations to senior management on the subject. His goal for the structure is to place the department where it will have the most effective impact on the company's overall performance. Ensuring effective impact also entails staffing the department with necessary talent and instilling motivation to perform comprehensive and thorough functions for the company. With the restructuring of the two new divisions (Hydrogen Power and Coal Power), Project Management has made an orphan of the computer section of its department. Absorption of this section seems likely, but the flow of paperwork within MISD does not work well with the types of projects handled by the Project Management department. Chris is not sure that having two project tracking mechanisms will be understood by user departments. Therefore, he is wondering if his department should take another form within the company, other than a "department."

MISD Internal Structure

Secondly, Chris is interested in shaping Management Information Services' internal organization to optimize its efficiency. An organizational structure change should also minimize conflicts within the department. He has mentioned an interest in dissolving one section of the department but is not certain where to transfer the associated workload. He wants to place the general supervisors strategically in positions where they will work best but also sees the value of giving the supervisors well-rounded exposure to all areas of the department. Redundant activities should be eliminated, and his high-priced experts should be given responsibilities comparable with their abilities. It is also important for Management Information Services to interact as smoothly as possible with other departments.

Chris is also concerned about the personnel situation in the department. He wants to continue rotating general supervisors through the department while keeping efficiency and effectiveness high. Further, he wants to reduce the tensions among Business Functional and Special Systems employees. Since Chris has taken over the Management Information Services department, he has found the goals and problems of the department to be quite a challenge, and very different from his experience in the Transportation department. He hopes that his decisions in the near future will reward him with the type of success he experienced as manager of the Transportation department.

QUESTIONS

1. Chris Timberlake does not intend to include system development or application maintenance in the charge-back system. What do you think will be the result of this decision? What would you include in the charge-back system?

2. Does the Information Systems Center appear to be doing a satisfactory job at Mid-States? If not, how would you change the Center?

3. Do you see any problems with the Office of the Auditor's Automatic Data Processing Standards? Explain your answer and describe actions you would take to increase the value of the document.

4. Describe a training curriculum you would propose for the company's programmers and include a schedule for the next three months.

5. Was Chris Timberlake the right person to head up the MIS department? Why or why not? If not, who would you favor as his replacement?

6. Assess the qualifications of the MIS staff. Who would you replace and why?

7. Is the automatic data processing coordination committee (ADPCC) performing its role effectively? If not, what would you change?

8. Evaluate the development process at Mid-States. Would you modify the procedures? If so, which ones and why?

9. What recommendation should Chris make relative to reorganizing his department? Include the external organizational environment, MISD internal structure, and personnel. Support your answer with organization charts and personnel policy revisions.

Appendix   Inventory of MSG&E Computers (abbreviated—9/13/86)

Quantity Manufacturer Model	Purpose/Function	Support/Group	Capital Investment (in thousands)	Monthly Expenditure (in thousands)
Company Systems				
1 IBM 3090	Company computer system	Various*		
2 IBM 3081	Large-company systems	Various*	$3,800	$90
1 IBM 8100	Employee services			
2 IBM Series 1	Portable meter reading	MIS-BF/SM		
4 HP 3000	In-house time-sharing	Various*	700	6
2 EK Komstars	COM microfilm	Various*		
2 AM Bruning (OP 17)	Microfilm duplication	Various*		
1 HP 21 MX (Scan Optics)	Customer billing	MIS-BF/O	325	4.2
2 Nixdorf (Entrex511)	Key entry	Various*		
1 DG Nova (READOC)	Customer billing	MIS-BF/O	95	3.2
Engineering Support				
1 DG Eclipse (S-130)	Reactor Schedule	HPD/Proj. Team (P)	140	.5
1 Computervision (Designer M)	CAD (drawing update)	Systems Maintenance		
2 Apple II	Nuclear power training	HPD Training		
3 TI-59	Dosimetry and leak rate calculations	HPD/Proj. Team (P)	5.8	.035
1 Wang 720C	Neutron count monitor	HPD		
1 IBM PC	Label control	HPD		
3 IBM PC XT	Media center and tubing/ chemistry analysis	HPD		
1 IBM PC XT	Information systems center	MISD		
1 Prime 400	Load flow studies	Elec. Opns. Plan.	180	1.8
1 HP 21 MX	Tape translation	CPD/Proj. Team (B)	80	.6
1 Westinghouse 2500	Tape translation backup	CPD/Proj. Team (B)		

*Various—Systems support provided by the Systems Maintenance section; applications supported by the Special Systems and Business Functional sections.

Appendix   *(continued)*

Quantity Model	Manufacturer	Purpose/Function	Support/Group	Capital Investment (in thousands)	Monthly Expenditure (in thousands)

Office Automation (OA)

Quantity Model	Purpose/Function	Support/Group	Capital Investment (in thousands)	Monthly Expenditure (in thousands)
1 NBI Sys/64	OA pilot in HPD	Office Systems/ MISD		
7 NBI 3000	Word processing (various purposes)	Office Systems/ MISD		
1 IBM Displaywriter	Word processing (simulator—HPD)	Office Systems/ MISD		
21 IBM (various)	MISD office systems products	Office Systems/ MISD		
2 Wang	Word processing(various purposes)	Office Systems/ MISD		$2.7
26 NBI 4000	Word processing	Office Systems/ MISD		
11 NBI 3000	Word processing	Office Systems/ MISD		
8 XEROX ETS 800	Word processing	Office Systems/ MISD		
5 Olivetti	MISD office systems products	Office Systems/ MISD		

Personal Computers

Quantity Model	Purpose/Function	Support/Group	Capital Investment (in thousands)	Monthly Expenditure (in thousands)
35 IBM 5150 PC	Various uses in various locations including: HPD (Training, License and Safety, Glow Curve Analysis, 1/M Data Collection), Electronics, QCD, and PMD.	Office Systems/ MISD		
37 IBM 5160 PC XT	Various uses in various locations	Office Systems/ MISD		
19 IBM 5170 PC AT	Various uses	Office Systems/ MISD		
10 Apple II	Various uses	Office Systems/ MISD		
2 Apple II +	Various uses	Office Systems/ MISD		
6 Apple Lisa	Various uses	Office Systems/ MISD		
1 HP 125	Building 200	MISD-SM		

Appendix   *(concluded)*

Quantity	Manufacturer Model	Purpose/Function	Support/Group	Capital Investment (in thousands)	Monthly Expenditure (in thousands)
		Time-Sharing Services			
1 CD Cybernet		Nuclear finance models	HPD/Proj. Team (P)		$10.5
1 CD Plato		Scientific training	HPD Training		23.0
1 Combustion Engineering		Reactor core models	HPD/Proj. Team (P)		11.0
2 GE		Time-sharing	HPD/Proj. Team (P)		1.750
1 INPO		Plant reliability DB	HPD/Proj. Team (P)		
4 Service Bureau Call		Budgeting	Distribution		3.500
1 Warren Selbert		Financial models	Corporate Planning		.265
1 Chase Econ.		Economic models	Economic Research		.375
1 Boeing Computer Service		STRUDL program	Electronics		
1 College Computer Service		Thermal analysis	HPD/Proj. Team (P)		
1 Dialog		Information retrieval	Corporate Communications		.080
1 Stoner Solutions Services		Gas stream analysis	Gas Resources		2.700

Sensor-Based Information Collection System and/or Process Control

These computers, more than 115, are located mostly at the Big Bluffs generating station, four other generating stations, and the Electronics Building (40 computers there alone). They were manufactured by over 20 different companies, including Univac, Westinghouse, Control Data, Hewlett-Packard, Digital Equipment, Tracor, Nuclear Data, Panasonic, NUS, Perkin Elmer, Data General, IBM, Gould, Fisher, Bolle, and Tennelec.

The purposes or functions of the systems include power plant monitoring, security access, gamma spectrometer, counter-dosimetry, reactivity processing, plant control simulation, data acquisition, energy management, production control, turbine control, MIDAS dose assessment, and many more.

Capital investment ranges — on the high side — from the $13,000,127 of the Control Data Cyber 170/730 down through $7,650,000 for the Perkin Elmer 3244 training simulator, $2,942,000 for Westinghouse's P-250 power plant monitor and control, $1,600,000 for Bolle's nuclear plant computer system, and $210,000 for the Gould/SEL 32/2705 power plant performance machines. Less expensive systems include Nuclear Data's ND 6620 ($57,800) — a gamma spectrometer system, and a $75,000 for Hewlett-Packard's 5451C fourier analyzer. Monthly expenditures can be as much as $7,000 per month for a Univac V77/600 to $150 per month for a Nuclear Data ND 66 portable gamma spectrometer system.

Chapter 8

Controlling Development and Implementation

INTRODUCTION

The life cycle of an automated system has many phases, including problem definition, development, implementation, installation, operation, maintenance, enhancement, and replacement. While controls must be in place during all phases, our focus here is control during development and implementation.

DEFINITIONS OF DEVELOPMENT AND IMPLEMENTATION

Development

The systems approach and life cycles, as noted in Chapter 7, have many definitions of development and implementation. Some definitions include implementation as a part of development; others use the word *implementation* to describe phases of the decision-making process, and suggest that IS should support management decision making.

For example, Parker names five activities in systems development: preliminary investigation, requirements analysis, system design, system acquisition, and system implementation.[1]

---

[1]Charles S. Parker, *Management Information Systems: Strategy and Action,* Chapter 15 (New York: McGraw-Hill, 1989).

However, Taggart and Silbey view decision making as having four phases: intelligence, design, choice, and implementation.[2] We particularly like their description of situation review; it consists of reviewing problems *and* considering opportunities. They suggest that thinking of opportunities may offer greater benefits than focusing on the very visible problems.[3]

Implementation

McLeod writes that ''The implementation phase includes all of the tasks necessary to convert the MIS design into a working system.''[4] If an organization regards the acquisition of software as part of implementation, then its managers should ask three questions:

1. Should we develop the application ourselves?
2. Should we purchase a proprietary package from a software house, computer manufacturer, or OEM supplier?
3. Should we try to find a firm in our business that is willing to sell us an application they developed?[5]

The answers depend on an organization's IS/IT resources, size, budgetary considerations, availability of programming staff, tolerance for risk, and amount of modification required if the application is not developed in-house.

DEFINING CONTROL

Looking initially at general management activities—plan, organize, staff, and control— ''*Control* refers to the process whereby steps are taken to recognize, assess, and (possibly) correct deviations from plan.''[6]

[2]William Taggart and Valdur Silbey, *Information Systems: People and Computers in Organization,* 2nd ed., Chapter 14 (Boston: Allyn and Bacon, 1986). Their four phases are an extension of the three phases of Herbert A. Simon, *The New Science of Management Decisions* (New York: Harper & Row, 1960), pp. 1–4.

[3]Taggart and Silbey, *Information Systems,* Chapter 8.

[4]Raymond McLeod, Jr., *Management Information Systems,* 3rd ed., Chapter 17 (Chicago: Science Research Associates, 1986).

[5]Taggart and Silbey, *Information Systems,* Chapter 8, p. 266, adapted from Figure 8–5.

[6]Parker, *Management Information Systems,* Chapter 3.

WHY IS CONTROL NEEDED?

In most organizations using computers today, development and implementation of new computer systems — or conversion from one system to a more advanced, powerful configuration — is a potential disaster. Budgets are not met, development schedules are delayed, users are not ready for the system, and the final system does not meet user expectations.

Formal control of the development and implementation phases assures closer adherence to plans, helps to track and optimize expenditure of funds, and provides checks on progress.

WHAT ARE THE FORMAL METHODS OF CONTROLLING?

The charge-back system is one method to control the costs and proliferation of computer systems, while restraining the functional user tendency to submit ever-growing wish lists. Costs to develop the systems and write the application programs are charged to the departmental or divisional budget of the requestor. However, to control in-house costs and provide competition for the IS/IT staffs, many corporations permit their functional groups to seek external bids.

Overall control of the total systems acquisition process, from problem definition through installation and implementation, can be a formal process in which the project manager must seek approval prior to leaving each phase. Milestones in time and events can be specified; documents and products for each phase must be evaluated prior to approval to proceed.

Information centers can control end-user computing but only when end-users seek assistance voluntarily or are required to show evidence of their efforts to secure and utilize the center's technical advice and assistance.

WHAT ARE THE PROBLEMS OF CONTROL?

Computer system (or IS/IT) control problems in most organizations come down to (1) control over the system acquisition process — which normally leads from problem definition through development to installation and implementation of a new or modified system, and (2) control over end-user computing (EUC).

Problems controlling the computer or automated systems acquisition process are no different from those of controlling any other acquisition process. Similar acquisition problems occur for military systems, which includes computer systems as well as aircraft, ships, and tanks; transportation systems such as San Francisco's Bay Area Transit Authority (BART); or construction projects such as the Alaskan pipeline.

Early estimates of total development cost, completion dates, and system performance invariably miss the mark by significant amounts — millions of dollars, months or years, and performance shortfalls, from total inability to meet approved system goals to acceptance of scaled back or reduced subsystem performance.

Causes of the failures include insufficient funds; vague requirements; unreasonably optimistic planners/designers; inexperienced personnel at all levels; uncontrolled changes to the design; lack of communication between the users and the developers; and high turnover of critical personnel.

IMPLICATIONS OF END–USER INVOLVEMENT IN DEVELOPMENT/ IMPLEMENTATION

The struggle for power in many organizations gained a new dimension when computers were first introduced. Functional area managers were held hostage by computer managers and operators; they lost control of their information resources. After over 20 years, and due to technological advances that produced microcomputers and ever-falling prices for computers, the end-users of information are regaining control over system development priorities, maintenance priorities, and day-to-day operations.[7]

CONTROL OVER END–USERS

Parker listed three critical areas[8] where control of end-user computing and development activities can cause serious problems; they are: *cost control* (functional departments, supported by their own budgets and not required to obtain purchase approval from IS/IT, may not know—or be particularly concerned about—how much they are spending on computers);[9] *product control* (users choose their own products without concern for availability of, or compatibility with, other equipment and applications; this leads to redundancy, unused capacity, and high training costs); and *data control* (end-users do not see security, checks and balances, system audit trails, documentation, and backup as high-priority matters).[10]

---

[7]James I. Cash, F. W. McFarlan, J. L. McKenney, and M. R. Vitale, *Corporate Information Systems Management: Text and Cases,* 2nd ed. (Homewood, Ill.: Richard D. Irwin, 1988).

[8]Parker, *Management Information Systems,* Chapter 18, p. 713.

[9]As early as 1982, Benjamin reported that EUC might soon account for 75 percent of computing resources at Xerox. Rockhart and Flannery, in their classic 1983 article, estimated that end-user computing represented 40 to 50 percent of all organizational costs in the large organizations they had surveyed. There is no reason to expect that estimates are less today.

[10]Parker, *Management Information Systems,* Chapter 18, pp. 713–14.

CASES: WILLOBY AND COMPANY, TUSCORA COUNTY HOSPITAL, PROTECTIVE SYSTEMS EVALUATION FACILITY, AND OMAHA–COUNCIL BLUFFS VISION CENTER

In Case 8–1, Willoby and Company, a producer of specialty foods, does not require its operating divisions to request hardware or software support from its Management Sciences division (MSD); top corporate management has received complaints about MSD's practice of contracting its services to outside clients in order to reduce MSD costs.

Tuscora County Hospital (Case 8–2) is a low-cost (compared to its nearby competitors) provider of in-patient services. While the hospital's patient care facilities have grown rapidly, its IS assets are meager. Recently, financial constraints have caused problems for the Materials Management department.

The productivity of three labs in the Protective Systems Evaluation Facility (Case 8–3) is falling; testing accuracy and quality are decreasing as workload has ballooned. Although one solution, to automate the test facility, seems to be on track, the director has called in a consultant to review PSEF's process and progress.

In Case 8–4, the Vision Center, a small, private practice, has been relatively successful, due mostly to the technical skills of the doctor/owner. The center purchased a computer system to improve its controls over administrative, business, and clinical functions. However, only one person has had experience with automated systems.

Case 8–1 Willoby and Company

THE SCENE—9:30 A.M.

Clark Donaldson has just completed a meeting with Brian Yeager. The subject of the meeting was two memos Clark had received relating to problems in the MIS systems at Willoby Development and the decision of Willoby Development not to use any MSD services. He directed Brian to return to his office and prepare

---

This case was prepared by Shary Vaile and Larry Gosnell. Names, locations, and financial data have been disguised.

a response to those memos for presentation to him by 11:30 A.M. today.

While he is waiting for Brian to get back to him, Clark has requested John Leach to stop in and give him additional background on the first of the two memos. This memo is from John to Brian and addresses problems with MIS systems at Willoby Development and is included as Appendix 1 to this case.

THE SCENE—10:00 A.M.

John's concerns are in three areas—deficiencies in current systems, PC support, and status of recommendations of the feasibility study. Regarding the deficiencies, John explained, ''I have listed several deficiencies in my memo, but let me expand on a couple. The current Property Management Accounting System (PMAS) has prior year data files. We cannot access those files. Also, although we input the rental requirements of our tenants over the entire lease term, we cannot automatically handle such a standard procedure as a rent escalation clause. Every time the rent increases, we have to physically change the monthly rental in the system. That means we have a manual tickler file to remind us to update our automated system. This strikes me as ridiculous. The other problems listed in my memo are similar in scope. I have separated them into two categories. The first is a list of existing problems with the system, while the second is a list of enhancements we need in order to be able to do our jobs in a useful and efficient manner.''

When Clark asked what John saw being done about these problems, he replied, ''I know Brian is discussing these problems with the vendor, and the vendor has promised to make the needed changes; but that was over six months ago, and we still have not seen even one change. I was hoping this new analyst Brian hired would help, but he doesn't seem to think writing or modifying programs is his job. Also, I am getting similar feedback from the Construction group. They have never gotten the billing portion of their accounting package to work properly in the two-and-a-half years since they installed it. That is causing a problem not only for them but also for my people.''

Regarding PCs, John explained that the only training his staff had on their PCs was what they could glean from each other. John was even being asked by other areas within Willoby Development to recommend appropriate software. He said, ''I don't have the time to be a PC guru for our company. I also know that MSD has an area devoted to just this type of thing. Maybe we should be looking to them.''

Clark then asked John to explain his comments on the recommendations of the feasibility study. John replied, ''We just seem to be far short of where I expected us to be this long after the formation of our MIS group. Some recommendations are only partially implemented, and some—such as the marketing prospect database—have never even been addressed. Maybe Brian needs more staff.''

COMPANY BACKGROUND

Willoby and Company, Inc., is a specialty foods manufacturer. The company was founded in Baltimore, Maryland, in 1889, to manufacture cereals and sell them to grocery stores. The founder of the company, Michael C. Willoby, and his sons controlled the company as a privately owned business until the corporation went public in 1925 and was listed on the New York Stock Exchange. During this period the company established a reputation for producing a high-quality product at a reasonable price. This reputation for quality continues into the present. Mr. Willoby's eldest son, Paul, took over control of the company in 1930 and led it through the Depression era with a combination of innovative management and personal leadership. It was during this period of national hardship that Willoby's developed its reputation as a concerned, people-oriented company.

After the Depression, Willoby's management recognized the dangers of limiting themselves to their current product lines, even though they were still very profitable, and so started to diversify. The diversification began with other consumer-oriented grain-based products. Divisions were set up to cater to the restaurant and industrial markets. As the century progressed, the company moved into new markets both related and unrelated to their original specialty foods business. Subsidiaries were bought that produced such diverse items as frozen breakfast foods and plastic-based packaging. In addition, the international marketplace was entered through both partnership/affiliations and acquisitions. By the 1950s, Willoby had grown into a multinational, multidivisional corporation in the Fortune 1000 with sales rapidly approaching $500 million per year. The growth process continues today through both introduction of new product lines in the grains-related fields and addition of new business ventures. Most of these new ventures in recent years have been through acquisition.

When dealing with its various divisions and subsidiaries, Willoby is a firm believer in autonomy. As long as divisions or subsidiaries are meeting their goals, the corporation leaves them to run themselves as they feel most appropriate. Because of this philosophy of divisional autonomy, the administrative corporate staff is rather small for a corporation of its size. The divisions and subsidiaries are loosely structured into groups for reporting and administrative purposes. An abbreviated organization chart is included as Exhibit 1.

Each year, the company sets a goal of 5 percent growth in both sales units and dollars. Both 1985 and 1986 were good years, and these goals were met (financial summaries are included as Exhibit 2). In 1985, Willoby was a member of the Fortune 500 with sales of almost $750 million. Although the corporation is diversified, the original Cereal Products group (CPG) continues as the largest contributor to total sales with 1986 sales of $444 million. CPG has a 1991 sales goal of $1 billion. However, 1987 is not such a good year. Final figures are not in, but it is known that most divisions and subsidiaries, with some notable exceptions, did not meet these goals. One of the exceptions is Willoby Development.

EXHIBIT 1 Abbreviated Corporate Organization Chart

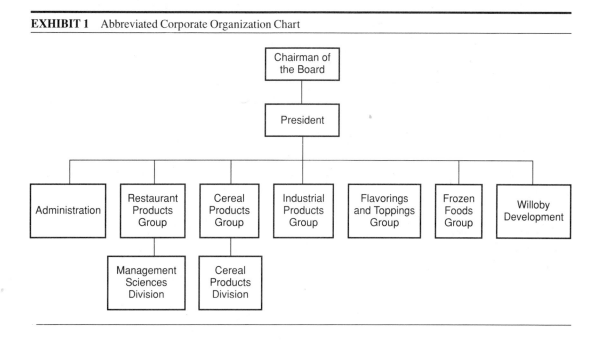

WILLOBY DEVELOPMENT

In the late 1950s, Willoby and Company decided to build a new manufacturing facility west of Baltimore. Research led them to believe they could build the facilities cheaper and more efficiently themselves rather than by hiring a contracting firm. Consequently, a 400-acre tract of land was purchased and a new subsidiary, Willoby Building, was spun off to build the new facilities.

After construction was completed, the new subsidiary was charged to develop and then hold some of this land for sale to other companies needing to expand. Willoby Development began to develop the remaining acres and had little difficulty in locating buyers and lessors. Soon other parcels of land around Baltimore were purchased and developed. Following these successes, Willoby Development began to purchase and develop areas outside the Baltimore metropolitan area, to include Washington, D.C., and areas within the Sunbelt region. Willoby Development became a well-known regional construction/development company.

Today, Willoby Development is a fully integrated real estate development company (see Exhibit 3). It is a fully owned, nonconsolidated subsidiary of Willoby and Company. It owns and operates commercial office and industrial buildings, performs design/build construction services, holds undeveloped land for sale, syndicates properties for outside ownership, and manages rental space for other owners. Willoby Development has over $200 million in assets and currently has

EXHIBIT 2   Historical Financial Summary

	1986	1985
Net sales	$788,359	$743,154
Cost of goods sold	503,046	464,275
Gross profit on sales	285,313	278,879
Profit from operations	65,161	66,725
Other income and miscellaneous expenses, net	(493)	(3,687)
Interest expense	(13,047)	(10,932)
Provision for income taxes	(24,830)	(25,744)
Share of income (loss) of unconsolidated subsidiary and affiliates	27,805	13,751
Net income	54,596	40,113
Preferred dividends paid ($5.00 per share)	14	14
Common dividends declared	13,979	10,996
Income reinvested	$ 40,603	$ 29,103
Financial position		
Current assets	$269,118	$228,428
Current liabilities	192,885	139,707
Working capital	76,233	88,721
Capital		
Current debt	44,786	18,286
Long-term debt	96,574	56,832
Total interest-bearing debt	141,360	75,118
Stockholders' equity	243,706	216,374
Total capital	$385,066	$291,492
Other information		
Property—net	$139,992	$128,527
Depreciation and amortization including intangibles	20,867	19,599
Funds provided from operations	50,705	50,209
Property additions	31,275	37,204
Assets	542,482	419,461
Average assets	464,411	402,208
Net income before financial charges, depreciation, and amortization	$ 81,986	$ 65,178
Average common shares outstanding	12,398	12,460
Average number of stockholders	7,991	7,693
Average number of employees	7,091	6,872
Key financial indicators		
Increase (decrease) over prior year		
Net sales	6.1%	3.5%
Net income	36.1%	60.7%
Net income before financial charges, depreciation, and amortization	25.8%	14.1%
Gross profit to net sales	36.2%	37.5%
Profit from operations to net sales	8.3%	9.0%

EXHIBIT 2   (continued)

Net income to net sales	6.9%	5.4%
Effective tax rate	48.1%	49.4%
Common dividends to net income	25.6%	27.4%
Current assets to current liabilities ratio	1.4	1.6
Interest-bearing debt to total capital	36.7%	25.8%
Return on assets	17.7%	16.3%
Return on equity	23.1%	20.6%
Per common share		
Earnings	$ 4.40	$ 3.22
Common dividends declared	$ 1.13	$ .88
Book value	$20.01	$17.25
Market price: High	$34.13	$35.50
Low	$28.50	$24.75
Price earnings ratio: High	11	18
Low	9	12

a goal of over $1 billion in assets by 1991. Although Willoby's investment in Willoby Development only represents 12 percent of the total corporate assets, Willoby Development in 1984 contributed over 50 percent of the net earnings and earnings per share for the corporation. This was accomplished through the sale of some of Willoby Development's stockpile of developed properties.

As Willoby Development grew in size and stature as a construction/development company, it became impractical to prepare proposal estimates by hand. Software was needed that would yield a product presentable to potential customers. The then current corporate MIS systems did not have appropriate software. To meet the need, a feasibility study was initiated in 1982 to determine whether to develop the system in-house, if such a system should run on the corporate computer, and if Willoby Development needed their own MIS department.

MIS AT WILLOBY

MIS at Willoby is a combination of centralized and decentralized systems. MIS began in 1971 with the hiring of Tom Jackson to create a department to bring in-house and consolidate all of the MIS systems being run at various places within the corporation. Tom formed a group that has evolved into a corporate MIS planning staff group with no computing power. The actual MIS department was formed in 1972 and was renamed the Management Sciences division (MSD) in 1974. MSD has two IBM mainframe computers, an IBM minicomputer, and several IBM PCs.

EXHIBIT 3   Abbreviated Willoby Development Organization Chart

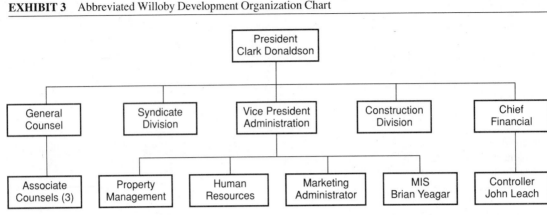

MSD functions as a nonprofit center. It is charged with breaking even each year. This is accomplished through a charge-out or charge-back system. Any division or subsidiary that wishes to use MSD's facilities or MIS expertise contracts for a certain amount of MSD services at a set rate (currently $425 per workday). MSD uses the revenue generated in this fashion to develop, maintain, and execute the systems desired by its customers. Any monies remaining at the end of the year are rebated to the customers at a rate proportional to the amount of MSD services purchased by that customer. Currently, MSD provides approximately 8,000 workdays of MIS support to the corporation each year. An abbreviated organization chart of MSD is included at Exhibit 4.

MSD has also just begun a new venture; it is selling excess computer cycles to outside companies. Other outside customers of computing power are being sought actively. The revenues from this venture will be used to reduce the charge-back rate MSD has to charge its corporate customers in order to meet its goals.

The divisions and subsidiaries are not required to use MSD's services or even their computer. There is only one corporatewide system, and that is payroll. Payroll became a corporatewide system at the end of 1984. Some divisions, such as the Cereal Products group (CPG), use MSD exclusively. Some, such as the Flavorings and Toppings group, use the MSD hardware but retain their own staff to perform the programming. Others, like Willoby Development, have their own MIS departments and use no services of MSD.

CAST OF CHARACTERS

Cal Tacy is the director of Systems Development for MSD. He is responsible for all of the development, maintenance, enhancement, and purchase of software within MSD. In addition, Cal was the person primarily responsible for the success

EXHIBIT 4   Abbreviated Management Sciences Division Organization Chart

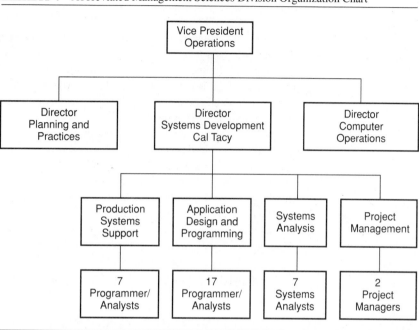

of the MSD venture into selling of excess cycles. He personally negotiated the original contracts and closed the first sale. Cal has been in MSD for nine years. He started as a junior programmer and progressed through the ranks to his present position. Cal believes strongly that all people are basically reasonable and that most things can be resolved by open discussion.

Clark Donaldson is the president of Willoby Development. He has been with Willoby for 10 years, first as a lawyer and later as the vice president of Administration. Clark has been very successful at running Willoby Development and is respected throughout the corporation.

John Leach is the controller for Willoby Development. He has been with the company for about four years, has a BS from the University of Maryland and an MBA from Loyola College. Before coming to Willoby Development, John was with MSD for one year.

Brian Yeagar has been the MIS manager for Willoby Development since the formation of the department in 1982. Before that time, Brian was in the Accounting department of Willoby Development for five years. Brian has a BS in Accounting.

THE SCENE—10:30 A.M.

Clark thanked John for his input, and John left. After allowing John's comments to sink in for a few minutes, Clark reread the second memo. This memo (see Appendix 2) was from Cal Tacy of MSD. The subject was the relationship of Willoby Development and MSD. As he read, Clark remarked on the points in the memo: "Cal is right; $425 per day is expensive if you only look at it as one person; but when you throw in a machine and a complete support staff, it becomes more reasonable. MSD responsiveness was one of our main reasons for starting our own MIS department; maybe now that our major crises situations have been handled, we could deal better with being scheduled in among the Big Boys. Of course, CPG will always get first choice of times and people as they are MSD's largest customer. Professionalism and good testing—those are definitely areas in which we could use some help. It's good to see that MSD is finally realizing that there are things other than large IBM mainframes. John is right about the end-user computing group; it sounds like they could definitely help us with our PC concerns." After rereading the memo, Clark commented, "Cal makes a good case for a better relationship with MSD even if we don't want to run systems on their computers. All that remains now is to see what Brian has to say."

THE SCENE—11:00 A.M.: BRIAN PREPARES HIS REPLY

Brian is sitting in his office with the two memos in question in front of him. He is trying to understand what these people are complaining about. He knows things are going as well as can be expected.

"Maybe if I review the history of MIS here at Willoby Development and the recommendations of the feasibility study, I will be able to understand what they perceive the problems to be and put their concerns to rest.

"In March 1982 I was chosen to perform an information systems feasibility study for Willoby Development. I was given Cal Tacy from MSD to assist me in this effort. The study was expanded to include the following topics:

1. Providing a three- to five-year computer-based information systems plan for Willoby Development.
2. Interfacing of information to the Willoby and Company parent company.
3. Integrating critical data, business processes, and organization structure.
4. Tailoring operational support systems to critical business requirements for operational decisions.

"At the conclusion of our study, we produced an eight-point recommendation. Cal returned to MSD, and I presented the proposal to our board of directors. They approved the recommendations, and the president appointed me manager of the new MIS department. I was allowed to bring an accounting clerk with me and hired a secretary. We have recently hired an analyst to assist us with managing the growing number of systems and making systems modifications. He has been with us for a couple of months and has really taken control of the system processing.

"I think I should review the original recommendations point by point:

1. Establish a systems support function at Willoby Development. We have certainly done that.
2. Purchase an IBM System 34 from MSD. We did this because of the number of software packages available for the machine that were directed toward our business area, such as PMAS. Of course, we have already had to upgrade to a larger machine, but that is only to be expected.
3. Implement a new accounting system for the Construction group. This system was supposed to provide on-line data entry for increased timeliness, project status on demand, automated committed cost reporting, and elimination of manual tracking of costs. We installed the CMAS system on the System 34, and it has worked very well. There is a flaw in that we cannot automate the billing, and this is causing the Construction group to keep manual records of progress billings, prior payments, and retainers withheld. We have been trying to get information about this from the vendor, but the controller doesn't seem to be in any hurry.
4. Evaluate and test land and building investment analysis models. These models were supposed to provide faster, more accurate, and detailed data for decision making, a standardized methodology for measuring performance, and faster evaluation of financing arrangements. To handle this, we have bought several IBM PCs and put them out in the user areas; 1-2-3 from Lotus is the primary tool being used. I don't know what all the software is that is on the PCs here. I don't have the expertise on my staff to deal with them. But that really hasn't been a problem, since the users use each other as sounding boards for problems or new applications.
5. Perform in-house employee computer concepts seminars to provide staff and managers with a good understanding of computers. We have not held any seminars, but most of our employees know their systems' capabilities and frequently make inquiries and requests for information. Therefore, I believe we did not need to implement this objective.
6. Install and maintain a marketing prospect database for the regional markets. The PMAS system has a database of existing tenants; however, a database of potential customers has not been implemented. We will be evaluating some PC software to fulfill this objective.
7. Evaluate property management software for future installation. We have installed the PMAS system; although we had some problems with the installation, the $425 a day that MSD was charging convinced us to correct the problem ourselves with whatever vendor support we could get. The vendor of this system is a small company, primarily dedicated to this package, so some problems were to be expected. The company did not have a training program or established support mechanism, and its procedure manual was quite limited.

This caused several problems with the installation. Because we did not parallel the old system, we did not find all the problems right away. There were also several automatic calculations the system was guaranteed to make. The vendor has now admitted that these calculations and several other special features do not work, but they are fixing the problem. I don't know all the capabilities of the system, and we are still experimenting with it; but I think our people now know how to handle most of the problems we encounter. I also think that they have learned a lot more by being forced to learn the system than they would have had we had more formal training.

8. Centralize word processing. All of the secretaries in the division now have access to a PC with word processing capabilities. We have had a few other minor problems. A year ago, we had to replace our System 34 with a System 36 because IBM was dropping support of our CMAS system on the System 34; the change allowed us to install the new PMAS system I was just talking about. The only other problem I can think of is with our new general ledger. The monthly ledger did not agree with the year-to-date ledger for about six months. However, we have corrected that problem, and I feel pretty confident it will not happen again.

"Basically, I feel we have come a long way in five years. Sure, we have a lot to improve on and evaluate but I think we've accomplished a great deal, and we'll continue to forge ahead without the help of MSD or outside consultants. Now, what more do I need to do to convince Clark that everything is under control?"

QUESTIONS

1. Are the present weaknesses noted in the information system by John Leach major or minor?
2. How serious are the Accounting staff morale problems John discussed?
3. To what degree, if any, should Willoby Development (WD) rely on MSD for support?
4. Is Willoby and Company vulnerable to security or confidentiality problems if MSD does become involved with WD?
5. What effect will getting assistance from MSD have on Brian's morale? How important is he to WD in the short term?
6. Is Brian capable of handling the position of MIS manager for WD over the long term, considering the company's growth objectives?
7. What happens if all the need dates cannot be met? What role does/should the user play in these decisions?
8. Will existing systems meet long-term goals?
9. What should Clark Donaldson do?

Appendix 1

To: Brian Yeagar

cc: Clark Donaldson

From: John Leach

Subject: MIS problems at Willoby Development

Over the past year my staff has compensated for deficiencies in the PMAS system. We have created personal computer applications and maintained duplicate manual records for information that is now inaccessible through PMAS. I think the time has come to correct these deficiencies. I have pushed my staff too far as it is.

For example, the system has prior year data files; however, the information cannot be printed on any reports. Also, we input into the system rental requirements for an entire lease but the system cannot properly use this data unless the lease is of the absolute simplest type. The following is a list of additional problems with PMAS:

1. Tenant rental adjustments for CPI are not being calculated.
2. Reversing journal entries do not work for months with other than 30 days.
3. Financial statements cannot be printed for a period until that period is completely closed.

Additionally, the following is a list of enhancements needed to process in an accurate and efficient manner:

1. All reports need to be dated and have the time of creation recorded on them.
2. The system needs to provide a listing of all tenants in each of the buildings and what percent occupancy the building has.
3. The listing of tenants should also be available in alphabetic order regardless of building location.
4. The ability to create a five-year summary report of future rental income is required.

In order not to overwhelm you, this is just a preliminary list of enhancements. We have many others but these are the ones we feel are the most important.

I know that you are discussing some of these problems and others with the vendor and the vendor has promised that later versions will correct the deficiencies. I, however, do not think that we can rely on the vendor any longer. These promises were made over six months ago and as yet no progress has been made. I know that there are quite a few RPG programmers who would love to do some work for us. I know that you recently hired a systems analyst who knows RPG, but if he is unwilling to do programming, his presence is not going to help the situation.

Maybe it would be worth getting MSD involved. I know that is like admitting defeat around here, but I know from my experience over there, they have a lot of very qualified people who would be more than willing to lend you a hand at getting our needs prioritized and helping you generate a plan of action. Also, their experience in dealing with vendors might help us estimate what we can realistically expect in the way of support from the PMAS vendor. Then, at least, we would know where we have to modify the system.

I also have a need for support in personal computer usage. I would like to have my entire staff trained in its usage. The marketing people are coming to me for a recommendation for a database system to provide tenant prospect information. I am not qualified to make a decision for them, but I know MSD has a group dedicated to personal computer support. We will have to start using them if your department cannot provide us with faster responses to our questions and needs.

I am not the only user who feels you have not been sufficiently supportive. The Construction group continues to complain that they cannot do automated billing with their CMAS system even after two-and-a-half years. This not only causes an extra effort but it also places an added burden on my already overloaded staff.

It seems to me we've fallen far short of the recommendations outlined in your feasibility study. I guess you really need more staff. I would be happy to discuss any of these items with you. My only interest is in making our information systems better and more efficient.

John

Appendix 2

To: Clark Donaldson

cc: Brian Yeagar

From: Cal Tacy — MSD

Subject: Relationship of MSD and Willoby Development

I have been reviewing the tasks accomplished by MSD in 1987. As I look through the list of projects and who they were done for, one thing stands out. While we have done much for the major divisions such as the Cereal Products group (a new order processing system) and the Restaurant Products group (a new inventory management system), we do very little for the other divisions and subsidiaries. Many of these have their own MIS departments and wish to have very little if anything to do with MSD.

However, the picture of MSD support for the other divisions and subsidiaries is changing. The Flavorings and Toppings group uses our computers even though they retain their own programmers to perform the work. The Frozen Foods group has developed interfaces jointly with MSD that allows their systems to talk to ours. We have just installed three non-IBM terminals in MSD to provide additional support to one of the West Coast groups. Finally, we have just completed the sales of excess computer time to an outside firm, showing once again that we can meet diverse needs.

Even when I was on the task force with Brian Yeagar that set up your MIS department, it was clear that Willoby Development wanted no part of MSD. We were tolerated when we helped put up your CMAS system. When the time came to install PMAS, we were allowed to help until the system was installed; then we were sent away before the testing could start. In the hope of furthering understanding, I would like to present the MSD responses to the standard "reasons *not* to deal with MSD":

1. MSD is *too* expensive. In 1985, we charged $330 per billable workday of effort expended. The rate has been rising at about 10–15 percent per year for the past several years. You must realize we are charged by the corporation to break even each year. We must charge a rate to our customers large enough to cover the expense of running a large MIS shop and to cover the cost of the nonbillable personnel such as the liaison people who deal directly with the customers. We get no money from corporate except when they desire us to do work on a corporate-only system. Therefore, all maintenance/enhancement of the systems hardware and software must be apportioned back to the customer. If the customers won't fund a project, we can't do it. We feel $425 per day is reasonable.

2. MSD is not responsive. We can only do the work customers contract us to do. Customers agree to pay for a certain number of workdays within a year, and we provide that amount of support. We cannot guarantee their project will be the first done in the fiscal year; we need to balance demand, just as you do; but if the customer contracts for the time, they will get it.

3. MSD takes too long. Many of the subsidiaries work from verbal specifications. We are a large professional shop and do things in a professional manner. We document requirements in writing and have formal review points at various stages throughout the project. We are currently installing a systems development methodology to help further define this process. This approach requires more work and time from both parties involved. We can't get a system up as fast as the subsidiaries can, but when it goes up it has a higher chance of being the system needed, of being without flaws, and of being maintainable and properly tested and approved.

4. MSD's machine can't handle us. We have excess computing power to the level where we are actually selling those excess cycles to an outside company on a time-sharing basis, and we still have a mainframe computer sitting on the floor not even turned on. In addition, we have minicomputer experience. The analyst you just hired from MSD had been working on our new System 38 order processing system.

Additionally, there are other services that MSD can provide that may not come to mind on first thought. These include:

1. End-user computing. Our EUC group provides PC expertise and training to all who want it. We can even train on specific software packages.
2. Negotiation skills. We negotiate with many vendors daily. The experience and skills we have gained through this constant exposure can aid you in your search for the best deal from the best vendor.
3. Weight. MSD is a large MIS shop; our requests for change carry more weight than that of a smaller shop. This can be of use when requesting corrections to a system you have already purchased.

I hope this memo clarifies the MSD position and the advantages to be gained by a better relationship with MSD. Call me if you have any questions or comments.

Cal

Case 8–2 Tuscora County Hospital

In February 1986, Joe Stadley, president of Tuscora County Hospital (TCH), was sitting in his office contemplating the letter he had just finished reading. It was the third letter he'd received that month written by a patient complaining about billing problems. Even though each of these patients had been on different floors at different times, the complaints were very similar—"wrong items charged," "pricing extraordinarily high," or items not used but still charged to the patient's account.

Joe is concerned—he wonders if the three letters are a tip-off to a bigger problem. If these patients are being billed incorrectly, what about the rest of the patients? Since all three complaints deal with inventory (nomenclature or pricing), is the inventory value correctly stated on the hospital's financial reports? How can all these errors be happening? After all, he's insisted on hiring only the most competent, hard-working managers. He leans back in his large, leather, heavily padded executive armchair and reflects on the current status of the hospital's management team, particularly those responsible for the billing problems identified by these patients' letters.

THE HOSPITAL

Tuscora County Hospital is a nonprofit, private community hospital in Happy Acres, Arizona, approximately 20 miles west of Phoenix and 70 miles northwest of Tucson. The 210-bed hospital provides a full range of acute-care services including medicine, surgery, psychiatry, obstetrics, gynecology, pediatrics, intensive care, and emergency care programs.

Tuscora County Hospital began its operations as an 80-bed acute-care hospital in 1975. Originally, the hospital was to operate solely as a provider of inpatient services for the participants in the Happy Acres Medical Plan, a prepaid group practice health-care plan created by the Arizona State University Medical Institutions and the Southwestern General Insurance Corporation. However, just prior to the opening of the hospital, the board of trustees decided to operate independently of the initial founders and to offer all of its services to the general public. The hospital was built without many ancillary services customarily found in hospitals. As a result, a variety of privately owned and operated ancillary services were established, primarily by local physicians, but outside the hospital.

The hospital itself had neither the time nor the foresight to create these necessary departments. Basic functions such as billing, accounts payable, and other ac-

---

This case was prepared by Matthew S. Hamp and U. R. Sunkara. Names, locations, and financial data have been disguised.

counting functions had to be created almost overnight within the hospital, since initially it was intended that Arizona State Medical would handle these responsibilities.

The hospital's utilization rate continued to grow during the next few years. It was evident that being located in Happy Acres, as well as being the only hospital in Tuscora County, significantly contributed to this growth. In 1983, a 130-bed addition was completed, giving the hospital its current 210-bed configuration.

A few key hospital statistics are as follows:

Occupancy rate	87%
Length of stay	5.4 days
Annual admissions	8,100
Total patient days	43,726

Physicians are eager to use the hospital as evidenced by the 220 doctors with privileges on the medical staff. All of the physicians have privileges at one or more hospitals in the area as well. Many of the physicians who utilize the hospital frequently have their medical offices located in close proximity to the hospital or are hired by the Happy Aces Medical Plan; the Medical Plan uses Tuscora County Hospital as its primary health-care institution.

The hospital is considered a low-cost hospital compared to other hospitals in the region. It has been operating in the black for the past five years. Long-range plans forecast continued high growth rates for both Happy Acres and Tuscora County. As a result, the current long-range plan projects 100–200 more beds within the next 10 years.

AREA OF SERVICE

Happy Acres, Arizona, was built as a planned community by the Hadley Builders Corporation and Southwest General Life Insurance. The city's population is approximately 35,000 people. Its residents are typically commuters to Phoenix and Tucson and other surrounding cities. The median household income is approximately $31,000, ranking within the top 80 cities in the United States. One of every five families has a member with a graduate degree. Happy Acres has several federally subsidized apartment complexes for lower-income families. Even though Happy Acres residents make up a majority of the hospital's patients, its service area extends to almost all areas of Tuscora County, as well as into neighboring counties.

Three other hospitals are located nearby. Wilson Hobbs General is approximately 20 miles to the east, while Greater Tucson Valley Hospital is about 35 miles to the southeast. St. Consuella Hospital, TCH's largest competitor, is a 320-bed tertiary care center located about 30 minutes northeast on the outskirts of Phoenix.

ORGANIZATIONAL STRUCTURE

Exhibit 1 shows a diagram of the Tuscora County Hospital Organization Chart.

President

Joe Stadley has been at TCH for four years, serving as president since he was hired. He is a Fellow in the Association of County Health Administration (ACHA) and also has a master's degree in Health Administration (MHA). His primary relationships are with the board, medical staff, and the vice presidents.

Vice President for Financial Affairs

Al Fisher, 46, has been at TCH since 1977. He has a CPA and MBA but no experience in Information Systems (IS). His responsibilities are identified in Exhibit 2.

Vice President for Operations

Charles Conrad, 37, has been at the hospital for five years and served as acting president in the interim before Stadley was hired. He has an MHA, seven years of experience in upper administrative positions, and no IS experience. His areas of responsibilities are vast (see Exhibit 3); he relies heavily on his department heads to keep him informed and to present problems to him when necessary.

Controller

Stan Sherman has been at TCH for eight years, having been hired almost immediately by Al Fisher when he came on board. Stan, 57, was one of the first systems specialists in Management Information Systems (MIS) in the early 1950s. He was involved in the production aspects of a major equipment manufacturer. He has been drawn to computers since his early days and prides himself on always taking the initiative to learn the benefits of a system right from the start. Stan has directed the patient billing, data processing, and accounting departments since their beginning at the hospital. His only previous position was at another hospital where he worked as a manager of patient billing. Stan feels the controller position is what he's been working toward and plans to hold it long enough to retire at TCH.

Director of Materials Management

John Lawson, 30, came from a similar materials management position at a 400-bed hospital in New York. He has been at TCH about 18 months. He has nine years of materials management experience as well as a bachelor's degree in Business Administration.

EXHIBIT 1   Tuscora County Hospital Organizational Chart

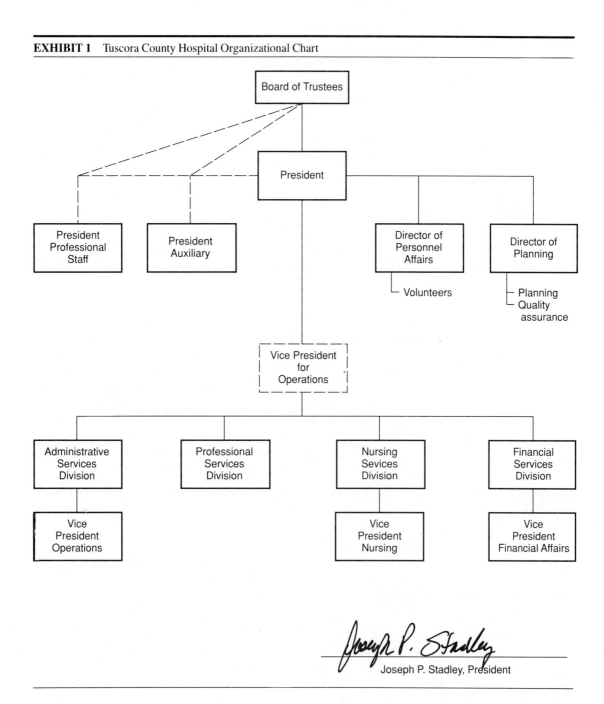

Joseph P. Stadley, President

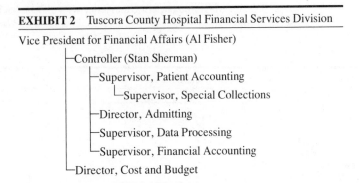

EXHIBIT 2   Tuscora County Hospital Financial Services Division

Vice President for Financial Affairs (Al Fisher)
- Controller (Stan Sherman)
  - Supervisor, Patient Accounting
    - Supervisor, Special Collections
  - Director, Admitting
  - Supervisor, Data Processing
  - Supervisor, Financial Accounting
- Director, Cost and Budget

Board of Trustees

The hospital's board was comprised of long-standing members of Tuscora County and Happy Acres. The trustees were representatives of the community. Yet many did not have business backgrounds—they were asked to join the board either for their political ties or community spirit. Most members were over 50 and had little background in health care.

HISTORY OF MATERIALS MANAGEMENT

Although TCH started out as a small, 80-bed hospital, with minimal space and storage, its poor design and rapid growth presented departments with supply storage problems. Materials management has always been a weak spot for TCH. The hospital had hired several managers, trying to get some sort of control system established for purchasing, inventory, and distribution, but because of the managers' lack of knowledge or experience, nothing ever worked as it should have.

Two-and-a-half years ago, the hospital contracted with Housekeepers, Inc.

EXHIBIT 3   Administrative Services Division

Vice President for Operations (Charles Conrad)

- Director, Security and Transportation
- Director, Communications
- Director, Dietary
- Director, Housekeeping
- Director, Medical Records
- Director, Plant Operations and Maintenance
- Director, Materials Management (John Lawson)
- Director, Medical Social Work
- Director, Medical Library
- Director, Pharmacy
- Director, Physical Medical Services
- Chief X-Ray Technician, Radiology
- Chief Technician, Anethesiology
- Chief Technician, Pulmonary Function
- Director, Clinical Laboratories
- Director, Cardiology Services
- Director, EEG Services

(HI), an outside management firm, to direct the Materials Management department. Managing materials was a new area of involvement for HI. However, since they already handled general housekeeping and linen distribution successfully, the move to oversee all materials and supplies was thought to be a proper decision. The company assured TCH that it would reduce inventories, establish a patient charge system, and would resolve all current materials-related problems.

A year later, the hospital's inventory had doubled, no patient charge system was in place, and supply costs were exorbitant. The contract was abruptly canceled, and the hospital began looking again for a director of Materials Management.

GREG WILSON

After a short search, TCH hired Greg Wilson, a specialized Materials manager. He clearly understood his priority when hired — to implement a hospitalwide automated inventory control system that would reduce inventory levels as well as provide accurate supply cost information. Within two months, he signed a two-year contract with Reynolds & Reynolds Company (R & R) for a turnkey computer system that would resolve the inventory problems. Greg had also convinced Charles Conrad, the vice president for Operations, that this system was the answer to the hospital's problems.

Al had been so overwhelmed with problems in his Materials Management sub-unit for so many years that this solution sounded reasonable. He approved the two-year agreement, since it was only $500 in lease costs. Also, approvals by other officers were not necessary per hospital policy (unless the cost was in excess of $1,000 per payment of a capital equipment outright purchase).

Two months after the implementation of the turnkey system, Greg Wilson, the Materials Management specialist, resigned. No one else knew the system's features or advantages or even how it worked!

Jeanne Munro, a purchasing buyer, was given temporary responsibility for Materials Management. She had no experience in computers but was enrolled in an evening Introduction to Data Processing course. Though she tried to keep the inventory and patient charge system going, it was a nightmare.

Meanwhile, Stan Sherman, the controller, found out about the turnkey stand-alone system and was furious. How could another computer system have been purchased without his knowledge? He was responsible for Data Processing; the director of Materials Management was not.

A meeting was held between the vice presidents for Financial Affairs and Operations; the president and controller also attended. Charles Conrad felt he had been well within his authority to approve the separate system. Even though he didn't necessarily feel this decision should have been made in a vacuum, the president supported Al.

Stan Sherman was outraged. This new computer system was a joke. It could not interface with the hospital's minicomputer system; the database was not even the same for charge codes, descriptions, and issue units. "Well," Stan thought, "it will be a cold day in July before I offer my assistance to straighten out this mess."

JOHN LAWSON

Meanwhile, John Lawson was hired as director of Materials Management. His years of experience included the implementation of a patient charge system and an in-hospital activated inventory control system as well. When he started at the TCH, everyone seemed receptive and cooperative.

Within the first few months, the Materials Management department finally started to stand on its own. Problems were resolved, inventory costs were down, and the systems were being organized. Yet John was unable to get the turnkey inventory computer system working properly. Stan Sherman was not helpful and could even be termed difficult to deal with. He made no attempt to improve the relationship and working atmosphere between Materials Management and Data Processing.

HISTORY OF MIS AT TCH

Unfortunately, typical of the health-care industry, TCH was far behind banks, manufacturers, retailers, and insurance companies in the utilization of computers to enhance various business applications. It was the 1980s, yet TCH was minimally automated. For many years, other businesses had been employing computers to increase efficiency in all areas of operations. TCH, until three years ago, had been on a completely manual record-keeping system for admissions, inventory control, patient billing, and various financial reports. It was then that the hospital contracted with a private automated data processing company to provide payroll services, which eventually broke the ice for other limited data processing duties.

STAN SHERMAN

Stan Sherman had always been a proponent of the computerization of various aspects of his assigned responsibilities yet could never convince his boss to fund their costs. True, the hospital had been strapped financially and had operated in the red for the past several years. It was not that the current hospital administration could not appreciate the value of computers. Rather, due to both TCH's size and financial constraints, the president felt the "financial risk" could not be taken at this time.

Stan was determined to establish a hospital information system (HIS). He was convinced that, due to the ever-changing computer industry, TCH should not buy an in-hospital computer but rather should use a time-sharing system. His reasons were as follows:

1. It would be difficult to find and retain capable software/programming personnel since the market was so competitive and the hospital's size could offer little advancement. High-caliber quality personnel would always be at a premium, and turnover would be high.
2. Buying a computer system would require high financial outlays. Due to the rapidly changing data processing environment, such a purchase would not be a wise investment, since new developments in both software and hardware were always occurring.

Eventually, Stan's persistence paid off. A contract was signed for a time-sharing arrangement with Pentamation, Inc. (PI). PI specialized in health-care information systems and operated nationally. TCH placed its Admissions department, accounts receivable, and patient billing on the Pentamation system. For every system automated, a manual system procedure was on file to assure appropriate backup and control. The two main areas not on the Pentamation system were inventory control and budget.

When the system was fully implemented in 1984, everyone in data processing thought the transition was very smooth, with few problems. Pentamation also stated that the start-up went very well. However, other department managers did not agree with these beliefs and felt that problems were experienced in patients' bills as well as other areas such as room assignments and correct patient information.

The inventory system at TCH is a separate, different problem. In the spring of 1983, the "specialist" (Wilson) hired to straighten out the Materials Management department entered into the two-year contract with the Reynolds & Reynolds Company. This hospital-computerized inventory system was a spin-off of the automobile industry's computer system. The contract was approved only by Greg Wilson, the new Materials Manager, and Charles Conrad, the vice president for Operations.

After Wilson resigned, Stan was asked by Joe Stadley to review the system's capability and determine the value of the system. Though he was still upset regarding his noninvolvement with the acquisition of the Reynolds & Reynolds computer system, Stan admitted the system had several strengths. Since Pentamation did not offer an automated inventory control system, Stan figured he should at least recommend maintenance of the R & R system; eventually, on expiration of the contract, he could install a system he preferred.

When Stan reviewed the system, he discovered the charge to the hospital was based on total items in inventory. Since the hospital used a multilocation system, each item in each system was considered a distinct item—even though it utilized the same inventory code, it had a different location. The initial estimate of $500 per month for leasing had skyrocketed to approximately $1,500 per month.

When the inventory system was implemented, the Pharmacy, General Stores, and Central Supply departments had been given the responsibility to assign inventory code numbers within a specified range for those items controlled by each department. For example, IV solutions would have code numbers 4450001 through 4450099. Once numbers were assigned, they were entered directly into the system by each department. No control master list was established, although the system would print off a current listing, either numerically or alphabetically, on an as-needed basis (see Exhibit 4).

When the system was first in place, it appeared to assist the Nursing staff greatly in ordering supplies and recognizing the distribution between similar supplies. Due to the apparent success of the system, the Nursing staff began to utilize these inventory code numbers for patient charge codes. When each patient used a supply item, the inventory code number was identified on a charge slip and sent to Data Processing on a daily basis. Eventually, the Nursing department established preprinted forms with the high-usage, most common supplies identified; thus, nurses would save time by marking only the quantity and the patient's addressograph plate for each day. The data entry operators were very pleased with this preprinted format, since it significantly reduced their keypunching time and provided the supposed "correct" supply usage information. This information was labeled on a daily basis, and a copy from Data Processing was sent to Ma-

EXHIBIT 4   Partial Current List of Inventory Code Numbers

B$, ITEM #	DESCRIPTION
4450001	2B0164 IV SOLUTION D10W 1000ML
4450002	2B0064 IV SOLUTION D5W 1000ML
4450003	2A5043 10% GENT 40, 9% NACL 500ML
4450004	2B0062 IV SOLUTION D5W 250ML
4450005	2B0061 IV SOLUTION D5W 150ML
4450006	2B1094 IV SOLN D5-0.25 1000ML
4450007	2B1093 IV SOLN D5-0.25 500ML
4450008	2B1074 IV SOLN D5-1/2 NSS 1000ML
4450009	2B1073 IV SOLN D5-1/2 NSS 500ML
4450010	2B1064 IV SOLN D5 NSS 1000ML
4450011	2B1063 IV SOLN D5 NSS 500ML
4450012	2B1324 IV SOLUTION NSS 1000ML
4450013	2B1323 IV SOLUTION NSS 500ML
4450014	2B1322 IV SOLUTION NSS 250ML
4450015	2B1321 IV SOLUTION NSS 150ML
4450016	2A1324 IV SOLN 1/2 NSS 1000ML
4450017	2B2324 IV SOLN L/R 1000ML
4450018	2B2323 IV SOLN L/R 500ML
4450019	2B2024 IV SOLN D5-L/R 1000ML
4450020	2B2073 IV SOLN D5-L/R 500ML
4450021	2B2064 IV SOLN D5-RING 1000ML
4450022	2B2063 IV SOLN D5-RING 500ML
4450023	2B5013 IV SOLUTION 6 DENTRAN 500ML
4450024	2A1353 IV SOLN 3 NACL 500ML

terials Management; Materials could then check what items were actually charged compared to supplies that had to be replenished.

PROBLEM OF CODE INCOMPATIBILITY

When Stan automated the patient billing system, all codes had a specific prefix to identify them, as either chargeable or nonchargeable, and type of supply (i.e., medical, surgical, or IV solution). It was discovered four months after the implementation of the Reynolds & Reynolds system that no consideration had been made for different supply classes.

As different nurses started to utilize the new inventory codes and forms, tenured nurses continued to use the charge codes they had utilized for years. Additionally, it was recognized that the same supply items could be obtained from either General Stores and/or Pharmacy, yet have distinctly different codes, descriptions ("IV tubing" versus "administration set") and costs. Since Purchasing was within the Materials Management department, only price changes they received were updated into the computer system. There was no system to inform the Billing department of price changes received by the Purchasing department. The hospital was purchasing about $1.5 million worth of supplies annually; the annual increase in the cost of these products (predominantly oil-based products and plastics) was 7–10 percent.

As each series of charge numbers was utilized, each department began to overlap into other series; for example, an IV solution that had always had a 445 prefix and now was assigned a 714 prefix.

The problems seemed all-encompassing, yet Stan Sherman claimed that John Lawson should "straighten out" this mess, since he was assigned inventory control responsibility. John stated that he knew of the problems and that it was impossible to correct them; he had no control over patient billing or the charge master. He reinforced this statement by submitting a copy of the inventory codes (see Exhibit 5) used in the most recent physical inventory, compared to the patient charge description master list (see Exhibit 6).

It is difficult to know who is at fault or even how the problem evolved. Immediate action has to be taken, however, to resolve the problems and establish the appropriate controls to avoid continuing patient complaints and lost revenue.

QUESTIONS

1. What are the major problems facing TCH's Materials Management department?
2. What part does Stan Sherman play in the current situation?
3. Can TCH continue to prosper with its present IS philosophy?
4. What must John Lawson do to improve the present IS situation at TCH?

EXHIBIT 5 Partial Physical Inventory Code List

RUN DATE   4

Page 1

PHYSICAL INVENTORY BY LOCATION AND PRICE EXTENSION AS OF 11/28/86

CATALOG NO.	U/M	DESCRIPTION	LOCATION	U/M	QTY	UNIT COST	TOTAL INV
016165	EACH	BEDPAN, DISPOSABLE, 50/CASE	AA 03	EACH	15	.89	10.35
010510	EACH	PILLOW, DISPOSABLE	AA 03	EACH	12	1.05	12.60
010750	EACH	UNDERPAD, DISPOSABLE, 17 1/2 X 24 300/CS	AA 03	EACH	435	.048	20.88
020220	EACH	DEODORANT, AEROSOL	AA 03	EACH	1	1.48	1.48
020370	EACH	ERG PAPER, SINGLE CHANNEL 2 RL/BOX	AA 03	EACH	4	1.97	7.88
020390	EACH	FILTER, KIDNEY STONE 100/CS	AA 03	EACH	16	.44	7.04
020495	EACH	PAD, DEFIBRILLATOR PADDLE 6 SET/BOX	AA 03	EACH	2	3.15	6.30
020790	EACH	URINAL, DISPOSABLE (FROM CSO) 50/CASE	AA 03	EACH	25	.38	9.00
030060	EACH	BANDAGE, GAUZE, ELASTIC (KLING) 3 INCH	AA 03	EACH	9	.24	2.16
030100	EACH	BANDAGE, RUBBER ELASTIC 3 INCH	AA 03	EACH	3	.45	1.35
030530	EACH	LUBRICANT, SURGICAL, SINGLE USE 144/BOX	AA 03	EACH	55	.04	2.20
040090	EACH	CANNISTER, SUCTION, SMALL	AA 03	EACH	1	1.53	1.53
040150	EACH	INFUSION SET, BUTTERFLY, 190A 50/BOX	AA 03	EACH	92	.39	35.88
040160	EACH	INFUSION SET, BUTTERFLY 210A 50/BOX	AA 03	EACH	75	.39	29.25
040180	EACH	INFUSION SET, BUTTERFLY 23 GA 50/BOX	AA 03	EACH	102	.39	39.78
040220	EACH	STOPCOCK, THREEWAY WITH EXTENSION TUBE 5	AA 03	EACH	10	1.03	10.30
040240	EACH	STOPCOCK, FOURWAY WITH EXTENSION TUBE 50	AA 03	EACH	51	1.04	53.04
040400	EACH	SYRINGE, IRRIGATING PISTON TYPE 125/CASE	AA 03	EACH	20	.30	6.00
040510	EACH	TUBE, CONNECTOR, 1/4 INCH 50/BOX (EA-CSD)	AA 03	EACH	5	.12	.60
050140	PAIR	GLOVE, SURGEONS, STERILE 6 1/2 50 PAIR/BOX	AA 03	EACH	25	.33	8.25
050150	PAIR	GLOVE, SURGEONS, STERILE 7 50 PAIR/BOX	AA 03	EACH	50	.33	16.50

Item	Unit	Description	Class	UOM	Qty	Unit Price	Total
050160	PAIR	GLOVE, SURGEONS, STERILE 7 1/2 50 PAIR/BOX	AA 03	EACH	45	.33	14.85
050170	PAIR	GLOVE, SURGEONS, STERILE 8 50 PAIR/BOX	AA 03	EACH	58	.33	19.14
050190	EACH	MASK, OXYGEN, ADULT WITH EXTENSION TUBE	AA 03	EACH	3	.70	2.10
050440	EACH	TUBE, EXTENSION, 33 INCH 50/BOX (EA-CSD)	AA 03	EACH	56	.44	24.64
050471	EACH	TUBE, FEEDING 5FR 15 INCH 50/CASE (EA-CSD)	AA 03	EACH	68	.67	45.56
050472	EACH	TUBE, FEEDING 8FR 15 INCH 50/CASE (EA-CSD)	AA 03	EACH	24	.67	16.08
050473	EACH	TUBE, FEEDING 8FR 42 INCH 50/CASE (EA-CSD)	AA 03	EACH	4	.41	1.64
060140	EACH	BOARD, ARM, ADULT	AA 03	EACH	3	.26	.78
060390	PAIR	CRUTCH TIPS	AA 03	EACH	2	.68	1.36
070220	EACH	GOWN, SURGEONS, STERILE, SINGLES 30/CASE	AA 03	EACH	2	2.67	5.34
110030	EACH	NEEDLE, HYPODERMIC 18 GA X 1 1/2 INCH 10	AA 03	EACH	179	.03	5.37
110050	EACH	NEEDLE, HYPODERMIC 19 GA X 1 1/2 INCH 10	AA 03	EACH	100	.03	3.00
110070	EACH	NEEDLE, HYPODERMIC 20 GA X 1 INCH 100/80	AA 03	EACH	100	.03	3.00
110090	EACH	NEEDLE, HYPODERMIC 20 GA X 1 1/2 INCH 10	AA 03	EACH	133	.03	3.99
110110	EACH	NEEDLE, HYPODERMIC 21 GA X 1 INCH 100/80	AA 03	EACH	100	.03	3.00
110130	EACH	NEEDLE, HYPODERMIC 21 GA X 1 1/2 INCH 10	AA 03	EACH	205	.03	6.15
110170	EACH	NEEDLE, HYPODERMIC 22 GA X 1 1/2 INCH 10	AA 03	EACH	50	.03	1.50
110190	EACH	NEEDLE, HYPODERMIC 25 GA X 5/8 INCH 100/	AA 03	EACH	318	.03	9.54
110411	EACH	NEEDLE, MYLOGRAM 18 FT 3 1/2 IN 10/BOX	AA 03	EACH	17	4.30	73.10
120200	EACH	RAZOR, SAFETY, DOUBLE EDGE, DISPOSABLE	AA 03	EACH	25	.22	5.50
120220	EACH	SCALPEL, DISPOSAL #11 10/BOX	AA 03	EACH	1	.34	.34
130330	EACH	MANOMETER TRAY 50/CASE (EA-CSD)	AA 03	EACH	13	1.90	24.70
130355	EACH	MYLOGRAM TRAY W/CAUTICO NEEDLE 20/CASE	AA 03	EACH	7	13.04	93.80
130520	EACH	SUTURE REMOVAL KIT	AA 03	EACH	1	.52	.52

EXHIBIT 6   Partial Charge Description Master List

CHARGE DESCRIPTION MASTER LIST   DATE: 08/01/86

SERVICE CODE	INS. CODE	PRICE	RELATIVE VALUE	BILLING DESCRIPTION	G.L. NO.	IND
4303260	71	4.70	.89	SFT, IRRIGATION BULB	430	00
4303262	71	42.91	8.10	TRAY, SPINAL, ANESTHES.	430	00
4303270	71	4.98	.94	SFT, IRRIGATION PIST	430	00
4303330	71	20.14	3.80	TRAY, MANOMETER 5/CS	430	00
4303350	71	132.45	25.00	LUMEN DOUBLE 7FR	430	00
4303351	71	17.42	3.29	CATHETER FOLEY, 20FR	430	00
4303352	71	2.48	.47	CATHETER, TEXAS	430	00
4303353	71	16.25	3.07	CATHETER, FOLEY, 26FR	430	00
4303354	71	95.36	18.00	CATHETER, SWAN-GANZ 8	430	00
4303355	71	83.53	15.77	TRAY, MYLOGRAM W/CAUT	430	00
4303356	71	185.43	35.00	LUMEN TRIPLE 7FR	430	00
4303357	71	336.42	63.50	BALECTRODE ELECATH	430	00
4303358	71	14.04	2.65	CATHETER, THORACIC 1	430	00
4303360	71	59.80	11.29	TRAY, NERVE BLOCK 10/	430	00
4303380	71	24.11	4.55	TRAY, PARACERVICAL/DF	430	00
4303381	71	23.21	4.38	TRAY, EPIDURAL ANESTH	430	00
4303400	71	2.74	.52	TRAY, SHAVE PREP 50/G	430	00
4303410	71	11.13	2.10	BATH, SITZ (EA-CSD)	430	00
4303420	71	5.83	1.10	TRAY, SKIN SCRUB 20/C	430	00
4303425	71	50.96	9.62	TRAY, SPINAL ANESTHES	430	00
4303440	71	2.58	.49	SET, SUCTION CATH-N-	430	00
4303450	71	2.58	.49	SET, SUCTION CATH-N-	430	00
4303460	71	2.58	.49	SET, SUCTION CATH-N-	430	00
4303470	71	2.58	.49	SET, SUCTION CATH-N-	430	00
4303475	71	2.96	.56	SET, SUCTION INFANT	430	00
4303479	71	7.00	1.34	BAG, URIN LEG	430	00
4303481	71	37.02	4.99	TRAY, INFANT LUMBAR	430	00
4303484	71	31.94	6.03	TRAY, THORACENTESIS I	430	00
4303485	71	37.02	6.99	TRAY, LUMBAR PUNCTURE	430	00
4303486	71	63.41	11.97	TRAY, PERITONEAL DIAL	430	00
4303487	71	42.22	7.97	TRAY, PERITONEAL LAVA	430	00
4303488	71	12.98	2.45	TRAY, I&D	430	00
4303489	71	19.33	3.45	TRAY, POST NATAL	430	00
4303490	71	55.63	10.50	TRAY, EXCHANGE TRANSF	430	00
4303491	71	37.51	7.08	TRAY, PED/INF LUMBAR	430	00
4303492	71	37.51	7.08	TRAY, PED/INF LUMBAR	430	00
4303493	71	37.02	6.99	TRAY, LUMBAR PUNCTURE	430	00
4303494	71	254.30	44.00	KIT, EMERGENCY TRANSF	430	00
4303520	71	2.58	.49	KIT, SUTURE REMOVAL	430	00
4303521	71	1.48	.28	SUCTION PLAIN 16FR	430	00
4303522	71	4.77	.90	MASKS, OXYGEN PEDIATR	430	00
4303523	71	6.47	1.20	TUBE, SALEM SUMP	430	00

EXHIBIT 6   *(concluded)*

4303525	71	26.92	5.00	LAVAGE SET, GASTRIC	430	00
4303530	71	43.01	8.12	TRAY, THORACENTESIS	430	00
4303531	71	122.91	22.80	PLEUR EVAC	430	00
4303532	71	9.19	1.75	TUBE, CANTOR	430	00

Case 8–3 Protective Systems Evaluation Facility

It was early September 1986 when Frank Fox, a new account manager for BLC Consultants, Inc., contemplated how he could best handle his first project, the Radar Service Center (RSC) job. He was anxious to make a good showing to prove to himself and his boss that he had "the right stuff." The RSC job involved one of RSC's eight divisions, the Protective Systems Evaluation Facility (PSEF) and was considered important since it could very easily lead to business with the other divisions. More importantly, the RSC contract could open up the possibility of attaining more government work through the close working relationships RSC had with several government agencies.

BLC Consultants had been called in by Jack Whitney, the Protective Systems Evaluation Facility's director, to ensure that the new computer and automated test system (for their test facilities for small engines, generators, and air-conditioning units) would be completed on schedule and perform as expected. This new system was needed desperately to alleviate growing problems and to provide improved capabilities. Now that the system was due to start up within a month, Jack wanted to be sure all bases were covered, so he hired BLC Consultants to double check the system, pick out any minor problems that could have been overlooked, and help devise solutions for them.

The PSEF project initially appeared to be a straightforward case of hardware/ software requirements evaluation, comparison of these requirements with action taken by RSC, and recommendation formulation. However, from the initial meetings Frank had with RSC personnel, he could tell that he was not coming into a cold case. A lot had happened before BLC was invited in; as a result, Frank found himself in a difficult situation. He wondered, with this case, whether he should step beyond the realm of his normal responsibilities to inform the clients that they were overlooking a very important aspect in the installation of their new system.

This case was prepared by Joseph Lyall, Kathy Considine, and James Bersani. Names, locations, and financial data have been disguised.

How could he make meaningful, objective recommendations regarding this oversight without alienating and upsetting his client? That outcome surely would not win BLC any return contracts or much job security for himself.

COMPANY BACKGROUND

The Radar Service Center is a private testing center established in 1939 to do testing of radar systems for the federal government. Since that time, the center has grown substantially and now has 10 separate test facilities that do testing work around the globe for several U.S. allies. Forty percent of RSC's work comes from the U.S. government, 20 percent from its allies, and the remainder from private industry. RSC has diversified horizontally into testing almost all types of equipment and electronic instruments. Overall business has a fairly stable volume of work that is relatively immune to general business cycles due to the diversity of work and clients. There are, however, fluctuations in the workload of individual test labs.

RSC employs 9,500 people throughout the world, and, in 1984, recorded sales of $698 million. PSEF recorded the second smallest amount of sales of the 10 facilities, $32.8 million, but had the next to the largest percentage increase in sales over the last three years at 17 percent (see Exhibit 1). PSEF's net income to sales was also the highest at 11.7 percent. PSEF employs 142 people. The low security test center for generators, small engines, and air-conditioning units, with 31 people, accounts for $16.7 million.

The PSEF is located in a 100-acre tract of land overlooking the Gunpowder River (see Exhibit 2). The main charter of PSEF is to test high-security components and to evaluate small engines, generators, and air-conditioning units for the U.S. Army. These three types of equipment are manufactured by a variety of companies. The small-engine and air-conditioning test labs are located at opposite ends of the #5 Building, while the generator test lab is in Building #34 at the far side of the facility. John Ford, the Low Security Test Center general manager (see Exhibit 3), has often griped about supervising installations that are so spread out. "Sometimes, it seems like I spend half of my time just traveling between labs," he notes. He has tried in the past to relocate the labs closer together in a cluster but without success. He thinks the new computer system should reduce that problem.

The equipment to be tested is brought in by truck or train or flown in to Harford Municipal Airport. Ford's office is next to the small-engine test lab. Often, as he looks out of his office window and sees the technicians setting up a test, he recalls how he had been hired right out of high school to run similar tests. "The company was young then," he remembers, "and a man did not need a college diploma to get ahead. I have worked hard to gain the respect of others, and it has won me a position usually reserved only for those with degrees." He has thought about going back to school but the pressures of the job and his family responsibilities

EXHIBIT 1   Radar Service Center, Inc., Sales (in thousands)

Division	Years Projected			
	1982	*1983*	*1984*	*1985*
Radar Support and				
Evaluation Facility	$172,900	$188,500	$207,200	$232,100
PSE Facility	24,500	28,000	32,800	38,700
Taiwan	81,500	93,700	108,000	124,200
Argentina	51,800	52,700	54,600	56,500
Australia	30,700	31,000	43,200	44,000
United Kingdom	39,200	42,700	46,700	52,500
South Korea	44,800	44,700	42,900	42,000
Japan	68,700	79,500	89,800	104,200
West Germany	21,400	25,300	31,800	41,200
Israel	30,100	32,200	37,600	42,700
Total	$585,600	$618,300	$698,400	$778,100

just do not permit it. Besides, he is confident in his abilities and has been promoted regularly over the years, without the degree.

Ford now supervises the three test labs that employ 30 people. Presently there are 6 technicians in the small-engine test lab, 10 in the generator facility, and 8 in the air-conditioning lab; an experienced manager and lead engineer have direct responsibility for each lab. The new engineer responsible for the generator lab is Tim Mark, a computer whiz, who graduated from Duke University only a year ago. Although he has a way of rubbing people the wrong way, Mark has done wonders ·by successfully installing the computer and controller in the generator test lab. He also helped Ford with the initial proposal for automating all three labs.

DATA PROCESSING AT PSEF

Data processing began at PSEF in 1968 with the lease of a UNIVAC 90/30 mainframe computer by the Accounting department, which wanted to automate the general ledger and payroll systems. The UNIVAC system was upgraded to a 110/50 in 1973 when the decision was made to automate accounts payable and receivable along with inventory control. Jim Tamburrino, who was at that time the general manager of Accounting and Finance, was given responsibility for the system.

Between 1973 and 1978, PSEF doubled in size, pushing the UNIVAC into obsolescence in favor of an IBM 4342/4381 mainframe. The IBM system was purchased outright, and all existing software was converted. An MIS department was formed with Tamburrino as the manager, 8 systems staffers, and 25 pro-

EXHIBIT 1   Chesapeake Mutual Insurance Company Organization Chart

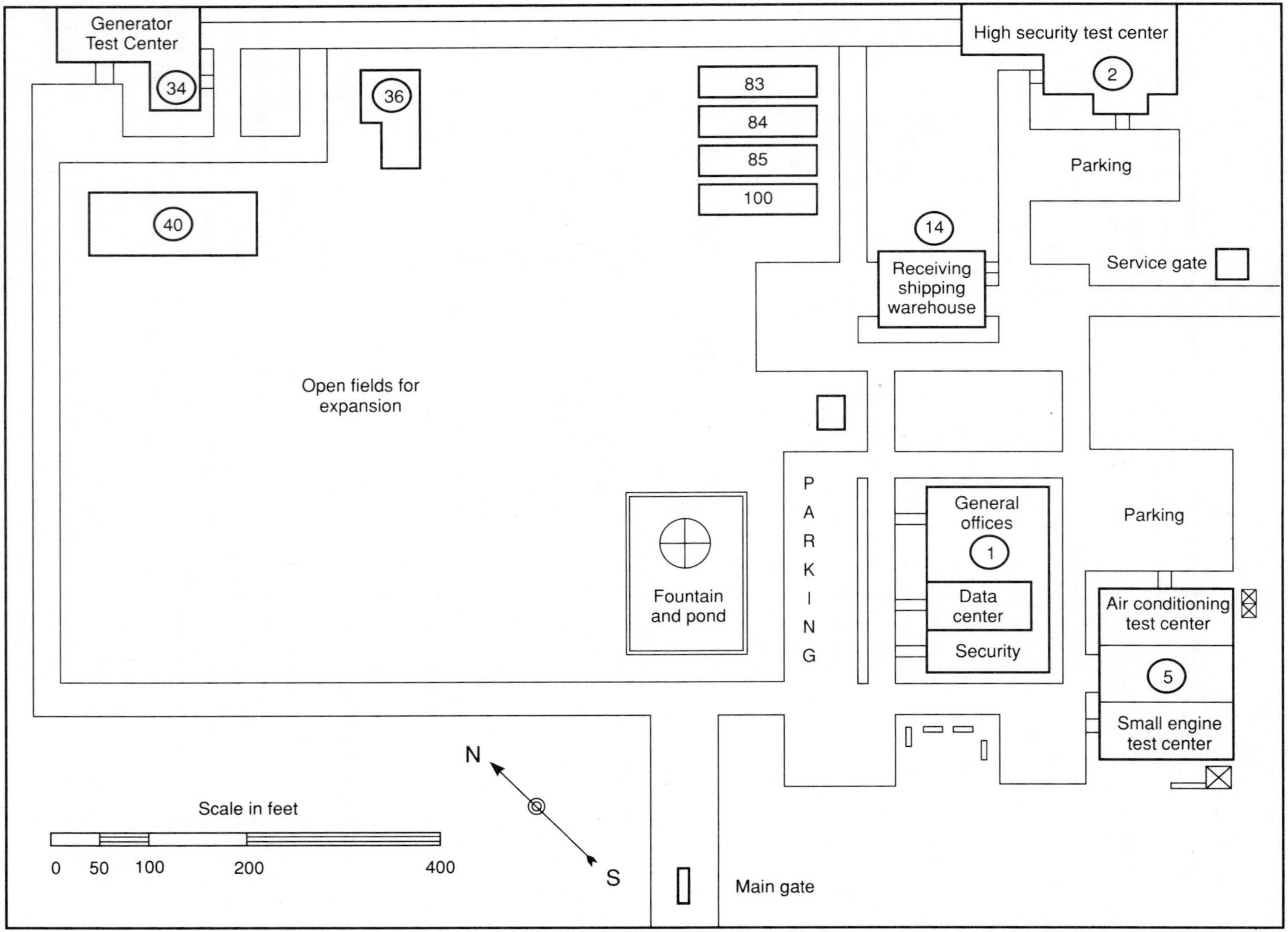

High security test center

(2)

Parking

Service gate

Parking

Air conditioning test center

Small engine test center

(5)

General offices

(1)

Data center

Security

Receiving shipping warehouse

(14)

83

84

85

100

P
A
R
K
I
N
G

Fountain and pond

Main gate

Open fields for expansion

(36)

Generator Test Center

(34)

(40)

Scale in feet

0   50   100   200   400

N

S

EXHIBIT 3 Radar Service Center, Inc., Corporate Organization

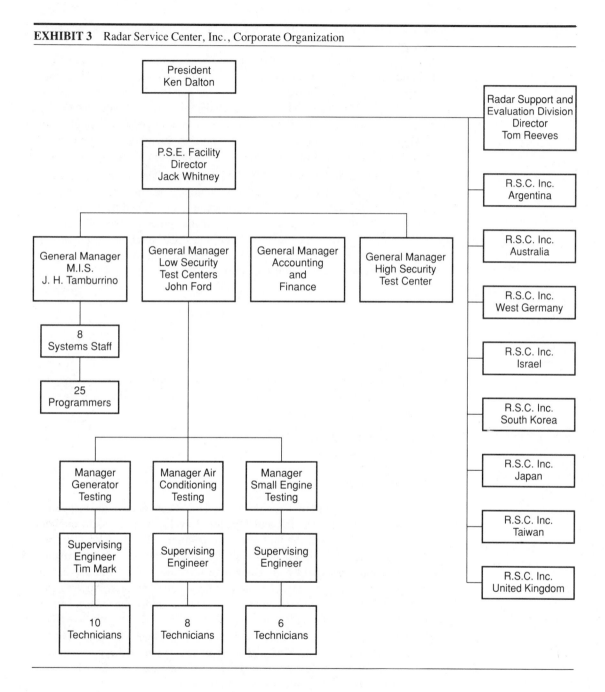

grammers. Both batch and on-line operations were performed, and priorities were assigned.

Due to a request from Ford in 1979, inspection data received was logged into the IBM on a batch basis. This was RSC's first attempt at an automated application of test center data; the results were so encouraging that PSEF "borrowed" a DEC VAX 11/780 in 1981 from its sister division, Radar Support and Evaluation (RSE). The VAX machine was used primarily for quality control and ran an application called Quality System. A large increase in report productivity was immediately realized and eventually led to a 30 percent decrease in report generation time.

In 1984, Tim Mark set up the first computer-controlled automated test of a generator using a desktop controller and programmable instrumentation. This was the first time actual equipment test time had been reduced, and by 50 percent at that. The successful generator test, along with the other successful computer applications, encouraged Ford and Whitney, the PSEF director, to pursue the purchase and installation of a dedicated computer system to do quality control analysis and automated testing for the entire test facility.

PRESENT QUALITY SYSTEM

Data collection at PSEF is presently collected at the inspection (receiving, in-process, final), test, and rework areas. The log sheets used by the inspectors to record the quality data include:

1. Inspection event log (IEL).
2. Reject report (RR).
3. Test event log (TEL).
4. Test failure report (TFR).

In the event of a unit failure, a unique RR or TFR is generated at the inspection or test area, respectively. The RR and TFR logs travel with the units throughout the in-process section, until the unit passes inspection. All IEL, RR, TEL, and TFR log data is later keypunched into the VAX 11/780 computer. The information is then stored and processed by the Datatrieve software package. Receiving inspection quality data is presently recorded on the receiver reports. Any rejected data will eventually (future use) be entered into the nonconforming material report (NCMR).

Quality data on incoming equipment from vendors is obtained from the material rejection invoice (MRI). The MRI and receiver report data is keypunched into the Data Analysis Information System (DAIS) software package, which resides on the IBM mainframe computer (VM operating system).

Current quality data reports are generated either manually or by the Datatrieve software on a daily, weekly, and monthly basis. The majority of the failure/reject reports are in tabular format. Bar graphs or other graphics failure reports are hand-plotted.

The present vendor analysis reports are generated from the DAIS software package.

PRESENT TEST PROCEDURES

All tests at the generator, air-conditioning, and small-engine unit labs are performed manually with the actual procedures differing very little from those used 30 years ago. A large variety of very specialized electronic measuring equipment is used to perform the testing; therefore, the person conducting the test has to be extremely well versed in a broad category of electronic test instrumentation. Even though technology has made monumental leaps during the last three decades, most of the gains have come in the digital world. The tests performed at PSEF are mostly analog. While technical improvements do help by defining better accuracies and smaller error margins, little gain has been realized in actual testing time. Therefore, while specific pieces of electronic gear have changed, the overall measurement procedures have not.

It was not until the mid-1970s that both the digital and analog worlds were joined. The first programmable electronic instrumentation was developed and gave users the capability to control the instrument with a desktop controller by means of a specialized interface. Problems arose, however, as different manufacturers built their own interfaces, and compatibility was impossible. In the late 1970s, the Institute of Electronic and Electrical Engineers (IEEE) picked a standard, and the compatibility problem was resolved. Advances in computer technology were applied to the desktop controllers, expanding their capabilities. Not only could electronic measuring instrumentation be controlled automatically, but powerful measurement routines and analyses could now be performed.

In 1983, PSEF purchased its first programmable instrument and controller at the direction of John Ford. Since PSEF had been using National Testers, Ltd., (NTL) test instrumentation in all of the test centers, the company decided to stay with the NTL programmable signal source and NTL 471X desktop controller. Tim Mark was given the responsibility of evaluating the system and analyzing the implications such a system would have on current test procedures.

PRESENT SITUATION

Productivity of the three test labs had been a concern for some time. Something had to be done. With many government contracts coming up, the workload on these test labs had increased substantially. As a result, a backlog was steadily building. It would not be long before service complaints would start coming down from above. To make matters worse, there were also indications that testing accuracy and quality were dropping off. This latter problem was believed to be the result of hasty testing procedures and the laxity of overworked employees who were expected to keep a lid on everything.

John Ford, with the help of Tim Mark and Jack Whitney, devised a plan to automate the test facilities through a stand-alone computer network. The system would control and run all test parameters, gather all critical test data, generate statistical information for quality control purposes, and prepare reports. Ford had done the initial investigation through several local computer supply houses and felt that a suitable system could be installed for $200,000. With equipment deliveries being quoted at four months and allowing only two weeks for installation and start-up, PSEF MIS staff felt they could be reaping the benefits of the new system by the end of August—just in time to relieve the annual end-of-summer surge in workload. They would be able to absorb this additional work without adding to their backlog and, once the surge was over, could quickly eliminate the backlog-associated overtime. Looking to the next year, and assuming efficiency with the system would increase, excess work force (created by the efficiency increase) could be deployed to other overworked test installations at the PSEF. The deployment would reduce overall costs and help position Whitney for further jumps up the corporate ladder.

In light of the very tight timetable required and the importance Whitney attached to the project, he decided to proceed with selling the computer network system idea to the president and board of directors in order to attain an appropriation of funds as quickly as possible. He realized that it could be risky proceeding with a fund appropriation before all the details were worked out, but he felt the benefits outweighed the risks. To cover himself, he requested a conservative budget appropriation of $300,000 with an October 15, 1986 completion date. The main benefits derived from these expenditures included improving the service position of the three test labs, freeing up capacity on the accounting system mainframe computer, and displacing 50 percent of the technicians by 1987. While the economics of the benefits were not outstanding, they were enough to sell the project. The fact that this was a high-technology area that the board of directors had been interested in for some time also helped in winning their support.

EXECUTIVE SUMMARY

The following is an excerpt from the letter Jack Whitney sent to the board of directors for justification of the system:

"Due to the continued large growth of the PSEF business and my concern that our present test procedures are nearing their limits in terms of quantity of tests run per day, I am presently investigating available quality management systems and automated tests to replace our existing Datatrieve software, which currently runs on a VAX 11/780. Our test procedures are constrained due to:

1. Lack of flexibility in report generation.
2. Lack of statistical graphics.
3. Lack of user-friendliness.
4. Lack of adequate system growth potential.
5. Lack of automated tests.

"PSEF recognizes that quality data must be organized into a clearly defined database if the data is to be accessible and usable. The database format stores and presents important information such as symptoms of failures, causes of failures, and possible remedies. In order to eliminate problems early in the process, the quality data must also be reliable and easily accessible to management. The ultimate goal is to produce a high-quality test environment so that products will meet customers' expectations but at minimum cost to RSC. The automated testing must include testing to reduce operator error and test time.

"The National Testers (NTL) solution (see Exhibit 4) would enable PSEF to (1) identify a product defect, (2) find the cause, and (3) implement a procedure to prevent recurrence of the defect. These three steps must be done in an automated environment, in order to maximize productivity and efficiency and to minimize error.

"PSEF's quality data systems objectives are:

1. Provide necessary hardware and software to replace the current quality Datatrieve system with improved flexibility.
2. Expedite system implementation.
3. Reduce cost of quality tools for quality cost assessment.
4. Provide a user-friendly system.
5. Improve accessibility of quality data for management use (quality and non-quality related).
6. Provide all present daily, weekly, and monthly reports.
7. Provide productivity measurement reports.
8. Eliminate duplication of effort in quality data collection and reporting by various departments.
9. Automate data collection with automatic test equipment.
10. Provide communications to IBM for future computer-integrated testing plans.
11. Provide flexible and timely ad hoc quality reporting capabilities (easy to query).
12. Provide the ability to transfer past Datatrieve data to the new system.
13. Minimize or eliminate quality log sheets.

"Because NTL can help us meet all of these objectives, along with the fact that we have been using NTL test instrumentation for the past 30 years with outstanding results, the solution I have included is composed entirely of NTL gear.

"Since time is money and PSEF is on the verge of its best year ever, I recommend that a decision be made as quickly as possible."

EXHIBIT 4 Proposed NTL System

Solution Components

- NTL 600 C500 Computer System
- NTL Quality Control Decisions (QCD)/600
- NTL Mirrorview/600 III
- NTL Distributed Computer Process System (DCPS)/600
- NTL RJE/600 III
- NTL QCD/600 HELPMATE

Solution Benefits

1. Improve response time to solve quality problems.
2. QCD/600 includes menu-driven user interfaces for easy configuration, modification, and system use by nonprogrammers.
3. Reduce retesting.
4. QCD/600 predefined database and configuration menus allow for shorter implementation time.
5. Easily accessible data for quality and nonquality reporting needs.
6. Improve methods of data collection.
7. Increase utilization of statistical techniques.
8. Reduce data duplication while providing testing traceability.
9. The C500's versatility to interface with a vast majority of instrumentation and test equipment for automatic test and real-time data collection.
10. Ease of system adaptation to other PSEF projects.
11. Provisions to ensure accurate data collection.
12. Allow measurements for product and process quality.
13. Provide system growth and communications interfaces for future networking plans.
14. Easy to produce ad hoc management and SQC reports.
15. Automatic generation of bar graphs, pie charts, histograms, $X-Y$ plots, and other graphic aids.

BLC'S ANALYSIS

The first thing Frank Fox did after Whitney called him to double check the new system that PSEF had purchased was to schedule a series of interviews with all the key people who would be involved with the day-to-day operation of the system (see Exhibit 5). He collected specific data on how the tests were presently being performed, expectations on how future tests would be performed, current data processing techniques and applications, future data processing needs and desires, facility layout, expansion plans, and current hardware and software—among other things. He cross-referenced this information with the proposal that Whitney and Ford had compiled to make sure that all the new hardware and software would

---

EXHIBIT 5   Interviews to Date

1. MIS
    Jim Tamburrino
    Karen Brown
    Bob Johnson
    Sharon Martin
2. Accounting and Finance
    Paul Zugell
    Kelly Bosic
    Joe Dyson
3. Generator testing
    Tim Mark
    Rico Martinez
    Alan Gilligan
4. Air-conditioning testing
    Eric Towner
    Jill Roos
    Larry Smith
5. Generator testing
    Bill Thorton
    Dan Thomas
    Rob Greer
6. Upper management
    Ken Dalton
    Jack Whitney
    John Ford

---

meet PSEF's present and future needs and expectations. The results were surprising.

Even though the automated test project was the first job of this stature for PSEF, and neither Ford nor Whitney were computer gurus, their proposal had been right on the money in terms of hardware and software. There were some mistakes but they were in the installation phase and minor. The estimated costs at completion would still fall within the $300,000 figure Whitney had budgeted.

Fox had been in the electronic equipment test marketplace for over 35 years and amassed a variety of degrees including a master's in Information Systems; he could not have picked a better package of hardware and software. He was truly impressed with Whitney and Ford. They had done a beautiful job in assessing PSEF's future needs and matching them perfectly with reasonably priced, compatible hardware and software.

However, one aspect of the plan bothered Fox. In all of the data that had been given him for analysis, there was no mention of a system implementation approach beyond the actual installation procedures. And even though Fox's job only involved the system hardware and software, he knew that—without proper planning —the implementation of any new system could be a disaster. The best hardware and software in the world would most likely become expensive paperweights if they were not implemented properly.

Should he risk opening up a can of worms by stepping outside the scope of his contractual responsibility? The question was meaningless, and he knew it. There was no way that his engineering background would allow him to ignore or overlook a potential problem, regardless of the situation. Fox decided to set up an appointment with National Testers to find out what, if any, implementation plans had been discussed.

Fox arranged a meeting with Harry Klie, the Automated Test Systems engineer at NTL who had helped PSEF with their proposed computer system. Fox and Klie had known each other for over 20 years and had met on a regular basis while Fox was a lead project engineer at Eastern Engineering. Fox had used NTL computers and instrumentation back then, and Klie had been invaluable in helping him to select the proper equipment for the application. Theirs had been a very good working relationship.

The following is an excerpt from their conversation: Fox spoke first.

"Anyway, Harry, I did what they hired me to do and double-checked the system from top to bottom. They didn't miss a thing. Now that I know that you were the one helping with the system, it doesn't surprise me. It bothers me, though, that little information exists on the implementation phase. Whitney was pretty hard-nosed about me checking only the hardware and software, so that's why I came to see you. Do you mind telling me what you two talked about in terms of what happens after the system is installed?"

Harry replied, "First of all, Frank, I can't take any credit for the system. They did their homework on what they needed and just about came in here with a final shopping list. All I did was help smooth out some of the rough edges. I couldn't have configured a better system myself. That Mark kid can be a cocky, obnoxious, smart-mouthed little SOB, but he really knows his stuff when it comes to automated testing. Hell, he made one of our desktops just about sing and dance. It's funny that you mention implementation, though. After the hardware and software was decided on, I started drawing up plans on how we would help them with training, project organization, defining the project charter, and so on, just like I used to do with you at Eastern Engineering. It's a standard practice, we both know, to include a postinstallation implementation package with any large computer and instrumentation system, especially when it's the customer's first one. You know as well as I do, Frank, that's always been one of our strengths. Anyway, before I got more than a half a dozen words in, Whitney cut me off and asked me how long the implementation phase would take. I figured it to be about two months before everyone is trained and the system is running smoothly, considering this would be their first attempt at this type of thing. He immediately said that was too long."

"Too long?" Fox asked. "I would have guessed closer to three months."

Klie continued: "I couldn't understand it either, so I asked him what was the rush? Why did the system have to be fully operational sooner than two months? I thought maybe we could take a phased approach to the implementation. He told me not to worry about it, that they would take full responsibility for the implementation of the system. He insisted they had the resources.

"You know, now that I think back, Whitney has been one of our best customers for the last 20 years, ever since he was an engineer up at the generator test area, and he has always turned down our offers to aid in training and implementation. In fact, he has always made a point of calling me up to let me know how he was using the equipment and how it was operating. I guess it was his way of saying that he had everything he needed.

"I tried to tell him that this was different, but he just laughed and said he'd cross that bridge when he came to it. I asked him to give me a call if he changed his mind, said we'd be happy to give them a hand. I even called him after we received the order for the hardware and software, to see if he had changed his mind, and he hadn't. He said Tamburrino, the MIS manager up there, would be handling the quality system implementation and that Mark would do all of the test automation. Ford would be the liaison between the two."

Fox added, "If that's the case, Harry, then Ford, Tamburrino, and Mark are in for a nice surprise. I just interviewed all three of them last week, and not one word was mentioned in terms of responsibilities of implementation. And I specifically asked them what their roles would be."

FOX'S VIEWPOINT

As Fox sat at his desk contemplating the possible repercussions of the letter that he now was preparing to mail, his thoughts drifted back to his drive home after the meeting with Klie. Angry, confused thoughts again filled his mind. Why had Whitney really called him in? Was it to check a system that Whitney had already known was complete? Or was it to bring an outsider into the picture, someone to blame when this thing blew up in his face? Hell, here Whitney was appropriating a large and very complex instrumentation and computer system composed of a variety of different hardware and software packages and throwing the responsibility of implementing it to a supervisor with only a high school degree and no computer training or experience, an over-confident college kid whose gills were so green leaves paled in comparison, and an MIS manager whose only concern was credits and debits.

Fox had seen it happen before. Managers would bite off more than they could chew and realize it too late; so they would call in someone from the outside to act as a scapegoat. If the news is bad, kill the messenger. Well, he wasn't about to let his name or that of BLC Consultants be tarnished if he could help it.

He had tried to contact Whitney directly to discuss his misgivings. Whitney didn't come on the phone but instead gave his secretary a message to pass along, asking him to send PSEF a letter, attention of J. Whitney, and stating the results of the study. Whitney would contact him if necessary.

Fox had to laugh to himself as these memories faded. A couple of good nights' sleep had enabled him to look at the situation objectively, and it seemed to be making a little more sense. Because Whitney has had such an outstanding career at PSEF and never once had problems incorporating new gear into the test labs, this appeared to be just another small challenge. Fox guessed that it was because of these past successes, along with the fact that no one up at PSEF had any real-world experience with a system of this magnitude, that Whitney kept shrugging off the offers to help with the implementation.

The poor sap didn't even know that he didn't know! The *incompetent incompetent* was a term Fox had once heard someone call it — a mind-set that affects most self-confident people the first time they try something new. Knowing Whitney's personality, Fox worded the letter accordingly. As he dropped the letter into the outgoing slot, he knew he'd done his best; that — come what may — BLC would not be to blame.

FOX'S LETTER

Whitney had to read this section of the letter again, it had caught him so off guard:

"and having finished a careful analysis of your hardware and software requirements, the system that you decided on proves an excellent match and is complete. Aside from the minor changes in installation diagrammed at the conclusion of this letter, the system should stay intact. Even with the changes in installation, the total cost of the system is $285,785, within your $300,000 window. Installation should be completed by October 16, 1986, leaving you 15 days for implementation and start-up.

"I would like to thank you for the opportunity to work with you and your people at PSEF on such a state-of-the-art computer/instrumentation network. Even though BLC's job is finished, our file on this system is unfinished. In order to close the file, I would like to meet with either you or one of your people and document your implementation phase of this project. I know that you must have spent a great deal of time analyzing what prerequisites are critical for the successful implementation of PSEF's quality data and automated test system. I would find the specifics to the following key ingredients most interesting:

1. Top management commitment and the allocation of qualified personnel and resources.
2. Project organization.
3. Education and training plan.
4. Defined project charter and objectives.
5. Goal-oriented implementation plan.

"I would also be interested in how you addressed the following elements:

- Defining the tasks required.
- Defining the expected results.
- Estimating effort and duration.
- Assigning specific responsibilities.
- Determining and balancing resources.
- Up-to-date reporting.

"Please contact me at your convenience as I understand that the next three weeks will be very busy ones for you."

Whitney's pulse quickened as he tried to make sense out of Fox's letter. He had never needed anything like this in all of the other projects he had accomplished. Granted they weren't as large, but still. . . . Was this what Klie had been trying to tell him earlier? If only he hadn't been so quick to cut him off and at least listened to what he had to say.

Jack Whitney was an authoritative and aggressive individual who was not ready to lose face to his superiors. He had been with the company for 25 years and firmly believed that a person had to make things happen if he wanted to succeed. He was 49 years old and was pulling for that next big promotion. He had started with PSEF as a supervising engineer in the generator test lab and, via the successful completion of quite a few new projects, had moved steadily up the management ladder. As director of the Test Center, he had single-handedly taken a division that had been in the red and turned it into the most profitable division (percentagewise) in RSC. Unfortunately, even with PSEF dominating the generator/small-engine/air-conditioning unit marketplace with a 75 percent share, it was still the smallest division in RSC.

Whitney had his eye on a position opening up in September in Cuppertino, California—director of Testing at RSC's largest division, Radar Support and Evaluation (RSE). That slot was one of the most prestigious positions within RSC. With the retirement of the current director, Tom Reeves, Whitney had the inside track. He would use this final project at PSEF as a springboard to launch himself into the land of sunshine and yogurt. His heart raced at the thought.

The job opportunity out in Cuppertino suddenly seemed very far away. As his Adam's apple swelled to the size of a golfball, Whitney's mind was consumed with one thought: "What do I do now?"

QUESTIONS

1. What are the main ingredients of the implementation phase of PSEF's quality data and automated test system project?
2. What were the key elements of the letter to Whitney? Why do you consider them to be key?

3. What additional information would you like to have about each of those key ingredients?
4. If you were going to add to the letter, what specific recommendations would you include? Why?
5. If *you* received the letter, what would you do?
6. Should Jack be concerned particularly?
7. What should Jack Whitney do?

Case 8–4 Omaha–Council Bluffs Vision Center

Dr. Jerry Creighton walked down the hallway of the Vision Center, passing within earshot of the unit administrator's office. "... and that computer was a waste of $20,000. It doesn't do anything," he remarked to one of the technicians. The unit administrator, Carl Weber, obviously overhearing the comment, was not surprised by the doctor's complaints. "What a wonderful year this is going to be," he thought.

Weber joined the practice in May 1986 to handle the business affairs of the Center; he saw immediately the need to upgrade the office systems. From the beginning, he had argued with the doctor, pushing for computerization.

Weber felt that with time, Dr. Creighton could be talked out of his negative feelings about computers. In the meantime, the information systems would be upgraded. The questions were:

1. How could this be done with the least disturbance to an ongoing enterprise?
2. What hardware system should be used?
3. What software capabilities should be introduced and in which order?

COMPANY BACKGROUND

The Omaha–Council Bluffs Vision Center was formed in 1969 as the private practice of Dr. Jerry Creighton. Creighton was a graduate of the University of Nebraska Medical School, had spent the required amount of time in the military, and then embarked on his private career. The practice developed a fine reputation, based largely on the doctor's skills as an excellent cataract surgeon.

This case was prepared by Timothy L. Cross. Names, locations, and financial data have been disguised.

In 1983, the practice staff included the doctor, two ophthalmologic technicians, and two clerical employees. At this point, the decision was made to create an outpatient surgical center. The surgical center would provide the surgeon with greater control over patient pre-op and post-op care, and would be a potential source of increased revenue. By 1986, the Outpatient Surgical Center (OSC) was completed and with that came a substantial increase in personnel and administrative requirements (see Exhibit 1).

Carl Weber was brought on board soon after the completion of the OSC. As unit administrator, he was responsible for managing all business functions including personnel, accounting systems, and operations of both the clinic and surgical units. It was not long before he recognized the potential for computers in the practice. To date, only manual systems had been used for accounting (accounts receivable, billing, payroll, etc.) and for clerical work (correspondence, patient scheduling, and medical charts). Weber believed that development of automated information systems would greatly improve efficiency and provide more information for management.

SYSTEM REQUIREMENTS

As of July 1986, the practice had over 8,000 patient charts and handled more than 4,500 patient visits annually. All patients were scheduled in a logbook, up to one year in advance. Scheduling was determined by the type of examination, and preference was given to potential surgical patients. Patients were reminded

EXHIBIT 1   Omaha–Council Bluffs Vision Center

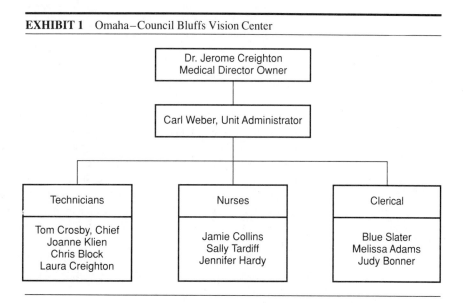

of their appointments by telephone on the day before they were scheduled. A medical secretary spent a large part of her day maintaining the schedule, calling patients, and searching the book for openings. Weber believed simple computer applications could reduce her scheduling workload significantly.

A more urgent need involved a severe cash flow problem. The practice, due largely to the administrative morass in the local medicare carrier's operation, had developed a serious accounts receivable problem. In the past year, receivables had risen from under 35 days payment time to an average 62 days. This increase in aging created a cash shortage that forced the doctor to defer his own salary on occasion.

Identifying and correcting the problems was difficult because of the manual system. It was evident that medicare was the prime culprit but statistical break-downs of aging and other support data were nearly impossible to acquire. Without such data, communication with medicare was an exercise in futility. Weber looked to computerized billing and accounting as the solution to what ailed the receivables account.

Medical charts and record-keeping presented another data headache and was an obvious target for Weber's investigation. With over 8,000 of these charts, all handwritten and filed in large vertical file cabinets, the potential for lost or illegible records mounted with each patient.

Finally, there were no general lists of patients from which to cull mailing lists or to use for quality assurance studies. Again, it seemed a computer would provide the solution. Having identified some areas for immediate remedy, Weber decided to approach the doctor at the practice's strategic planning meeting, to be held in December. He felt that there was sufficient reason to computerize. At the meeting, he intended to present his recommendations for a system and inform the doctor of the expected value of this addition to the office. In the meantime, Weber began the search for the required equipment.

THE SYSTEM

Weber developed a shopping list of requirements for the office computer system. Listed were necessary items of hardware and software as priorities and then what Weber considered luxuries. He knew that cost would be a major factor in the search, as it would be a prime concern to the doctor. Swallowing the pill of computerization would be hard enough for him without adding the bad taste of a large capital outlay. Medical management articles and discussions with other medical administrators provided Weber with a ballpark figure of between $15,000 to $20,000 for the total package. With this estimate and his shopping list, the search began.

Exhibit 2 displays the results of the search and the options from which Weber had to choose. Proposals were elicited from all vendors following full operational demonstrations of the equipment.

EXHIBIT 2 Hardware and Software Systems Considered by the Omaha–Council Bluffs Vision Center

1. Nielson Computer Company, Wilmington, Delaware
   - Hardware: Altos 50 MB drive (file server).
     - Wyse terminals, fully networked.
     - Printer (letter-quality, high-speed).
   - Software: Nielson proprietary software for general medical usage. Operated on the AT&T's XENIX DOS.
   - Functions: All accounting, records, scheduling. Fully integrated. Very complete.
   - Capacity: 10,000 + patients, easily expandable to handle any conceivable growth in the practice.
   - Cost: $50,000 all inclusive.
2. Ivy Technologies Company, St. Louis, Missouri
   - Hardware: IBM PCs and XTs (20 MB system master), fully networked.
     - Printer (dot-matrix, very-high-speed).
   - Software: Ivy Technology proprietary software. Developed by an ophthalmologist for use exclusively in ophthalmologic practices. Operates on PC–DOS.
   - Functions: Billing, accounts receivable, records, scheduling. Not a full accounting package. Special ophthalmologic applications.
   - Capacity: Handles 10,000 patients.
   - Cost: $19,200.
3. Data Systems Corporation, Omaha, Nebraska
   - Hardware: IBM PC XT, no network.
     - Printer (dot-matix, high-speed)
   - Software: DSC proprietary. Operates on PC–DOS. General medical office system.
   - Functions: Accounts receivable, billing, scheduling, records. Not a full accounting package.
   - Capacity: 6,000 patients.
   - Costs: $12,500.
4. Advanced Software Company, Sioux City, Iowa
   - Hardware: IBM PC AT, IBM PCs.
   - Software: ASC software proprietary. Full accounting package adapted for medical use.
   - Functions: All accounting functions.
   - Capacity: 5,000 patients.
   - Cost: $11,000.

The selection process involved analysis of several other manufacturers and their systems. However, only the four listed in Exhibit 2 displayed the minimum requirements for the practice. Because of the doctor's tenuous approval of the computer, Weber felt it imperative that he get the minimum capabilities at the lowest price. This immediately eliminated the Nielson system. It was a total package with tremendous expansion capability but was simply too expensive for the practice.

The Data Systems Corporation (DSC) system was not a networked system. The company was developing a network for its system that was due out before the practice was set to purchase. A new network would almost certainly have numerous kinks to work out. The doctor would be sensitive to any perceived faults. Weber could not risk the untried product. The DSC system was deleted from the list.

Advanced Software Company (ASC) made a strong presentation but was simply not able to provide the full medical support necessary. In addition, ASC was a small concern backed by a CPA firm. Weber wondered about the company's ability to stay afloat in this competitive market. He needed the assurance of a stronger organization.

Ivy Technologies seemed to meet all the requirements for the Vision Center. Ivy was developed by an ophthalmologist in St. Louis for his own practice. It was marketed nationwide by a very strong organization with a 10-year track record. The recommendations for the system were encouraging in all areas — software, hardware, training, and support. The system was able to meet the practice's needs and allow for expansion. Weber was further pleased with the component nature of the software. With Ivy, he would be able to purchase different modules as he required them. This would keep the initial outlay down to a reasonable — and palatable — level.

Following a month of negotiating, the Center purchased the Ivy system. The entire process had taken over four months and involved a great deal of the administrator's time. It was hoped that now the staff could be trained to get the system moving along successfully. The efficiency of the practice should begin to pick up.

The search for the system had emphasized hardware and software acquisition. Little thought had been devoted to integration of the information system and the practice. The simple placement of computer equipment onto the staff members' desks had only been the beginning of the struggle.

Carl still had to develop a plan for building an information system without disrupting the flow of the medical practice. The staff at the O–CB Vision Center had no previous experience with computers — not even home PCs. Weber was the only one with any background in this area.

THE STAFF

The practice administrative staff was small, yet they would be the ones utilizing the system. The medical technicians would have little use for the computer except in isolated circumstances.

The practice had always been run on manual systems and relatively successfully at that; it was evident that there would be resistance to the changes brought about by the new equipment, and the level of resistance would vary.

MELISSA ADAMS

Melissa Adams was the accounts receivable clerk and had been with the practice for nearly two years. She had been doing billing and receivables work at different practices for over 10 years, however, and was very competent. The problem for the practice, as mentioned earlier, was that information on the receivables aging and outstanding accounts was difficult to obtain and was very time-consuming to extract. Weber would wait for days to get aging information, and even then it was vague. Data on amounts due was the most vital need of the practice and the main reason for purchasing the computer system. The billing process would also be streamlined with the computer, hopefully eliminating the manual statements that were generated each month. Probably most interesting for the future was the ability to automatically transmit claims to medicare; that feature alone should reduce the account turnover by weeks and end the need for Adams to mail claims to medicare.

Adams was silent about the entire plan but was obviously not thrilled with the advent of the computer. She said that she would try to work with it; she was very dedicated to her work and conscientious. Weber felt that he could depend on her but was hoping to see more enthusiasm from the person whom the system would benefit most.

BLUE SLATER

The practice's medical secretary, Blue Slater, was the strongest supporter of computerization. Slater was enthusiastic from the first and participated in many of the discussions about the system. She saw the value of the system for scheduling, a task she performed, as well as word processing. Slater attended college at night and was majoring in Management. She felt that the computer experience would help her significantly in other areas.

JUDY BONNER

The practice receptionist, Judy Bonner, was the least involved in the computer selection and installation. She was senior to the others in age and showed little interest in automation. If anything, she seemed fearful at the first sight of the boxes. However, Bonner would have to learn how to operate the computer, since she was the backup to Adams and Slater when either was out of the office. Weber noticed almost a belligerence on Bonner's part when she—or anyone, for that matter—discussed the computer. He felt that she would be the most difficult to sway in her opinion of the system.

THE PROBLEM

In January 1987, the system was delivered to the office in boxes. A training technician was sent the following day to set up the system and train the office staff for two days. All went well in the installation and training. The system worked well from the start and training, although only an overview of the major functions and operations, seemed to pique some interest from all in attendance. Weber felt that "things were going to be just fine."

Shortly after the training technician returned to St. Louis, the system was fully operational, and Weber realized that there was a gap in his planning. Now that it was here, what would he really get from the computer? The questions started to flow. What reports should he have? What backup procedures should be followed? Who would be responsible for what operations? Weber had already spent far too much time in getting the system to this stage. He had neglected many other areas of the practice. Marketing was behind schedule. His dealings with Medicare had been delayed. Plans for developing satellite offices were waiting in the wings. And the doctor was asking, every day, why Carl spent so much time at the computer.

Weber had come to the practice from a much larger medical instrument distributor. He had supervised managers who implemented an IS plan. But now, with a much smaller staff with limited computer know-how, how was he to continue the implementation? He was not certain of the steps to follow in the small office environment.

The other nagging problem was the direction of future development of the system. Which areas should be addressed and in what priority? Weber believed that, in order to really sell the system to the doctor and his staff, the system's full capabilities had to be demonstrated.

It was time to begin full implementation of IS at the Omaha–Council Bluffs Vision Center. But how?

QUESTIONS

1. Do the case facts indicate that Weber did an adequate research job before he purchased the system?
2. How should Weber gain the users' support, since he did not have their participation during the system definition and acquisition?
3. Who should determine what reports the system is to generate and when should that decision be made?
4. What can Weber do now in the way of internal marketing? Who must he sell the system to, and how can he do it? What are his alternatives?
5. Should the Vision Center hire an assistant for Weber? If so, what should be the qualifications for the position and its responsibilities?

6. Relate the case facts to the articles by Cyrus F. Gibson and Richard L. Nolan, "Managing the Four Stages of EDP Growth," *Harvard Business Review,* January–February 1974, and by F. Warren McFarlan and James E. McKenney, "The Information Archipelago—Maps and Bridges," *Harvard Business Review,* September–October 1982.

Chapter 9

Audit and Security

INTRODUCTION

Much of what we read about the effect of a changing environment on IS emphasizes technology and hardware. Management areas that have been equally affected are the auditing of information systems and security of information systems—their data, the hardware itself, and access to the systems.

AUDITING OF INFORMATION SYSTEMS

Most large organizations use two types of IS auditors whose roles are quite different, although both are considered independent evaluators, and both perform similar tasks. The two are: (1) independent, or external, auditors whose primary interest is that organization financial statements be impartial and fair, and (2) internal auditors (employees of the company) who do evaluation, auditing more detailed than usually performed by external auditors, and frequent testing of data processing. If computers are used to generate information for the general ledger, and to prepare income statements and balance sheets, then the external auditors must review internal controls of the corporation's DP and IS systems.[1]

External Audits

The external auditor's procedures normally entail: (1) preliminary review of the computer's contribution in the building of financial statements; (2) complete evaluation of DP internal controls, including reviewing checklists and documentation

---

[1]Gordon B. Davis and Margrethe H. Olson, *Management Information Systems: Conceptual Foundations, Structure, and Development,* 2nd ed., Chapter 19 (New York: McGraw-Hill, 1985).

and interviewing key members of the DP/IS staffs; (3) tests of the controls (required signatures and approvals, totals comparisons, and other records) to be certain that control procedures are being followed correctly; and (4) tests of reliability of internal DP controls, using manual substantive tests and auditor- and company-supplied software. Although these procedures will not guarantee that minor frauds will be uncovered, they should detect evidence of major swindles or misconduct.[2]

Internal Audits

Internal audits, if they are to be effective, must be performed by company employees who do not report to (or are not required to be responsive to) executives in the organization being evaluated. Their audit is usually more detailed than that of the external auditor and looks closely at the entire computer system, to be certain that "the completed system embodies adequate internal controls and that the system and its output can be audited."[3]

Therefore, they examine and analyze internal controls and output. Davis and Olson[4] describe three types of controls "associated with information processing: general controls procedures for system operations, controls for a specific application, and application development controls. . . . General control functions internal to information system operations ensure that applications are run correctly and that the facilities are operational. These controls include the following:

- Scheduling control for on-line systems, internal time-sharing, and production batch systems.
- Library control for program and data files and documentation.
- Database control for creation, updating, and use of databases.
- Access control for physical access to computers through terminals.
- Backup and recovery procedures."

Internal auditors also study the audit trail[5] and system products (documents, transactions, and records) to be assured that it is possible to track transactions through the system.

---

[2]Davis and Olson, *Management Information Systems,* Chapter 19.

[3]George M. Scott, *Principles of Management Information Systems,* Chapter 14 (New York: McGraw-Hill, 1986).

[4]Davis and Olson, *Management Information Systems,* Chapter 5.

[5]"An audit trail should always be present. Its form may change in response to computer technology, but three requirements must be met: (1) Any transaction can be traced from the source document through processing to outputs and to totals in which it is aggregated, (2) any output or summary data can be traced back to the transactions or computations used to arrive at the output or summary figures, and (3) any triggered transaction (a transaction automatically triggered by an event or condition) can be traced to the event or condition." Davis and Olson, *Management Information Systems,* Chapter 5.

COMPUTER SYSTEMS SECURITY

Systems security is the sum of methods, activities, and controls directed toward safeguarding hardware, software, data, procedures, and people. In today's environment of computer crimes and viruses, computer security can be as important as accounting, inventory control, or production methods in saving thousands or even millions of dollars. One important difference—if we temporarily set aside criminal acts such as deliberate attempts to embezzle or to destroy data—is that one person's absentminded, preoccupied oversights can be expensive. People can "forget to prepare backup copies that turn out to be needed, accidentally erase or alter company records, or commit blunders in operating the hardware."[6]

One goal of an IS organization is to avoid costly delays and user frustration by trying to control the development and implementation processes; another goal is to operate systems that are precise and reliable; safe from threats, both external and internal; and protective of individuals' rights to privacy.

The use of tapes and diskettes to back up files is a security measure, as is the use of dual processing or hardware redundancy.

The advantages of using telephone lines and modems to permit access to the system from employees' homes or from traveling salespeoples' portable microcomputers must be balanced against the inherent security risks. Use of passwords, automatic callback, automatic disconnect devices, and lockouts (when password entry fails successively) are means to provide teleprocessing security.[7]

MIS ASSESSMENTS AND EVALUATIONS

Executives frequently question whether the value received from computer systems is worth their costs. Many are concerned because large amounts of the organization's assets and resources are devoted to computers and automation, and it may appear sometime that the return does not match the investment.

Some of the same methods used to audit the systems and to provide secure systems are used in MIS assessments. Many of the same people are involved and include systems analysts, programmers, computer systems managers, information systems users, user representatives, systems consultants, vendor representatives,

---

[6]Jerome S. Burstein, *Computers and Information Systems,* Chapter 17 (New York: Holt, Rinehart & Winston, 1986).

[7]Burstein, *Computers and Information Systems,* Chapter 17.

top executives of the organization, internal auditors, database administrators, and members of the steering committees.[8]

Often, the assessment or investigation report will point to communications problems and people problems. The latter often reflect resistance to change, embarrassment, commitment to the old system, fear of being a scapegoat, fear of job loss, key personnel lack of interest, territorial instincts, and conflicting goals and objectives.[9] It is interesting that the same people problems that may have slowed a system's development or degraded its operations after installation may also have impeded or biased the evaluation or assessment.

CASES: CHESAPEAKE MUTUAL INSURANCE COMPANY (CMI) AND GREATER METROPOLITAN SAVINGS AND LOAN

Chesapeake Mutual has doubled the number of its field/district offices in the last 20 years. As a result, the vice president of Information Systems Planning has approved a plan for replacing field organizations' video display terminals with IBM-compatible microcomputers. The newly hired security officer has submitted a lengthy report and recommendations to the vice president of Corporate Operations.

Greater Metropolitan Savings and Loan is a large, multimillion dollar, conservative organization that has recently purchased a small number of microcomputers. The auditor, currently working on an audit of the Appraisal department, has been asked to review the S&L's compliance with the latest Fedral Home Loan Bank Memorandum R 67-1 (subject—end-user computing risks).

---

[8]Scott, *Principles of Management Information Systems,* Chapter 14.
[9]Scott, *Principles of Management Information Systems,* Chapter 14.

Case 9–1 Chesapeake Mutual Insurance Company (CMI)

It was mid-June 1986, and Peter Matthews, vice president of Corporate Operations for CMI, was wondering whether he should work late. It was already 6 PM, and his wife would be expecting him for dinner at any minute. In his 15 years with Chesapeake, he had only come home late about 20 times, all within the past two years. He hoped that when the claims modernization project (CMP) was complete, the demands on him would lessen. CMP, by the way, is an expansion of the system modernization plan (SMP) already underway at CMI; the goal of the earlier project, SMP, is to strengthen management of the company's growing insurance business by adding new central processors, thereby capacity, to the total system.

Charles Dey, vice president of IS Planning and Consulting, (see Exhibit 1) had led the development and design of the CMP and was very enthusiastic about it. Over lunch a month or so ago, Charles had told Peter how pleased he was with the security committee's plan for CMP.

Charles's attitude had instilled confidence in Peter; Charles was positive that the implementation of the CMP would be successful and that its security plan would be adequate. After all, Charles had been with the company almost as long as he had and had considerable DP experience prior to joining CMI. He was highly respected at CMI and had directed development of the first claims processing system, which was operating smoothly and without hard evidence of any major security problems.

Nevertheless, for the first time, Peter was having doubts about the modernization plan's security. Following completion of CMP's analysis and design phases, and the start of its implementation, concerns about the plan's security features had begun surfacing; some were rumors, hard to track down; others were solid and direct. Clete Carr's input was probably most disturbing of all.

Clete, VP of Data Processing, had first approached him just 2 weeks ago. Clete didn't feel CMI's information system even needed modernization. To Clete, the current system "provided more than enough information and supplied it in plenty of time to process claims." In addition, Clete felt the company would be tying up too much money and staff evaluating the new system and its inherent security problems. To be fair, it should be noted that systems security planning for CMP is not complete; so far, it is limited to the use of personal identification numbers.

Clete was not the only one to express his concerns up front. Ralph Spencer was another. Ralph, Claims district manager of one of the CMP software test offices, did not like the additional paperwork that the new security plan demanded. Also, Ralph thought the assessment questionnaire would only be a waste of valuable time.

This case was prepared by Mary Sasscer, Claire Willey, and Jennifer Austin.

o

EXHIBIT 2   PSEF Physical Layout

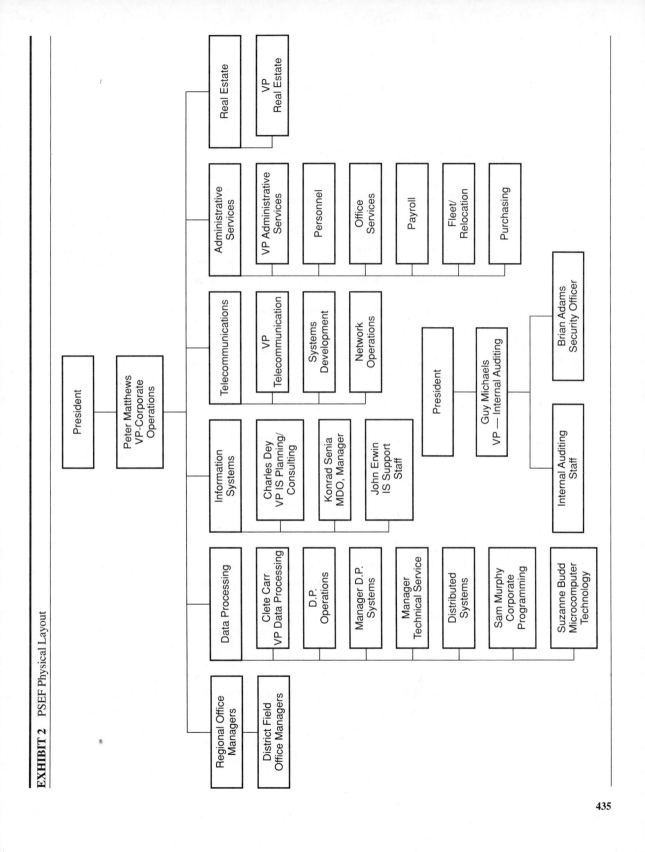

Peter appreciated these different opinions, as they gave him tools for identifying potential problems, but the point of view that really disturbed him was that of the newly hired security officer, Brian Adams. Brian had just delivered his concerns about security—personally, formally, and in writing. Now, Peter probably should stay late, review the extensive list, and decide on the ultimate plan.

HISTORY AND GENERAL BACKGROUND OF CMI

Chesapeake Mutual Insurance Company (CMI) had its debut in Clarksburg, West Virginia, when William F. Chesapeake and his cousin, Herbert A. Chesapeake, opened a small insurance office in the early 1890s. In 1901, when Herbert drowned in a flash flood, William's brother, Charles B. Chesapeake, joined the firm.

In 1914, the brothers landed the Baltimore and Ohio (B&O) Railroad as a client, and William moved to Baltimore to handle the account. A few years later, Charles also moved to Baltimore, and that city became CMI's home base.

In 1923, CMI incorporated in Maryland. For the first time, ownership and management extended beyond the Chesapeake family. However, the bylaws stated that only active company managers could share in the ownership of the firm. In 1969, CMI went public and offered company stock to the general public.

Today, CMI is one of the top 30 insurance companies in the world and employs 11,200 people. Insurance service revenues have been decreasing over the years, due to lower interest rates (see Exhibit 2). Approximately 1 million claims are processed each year.

CLAIMS CONTROL FLOW: OLD SYSTEM

Chesapeake Mutual Insurance Company (CMI) enlarged its claims operation to 40 field offices in the early 1960s. The company has expanded to 104 field/district offices during the last 10 to 15 years, with 7 regional offices throughout the United States. The regional offices oversee claims processing by the field operations. CMI's basic insurance business involves claims processing of workers' compensation and automobile, homeowner, medical, and public liability benefits. Each field office also has a staff of 5 to 10 adjusters in the claims verification unit to establish liability of the claims through field investigation.

To manage the large claims operation, CMI established an automated system in the Data Processing department for controlling and paying all claims for benefits. The payment or disallowance action is a product of a claims automated processing system (CAPS) action, or a manual adjustment, credit, and award process (MADCAP). A claim is processed by the establishment of an initial claims orbit, creating a record of identification for each claimant. The CAPS or MADCAP

EXHIBIT 2   CMI Statements of Consolidated Income

Chesapeake Mutual Insurance Company
Statements of Consolidated Income
For the Three Years Ended December 31, 1985
(millions of dollars)

	1985	1984	1983
Operating revenues:			
Insurance services	$468.6	$470.4	$488.3
Employee benefit and management consulting	66.0	63.2	58.0
Other	15.8	17.3	12.9
Total	550.4	550.9	559.2
Operating expenses:			
Salaries and benefits	320.3	319.1	326.3
Other*	188.5	185.4	179.1
Total	508.8	504.5	505.4
Operating income	41.6	46.4	53.8
Equity in unconsolidated operating	6.5	6.6	6.4
Other income (expenses):			
Investment income	25.6	22.6	40.0
Interest expense	(18.0)	(22.5)	(26.3)
Amortization of intangible assets	(7.9)	(8.0)	(6.2)
Other	(3.2)	(1.6)	2.5
Total	(3.5)	(9.5)	(10.0)
Income from continuing operations before income taxes	44.6	43.5	70.2
Income taxes	18.7	27.6	36.1
Income from continuing operations	25.9	15.9	34.1
Loss from discontinued operations	(77.1)	(22.1)	(18.8)
Income (loss) before extraordinary items	(51.2)	(6.2)	15.3
Extraordinary items	1.6	6.9	(40.0)
Net income (loss)	(49.6)	0.7	(24.7)

*DP expenses equal $3,890,415.

operation results in a final payment or denial notice for the claim. The claims control system tabulates a record of the number of claims submitted and reimbursed or denied (see the claims control flow diagram and narrative in Exhibits 2a and 3 for a detailed explanation of this process).

EXHIBIT 2a   Chesapeake Mutual Insurance Company Claims Control Flow

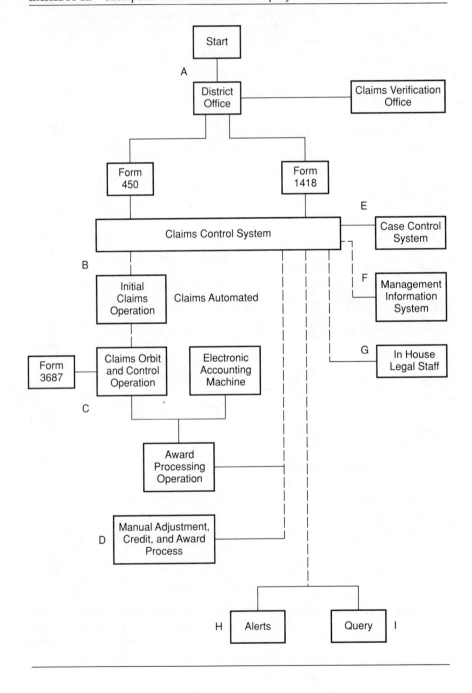

EXHIBIT 3   General Description of the Claims Control Flow as It Involves the Claims Control System

---

1. The initial step in the process begins with the field/district office (FO/DO) taking an application for an insurance claim. From the application for benefits, information is coded on either Form 450, Form 1418, or Form 3687, and that data is transmitted to the claims control system.

- Form 450 is completed whenever an initial claim is taken. This establishes an initial computer orbit for the claim with identification of the claimant involved coded.
- Form 1418 is completed in order to maintain a record of the exact number of claims received and processed by the system. It also establishes a computer record of the location of a claim by field offices and the legal staff.
- Form 3687 is completed in order to finally process a benefit claim for actual payment. A check from CMI in the amount of the claim settlement is issued by this input.

2. ICO, initial claims operation, is the operation that determines the payment amount on each insurance claim after information is obtained from the Claims Verification office approving the settlement.

3. The award processing operation (APO) is the operation that processes the insurance benefit payment on receipt of FO/DO authorization, prepares the beneficiary notice, and passes data to the master beneficiary record (MBR), a record showing a history of all claim payments for each beneficiary. APO is comprised of the claims automated processing system (CAPS) and the electronic accounting machine (EAM) operation.

- CAPS is the process that gives the FO/DO the ability to adjudicate claims in a more cost-effective process. EAM is the process that gives the FO/DO the ability to process claims not processable via CAPS due to the complexity of issues involved.
- Within CAPS is a process called the claims orbit and control operation (COCO). This operation maintains the data transmitted via Form 450 and the data accumulated from ICO. It is maintained until the claim in CAPS is adjudicated.
- APO also gives the claims control system records as to the claim's movement, completion, and rejection from the CAPS process.

4. The manual adjustment, credit, and award process (MADCAP) is the process used by the FO/DO for claims that cannot be processed through APO. There are exceptions to CAPS processing due to computer incapability that must be processed by MADCAP.

5. The case control system (CACS) receives data and also sends data to the claims control system.

- The claims control system generates a CCS monitor record for each establishment record.
- CCS gives the claims control system a record whenever it receives an initial claims record.

6. The department of Information Systems receives the complete claims control master file. It uses the data to create a wide variety of management reports.

7. The legal staff gives the claims control system a record of the movement of claims and the decision on the claims being appealed through court actions.

8. The claims control system generates alerts at specified intervals to any office that has a claims controlled system case.

EXHIBIT 3   *(concluded)*

---

9. The claims control system also makes available, via the telecommunications network, a query facility. This facility gives the various users the ability to determine the status on any claim being controlled by the claims control system.

FIELD/DISTRICT OFFICE COMPUTER OPERATIONS

The following section is a brief description of CMI's existing (mid-1986) computer facilities in the field/district offices. The system in each field office includes a video display terminal with keyboard, a modem, a printer, and a small computer (a Paradyne 8400) called the controller.

The field offices access the data acquisition and response system (DARS), an advanced data communications system designed for CMI. DARS provides rapid communication between field/district offices and the Central Computing Facility (CCF) in the Baltimore main headquarters. The DARS network has several components, including the CCF (the nucleus of this system), and a small computer —the concentrator—(an IBM 360/65 system), also located in the Baltimore headquarters. At the Central Computing Facility and concentrator sites, personnel and equipment maintain technical control of the entire CMI system. Both facilities edit messages entered in the system to ensure accuracy of data.

High-speed telephone lines connect the CCF to the headquarters concentrator, and voice grade telephone lines connect the concentrator to terminals in the field/district offices. Messages come to the concentrator first, which performs edit functions, and then are passed to the CCF, where the messages enter the host computer (an IBM 3031 system). The host computer directs the message responses back through the concentrator to the video display terminals in the field offices, through the field offices' controllers.

ONGOING SECURITY MEASURES AT CMI

In order to monitor the security of computer facilities in the field offices, one manager, usually a field office supervisor, is appointed as the security officer for each field/district office. There is no overall systems security officer to police the field offices or to establish policy. The supervisor in each field office follows a system security manual issued in the early 1970s by Peter Matthews. The manual established the system security policy to be followed by all field offices and sought to make both ADP and manual processes more secure. The manual is updated periodically in a routine fashion but it has not been revamped seriously to adapt to the problems encountered during and since the major growth sustained by the company in the last six years—since 1980.

CMI has no systems security audit function (or automated program) to evaluate the effectiveness of the safeguards currently published in the security manual. Also, CMI has not resolved how to measure the effectiveness of its current security plan; no individual has been appointed to conduct on-site security facility reviews and to measure adherence to the security guidelines in the manual.

Top management did not believe originally that a systems security officer was crucial to the safe operating of this company. During the last few years, however, increasing expansion and implementation of a new claims system triggered security problems. The onset of problems was due partially to the field offices' inability to conduct electronic security audits; they did not have the necessary automated equipment.

Many functions were still manual to some degree, requiring end-of-line reviews by managers on all claims processed. As a result, authorization for payment of claims was tightly controlled by the managers of the field offices or the regional offices, depending on the dollar amount of the settlement involved. In addition, the current system did not have dial-up ports or terminals in the benefit payment operation, which would limit access control to the data. At the same time, the company did have a system of edits and alerts in various stages of claims processing; these required accurate processing and reduced employee omission and error.

Nevertheless, the field offices did comply closely with certain guidelines established in the security manual, particularly those relating to the computers in the field operations. As previously mentioned, each office was supplied with a keyboard, a video display terminal, and a small computer (controller). The terminals were locked and unlocked each day with a password known only to the security officer (a supervisor) in each field office. In addition, each terminal was locked and unlocked with its own key for additional safety.

In each field office, there were only three to four data entry employees who were authorized to enter data transmissions on all claims being processed. Each of these data entry operators was assigned a personal identification number (PIN), allowing access to the terminals. The operators also followed a log-on, log-off procedure each time they transmitted data. This procedure blocked other users from accessing the terminals while the data operators were transmitting data. The log-on process established a positive identification of the terminal entry operator to ensure accuracy of payment and to prevent internal fraud and theft. No other employees were authorized to enter data into the terminals.

The above procedures were considered adequate but still left the company in a vulnerable position at times. The claims adjusters and representatives (along with the data entry operators) were limited by various access controls through an editing procedure but were still responsible for the control of benefit payments. For example, they could establish fictitious claim accounts by reactivating claims with no benefit payment history over the last few years, due to a death of the beneficiary or an unknown address of the beneficiary. The only controls to inhibit this type of internal fraud were through security audits and good record-keeping.

However, at present, there was no auditing function, even though the managers reviewed claims of their field/district offices once every five years in a general review. There were also some very sporadic field contacts, with actual claimants taken from a small sample of the population to verify the genuineness of these claims.

However, these measures were very limited and resulted in an uneven evaluation of the security in the claims process. With continued growth in insurance claims, better controls were needed. In addition, the new claims modernization project, by introducing microcomputers in the field offices, could cause further difficulty with the security function.

THE CLAIMS MODERNIZATION PROJECT (CMP)

Charles Dey, vice president of Information Systems Planning and Consulting, is one of a group of employees in the Information System department charged with designing a faster—yet secure—claims processing computer system. His group has developed a software system that will replace the current manual application-taking process, bypassing the regular DARS network, and creating output that can be processed by the existing (CAPS) software.

According to Charles Dey, "The one aspect, which I think field staff can appreciate, is the creation of screens on the computer that will be used by the field office employees to replace entering data on paper applications. After creating these screens, one of our more difficult tasks was to create software to make the data coming through the screens on the new computer terminals look like normal DARS traffic to the existing CAPS system." In spite of the difficulties, Charles Dey and his team completed the claims modernization project (CMP).

A follow-on project—Field Office Special Enhancement (FOSE)—will replace the existing video display terminals with Eagle or other IBM-compatible microcomputers and will be used by all field office personnel. The new FOSE system will allow CMI to establish, maintain, and update customer accounts accurately and quickly; also, it will provide automated input/processing/output and information retrieval systems, which will minimize manual processes and systems exceptions, among other things. FOSE will also standardize data so that all databases have some duplicate data elements, which will possibly permit integration of databases downstream.

CLAIMS MODERNIZATION PROJECT—FIELD OFFICE SPECIAL ENHANCEMENTS (CMP–FOSE)

In April 1985, Charles Dey, VP of IS Planning and Consulting, decided to meet with members of his department and several from Data Processing. He wanted to discuss ways of improving the company's level of service to its customers, notably by automating functions to provide better support to field operations.

As the meeting began, Dey elaborated on the strategic plan that he had conceived for modernizing CMI's information systems.

"I am interested in improving data collection and coding, workload control, and payment of insurance claims. When I developed the system modernization plan (SMP) to expand existing computer facilities, it became apparent that broader, on-line programmatic processing capabilities were needed. Additional programming support had to be tied to other SMP programs already underway, such as database integration, capacity upgrade, and data communications.

"As a result, I am taking a technical approach to employ the increased capacity of our new central processor for this CMP. I am also looking into the capability of migrating to distributed processing should that be needed in the future.

"As we all know, the present claims process is generally acknowledged throughout the company to be in critical need of modernization. Any person visiting our field operations can see that our field offices are not equipped with comparable data entry/retrieval capabilities. A similar visit to our regional offices would reveal the same general lack of state-of-the-art technology. While the Data Processing department is implementing the current technology, the claims processing system and software programs have not been redesigned to take advantage of the newest technology. Therefore, in time, we plan to install microcomputers with new software to aid field employees with their claims processing."

Clete Carr, VP of Data Processing, questioning Dey on the capabilities of the new system, asked, "Charley, just what will be achieved by overhauling our current system of data entry using terminals to a system consisting of microcomputers? Also, who will be operating the micros in the field?"

Charles responded. "Clete, this microcomputer project, called FOSE, is amazing in terms of claims processing. First, it allows immediate data entry, edit capability, and system generation of application documents. Any claim taken by telephone or in person will be automatically entered into the micro for further processing and payment of insurance benefits. We'll reduce our processing time for large insurance claims and medical payments from three or four weeks to a one-week period. The system will be used by all field personnel such as claims adjusters and service representatives.

"Secondly, FOSE allows our field office managers to generate on-line management reports needed for work measurement, statistical purposes, and performance evaluations. FOSE also enables the field employee to retrieve an immediate record from the master beneficiary record (MBR); MBR provides availability of payment and benefit and/or transaction history on all insurance claims taken and paid.

"Third, FOSE provides standardized claims documentation output and an improved process for generating understandable customer notices and payment determinations. It also provides improved information-gathering and data entry techniques, including immediate error detection.

"FOSE also establishes control mechanisms that will support audit and management information functions and system security requirements."

"This all sounds great, but, speaking of security," Clete exclaimed, "won't FOSE pose problems concerning physical and software security? Further, doesn't availability of this data to all field office personnel present numerous access control problems we don't have today?"

Charles had an answer here, too, saying, "Clete, we are aware that controls must be placed to limit or monitor access to insurance claims data. I am currently working on security controls with Peter Matthews (VP of Corporate Operations). Peter has formed a security committee to address your concerns. He has appointed me, Donald Mack (manager of the Mid-Atlantic regional office), John Erwin (chairman of the new field/end-user committee), and two district managers for claims (Wendy Williams and Ralph Spencer) from our PC pilot offices representing the end-users. Peter also requested that you be an integral part of our committee to assist us in systems security implementation.

"Our report on security problems and solutions will be sent to Peter on completion. The security committee will also establish a planning schedule to provide dates for evaluation of security measures proposed."

Clete Carr again confronted Charles Dey: "Then, how are you going to implement this massive modernization project in 104 district offices? I do not see how your security committee can possibly manage all the security precautions necessary to allow for a safe operating environment. You are allowing the end-users, namely, claims adjusters and field service representatives, to manipulate and process benefit payment data. Controls on access to sensitive data must be maintained. Our current system provides this control now by limiting access to only a small number of data entry personnel."

"Clete," Charles replied, "your concerns are well founded, but rest assured that we will not release micros to all offices at once. We are taking things slowly and exploring all facets of systems security. First, we are establishing a model district/field office (MDO) at our main headquarters to serve as a user validation and acceptance facility. Equipment and furnishings have been purchased and demonstrations of MDO-CMP software have begun. By January 1986, the MDO software will be extended on a limited test basis to 15 field offices and two (Mid-Atlantic and Pacific) of the seven regional offices.[1] A limited amount of equipment will be installed in these offices to provide for further development and evaluation as well as for local staff orientation.

"In July 1986, our 17 STOs will begin using CMP-FOSE[2] in a 'live' environment. The initial systems enhancement, which will have been tested and validated, will be implemented at that time. A phased implementation, one block every 2 months, of subsequent enhancements is planned. Nationwide implemen-

---

[1] Referred to collectively as Software Test Offices (STO).

[2] When used in a live environment (after testing in the 17 STO's), MDO-CMP becomes CMP-FOSE.

tation of CMP–FOSE is not expected to be phased in until 1988. This allows sufficient time to implement proper security measures to control our data. We'll have to come up with some method to prohibit access to sensitive data kept on the mainframe.'' (See Exhibit 4 for an interim plan devised by Charles Dey for the phased implementation of CMP–FOSE. See Exhibit 4a for an explanation of the implementation plan.)

''Charley, you still will have a problem in preventing the end-users from writing their own applications and validating their data. What types of controls are you establishing?'' Clete asked.

''Clete, I previously mentioned that a field end-user committee, headed by John Erwin of our IS support staff, will be part of our security committee. However, I failed to explain to you what this committee's duties will be in this project. The field end-user committee (FEUC) will determine if programs written by field office personnel can be distributed to other field offices. The FEUC will be attempting to draw up standards of compatibility to be used if a field office develops a good application on the micros. The FEUC will meet with user groups from the software test offices once every three months to evaluate new uses of the system.

''Questionnaires will be given out to the field offices to assess security plans in effect. FEUC hopes to validate all applications written by field personnel. FEUC will report quarterly to Peter Matthews on their findings.''

''I am not satisfied that you have addressed all of the security concerns, Charley, but I am willing to try your pilot program,'' Clete promised. ''I still believe that the FEUC will not be able to control all uses by field personnel on the micros.''

''With these problems addressed,'' Charles concluded, ''if no one has any further comments, I would like to close this meeting, with the understanding that many more meetings of this kind will be needed.''

Clete just shook his head, continuing to resist, and arguing, ''It's not going to work, Charley.''

FEUC'S FIRST MEETING

On June 4, 1985, John Erwin convened the first meeting of FEUC. Present were security committee members Charles Dey, Donald Mack, Clete Carr, Ralph Spencer, and Wendy Williams. As he spoke, John thought of the monumental task ahead.

''I want to thank you all for attending this important meeting. As you know, the security committee has developed a security plan for us to implement. I wish to welcome all the members of the security committee who are with us today. Our objective today is to acquaint you with the different stages of the plan.''

Erwin passed out a mimeographed document (Exhibit 5) and continued, ''The first step has already been done for us by the security committee. This is our Information Security Charter Statement, which will set the ground rules for our security plan. Please notice that it has addressed information as a corporate asset.

EXHIBIT 4 CMP–FOSE Implementation Strategy

Software

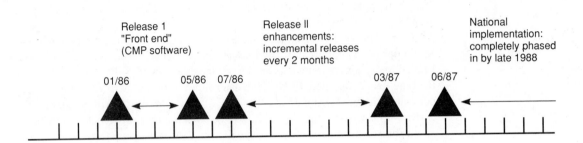

Release 1
"Front end"
(CMP software)

Release II
enhancements:
incremental releases
every 2 months

National
implementation:
completely phased
in by late 1988

01/86   05/86 07/86   03/87   06/87

Data Communications Utility (DCU)

— A new telecommuncations system

— Replaces DARS and existing concentrators

— Increased number of circuits

— Faster response time

DCU   DCU "Backbone"

10/86 — 01/87

The first thing we have to do is to classify our information assets according to
their sensitivity and importance to CMI. We must then advise employees and
managers as to which types of information are considered more sensitive and

---

EXHIBIT 4a   Explanation of Exhibit 4

Release I (CMP) software would interface with the existing batch process for some claims workload via a conversion program. Software was implemented on March 28, 1985 for the model district office.

Thirteen claims were processed as a trial run.

Release II (CMP) is defined as the ability to electronically collect the data necessary to establish claims and to receive immediate notification of errors. All transactions are sent through a conversion program for entry into the existing claims automated processing system (CAPS) for processing of the claim.

Features of CAPS include:

Standard surface edits.

Logical sequential screen presentation.

Data propagation.

Automated receipts.

Delete facility.

There is also a schedule (bottom of Exhibit 4) for the implementation of the new data communications system, DCS.

---

how CMI wants this information handled. I have copies of a Self-Evaluation Checklist that I'll pass out in a minute; it will be the basis for classifying our assets. We should expect a lot of employee resistance and red tape, but senior management would like this step to be completed by November of this year.

"Our next step will be to create a new security manual. This manual is to include the following: ownership of information, user information security responsibilities, the Information Security Charter Statement, the information classification system, segregation of duties, business resumption planning requirements, and risk assessment. This manual should be completed by December 1986."

Erwin stopped and passed out another form (see Exhibit 6).

"You all have Peter Matthews' memo on security (Exhibit 6). The Security Committee had a consultant develop this Checklist for Evaluating Computer Security Activities, which is an enclosure to Peter's memo. This form is a tool to help managers become more aware of security. Since it is to be filled out quarterly, it requires managers to assess the security in their areas every three months. It also allows managers to document security problems in their areas. The final forms are to be distributed on September 5, 1985 and must be returned to us no later than October 1, 1985.

"The final step will be for us to develop an ongoing maintenance and enforcement program. This is necessary because of the very rapidly changing data processing and information security environments.

EXHIBIT 5   Security Committee's Information Security Charter Statement

May 28, 1985

CMI Information Security Charter Statement

Charter

The mission of the Information Security function is to direct and support CMI in the protection of its information asset from intentional or unintentional disclosure, modification, destruction, or denial through implementation of appropriate information security and business resumption planning policies, procedures, and guidelines.

Responsibilities

The information security function shall be responsible for development and administration of information security strategic and tactical plans that address the following:

1. Development of security policies, procedures, and guidelines that are in compliance with CMI policies and generally accepted data processing control requirements.

2. Implementation of a security program that includes classifications of information and a management information self-assessment process to be conducted quarterly.

3. Development and maintenance of a companywide information security awareness and education program.

4. Development and maintenance of overall minimum guidelines for administration of access control software and procedures for both mainframe and microcomputer systems.

5. Development and implementation of information security review procedures and work programs that support CMI policies, procedures, standards, and guidelines.

6. Insuring that information security requirements are incorporated in automated applications through participation in systems design and development.

7. Coordinate CMI information security information dissemination and provide technical assistance to operating organizations as required.

8. Selection, implementation, testing, and maintenance of an appropriate business resumption planning methodology for each organizational location responsible for processing critical automated applications.

9. Other information security responsibilities as deemed appropriate.

"There are many tasks which will require the attention of a Security Officer, but implementation of such a program will provide a framework for building an effective and secure information environment.

"This will not be an easy assignment by any means, but I'm sure that you are all aware of our critical need for a security program for our new system. If we all work together, I'm sure that we can make this program a success. I'll be speaking with each of you individually as to what I'd like you to do specifically."

Erwin announced the next meeting date of September 2 and asked whether there were any questions. Clete Carr spoke up: "John, I'd like to know when this company is going to get a security officer. All these plans are great, but we'll need someone to monitor the program in the future."

Erwin checked his watch and responded. "Well, Clete, I understand that Peter Matthews is conducting an extensive search for an experienced security officer but he hasn't found anyone yet. You'll have to excuse me now; I have to run."

EXHIBIT 6   Memo Regarding Security

June 1, 1985

TO: All management personnel

FROM: Peter Matthews, Vice President of Corporate Operations

RE: Security

Security is not a technical problem.
Security is a people problem.

This basic misunderstanding has been the basis for problems in the computer profession since the beginning of computers. The technician insists on ignoring people in the solution, and those ignored people sabotage the effectiveness of the computer system, intentionally and unintentionally.

The technical problems of computer security can be solved by technicians. The human problems of attitude and behavior cannot be solved by technicians. The people problems are only solvable by management because it alone can establish direction and priority within the organization.

Computer security is definable, specifiable, measurable, and achievable. All it takes to make computer security work is the direct involvement of managers in assuming responsibility in their areas and instilling an attitude in their people that they are responsible for the security over their own activities. Without the cooperation and support of each one of us, no strategy will work.

One of the initial steps in the development of our new comprehensive security plan is the enclosed Self-Assessment Checklist. Use these forms as rough drafts that you can mark up as you please between now and the end of September. At that time, you'll receive another set that you can fill in as your final submittals. Complete these final forms thoroughly by 10/1/85 and return them with all comments to FEUC chairman John Erwin. These forms will be sent to you periodically depending on your involvement in FEUC and the level of your individual security preparedness.

The solution to computer security is through people.

Gaining cooperation for computer security is a management problem.

Self-Assessment Checklist for Evaluating Computer Security Activities

	Yes	No

Central

1. Has a formal change control procedure been established over changes to application systems?
2. Does someone in Data Processing management review the controls installed and deleted from vendor-supplied operating software?
3. Has the confidentiality or sensitivity of each piece of information been identified?
4. Has a formal method been adopted for developing application systems?
5. Has all information within your area of control been classified?

EXHIBIT 6   *(continued)*

	Yes	No

Regional and Central

1. Have procedures been developed defining who can access the facility, and how and when that can occur?
2. Have procedures been developed on the handling of programs and data?
3. Have procedures been established to positively identify all transactions?
4. Do you have a full inventory of equipment by serial number, user(s), custodian, and location?
5. Have you noted and documented any security exposures not previously attended to?
6. Is the level of protection periodically reviewed to insure adequacy?
7. Are employees periodically informed of their information security responsibility?
8. Is the security environment regularly reviewed and records and procedures updated?
9. Is a log maintained of access to computer resources?
10. Do nonemployees have access to facilities? To computers?
11. Is a log maintained of security violations so that the type and magnitude of problems can be monitored?

Personal Processing

1. Have procedures been established for providing physical security over microcomputers and the data processed by them?
2. Has the ownership of microcomputer programs and data been defined by the group?
3. Have procedures been established regarding protection of data within the custody of the micro user?
4. Have alternate means of processing been established in the event either the individual or the personal computer is lost?

Communications

1. Can the identification of the initiator of processing be determined prior to authorizing processing?
2. Can data being transmitted or processed be reconstructed in the event either main processing or remote processing loses integrity?
3. Are processing actions restricted based on point of origin or individual making requests?

Office Systems

1. Is there a security procedure for information processed by office equipment?
2. Does appropriate backup exist for data stored electronically in the event the integrity of the office processing is lost?
3. Have provisions been made to destroy sensitive information controlled by office systems?
4. Are records maintained of the types of computer-processed data that are utilized in office systems?

EXHIBIT 6   (*continued*)

	Yes	No
Disasters		

1. Has equipment been provided to deal with minor disasters such as fire and water?
2. Have alternate processing arrangements been made in the event of a disaster?
3. Have simulated disasters been conducted to ensure that procedures work?
4. Are critical programs and data retained in off-site storage locations?
5. Have users been heavily involved in the development of disaster plans for applications that affect their areas?

Employee Perpetrators

1. Are formal reports required for each reported instance of computer penetration?
2. Are records maintained on the most common methods of computer penetration?
3. Are records maintained on damage caused to computer equipment and facilities?
4. Is one individual held accountable for each data processing resource?
5. Is management evaluated on its ability to maintain a secure computer facility?
6. Are food, smoking, or drinks in the vicinity of computer hardware prohibited? Is this enforced?
7. Are all diskettes properly labeled and secured when not in use?
8. Is after-hours access to facilities controlled?

Nonemployee Perpetrators

1. Are the activities of all nonemployees monitored?
2. Is control to computer areas monitored?
3. Are marketing personnel and other individuals performing business regularly outside the company premises instructed to monitor situations for potential compromise of confidential information?
4. Are procedures installed to restrict nonemployees from gaining access to computer program listings and documentation (confidential trash areas)?
5. Do procedures require management approval before performing non-routine tasks?

People Errors and Omissions

1. Are all diskettes properly labeled and secured when not in use?
2. Are errors made by computer personnel categorized by type and frequency?
3. Are records maintained on the frequency and type of errors incurred by users of data processing systems?
4. Are users provided a summary of the frequency and types of user-caused errors identified by the application system?
5. Are losses associated with data processing errors quantified?

EXHIBIT 6   *(concluded)*

	Yes	No

6. Are records maintained on the frequency and types of problems occurring in operating systems?

7. Are computer software abnormal program terminations summarized by type and frequency so that appropriate action can be taken?

CMP As Viewed by a Headquarter's DP Manager

Installation of the claims modernization project is certain to prompt a loud to-do among the Data Processing department and field office employees, although reaction to this project is, for the most part, enthusiastic. In fact, Suzanne Budd, manager of microcomputer technology in Data Processing, could not wait to inform her friend, John Stanhagen, a field office manager, of the new system. Exhibit 7 shows Suzanne Budd's letter explaining FOSE and FEUC to John Stanhagen.

THE SEARCH FOR A SECURITY OFFICER

It was now March 1986. The initial stages of the security plan had been undertaken, and, to Matthews' knowledge, there had been no major problems. Matthews had indeed conducted a very extensive search for a security officer. It began with a memo to Personnel (see Exhibit 8) that specified exactly what he was looking for. Personnel had sent him several candidates, and he had decided that one of them, Brian Adams, possessed the right qualifications. Because CMI had a contractual relationship with the National Security agency, Matthews had to order a federal security clearance search on Adams. Happily, Adams had a clean record; he was finally cleared and hired on March 30, 1986.

BRIAN ADAMS

Brian Adams received his undergraduate degree in Business Administration from Georgetown University in 1978. He received his graduate degree from Duke University in 1980. He had spent the last five years at North Carolina National Bank (NCNB). He started as a Policy Review analyst in the IS department and had worked his way up to assistant Security director, a job he had held for the last 18 months. He had helped develop security policies for NCNB in that position. Adams saw the position of security officer at CMI as the opportunity he had been waiting for, a chance to make a name for himself. His first assignment as security officer was to review both the existing security policies and the security plan. He promised Matthews a report by the end of May.

EXHIBIT 7   Suzanne Budd's Letter to John Stanhagen regarding the FOSE and FEUC

September 14, 1985

Dear John,

How are things in the district office? A memo just came across my desk that you will just love. First it was the claims modernization that is heading your way, and now it looks like more field managers are going to be getting personal computers, too! No kidding— PCs. Those same machines you see in ads for the perfect Christmas gift will be coming to more offices sometime in the next couple of years if the pilot project is successful.

You've probably heard about the Compucorp word processors out there in the field, but I am not talking about them. Offices are benefitting from what the Compucorp equipment offers—with its letter-quality printer and word processing software. But the PC can take advantage of an almost unlimited variety of business software to handle a greater variety of administrative and managerial tasks. Some of our people are already testing the PCs in field offices (called PC pilot offices) in 18 locations. All regions have at least two offices participating.

Right now, the thinking is that we're going to start slowly with a few applications, and then move on from there. You know, the PCs use regular commercial software, the kind that is available at your neighborhood computer store. Of course, we won't have to worry about this because the software is provided with the PC.

A special group, the field/end-user committee (FEUC), is serving as a focal point or clearinghouse for all uses of the PCs in the 18 PC pilot offices, and boy, have they been working hard. Some of the jobs the PCs have been programmed to handle are a payroll check recordation program, a mailing list management system, an information retrieval system, a district office weekly report, and an equipment inventory system.

If this list impresses you, rest assured that I copied it from one of the memos in my in basket. But if there's one machine I know how to use well, it's the old rotary dial Graham Bell. So, I called the author of most of the memos, FEUC chairman John Erwin from the IS Support staff, and asked him what the list really means.

Well, this is what he told me: The payroll check recordation program automatically assigns payroll check serial numbers. The information retrieval system records multiple instructions on similar subjects, making it simpler to deal with multiple issuances such as regional updates. The district office weekly report system performs all of the math functions and prepares the summary listing for all employees in the office, along with a list of all pending and new claims. And the capitalized equipment inventory program is designed to control both capitalized and noncapitalized equipment. Equipment records can be easily updated and can be sorted by several categories, such as by item name. If that is not enough, the FEUC actually has many more ideas about automating the way we do business, but I do not want to get too technical here. John Erwin told me, "The goal of this project is to evaluate the use and benefit of putting personal computers in our field offices."

When someone in one of the 18 PC pilot locations decides to use the commercial software and the PC to handle a new job, he or she registers it with Sam Murphy's office, and we keep track of its progress. That way, we hope to avoid two people working on the same automation program. If someone calls us with an idea already being worked on, we refer the person to the one to whom it's registered. Programs judged to be beneficial by the user group are reproduced and shared with all 18 locations.

The FEUC is also evaluating all of the projects. Those involved in automating a particular task, function, or report or application on the PC are filling out evaluation forms. The

---

EXHIBIT 7 *(concluded)*

---

forms take into account such facts as development time, frequency of use, cost, and benefits.

Our expectation is that this information will clearly show the benefits of this equipment in a field office. If this happens, the results will serve as the basis for getting more PCs, with the ultimate goal of having them in many more field offices. So, John, get ready to fly with whichever PC comes your way!

Your HQ buddy, Suzanne

MATTHEWS'S DILEMMA

Matthews read Adams's report (see the appendix to this case) with a growing sense of trepidation. He hadn't realized that IS security had such a broad scope. He wondered if Adams wasn't going a bit overboard; after all, CMI wasn't a USF&G or an Alexander & Alexander. All this security sounded expensive. CMI had incurred losses, and he might have some trouble getting his superiors to approve any increases to the IS budget.

Adams seemed to want to control every aspect of security at CMI. That much control in the hands of one person made Matthews a bit uncomfortable.

Several employees had complained about the restrictions and red tape associated with the existing security plan. Matthews imagined the uproar that would follow some of the suggestions that Adams had made. Adams seemed to like stepping on toes. Konrad Senia and Clete Carr had both complained about the way Adams had come across to them and their employees.

Still, some of Adams's suggestions made sense to Matthews at first glance. After all, he had hired Adams because he was an expert. Matthews wondered what he should do.

QUESTIONS

1. What is happening at Chesapeake Mutual?
2. Does Brian's report — or any part of it — seem extreme? Which parts and why? Is he asking for too much?
3. Which parts of Brian's report would you implement? Why?
4. *If you were Peter Matthews,* what would you do with Brian's report? What would you do with Brian?
5. Do you agree with Clete when he says the system is poor? Why or why not?
6. Charles Dey says everything is fine, while Brian claims everything is terrible. How do you explain this inconsistency? Does it require any action from Matthews? If yes, what? If no, why not?
7. Support your opinion on Charles's implementation schedule.
8. Should the field/end-users committee be changed? If so, how and why?

EXHIBIT 8   Memo Regarding the Hiring of a Security Officer

May 2, 1985

TO: Personnel Office

FROM: Peter Matthews

The employment of a security officer is required. The holder of this position will have basic responsibility for the physical and logical security of operational, procedural, and descriptive data and all other information systems resources using data. He or she will report directly to the vice president for Corporate Operations. The security officer will administer the data security program necessitating direct contact and awareness of activities with:

Suppliers of services.

Owners/users.

Management.

Outsiders—consultants, legislative/regulatory agencies, security products vendors, and data security organizations.

Auditors—internal and external.

Legal—internal and external.

Duties and Responsibilities

The holder of this position will:

1. Provide direct administrative support for installed security systems to ensure the secure use of all on-line and information systems.

2. Set up objectives for future development and updating of security systems for evolving systems.

3. Determine special resource requirements such as personnel, training, and equipment and development plans, schedules, and cost data relative to various security responsibilities.

4. Negotiate with multiple levels of programming support management to assure integration of assigned security objectives with the long-range data processing strategy.

5. Continually review and evaluate security alternatives to determine courses of action based on technical implications, knowledge of business objectives, and corporate asset protection policy, procedures, and requirements.

6. Assure that assigned projects meet corporate security objectives and are completed according to schedule within committed costs; inform management as early as possible of problems that could materially affect objectives, schedules, and costs; recommend alternate solutions.

7. Monitor the use of all systems to detect and act on unauthorized access and use of proprietary business data.

8. Conduct security audits, participate in security evaluations, and provide guidance and assistance to facilitate the implementation of data processing asset protection programs.

9. Supervise documentation efforts associated with various internal security systems.

Capabilities

The holder of this position must be capable of:

EXHIBIT 8   (*concluded*)

Recognizing actual and potential security exposures.

Developing solutions in a constantly changing environment of computer technology.

Correlating highly specialized confidential data to real-time as well as batch security systems.

Setting security design standards for application programs.

Establishing administrative procedures and programming development criteria for future security systems.

Negotiating and influencing middle and senior management on risk analysis issues concerning security versus utility of computer resources.

Such a position demands highly innovative action with little dependence on past experiences. The holder of this position must have the self-confidence and initiative necessary to perform required functions using only broad management guidelines in determining both day-to-day and long-range goals.

Appendix

TO: Peter Matthews

FROM: Brian Adams

Your decision to implement formal micro-to-mainframe links puts CMI in the 46 percent of the largest U.S. corporations that are currently implementing such links. Another 44 percent are conducting studies or pilot programs to do so (International Resource Development survey). Forty-four precent of the IS managers responding to a survey of Newton-Evans Research Company in Baltimore said that their largest fear was the possibility of privacy/security breaches resulting from this use of micros. Therefore, CMI is in the forefront of this new wave; and you are not alone in your concerns for security.

It's time to get going with concrete security plans. Your security committee is three-tiered, with corporate, regional, and field managers, which is good representation, but I don't think they've done much so far.

I've reviewed the classification of information assets dated November 15, 1985, and, although it does identify those records vital to the organization's continued operation, it fails to address the problems of protecting them, on- or off-site. It also fails to develop update cycles to keep procedures current or establish a means to reconstruct data. I need to see an information flow analysis so that I can have a clear understanding of how the information flows throughout the system, the interfaces for that information, and how it is being stored.

I'll need a technical assistant familiar with the current programs and the new programs of CMP–FOSE. Since I was assigned no staff other than a secretary, I assume that you will assign the necessary people to me for the necessary periods. Initially, I will need this assistance for about a month. Clete Carr has been unable, or unwilling, to walk me through the present system. He refused to show me his log of security violations so that I can get a feel for the present problems. I suspect that he hasn't kept it current, if he ever kept one. He wouldn't even discuss the details of the present mainframe security. I suggest that you set him straight.

I have reviewed the CMI security manual, which hasn't been updated, I'm told, since 1980, and the draft of the new manual, which still has lots of holes. One of these is the area of access control, which encompasses the following:

1. Facilities

There are all kinds of devices, from dead bolts to sound and motion detectors, coded badges, magnetic card and hand-print systems, security guards, and TV surveillance systems. This includes everything from the vulnerability of your air-conditioning system to multiple security control points and door and window security.

2. Hardware

a. We need an inventory of equipment by serial number. This should include where it is located, who is responsible, and what modifications have been made to the equipment.

b. Security devices run from basic equipment covers (to protect against airborne contaminants) to lockdown devices. Lockdown devices are available from many manufacturers (e.g., Anchor Pad Services in Silver Spring, Maryland). These devices glue or bolt the equipment to a desk or table. I've used the "Huggy System," which is essentially a bolt with a two-piece nut; once the computer is bolted down, part of the nut is removed, and the bolt cannot be removed without reinstallation (National Field Sales, Inc., Broomal, Pennsylvania). There are available lockable equipment enclosures that consist of a series of sized boxes that secure to each other and then to the desk. Crystal oscillators can be embedded in the equipment to trigger an alarm when the equipment is moved. There are secured pads and alarms that sound when the equipment is disconnected from the wall and software that sounds an alarm at the mainframe when the micro is disconnected without advance notice.

3. Data

Data access can be controlled in many ways. Hardware such as the APX286 microprocessor is one approach.

a. Limit access to terminals. This is done by passwords or levels of passwords or more sophisticated built-in mechanisms for automatic checking of privilege levels, access or rights validation, controlled data sharing, and code transitions through gates.

b. Limit access to diskettes. There are all kinds of programs that "rejuvenate" even "erased" data. Hard disk data can be rejuvenated, too.

c. Limit access to signals. Since data will be transmitted over communication lines, methods of preventing someone from intercepting the signal or masquerading as someone authorized access will have to be considered.

Your micros are more vulnerable than mainframes, since they generate a clearer signal to tune into. The electrical power line or the computer can be tapped. A very high level of protection can be achieved with Tempest. Tempest specifications, developed by the National Security Agency, specify protective shielding levels that protect against intentional eavesdropping on electronic signals.

This is very expensive; it triples the cost of a micro and is ugly. Printers, cables, and all other peripherals devices that broadcast radiowave frequencies would need this protection. You don't need Tempest, and elastomers are probably also going rather far for CMI. (Elastomers are conductive plastics and electrically conductive paints that absorb radio emissions.)

d. Encryption. Prices for software and hardware devices for data encryption are coming down.

There is no emergency response plan setting forth immediate responses to threats, whether from acts of God or acts of humans. Its purpose is to limit critical resource damage as well as preserve the business capability. This should be an action plan to mitigate, if not avoid, loss of business essentials at the moment of occurrence. Related but separate is a restoration plan, also lacking. This plan should include provision for off-site storage of backups, joint use agreements with other organizations, and/or a loaner arrangement with a local vendor in case of emergency.

I've reviewed your Self-Assessment Checklist for Evaluating Computer Security Activities and frankly, Pete, it sounds to me as if you expect the regional people to do their own access security. This will never work. If they all go off on their own, we'll have invented the wheel in each of the 104 field offices. Most of these "inventions" will be unsatisfactory.

Granted, the different facilities used by the various offices present different problems; however, this can be handled by my good friend Joe Elliott at Honeywell. They've been installing, monitoring, and maintaining security systems nationwide for 25 years. We'll deal with one representative who'll work with me to establish uniform security standards for all locations. We'll need blueprints of the 15 field and 2 regional offices in the STO group to get started.

As you now know, I paid a visit to the MDO the other day. What a disaster. Konrad Senia (manager of the MDO) has completely ignored any physical security. Anyone can walk right in; I did, and used the PC for about five minutes before the sweet young thing whose desk I was sitting at asked me if she could "help" me. She found out what kind of "help" I wanted. I'd have fired her on the spot. Konrad gave her a Kleenex for her tears and ushered her into his office. The equipment was running and was just sitting there on the desk unattended.

Keyboards and peripheral equipment including printers, disks, and modems have a nasty habit of disappearing, since they are compatible with home equipment. Purses, briefcases, or coat pockets accommodate many components. "Trusting" your people is beside the point and naive. You may not be aware of it, but there is a flourishing black market for "hot " microcomputer parts with street values as high as 50 percent of market value. Other items to be considered are:

1. Antistatic mats or antistatic sprays. Ten or 15 volts can damage a micro or erase all memory. Ten thousand volts can be generated by simply walking across a carpet.

2. Fans. Although heat buildup is more a problem with large computers, stacking of various peripherals and restricting the air flow can cause heat to build up and ultimately damage the equipment and/or alter data or programs.

3. Air filters and vacuum cleaners. Dust, human hair, and lint or ashes in a disk drive can have the same effect as trying to clean a phonograph needle with a wire brush.

4. Fire extinguishers. Halon is the best agent for use around electronic equipment as it is the least damaging and least toxic. It is usually mixed with nitrogen, which can be toxic in heavy concentrations. APS International, Inc., of Cleveland Tennessee, markets the American Safety Products portable extinguisher that uses two different types of Halon for a blend that is absolutely nontoxic; I've used this often.

5. Power surge protectors. Power surges caused by other electrical motors operating on the circuit, load switching by the power company, or lightning, can destroy circuits, memory, and/or data. I've purchased surge and spike protectors from Sola in Elk Grove Village, Illinois.

6. Uninterrupted power source. An auxiliary unit or battery can be placed on the line to kick in when the normal source is out.

The selection of security devices and procedures is basically a matter of cost-effectiveness. I still don't know my budget amount. Two to 3 percent of the annual data processing budget is fairly standard for ongoing security support. However, there is no way that we can develop and install the necessary equipment for even 2 to 3 percent of the overall cost of the new system. Most firms have no idea what their information is worth. As a rule of thumb, you can start with an estimate of how much business could be lost if files are damaged, add the cost to reconstruct the data, plus any law suits that would result from the exposure of confidential data, plus the possible loss from misappropriation/ alteration of data. In short, you're very vulnerable. It's your decision. But I need an approximate dollar amount before I start talking to vendors.

At present my hands are tied. I can't do this job alone. I need the authority to purchase devices and enforce security precautions.

I also need to start training and education sessions with the managers of your STO offices. I'd like to have them all here for a training session as soon as possible. I'm sure that, like most people here at CMI, they are completely unaware of the full range of the vulnerabilities of their assets (hardware, supplies, software, and data) and the multitude of threats (system denial, loss of data integrity, compromise of data) from various sources —the environment and humans. I can't overemphasize the need to get moving on security *now.*

Case 9–2 Greater Metropolitan Savings and Loan

Jan Paules was busy working on the Appraisal department audit when Harry H. Dicker, president, walked into her office and asked her to report back to him on the Association's compliance with the new Federal Home Loan Bank Memorandum R 67-1 (see Appendix A). Compliance work was nothing new to Jan, as it was a regular part of her job as assistant vice president/internal auditor.

She quickly glanced at the new coversheet entitled End-User Computing (see Exhibit 1). It appeared to deal with personal computers, word processors, and their security. "It is about time," she thought. "We have a tremendous amount of strategic information for the savings and loan with very little in the way of an established security system."

Jan did not have a PC in her office, nor did she use one for her audits, but the president wanted to know the situation at hand, so she knew she was going to learn quickly.

EXHIBIT 1   Federal Home Loan Bank of Atlanta—Supervisory Bulletin

4th District
1475 Peachtree Street, N.E.
Atlanta, Georgia 30309

April 1, 1988

End-User Computing

Memorandum R 67-1, dated March 22, 1988, contains a joint issuance by the Federal Financial Institutions Examination Council (FFIEC) on end-user computing risks. End-user computing refers to the development and operation of data processing applications by the traditional end-users of data processing systems rather than by a centralized Information Services staff. This joint issuance is meant to provide guidance to management for evaluating potential risks, and for implementing adequate control practices and responsibilities in end-user computing environments. The memorandum notes that the management of each FSLIC-insured institution utilizing end-user computer systems is expected to implement controls consistent with the guidelines offered in the joint issuance. Memorandum R 67-1 is attached.

SB-13-1988
With attachment[1]

This case was prepared by Isabel M. Cumming and updated by Keith Zumbrun. Names, locations, and financial data have been disguised.

[1]See Appendix A.

BACKGROUND

Greater Metropolitan Savings and Loan (the Association) was established in the 1920s. It was founded by a group of men in the same card club who wanted to pool money together to help one another buy houses. From those humble beginnings, it has grown into a $500 million institution, the 12th largest savings and loan in Ohio. It has had federal insurance since the 1960s, so the Ohio savings and loan crisis did not adversely affect the firm, which is *very* conservative.

Everyone in management at the S&L had been a teller at one point and progressed from there. The first "outside" person ever hired for a management position by Greater Metropolitan is Jan Paules, the internal auditor. Jan was an accounting major from James Madison University in Virginia. She had a strong leadership background, having been the president of the student body at JMU. She worked two years for the "Big Eight" accounting firm of Peat, Marwick, Mitchell & Co. before being hired by Greater Metropolitan to start the internal audit program.

The remainder of the management personnel are men who have been at Greater Metropolitan for an average of 20 years.

PCs AT GREATER METROPOLITAN

The first thing Jan did was develop a questionnaire regarding issues discussed in Memorandum R 67-1 (see Exhibit 2). As a result of the questionnaire, Jan discovered that there were 11 personal computers, 12 word processors, and 2 standing mainframes at Greater Metropolitan. In 1986, there was only one IBM PC, so the use of PCs has grown significantly in the last two years.

EXHIBIT 2   Questions for Personal Computer Audit — Memorandum R 67-1

---

1. Is there a manual available on how to operate your computer?
2. Does anyone else have a working knowledge of the personal computer (i.e., does anyone else know how to access, change, and input data)? If yes, who?
3. If something should happen to the chief user, are all steps documented: how to access the computer, file codes, and so on?
4. Where are the disks stored? How often is the material backed up? Are security measures used?
5. If your computer has a direct monetary impact on the Association, is there segregation of duties between the input of information and the review of that information into processed form?
6. Are there adequate restrictions over physical access to hardware?
7. How is the password controlled? How often is it changed?
8. Before a program is changed, is there a thorough testing of the new system?
9. When a program is changed, are records kept describing the change, the reason for the change, and the individual responsible for the change?

During the questioning process, it became apparent that security was lax; no one felt personally vulnerable nor concerned about the catastrophe that could happen. No one felt his or her information was critical, although middle management data was the basis for much of the information presented to the board of directors.

Jan submitted a summary of the questionnaire results to President Dicker's office. Within half a day, he was on the phone, telling Jan that he wanted an end-user security policy developed for Greater Metropolitan, a policy that would protect the S&L from the security risks that seemed endemic to the microcomputer environment. On May 5th, the president sent a brief memo to Paul E. Kain, senior vice president, and Gerry T. Maloney, assistant vice president/controller, appointing them committee members with Jan to develop a personal computer security policy that would comply with R 67-1. Jan was to be the chairperson; Dicker expected to see a draft statement in 30 days (30 was underlined in the memo). Paul and Gerry were both computer literate and had well-used PCs in their offices.

Paul Kain was 35 and had received an MBA from the University of Cincinnati in 1987. Paul, with an undergraduate degree in English, had joined Greater Metropolitan in 1975. He has moved up very quickly, being the youngest senior vice president. He enjoys dominating meetings and is known as the "Golden Boy," mostly because of his personal and social relationships with President Dicker, his next-door neighbor. Paul, who runs the computer operations for the savings side of the house, was the first one at the Association to use a personal computer.

Gerry Maloney is the assistant vice president/controller. He started with the Association in 1977. Gerry is attending night school now to finish his BS degree. He has a real estate license. His department has one of the Association's two standing mainframes and two personal computers. His manner is very low key but his reputation for hard work is legend.

THE COMMITTEE

President Harry Dicker appointed Jan to chair the committee; Paul and Gerry were to report to her. Harry wanted a policy within 30 days. Jan immediately contacted both men to arrange a meeting.

Paul claimed that he was too busy that week and requested that they meet the following week. He told Jan to inform the president that the delay was his fault. Jan did so and also asked for a 15 to 45-day extension, which Dicker granted.

The First Meeting—May 11, 1988

Jan went ahead with the first meeting in spite of Paul's absence. She and Gerry decided to review Memorandum R 67-1 and look for overlaps between the R 67-1 and the responses to Jan's personal computer audit. Then, the committee could focus its efforts of the areas where Greater Metropolitan was weak.

Although both Jan and Gerry had read R 67-1 before coming to the meeting, they took about 15 minutes to glance through it again and to review the notes they'd written. Gerry spoke first.

"I can certainly see a couple of conceivably very serious problems already, Jan. Did you notice, in the section called Program Changes—the *most important* requirement, is for thorough testing of modified systems? We certainly don't have a capability to do that.

"And look at the next paragraph under Documentation. Our end-user operators are all guilty of making personal changes that never show up in the update of our users' manual. What was the date of the last revision, by the way?"

"You have me on that, Gerry, but it's a good question, and I'll find out. I'm still back on the section called Program Development and Testing. I think one of our difficulties has been that we haven't paid enough attention to our very specific needs when we purchased those bundled software packages. We should be looking not only for the best solution but for the best system.

"I guess part of the problem with assuring that the new system is easily modified and maintained is that the program development and design of those purchased packages is done by the software suppliers; I think sometimes their interests are much shorter term than ours."

"No question about that, Jan; they are interested in the sale, in shipments out the door. Did you see in the paragraph just above that, the comment about redundancy and compatibility? I would think we could almost lift that last sentence verbatim and put it near the top of our charter.

"Do you know what I think, Jan? I think we should go ahead and pick out a few more major areas for the committee to work on, draft up some meeting minutes, and then call it a day. I have a million things to do, and we're only going to be spinning our wheels until Paul gets involved. As soon as we can sit on him long enough to get some agreement on who's going to cover what, we can go our separate ways and really grind out some policies. Does that sound reasonable to you?"

"Sure; why not," Jan answered.

The two worked on for another half hour, prepared the meeting minutes, agreed to try to meet again on May 16th, and then left the meeting room (see the Minutes, Exhibit 3).

The Meeting of May 16th

Everyone was present at the second meeting. Paul dominated—as expected. He felt the project should be broken into three areas: (1) hardware, (2) applications, and (3) software. Therefore, the committee's total work was broken down into the three areas by individuals: Paul—software and applications; Gerry—minicomputer and network system; and Jan—training and hardware. Jan asked that all work be completed by the next meeting of May 24, 1988 so that she could start putting the information together (see the Minutes, Exhibit 4).

EXHIBIT 3 Minutes of the Memorandum R 67-1 Committee Meeting

GREATER
METROPOLITAN
SAVINGS

A Memorandum R 67-1 committee meeting was held on Wednesday, May 11, 1988, at 10:00 A.M. In attendance were Jan D. Paules and Gerry T. Maloney. Mr. Kain was excused from the meeting.

The first order of business was to review the actual memorandum and the various responses from the audit inquiries.

Mr. Maloney felt the areas that were lacking included (1) management controls; (2) data/file storage and backup; and (3) data security. While reviewing the memorandum, we agreed that it covered the stand-alone mainframe, the personal computers, and the word processors. The difficulty is that the systems are not consistent.

Mr. Maloney will investigate the cost of using DataVault and the usage of a disk program called Fast Back. The possibility of using more passwords will also be investigated.

Mr. Maloney also noted that in the future, the Association will be using a shared database. Appraisal, Accounting, and Mortgage Servicing will be using the same database in regard to the SLIMS Construction Loan Package. This will place an emphasis on management controls.

The next meeting will be held on May 16, 1988 at 10:00 A.M. in the dining room.

There being no further business, the meeting adjourned at 11:00 A.M.

Jan prepared a four-page overview on training and hardware and was looking forward to ending the meetings and starting to compile information. However, the third meeting did not start out on the right foot.

The Meeting of May 24th

Paul Kain walked in, 30 minutes late, and announced, "Sorry to have to leave you all in the lurch like this, Jan, but I just don't have the time. I don't have anything for you and won't be able to make any really meaningful contribution."

Jan and Gerry glanced at each other very briefly. Jan replied, asking, "Darn it all, Paul, why did you wait 'til the last minute to drop this bomb? I must have stopped by your office at least once a day in the last week to remind you of the meeting today. We were really counting on your input."

Paul did not answer.

"Okay," Jan continued, "we only have about 15 days to finish our report and get it on Harry's desk. I'll put you in an advisory role, Paul, because we've got to get cracking; we really need results right now. Send me whatever you've managed to put together as soon as possible, please."

EXHIBIT 4   Minutes of the Memorandum R 67-1 Committee Meeting

A Memorandum R 67-1 committee meeting was held on Monday, May 16, 1988, at 10:00 A.M. In attendance were Jan D. Paules, Gerry T. Maloney, and Paul E. Kain.

The first order of business was to review the mission of the committee: to develop written policies and procedures defining the steps necessary to protect the institution's microcomputer system.

Mr. Kain felt that we needed to break the project down into three areas: (1) hardware, (2) application, and (3) software. The committee felt this would be the best approach.

The backup of disk information was discussed. Mr. Maloney suggested the use of the Fast Back package to aid in backing up data. It was mentioned that the Association could use Data Vault to store backup disks so that the original disks would be in off-premises storage.

It was also suggested that the vault in Mortgage Servicing could be used for daily disk storage.

Mr. Maloney informed the committee that passwords could be incorporated into all personal computers with a program at minimal cost to the Association. The committee felt this would be a worthwhile investment.

The committee decided to break the work down to three areas: Paul will concentrate on software and application; Jan will concentrate on training and hardware; and Gerry will concentrate on minicomputer and network. Each individual is responsible to develop the policy for his or her area.

The next meeting will be held on Tuesday, May 24, 1988, at 10:00 A.M., in the executive dining room.

There being no further business, the meeting adjourned at 11:45 A.M.

She reached across the table and picked up the fat folder Gerry slid toward her, thanked him for his help, and promised him she'd get back to him shortly.

Back in her office, she wrote a memo to the president, informing him that she had placed Paul in a new, advisory role at his request (due to the press of other commitments); she and Gerry would assume Paul's committee assignments and submit the draft statement on time.

Two days later, Jan received Paul's synopsis. She reviewed it (see Appendix B) and concluded it was merely a lesson on personal computers, including their components, and not helpful to the committee.

"Now what do I do?" she thought. "Only 12 days left and still no policy." Jan headed down the hall toward Gerry's office.

POLICY STATEMENT TOPICS

She interrupted Gerry who was hard at work on another project and pleaded with him to share Paul Kain's areas of responsibility with her in order to get the committee report to the president on time. He agreed under protest but told Jan with a rueful smile that she had just learned a valuable lesson in office politics from an expert.

"To hell with politics," she answered. "We need a personal computer security policy in 10 days or it will be *my* fault, not Paul's. Do you know what our problem is? This is a job for an EDP auditor, and we don't have one, darn it all. It shouldn't be my job or yours. We never could have prepared that Panaudit purchase proposal without the consultant. Oh damn, let's just sit down and get on with it; we'll develop Association policies for each major element of the R 67-1 memorandum."

"Right on," Gerry responded, enthusiastically. "That means we have to address each of the following eight points:

1. Management control.
2. Data security.
3. Documentation.
4. Data/file storage and backup.
5. Systems and data integrity.
6. Contingency plans.
7. Audit responsibility.
8. Training.

"First, in the area of management control, we should have a steering committee that would handle all new requests and review existing systems.

"And data security has to involve incorporating passwords on all systems. Physical security includes locking keyboards and using power surge suppressors."

"Okay," Jan joined in, "under documentation, all the users must be required —as a minimum—to develop procedures that show how their machines operate and what information they store. We need more emphasis on data backup. I don't think it's too much to say that after 20 minutes of continuous use, backup is required.

"As for data storage, I think we should use off-premises storage for all templates and original program files. Nightly storage will be in the Association's fireproof vault. And we'll continue the contingency plan that's been in effect with the SLIMS Corporation for disaster recovery. How are we doing so far? Great, huh?"

"You betcha," allowed Gerry, with a grin. "Now, for audit responsibility; that's your area of expertise but let me tell you what I think, anyway. It seems to me that Internal Audit should be responsible for reviewing logs, documentation, and procedural manuals for compliance."

Jan concurred, saying, "No argument there. That leaves the final area—training. We've got to incorporate all these policies, once we get them fleshed out, into future training manuals. Also, I'm going to suggest that all individuals attend a computer training class for at least one day. Buy that?"

"Absolutely," said Gerry. "Now, let's take a couple more days to include some of the specifics, then finalize all this, and get together one last time on the 25th."

"Darn it all," exploded Jan, "I just thought of something! Do you remember that proposal we submitted two months ago on the Panaudit software package? We've got to be sure that we include in our policy all the points we made in the proposal."

"You're right," agreed Gerry. "Wouldn't we have looked dumb if the two weren't consistent? Do you have a copy handy?"

"Yes—got one right here in the bottom drawer. Here you are (see Appendix C). Well, I can't put any more time on it today. I've been asked to be a guest speaker at U.C. tonight. Miles Wilson wants me to give a presentation to his MBA majors on issues and problems with IS and auditing. By the way, did you know he's a former MIS manager and just finished his CPA? He did it part-time while he was teaching full-time. Anyhow, want to come along, Gerry?"

"Gee, I sure appreciate your giving me the opportunity, Jan. With friends like you, who needs enemies? Actually, I'm already on the hook with him for his class two weeks from tonight. I don't want to be accused of overexposure. But thanks, anyway."

JAN'S PRESENTATION TO THE MBA CLASS

Miles and his students had just returned to the classroom after their break. Miles had given a brief introductory lecture covering some of the regulatory history of auditing before the break (see Appendix D). Everyone took a seat, including Jan. Miles gave a brief background on Jan and then turned the class over to her.

Jan rose from her seat at the front of the class, set her notes on the professor's desk, and turned to face the class.

"Thank you, Miles, for the kind introduction and for the opportunity to talk to your class. Greater Metropolitan wants to contribute to the community, to be considered a good corporate citizen; so we are delighted to have opportunities such as this one tonight to repay local organizations and people who helped make us a success. I hope all of you will think of Greater Metropolitan for any personal needs you may have."

As the students grinned at her straightforward commercial, Jan smiled back and then continued.

"Let's move on to issues and problems with auditing and computers."

Introduction

"I assume that you all have been exposed to auditing in your accounting and finance classes, but I am going to review some introductory material anyway, so please bear with me.

"First, auditing is a major duty or obligation of the finance/accounting people in any firm. I am in the midst of an audit—call it an inspection—of our Appraisal department. What I want to know is very simple, just two things, really: (1) are we using our computer systems in accordance with our corporate procedures, SOPs, and guidelines? And (2) are the processes really working the way our people say they are?

Internal and External Audits

"As you know, there are two types of audits—internal and external. My job with the Appraisal people is **internal.** We are required to take part in regular security and backup reviews. We also look into more detail than external auditors and do quite a bit of data processing evaluation, mostly using special software called Panaudit Plus, which we've only had for a couple of weeks. I have some handouts on it for you.

"An internal **financial** audit attempts to validate the accuracy of the corporation's financial accounting records, while an **operational** audit—which an EDP auditor does with computer systems—is a check on whether the automated processes and methods achieve what they are supposed to accomplish.

"**External** audits are usually financial and are done by CPAs from outside your own organization; their major products are income statements and balance sheets.

"The 'outside your own organization' point is important because independence of the evaluators is critical with all auditing, internal as well as external. It is more difficult to maintain the degree of independence desired with internal auditing, particularly when we get involved with system design and maintenance, but it is mandatory. What we want is a reporting relationship up the hierarchy of the organization that assures us of independence (a shield, you say?) from those we are auditing.

Functions of the Auditor

"Any questions so far? None? Alright, I'll move right along. Let me ask you a question and then answer it myself. What are the functions of an auditor? There are basically three:

1. We want to be certain that standards for development and operation of IS have been prepared and circulated for action.
2. We then want to ensure that the standards are being followed by the operational groups, the functional business areas.
3. Finally, we want to guarantee that we are actively participating in the design of systems, so that the systems, when installed, can be audited—and maintained in a way that doesn't generate new problems.[2]

---

[2]James I. Cash, F. W. McFarlan, J. L. McKenney, and M. R. Vitale, *Corporate Information Systems Management: Text and Cases,* Chapter 7, 2nd ed. (Homewood, Ill.: Richard D. Irwin, 1988).

Controls and Auditing

"Let's spend a little time now on controls. With information systems evolving and proliferating as they are, companies must have controls.

"There are three types of control in IS—general for system operations, specific for applications, and those for application development. I'm not going to discuss general controls other than to say they include scheduling use of systems, library files and documentation, use and creation of databases, physical access to computers, and recovery and backup. I'm sorry that we don't have time to get into application development controls, either.

"As for controls for specific applications, the goal is to be certain that data is not lost, misappropriated, or mishandled, and to be sure that the number crunching and data processing is exact and reliable. And most importantly, *there should be an adequate audit trail.*

Audit Trail

"So you'd like a definition of an audit trail? An **audit trail** 'is the trail of references (document numbers, batch numbers, transaction references, and so on) which allows tracing of a transaction from the time it is recorded through to the reports in which it is aggregated with other transactions, or the reverse, tracing a total back to amounts on individual source documents.' That quote's from Davis and Olson, *Management Information Systems: Conceptual Foundations, Structure, and Development,* page 139, if anyone is interested.

"It's unfortunate but true that most users leave out audit trails because they don't understand or appreciate why they are needed. The point is that any report figure should be traceable back to its source. The way to assure that is to use pointers and intermediate outputs with your models. That way, others can check the flow of data through the system and can weigh the model's assumptions themselves.

Auditing Software

"Any questions? No? Let's return to auditing software. We just bought some so we looked at several auditing software packages on the market today. Most of them are generalized packages that can be used in an audit of a variety of automated accounting systems. What they do is give you access to the computers' files. They also create their own files and permit the auditors to analyze, sort, and summarize the system's data; they also will create reports. Panaudit Plus is typical of many. I have a handout that you can take as you leave tonight; it gives a very good description of the package.[3]

---

[3]Robert Schultheis and Mary Sumner, *Management Information Systems: The Manager's View,* Chapter 8 (Homewood, Ill.: Richard D. Irwin, 1989).

Auditing Techniques

"Next, techniques of an auditor. We used to look only at business accounts, frankly looking for discrepancies and evidence of fraud. Now, we have to check out the software, data security, and even how many users ask how often to see what sensitive data. Growth in the use of microcomputers and local area networks has added an entirely new dimension to our jobs, especially with respect to security concerns.

"We look at everything, from the forms used by data entry people to input data to the reports that are the final product. We trace audit trails on cash and documents. We create test data to use when we run the system to check actual processing; if the processing is correct, the outputs should also be correct. We even run some of our checks at the same time that users are inputting data or querying the systems. It's almost gotten to be a case of auditing going on continually rather than being done during a surprise one-week visit, as it used to be in the past.[4]

Guidelines for Auditing

"Here are two short lists; one is general guidelines for audits; the second is general steps to take that help prevent computer crimes. Both of these came from a book that's due to be published next year; I reviewed part of a chapter on auditing and got the author's OK to use these myself. Let me pass them out (see Exhibits 5 and 6).

"Why don't you take a minute to read over those? I think they're all pretty much self-explanatory. But I'll answer questions if you have any.

"Has everyone had a chance to read through the lists? Good. Questions? None? Let's move on now to the last section, and that's short. After that, I'll answer questions and be on my way. Is that alright, Miles? Great; then that's what we'll do.

Audit Problems

"I've discussed several topics. They all probably seem simple enough. However, it's one thing to explain what we do; it's something else to do it. Actually the doing turns out to be very difficult in many instances. And the problems may be quite different from what you might guess they'd be.

---

[4]Jerome S. Burstein, *Computers and Information Systems,* Chapter 17 (New York: Holt, Rinehart & Winston, 1986).

"First is the problem of retaining and updating the actual auditing skills. Auditing and IS/IT are separate disciplines that require many years of education, training, and experience; yet what we are asking, when we advertise for positions, is someone who is expert in both. It's hard to find those people and it's hard to keep them.

"Second, and this one is somewhat related to the first problem, IS/IT is advancing so quickly that it's hard for EDP auditors to keep up. Just when they thought they had all the batch processing techniques defined and refined, along came databases, electronic spreadsheets, microcomputers, downloading data from mainframes to micros, and local area networks. Keeping up is a significant challenge.

"Third is the question of top-level support, and this applies to anything in business. Right now, many top-level executives are ambivalent about how to acquire DP auditors. Do they train financial auditors to be DP auditors, do they train experienced DP people to be auditors, or do they go outside and hire someone who supposedly already has all the skills they need? From what I hear at conferences these days, most firms are opting to try to teach their financial auditors what they need to know about DP.[5]

"There's something else I should mention to those of you who may be considering auditing, any kind of auditing, as a career. There are some jobs, very honorable and extremely satisfying, that are not well liked. Auditing is one of them. People are often not really sure of what you're doing. They do know that you're going to write a report that will result in additional work for them, point out discrepancies, and probably give details on how some people were failing to do their jobs properly. Some individuals will feel threatened. Sure, they kid about how they understand you're really there to help them, but that doesn't mean they have to like it, and most don't.

"Fortunately, most managers realize we try to minimize exposure to risk with possible losses. We find few cases of exposure with low degrees of risk. We don't expect to find all the problems, but we know, and management knows, that we lower the likelihood of loss.

"That concludes my presentation. Thank you again for the opportunity to come here tonight and talk about issues and problems for the EDP auditor. Now, are there any questions?"

Only one student raised her hand and then asked, "If it's so hard to find these people, the jobs must pay really well. Why is it so hard to hold them?"

"Good question. Of course, the answer is that the pay hasn't been spectacular. It's getting better though, as companies realize that a good EDP auditor can save them hundreds of thousands of dollars, even millions, if we believe the stories of computer fraud that we've been reading.

"Most firms still don't seem to accept auditing as a solution to computer fraud

---

[5]Cash et al, *Corporate Information Systems Management.*

EXHIBIT 5 Audit Guidelines

- Are administrative security procedures documented?
- Are administrative procedures for hard disk and diskette backup documented?
- Are administrative procedures for off-site backup and storage documented?
- Does a written policy state when the user-based system is to be signed on and off and by whom?
- Are there written procedures to control the use of sensitive documents?
- Are there written departmental policies and procedures stating how and what to document for in-house–developed applications?
- Are eating, drinking, and smoking prohibited in the immediate computer area?
- Is there a procedure for informing employees that corporate policy forbids the copying of copyrighted software, except for backup purposes?
- Is there a written policy in place regarding the removal of hardware and/or software from bank premises?
- Is there a written policy regarding the reformatting of the hard disk on leased or rented computers when that computer is to be returned to the lessor?

Source: Charles S. Parker, *Management Information Systems: Strategy and Action* (New York: McGraw-Hill, 1989), Figure 20–4, p. 786.

---

problems. They don't realize how much of that is going on because companies hush up the stories when it happens to them. Maybe an even more important point is that EDP auditing has seemed to be a dead-end job as far as a career is concerned. But corporations are working to improve that, also.''

Jan picked up her notes and returned to her seat. There was a polite round of applause from the class and Miles, but no more questions. Miles dismissed the class and offered to take Jan out for pie and coffee and a short discussion about EDP auditing. She accepted quickly, and they left.

CONCLUSION

All policies were incorporated into a policy statement given to the president on June 27th, the final day of the deadline (see Appendix E). The president was concerned over the individuals selected for the committee and the cost involved. Jan sent the answers to his questions in an additional memo (see Exhibit 7).

The president then sent the proposal to the senior vice presidents (Keith G. Bowen, executive vice president, and the four senior vice presidents: Paul E. Kain, Clark S. Stein, Jim Y. Tyree, and Van F. Weaver) for feedback. Paul Kain submitted a one-and-a-half page critique (see Exhibit 8) of the proposal; no other senior vice president responded.

Back in her office the next morning, Jan was waiting for word from President Dicker. She was thinking about the MBA's Information Systems class she had

EXHIBIT 6   Preventing Computer Crime

- Hire carefully.
- Beware of malcontents.
- Separate employee functions.
- Restrict system use.
- Protect resources with passwords or access cards.
- Encrypt data and programs.
- Monitor system transactions.
- Conduct frequent audits.
- Educate people in security measures.
- Educate people on ethical considerations.

Source: Charles S. Parker, *Management Information Systems: Strategy and Action* (New York: McGraw-Hill, 1989), Figure 20–3, p. 783.

attended a few nights previously. The instructor, Miles Wilson, a former MIS manager and recently CPA, had pressed her about EDP auditing and mainframes. She reviewed her class notes to see if there was anything that might prepare her for possible questions. What would she say if President Dicker asked her, "Based on your experience looking at the microcomputer security policy question, do you have any concerns about EDP auditing in general?"

Back in her office, 30 minutes after President Dicker had called personally to say he was approving the microcomputer security policy paper as she and Gerry had proposed it—without changes—Jan was beginning to have misgivings.

"Damn, it's great to win one, but we really were under an awful lot of pressure to meet the deadline. I wonder if we missed anything. Sure, he approved it with no changes, but he's not expert in this area. We are. And then there's that critique memo from Kain. I didn't see anything world-shaking there, but I think I'm going to try to get Gerry to put in just a couple of more hours to help me compare our policy statement (Appendix E), Memorandum R 67-1 (Appendix A), and Kain's comments (Exhibit 8).

QUESTIONS

1. Should the middle managers have been concerned about security risk to their data? Why or why not?
2. What is your opinion of Paul Kain's actions?
3. Should Jan have accepted his cop-out so readily? What were her options?
4. Did you agree with Paul's critique of the microcomputer security policy statement (Exhibit 8)? Why or why not?
5. Did the committee's cost and schedule estimates appear reasonable?

6. What revisions or additions would *you* make to Jan and Gerry's policy statement?
7. Compare Professor Wilson's lecture (Appendix D) with Jan's presentation. Point out the inconsistencies, if any.
8. Compare the Panaudit Purchase Proposal (Appendix C) with the microcomputer security policy statement (Appendix E) that Jan and Gerry wrote. Are they consistent? If not, submit—in writing—changes you suggest should be made to the policy statement. Support your proposal.
9. What should Jan do now? Why?

EXHIBIT 7   Jan Paules's Memo to President Harry Dicker

MEMO: June 29, 1988

TO: Harry H. Dicker, President

FROM: Jan D. Paules, Assistant Vice President/Internal Auditor

RE: Memorandum R 67-1

The estimated <u>annual</u> cost associated with the policy will be zero. The initial cost, however, will include the following:

$250   Password programming

200   Surge suppressor

The cost of the two tape backup systems will be investigated by the committee.
The members of the committee were selected for the following reasons:

Gerry T. Maloney—His department controls two personal computers and the standing mainframe.

Hal C. Ross—His department has two personal computers and will be obtaining the network system.

Bill G. Forrest—He is in charge of requisitioning supplies.

Jan D. Paules—I oversee internal controls within the Association.

We really did not consider rotation of the members of this committee. If you would like to incorporate rotation into the provision, we have no objections. In addition, if you feel anyone else should be selected as a member, please notify me.
Should you have any further questions concerning this matter, please contact me.

JDP:jnm

EXHIBIT 8   Paul Kain's Response to the Proposed Security Policy Statement

Management Control

Suggest expanding the scope of the standing committee to include sharing and distribution of software and templates. This will encourage effective use of existing programs and template applications, compatibility of equipment, and equipment standards.

The committee should include representatives from all departments of the Association including:

Branches.

Savings.

Lending.

Internal Audit.

Accounting.

Marketing.

Members on the committee should have experience or attend the outside training discussed in the training section.

Data Security

How will the password software be incorporated into the floppy disk–based PCs? Generally, the DOS "COMMAND" file is attached to the software to be booted. Would the program, then, prevent use of particular software or equipment? Could it be overridden by using other operating system software?

Physical Security

Surge suppression will prevent losses to valuable equipment and should be used for all PCs and electronic equipment. UPS (uninterrupted power supply) systems could be considered for key PCs such as in personnel or the master terminal for the upcoming network. This would prevent loss of volatile data.

Data Backup

Tape backup systems are compatible for hard disk systems. Marketing's PC is floppy based. Procedures for documentation backup, and storage should be sufficient to protect the data.

Data File Storage

Access to files at DataVault is assigned to individuals. Who will assign and monitor access cards and register individuals with DataVault? Branches will have access to obtain operating disks for the Olivetti processors.

Systems and Data Integrity

The greatest threat to computer systems is internal (80 percent of security breaches) through errors, omissions, and deliberate actions by individuals with authorized access. Systems are vulnerable through power lines, communication lines (another point for surge suppressors), and software commands. A single command can be placed in the AUTOEXEC.bat command file that will erase the directory for stored files. These viruses can be prompted by the loading procedure or any time by the PCs internal clock. Software written by unknown sources and downloaded from other networks (via modem) should not be run on the Association's PCs and should be policy. This would also apply to pirated copies of software.

Appendix A   Memorandum R 67-1

FEDERAL HOME LOAN BANK SYSTEM
OFFICE OF REGULATORY POLICY, OVERSIGHT, AND SUPERVISION

M E M O R A N D U M   R 67-1

TO: Professional Staff—   March 22, 1988
    Examinations and Supervision

FROM: Darrel W. Dochow   End-User Computing

Attached is a joint issuance by the Federal Financial Institutions Examination Council (FFIEC) on End-User Computing Risks. End-user computing refers to the development and operation of data processing applications by the traditional end-users of data processing systems rather than by a centralized Information Services staff. The increased power and capabilities of microcomputers, small mainframes, and/or other computer activities terminals have encouraged the growth in end-user computing activities and have made them a key component of information processing in many financial institutions.

The implementation of these new information delivery and processing activities has often outpaced the implementation of adequate controls. This issuance is meant to provide guidance to management for evaluating potential risks, and for implementing adequate control practices and responsibilities in end-user computing environments.

It is expected that management in each FSLIC-insured institution utilizing end-user computer systems will implement controls consistent with guidelines offered in this issuance.

Roberta Wagner for
Executive Director

Attachment

Please distribute to State supervisory authorities.

Federal Financial Institutions Examination Council

1776, G Street, NW, Suite 701 • Washington, DC 20006

Joint Interagency Issuance on
End-User Computing Risks

TO: Chief Executive Officers of all Federally Supervised Financial Institutions, Senior
Management of each FFIEC Agency, and all Examining Personnel

PURPOSE:

The purpose of this issuance is to alert management of each financial institution of the
risks associated with end-user computing operations and to encourage the implementation
of sound control policies over such activities.

BACKGROUND:

In recent years, microcomputers, or "personal computers," have become more prominent
in the business environment. They are now being used, not only as word processors and
access devices to other computers, but also as powerful stand-alone computers. As such,
information processing has evolved well beyond the traditional central environment to
distributed or decentralized operations. This trend has offered substantial benefits in productivity, customization, and information access. However, it also has meant that those
control procedures, previously limited to the central operations, must be reapplied and
extended to the "end-user" level.

CONCERNS:

Technology, using microcomputers as end-user computing devices, has taken data processing out of the centralized control environment and introduced the computer-related
risks in new areas of the institutions. However, the implementation of these new information delivery and processing networks has outpaced the implementation of controls.
Basic controls and supervision of these computer activities often have not been introduced,
or expected, at the end-user level. The technological advantages, expediency, and cost
benefits of end-user computing has been the primary focus. Recognition of the increased
exposures and the demands for expanded information processing controls has lagged. These
concerns for data protection and controlled operations within the end-user environments
must be addressed to minimize risks from:

- Incorrect management decisions.
- Improper disclosure of information.
- Fraud.
- Financial loss.
- Competitive disadvantage.
- Legal or regulatory problems.

End-user computing is recognized as a productive and appropriate operational activity. However, control policies for data security and computer operations, consistent with those for centralized information processing functions, need to address the additional risks represented in the end-user computing operations.

Institution management is encouraged to evaluate the associated risks with its end-user computing networks and other forms of distributed computer operations. Control practices and responsibilities to manage these activities should be incorporated into an overall corporate information security policy. Such a policy should address areas such as:

- Management controls.
- Data security.
- Documentation.
- Data/file storage and backup.
- Systems and data integrity.
- Contingency plans.
- Audit responsibility.
- Training.

Responsibilities for the acquisition, implementation, and support of such networks should be clearly established.

The appendix to this issuance provides more detail regarding the risks and suggested controls for end-user computing and other computer-related activities. Additional control recommendations can be referenced in the FFIEC EDP Examination Handbook.

POLICY:

It is the responsibility of the board of directors to ensure that appropriate corporate policies, which identify management responsibilities and control practices for all areas of information processing activities, have been established. The existence of such a "corporate information security policy," the adequacy of its standards, and the management supervision of such activities will be evaluated by the examiners during the regular supervisory reviews of the institution.

APPENDIX
RISKS AND CONTROLS IN END–USER COMPUTING

Microcomputers, in the end-user computing operations, are being used basically for three purposes:

1. As word processors.
2. As communications terminals with other computers (to transmit or receive information in their databases).
3. As stand-alone computer processors.

These three functions require different control objectives, based on the risks associated with the activity. Each function requires certain operational type controls such as physical security, logical security, and file backup. However, the more pronounced risks involve those operations using microcomputers as stand-alone processors.

While word processing and terminal communications also require strong controls, programming support for the operating software and applications systems generally remains centralized or is a vendor responsibility. In end-user computing, the user is often engaged in program development, in addition to information processing. This may involve the creation of programmed software from an original design or building customized routines from specialized vendor software. Regardless , the control techniques for the programming, its testing, and its documentation are necessary to ensure the integrity of the software and the production of accurate data.

In addition to the programming activity, the end-user environment supports computer processing, which may be totally separate from centralized controls. Information may be downloaded from the main databases and reprocessed by the end-user. Data may also be originated for processing in this structure. Regardless of the source, the resulting information is relied upon by management for decisions impacting corporate strategies and customer relationships. The integrity of the data becomes no less important than had the data been produced through more sophisticated computer processes. Likewise, the need for control at the micro level remains equally important.

IMPACTS

The failure to properly implement a uniform set of controls on the end-users of microcomputers, consistent with those controls required in a mainframe data center, can create two broad categories of risks:

1. The corruption or loss of data and/or program software.
2. Impediments to the efficient operation and management of the institution.

The quality of data is paramount to the successful management of any institution. Should the data, or the systems which produce that data, be corrupted, whether intentionally or unintentionally, financial loss is highly probable. Data corruption could result from three basic causes: error, fraud, or system malfunction.

In addition to accuracy, management requires the timely availability of data. Inefficiencies, caused by poor operational controls, can further impede the production of information and result in financial loss. Regardless of the source, poor quality information and operations can adversely impact the institution in a number of ways:

- Management Error — Inaccurate or incomplete data can adversely influence institution management decisions. Delays in information availability can also adversely impact corporate strategies.
- Inadvertent Disclosures — Human error, fraud, or system malfunction may result in proprietary institution data, customer data, or program software being disclosed to unauthorized persons.
- Competitive Disadvantage — Problems in the production of accurate and timely information can place the institution at a competitive disadvantage. Delivery of services, customer confidence, and management decisions could be impaired.
- Legal Problems — Errors in the production of data or wrongful disclosure of data may result in legal actions against the institution by its customers, consumer groups, competitors, and regulators.
- Regulatory Problems — Failure to produce timely and accurate data can cause the institution to be in violation of regulatory requirements, subjecting the institution to regulatory penalties.
- Monetary losses to the institution can arise from deliberate manipulation of the data

(fraud), missing or erroneous data (leading to costly incorrect decisions), or various inefficiencies in the operation of the system.

CONTROLS

There are basic controls that should be present in any level of computer operations. These controls should already be present at the centralized data center. The evolution of microcomputer-based systems has not eliminated the need for these basic controls, but has shifted the focus of control to the end-user level.

Some of these basic control standards that need to be implemented in microcomputer-based systems are:

Policies and Procedures

Control requirements for microcomputer use need to be addressed by management in its internal policies and procedures. Policies and procedures should be in writing and should define what steps are to be taken to protect the institution's microcomputer systems. Management should also designate responsibility within the institution to monitor microcomputer system acquisition and use. The purpose of this function should be to help prevent redundant uses of microcomputer systems and to ensure that there is the required degree of compatibility among hardware and software systems in use throughout the institution.

Program Development and Testing

Before a new system is developed or purchased, the user should have a clear understanding of the specific needs being addressed by the proposed new system. Alternatives should be reviewed by the user and analyst to ensure that the best solution is selected. Development should be done with the aim of producing a system that is easily modified and maintained by someone other than the original developer. Finally, the completed system should be subject to rigorous testing to provide assurance that the results produced are valid and reliable.

Program Changes

Just as with larger systems, microcomputer systems must be adapted to meet changing requirements and circumstances. Modified programs should be subject to many of the same controls as newly developed systems. Most important among these is the requirement that there be thorough testing of the modified system. In addition, accurate records should be maintained describing the change, the reasons for the change, and the person responsible for making the change.

Documentation

Documentation is a potential problem in microcomputer-based systems. There is a tendency for these systems to be highly personalized, with one person fully responsible for the development, testing, implementation, and operation of a set of programs. The successful use of a microcomputer-based system and the production of specialized data may depend on the continued presence of this one person. An adequate level of documentation helps to prevent an overreliance on the knowledge of this one person. This is particularly needed should revisions to programs be required. Documentation standards should define acceptable levels of program, operating, and user documentation. In addition, there should be an enforcement mechanism to guarantee compliance with standards.

Data Editing

The development or purchase of microcomputer systems should be done with adequate attention given to the need for data-editing routines. These routines are important to help ensure that data entering the system is error-free and not likely to result in erroneous output. This control is important whether the data is being manually entered into the microcomputer or electronically transferred or downloaded from another system. In the case of the data being uploaded to a mainframe, additional controls may be required at that level to guarantee the integrity of the data being transferred.

Input/Output Controls

Microcomputer systems that are used for the processing of information with a direct monetary impact on the institution or its customers may require that additional data controls be established. At a minimum, these controls may include the requirement that there be a segregation of duties between the input of information and the review of that information in processed form. This control may be extended to require that a formal reconcilement be done by the reviewer of the processed information. In more sensitive situations with a significant dollar impact, there may be a requirement that certain functions be performed under dual control. The need for these types of input and output controls should be established during the early stages of program development. These special requirements need to be described in detail in the program documentation package.

Physical Access Restrictions

The location of microcomputer systems outside of a physically secure data center can permit unauthorized access to programs and data files used on these systems. The use of physical access restrictions complements the logical access restrictions discussed below. Basic steps would include the secure storage of diskettes or other magnetic media containing the programs and data for a particular system. In addition, since documentation on what a system does and how it is being used can provide important information that can be used to compromise system security, this information should also be secured. Finally, there should be adequate restrictions over physical access to the hardware itself, so that it is protected from unauthorized use, vandalism, and theft.

Logical Access Restrictions

Just as in larger application systems, the need exists to identify those individuals who will be permitted access to the microcomputer system's capabilities. In addition, there may be the need to differentiate between functions allowed for certain individuals, ranging from an inquiry capability for many persons to an override and correction capability for a few supervisory personnel. Normally, these restrictions will be in the form of password controls. Standard password-related control procedures such as frequent changes and reporting of exception conditions need to be established to provide for effective access restrictions.

Backup and Contingency Planning

For each operational system, adequate plans should be made and precautions taken to ensure that users can adequately recover from damage to the hardware, software, and data. For some systems, inability to process during recovery may mean that work can be held for later processing. For other systems, a manual backup may be appropriate. For some time-critical, highly automated systems, arrangements may have to be made for data reconstruction or for processing on other hardware. At a minimum, for all systems, there should be secure and remote backup storage of data files and programs. Beyond this, the backup and contingency requirements for individual systems may differ and need to be addressed separately.

Audit

The audit area should serve as an independent control reviewing microcomputer use throughout the institution. Audit involvement in microcomputer systems may begin at a general level with a review for compliance with the internal policies and procedures discussed above and may extend to detailed testing in particular areas such as the use of logical access controls. Audit procedures and work programs should be expanded to provide for adequate coverage of microcomputer systems. Responsibility for microcomputer auditing should be clearly assigned and plans for microcomputer audits should be built into the audit schedule.

It should be recognized that this list of controls is not all-inclusive of methods to manage risk. Each computer operation, whether centralized or end-user, possesses different characteristics and possibly some specialized risks. Control practices must be sufficient to minimize such risks. These recommended control features are considered <u>fundamental</u> to sound information processing.

Appendix B   Paul Kain's Committee Contribution

Memorandum R 67-1 indicates that the management of each FSLIC-insured institution is expected to implement controls for the development and operation of data processing applications by the traditional end-users of data processing systems. The controls in the form of a policy should address areas such as:

1. Management controls.
2. Data security.
3. Documentation.
4. Data/file storage and backup.
5. Systems and data integrity.
6. Contingency plans.
7. Audit responsibility.
8. Training.

The appendix to the memorandum notes that microcomputers are used for three purposes:

1. Word processing.
2. Communications with other terminals.
3. Stand-alone computer processing.

It further states that: "the more pronounced risks involve those operations using micro-computers as stand-alone processors."

It is difficult to discern what is meant by stand-alone computer processing, since all microcomputer or PC computing involves stand-alone processing. Stand-alone computer processing of data for individuals is the reason for the increasing use of PCs. The contents of the memo are generally vague or overbroad in the discussion of computer application, risks, and controls. Consequently, the memorandum cannot support the basis for policy.

A general knowledge of system components is necessary in order to establish an effective policy that addresses the risks of microcomputer processing and provides realistic controls. The overview that follows discusses the microcomputer system in terms of its components and applications.

END–USER COMPUTING

A computer is a system composed of three basic components — input, processing, and output. An input device is used to enter data, which the system processes according to instructions contained in a program. Then the computer produces some usable output, which can be either displayed on a CRT screen, printed, or saved on permanent media such as floppy disks.

INPUT DEVICE

An input device is used to enter both data and programs into the computer in a form recognizable by the computer. The two most common input devices are keyboards and disk drives. The keyboard is similar to a typewriter keyboard, except that it has additional keys required for computer operation. A disk drive provides permanent storage for data and programs on a magnetic medium.

An operating system is necessary to get the computer to interact with input and output devices. A small program stored in permanent memory and installed by the manufacturer automatically loads the operating system. The operating system is a series of programs used by the computer to manage its own operation as well as allow the user to interact easily with the computer through various input and output devices such as disk drives, printers, monitors, and keyboards.

PROCESSING

The processing of data is accomplished through an application program, which consists of a series of instructions that interact with the operating system and the various hardware components. The application program must be loaded into the computer's memory after the operating system.

Processing of data is accomplished through a microprocessor, which is the heart of the computer system. It stores the program instructions in its own language into memory and then processes all the data that arrives through the input device. Processing operations involve mathematical calculations and logical operations.

There are two types of memory: ROM (read only memory) and RAM (random access memory). Memory consists of a number of silicon chips containing thousands of electric circuits. Data and program instructions stored in ROM cannot be altered by the user. RAM is the primary storage of the computer. The more memory the computer has, the larger the applications programs can be and the more work the computer can process at any one time. The major problem with RAM memory is stored data is lost when the current is turned off.

OUTPUT.

Data is usually in the form of meaningful information once it has been processed. Processed data is printed as hardcopy and is usually stored for future use on magnetic media. The most common output devices are printers, disk drives, and video monitors.

THE BASIC SYSTEM

The basic computer system consists of three components: a central processing unit (CPU), a keyboard, and a monitor. The actual processing of data occurs in the CPU. The CPU performs all processing and calculations and controls all other functions. The CPU consists of three main parts: primary storage, or memory; the control unit; and the arithmetic and logic unit. The keyboard is the main input device for data that has to be entered manually. It has three distinct parts: alpha keys, including some special keys; numeric keys, and function keys. The video monitor (VDT or CRT) is the least critical part of the basic system. The monitor shows the keyboard input and is used by the software to prompt for data input and displays the output generated by the CPU. Video monitor output is referred to as softcopy output because it is temporary and available only to the end-user.

HARDWARE PERIPHERALS

Printers

Serial Printers.   Serial printers form one character at a time as the print head moves across the paper. Printing can occur in one direction or in both directions. Types of serial printers are:

1. Dot-matrix.
2. Daisy wheel.
3. Ink-jet.
4. Thermal.
5. Laser.

Line Printers.   Line printers form one line at a time.

Page Printers.   Page printers are high-speed nonimpact printers capable of printing a page at a time.

Buffers

A buffer consists of memory chips that hold data from the computer before it is printed. A buffer allows the CPU to engage in more computing time because it does not need to supply output in conjunction with the slower speed of the printer.

Cables

Ribbons

Covers

Disk Drives

Disk drives are peripheral devices used for secondary storage of programs and data and are connected to the computer.

Floppy Disk Drives.   Floppy disks are manufactured in 3-inch, 5-inch, and 8-inch sizes. They are made of mylar plastic and shaped like a 45-rpm record. A floppy disk is encased in a jacket with a hole in the center where the disk mounts on the driving device. A smaller hole near the center is used as a timing mechanism.

RAM Disks.   RAM disks allow the partitioning of the RAM to use as an equivalent to a floppy disk. This pseudodisk increases operating speed significantly as the program does not have to swap data between the disk drive and the memory. The main drawback is that all information is lost when the power is turned off.

Hard Disk Drives.   Hard disk drives are similar to floppy disks but are a more permanent form of storage device. Hard disks usually remain in the computer and data and programs are almost instantly available. They have more storage capacity and are found in sizes of 5 megabytes, 10 megabytes, 20 megabytes, and larger. The disadvantage of the hard disk is that it cannot be taken out of the computer to use on another computer.

Tape Drives.   Tape drives are secondary storage devices that closely resemble a tape recorder. Information is placed on them in sequential form and retrieval of the information is slow and cumbersome. Tape drives are commonly used for backup of data and programs on a hard disk. A streaming tape drive, which runs at high speed, creates a mirror image on tape of the data on the hard disk. This procedure takes approximately four minutes for 10 megabytes of data. This method of backup is relatively inexpensive.

RAM Expansion Cards

Input Peripherals

Mouse.

Touch-Sensitive Screen.

Optical Character Reader.

Modems.   Modems are used for communicating between computers. Short for modulate and demodulate, they translate digital signals from the computer to analog signals for telephone communication, and then back again.

APPLICATION SOFTWARE

Word processing
Electronic spreadsheets
Database management systems (DBMS)
Business software
    Accounting systems
    Inventory control
    Personnel management
    Mortgage processing
    Training
    Transaction processing
    Platform automation
    Time management
    Data communication
    PC networks
        Wide area networks
            CompuServe
            FHLB
            Dow Jones News/Retrieval
        Local area networks (LANs)
    Financial analysis

POLICY DEVELOPMENT

The variety of uses that a single PC can handle poses the greatest difficulty in establishing a specific policy. For example, one PC could perform all of the above listed functions in a day. Applications can be changed by loading different software. Integrated software allows changes to applications to be activated through a series of keystrokes. However, there are common activities, and it is these activities that the policy should address:

1. Software for operating systems and applications are generic. Only one in-house written program exists (LIP program written in BASIC). This program is being phased out in favor of a vendor supplied program.
2. PCs are used for more than one application or have the ability to be used for more than

one application. User familiarity with the operating systems and application software will result in multiple applications for all PCs.

3. All PCs are IBM PC compatible but little other commonality exists. This is true in regard to CPU, memory, storage, and peripherals.

4. Software applications are loaded from floppy disks or hard disks depending on application.

5. Data is stored on hard disk and/or floppy disks.

6. Spreadsheet template software is used for both individual processing of information and institution reports. However, personal processing of data is the most common use.

7. The operating system is Microsoft DOS; however, the versions vary from 1.0 to 3.0. Software designed for one version may not operate with another.

8. There is no central management information systems (MIS) individual. Systems and applications are purchased and managed independently. Consequently, there are no controls over copyright protection, no benefits from the learning curve, and no interaction among users.

Central control will require maintaining a list of (1) applications and software used with each PC; (2) the individuals using the particular PCs; (3) the application software used by each individual; (4) the peripherals connected to each PC; (5) copies of the user agreements for each vendor supplied program; (6) all reports provided for general department and/or Association use; and (7) location and description of each basic system including the total memory, internal cards, and storage devices.

Data similar to the above should also be compiled for the dedicated word processors, Olivetti processors, and SLIMS minicomputer.

This data should be confirmed and updated quarterly. It will provide for monitoring of:

1. Hardware security.
2. Copyright adherence.
3. Reporting scope and integrity.
4. Individual access.
5. Applications.
6. PC processing requirements.
7. Storage devices and backup required.

Appendix C   Proposal for Panaudit Plus Software

Software/Vendor Overview

Panaudit software was released by Pansophic Systems, Inc., in 1979 as a general software package for auditing. Auditors used the product to extract, evaluate, and validate data from computerized files during financial, operational, and data processing audits. Panaudit Plus was released in October 1984 as an upgrade of Panaudit and today is considered one of the leading audit software packages (see Attachments 1 and 2).

Panaudit Plus consists of prewritten auditing routines and the Easytrieve Plus lan-

ATTACHMENT 1 Fortune 1000 Market Share Audit Software

Supplier (Product)		Non F1000 Installed Sites		Fortune 1000 Installed Sites	
		Number of Sites	Percent*	Number of Sites	Percent*
Carleton	(Auditec)	17	5	7	4
Cullinet			21		32
	(Auditor)	22		18	
	(EDP-Auditor)	46		49	
Dylakor	(DYL-Audit)	30	10	26	12
Pansophic	(Panaudit)	170	54	95	45
TSI	(Audit-Analyz)	19	6	11	5
Other			4		2
Arthur-And	(Audex)	5		1	
Informatics	(MarkIV/Audit)	1		1	
Sage	(Cars)	7		2	
Total sites		317	100	210	100

*Basis for graphic representation.

August 1985
CIG-8510

Source: *The Intelligence Report,* Computer Intelligence Corp., La Jolla, Calif., August 1985.

guage. The auditing routines (MACROS) include statistical sampling, generalized audit, and computer system analysis; all are easy to use and provide a wide variety of report formats (see Attachment 3). These factors greatly simplify routine audit tasks and reduce the time required to perform the tasks manually. The Easytrieve Plus language permits the auditor to create customized programs for unique audit tests. Easytrieve Plus is user-friendly and does not require the use of extensive commands nor rigorous formats. Hence, nontechnical auditors can write their own programs. With our on-line capability, the Audit department will control the activities of the Computer Assisted Audit Technique. In addition to the audit function use of Panaudit, data processing could produce reports more efficiently for current department user requests. Also, Pansophic has a product, EZ/KEY, to prompt users of Panaudit Plus for the correct commands; it provides faster results for infrequent or inexperienced users.

The biggest advantage of using audit software is that less time is required to evaluate, select, and validate transactions. The time saved can be spent interpreting test results and developing workable solutions to improve control.

Audit findings could lead to substantial dollar savings and/or increased productivity. Direct savings will be realized from audit findings that would have been too expensive and time-consuming without audit software.

Software Selection

There are several audit software packages available; however the two most popular are EDP Auditor/Culprit[1] versus the Easytrieve Plus from Pansophic. Therefore:

---

[1]Culprit is a report generating language that eliminates the need to manually prepare reports of EDP auditor's findings.

ATTACHMENT 2   Fortune 1000 Market Share Audit Software (graph)

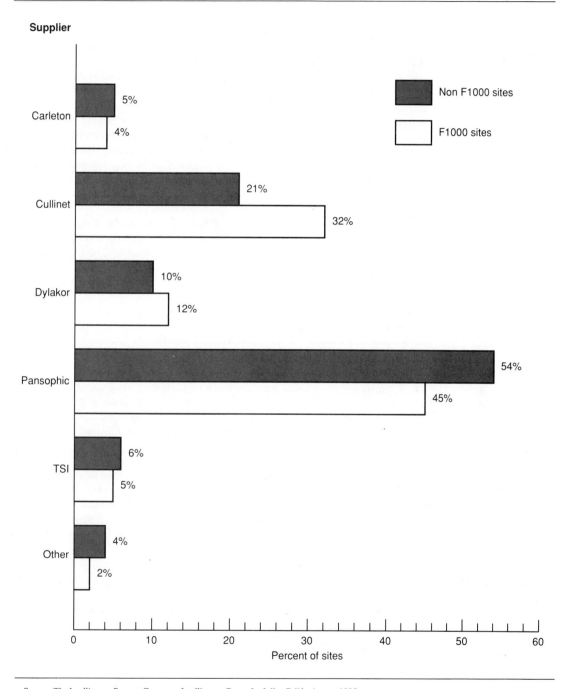

Source: *The Intelligence Report,* Computer Intelligence Corp., La Jolla, Calif., August 1985.

ATTACHMENT 3 Summary of Prewritten Audit Routines

Generalized Audit Routines	*Statistical Sampling Routines*
• Integrity tests: Assist the auditor in verifying the validity of computerized files. An example would be duplicate transactions testing. • File comparisons: Allow comparison record by record. When a mismatch occurs, both records are printed to an exception report. • Date and time: Provides for computations of elapsed time and conversion to numerous date formats. • Numeric: Performs mathematical functions such as exponentiation, calculation of square root, standard deviation, and generation of random numbers. • Testing data generation: Provides the ability to create test data in user-defined formats. • Miscellaneous: Perform various functions such as aging analyses and data conversions.	• Distribution analysis: Determines the frequency of occurrence of specified values or transaction types. Graphic reports illustrate the results to facilitate sampling design and selection methods. • Statistical sampling: Performs various statistical sampling methods including attribute, variable, discovery, interval, random, and stratified. These methods conform to generally accepted auditing standards (GAAS) established by the American Institute of Certified Public Accountants (AICPA). • Statistical forecasting: Uses both linear and multiple regression as the basis to determine estimates. These methods are useful to accurately evaluate populations with a large number of small transactions.

---

1. We reviewed results of a benchmark test of Culprit versus Easytrieve Plus by a PULSE (Pansophic users learning and sharing exchange) users group member. The test compared performance when processing large volumes of data. Results showed that Easytrieve Plus was easier to use and more flexible; also it took less time to create and process the test program.

2. We reviewed the Datapro Research Corporation evaluation of Panaudit Plus software; Datapro is the *Consumer Reports* of data processing. Panaudit scored well in all three areas considered: synopsis, analysis, and characteristics. Generally, Panaudit Plus operates on any data maintained on a mainframe. Data must be defined by creating a dictionary that Panaudit Plus can understand; our Data Processing group has agreed to develop a dictionary because they need one if they are going to use Easytrieve Plus.

Software Benefits

Computer-assisted audit techniques increase the auditor's productivity. Panaudit Plus allows the Internal Audit staff to perform computer-assisted audits for the external audits, saving time and reducing the audit fee.

Audit software, when used effectively, can:

1. Help the auditor evaluate and select more accurate test samples.
2. Reduce the need for manually intensive tasks such as comparing and sorting.
3. Help the auditor evaluate and quantify errors and audit findings.
4. Eliminate the need to manually prepare summary documents, reports, and conformation letters.
5. Improve the ability to monitor sensitive systems for unusual transactions.

Recommendation and Costs

Panaudit Plus/Easytrieve Plus seems to be easier to use and requires less computer time than EDP Auditor/Culprit so we recommend Panaudit Plus/Easytrieve Plus. The department's objective is to provide every internal auditor (financial, EDP, and operational) the opportunity to maximize their productivity using computer-assisted techniques. The audit staff is more likely to use these resources if they are simple to implement and provide accurate results. The Pansophic products seem to meet these goals. Total cost is $30,000 plus $4,500 (15 percent) annually (beginning the second year) for maintenance.

Appendix D   Miles Wilson's Comments to the MBA Class before Jan's Arrival

"EDP auditing grew from quality control sections within Information Systems departments and from external requirements. The origin of the audit function often controlled the audit structure in many organizations. Those that originated from quality control were more active in systems development, usually reported to the head of IS, and most often came from a systems and programming background.

"Among the major reasons for an externally imposed EDP audit function were regulatory requirements, the Foreign Corrupt Practices Act, *Statement on Auditing Standards No. 48,* and the increased negligence liability exposure after the equity funding scandal. Auditors, whose functions originated from external sources, were most often financial auditors with additional computer training or experience, were not involved in systems development, and reported to the board of director's audit committee.

"You recall that earlier in the course we had a panel of five information executives from large corporations speak to us; they were unanimous in their recommendation of EDP auditing as a career field—none recommended it! They felt that it was too limiting and did not have good advancement potential. Of 30 firms in the local area I surveyed last semester, asking about the requirements for an EDP auditor, one executive felt that the professional designation CISA (Certified Information Systems Auditor) was desirable in conjunction with the CPA, while 17 felt that the CPA alone was desirable. CISA exam components are in a handout I'll distribute after class (see Attachment 1).

"EDP auditing may be difficult to staff if the role of the auditor extends beyond

---

ATTACHMENT 1   CISA Exam Components

Category	Weightings (percent)
1. Application systems controls review.	19
2. Data integrity review.	13
3. Systems development life cycle review.	5
4. Application development review.	9
5. General operational procedures controls review.	12
6. Security review.	14
7. Systems software review.	5
8. Maintenance review.	6
9. Acquisition review.	3
10. Data processing resource management.	5
11. Information systems audit management.	9
	100

---

compliance auditing to operational auditing. Operational auditing requires an assessment as to whether the procedure could have been accomplished more efficiently or effectively and requires very experienced and knowledgeable auditors with significant business know-how. The responses of the executives in my survey lead me to doubt that many organizations would be able to find or compensate employees with the skills needed to be operational EDP auditors.

"Applicants with the CISA would have an interest in EDP auditing; therefore, the CISA association, Electronic Data Processing Auditors Association, may be a good source of prospective employees. If one was to train an auditor internally, the question becomes, should I select a financial auditor (CPA) and give that person additional computer training, or vice versa? To be able to perform operational audits, a DP expert would need extensive cross-training in auditing plus some work in functional areas. Auditors must be able to move from auditing to management positions, or the type of person likely to be a successful auditor will not apply.

"I recommend most entry level EDP auditors come from a financial auditor (CPA) background with computer science—not MIS—training. I prefer computer science training to MIS because the job requirements relate more to hardware and software technical requirements and financial controls. An EDP auditor would have to move to a functional area and back to auditing to develop skills necessary for middle-level EDP auditing.

"The external auditor (CPA audit firm) is concerned with adherence to *SAS 48*, which requires answers to four major questions:

1. Are there adequate internal controls, and can the auditor rely on the system output?
2. Can the independent auditor rely on the output, in lieu of other costly and time-consuming audit procedures?
3. Does the function generate data and produce reports that truly serve management's current information needs?
4. Is the IS function efficient and effective in terms of both cost and utility?

"In addition, the Foreign Corrupt Practices act requires that companies subject to the SEC Act of 1934 maintain an adequate system of internal controls. The act requires reasonable assurance that:

1. Transactions are executed in accordance with management's authorization.
2. Transactions are recorded so as to permit preparation of financial statements in accordance with GAAP or other criteria applicable to such statements and to maintain accountability for assets.
3. Access to assets is permitted only in accordance with management's authorization.
4. Recorded assets are compared with existing assets at reasonable intervals, and appropriate action is taken with respect to any differences.

"More progressive companies audit information systems to verify their costs, benefits, and user acceptability. Generally, interest by senior management motivated these audits; their objectives were to have a more efficient and effective IS department and a record of cost estimates.

"That concludes my introductory lecture. Let's save your questions until after Miss Paules finishes her presentation; I expect she'll go into quite a bit of detail and will answer many questions you have at this point. Please be back here in 10 minutes."

Appendix E   Proposed Security Policy Statement

MEMO: June 27, 1988

TO: Harry H. Dicker, President

FROM: Jan D. Paules, Assistant Vice President/Internal Auditor, and Gerry T. Maloney, Jr., Assistant Vice President/Controller

RE: Memorandum R 67-1

The R 67-1 committee has developed the following policies and procedures concerning personal computers and the minicomputer.

We are recommending that the following individuals serve on the standing committee:

Gerry T. Maloney

Jan D. Paules

Hal C. Ross

Bill G. Forrest

As stated in the policy, this committee would review any new requests for computers as well as review procedures manuals on existing computers.

We recommend the following implementation schedule for items addressed in the policy and procedures memorandum:

1. Developing passwords — three weeks after spending approval.
2. Developing individual operating procedures — September 1.
3. DataVault storage — August 1.

·4. Data backup (tape system) — September 1.

5. Training — September 1.

We are including the original memorandum with the procedures.

As indicated in R 67-1, management of each FSLIC-insured institution is expected to implement controls for the development and operation of data processing applications by the traditional end-users of data processing systems. The controls in the form of a policy should address areas such as:

1. Management control.
2. Data security.
3. Documentation.
4. Data/file storage and backup.
5. Systems and data integrity.
6. Contingency plans.
7. Audit responsibility.
8. Training.

We believe all items have been addressed.

Policies and procedures will be updated when the SLIMS Construction Lending/Project Control System is placed into effect. Implementation of this system is set for August 1. We also recommend a yearly reevaluation of this memorandum to ensure Association compliance.

If you have any questions, please do not hesitate to call.

JDP/GTM:jnm

Management Control

The memorandum states that management should designate responsibility within the institution to monitor microcomputer system acquisition and use. A standing committee should be formed to review any new requests for computers. The committee would question the individual and evaluate the purchase to insure the best compatibility with the user.

Data Security

Passwords will be incorporated on all personal computers as an internal control to restrict unauthorized use. A software package will be purchased and incorporated with the operating system of each PC. Managers will be responsible for assigning passwords for the systems under their control. It is recommended that passwords be changed every calendar quarter.

The security for the SLIMS software, that is, Financial Management System, Accounts Payable System, Lending Management System, and Micro Correction, is performed on two levels. First, specific terminals are prevented from performing applications within the software. Secondly, individuals are prevented from performing functions within the applications system. The security system consists of two parts: a user ID and a password. The user ID identifies a specific individual. In order to sign on to any applications system, a valid user ID must be specified. Once a valid user ID has been entered, the operator must then enter a password to access the specific routine desired. Currently, both a user ID and a password are being used in the software applications for accounting and lending. Security over the passwords can only be accessed through one terminal in the controller's office. This master list of user IDs and passwords are only accessible in hardcopy through this terminal.

Physical Security

Systems with security features, that is, locking keyboards, should be utilized on a daily basis. All future systems purchased should be required to have this minimum security feature. It is further recommended that all PCs currently in use be equipped with surge suppressors to prevent loss of data.

The Burroughs B900 hardware is secured in a locked room in the Accounting department. The system is powered off on a daily basis to prevent unauthorized use during off hours.

Documentation

All individuals with personal computers will be required to develop procedures that show how their machines operate and what type of data they are storing. All procedures should be reviewed by the standing committee to assure Association uniformity and completeness. A model procedures manual will be developed to aid association personnel in completing this requirement.

Data Backup

Employees should be aware that Association policy recommends backup after 20 minutes of continuous use. Backing up data during daily usage will be either on floppy disks or hard disks, depending on the type of equipment.

The committee recommends a tape backup system for those PC systems that are the most critical to the Association. The systems are Accounting department (2 systems); Loan Servicing (1); Personnel (1); and Marketing (1).

In regard to the standing mainframe, the Accounting department is responsible for the daily backup of financial data. The Lending department is required to perform daily backup of the lending data. All backup performed should be logged. This should include the current day's date, tape number, date of the work being backed up, and the operator's initials.

Data/File Storage

An important consideration is off-premises data storage. All Association personnel should store all templates and original program files at DataVault. Data files will be picked up on a weekly basis by DataVault. The importance of correct labels and the maintenance of proper logs of the material that is sent to DataVault must be stressed. The labels should include department, individual using, and summary of the information stored. The logs should include when the disk was sent. Internal file documents will be developed so that the Association will have an audit trail to follow. These should be kept with the logs.

The daily backup should be stored at night in the Mortgage Servicing vault. This will keep the disks in a fireproof environment when they are not being used.

Systems and Data Integrity

Software documentation and program enhancements are tested by the software vendor. We do not develop in-house programs. At the current time, this section was not applicable to Greater Metropolitan's system.

Contingency Plans

Greater Metropolitan has a written contract with SLIMS Corporation for disaster recovery. This agreement provides for installation of backup hardware, operating software, and the most current month-ending file backup.

Greater Metropolitan also has a written contract with DataVault for off-premises storage of disks and files.

Audit Responsibility

It will be a future audit function to perform annual audits on compliance of the Association's policies and procedures concerning personal computers. The audit will review computer logs, proper documentation, and all procedures manuals.

Training

It should be an Association policy that all individuals acquiring a personal computer attend for at least one day an outside training class or seminar relating to computer use. The Association's polices on security, use, and storage of data with a personal computer or word processor should be incorporated into the training manual.

Chapter 10

Multinational IS Issues

INTRODUCTION

"The rate of change in technology has been almost exponential since the 1950s, and particularly since the 1970s. . . . their [businesses'] survival depends on their ability to adapt to technological change."[1]

New competitors, especially Japan, have capitalized on low wages and costs and are now competing very successfully on the basis of technology. American firms—such as IBM and DEC—are collaborating to meet the threat.[2]

Many other American companies are exploring foreign markets, using information gathered from various sources (international organizations, foreign government agencies, international publications, and U.S. Department of Commerce publications).[3]

KEY ISSUES

Securing large markets overseas, to replace lost market share at home, is not easy; issues to be decided include the following from Cash, McFarlan, McKenney, and Vitale:[4]

---

[1]Tammy A. Wallett and Kumar Chittipeddi, "Global Competitiveness and the Japanese: Strategy Implications for U.S. Managers" (Northeast DSI 1989 Proceedings, 18th Annual Regional Conference, Baltimore, Maryland, March 30–31, 1989), p. 108.

[2]Wallett and Chittipeddi, "Global Competitiveness," p. 108.

[3]Wallett and Chittipeddi, "Global Competitiveness," p. 108.

[4]James I. Cash, F. W. McFarlan, J. L. McKenney, and M. R. Vitale, *Corporate Information Systems Management: Text and Cases,* 2nd. ed., Chapter 10 (paragraph subtitles) (Homewood, Ill.: Richard D. Irwin, 1988).

Diversity Between Countries.   Sociopolitical, language, local constraints, economic, currency, autonomy, and national infrastructure.

National IT Environments.   IT professional staff availability, central telecommunications, national IT strategy, level of IT sophistication, size of local market, data export control, technological awareness, trade union environment, and border opportunities.

Corporate Factors Affecting IT Requirements.   Nature of firm's business, strategic impact of IT, corporate organization, company technical and control characteristics, effects of geography and size of company, economic analysis, and other considerations.

Multinational IT Policy Issues. Communication and data management standards, central hardware/software concurrence or approval, central software development, IT communications, staff planning, consulting services, central IT processing support, and technology appraisal program.

PROBLEMS OF MULTINATIONAL IS

Our cases, up to now, described real situations with real problems, such as inexperienced IS/DP managers; confrontations between users and developers; conflicts between headquarters and field organizations; disagreements between vendors and clients; and battles over computer system development priorities between functional area VPs.

On the international scene, we now add difficulties inherent to differences in language, culture, political climate, laws and customs, standards, economies, staffing, and workday.[5]

JAPAN—VALUES AND CULTURAL TRAITS

Since Japan is considered a major competitor by the U.S. electronics industry (which includes computers, computer parts such as memory chips, television sets, and VCRs), it might be useful to review key Japanese values and cultural traits different from our own. Included are group affiliation and teamwork, commitment to long-term relationships, intense nationalism, patience, respect for individual dignity or face, emphasis on education, and the preeminence of work over rec-

---

[5]Charles S. Parker, *Management Information Systems: Strategy and Action,* Chapter 20 (New York; McGraw-Hill, 1989).

reation. Decision making in corporations emphasizes participation, both top-down and bottom-up. When negotiating with external businesspeople, the Japanese put more faith and trust in long-term relationships than in written agreements or legal precision.

And finally, "The history and culture of Japan emphasize a spirit of collectivism, a propensity toward making long-term decisions, an unusual sensitivity to preserving individual dignity, and a fierce competitiveness that has precluded the participation of women in the higher echelons of corporations."[6]

CONCLUSIONS

"To operate effectively, a corporation must have good information sources and excellent communications. . . . [L]eased-line networks, electronic mail, video-conferencing, voicegram systems, and computer links will become an essential facility of global corporations, vital to their fast, efficient functioning."[7]

As might be expected, however, the spread of networks, IS services, and corporate data across national boundaries will likely produce the same international IS/IT controversies that were encountered previously within national borders.

There will be some new controversies, however, such as free flow of information across borders versus international controls of information distribution.

It may be years before we truly have a "wired world,"[8] with equal communications to all peoples, because the barriers of history, tradition, culture, fear, and distrust are high and solid.

CASE: NIHON TELECOMMUNICATIONS EQUIPMENT COMPANY

In Case 10-1, Nihon, one of the Far East's largest independent data communications manufacturers and suppliers, has recently acquired an American firm, Hightech. Japanese executives, assisting in new system implementation, favor NEC, which they use in the Japanese home office; Hightech's IS manager prefers IBM.

---

[6]Wallett and Chittipeddi, "Global Competitiveness" p. 108.

[7]James Martin, *Telematic Society: A Challenge for Tomorrow,* Chapter 23 (Englewood Cliffs, N.J.: Prentice-Hall, 1981).

[8]Martin, *Telematic Society,* Chapter 23.

Case 10–1 Nihon Telecommunications Equipment Company

Harry Santura, IS manager of Nihon Telecommunications Equipment Company (NTEC), is concerned about the forced conversion and implementation problems caused by the changeover to a new hardware and software system. NTEC is a subsidiary, newly acquired by Nihon Telecommunications, Inc. (NTI), of Japan. Ever since NTI took over NTEC (formerly Hightech) in December 1984, it seemed that nothing but problems had occupied his time.

Recently, Nakamura (Harry's boss's boss) had been on him about the sad state of their DP audit capability. Santura had always known that a real audit function would be needed eventually, and he would have advised management of their shortcomings—with recommended changes—had he been asked.

Above all, Santura was disturbed by his loss of status within his own division. He felt it, and his employees sensed it. He didn't know how to deal with his damaged ego. He had to work with and try to manage his people as he had before the acquisition, while knowing he was no longer really in charge.

The IS staff used to feel like a vital part of the team. They were usually well informed about their department's goals and responsibilities. The involvement, "togetherness," and camaraderie was a thing of the past, in Harry's opinion.

Nor was he used to the constant feeling of pressure.

INDUSTRY SALES

Nihon (NTI), based in Japan, is a multinational company that manufactures data communications equipment. NTI purchased Hightech (now called NTEC) to facilitate its expansion overseas. Data communications equipment is one of the fastest growing segments of the telecommunications industry. Total sales for data communications equipment were $2.1 billion in 1984, which reflected a growth rate of about 30 percent during each of the previous two years; industry growth in the succeeding two years (1985 and 1986) was slightly higher. Data communications equipment sales are expected to exceed $5.4 billion by 1989 (see Exhibit 1).

This case was prepared by Pam Kues, Paul Biser, and Charles H. Devaud, Jr. Names, locations, and financial data have been disguised.

EXHIBIT 1   Data Communications Industry Projected Growth, 1982–1989

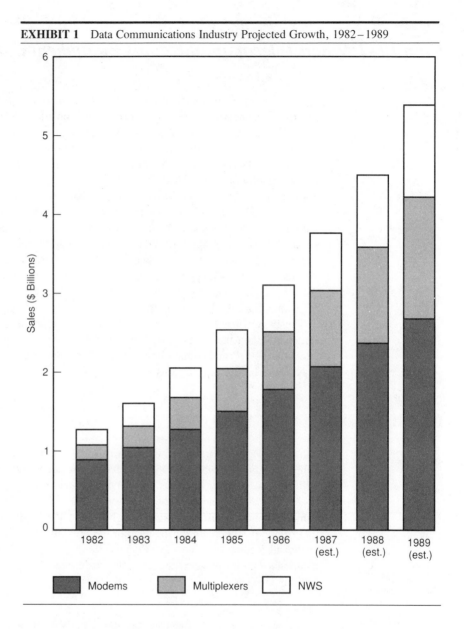

DATA COMMUNICATIONS EQUIPMENT (DCE)

The three main components of data communications equipment are modems, multiplexers, and network management systems (NWS).

A modem is a device used to convert digital signals from computers and their terminals to tone (analog) signals suitable for transmission over a telephone network. At the receiving end, the tone signals are converted back to digital signals by another modem.

A multiplexer allows two or more data messages to be transmitted simultaneously and received over a single transmission line.

A network management system continually gathers and analyzes information about all the characteristics of a network, converts the data into usable form, and enables an operator to actively manage the network. Modems accounted for about $1.3 billion of data communications equipment sales in 1984, increased about 15 percent in the following two years, and should increase by at least 20 percent annually between 1987 and 1990. Multiplexer sales totaled close to $405 million in 1984 and could be up as much as 30 to 35 percent per year through 1989. Network management systems represented $375 million in 1984 sales and should be 25 to 30 percent of total DEC revenues by the end of the decade.

INDUSTRY BACKGROUND

The data communications industry is not monopolized by any one company. The market is controlled by a half dozen companies with established positions. However, there are more than 70 modem companies and about 30 multiplexer vendors. After-tax margins for most companies in the industry are between 10 and 15 percent. Year-end returns on equity are generally between 10 and 20 percent.

Most companies should be able to achieve five-year earnings growth rates of 25 to 30 percent per year. The rewards are many, but companies in the data communications industry face a number of key risks. The first is failure to react to changes in the marketplace and to evolve new products; the result can be obsolescence and gross margin erosion.

Declining prices and increased competition are other risks to the industry. Failure to offer a broad product line and to manage growth round out the list of key risks. There are certain critical factors required for success in the data communications industry. Technological innovation in product development and cost-competitive manufacturing are very important. A successful data communications company must have strong distribution channels and services. Another key factor is a broad line of high-quality, reliable products. Finally, a large installed base of equipment is necessary if a company is to grow and prosper in the long run.

COMPANY BACKGROUND

Nihon Telecommunications, Inc., one of the Far East's largest independent data communications manufacturers and suppliers, is rapidly becoming a major force in the United States, which is the world's largest single marketplace for data communications equipment. NTI's network equipment provides a total networking capability, ranging from simple point-to-point connections to multinode, switching networks that can span a country, a continent, or the world. NTI also offers a broad range of modems, multiplexers, and network management systems.

NTI was founded in 1965 by Kesi Mashita, Hideri Shigatsu, and Saburu Nakamura, all directors of the company. Mashita is chairman of the board, Shigatsu is managing director, and Nakamura is the chief financial officer. NTI became a publicly listed company on the Tokyo Stock Exchange in 1976.

Initially, NTI sold factored communications and computer peripheral equipment. The company then established sales and customer engineering operations throughout Japan. In the early 1970s, the company began to design, develop, and manufacture its own innovative data communications systems.

These products were very successful. NTI grew rapidly and began to move into new markets. The company now has systems operating in more than 44 countries.

In the rest of the Far East, NTI operates through a network of distributors who provide the necessary sales and customer support to cover the diverse market. NTI has a 30 percent share in Nihon Telecon Systems (NTS) of Singapore, which was established in 1976.

A London office was authorized in 1980 to exploit the European markets.

HIGHTECH (NOW NTEC)

The Hightech philosophy centered around employee involvement, as the old company was committed to fully involving employees in the affairs of the company. There was freedom of information at Hightech. All employees were encouraged to take a close interest in the performance of the company, and there was an open-door policy at all levels of management. Today's management experts would say that Hightech employed a bottom-up approach to management.

Hightech Company was organized in 1950 to develop and manufacture custom electronic equipment. In 1954, Hightech began to manufacture modems and entered the data communications industry. The company was purchased by Jordan Chamblis in 1972. NTI purchased Hightech from Chamblis in December 1984. Hightech became Nihon Telecommunications Equipment Company (NTEC), a wholly owned subsidiary of NTI.

Currently, NTEC is concentrating on marketing. Before being acquired by NTI, Hightech's main focus was manufacturing. This shift from manufacturing to marketing is needed for successful penetration of the U.S. market. The sales force at NTEC has almost tripled since acquisition.

NTEC also has a strong commitment to research and development and invests approximately 10 percent of sales revenues in R&D.

NTEC employs approximately 1,400 people throughout North America. The sales and marketing headquarters of the company are located in Houston, Texas. The manufacturing facility is a short distance away in Galveston. A new 210,000 square foot manufacturing plant—in Houston—is scheduled for completion in late 1988. NTEC has 38 sales offices and 47 field service operations located in the United States and Canada.

The acquisition of Hightech should prove beneficial to both companies since their products are complementary. NTI is especially strong in multiplexer technology and NTEC in modem technology. With the United States representing about 50 percent of the total worldwide data communications equipment market, NTEC provides NTI with a manufacturing facility in the United States plus an entrenched sales and service network covering most of the United States and Canada. NTEC will be able to use NTI's well-established distribution channels to market its products outside of North America. Exhibits 2 and 3 show the financial results of NTI and Hightech for fiscal years 1983 and 1984. NTI (Japan) had sales of $114 million and net income of $8 million in fiscal 83/84. Total assets were $123 million at the end of that year. Hightech Company had net income of $5 million on sales of $76 million in fiscal 1984. Total assets were $82 million at the end of that year. The combined net income was $14 million on sales of $190 million. Combined total assets were $206 million. Similar figures for 1985 and 1986 were not provided by NTI.

IS AT HIGHTECH (PRE–NTEC)

The IS department of Hightech, before NTI took over, consisted of 16 employees (see Exhibit 4). The department was headed by Harry Santura, who reported to Karl Weber, the director of Finance. Santura's staff consisted of three administrators (Telecommunications), two senior programmer/analysts, three programmer/analysts, three programmers, one PC coordinator, one computer operations supervisor, and two computer operators.

The IS budget, $1,661,000, was approximately 2.2 percent of sales. All training was done internally. The training budget was $83,000, or 5 percent of the IS budget. The hardware was an IBM 4381, which was underutilized. Santura felt the system could handle the growth anticipated over the next five years. There was no formal DP audit function.

The software used by Hightech was varied. Most of the programs were developed in-house. However, some of the applications were purchased from outside vendors. The software was arranged in four groups: financial, sales, manufacturing, and inventory.

Two of the financial systems were purchased from outside vendors: the general ledger system was developed by McCormack Corporation and the payroll system was supplied by Payroll Plus, Inc. Accounts payable, accounts receivable, and fixed asset systems were developed in-house. The sales order system was an in-house system, also. In contrast, the complete manufacturing inventory system was purchased from National Software, Inc.

The systems that were bought from outside vendors had been modified to meet

EXHIBIT 2   NTI Income Statement

NTI
Combined Income Statement
Fiscal Years 1983 and 1984
(in thousands)

	1984			1983		
	Total	*NTI*	*Hightech*	*Total*	*NTI*	*Hightech*
Sales	$190,280	$114,168	$76,112	$124,134	$74,480	$49,654
Cost of sales	101,178	60,707	40,471	72,480	43,488	28,992
Gross profit	$ 89,102	$ 53,461	$35,641	$ 51,654	$30,992	$20,662
Period expenses:						
Research and engineering	$ 20,456	$ 12,274	$ 8,182	$ 9,870	$ 5,922	$ 3,948
Marketing and selling	35,234	21,140	14,094	18,538	11,123	7,415
General and administration	13,904	8,342	5,562	8,712	5,227	3,485
Total expenses	$ 69,594	$ 41,756	$27,838	$ 37,120	$22,272	$14,848
Operating income	$ 19,508	$ 11,705	$ 7,803	$ 14,534	$ 8,720	$ 5,814
Other income (expense)	1,494	896	598	(42)	(25)	(17)
Income before taxes	$ 21,002	$ 12,601	$ 8,401	$ 14,492	$ 8,695	$ 5,797
Taxes	7,372	4,423	2,949	4,824	2,894	1,930
Net income	$ 13,630	$ 8,178	$ 5,452	$ 9,668	$ 5,801	$ 3,867

the specific needs of the users; those developed in-house were designed specifically for Hightech. The overall automated system was not fully integrated due to the variety of applications.

IS AT NTEC

Shortly after the acquisition of Hightech, a decision was made by NTI to install a new computer system within Hightech, identical to the one used by NTI in Japan. Hightech's IBM mainframe was superseded with a NEC supermini. The various software systems were replaced by an integrated software package trademarked Informationflo™.

The IS department has changed a great deal since the Nihon (Japan) acquisition, adding three programmer/analysts, a conversion project leader, and a telecommunications manager (see Exhibit 5).

Daichi Ito and Sachiko Natijoi were loaned by NTI to help with the conversion. Santura now reports to Daichi Ito. Ito reports to Saburu Nakamura, also loaned from NTI.

EXHIBIT 3   NTI Balance Sheet

NTI
Combined Balance Sheet
Fiscal Years 1983 and 1984
(in thousands)

	1984			1983		
	Total	*NTI*	*Hightech*	*Total*	*NTI*	*Hightech*
Assets						
Current assets:						
Cash and ST investments	$ 25,952	$ 15,571	$10,381	$ 24,890	$ 14,934	$ 9,956
Accounts receivable—customers	61,010	36,606	24,404	39,696	23,818	15,878
Inventories	49,832	29,899	19,933	27,876	16,726	11,150
Total current assets	$136,794	$ 82,076	$54,718	$ 92,462	$ 55,478	$36,984
Total long-term assets*	$ 68,982	$ 41,389	$27,593	$ 83,612	$ 50,167	$33,445
Total assets	$205,776	$123,465	$82,311	$176,074	$105,645	$70,429
Liabilities and Equity						
Current liabilities:						
Accounts payable—suppliers	$ 75,567	$ 45,340	$30,227	$ 63,513	$ 38,108	$25,405
Employees/other payables	25,189	15,113	10,076	21,171	12,703	8,468
Total current liabilities	$100,756	$ 60,453	$40,303	$ 84,684	$ 50,811	$33,873
Long-term liabilities	$ 442	$ 265	$ 177	$ 442	$ 265	$ 177
Stockholders equity:						
Common stock	$ 25,326	$ 15,196	$10,130	$ 25,326	$ 15,195	$10,130
Paid-in capital	44,676	26,805	17,870	44,676	26,806	17,871
Retained earnings	34,576	20,746	13,831	20,946	12,568	8,378
Total equity	$104,578	$ 62,747	$41,831	$ 90,948	$ 54,569	$36,379
Total liabilities/equity	$205,776	$123,465	$82,311	$176,074	$105,645	$70,429

*This line contains only property, plant, and equipment.

SABURU NAKAMURA

Nakamura is the chief financial officer of NTI (Japan). He was one of the original founders of the company and has been a driving force throughout his career. With a stubborn, strong, hard-nosed attitude, he was used to getting his way. Nakamura was often heard to say, ''My way or no way.''

Nakamura's tight controls over NTI's financial operations were not challenged because he had the knowledge and experience required to keep NTI in good financial condition. He was one of the most respected and feared members of

EXHIBIT 4   Hightech IS Department Organization Chart

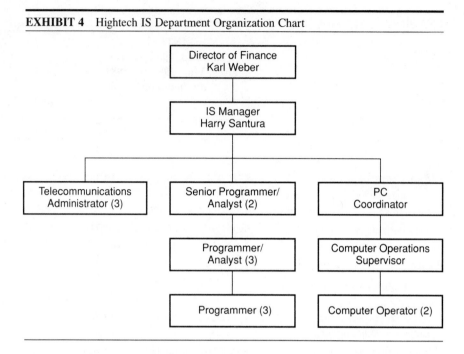

senior management, responsible for audit procedures, mergers and acquisitions, financial reporting, and the data processing operation. He oversaw the committee that chose the computer system and managed the installation of NEC computer equipment in the firm's headquarters in Tokyo.

Nakamura also was the main force behind the acquisition of Hightech. When NTI decided to expand into the U.S. market, it was no surprise that he was in charge of Hightech's conversion from IBM to NEC.

Nakamura was loaned to NTEC for two years. The company bought a house for him but his family did not move from Tokyo. They spoke frequently by phone but saw each other only on major holidays. This caused some emotional strain for the 50-year-old executive. Nakamura wanted to get the conversion completed as quickly as possible. He went about this task in his usual brusque manner.

BUDGET CHANGES

The IS budget was increased to $2.1 million, 2.5 percent of planned sales. Training was $210,000, 10 percent of the IS budget. Outside training represented a large part of the training budget. A DP audit function was in the final planning stages. Nakamura expected the audit department to be established within a year.

EXHIBIT 5   Nihon MIS Department Organization Chart

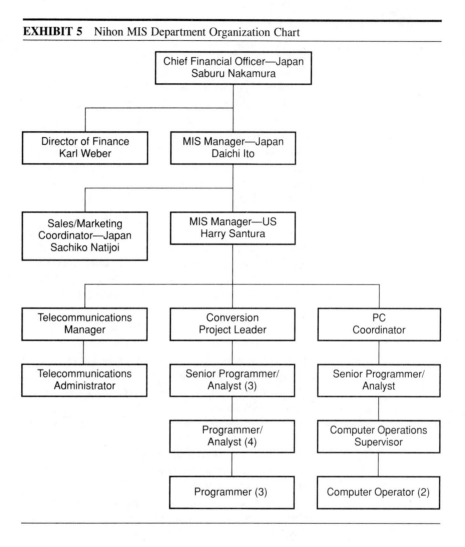

HARDWARE CHANGES

The new hardware was a NEC 8700, a high-performance, interactive supermini. The system is ideal for computational, commercial, office automation, or CAD/CAM/CAE applications in stand-alone or distributed environments. The NEC has about the same capacity as the IBM 4381 (being replaced). Santura knew that the IBM processed data much faster than the NEC.

INTERACTION, INC. (I.I.)

The new software was provided by Interaction, Inc. Interaction designs, develops, sells, installs, and supports turnkey business information systems and specializes in business systems for the distribution, manufacturing, and interconnect industries. Interaction's Business Information System, called Informationflo, is an integrated, interactive, real-time system. It is the software system used by many of NTI's international subsidiaries.

Interaction, begun in February 1975 as a software applications firm, has a solid foundation of technical people with many years of experience. Based in San Diego, the company has branch offices in Los Angeles and London. Its systems are installed in over 150 sites around the world.

Interaction's products are in three categories: equipment, application software, and services. The company's equipment products include complete computer systems and peripheral equipment (from computer manufacturers such as Honeywell, DG, Microdata, and NEC). Interaction's software products are based on Informationflo; its services include systems analysis, systems design, and programming for clients who desire modifications to their existing systems.

Interaction assists in all phases of implementation and provides preinstallation service to ensure that the computer facility is physically prepared prior to the arrival of equipment. Interaction is also involved in product orientation; regular meetings are scheduled to explain the installation, capabilities, and features of each system. Initial meetings are held with top-level management. Subsequent discussions are with middle managers and those responsible for supervising the various applications.

Interaction routinely develops a systems survey. The survey report identifies necessary and/or desired modifications to the base system. Interaction training for operators and users includes operation of the various pieces of equipment, a review of the operating system software, and the use of various utility programs.

The computer equipment is installed by a NEC field engineer, who then runs diagnostic tests to verify the proper operation of the system. After the basic Informationflo system is installed, the field engineer implements the operational subsystems in a phased schedule over a period of time.

Interaction, Inc., has the resources to coordinate NTEC's conversion and write any needed conversion programs. Its staff provides continuing monitoring and support on a weekly basis during and following conversion and will isolate and correct any program logic errors. Interaction also assists in the definition and planning of enhancements or new applications afterwards. The above activities are included in the services portion of every Informationflo contract.

INFORMATIONFLO

Informationflo is a very large software package consisting of approximately 200 files and 700 programs. All subsystems that provide information to the general ledger do so automatically and are in four classes: financial, sales, manufacturing, and inventory (see Exhibit 6).

The financial group includes general ledger, accounts receivable, accounts payable, asset management, and payroll. The general ledger subsystem provides for the maintenance of the financial database. The accounts receivable subsystem enables users to maintain customer accounts receivable data on an open-item basis. The accounts payable subsystem accommodates data entry and maintenance of vendor and accounts payable data. The asset management subsystem accepts data entry and facilitates management of the fixed asset database. The payroll subsystem maintains on-line payroll and personnel data.

The sales group includes job order processing, sales order processing, and service order processing. The job order subsystem facilitates the entry of the initial order, using the product definition module to calculate sales price and total manufacturing costs. The sales order subsystem assists users in the maintenance of the sales order database. The service order processing subsystem allows the users to record, dispatch, invoice, and analyze work associated with the servicing and repair of installed equipment.

The manufacturing group includes requirements planning, product definition, and production/costing. The requirements planning subsystem permits user/operators to create and maintain production and purchasing requirements. The product definition subsystem allows for the entry and maintenance of product structures, operation standards, and assembly routings. The production/costing subsystem assists users in maintaining the shop order database.

EXHIBIT 6　Informationflo — Overview of Subsystems

Financial	Sales/Marketing	Manufacturing	Inventory
General ledger	Job order processing	Requirements planning	Purchasing
Accounts receivable	Sales order processing	Product definition	Inventory control
Accounts payable	Service order processing	Production/costing	
Asset management			
Payroll			

The inventory group includes purchasing and inventory control. The purchasing subsystem facilitates maintenance of the purchasing database on an open-item basis. The inventory control subsystem provides for the entry and maintenance of the inventory database.

HARRY SANTURA

The Nihon (Japan) management needs Harry Santura's know-how to make the transition from IBM to NEC. Even so, both Nakamura and Ito have heard from other personnel that Harry is unhappy with the switch to NEC; they are worried that opposition or ''foot dragging'' on his part may cause added difficulties.

Harry Santura, in his late 50s, was the first Mexican-American hired to fill a professional slot at Hightech; he had been with Hightech since 1960. He started as an assistant programmer and worked his way up to his position as IS manager. He is a very methodical person, who ensures that all major IS decisions are carefully planned. He has been involved in all major IS projects of the last 15 years. As project manager for the selection and installation of the current IBM system, he performed a detailed feasibility study to be certain the new system would be flexible, compatible with most major software, and expandable; he even researched the vendors' experience and reputation, trying to measure reliability and long-term support. Subsequently, he was a major force in the decision to buy the IBM system.

Harry recently updated his education by completing a master's degree in Computer Science at the University of Houston's part-time evening program. He has no experience in DP auditing but has read many books, reports, and journal articles on the subject.

Santura enjoys his powerful position as manager of IS and feels his position is threatened by the Hightech buyout.

HARRY'S MISGIVING

The Nihon (Japan) management presented Harry with a timetable for the installation of the Informationflo software system (see Exhibit 7). As Santura examined the schedule, he questioned several factors and became more and more agitated. He wondered how his IS staff was going to react to all these projects that needed to be completed in such a short time. It had taken years to gather and train his current staff, and he worried that this major system overhaul would create heavy turnover. He also doubted that all of his current people could be easily taught to work with the new hardware and software. He would hate to fire part of this excellent staff and hire new people.

Santura was especially undecided about where he might find additional programmers and analysts sufficiently experienced with NEC to handle the expansion

EXHIBIT 7   NTEC Informationflo Installation Schedule

Subsystem	Estimated Starting Date	Estimated Ending Date	Actual Finish	Percent of Completion
Accounts payable/ purchasing*	06/01/85	09/01/85	08/30/85	100
General ledger	06/01/85	11/01/85	11/01/85	100
Asset management	11/01/85	11/15/85	11/25/85	100
Sales/marketing	09/01/85	11/30/85	—	50
Manufacturing	01/01/86	03/01/86	—	—
Leasing	04/01/86	04/15/86	—	—
Payroll	05/01/86	06/01/86	—	—

*When he was given the installation schedule, Harry was told to treat accounts payable and purchasing as one system and to "bring them along together."

and conversion. NEC was not used extensively in the United States, and such people would be very hard to find and expensive to hire and retain.

Harry's other major reservation was servicing. IBM had always given outstanding service in the past but NEC's nearest service center is in Oklahoma City. Interaction does have a toll-free 800 number to help solve software problems. "I hope there's a solution to this dilemma," Harry thought, "or all my past efforts will have been wasted."

Another trouble for Harry was conversion costs. Ito gave him the estimate shown in the accompanying table.

Conversion Costs

New NEC hardware	$ 549,100
Software package	67,500
Additional training	100,000
Four additional programmers	120,000
Data transfer (hiring of temps)	80,000
Conversion project supervisor (new)	55,000
Telecommunications manager	55,000
Temporary housing for Japanese personnel	100,000
	$1,126,600

Harry thought about all the things he could have done with the additional $1 million in his IS department. He couldn't understand why these headquarters types were so hardheaded. "Why even switch to NEC if NTEC will still act as a separate, decentralized entity?" he asked himself.

Santura calculated that if the conversion did not take place and only an expansion occurred, NTI would have spent only $250,000. The $250,000 total included three additional programmers at $90,000, a telecommunications manager for $55,000, and other costs at $105,000. Why wouldn't the Japanese managers listen to him? He had prepared a rough feasibility study for them, as shown in the accompanying table.

Feasibility Study—IBM versus NEC

Category	IBM and Software	NEC and Informationflo
Cost of conversion	$250,000	$1,126,600 (including expansion)
Vendor reliability	IBM very reliable; Number one in market	NEC – medium-sized firm; small market in United States; Interaction – small firm with little capital
Performance	Very good; excellent support and servicing	Good performance; servicing weak; vendor help good
Output	Good output for user; very flexible	Very good output; flexible
Programmer availability	Many available	Few available
Expandability	Handle projected growth for up to five years	Handle projected growth for up to three years

In addition to preparing the feasibility study, Santura collected user feedback. Mechiko Mitsubi, financial analyst, examined a sample of the Japanese financial package. She said the output was not as detailed as IBM's, and the general ledger package did not seem to be as flexible. The major problem with the financial package was the payroll system, which needed major modifications. However, Mechiko did feel the accounts payable subsystem was a bright spot within the financial package. It provided better summary reports and had on-line capabilities.

Karl Weber, director of finance, felt both the new and old software packages were adequate for his needs. He said, ''I just have a problem justifying all the additional expense. Converting all my U.S. dollar figures into Japanese yen and converting my statements to support U.S. accounting policies is going to be challenging, to say the least.''

Harry also received feedback from the Marketing department. Helen Willoughby, U.S. Sales manager, added the following: ''From the preliminary report, it appears the NEC output is going to be just what we need. Now that our sales force has more than doubled, and we're expanding into new areas, we are going to need the marketing data they propose. I just hope they can deliver the package soon because the market for multiplexers, modems, and networking systems is hot, and we can't afford to miss it.''

Next, Harry spoke with Mal Tempkin, Materials manager, who asserted, ''The manufacturing/inventory package I saw in Japan is far superior to the one we're using now.''

Also, the Purchasing manager claimed the Informationflo purchasing package was excellent; it had on-line capabilities and was very flexible, an important characteristic the old IBM package lacked.

DAICHI ITO

Each of the people Santura spoke with also voiced reservations about working for Ito.

Daichi Ito is 38 years old and is in the United States for two years. He will be directing Harry Santura in the conversion of the systems. Ito has an extensive, impressive data processing background, including:

- Eight years as a computer auditor for Coopers & Lybrand, Tokyo (a Big Eight accounting firm).
- Six years as a data processing manager for a multinational insurance company that used NEC (Fujisu of Tokyo).

Three years ago, NTI originally hired Daichi away from Fujisu of Tokyo to help install the NEC system in Japan. Daichi has always been reserved, task-oriented, and technically strong. He gets the task at hand accomplished and is not deterred by obstacles or concerned about anyone standing in his way. He is also highly regarded and respected by NTI's top management.

SACHIKO NATIJOI

Ito brought his best assistant, Sachiko Natijoi, with him to the United States. In only four years at NTI, Sachiko had become a rising star—quite a rarity for a woman in Japan, particularly for someone as young as she was, in her mid-30s. Natijoi was open-minded, objective, and inclined to speak up when she did not agree with policy or procedures—another rarity among Japanese women.

She had made her mark as a sales and marketing specialist at NTI's home office. Subsequently, Natijoi became an important liaison link between production and sales in a company that, at that time, needed more emphasis on sales. However, neither her undergraduate studies in Computer Science nor her Harvard MBA had prepared her for the difficulties she faced at NTEC.

Sales training, marketing studies, and strategic planning had been low-priority activities at NTI when Natijoi arrived. Under her direction, a full-fledged sales and marketing plan was formulated. Partially as a result of Sachiko's efforts, in recent years emphasis by NTI had turned from production to marketing.

Sachiko had also developed an information system to keep her sales staff up-to-date on new products and sales results. Progress of the marketing effort against the marketing plan could be checked quickly by calling up sales and production statistics; this ''how goes it'' management tool enabled NTI to match its production to sales estimates and market needs.

Early in 1984, several U.S. managers had been invited to NTI's headquarters to review the NEC system. Because their reception of the NEC conversion plan was mixed, Natijoi was drafted to act as a liaison between NTEC U.S. managers and NTI's loaned Japanese managers.

Appreciative of Natijoi's training and interpersonal skills as a liaison link, Daichi Ito had requested that Natijoi be part of the U.S. conversion team. As Ito's right hand, her job was to strike a balance between the way things were done at NTI as opposed to the American way of doing business.

PROBLEMS SIX MONTHS INTO THE CONVERSION

Six months into the conversion, only the accounts payable/purchasing, general ledger, and asset management systems were running satisfactorily. The sales/marketing system was well behind schedule. That the parent corporation, NTI, did not have its marketing software complete was a contributing factor to the software schedule slippage.

NTEC had been rapidly expanding its sales force. Having up-to-date sales, marketing, and production data was essential to operations. As the sales force increased from 30 to 85, the training of the new salespeople was seriously handicapped. The slow training, as well as the dismissal of many long-term sales personnel, did not help NTEC's marketing efforts. Customers used to dealing with certain sales personnel were turned off by the more aggressive, newer sales staff. The new salespeople appeared more interested in a sale and their own performance than in the customer's true needs. Delayed reports — sales, marketing, and production — had caused mistakes in promised delivery schedules. Some customers had to wait nearly twice as long as promised.

There had been no consideration given to the differences between programming IBM and programming NEC equipment. NTI management assumed there would be no problems in the software conversion until the programmers began to complain about lack of familiarity with NEC. The sales/marketing software in particular was more complex and was taking far longer to customize than had been estimated.

Prior to the takeover, data processing staff turnover had averaged 15 percent. Over the last six to seven months, it had nearly doubled to 29 percent. After a little research and several postemployment interviews with former NTEC programmers, Santura uncovered two primary reasons for the turnover upswing. The most important reason was career misgivings. In addition, the IS system staff had been keeping pace with rapid sales growth through frequent overtime and 70-hour workweeks. The effort to keep up with the booming sales and the unrealistic conversion schedule were cited as additional reasons for leaving.

The IS personnel were not accustomed to working under conditions of confusion and constant pressure. The chaotic environment implied poor planning and an obviously altered management style from the "good old days" at Hightech.

Poor planning was revealed when staffers were told that several programmers would be hired in order to get the conversion schedule back on target. Also, because a technical staff, familiar with NEC, was not easy to locate (contrary to expectations), two programmers from the corporate headquarters in Japan had to be borrowed—and housed at NTEC expense.

Santura, usually well thought of as a manager, was blamed by his people for the changes. The IS staffers believed he was now merely safeguarding his IS manager position instead of protecting them—which he had done so well in the past.

Actually, Santura had been excluded from the new planning and could not advise his staff. If he had been included, at least in the discussions about the conversion, he might have been allowed to describe potential major problems with top-level managers. For example, the software packages were written in different languages; all programmers were not familiar with the Interactive software, and the IBM system had excess capacity, which would have allowed the firm to continue using the older system until the data processing staff had been properly trained.

Beyond that, the training was backwards; end-users were being trained before the DP staff. The end-users had been sent to San Diego for training by Interactive personnel. Well aware of the typical burden on his IS staff, Santura could have warned management about the tightness of the conversion schedule and expressed his doubts about its timely completion. Instead, NTEC was having to pay for the services—and board—of two programmers from Nihon (Japan).

Since Saburu Nakamura was a stickler for DP audit controls, NTEC had been forced to contract with outside auditors. Serious control problems were uncovered. Inadequate DP costs checks, inaccurate user DP time charges, security leaks, skimpy performance measures, and flawed budgetary controls were only a few of the many deficiencies revealed.

Nakamura insisted on implementing audit functions immediately, as part of the conversion; the impact, of course, was an added interruption and extension of the original conversion process; the IS staff found themselves even further "behind the eight ball"; the scheduled completion date slipped a few more months.

Santura and Ito were having problems. They disagreed about almost everything —plans, procedures, processes, and personnel; their relationship appeared to be the classic personality conflict; Ito intended to wield his power as overseer of the conversion.

Santura didn't like the blitzkrieg approach—he sensed more could be accomplished through planning and cooperation. But Ito's temperament didn't allow for time to be wasted on what he thought were unnecessary trivia. On several occasions, Ito commented that Hightech would not have been acquired if its people had spent more time doing, rather than planning. His was a short-run view, while Santura took the long-run outlook.

Ito knew what his responsibilities involved because he had received specific directions from Nakamura. Since both men had worked together before, each knew how the other thought.

Santura, on the other hand, was left out in the cold. He was given no guidelines, other than a schedule, and ordered to meet it. Deadlines seemed to be the only thing Nakamura and Ito understood.

Sachiko Natijoi was about the only person in the Japanese takeover team who seemed to appreciate Santura's quandary. Because of her involvement in the sales and marketing realignment of NTEC, she began to suspect that the home office team's style might not be the most efficient.

Natijoi felt and expressed some sympathy for Santura's plight but she encouraged him to give consideration to what NTI wanted to accomplish. During several short discussions, Santura had told Natijoi, "I've lost control of my department. Daichi Ito has stepped in and taken over. Thank God, the man is technically strong, because he is so arrogant," and "It appears that my study heavily favors the use of the existing IBM system. Why didn't they even consider it?" Santura also repeated some critical end-user comments about Ito's heavy-handed management methods. Natijoi agreed to approach Ito on Harry's behalf.

Late in October 1985, Ito listened to Sachiko's comments and even made some notes. But he quickly ended the discussion, saying he did not have the time to respond immediately.

FINAL MEETING

During the first week of January, a meeting was called by Nakamura to check NTEC's progress against the conversion plan's deadlines. Ito, Natijoi, Santura, and Willoughby (NTEC's U.S. Sales manager) attended. It wasn't until Ito and Santura met face-to-face that their differences were confronted directly. The small talk eventually turned to angry discussions, supposedly about business. This time, the hostility between Ito and Santura erupted and shattered the conventional courtesies; their mutual dislike was evident. Ito blamed Santura for the delayed schedule and poor management. Santura accused Ito of being pigheaded, unrealistic, and a poor planner. He couldn't understand why Ito failed to act when Natijoi had talked to him over a month ago.

Nakamura suddenly realized he had a major problem. He wondered if and how he could get these people to work together. Maybe they should have done some things differently.

QUESTIONS

1. What is your opinion of the project implementation strategy and timetable? What changes, if any, would you make and why?
2. Can Interaction, Inc., be of any assistance to Nakamura?
3. Is Santura unduly concerned about the NEC system? What should his role be during the conversion? After the conversion? Should Santura be fired? If so, why, and who should take his place?
4. Being only six months into the conversion, should Nakamura do a turnabout and return to the IBM system?
5. With respect to the new sales/marketing package, which parts:
   a. Are essential?
   b. Impact on other systems?
   c. Could be delayed for six months? one year? two years?
6. Should the training budget for the MIS staff be increased? If so, why and by how much?
7. How can Nakamura:
   a. Complete the conversion process?
   b. Improve the morale and environment within the MIS group?
   c. Get Ito and Santura to cooperate with each other?

Chapter 11

Capstone Case

INTRODUCTION

In these chapter opening sections, we have tried to summarize subject matter, without specifically highlighting material that applies directly to the cases that followed. The introductory pages have touched on much of the information that we would include in an IS upper-division capstone or graduate-level survey course. But we have barely alluded to some areas that are important today; they include: conversions, decision support systems (DSS), and controls imposed by outside agencies, both state and federal.

THE IMPACT OF CHANGE

The three—conversions, DSS, and controls by outside agencies—are typical of the impact of change on IS/IT; conversions are the result of management decisions to change from one system to another; DSS reflect the need to change the source of management information from pure data processing application products to models and databases especially designed to meet managers' needs; and the changing state and federal laws and regulations—themselves responding to changes in our society—force organizations to modify their systems to provide information for reports.

SYSTEM CONVERSION

Burstein's definition of system implementation includes conversion, training, and the acceptance test. He writes, "Conversion entails not only putting the new software and hardware to work successfully, but also changing the data structure as required.''[1] Four techniques for changing from the old system to the new system are: direct cutover, parallel, phased, and pilot.[2] The major differentiating factors are: (1) the degree of risk, which is highest for the direct cutover and lower for the other three, (2) cost, which is higher when two systems are running concurrently than with direct cutover, and (3) time to complete conversion, which is least with the direct cutover.

DECISION SUPPORT SYSTEMS (DSS)

Some students have asked, ''Isn't any system that supports decisions a decision support system?'' A rudimentary acquaintance with the English language might suggest an affirmative answer. However, the correct answer is, ''No.''

According to Licker, a DSS ''supports management decision making by providing data, graphics, and decision-making tools to a relatively sophisticated manager. The components of a DSS are a **corporate database,** a **model base,** and a **dialogue manager.** The dialogue manager allows the manager to converse with and access models''[3] and databases to answer ''what if'' questions. A financial DSS, for example, using uncontrollable variables (assumed forecast values), controllable variables (select values), and a financial planning model, produces income statements and balance sheets for the financial manager's use in reviewing alternatives.[4]

CONTROLS IMPOSED BY OUTSIDE AGENCIES

Many business data processing and information systems, whose primary roles are to support business functions such as accounting, personnel, finance, and sales have been modified to comply with state and federal regulations and to furnish the government agencies with the reports they require. For example, personnel systems produce reports (concerning employee payrolls, positions, evaluations, and promotions) that are mandated by the affirmative action and equal employment opportunity laws. The Immigration and Nationality Act requires that records be kept on the citizenship of employees. The Occupational Safety and Health Administration (OSHA) has rules about reporting on accidents

---

[1]Jerome S. Burstein, *Computers and Information Systems,* Chapter 15 (New York: Holt, Rinehart & Winston, 1986).

[2]Burstein, *Computers and Information Systems,* Chapter 15.

[3]Paul S. Licker, *Fundamentals of Systems Analysis with American Design,* Chapter 17 (Boston: Boyd and Fraser, 1987).

[4]William Taggart and Valdur Silbey, *Information Systems: People and Computers in Organizations,* 2nd ed., Chapter 16 (Boston: Allyn & Bacon, 1986).

or illness at the work site and about the health and safety of all employees of a firm. Some jobs are so critical to the health and safety of the general public that employees must be tested for drug abuse and reports submitted to appropriate agencies. Systems that are too effective could generate unwelcome state and federal intrusion to quiet charges of unfair competition.

There are also strict state and federal controls on the transportation and sale of explosives. At the same time, much of that same information is useful to the companies who wish to analyze accident rates, cost of accidents, time lost due to accidents and illness, and so on.[5]

THE FIVE COMPONENTS OF AN INFORMATION SYSTEM

Whether we are discussing, designing, developing, or implementing a data processing system, management information system, decision support system, or executive information system, we must consider carefully the **hardware, software, data, procedures,** *and* **people.** If any one of the five is neglected, problems will multiply, schedules will slip, cost will increase, and system performance will be disappointing.

CASE: HILL EXPLOSIVES

The Hill Explosives case (Case 11–1) describes a company that was converting from a manual inventory control and tracking system (no longer adequate) to an automated system. Following a lengthy development and implementation process, Hill asked Stroud, the consultant, for a proposal to develop a general ledger system; after reviewing the proposal, Hill decided to develop the system in-house.

Case 11–1 Hill Explosives

It was a cold, damp, and dreary November day as George Stroud drove home from his meeting at Hill Explosives. George had done many conversions in the past but he just couldn't figure out where this one had gone wrong. In fact, until

---

This case was prepared by Gurney E. Strouse and Thomas R. Taylor.

[5]Robert Schultheis and Mary Sumner, *Management Information Systems: The Manager's View,* Chapter 11 (Homewood, Ill.: Richard D. Irwin, 1989).

about six months ago, the entire conversion had been an outstanding success. As the mist from the trailer truck ahead clouded the automobile windshield, Stroud reached for the windshield-wiper control and began to rethink the entire process.

A little over a year and a half ago, George's firm was approached by Sam Merrick, vice president of Hill Explosives. For some time, Merrick had been wondering if it would be possible to automate some aspects of Hill's operation. A meeting was arranged to discuss the possibility. At the meeting, Merrick and Ron Dennison, president of Hill Explosives, outlined the problem. What Hill Explosives needed, they said, was a decision support system for senior managers and employees to control the inventory and distribution of explosives, blasting equipment, and black powder.

Due to the hazardous nature of the business, the company's operations come under stringent controls mandated by the state and federal government. One predominant guideline mandated quick tracking of all sales and deliveries of the hazardous materials (information frequently requested by the Bureau of Alcohol, Tobacco, and Firearms of the Treasury Department).

Merrick had searched unsuccessfully for a canned computer package. In addition, he knew of several other explosives firms that had been working on similar systems for some time. As far as Merrick knew, no workable system had been developed. One firm that had been working on developing such a system for the last five years had not progressed past automating receivables, payables, and a general ledger. Stroud suggested that a detailed analysis of the system be conducted to determine if automation was feasible.

BACKGROUND ON HILL EXPLOSIVES

Hill Explosives is a central Pennsylvania explosives firm distributing its products from the Pennsylvania-Maryland line to the Canadian border. The firm also performs custom blasting for mines and quarries in the central Pennsylvania area.

Business is booming, although Hill supports a limited customer base (approximately 700–1,000 customers). Two years ago, before Sam took over as vice president, sales averaged about $500,000 per month. Lately, Hill's monthly sales have been averaging over $1.25 million and, as Sam stated, "the potential for continued growth is obvious."

Hill operates two large magazines (storage sites for explosives) with several inventory personnel at each site. The inventory operations are managed by Terry Dudman, a capable and conscientious inventory operations manager. Blasting personnel consists of 6 blasters who double as site analysts, 14 blaster assistants, and several laborers. The blasters, assistants, and laborers work out of specialized trucks that are used to transport explosives and blasting equipment from the magazines to the blast site and back. Accounting and document preparation and tracking are under the control of Grace Strickler, a hardworking office manager.

Grace believes her people are handling the documentation as efficiently as possible; but even with the two clerks she has added recently, keeping up with the paperwork is impossible.

HILL'S INFORMATION SYSTEM

The firm operates a manual inventory and sales tracking system that requires extensive employee effort to comply with various laws. Accounting and document preparation are also manual. Over the past two years, business has expanded so rapidly that the manual system has become a detriment to the firm's overall performance.

In their initial meeting, Sam had told George, "Our inability to obtain information using varying parameters on inventory, distribution, sales, and finance is hindering continued growth. We need to develop a system that can answer all the inventory tracking problems and provide information instantly, whenever desired, without any programming. If we don't do something soon, our competitors will."

TERRY DUDMAN

Like all Hill personnel, Terry Dudman, the Inventory System manager, had never worked with an automated system and so had designed Hill's inventory system to be maintained entirely on cards. Detailed information for each item (nomenclature, identification code, product code, hazardous code, hazardous shipping placard requirements, Department of Transportation shipping code, unit of measure, weight per unit of measure, standard pack, and reorder point) was maintained on the front of the card. Lot information (federal identification code for each lot, the location of the lot, the date received, the expiration date, if any, quantity initially received, and the quantity on hand) was maintained on the back. Although somewhat skeptical about computerization, Dudman recognized that current end-of-month inventory valuation procedures were slow. The Inventory System manager also knew it had become very difficult to keep up with inventory changes, especially since the business had begun to expand.

Federal lot code tracking had become almost impossible. The federal government requires that any firm selling explosives sell only to authorized licensed firms/individuals; each sale from each lot or group of lots must be tracked by lot and also by quantity (in case explosives are stolen or used for unlawful purposes). Each day, in the manual method of lot tracking, inventory staff checks the inventory cards and then looks through all the invoices typed on that day to find the invoice or invoices showing that lot. Having pulled all the invoices, they then group all sales by lot, by purchaser, and by date, indicating the quantity sold on that date.

Before the sales increase, Terry could track down a lot in an hour or two. Now, an entire day might not be enough time.

GRACE STRICKLER

Grace, the office manager, had no hands-on experience with computers—in fact, little exposure to them at all. She had, however, received computer-generated output from an accounting firm that managed Hill's books. This output was based on the month-end figures that Strickler gave the accounting firm.

Once compiled, the information could be used as a rough indicator on how the firm was doing. The problem with this procedure was that it usually took a week to 10 days to accumulate, compile, and type the month-end accounts information. It was another three days to a week before the accounting firm actually received and began working on the data. Processing at the accounting firm took between one and two weeks. The total delay usually left Hill about a month behind in actual status of the business. Further, the prior month's accounting figures could not always be reconciled because Strickler could not determine how the accounting firm calculated some of their entries.

Recently, problems in verifying available inventory, coupled with the length of time it took to prepare delivery tickets and hazardous cargo manifests, had caused delays in moving explosives from the magazines to the blasting site. These delays resulted in lost time and customer dissatisfaction. One error in typing a hazardous cargo manifest had almost resulted in a license suspension when a state policeman stopped one of their trucks to check for proper documentation.

THE ANALYSIS

Analysis began with an extended interview (by one of Stroud's senior analysts) with the president and the vice president of Hill Explosives. The purpose of the interview was to ascertain the strategic relevance of the project as well as to describe Dennison's and Merrick's perceptions of the corporate culture. Dennison and Merrick immediately pointed out that automation of the information system was essential to continued growth. In fact, they both indicated that several areas of operation—such as the preparation of delivery tickets, hazardous cargo manifests, and invoices—were causing delays in normal operations. Further, the firm's inability to process inventory valuation, track receivables, earn payables discounts, and respond quickly to federal tracking requirements was severely hampering continued development and expansion.

Dennison had reservations about automation, in general. It appeared that he was willing to computerize only out of necessity because the manual system simply couldn't keep up.

Merrick, on the other hand, was very excited about the idea of automation and envisioned much broader applications of computers than Dennison did. Merrick saw inventory control and order entry as just two parts of a wholly integrated information system. He felt that if an integrated inventory and order entry system could be developed, he would be able to convince Dennison, the company's president, to expand the information system throughout the business. Merrick realized that the manual system was already outpaced by growth, and the situation could only get worse. It was obvious that the recent growth was due to Sam's influence.

Overall, the atmosphere of the business was informal with a concentration on professionalism. Approval to automate the federal tracking requirement was management's major concern. If approval could not be obtained, the impact of automation would be limited.

The local representative from the Federal Bureau of Alcohol, Tobacco, and Firearms (ATF) was contacted concerning automation of the hazardous cargo manifest and lot tracking requirements. As far as could be ascertained, no one had ever automated these procedures before. The ATF representative was willing to help in directing and evaluating the process. With the ATF's blessing, Hill's top management decided to automate—*if* the analysis demonstrated feasibility.

ANALYZING THE EXISTING SYSTEM

Stroud and a couple of the firm's analysts decided to develop data flow diagrams of the existing order processing and delivery systems and agreed the best analysis method would be a procedural walk-through. The actual design procedure began with a detailed interview of the Accounting and Inventory managers (see Exhibits 1 and 2).

Orders were usually phoned in, but occasional mail and walk-in orders were encountered. The methodology used for processing phone, mail, or walk-in orders was basically the same. Initially, an informal loading manifest was prepared. Orders were then checked against the existing inventory card system for proper identification by item number, lot number, federal code, location, and quantity. If the items verified and quantity was available, a two-copy loading manifest was prepared. One copy was placed in the pending file, and the other was sent to the magazine for stock selection.

Inventory personnel at the magazine verified the item numbers, lot numbers, and federal codes. The verified loading manifest was then returned to the main office to be matched with the pending copy. At this time, an eight-part delivery ticket/invoice package was prepared; Invoice #1 (white) was immediately sent to the customer file.

Depending on order size, order processing and inventory people could take anywhere from a few hours to an entire day completing the above tasks. Much time was spent on the phone trying to verify items, codes, and locations.

EXHIBIT 1   Order Processing System

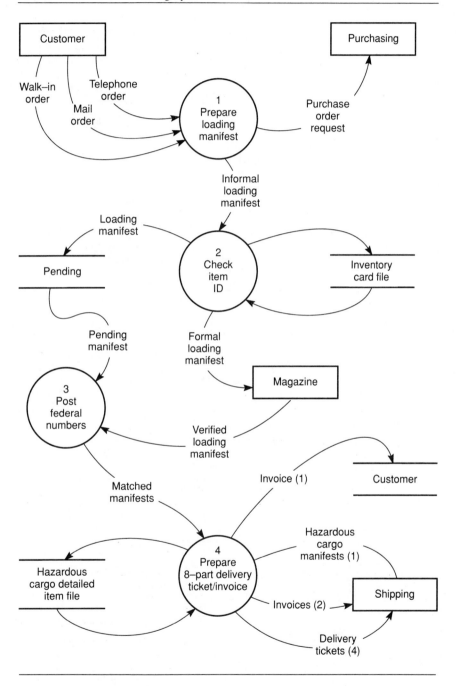

EXHIBIT 2   Delivery Procedure (delivery and blasting by Hill)

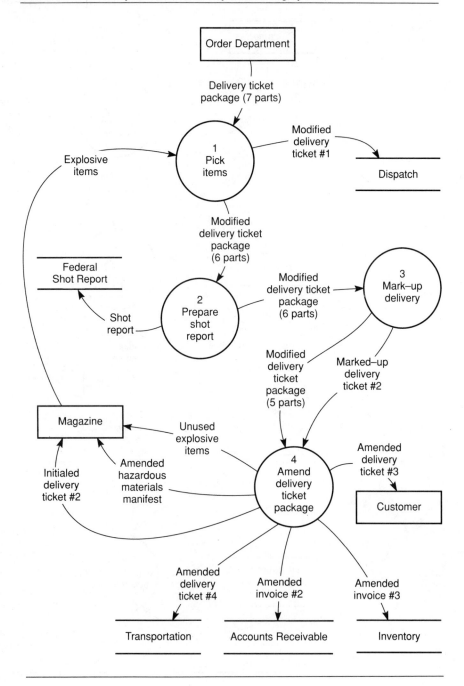

Just typing the delivery ticket/invoice was a real problem. Since part of the delivery ticket package was used as a hazardous cargo manifest, it was essential that all data pertaining to hazardous codes and shipping information be correct. Otherwise, if a company vehicle moving explosives was stopped by local police or state highway patrol, the company could be heavily fined and would risk losing its operating license.

In many cases, the hazardous cargo manifest required detailed item descriptions; some were between 80 and 90 characters long. In addition, the hazardous class often changed. For example, if the firm shipped only a few blasting caps, the hazardous cargo class designation would be relatively low. However, shipping a much larger quantity called for a higher hazardous classification. The stringent controls and high demand for accuracy not only placed stress on the individuals involved but often caused the operation to grind to a halt while waiting for documents to be completed.

The delivery procedure was no easier. Besides having extensive controls and regulations on the storage and movement of explosives, both seller and buyer have to conform to the minimum requirements. Dealers in explosives must:

1. Have a federal license.
2. Have proper storage facilities.
3. Keep accurate and complete records.
4. Verify that each out-of-state buyer has a federal permit.
5. Have nonlicensees and nonpermittees execute Form 5400.4, Explosives Transaction Record.
6. Have employees of buyers or carriers, to whom delivery is made at a distributor's premises, execute Form 5400.8, Explosives Delivery Record.
7. Verify buyer's identity.

If the customer picked the items up, the procedure was relatively straightforward. It required special state approval in addition to meeting the above federal criteria. The customer would pick up the delivery ticket package (seven parts), go to the magazine, receive the items, sign all parts of the delivery ticket, and pull the hazardous materials manifest (pink)—as authorization to transport the cargo—and delivery ticket #3 (orange)—for the customer's own records. If delivery was involved, which was normally the case, an even more convoluted procedure was required.

After satisfying the ordering process, the inventory personnel at the magazine would usually pull the items and load them onto one of the trucks the night before shipment was to be made. The driver would deliver the items the following day. If the customer did the blasting, one of the customer's shipping/receiving clerks would sign the six parts of the delivery ticket package, retain the orange copy as a customer record, and receive the explosives.

In most cases, however, the blast was performed by the explosives company. In this case, Shipping always sent an adequate supply of explosives—to preclude having to make two trips—and modified all parts of the delivery ticket to show the actual amount loaded. Dispatch gets the modified delivery ticket #1 (blue). The blaster would use the explosives required, prepare a federal shot report, and mark up and initial delivery ticket #2 (yellow). The driver would then amend all other parts of the delivery ticket package (including invoices and the hazardous cargo manifest) and initial delivery ticket #2, confirming agreement with the actual amount of explosives used, as well as the amount returned to the magazine. The customer at the site was given delivery ticket #3 (orange) as a customer record. The unused explosive items—plus delivery ticket #2 (yellow) and the hazardous materials manifest (pink)—would then be returned to the magazine and the amended parts of the delivery ticket returned to the main office. One copy, invoice #3 (gray), was used to update the cards in the inventory file; another copy, delivery ticket #4 (green), was filed in the transportation log; and another, invoice #2 (canary), was sent to accounts receivable, thereby starting the billing process.

The above procedures caused three major problems:

1. Delivery ticket items varied, allowing little or no standardization in preparation.
2. Although a customer's federal permit number always remained the same, the state permit number would often change, depending on job and site.
3. Inventory that was loaded the night before a shot was to take place, and that was not used/consumed by the shot, often did not get unloaded and restocked until the day after the blast. Consequently, stock that was no longer in its assigned warehouse location (where it would be available for issue) was being listed on the inventory cards as "available." This incorrect entry created many inventory problems in an industry where inventory problems are absolutely not allowed.

It was also noted that, due to the size of the inventory and the number of items involved, inventory valuation would often take from 8 to 10 working days. This excessive amount of time complicated month-end accounting procedures and often made inventory reordering a hit-and-miss affair.

As the firm expanded, it became obvious that information was a strategic resource; its timely management was essential and slipshod practices could not continue.

SYSTEM DEFINITION

System definition began with in-depth interviews, lengthy observations of work in process, and the gathering of detailed information pertaining to invoice/shipping specifications, inventory lot sizing, federal and state tracking requirements, accounting procedures, customer data, pricing specifications, and so on. Unique requirements, like mandatory 11-digit item identification numbers, 14-digit federal lot numbers, and up to 90-character mandatory item descriptions, became commonplace. Special physical situations also carried over to logical system concepts. The federal requirement for maintaining segregated lots mandated that lot integrity be carried throughout the system.

In addition, each newly acquired lot of every item could have a different item cost, impost (tax or duty) cost, sale price, and sale impost. However, when billed, a standard charge must be made for the item and the unit of measure price; and the unit of measure impost must be stated. The price billed for both federal impost and item cost is calculated in the form of sale price and impost price less customer discount, if any; that figure is then multiplied by the quantity purchased.

Automation of the above invoice charge calculations became complex. For one thing, the unit of measure may vary among manufacturers (i.e., one may ship in 25-pound bags, and another may ship in 50-pound bags). Secondly, items may be issued in less than unit-of-measure standard pack quantities. As a result, the system designers reluctantly decided to carry all three prices (amount to acquire or purchase price, unit of measure cost, which related to cost of a standard pack, and sale amount) for both item cost and federal impost. The valuation of inventory was based on the purchase quantity and price of newly acquired inventory averaged with current quantity and price of on-hand inventory.

Varying management requirements, such as preparing and completing ad hoc queries, and analyzing specialized sales data and service profit analysis, almost mandated the use of a database environment.

Dennison and Merrick knew Hill Explosives needed an automated information system; yet, neither had been able to find one. They found several companies that were trying or had tried, with little or no success, to develop automated systems; most firms had implemented receivables and payables but had failed to integrate inventory management and federal tracking. Stroud believed the other companies failed because they had based their systems on accounting procedures/programs, rather than on inventory control.

Aside from Stroud's system-basing conclusion, Hill's objective was to implement a system without exceeding cost constraints. Therefore, management and designers agreed that an initial configuration of three to eight terminals and two printers would adequately provide the required access. Expansion capabilities were necessary, but, if inventory and receivables could be even marginally automated, growth could be maintained. Taking these factors into consideration, the data requirements analysis began.

DATA REQUIREMENTS ANALYSIS

The data requirements analysis of the system definition followed a somewhat traditional approach. Stroud decided that a seven-step procedure would be used to define data requirements. The steps were:

1. User views were to be defined for each system function. A user view form was developed for this purpose. Approximately 35 user views were constructed (see Exhibits 3a and 3b).

EXHIBIT 3a   User View Form—Example 1

USER VIEW

USERVIEW # _____1(a)_____   NAME: _____Inventory Item Data_____

DESCRIPTION: _Used as an overview of inventory items. Maintained in a card file_

side of 1 of card.

SPECIFICS

PRIMARY USER: Inventory Control

LOCATION: Inventory Section

PURPOSE and POSSIBLE LINKS TO OTHER VIEWS: _Card contains general_

inventory information.

DATA ELEMENT INFORMATION

NUMBER	NAME	TYPE	LENGTH	COMMENT
1	Item ID	AN	11	Required Fed Item Identifier
2	Description	AN	up to 90	Required Fed Description
3	Hazardous Code	AN	2	Fed Hazardous Code
4	Unit of Measure	AN	4	Item Unit of Measure
5	Item Weight	Real	5	Weight based on lowest sale unit
6	Quantity on Hand	Integer	9	Quantity on Hand from All Lots

AN = Alphanumeric

EXHIBIT 3b   User View Form—Example 2

ÚSER VIEW

USERVIEW # _____1(b)_____   NAME: __Lot Nr Inventory Data__

DESCRIPTION: __Used to represent specific transactions on individual inventory lots__

   __side 2 of inventory card.__

SPECIFICS

PRIMARY USER: __Inventory Control__

LOCATION: __Inventory Section__

PURPOSE and POSSIBLE LINKS TO OTHER VIEWS: __Contains detailed inventory item__

   __data on each lot. Possible link to receivables and sales history.__

DATA ELEMENT INFORMATION

	NUMBER	NAME	TYPE	LENGTH	COMMENT
	1	Item ID	AN	11	Required Fed Item ID
	2	Description	AN	30	Short Description
	3	Federal Lot Nr	AN	14	Required Fed Lot Code
	4	Location	AN	7	Item Location
	5	Date Recvd.	AN	8	Lot Receipt Date
	6	Qty. Recvd.	Integer	8	Quantity Received
Many	7	Customer	AN	25	Customer Name
	8	Issue Date	AN	8	Issue Date
	9	Issue Quantity	Integer	8	Quantity Issued
	10	Quantity on Hand	Integer	8	Quantity Remaining after issue

AN = Alphanumeric

2. An Entity-Relationship (E–R) diagram was to be developed that would establish the functional relationships within the system. Because of the unique relationship that existed between the delivery ticket and the invoice (receivable), an aggregation-type relationship was used (see Exhibit 4).
3. Conceptual data models were to be developed and normalized using the user views and the E–R diagram (see Exhibit 5).
4. Logical Access Maps (LAMs) were to be designed indicating access methodology (see Exhibit 6).
5. A composite frequency table indicating the type of access and the relative load the basic access activities would place on the system was to be developed (see Exhibit 7).
6. Physical record/tuple layouts were developed with optimization in mind (see Exhibit 8).
7. Storage requirements were estimated based on current and projected activity.

After considering the data requirements and system configuration, Stroud presented several alternatives to Hill management. Dennison and Merrrick decided to use a DEC MicroVax II with 4 MB RAM, two 71 MB hard disks, four terminals, and two printers. They based their decision primarily on performance, speed, cost, and dependable local service. The accompanying software would be Sculptor, a file manager–type database with a programming interface.

EXHIBIT 4   Entity-Relationship (E–R) Diagram

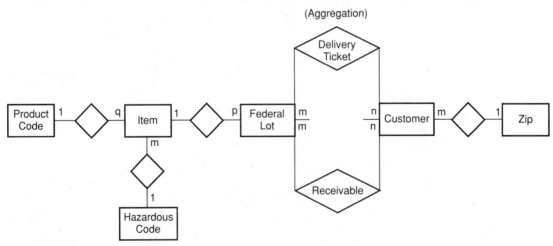

q = approximately 12
p = approximately 7

1. All 1–M relations are null relations in the database with the relationship defined by a foreign key carried in the M-side entity relation.
2. Elements contained in conceptual data models.

EXHIBIT 5   Conceptual Data Model

Item Data   **600 Occurrences**

Item ID	Description Number 1	Description Number 2	Description Number 3	Hazard Code	DOT Code	Unit Measure	Weight

Standard Pack	Minimum Order	Purchase Price	Purchase Impost	Sale Price	Sale Impost	Unit Price	Unit Impost

Lot Data   **7 Occurrences per item (on average)**

Item ID	Federal Lot Number	Lot Location	Lot Receipt Date	Lot Expiration Date	Lot Quantity Received	Lot Quantity on Hand	Lot Quantity Out on Site

(Concatenated Key)

SYSTEM IMPLEMENTATION

A modular system development technique was used to create the system. Stroud felt that if the system were developed and implemented in modules, the users, who had no prior computer experience, could more easily assimilate system exposure. Throughout the implementation, users were kept closely involved, to help tailor the system, insure it provided the necessary functions, and foster a sense of participation. Because the users had little computer experience, the system climate had to go beyond user-friendly; in a sense, it had to be user-seductive.

To be certain that the system would encourage users, Stroud's people developed easy start-up procedures, menu-driven routines, and fill-in-the-blank screens (see Exhibits 9 and 10). In addition, Stroud insisted on detailed documentation of all products, even down to an automated daily backup procedure that used different color-coded disks for each day of the week. As an example of the documentation detail, using the disk backup procedure, the system would prompt the user to obtain Monday's red backup disks. After the user had inserted the proper disk and keyed "Return," the system would check the disk label to insure it was indeed Monday's first disk, prior to initiating the backup procedure.

Training was conducted on the use of each module as it was implemented.

The data access modules were developed first. The LAMs, the composite access frequency table, and the projected storage requirements were used to compare access requirements to the physical capabilities of the system. The decision was made to index the outstanding delivery tickets table, customer table, and inventory tables. The ZIP code table was optimized up one normalization level into the customer table. The transaction history table was not indexed. Once the

EXHIBIT 6 Logical Access Maps (LAMs)

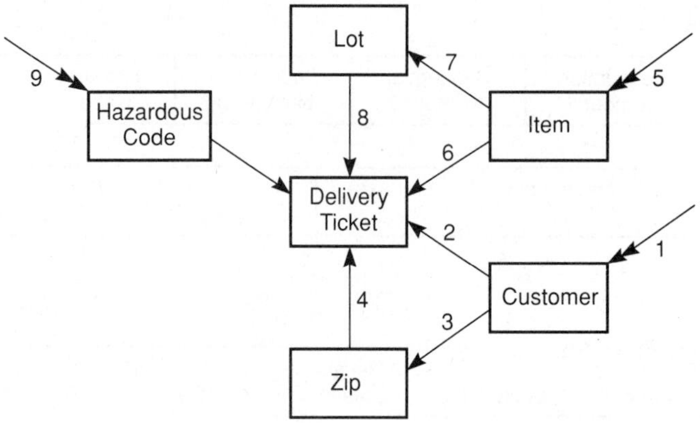

Transaction
1 Access Customer using Customer Number — Frequency: 150 per month
2 Getting Name, Address, Zip, Terms, Price Category, State Permit Number, and Federal Permit Number
3 Access Zip using Zip
4 Getting City and State — (Item Data, Flag Loop)
5 Access Item using Item-ID
6 Getting General Item Data
7 Access Lot Select ALL where Item-ID = Item-ID
8 Getting Lot Data (Use Oldest First) — (Lot Data Quantity, Loop)
9 Access Hazardous Code (If change required)
10 Getting Placard

Item Data, Flag Loop — 1400 per month
Lot Data, Quantity Loop — 2500 per month

data access modules were working, a screen program was written that accepted inventory item data. The screen program would accept the data and use the access modules for storage and retrieval.

INVENTORY MODULE

Next, the programmers coded the start-up procedure module, which contained the main menu. As soon as data access and startup procedure modules were working, Stroud and Merrick decided to implement them and have inventory personnel begin entering inventory data. At this time, Stroud's people wrote an informal inventory listing query that furnished inventory lists, allowing Inventory staff to verify data after it was entered. No formal reports menu had been developed.

The inventory module used a two-screen entry system. One screen was for

EXHIBIT 7   Composite Access Frequency

RUDI*
(per month of activity)

Table	Action	Frequency	Percent
Customer	Read	1300	99.769
	Update	1	0.067
	Delete	0	—
	Insert	2	0.150
Zip	Read	1300	99.923
	Update	0	—
	Delete	0	—
	Insert	1	0.077
Inventory data	Read	2932	99.863
	Update	2	0.068
	Delete	1	0.034
	Insert	1	0.034
Lot data	Read	18024	78.066
	Update	5000	21.656
	Delete	32	0.139
	Insert	32	0.139
Delivery ticket	Read	150	33.333
	Update	0	—
	Delete	150	33.333
	Insert	150	33.333

High frequency of read only accesses on Customer, Zip, and Inventory data sets.

*Acronym for "read, update, delete, and insert."

general data that pertained to the item itself (see the completed inventory screen examples in Exhibits 11 and 12). The other screen held specific lot data.

As stated previously, one of the major inventory problems was knowing how much inventory, by lot, was really available for issue. The system designers addressed this problem by establishing an on-job quantity that would indicate how much of the particular lot had been sent out on blasting jobs.

It was a short, easy step to convert the inventory modules to customer data modules (see Exhibit 13).

STANDARDIZATION

By using the same base modules, standardization began to appear. The screens had the same basic appearance. The menus, customer/inventory editors, and general functioning of the system looked the same, worked the same, and had the

EXHIBIT 8   Physical Record/Tuple Layout

RECORD LAYOUT AND TEST DATA

Concatenated Key							
Item ID	Fed Lot Nr	Location	Receipt Date	Expiration Date	Qty Recd.	Qty On Hand	
11 (x)	14 (x)	7 (x)	8 (x)	8 (x)	Num	Num	

RECORD NO

RECORD DESCRIPTION   Lot Data

Tuple

x = alphanumeric   Num = packed numeric — 5 bytes required

EXHIBIT 9 Fill-In-the-Blank Screen—Example 1

EXPLOSIVES MANAGEMENT SYSTEM   87/06/30   INVENTORY EDITOR

*** MODIFY INVENTORY ***

ID CODE: _____

DESCRIPTION: _____

_____

_____

PRODUCT CODE: _____

HAZARD CODE: _____

'X'-FLAG: _____

D.O.T. CODE: _____

UNIT OF MEASURE: _____

WEIGHT: _____

STANDARD PACK: _____

REORDER POINT: _____

QUANTITY ON HAND: _____   VALUE: $ _____

PRICE (COST): $_____   (SALE): $_____   (UM): $ _____

IMPOST (COST): $_____   (SALE): $_____   (UM): $ _____

ESC 7 END DATA ENTRY

ESC 7 = = Depressing escape and the number 7 ends data entry

Items can be viewed by either initially entering an ID CODE or the first record in the table can be obtained by striking return on an empty ID CODE field.

Depressing the down arrow allows paging through the table sequentially

Depressing right and left arrows moves the cursor to the next or previous field

same reliability. By the time the customer module was ready, everyone who was to use the system knew that inventory personnel had entered a large volume of the inventory data successfully. The once-skeptical prospective users were now anxious to get started.

EXHIBIT 10   Fill-In-the-Blank Screen — Example 2

| EXPLOSIVES MANAGEMENT SYSTEM | | 87/06/30 | | | | INVENTORY EDITOR |

*** MODIFY INVENTORY ***

FEDERAL ID#	LOCATION	REC DATE YY/MM/DD	EX DATE YY/MM/DD	RECEIVED	ON HAND	ON JOB
_____	_____	_____	_____	_____	_____	_____
_____	_____	_____	_____	_____	_____	_____
_____	_____	_____	_____	_____	_____	_____
_____	_____	_____	_____	_____	_____	_____
_____	_____	_____	_____	_____	_____	_____
_____	_____	_____	_____	_____	_____	_____
_____	_____	_____	_____	_____	_____	_____
_____	_____	_____	_____	_____	_____	_____
_____	_____	_____	_____	_____	_____	_____
_____	_____	_____	_____	_____	_____	_____

ESC 1 — PAGE   ESC 7 END DATA ENTRY

ESC 1 = = Depressing escape and the number 1 pages back to the first screen

ESC 7 = = Depressing escape and the number 7 ends data entry

Depressing right and left arrows moves the cursor to the next or previous field

The standardization of the system provided an additional benefit: If any problems arose as new users were added, the more experienced users could be consulted for advice.

INTERFACING

After the inventory and customer modules had been completed, programmers added delivery ticket preparation and invoicing. Both these modules interfaced with the inventory and customer tables. Notice that the delivery ticket module would adjust the on-hand (that is, the amount available for issue) and the on-job quantities of the inventory record/tuple while the delivery ticket was being generated. Thus, Inventory personnel could determine the amount of stock actually

EXHIBIT 11   Completed Inventory Screen—Example 2

EXPLOSIVES MANAGEMENT SYSTEM	87/06/30	INVENTORY EDITOR

*** MODIFY INVENTORY ***

ID CODE: AANFO0000SL

DESCRIPTION: ANFO-SL _____

AMMONIUM NITRATE FUEL OIL ____

MIXTURE, BLASTING AGENT _____

PRODUCT CODE: 30

HAZARD CODE: BA

'X'-FLAG: X

D.O.T. CODE: _____

UNIT OF MEASURE: CTW__

WEIGHT: 1.000

STANDARD PACK: 50.

REORDER POINT: 35000.

QUANTITY ON HAND: 33100.   VALUE: $3558.25

PRICE (COST): $.1075   (SALE): $.1500   (UM): $15.0000

IMPOST (COST): $.0035   (SALE): $.0060   (UM): $ .6000

MODIFY THIS INVENTORY RECORD? (Y OR N): _____

ESC 1—PAGE   ESC 7 END DATA ENTRY

ESC 7 = = Depressing escape and the number 1 pages to the next screen

ESC 7 = = Depressing escape and the number 7 ends data entry

Items can be viewed by either initially entering an ID CODE or the first record in the table can be obtained by striking return on an empty ID CODE field.

Depressing the down arrow allows paging through the table sequentially

Depressing right and left arrows moves the cursor to the next or previous field

EXHIBIT 12 Completed Inventory Screen — Example 2

EXPLOSIVES MANAGEMENT SYSTEM		87/06/30				INVENTORY EDITOR

*** MODIFY INVENTORY ***

FEDERAL ID#	LOCATION	REC DATE YY/MM/DD	EX DATE YY/MM/DD	RECEIVED	ON HAND	ON JOB
AC86NOVV7__	TRL15___	86/11/11	_____	35000.	1300.	15000.
AC86NOV20_	TRL20___	86/11/22	_____	30000.	6800.	4800.
AC86DEC5__	TRL22___	86/12/06	_____	25000.	25000.	0.
_____	_____	_____	_____	_____	_____	_____
_____	_____	_____	_____	_____	_____	_____
_____	_____	_____	_____	_____	_____	_____
_____	_____	_____	_____	_____	_____	_____
_____	_____	_____	_____	_____	_____	_____
_____	_____	_____	_____	_____	_____	_____
_____	_____	_____	_____	_____	_____	_____

ESC 1 — PAGE			ESC 7 END DATA ENTRY	

ESC 1 = = Depressing escape and the number 1 pages back to the first screen

ESC 7 = = Depressing escape and the number 7 ends data entry

Depressing right and left arrows moves the cursor to the next or previous field

available. The final inventory adjustments did not occur until after the delivery ticket, with the actual quantities used, was returned from the blast site.

The invoice module would access the outstanding delivery ticket record/tuple and allow the actual amount used to be entered, along with any pricing variations or service charges. Individual inventory lot data was updated. The lot on-job quantity was reduced by the total amount sent out to the job site, and the on-hand quantity was adjusted to reflect the actual amount consumed. In addition, a transaction history record/tuple was written to show the exact amount of the issue and all required federal tracking data. The efficient functioning of these modules was crucial to a successful system.

When these new modules came on-line, the speed of the order processing and delivery functions took a quantum leap. Delivery ticket preparation dropped from hours to a matter of minutes.

The federal tracking module was developed about the same time the invoicing

EXHIBIT 13   Customer Screen

EXPLOSIVES MANAGEMENT SYSTEM	87/06/30	CUSTOMER EDITOR

*** MODIFY CUSTOMER ***

ID CODE: ____

NAME: _____

ADDRESS: _____

CITY: _____

STATE: ____

ZIP: ____

TERMS: _____

PHONE: _____

CONTACT: _____

PRICE CAT.: ____

STATE PERMIT#: _____

FEDERAL PERMIT#: _____

ESC 7 END DATA ENTRY

ESC 7 = = Depressing escape and the number 7 ends data entry

Customers can be viewed by either initially entering an ID CODE or the first record in the table can be obtained by striking return on an empty ID CODE field.

Depressing the down arrow allows paging through the table sequentially

Depressing right and left arrows moves the cursor to the next or previous field

module was being completed. After the installation of the federal tracking module, the ATF representative evaluated the system's tracking capabilities.

IMPLEMENTATION SIDE BY SIDE

Until this time, both the automated system and the manual system were being run side by side. Since none of the physical documents had been removed from the procedure, the basic capability to track and verify system output was unaltered.

In addition, should the system fail, the sale of explosives could still be tracked the old way. The old manual procedure of tracking explosives required going to the inventory cards for that item, checking the issues for that federal lot number, and searching through all the delivery tickets and invoices for each day that a sale of that particular lot occurred. The process could take an entire day.

With the automated system, a detailed listing could be produced for any item lot, even those that would eventually be archived in just a matter of minutes. The ATF representative was so impressed with the results of the test that he not only approved of its use but recommended the system to others in the business.

IMPACT OF USER ENTHUSIASM

By this time, the users were so pleased with the system that they began clamoring for applications. It was as if the procedure was moving through Nolan's stages of development at an accelerated pace. What had begun as a top-down approach was now being driven from lower levels of the organization. Every time two or more users got together, they would think up ideas for new applications. Each time a new module was installed, the users would gather around and ''watch it run.'' A continuous barrage of questions would be posed, most in the form of: ''Oh, do you think the system could do this or that application?''

Merrick was so excited about the new system's capabilities that he began to translate the various user requests into formal demands. Stroud remembered discussing that tactic with Sam. In fact, when Stroud had explained why it would be better to complete the original system design specifications, prior to trying to implement any further changes, Merrick had agreed.

CODING THE FINAL MODULES AND REPORTS

After formalized menu-driven backup and data archive procedures were finished, the Stroud programmers wrote a reports menu. Creating that menu allowed them to change informal inventory and customer list queries into callable modules that provided customer and inventory listing reports. Next, they wrote the receivables module. In addition to generating invoices, the invoicing module added a tuple/record to the database receivables table. Now, it became relatively easy to write payments and credit adjustment modules. With these last two modules in place, the next step was receivable aging.

The receivables menu was altered to allow a user to call for an aging menu. The aging menu was written; then, the programmers developed modules for individual customer aging, an overall aging recapitulation report (see Exhibit 14), and the preparation of statements. The individual customer aging module furnished either screen or printed output of all outstanding invoices and their value for the customer requested. The recapitulation report would print the 12 most

EXHIBIT 14 Aging Recapitulation Report

ACCOUNTS RECEIVABLE REPORT—6/30/87

ACCOUNT	1986	MAY	JUN	JUL	AUG	SEP	OCT	NOV	DEC	JAN	FEB	MAR	APR	June 30, MAY	Page 1 JUN
Restricted Account															1150.01
Adams Excavating															3022.33
Bellkirch Ammunition															33228.21
Baker Quarry														5241.13	44768.62
Calcite Blasting							48.91		38.51				29.47		1965.01
County Mines															7813.43
Decker Associates													947.57	14.21	14.21
Eastern RR Const.	156.06		8.21	8.21	−16.43	4.5									
GAF Inc.															23512.16
General Const.								1805.34	1035.19	45.28	60.45	42.33	42.33	42.33	42.33
Horn Quarry															15715.92
Knisley Const.			2.92	5.8											
Mahoney Mines															519.67
Marcona Quarry											18457.13	6526.37	5144.67	4552.77	3336.97
Martin's Quarry													2538.39	10032.02	
McCraig, Inc.												7762.75	22610.46	4967.28	455.59
New Eaton Stone							281.74	371.33	322.92	266.91	376.01	100.82	396.57		
PAS, Inc.															27436.42
Penn Supply, Inc.												21218.01	15027.28	861.06	
Pequay Const.															4304.51
Quarry Stone, Inc.								2562.75		38.44		38.44	38.44	38.44	
Smith Quarry															−416.75
U-Value Const.														61.74	4409.61
Valley Const.										60.83					
Watertown Quarry								59.76		11.15					
Winter's Blasting															4306.78
York Quarry														8343.31	1950.01
TOTAL	156.06	0	11.13	14.01	−16.43	4.51	335.15	4799.18	1396.62	422.61	18893.58	14470.71	52965.91	43767.72	178396.05
% of TOTAL	0.0005	0	0	0	0	0	0.0011	0.0158	0.0046	0.0015	0.0625	0.0478	0.1752	0.1448	0.5903

recent months of activity for all customers, indicating any amounts still outstanding in the month the invoice was written. Statements listed outstanding balances and interest charges. Amounts were displayed for 30-, 60-, and 90-or-more–days overdue.

Management reports could track outstanding delivery tickets and provide a daily delivery ticket and invoice transaction register. A new inventory valuation report reduced month-end inventory valuation procedures of 8 to 10 days down to about 35 minutes. An inventory reorder report provided a list of items below reorder point. In addition, a customer mailing list module furnished mailing labels.

After these reports had been installed, Stroud's programming staff wrote a payables menu (see Exhibit 15 for a full menu representation) to call for a payables entry/edit and payables report module. The payables entry/edit module allowed the entry of any payable requiring tracking. The payables report was basically a tickler program that searched payable entries for required activity dates and displayed or listed those payables not yet satisfied as of that date.

The ability to generate queries on the transaction history table allowed management to analyze inventory usage and volume by customer and general location. Managers could then accomplish a better site selection evaluation for an additional magazine location.

The ready availability of delivery ticket/invoice package data allowed for a monthly comparison of blast yields versus the expense involved, presented on a spreadsheet by customer and type of blast, yield, and cost. The information allowed the Hill managers to give detailed information to each customer on how to maximize yield. Hill's ability to supply that information became a great sales tool because it gave customers specifics on how to decrease costs.

SYSTEM BENEFITS

Stroud thought about the benefits the new system had given Hill. Some of the benefits were tangible, but many—perhaps more—were intangible. The tangible results appeared primarily in the area of office automation. The intangible results were reflected in increased business performance and better management overview and control; but most importantly, the system provided the capacity for continued expansion. As he was driving, George considered the benefits one by one:

- The reduction of delivery ticket preparation time from several hours down to 10–15 minutes greatly enhanced business performance while reducing costs.
- The time required to prepare invoices was not only reduced but the steps of manual inventory posting were totally removed from the process.
- End-of-month inventory valuation time was reduced from 8 to 10 days to approximately 35 minutes.
- The automated generation of month-end statements totally eliminated an entire day of typing.

EXHIBIT 15 System Menus

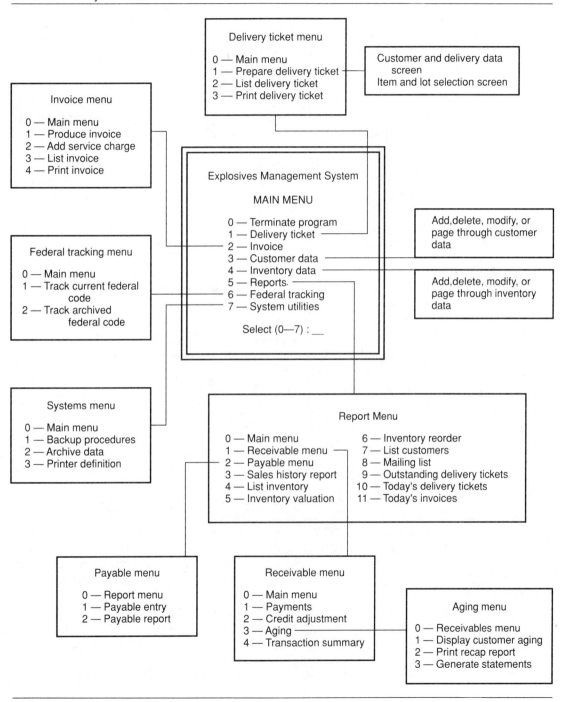

- Receivable aging provided a methodology for managing receivables and increasing cash flow.
- The addition of the ability to track on-hand and on-job inventory furnished a better methodology for inventory allocation and management.
- The automatic generation of inventory reordering reports helped preclude stockouts.
- The implementation of a payable tracking capability allowed the realization of discounts that had previously been missed.
- The speed and dependability of federal tracking was enhanced to a level previously unattainable.
- The ability to use the system to answer unique questions and provide both detailed and summary analysis (see Transaction Summary Report*, Exhibit 16) of sales, service history, and item use opened new avenues of business evaluation.
- The ability to analyze customer transactions provided new sales tools that enhanced sales and increased productivity.

THE NEW PROBLEM

The system was so accurate and so successful that the time between total physical inventories was changed from monthly to quarterly. Further, during one of the month-end closings, Merrick discovered that the outside accounting firm's figures did not agree with those the computer had provided. He contacted Stroud; after they ran several reports and queries and verified the numbers, they proved the accountant had carried the amounts incorrectly.

Their discovery of the accountant's error provided great credibility for the system but caused another problem. Strickler, the office manager, asked for a meeting with Dennison and Merrick and suggested that a general ledger package be integrated into the existing system. Strickler argued, "If we had our own general ledger package, we could cut our monthly accounting costs, and I mean significantly."

After the experience with the accountant, Dennison decided to become involved and asked Merrick to contact Stroud and arrange a meeting. During the meeting, Dennison asked Stroud if it would be possible to develop an integrated general ledger package. Stroud pointed out that, although it was possible, now was not the time to embark on this effort. It would be better, Stroud continued, to finish the project as originally defined and to look into implementing a general ledger package later.

Stroud remembered trying to explain that it might even be better to purchase a generic general ledger package and transfer the data, rather than trying to develop one in-house. Both Dennison and Merrick felt that suggestion was nonsense.

Dennison asked, "Haven't we just developed and implemented a system that

EXHIBIT 16   Transaction Summary Report

Transaction Summary Report*

COST PRICE	COST IMPOST	SALES PRICE	SALES IMPOST
131412.36	11427.16	168400.28	19546.46

TOTAL COST	TOTAL SALES
142839.52	187946.74

TOTAL SALES—TOTAL COST

45107.22

others have been trying for years to develop? Surely, we can write a simple general ledger program! I feel you're being uncooperative, and I don't know why.'' Without further discussion, Stroud agreed to prepare a cost proposal for writing and implementing a general ledger package.

After receiving and reviewing Stroud's proposal, Hill's top management decided to hire a programmer to develop the general ledger package in-house. Meanwhile, having received no immediate reply from Hill following their acknowledgement of receipt of his proposal, Stroud waited a month and then called. Merrick told the consultant that the proposal cost estimate ($15,000) to develop the general ledger package was too high.

CONCLUSION

Stroud recalled, ''Sure, there had been some problems. When the system was initially envisioned, the company had no prior computer or automated information system experience. There was a great deal of recalcitrance and skepticism on the part of managers and personnel. In order to overcome this, it was essential that the system 'fit' the business. Therefore, I had to devote an awful lot of time to analysis, system definition, and user involvement.

''If the system was to work at all, it had to be accepted. In order to gain system acceptance, I had to make everyone feel involved. The system was installed in small, manageable modules that were totally, or as much as possible, assimilated before the next module was added.

''They simply didn't understand how far they had gone in such a short period of time. After all, what could you expect when you took a zeroth-generation manual system to a fourth-generation, query-based system in one jump? I realize we didn't have time to touch all the bases, but where did we go wrong?''

---

*The Transaction Summary Report prints total cost, total sales, and the difference between total cost and total sales for the period from the date entered to present. Output can be printed or displayed. The user is prompted for a starting date, then asked where the output is to be directed. The transaction summary report can be run for any period not yet archived.

QUESTIONS

1. What changes, if any, would you make to Exhibits 1 and 2? Supply your corrected version of the two data flow diagrams.
2. Turn in a data flow diagram of the manual inventory control procedures at Hill.
3. Do you agree with the system configuration selected by Dennison and Merrick? If not, how would you change it, and why?
4. What changes would you have made to the systems definition, data requirements analysis, and system implementation processes followed by Hill? Support your answer.
5. Explain the advantages and disadvantages of the four main techniques for conversion—direct cutover, pilot, parallel, and phased? Do you agree with Hill's selection of the module-by-module (phased) technique?
6. Explain Hill's disapproval of Stroud's general ledger proposal.
7. Considering the entire consulting assignment, what should Stroud have done differently? What would you have done differently?
8. What should Stroud do now?

Glossary of Terms

The following glossary is not comprehensive since it omits most basic terms used in introductory data processing texts. The definitions are compatible, in many cases identical, with those used in official sources and other texts. These definitions are not intended to have the precision required by professionals in the computer and information systems fields; however, they will be useful to upper division undergraduates and graduate students.

The sources for this glossary include:

- James A. O'Brien, *Information Systems in Business Management,* 5th ed. (Homewood, Ill.: Richard D. Irwin, 1988).
- Charles S. Parker, *Management Information Systems: Strategy and Action,* (New York: McGraw-Hill, 1989).
- Mary Lou Sigler, S. Hornberger, and P. Clark, *Glossary* (''MSP and the LAN'') (MBA paper, Loyola College, Baltimore, Md., 1986).

access time   Time interval between the instant the CPU requests a transfer of data to or from a storage device and the instant the operation is completed.

Accunet T1   Customer-controlled private data, voice, or video transmission line offered by AT&T as a regular service; customer billed monthly for each circuit used.

acoustic coupler   Modem that converts digital data into a sequence of tones that are transmitted by a conventional telephone hand set to a receiving modem; then, it transforms the data back to digital form.

action diagram   CASE tool that helps programmers create structured program code.

analog signal   Refers to transmission in which the data are sent as continuous wave patterns. Contrast with **digital signal.**

APL   Acronym for A Programming Language. A highly compact language that is primarily used to code applications quickly.

application development system   System of computer programs that provides interactive assistance to programmers in developing application programs.

applications software   Programs containing logic that perform work directly related to the needs of end-users.

ARPANET   One of the original private networks, it was a packet-switched, digital system funded by the Advanced Research Projects Agency of the Department of Defense. It was designed to link the host computers at various government installations.

artificial intelligence (AI)   Area of computer science attempting to develop computers that can hear, walk, talk, feel, and think. Major thrust is the development of computer functions normally associated with human reasoning, inference, learning, and problem solving.

asynchronous transmission   Transmission in which data are sent through a medium one character at a time. Contrast with **synchronous transmission.**

audit   Inspection to certify that claims made are true.

audit trail   Presence of data processing media and procedures that allow a transaction to be traced through all stages of data processing, beginning with its appearance on a source document and ending with its transformation into information on a final output document.

automated office systems   Automated office systems combining word processing, data processing, information systems, and telecommunication systems technologies. Also called office of the future or electronic office systems.

automatic teller machine (ATM)   Special-purpose, intelligent terminal providing remote banking services.

auxiliary storage   Storage supplementing primary storage of the computer. Same as secondary storage.

bandwidth   Relative range of frequencies transmitted, or the difference between the highest and the lowest frequency. Example: a TV set bandwidth is 6 MHz.

baseband   Transmission of signals without modulation. In a baseband local network, digital signals (1s and 0s) are inserted directly onto the cable as voltage pulses. The entire spectrum of the cable is consumed by the signal.

BASIC   Acronym for Beginner's All-purpose Symbolic Instruction Code. BASIC is a beginner's programming language that is easy to learn and use.

batch processing   Method of updating whereby transactions are collected in a group before being processed. Contrast with **real-time processing.**

benchmark test   Simulation, conducted prior to purchase or lease, used to determine how well a hardware or software system will perform when implemented. System performance usually tested against specifications of the buyer or lessor.

bottom-up systems development   Systems development approach in which the existing organizational systems are a major variable in the consideration of information needs and new systems. Contrast with **top-down system development.**

bps   Bits per second.

bridge   Device that links two homogeneous, packet-switched local networks. Accepts all packets from each network addressed to devices on the other and retransmits them to the other network.

broadband   Use of coaxial or fiber-optic cables to transfer data by analog or radio frequency signals. Digital signals are passed through a modem and transmitted over one of the cable frequency bands.

bundling Inclusion of software, maintenance, training, and other DP products or services in a computer system price.

bus (or bus network) System configuration in which several devices tap off a single cable called a bus.

business information system Information system within a business organization that supports one of the traditional functions of business such as marketing, finance, or production. Business information systems can be either operational (data processing) or management information (support) systems.

business system planning (BSP) Comprehensive, enterprisewide approach to systematic strategic planning; was developed and marketed by IBM.

byte Configuration of eight bits, used to represent a single character.

C Low-level, structured language developed by AT&T–Bell Laboratories. Resembles a machine independent assembler language; popular for system software programming.

CAD: computer-assisted design Use of computers and advanced graphics hardware to provide interactive assistance for engineering and architectural design.

CAM: computer-aided manufacturing Use of computers to automate the operational systems of a manufacturing plant.

carrier sense multiple access (CSMA) Medium access control technique for multiple access transmission media. A station wishing to transmit first senses the medium and sends only if the medium is idle.

carrier sense multiple access with collison detection (CSMA/CD) Refinement of CSMA; station ceases transmission if a collision is detected.

central processing unit (CPU) Device in a computer system that processes inputs into outputs. Also known as a computer.

channel Path along which signals can be sent. In some cases, a small, special-purpose processor that controls the movement of data between the CPU and its input-output devices.

character printer Slow-speed printer that prints serially (one character at a time) as typewriters do. Contrast with **line printer.**

chief executive officer (CEO) Highest ranking operating official within an organization. Often referred to as the organization's president.

chief information officer (CIO) Generic title used to refer to the highest ranking IS officer in an organization. Sometimes called the corporate information officer.

coaxial cable Electromagnetic transmission medium consisting of a center conductor and an outer, concentric conductor.

COBOL Acronym for COmmon Business Oriented Language. COBOL is the principal language used to develop transaction processing systems in businesses.

coding Writing the programming language instructions that direct a computer to perform a data processing assignment.

collison Condition in which two packets are being transmitted over a medium at the same time; their interference makes both unintelligible.

communications carrier   Organization providing communications services to other organizations and the public; authorized by government agencies.

communications control program   Computer program that controls and supports communications between computers and terminals in a network.

communications controller   Data communications interface device (frequently a special-purpose mini or microcomputer) that controls a network's terminals.

communications monitors   Computer programs that control and support communications between the computers and terminals in a network.

communications processors   Multiplexers, concentrators, communications controllers, and cluster controllers that allow a communications channel to carry simultaneous data transmissions from many terminals; may also perform error monitoring, diagnostics, and correction; modulation-demodulation; data compression; data coding and decoding; message switching; port contention; and buffer storage. May be used as an interface to satellite and other advanced communications networks.

communications satellite   Earth satellites placed in stationary orbits above the equator; they serve as relay stations for communications signals transmitted from earth stations.

computer application   Use of a computer to solve a specific problem or to accomplish a particular job for a user. Common business computer applications include order processing, inventory control, and payroll.

computerized branch exchange (CBX)   Local network based on the digital private branch exchange architecture. Provides an integrated voice and data switching service.

contention   Condition when two or more stations on a network attempt to use the same channel at the same time. Opposite of polling. The peripheral device asks the computer if the medium is free (available) for transmission. Contrast with **polling.**

control   Process whereby steps are taken to recognize, assess, and (possibly) correct deviations from plan.

controller   Specialized computers whose purpose is to relieve (replace) the host CPU in communicating with a large number of low-speed peripheral devices.

corporate culture   Social energy that drives or fails to drive an organization; includes values of the executives, ''the way we do things,'' and traditional approaches to problems.

critical success factor (CSF)   Task whose importance is so great that the survival of the enterprise depends on whether it is carried out successfully.

cyclic redundancy check (CRC)   Numeric value derived from the bits in a message. Transmitting station calculates a number that is attached to the message. Receiving station performs the same calculation. If the resultant values differ, there is an error in one or more of the bits.

data   Collection of unorganized facts.

data administrator   Person or people in charge of setting up and maintaining large, enterprise-level databases. Sometimes called a DBA (database administrator).

database Nonredundant collection of logically related files or records that consolidates many records previously stored in separate files. Provides a common pool of data records and serves as a single central databank for many processing applications.

database management system (DBMS) Generalized set of computer programs controlling the creation, maintenance, and utilization of an organization's databases and data files.

data communications system Electronic data processing system that combines the capabilities of a computer with high-speed electrical and electronic communications.

data dictionary Integrated collection of facts about an application or processing environment, including detailed descriptions of data elements and their permissable use, descriptions of programs, and so on.

data flow diagram (DFD) Graphical modeling tool that provides a logical description of a system.

decision support system (DSS) Information system that uses decision rules, decision models, a comprehensive database, and a decision maker's insights in an interactive computer-based process, leading to a specific decision by a specific decision maker.

dedicated computer General-purpose computer that has been committed to a particular data processing task or application.

desktop publishing Use of desktop microcomputer systems, equipped with special hardware and software features, to produce documents that appear to be the products of a professional print shop.

digital signal Transmission in which data are sent as 0 and 1 bits. Contrast with **analog signal.**

digital switch Star topology local network that handles data only, not voice.

disaster recovery Measures taken by a firm after catastrophic events have interfered with IS operations.

distributed databases Distribution of databases, or portions of a database, to remote sites where the data is referenced most frequently. Data sharing is possible because a network interconnects the distributed databases.

distributed processing Also called DDP (distributed data processing). Major form of decentralization of information processing made possible by a network of computers dispersed throughout the organization. User applications are processed by several computers in a data communications network. Does not rely on a large centralized computer facility or on the decentralized operation of many independent computers.

documentation Comprehensive, written narrative describing a program, system, or procedure.

DSS generator Package of related hardware and software enabling one to build a DSS quickly and easily.

DSS tool Hardware, software, procedure, or data element that allows one to build either a specific DSS or DSS generator.

dual cable Broadband cable system using two separate cables, one for transmission and one for reception.

duplex   In communications, pertaining to simultaneous, independent transmission in two directions.

EDP auditor   Computer professional who certifies that computer system data are accurate, reliable, and not subject to abuse.

EFT: electronic funds transfer   Banking and payment systems that transfer funds electronically instead of using cash or paper documents such as checks.

electronic mail (E-Mail)   Hardware/software system that facilitates sending letters, memos, and documents from one device to another.

emulation   Imitate one system with another so that the imitating system accepts the same data, executes the same programs, and achieves the same results as the imitated system. Contrast with **simulation.**

end-user   Person who uses information technology to do a job or do it better.

end-user computing (EUC)   (1) Term covering development and computing activities performed by end-users. (2) Hands-on use of a computer system by an end-user.

environment   Collection of elements that surrounds a system.

exception report   Report issued when something unusual occurs requiring the attention of management.

executive support system (ESS)   Decision support system especially targeted to the needs of executives. Frequently called an executive information system (EIS).

expert system   Software systems that provide advice normally expected from human experts.

external environment   Environment consisting of all outside forces that affect an organization.

facsimile   Transmission of images and their reconstruction and duplication on some form of paper at the receiving station.

feasibility study   Part of the process of systems development that compares the information needs of prospective users with the organization's objectives, constraints, basic resource requirements, cost/benefits, and attainability.

fiber-optic cable   Thin filament of glass or other transparent material through which a signal-encoded light beam is transmitted by means of total internal reflection.

field   Collection of related characters.

fifth-generation computer   New type of computer that is able to see, hear, talk, and think. Depends on major advances in computer processing speed and flexibility, user input/output methods, and artificial intelligence.

file   Collection of related records.

file maintenance   Keeping a file up-to-date by adding, changing, or deleting data.

flowchart   Graphical representation using symbols to represent operations, data flow, logic, and equipment. A program flowchart illustrates the structure and sequence of operations of a program; a system flowchart illustrates the components and flows of data processing or information systems.

FORTRAN   Acronym for FORmula TRANslator. FORTRAN, perhaps the oldest high-level language, is used mostly for scientific, mathematical, and engineering applications.

fourth-generation langauges (4GL)   Programming languages easier to use than high-level languages like BASIC, COBOL, or FORTRAN. Known as nonprocedural, natural, or very-high-level languages.

front-end processor   Computer added to the front end of another computer system, to perform control functions and preliminary processing.

gateway   Device that connects two systems, especially if they use different protocols. Examples: a gateway is used to connect two independent networks, or to connect a local network to a long-haul network.

general-purpose application programs   Programs that can perform common information processing jobs for users from all applications areas. Examples are word processing, electronic spreadsheets, and graphics.

general-purpose computer   Computer designed to process a wide variety of problems. Contrast with a **special-purpose computer.**

graphics   Symbolic input or output — such as lines, curves, and geometric shapes — from a computer system. Uses video display units or graphics plotters and printers.

hard disk   Rigid platter, coated with a magnetizable substance, widely used for secondary storage on large and small computers.

hardware   Computer system and communications equipment. Contrast with **software.**

hertz   One cycle per second. The frequencies of many computers and communications devices are measured in megahertz (MHz), or millions of cycles per second.

hierarchical data structure   Data structure in which the relationships among data are modeled in the form of a tree; the relationships among its data elements are always one to many.

hierarchical network   Treelike configuration of hardware devices. In a common form of such a network, the topmost device is a host computer; beneath the host are computer controllers and communications terminals.

high-level langauge   Class of procedural-oriented languages, evolved during the third generation of programming languages; includes BASIC, COBOL, FORTRAN, PL/1, Pascal, and APL.

HIPO chart (hierarchy + input/processing/output)   Also known as an IPO chart. Design and documentation tool of structured programming; records input-processing-output details of hierarchial program modules.

host   Collection of hardware and software attached to a network; uses that network to provide interprocess communication and user services.

host computer   Main telecommunications network computer.

IEEE 802   Committee of IEEE organized to produce a LAN standard.

impact printers   Printers that form images on paper through the pressing of a printed element and an inked ribbon or roller against the face of a sheet of paper.

index file   Secondary-key access strategy in which an index is set up for a secondary key, providing direct access to records through that key. Also called an inverted list.

index sequential   Method of data organization; records are organized sequentially. When used with direct access file devices, known as index sequential access method (ISAM).

information   Data processed into a meaningful form.

information center   Support facility for computer users of an organization. Allows users to develop their own application programs and to accomplish their own data processing tasks. Users are provided with hardware support, software support (in the form of 4GLs), and people support (trained user consultants). They may also be given advice on purchasing and pricing hardware and software.

information resources management (IRM)   Concept that recognizes information as a key asset that should, like any vital resource, be managed properly.

information retrieval   Process of fetching meaningful data from computer memory.

inquiry   Requests information from a computer system.

installation   (1) The process of installing new computer hardware or software. (2) Data processing facility such as a computer installation.

instruction   Grouping of characters that specifies the computer operation to be performed and the value or location of its operands.

integrated package   Software combining ability to do several general-purpose applications (such as word processing, electronic spreadsheet, and graphics) in one program.

Integrity   Term used to refer to data that are accurate, reliable, and consistent; data that are representative of the phenomena they are supposed to depict.

intelligent terminal   Terminal with microcomputer capabilities; can perform many data processing and other functions without accessing a larger computer.

interface   Shared boundary, such as the boundary between two systems. Example: the boundary between a computer and its peripheral devices.

international standards organization (ISO)   Voluntary organization of national standards committees of each member nation; coordinates nations' activities on common issues; establishes standards on encryption, data communication, and other interest areas.

internetworking   Communications among devices across multiple networks.

job-shop production   Production process in which labor and materials can be traced back to and charged to individual work requests.

Just-in-time (JIT) production   Production planning methodology in which materials arrive at a factory or a production process just prior to the time they are to be used.

kilobyte (KB, K, or K-byte)   Approximately one thousand bytes; specifically, 2 to the 10th power.

large-scale integration (LSI)   Method of constructing or producing electronic circuits; thousands of circuits set on one semiconductor chip.

line printer   Device that prints all characters of a line as a unit. Contrast with a **character printer.**

load   In programming, to enter data into storage or working registers.

local area network (LAN)   Communications network typically using coaxial (or fiber-optic) cable to connect computers, word processors, mass storage devices, terminals, printers, electronic copying machines, and dictation systems within a limited physical area such as an office building, manufacturing plant, or other work site.

log   Record of operations of a data processing or management information system.

logical description   Representation of a system that does not specify how essential abstract system features will be implemented physically. Contrast with **physical description.**

magnetic disk   Secondary storage medium that consists of rotating platters; data are stored magnetically on concentric tracks.

magnetic ink character recognition (MICR)   Technology of the banking industry; uses a special character font for rapid encoding, sorting, and processing of checks.

mainframe   (1) Same as central processing unit. (2) A larger-sized computer system, typically with a separate central processing unit, as distinguished from microcomputer and minicomputer systems.

maintenance   Refers to keeping current stock of programs and systems in working order.

management information system (MIS)   System providing the information needed to support management functions.

management by objectives (MBO)   Management style used with workers who are capable of supervising themselves; workers establish their own performance standards and goals.

mass storage   (1) Devices having a large storage capacity, such as magnetic disks or drums. (2) Secondary storage devices with extra large storage capacities (in the hundreds of millions of bytes) such as magnetic strip and card units.

materials resources planning (MRP)   Production planning methodology, often found in batch-oriented production environments; a production schedule is established, materials needs are identified, and materials are scheduled for delivery in a cost-minimizing manner.

megabyte (MB)   Approximately one million bytes; specifically, 2 to the 20th power, or 1,048,576 in decimal notation.

menu driven   Characteristic of most interactive processing systems; provides menu displays and operator prompting; these assist a terminal or computer operator in performing a particular job.

microcomputer   Very small computer, ranging in size from a "computer on a chip" to a small typewriter-sized unit.

microcomputer system   Computer system powered by a system having a microprocessor CPU. Often referred to loosely as a personal computer (PC), microcomputer, or a personal computer system.

micrographics   Use of microfilm, microfiche, and other microforms to record data in a greatly reduced format. Use of computers involves computer output microfilm (COM), computer input microfilm (CIM), and computer-assisted retrieval (CAR).

minicomputer   Generally a medium-sized computer, usually too large to be placed on a desk.

modem   Device that transforms a digital bit stream into an analog signal (modulator) and vice versa (demodulator). The analog signal may be sent over telephone lines, as radio frequencies, or as lightwaves.

monitor   Software or hardware that observes, supervises, controls, or verifies the operations of a system.

Multiplex   To interweave or simultaneously transmit two or more messages on a single channel.

multiplexer   Electronics device allowing a single communications channel to carry simultaneous data transmission from many terminals, by dividing a higher-speed channel into multiple lower-speed channels.

natural language   Language — such as English, French, Spanish, or Japanese — that is used in human-to-human communication.

network   Interconnection of computers, terminals, mass storage devices, and communications channels and devices (such as modems and printers).

network interface unit (NIU)   Micro-based device that acts as a communication controller to provide data transmission service to one or more attached devices. The NIU transforms the data rate and protocol of the subscribing device to conform to the local network transmission medium and vice versa.

original equipment manufacturer (OEM)   Firm that manufactures and sells computers by assembling components produced by other hardware manufacturers.

office automation (OA)   Wide variety of computer-based technologies that make office workers more productive at their jobs.

open system interconnect (OSI)   Data communication standard developed by ISO; establishes a framework for defining standards for linking heterogeneous computers.

operating system   Software that controls the execution of computer programs; may provide debugging, scheduling, accounting, compilation, input/output control, storage assignment, data management, and related services.

optical character recognition (OCR)   Identification of particular characters and codes by optical reading devices.

optical scanner   Device that optically scans printed or written data and generates their digital representations.

packet   Group of bits; includes data plus source and destination addresses. Usually refers to the network layer of the ISO/OSI protocol.

packet switching   Transmitting messages through a communications network, in which messages are divided into short packets. The packets are then transmitted as in message switching, although packet switching is more efficient and rapid.

Pascal High-level language commonly used as a teaching vehicle to demonstrate structured programming practices.

password Group of characters that, when input to a computer system, allows access to certain hardware, software, or data.

peripheral equipment In a data processing or management information system, any unit of equipment, distinct from the central processing unit, that may provide the system with outside communication.

personal computer (PC) Term used to refer to a microcomputer system. In some contexts, the term is used to refer to a specific system unit, the IBM Personal Computer (IBM PC).

physical description Representation of a system that specifies how essential system features are implemented. Contrast with **logical description.**

PL/1: Programming Language 1 Procedure-oriented, high-level, general-purpose programming language designed (by IBM) to combine the features of COBOL, FORTRAN, and ALGOL.

polling Protocol in which a computer (acting as controller) asks several terminals (or microcomputers), in a serial fashion, whether they have any messages to send. Contrast with **contention.**

postimplementation review Follow-up evaluation of a system, after it has been implemented.

private branch exchange (PBX) Privately held telephone exchange on the user's premises that provides: (1) a switching facility for telephones on extension lines within the building, and (2) access to a public telephone network. It may be automatic or manual.

procedures Sets of instructions used by people to complete tasks.

program development life cycle Program-building process consisting of establishing software requirements, program design, program coding, program debugging, program testing, and program maintenance.

protocol Rules governing the exchange of data between two entities.

prototype Usable system or system component that is built inexpensively and quickly, with the intention of being modified or replaced.

pseudocode Program design tool that uses Englishlike statements as a proxy for actual program code.

query Request for specific data or information.

query language High-level, Englishlike language provided by a database management system; enables users to easily extract data and information from a database.

real-time processing Performance of data processing during the actual time a process transpires so that the results of the data processing can be used in guiding the system.

relational data structure Data structure with data elements placed in tables, which are logically equivalent to files. Rows of such tables are logically equivalent to records; the columns, to fields.

remote job entry (RJE) Entering jobs in a batch processing system from a remote facility.

repeater Device that receives data on one communication link and transmits it, bit by bit, on another link as fast as it is received, without buffering. An integral part of the ring topology, it is used to connect linear segments in a baseband bus local network.

request for proposal (RFP) Document sent to hardware, software, and services vendors; outlines organization systems needs and requests that interested organizations submit a formal proposal showing in detail how they intend to satisfy such needs.

request for quotation (RFQ) Document sent to hardware, software, and services vendors; specifies and describes the precise types of system resources needed by an organization and asks for a price on those resources.

requirements analysis Stage in systems development process in which the needs of the user are assessed.

ring Topology with stations attached to repeaters connected in a closed loop. Data are transmitted in one direction around the ring and can be read by all attached stations.

robotics Branch of artificial intelligence concerned with design, manufacture, and implementation of robots.

schema Overall conceptual or logical view of the relationships between the data in a database.

semistructured decision Decision having properties of both a structured and an unstructured decision.

service bureau Organization providing information processing services to other firms.

simulation Representation of certain features of behavior of a physical or abstract system by the behavior of another system. Contrast with **emulation.**

software Set of computer programs, procedures, and possibly associated documentation concerned with the operation of a data processing system. Contrast with **hardware.**

spreadsheet Software package that divides the display screen into a large grid — similar to columnar accounting paper — into which labels and values may be entered and manipulated.

star Topology with all stations connected to a central switch. Any two stations communicate via circuit switching.

steering committee Group of executives charged with overseeing the development of information systems within an organization.

strategic planning Planning process in which the current state of the organization is assessed; some broad, long-range targets are identified; the targets are translated into measurable objectives; and a "game plan" is established to achieve the objectives.

structure chart Graphical program development tool; shows the hierarchy of major program tasks.

structured analysis Use of structured techniques in the requirements analysis process. In practice, most closely associated with preparation of data flow diagrams.

structured design   Use of structured techniques in the program or system design process. Three widely used structure design tools are **structure charts, HIPO charts,** and **data flow diagrams.**

structured programming   Programming approach that adheres to such practices as limited program control structures, top-down design, structured walk-throughs, and other methodologies.

structured query language (SQL)   Example of information-retrieval languages used with relational database systems.

structured walk-throughs   Structured programming methodology that requires a peer review by other programmers of the program design and coding; intended to minimize and reveal errors early in programming.

synchronous transmission   Transmission in which data are sent, a block of characters at a time, along a medium. Contrast with **asynchronous transmission.**

system   Set of related elements that collectively form a unified whole; in information systems, it includes hardware, software, data, procedures, and trained people.

system flowchart   Graphical modeling tool providing a physical description of a system.

systems analysis   (1) Analyzing in detail the requirements and components of a system. (2) Analyzing in detail the information needs of an organization, the characteristics and components of existing information systems, and the requirements of the proposed information systems.

systems analyst   Computer professional whose primary duty is to design and build systems.

systems development life cycle (SDLC)   System-building process in five phases: preliminary investigation, requirements analysis, system design, system acquisition, and system implementation.

telecommunications   Transmission of signals over long distances, including not only data communications but also the transmission of images and voices, using radios, television, satellites, and other communications technologies.

telecommuting   People using communications technology to perform work at home or in a remote city; avoids the physical commute to work.

teleconferencing   Meeting that takes place among people who are at different sites, through the use of telecommunications technology.

terminal   Collection of hardware and software that provides a direct user interface to a computer or network.

token bus   Medium access control technique for bus/tree. Stations form a logical ring around which a token is passed. A station receiving the token may transmit data and then must pass the token to the next station in the ring.

token ring   Medium access control technique for rings. A token circulates around the ring. A station may transmit by seizing the token, inserting a packet onto the ring, and then retransmitting the token.

top-down control   Control mechanism with higher-level modules controlling the activities of lower-level modules.

top-down design   Methodology of structured programming; a program is organized into functional modules, with the programmer designing the main module first and then the lower-level modules.

top-down systems development   Systems development approach in which the organization's needs are viewed from a strategic perspective, and systems are proposed that best meet that perspective. Contrast with **bottom-up system development.**

topology   Structure, consisting of pairs and switches, that provides the communications interconnection among nodes of a network.

turnaround time   Elapsed time between the submission of a job to a computing center and the return of the results.

turnkey system   Complete, ready-to-go system that is purchased from a single outside vendor, as opposed to being built in-house from hardware and software acquired from a number of outside vendors.

twisted-pair   Electromagnetic transmission medium consisting of two insulated wires arranged in a regular spiral pattern.

update   To incorporate changes reflecting the most current status of the records in the master file.

unstructured decision   Decision involving a high degree of latitude, creativity, and intuition, as well as little precedent.

user-friendly   Characteristic of human-operated equipment and systems that makes them safe, comfortable, and easy to use.

value added carrier (VAC)   Company that leases communications facilities from a Federal Communications Commission licensed common carrier such as AT&T; then, it augments these facilities with additional services and offers the combined services to the public.

value added network (VAN)   Publicly available common carrier that can send and receive information over publicly or privately owned systems. The networks provide computer services and access to databases, but, unlike WANS, they change the characteristics or enhance the information.

vendor rating system   Formal, highly structured procedure used to make choices among vendors of hardware, software, and services.

very-high-level language   Problem-specific language that is usually easier to learn and use than a high-level language such as COBOL, FORTRAN, or PL/1. The terms *fourth-generation language* and *nonprocedural language* may be used as synonyms for very-high-level language.

voice mail   Variation of electronic mail in which digitized voice messages, rather than electronic text, are accepted, stored, and transmitted.

volume   Amount of activity taking place on a hardware device or a computer system at any one time.

Warnier-Orr diagram   Program planning tool that can be used to show a program's organization and its processing logic.

what-if analysis   Nonprobabilistic simulation technique; enables users to reformulate a problem over and over, getting useful information and a new end result each time.

wide area network (WAN)   Publicly or privately owned geographically dispersed network able to send and receive information, access databases, and provide computer services without significant enhancement or change in character to the data.

word processing   Automation of the transformation of ideas and information into a readable form of communication. Typically involves the use of computers to manipulate words, characters, sentences, and paragraphs in order to produce office communications—letters, memos, messages, documents, and reports.

word processing systems   Office information processing systems that rely on automated and computerized typing, dictation, copying, filing, and telecommunications systems.

X.25   Protocol that addresses the third layer (network layer) of the ISO/OSI model. Was developed by CCITT, and is used by AT&T's 9.6 K bps WATS-like data transmission services.

Case Index

Index

Q

R

S

T

U